LIBERTY

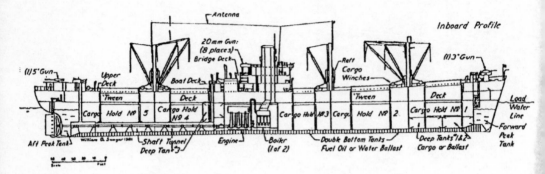

Cutaway drawing of the Liberty ship *Jeremiah O'Brien*.

LIBERTY

The Ships That Won the War

Peter Elphick

NAVAL INSTITUTE PRESS
Annapolis, Maryland

Dedication

This book is dedicated to the memory of Robert Cyril Thompson, who started it all, Harry Hunter, his principal co-partner, and William Bennett and John Heck, all of the British Shipbuilding Mission to the United States in 1940

It is also dedicated to the only surviving member of that Mission, Sir Richard Powell.

First published in Great Britain by Chatham Publishing, 99 High Street, Rochester, Kent ME1 1LX

Published and distributed in the United States of America and Canada by the Naval Institute Press, Beach Hall, 291 Wood Road, Annapolis, Maryland 21402-5034

Reprinted 2002

Library of Congress Catalog Card No. 2001089745

ISBN 1-55750-535-7

Manufactured in Great Britain

Contents

List of Illustrations

Acknowledgements

The research for this book has benefited enormously from the generous help given by close to 400 people from around the world. Indeed, without that help the book would have ended up being a very different one. Some of the help has been in the form of a name to contact or a telephone number to ring; but most of it has been much more extensive than that. It has not been possible to make direct use of all the material received, but everything has added colour and background to the narrative and has enabled the author to build up what he believes to be an overall picture of the birth of the Liberty ship and its role in war and peace. If the Liberty lives again in these pages, it is very largely due to the scale of this input. That having been said, the author alone is responsible for the way in which some of the input has been interpreted.

An alphabetical list, country by country, of all those who have helped is given below. If any name has been accidently omitted, the author proffers his sincere apologies. Some of the help has been very considerable indeed, the people concerned having given extensively of their time and their own records and research material, and it would be quite wrong not to give them a special mention.

They are Professor Frank Bull (Australia), John Hill, George Monk, Tom Scott, Patrick Thompson, and Stuart Walker (Britain), Kapitanleutnant Dirk Steffen (Germany), Baard Haugland (Norway), Kalevi Olkio and Captain John E. Simms (USA), and Vladimir Chepelev (Russia). Several members of that group have also helped with illustrations for the book. Others who have helped in that sphere are Eric Berryman in the USA, and Arthur Credland in Britain.

The author of any book on Liberty ships must play tribute to the pioneering research work of L.A. Sawyer and W.H. Mitchell in their *Liberty Ships*, which is a catalogue of the ships without peer.

Quotations from documents under Crown Copyright at the Public Record Office, Kew, appear by permission. The same applies to documents held at the Imperial War Museum, the Militargeschichliches Forschung Samt, Potsdam, and other official archives.

Australia
Mike Bartlett, C. Buhagiar, Rev. Ted Cozens (Mission to Seafarers, Melbourne), Richard Farquhar, Rev. Frank R. Roe (Mission to Seafarers, Esperance), Maurice de Rohan (Agent General, South Australia, London)

Belgium
Major B. Cambrelin (Centrum Voor Historische Documentatie, Belgische Krijgsmacht), Riet De Block (Archivist, Cie Maritime Belge, Antwerpen), Captain A Kockx (Defence Attache, Royal Belgium Embassy, London), G. Renard (President, Koninklijke Verbroedering der Belgiische Zeelieden ter Koopvaardij van de oorlogen)

Canada
Captain David B Crabb, Graham Deere, Bill Ellis, George Evans

China
H.M.G. Forsgate (Hong Kong)

France
Frederique Chapelay (Conservateur adjoint, Musee de la Marine, Paris), Jacques Chaveau, Senator Louis de Catulan, Jack-Philippe Maitre Ruellan (Commissaaire-Priseur, Vannes)

Germany
Horst Bredow (Director, U-boot Archiv, Cuxhaven), Admiral H. Hass and Warrant Officer Bernd H. Muller (Defence & Naval Attaché Office, German Embassy, London), Professor Jurgen Rohwer, Wolfgang Siegert

Great Britain
John Airey, David Allen, Sid Anning, Marjorie Bain, Michael Baker, David Balme, Roy A Barclay, Arthur Barnes (Secretary, London Branch, MRA Association), Eric Barnes, J.C. Bellaby, Frank W Berriman, Lynne Bowden (Heritage Department, Folkestone Library), Kevin Brown (Sonar Research & Development Ltd.), Natalia Bull (for Russian translations), John Burtt, Robert N. Cairns, Rev. Roy Chalkley, Lieutenant B.C. Cambray RNVR, Frank Carter, Captain John W. Chapman, Charlie Chater. Alex Clarke, John H. Coe, R.J. Coe, Derek Collins and the crew of *Medway Ranger,* David Cornes, Reg Crang, Arthur Credland (Hull Maritime Museum), Mike Crowe, Captain Kenneth Cummins, Rosemary Cummins, Captain Mike Curtis, Charles Dallas, John David (Porthcawl Museum), Captain Dawkins, Captain William C Dawson (The U-boat Association), Dr Danuta Dean (for translations from the Russian), R.C. Derham (T.S. *Vindicatrix* Association), R. F. Dobb (General Manager,

Corporate Department, Corporatiion of Trinity House, London), Christopher Dobbs, Captain Michael Dodds, Captain Norman Donovan, Captain A.C. Douglas (Editor, *Sea Breezes* magazine), Colin Douglas, Ken Douglas, Lieutenant Commander W. Dungate, Ron Elliot, Bert Elphick, Lieutenant Colonel Patric Emerson (Secretary, Indian Army Association), E.W. Evans, Graham Everitt, Len Farnham, Captain Tom W Flack, Marjorie Fuller, Jim Gates, Tom Gay, Richard Gerard, Jeremy Glen (Curator South Wales Police Museum), John Goddard, Roy Gould (Marine Manager, Medway Ports Authority), T.M. Govier, James Thomas Grieve, Captain Arthur Griffith, Peter John Guy, Ann Haines (Registrar, The Missions to Seamen, London), Phil Hall (Local Studies Centre, Central Library Sunderland and staff members Heather Wishart & Joan White), R. Hammond, John Hampson, Captain John Hannay, Sam Harper, A.L.G. Harrison, Captain Arthur Harvey, Leon Hawksbee, David Helyar, R. Herbert, Rear Admiral J.B. Hervey, Colston Hicks, Peter Hicks, Anthony J Higgins, June Hockley, F J Honisett, Don Hooper, Peter Hubble & Fran Green (Powers International Ltd), Mrs Lansdale Humphreys, Harry Summers Hunter, Captain Alan Jones, Barbara Jones and Emma Taaffe (Lloyd's Register of Shipping), Ian Jones, Pat Jones, Fred Kemp, Arthur King, Ian Laing, Noel Lamb, Cedric Lark, Geoff Larney, Ken Le Page, Alan Lewis, Mike Lewis (Swansea Maritime & Industrial Museum), Lieuenant Commander R.F. Linsell RNR, D.S. Lomax, Don Lyford, Captain T.J. Lyons, Con McCarthy, Colin MacDonald, Lieutenant Colonel C.H.T. MacFetridge, Captain C.S. Mackinnon, Mrs. Pat McKenna, Captain A.J. 'Sandy' Mackenzie, Walter McKenzie, Chief Engineer Norbert McManus, Ian N. Malcolm, Lynn Mallet, Captain Ken Maguire, J. Main, James Marr, Jack Marrable, Allison Marsh (Discovery Museum, Newcastle-upon-Tyne), George E Maskell (Public Relations Manager, King George's Fund for Sailors), Colin Menzies, Kevin Middis, Dave Molyneax (Blue Funnel Association), Donald B. Moncrieff, Captain Ian Nash, Professor Bernard de Neumann, Michele Nevard (London Office *Baltimore Sun*), Brian Nicholls, Captain Sam Nicolson, G.W. Noble, Sean Nugent, Richard Oliver (Librarian, Royal Institute of Naval Architects), Geoff Oxley (Hull City Archives), Harry Palmer, R.B. Patterson, Captain Dennis Pearce, Douglas Peel, Sid Penton, Ken D. Pizey, Peter Poston, Sir Richard Powell, Paul Quinn, Stephen Rabson (Librarian, P&O Group), Joe and Houston Rath, E.A. Rees & Kathryn Taylor (Tyne & Wear Archives), Len Reed, Thomas Reed, Jon Reeds, G.B. Reid, Irene Richmond, Don Riddle, Paul Ridgway, Veronica Robbins (Receiver of Wreck, Maritime & Coastguard Agency), Bob Robinson, John Robinson, Dennis Roberts, Neil Roberts, Ted Robson, Les Rowe, Paul Rowlands, George Ruck, D.Y.S. Russel, R.J. Scott, L. Shannon, J.P. Mallmann Showell, Andrew Sinclair (one-time Chief Surveyor, Salvage Association), David Sinclair, Ronald H. Singleton, Captain

Alan Smith, Captain Gerald Smith, Joe Stevens, Derek Stretton, Roderick Suddaby and David Penn (Imperial War Museum, London), Paul Sands, John Stewart, Sue Sullivan, Len L. Sutton (HM Rescue Tug Asociation), Captain R.L. Sutherland, Captain George Swaine, Roy Sweetland, Fred Taylor, Brian Tebbutt, Captain L.J. Thompson, Keith Townsley, Alf Trafford, John Waite (Chief Surveyor, Salvage Association, London), Frank Walker, Captain Peter White, David L. Williams, J.A. Williams, Christopher J. Willis (Association of Old Worcesters), Andy Wilmore, Captain Norman L. Wilton, Jason Winstanley, Ray Witt, Phil Woodgate, Victor Worton

Staffs at National Maritime Museum, Greenwich; Glamorgan Archives, Cardiff; Essex Record Office, Southend -on-Sea; Guildhall Library, London

Greece
Captain Babis Charalambides, Christos Dounis, Captain I.M. Fournarakis (Maritime Section, Greek Embassy, London)

India
Captain Rajan Vir, IN (retd)

Mexico
Herman Arbitter

Netherlands
Simon J. Loos, Dick Schouten

Norway
Turid Andreassen, Leif Fosse, Sverre Hansen, Arne Hartmark, Kornelius Korneliussen, Tore L. Nilson (Bergen Sjofartsmuseum), Commander Marcus Osen RNN, Leif Vetlesen, Ingvald Wahl

Russia
Andrey A. Berezkin (Adviser to the Vice-Governor, St. Petersburg), Y.D. Mozchil (Lloyd's Register of Shipping, Moscow), Ledezkiy Vladimir Platonovich, Astahova Irina Valerievna

USA
Gene Anderson, Commodore Henry H. Anderson, Steve Antos, Captain William M. Ayers, Mose Barker, the late Bill Bailey, Commander Eric Berryman USNR, Phil Bichler, Derek Brierley, Norman Brouwer (South Street Museum, New York), Captain Dean K. Bruch, Joan Burke (Newletter Editor, Project Liberty Ship), Neville Bryant, Captain

Acknowledgements

Jefferson Carey, Joseph G. Chaet, Mrs Midge Crittenden *née* Elphick, Hans Dahle, George E. Emmerson, Herk Esibill (Secretary, Project Liberty Ship), Albert A. Faulkner, Bill Flury, Hubert Fulmar, Pastor Greg Garis, Robert W. Gifford, Joe Glick, Pete Goodman, N.S. Gurnell, Edward M. Haake, Alan Harvie, Romuald P Holubowicz, Captain Brian Hope, Jarvis T. Hughes, Captain John Hughes, George Hurley, Ingolf M.Iverson, Dr. Erwin R. Jennings, Jan Jones (Dept of Transportation, Washington), Lawrence D. Kelsey, Allen I. Kinsinger, Oddvin Liseth, Charles A Lloyd (National Chairman, US Naval Armed Guard Veterans), Chief Engineer John M. Lockhart, Alex Lombardi (Chairman, North East Chapter, US Naval Armed Guard Veterans), Lieutenant Commander E.M. MacCutcheon USNR, Michael R McKay (American Maritime Officers), Melissa Mantel (Assistant Librarian, *Houston Chronicle*), Captain Frank Medeiros, Joe Milcic, Ian A. Millar, Raymond D. Moloney, Rita Orsini, Paul Porter, Jeff Price (Foreign Editor, *Baltimore Sun*), Sarge Ransome, Donald E. Robertson, Stan Rothman (Personnel Dept. Gibbs & Cox, New York), Peter Salvo, Robert J. Scott (President, Gibbs & Cox Inc.), Captain Ralph E. Smith USNR, Peter Stanford (National Historical Society of America), Chief Engineer James R Stevenson, Alfonsas Urbelis, Vito Virzi, Edward Von der Porten, Kline Wilson, Carl Winder, Mary Woodward (National Liberty Ship Memorial).

Introduction

Wars and battles are never won only by the skills and bravery of fighting men. Without logistics, which is the art of transporting military units and keeping them supplied, no amount of fighting spirit could prevail. In a global war, even in smaller ones that require the large-scale movement of men and equipment over vast distances as in the Korean War and the Falklands conflict, it is the merchant ship, manned by civilian seamen, that carries out most logistical movements. This was a particularly marked feature of the Second World War, the greatest of the two global conflicts. The contribution made by Allied merchant fleets during that war is perhaps best illustrated by the fact that the average-sized freighter then in use was capable of carrying 10,000 deadweight tons of cargo, a figure far, far in excess of the capacity of any aircraft.

Another marked feature of the Second World War was that the part played in it by Allied merchant fleets was never appreciated in the same way as were the roles of the fighting services; and it has remained so ever since. To be sure, political and military leaders of the time paid fulsome tributes to merchant seamen and their ships, but in general the crucial roles they played never really made the same sort of headlines as did the deeds of the more fashionable military, naval and air forces. In his 1945 Proclamation of National Maritime Day, President Roosevelt said, 'our ships, sailing every ocean, have been manned by courageous officers and seamen all of whom have left the security of their firesides and many of whom have given their lives for the land of their allegiance', while towards the end of the war Winston Churchill said, 'We never call on the officers and men of the Merchant Navy in vain'. He followed that up in his Victory in Europe broadcast in May 1945 with, '. . . when our minds turn to the North-western approaches we will not forget the devotion of our merchant seamen . . . so rarely mentioned in the headlines'. During and after the war, other leaders weighed in with similar fine words, including Field Marshal Montgomery and Generals MacArthur and Eisenhower. General Dwight D. Eisenhower, speaking in London in 1944, the year of the D-Day landings, said, 'When final victory is ours there is no organization that will share its credit more deservedly than the American merchant marine'. General MacArthur recognised the important contribution made by the American merchant marine when he noted, 'They brought us out lifeblood, and paid for it with their own.' Notwithstanding all those fine words it is true to say that the men, ships and deeds of the Allied merchant fleets have been largely ignored by historians and almost wholly forgotten by the man in the street.

This historical neglect goes even deeper than has been indicated above. Developments in aeronautics, radar, weaponry and cryptography have all been credited with having an important part in winning the war, and quite rightly so. However, comparatively little attention has been given to the development of a class of merchant ship, part of the largest shipbuilding programme the world has ever seen, without which the Second World War could not have been won notwithstanding the many important developments in other fields. This book sets out to tell the story of how that ship came to be born, its impact on the war, and its importance to the merchant fleets of the world for many years after the fighting was over. Although the ships were built in the United States, the story begins in Britain.

At the start of the Second World War Britain owned 17 million tons of merchant shipping, by far the largest merchant fleet in the world. It was just as well, for there was to be no so-called 'phoney war' period at sea. Within nine hours of Prime Minister Chamberlain's broadcast to the British people on 3 September 1939 in which he declared that a state of war existed with Germany, the liner *Athenia* (Donaldson Atlantic Line) was sunk by the submarine *U-30*. Over a hundred lives were lost including nineteen members of the crew, amongst them the ship's four stewardesses. Total war, with all that those words entail, began very early on the oceans. By the end of August 1940, when the story related in this book really begins, British shipping losses had reached staggering proportions. During those first twelve months of war, a total of 385 British ships amounting to 1.7 million gross tons, 10 per cent of the September 1939 total, had been lost, primarily as a result of the German U-boat campaign. In just one month of that period, May, which opened with Prime Minister Chamberlain trying to explain away his earlier statement that Hitler 'had missed the bus' over the conduct of the war, and ended with new Prime Minister Churchill famously offering the British people nothing but 'blood, sweat and tears', Britain lost thirty-one ships amounting to over 82,000 tons, an average of one a day. Another six had sustained damage from aircraft, submarine attacks and from shellfire from shore batteries.

That was not all, for many ships of the other Allied nations had also been sent to the bottom, together with more than a few neutral ones. Some of the neutral ships sunk were on charter to Britain and therefore fair game, but others were going about their lawful but, as it turned out, not so peaceful occasions, and just happened to wander into the line of fire. One of these was the Japanese *Terukuni Maru* which sank after striking a mine off the British coast on 21 November 1939. Another and rather later neutral victim of mine warfare was the American *City of Rayville* sunk by a German mine off the Australian coast on 8 November 1940. This sinking, during which Third Engineer Mack Bryan lost his life, is frequently cited as being the United States' first casualty of the Second World War although it took place over a year before Pearl Harbor. A more calculated and tragic sinking of an American ship took place only a few days prior to the attack on Pearl Harbor. The Socony-Vacuum Oil Company tanker *Astral*, Captain Chris Alsager, was on a voyage from Aruba to Lisbon when she was torpedoed and sunk by a submarine on 2 December 1941 with the loss of all thirty-seven members of her crew. The first American loss after that country entered the war, on the very day of Pearl Harbor in fact, was Olson Line's *Cynthia Olson*, sunk with all hands by a Japanese submarine on 7 December 1941 whilst on a voyage from Tacoma to Honolulu with lumber.

The Germans were sinking ships faster than the combined efforts of British and Commonwealth shipyards could replace them, three times as fast in fact, and a large attrition gap had developed. Those British shipyards not engaged in building warships were doing their best under the most trying conditions to maintain the flow of merchant ships down the slipways. In order to speed up building times, and with only a few exceptions, ships were no longer being built to the individual requirements of shipowners, but instead to certain British Admiralty approved designs. (The Admiralty, through its Controller of Merchant Shipping and Repairs, also had a purview over all ship repairs.) The general pattern was for these standard ships, as they were called, to be built on a one-yard-one-design basis, usually a design that the yard was used to building. But that was never a hard and fast rule for from time to time a yard could be ordered to switch to another type of ship. The overall guidelines were speed of construction and the cargo-carrying capacity of the ship. There were several reasons why this tendency towards shipbuilding conformity was never carried through to its logical conclusion in Britain, *ie* that of getting all yards to build to only two or three basic designs, which, as the Americans were to show, would have brought about the many benefits that accrue to near-complete standardisation. The reasons why this course was not pursued in Britain include the historical layout of yards, the varying sizes of slipways, and the valuable and not to be lightly discarded local shipyard expertise that had been built up over many years. Nevertheless, the degree of standardisation that was achieved did help to reduce average shipbuilding times, and did result in the standardisation of most shipboard machinery, equipment and accessories. Many British yards were old and had been built in places no longer open to expansion; not only did that prevent new slipways from being constructed, it also meant that except in rare cases, no adjacent spaces were available for such techniques as pre-fabrication. That was not all. Materials were in short supply, for many ships carrying iron ore for Britain's steel works were amongst those being sunk. The steel being produced at home together with that being imported, mainly from the United States, had to be rationed between competing demands. Manpower was also in short supply, the armed services taking most that was available. Traditionally, most ships built in Britain were riveted rather than welded and, although as the war went on there was a move towards the faster technique of welding, it was decided that it would not have made sense in those days of crisis to waste the services of all skilled riveters and to re-train them. Perhaps the worst handicap of all to the industry in Britain, however, was the blackout, for to have worked the yards after dark under floodlights, especially during the long winter nights, would have been to invite the ministrations of the *Luftwaffe,* and German air attacks were quite bad enough without soliciting more.

By August 1940 the situation was already critical. A new source of ships was needed and for that purpose British eyes turned to the still neutral United States of America. The British authorities knew that despite the scheduled increase in the number of convoy escort ships coming out of British yards, the shipping casualty situation would get worse before any new American-built ships could came on stream. That judgement was correct, except that the scale of future losses was rather under-estimated. Over the next fourteen months to October 1941 when, as we shall see, the first of the new American-built ships was delivered, a further 830 British ships were sunk amounting to over 3.5 million tons.

The British had good reason to be hopeful that they would not look across the Atlantic in vain, even though America's official entry into the war was still fifteen months away. But a positive response was far from certain. President Roosevelt was sympathetic to the British cause but he was in the middle of a re-election campaign and, on top of that, was having to tread warily under the watchful eyes of the many isolationists in his country. That situation is perhaps best illustrated by the 'destroyer affair'. On 15 May 1940, five days after he became Prime Minister, Churchill wrote to Roosevelt pointing out that 'a completely subjugated, Nazified Europe' might be 'established with astounding swiftness, and the weight may be more than we can bear'. He then asked for the loan of 'forty or fifty old destroyers'. In his reply Roosevelt pointed out that it would not be politically wise for him to ask Congress 'at this moment' for authorisation for such warship transfers, adding a rider to the effect that America's own defence requirements raised doubts over whether the destroyers could be spared anyway. (See *Roosevelt & Churchill, Their Secret Wartime Correspondence,* by Francis L. Loewenheim and others.) Although a deal over the destroyers was eventually struck in return for British territorial concessions in the Caribbean, the ships were not 'officially' made available to Britain until early 1941, a month or two after Roosevelt's re-election even though, in one of those pieces of political legerdemain that characterised many of the Roosevelt/Churchill dealings of that time, some of the destroyers which were then under refurbishment in American shipyards were 'unofficially' handed over to skeleton Royal Navy crews from September 1940. That notwithstanding, in August 1940, with the President preparing for the November election, the British could not be sure that the United States would co-operate by building merchant ships to order for them.

As an interim measure, British losses were partially offset during 1940 by the United States authorities sanctioning the purchase of over 100 existing merchant vessels in individual commercial transactions with the American shipowners concerned. This measure was far from ideal, for the ships concerned were old and obsolete, many dating from the First World War and which had been laid up in American rivers and estuaries for some years. Not only that, despite their maturity the ships did not come cheap, the average price per deadweight ton being between $40 and $45. The *Patrick Henry*, a ship name the reader will come across again in the pages that follow, was purchased in May 1940 from Lykes Lines, a firm that did particularly well out of these British transactions, and renamed *Empire Steelhead*. Dating from 1920 and with a deadweight of 12,650 tons, she cost well over half a million dollars, a currency of which Britain was running short. These high selling prices were in part due to other nations being in the market as well as Britain. One of those nations was Japan, the *Wall Street Journal* of 5 September 1940 noting that 'second-hand price pressure was upwards because of recent Japanese purchases'. On top of that, the British showed little interest at that time in turbine-engined vessels with watertube boilers and twin screws because British engineers were not used to working them; this resulted in no British offers being made for laid-up ships of this type – many ships of the Luckenbach fleet for example. This was another factor which caused market forces to push up the price of the ships that Britain was interested in. There was another difficulty quite apart from the costs involved, for even these ordinary commercial transactions were subject to considerable opposition in America from isolationist elements and from maritime trade unions – not always distinguishable the one from the other. In a letter he wrote to the head of the United States Maritime Commission dated 26 May 1941, Frederick Myers of the National Maritime Union of America, after saying that his organisation was 'opposed to further transfers of American tonnage to Great Britain or to any other country until such time as our own depleted merchant marine is built up', ended with a long diatribe against Britain and its maritime interests.

Before leaving American ports with British crews on board, these purchased ships were repaired and made serviceable to avoid the need to use the already overstretched British shipyards for that purpose. On reaching the other side of the Atlantic the ships were renamed and given an *Empire* prefix, all, that is, except for four which were torpedoed and lost en route. Despite this influx of tonnage, a huge attrition gap remained, and it was not until the Americans really got into shipbuilding mode in early 1943, a year after that country entered the war, that the gap disappeared, a situation helped, of course, by improvements in Allied convoy escort performance and techniques against the U-boat.

Between October 1941 and the end of the war some 5000 merchant vessels slid down the ways of American yards in that country's emergency shipbuilding programme. Well over half of them, 2710 to be precise, were of one type called the Liberty ship. Writing in 1962, Professor S.G. Sturmey, the noted British authority on matters maritime, said that the American wartime shipbuilding programme had been 'of crucial importance to the prosecution of the war.' In 1990 another British authority, Dr Ronald Hope, noted that the Liberty 'played a large part in ensuring victory for the Allied forces'. Professor Sturmey recorded the figure for British and Commonwealth ship losses during the entire war as 11.9 million gross tons. A further 9.8 million gross tons of other Allied and neutral ships were lost, giving a grand total of 21.7 million. When the total gross tonnage of the Liberty ships, 19.4 million tons, is set against that overall figure, it is clear that the Liberty, far and away the largest and most important class of ship ever constructed, almost of itself filled the attrition gap. As the war went on, Liberty ships became the maritime workhorses of the Allies and were to be seen, often massed together in large numbers, on every sea and ocean. They served in Arctic convoys to Russia, and in the Allied landings in North Africa, southern Europe, and Normandy. From late 1943 they formed major parts of most North Atlantic convoys. They became the backbone of General MacArthur's island-hopping campaign in the Pacific, and were essential parts of American fleet-trains. Over every ocean route they transported planes, tanks, landing craft, airfield equipment, ammunition, fuel, food and all the other supplies and equipment needed by armies in the field. Some were converted to carry troops, some into hospital ships, and a few were even used to transport mules for Allied forces operating in Burma. So many Liberty ships were constructed and so varied and vital were their tasks and roles in Allied maritime logistics, that it can truly be said that the Second World War could not have been won without them.

During the war by far the great majority of Liberty ships sailed under the Stars and Stripes, mostly as units of the American Merchant Marine but some as ships of the United States Navy and Army. About 300 Liberty ships were handed over to other Allied nations under Lend-Lease arrangements with the condition that those that survived the war would then be either handed back to the Americans. One hundred and eighty-seven of these were allocated to Britain (together with thirteen additional 'hybrids' of slightly shorter length). Forty-three were allocated to Russia and smaller numbers sailed under the Norwegian, French, Dutch, Greek, Belgian, and Chinese flags.

The importance of the Liberty ship did not end with the defeat of the Axis partners in 1945. So great was the need for shipping tonnage as the countries of the world dragged themselves back to normality after the war, that for many years after the conflict ended, the approximately 900 Liberty ships which were purchased from the United States at the end of the war, played key roles in the reformation of merchant fleets every-where. (The statement is often made that the Liberty ships loaned to the USSR were neither handed back nor purchased. That is not strictly true, for three of the on-loan ships, the three designed to carry oil, were handed back in 1948.)

So famous was the ship in its heyday and so familiar a sight did it become in every port of the world, that it is perhaps surprising that even today, nearly sixty years after the first Liberty ship was launched from its yard, that there are still many people in Britain, America and elsewhere, including some seamen who actually sailed in the ships, who are unaware that the Liberty ship stemmed from a British rather than an American design. Or perhaps it is not so surprising, for during the war and imme-diately after it, according to Admiral Emory Scott Land, various spurious claims were made in America over the Liberty plans. Admiral Land, who throughout the war years headed the United States Maritime Commis-sion, the body which initiated the ordering of the ships and which con-trolled their building along with all the other merchant ships built in the States, attempted to put the record straight in 1960. In an article in the *Proceedings* of the United States Naval Institute, he wrote,

> The contract plans and many others for the Liberty ship were obtained from the British . . . Various claims for the Liberty ship design have been made by U.S. citizens, even a gold medal was awarded for one, but they were erroneous and no award was deserved.

It was Admiral Land who recorded one version of how the Liberty gained its most famous nickname, 'Ugly Duckling'. Land said that when in 1941, President Roosevelt first saw the profile plans of the ship, he commented, 'Admiral, I think this ship will do us very well. She'll carry a good load. She isn't much to look at though, is she? A real ugly duck-ling.' If he did use that expression then, as a one-time Secretary of the Navy, President Roosevelt should have known better, for the ship's lines were not all that bad. Another version of the story is that the President called the ships 'dreadful looking objects', which was even worse, following which *Time* Magazine dubbed them with the 'Ugly Duckling' sobriquet. Whatever the truth of that matter, President Roosevelt more than made amends later when he credited the Liberty ship with the saving of Europe. The disparaging sobriquet was even used in British official correspondence. The author of an internal Ministry of Shipping memo dated 6 June 1941 said;

> I enclose the General Arrangement Plan of the ships building for the U.S. Maritime Commission under the Emergency Programme and which I understand are of the ugly duckling type.

A little later parts of the British press were even more insulting than their American counterparts. London's *Daily Mail* for example, ran an artist's impression of the ship over the caption 'U.S. Mass-Produces Sea Scows to Carry "The Tools" to Britain'. The 'tools' referred to were those Churchill had told the British people, in a broadcast made on 9 February 1941, he was going to ask President Roosevelt for, in the now famous phrase, 'Give us the Tools and we'll finish the Job'. Winston Churchill who, like Roosevelt, was a man with nautical pretensions, having been First Lord of the Admiralty, was kinder to the Liberty, calling the ship 'marvellous'. However, it was the Roosevelt/*Time* description that stuck with the American press, who later also called the ships the 'expendables' for it was said that they paid for themselves with one successful North Atlantic crossing. On that basis, some of the expendables were to pay for themselves, many, many times over. The United States Maritime Commission itself never considered the ships to be ugly ducklings, sea scows, or expendables. To a gathering of the American Press in June 1941, six months before Pearl Harbor, John L. Demsay, a member of Admiral Land's Commission, set out to describe the vast U.S. ship production programme then in progress, which included the placing of an initial order for 200 Liberty ships. He predicted that Liberty ships would contribute 'no small part to the necessary functions which will determine the success or failure of our huge defense effort'. Events were to prove just how right he was. A Press Release by the Commission later in 1941 said;

> The Liberty ship will present a trim, sea-going appearance.Riding low in the water, with its long sharp prow and its simple, straight-lined superstructure, it will knife its way through the water as gracefully as any vessel afloat.

That may have been overstating it a bit, for this ugly duckling never grew up to be a swan. Nevertheless, that having been said, most seamen from the age of the Liberty ship will agree that the vessel was far closer to being swanlike than the ugly box-like structures that now sail the seven seas.

From early on in the Commission's shipbuilding programme, ugly rumours developed over the safety of the ships being constructed. Most of these rumours concerned Liberty ships because more of them were built than any of the other types. The rumours had it that these welded ships were suspect in both design and construction, and that they were likely to break up at sea. Authorities on both sides of the Atlantic attempted to suppress the rumours and 'enemy agents' were blamed for initiating them. It is likely that enemy agents in America did help to disseminate the rumours but, as we shall see, the stories had a substantial basis in fact for many ships were suffering unexpected damage during normal usage. In an official U.S. Government report published after the war it was stated that the structural failures in merchant ships posed the second greatest threat to the transatlantic supply line after the U-boat menace. So desperately serious was the problem – hundreds of ships were affected – that teams of engineers and scientists were formed in the United States and Britain to try to discover why the structural failures were taking place. One part of the British effort was headed by Professor Frank Bull who has written that the failures at first cast grave doubts over the entire American shipbuilding programme. He said that the big question was, 'could the ships be used with any degree of confidence? If not, then final victory in the war could be set back by years, perhaps for ever. The fortunes of war were tied to these ships.' A few years after the war, in 1952, the man in charge of the US Coast Guard's Office of Merchant Marine Safety, Rear-Admiral H.C. Shepheard, described the wartime construction of ships as a 'calculated risk'. He went on, 'We would still be fighting the war if we had not taken that risk'. The only criticism one can make over the admiral's words, is his use of the word 'calculated' for it implies a significant element of predetermination, when in actuality the nature and scale of the problem came as a great shock to all.

We shall see that the principal cause of the failures was finally identified and some remedial action taken (although the problem was never entirely eliminated). However, even today, nearly sixty years on, at any gathering of old salts one is still likely to hear incorrect statements made about this issue and about the consequent dangers – dangers that had nothing whatsoever to do with war risks – of sailing aboard these ships. These statements, anecdotes may be a better word, have been voiced so many times since the war that they have acquired those barnacles of exaggeration which stick to every well-voyaged nautical tale. The grossest of all the exaggerations concern the loss of life involved; to be sure some structural failures did result in loss of life during the war but the overall figure of deaths directly attributable to this cause was tiny when compared with the total number of men who sailed in these ships.

(The tellers of those tales invariably mention that so dangerous were these ships considered to be, that they, the tellers, would under no circumstances have ever sailed in one! In other words, the story-tellers are not speaking from first-hand knowledge.)

This book sets out to tell the story of the Liberty ship from its very beginnings and in order to do that it has been necessary to delve back into the design and construction of the British-built prototypes. It has also been necessary to tell, in some detail, the story of the Ocean class of ships built in the United States to British order, ships which were the Liberty ship's immediate predecessors. Mention is also made of the Canadian-built Fort and Park classes of ships, half-sisters to the Liberty. Some British mariners include the Oceans and the Canadian-built ships under the generic name 'Liberty', but that is quite incorrect. Official documentation of the time in British, American, and Canadian archives, always differentiated between the classes. In fact the only government to lump all the wartime-built Allied tonnage together was that of Germany. In official German documents all were referred to either as *Neubaudampfer, Standardfrachtsciffe* or *Notdampfer,* which respectively translate as new construction steamers, standard freighters, or emergency steamers.

The early chapters of this book are largely based on the written and oral recollections of people who, in one way or another, were concerned in the design, planning and construction of the ships. Later chapters are based on the reminiscences of seamen of many nations who sailed in them either during the war or after it; the book is written by one of the latter. Wartime exploits have in general been recorded separately from peacetime exploits, although for the sake of narrative, in some instances they have been allowed to overlap. The points of view of those who did their best to sink the ships during the war have not been neglected. German sources are quoted on the effect of what by mid-1943 must have seemed to U-boat commanders and their superiors ashore, to be an unending line of *Neubaudampfer* crossing the Atlantic; sink one and another with exactly the same silhouette hove up over the horizon to take her place. In recent years Russian archival material has become available to researchers. As a result of this, for the very first time in the English language, this book presents some details of the operational histories of the forty-three Liberties that were handed over to the USSR, together with their ultimate fates.

The last working Liberty ship, apart from a few altered and almost unrecognisable ones still being used as storage facilities, went to the breaker's yard in late 1998. However, the story of the ship that won the war is not yet over thanks to the magnificent efforts of two bands of dedicated people in the United States. For, in addition to a few hulks and wrecks still to be found around the world, two of the class have been restored and preserved for posterity, one at Baltimore and the other at San Francisco. The stories of these ship preservation efforts are to be found at the end of this book.

Author's Note
British rather than American spellings are used throughout this book except in direct quotations from American sources. The spelling 'Harbor' rather than 'Harbour' is used in reference to American ports. The observant reader will also note that in the United States the form 'Coast Guard' is used whilst in Britain it is 'Coastguard'.

Japanese personal names are presented in the old form of surname first. Chinese names are shown with the anglicised spellings in use at the time.

PART I: IN THE BEGINNING

CHAPTER 1

The Parentage of the Liberty Ship

As Admiral Land intimated in the 1960 article referred to in the Introduction, one will not find the true parentage of the Liberty ship in the United States of America although that is where all of them were built. Instead, it is necessary to travel to the other side of the North Atlantic, across those waters over which so many of the type sailed and under which, from a variety of causes, not a few of them lie. As we shall see in the next chapter, those same waters also very nearly provided the last resting place of the man who can truly be called the father of the Liberty. To be precise, to find the true origin of the ship we must look to the port of Sunderland on the north-east coast of England, then to a particular shipyard there, and finally to the man himself, Robert Cyril Thompson.

In its heyday Sunderland could justifiably lay claim to being the largest shipbuilding town in the world. Lying at the entrance to the River Wear, its claim was based on the fact that all the Wearside shipbuilding yards, and there were a number of them, were to be found within the boundaries of a single county borough. (In recent years Sunderland has been granted city status.) Sunderland folk like to point out that in comparison, the shipyards of the Tyne and the Clyde, two other great British shipbuilding centres of the past, were scattered along those rivers and over a number of towns. Sunderland shipbuilding dates back many centuries though it can be said that the industry came of age there towards the end of the seventeenth century by which time a large proportion of the townspeople were directly or indirectly engaged in it, with shipwrights, boatwrights, sail, block, anchor and rope manufactories being among several thriving industries by that period. From the mid-nineteenth century marine engineering works appeared, the earliest of all being that of George Clark which just before the Second World War merged with the slightly younger but equally famous North-Eastern Marine Engineering Company, a Tyneside firm but with a large presence in Sunderland.

The period from the late eighteenth to the early nineteenth centuries produced many family firms on the River Wear which were to become famous in the annals of British shipbuilding. Laing, Pile, Crown, Austin, Bartram, Pickerskill, Priestman, Doxford and Short are all names to conjure with in this context. So is Thompson, the yard on which we shall centre our attention. Robert Thompson, son of a master mariner, worked on and off at various boat building yards on the Wear from 1819. In 1846 he set up for himself, and with the help of his three sons founded the firm which at first bore his name. The family embarked upon a shipbuilding venture at North Sands on the northern bank of the river close to its mouth. The very first of the company's ships was the *Pearl* of 1846, a brig of 226 tons. Over the following years the name 'North Sands' was to become synonymous with shipbuilding excellence In 1871 the firm became Joseph L. Thompson, the name under which it traded until it ceased shipbuilding in 1979. Passing through a wooden ship phase from 1846 to 1870 and an iron-ship phase from 1870 to 1886, from the latter date all Thompson ships were made of steel. (Over the years several authors have written that the Liberty ship stems from a Thompson-designed ship of 1879. The latest such reference was in the Winter 1999-2000 edition of the prestigious American publication *Sea History*. It is difficult to pin down the original perpetrator of that story which is, of course, utter nonsense. In the early part of the twentieth century Britain was at the forefront of ship design, and no British yard, let alone Thompson, was producing ships anything like those of the late nineteenth century. Thompson built sixteen ships in the years 1879/1880, the largest of which was the *Sybil* of only 2720 tons. Neither *Sybil* nor any of the others bore the slightest resemblance to the Liberty ship except in so far that they all had engines and floated on water.)

Throughout its existence and in common with all other shipbuilders, Thompson passed through good trading periods interspersed with bad ones. The company had an active First World War during which seventeen 'standard' cargo vessels were constructed at North Sands in addition to a series of barges for the Admiralty. One Thompson-designed ship of the time was adopted by the Admiralty as its standard 'F' type vessel. In contrast to those war years, the early 1920s brought a slump in orders and there were no launchings at all from the yard during 1923. Business picked up thereafter and by 1930 the company had completed its 571st ship, the *Vigdis* of 9100 tons. Then along came the disastrous early years of the 1930s. The early 1920s had been bad enough but that slump paled into insignificance when compared with the years 1931-4 during which no launchings at all took place at North Sands, and only a skeleton staff was retained. The firm was not quite dead, however, for those years were used to remodel the yard layout, some old machinery being discarded and some investment made in new plant. A handful of small non-shipbuilding contracts were undertaken, including the construction of a small bridge over the Wear upriver from Sunderland. However, to all intents and purposes the yard lay virtually idle for four years though behind the scenes much research work was being carried out.

During those dormant years shipbuilders and engine-makers in general came to realise that if the shipbuilding industry was ever to get back on its feet, ways must be found to reduce production costs, improve construction methods, and raise the performance capabilities of new ships. Throughout the industry research was directed towards producing a cheap and economic-to-run ship, one with a cargo-carrying capacity of the order of 10,000 tons, that would help break the depression. Perhaps of all the yards in Britain none took that more to heart than did Thompson. Under the direction of Major (later Sir) Robert Norman Thompson and his two sons, Robert Cyril and John Victor, the company embarked upon what was to turn out to be a remarkable development programme.

At the centre of this programme was Robert Cyril Thompson, a larger-than-life character always known as 'RC' or Cyril by friends and associates. His workforce knew him as 'Mr Cyril', the form of address being symptomatic of the master-and-man relationship that pervaded the British shipbuilding industry in those days and especially in the north-east where the impact of cyclical downturns in employment always seemed to have a worse effect than anywhere else. Yard owners and yard workers held each other in mutual respect but there was nothing democratic about the two-way flow. Respect travelled vertically upwards and vertically downwards, and very much in that order of precedence. The upward movement was of the doff-your-cap-the gaffer's-here variety, and the downward movement was paternalistic. Cyril was to become one of the unsung heroes behind the Allied victory in the Second World War, arguably *the* unsung hero in view of the huge importance of his contribution and the rather less than proportionate recognition it received. He was born on the last day of May 1907. He attended Marlborough School before going on to Pembroke College, Cambridge, where he was to earn his BA. During vacations from Cambridge and after leaving university, he embarked on an apprenticeship with Sir James Laing & Sons, a Sunderland company with which Thompson's always had close connections. A large man standing 6ft 3in in his socks and broad with it, Cyril was a keen rugby union player. Ken Douglas, younger than Cyril but whose career his own somewhat mirrored, and who after the war came to know Cyril well, says, 'it was difficult to get an apprenticeship with Laings unless you were prepared to play rugger for the firm's team. It was almost a condition of employment'.[1]

---

1. Kenneth Douglas b.1920, gained a Diploma in Naval Architecture at Sunderland Technical College, and was Deputy Shipyard Manager at Vickers Armstrong Naval Yard from 1946 to 1953. Then became Director and General Manager, William Gray & Company, 1954-6. Appointed Managing Director, Upper Clyde Shipbuilders Limited in 1969. Held many other senior appointments in shipbuilding and associated industries until his retirement.

By 1930 Cyril had joined the family firm, becoming a director the following year at the age of twenty-four. Over the next few years he made
several business trips abroad, held down the post of technical adviser to
Silver Line one of the firm's best customers, and even managed to fit in a
short spell at sea as a Junior Engineer Officer. In 1934 he joined the board
of Sir James Laing and in September of that year married Doreen Allen.
In 1935 he was awarded the Gold Medal of the North-East Coast Institute of Engineers and Shipbuilders for a paper he presented on the
modifications he had advised upon which increased the service speed of
two existing Silver Line vessels. The firm of Joseph L. Thompson may
not have been busy in the first half of the 1930s, but Cyril certainly was,
and we have not heard the half of it yet. He was one of those men who
possess a built-in and highly-tuned self-motivation mechanism.

It was during those same years that Cyril led the Thompson drawing
office staff in a series of experiments with models of varying hull forms,
using the National Physical Laboratory's testing tanks at Teddington for
the purpose. After a number of experiments Cyril was satisfied that a hull
form had been evolved which would, when associated with an improved
design of engine, produce efficiency and economy in service because pro-
portionately less power would be required to maintain a given service
speed. The hull form chosen was distinctive and highly unusual for the
times. At its forward end an appreciably sloping bow was associated with
a rare fullness, whilst at the stern the lines were quite fine, the cruiser stern
being more of a 'V' than the more common 'U' section. To further reduce
drag, the firm designed a built-up, semi-balanced rudder. The improved
engine design that was required came from the North-Eastern Marine
Engineering Company. Cyril was pleased with and proud of the overall
design of the ship and thought it could meet that much sought-after
financial parameter, that of keeping the ship's final cost under £100,000.

The firm's research was rewarded when the first ship built to the new
design, moreover the first ship to be constructed by the company since
1930, was launched in 1935. She was the *Embassage* with a deadweight
carrying capacity of 9100 tons and built to the order of Hall Brothers of
Newcastle. She was the first vessel to benefit from North-Eastern's
'Reheater' type of engine.[2] *Embassage* was the first of the trio of vessel
designs which were eventually to evolve into the Liberty ship. On her

---

2. James Hall, the founder of Hall Brothers, was the true instigator of the Load Line for merchant ships, rather than Samuel Plimsoll who knew nothing at all about ships before he met
Hall. The loss of the *Royal Charter* in 1859 had raised Hall's concern over overloaded ships,
and during the following years he wrote a series of letters to the *Times* of London on the
subject. He gave a talk on it in London in 1870, a member of the audience being Samuel
Plimsoll, the newly-elected MP for Derby who was out to make a name for himself. Plimsoll subsequently travelled to Newcastle to be briefed by Hall, and the end result was the
Load Line Rules contained in the Merchant Shipping Act of 1875 for which Plimsoll
received all the credit.

maiden voyage with a full cargo of coal she averaged 10kts, which may not sound much but she did it with her reheated triple-expansion engines developing 1500 IHP on an average fuel (coal) consumption of between 16 to 17 tons a day, a remarkably low figure when compared with the average 25 tons of the times. The economics of the achievement were impressive and the design created great interest in shipping circles, more so as North Sands had been able to build the ship for only £95,000. The firm received further orders resulting in the building of seven sister-ships. The efficiency of the design greatly impressed the Admiralty when it was brought to its attention. *Embassage* was to meet a tragic end during the coming war. As part of Convoy OS-4 and under the command of Captain W.E. Kiddie, she was on a voyage in ballast from Leith to Pepel in Sierra Leone to load iron ore when she was torpedoed and sunk by *U-557*, (Lieutenant Paulshen) on 27 August 1941 when the convoy was about 100 miles west of Achill Head, County Mayo, Ireland. Captain Kiddie and thirty-eight members of his crew went down with the ship. There were only three survivors, the Bosun and two seamen who managed to jump overboard and swim clear as the ship went down. The three men clung to an upturned boat and were rescued on the fourth day. The Bosun reported that the ship had 'ploughed under within sixty seconds'. *U-557* made three more kills from that same convoy, and her sister submarine *U-558* (Lieutenant Commander Krech) gained another victim.

The second of the trio of prototypes was the *Dorington Court* built for Court Line of London. Her keel was laid on 8 September 1938 and she was launched exactly six months later on 7 March 1939, not at all a bad building rate for those days. She was 10ft longer and 18in wider than *Embassage,* the hull dimensions being a step nearer to those of the Liberty ships to come. This ship was fitted with one of the first of a type of 2500 IHP engine developed by the North-Eastern Marine Engineering Company, which produced a speed of 11kts. Like the *Embassage* before her, *Dorington Court* impressed My Lords Commissioners of the Admiralty, especially as by the time the ship sailed from the River Tyne on her maiden voyage on 4 May 1939, the tocsin bells were sounding in the corridors of power in London; although nobody knew it then, the declaration of war with Germany was a bare four months away. Three sister-ships to *Dorington Court* were later constructed. The workforce at North Sands built *Dorington Court* without knowing, of course, the ship's significance as one of the forerunners of the most important class of merchant ship in world history. When, in 1939, twenty-one year-old engineer Thomas Reed worked at the yard on the ship's 'skin-fittings' – the ship's outside valves – and then helped to bore out its stern frame, he had no idea of the importance of the ship in the great scheme of things. 'Neither had anyone else', he says. 'That knowledge only came to us after the war, and even then we didn't think about it much. It was all part of the war effort.'[3] Tom Reed, who began his engineering career as an apprentice with the North-Eastern Marine Engineering Company, is one of a rare breed. Not only did he participate in the construction of the ship and, after its launch, work on installing its main engines, but he then sailed on the ship for her first two voyages in the capacity of Fourth Engineer Officer. He says *Dorington Court* set out on her maiden voyage with a 'guaranteed' chief engineer in charge of the engine-room in the form of another Sunderland man, Thomas 'Tommy' Collins. 'A guaranteed chief,' Tom Reed explains, 'is one who though employed by the shipping company, is selected in part by the engine builder and who is required to send in to the builder regular reports on the engine's performance. Guaranteed chiefs are always associated with new or newish engines still undergoing refinements.' *Dorington Court*'s engines were called the North-Eastern Reheater Type, and had been developed in 1938 when two ships, the *Lowther Castle* and the *Lancaster Castle,* were fitted with them. The engine was described in its maker's literature as being of the 'reheater, poppet valve, triple-expansion type'. (For the technically-minded the engine achieved extra fuel economy by use of a reheater which raised the temperature of the steam as it passed from the high-pressure to the intermediate-pressure cylinders by leading it, via a special system of poppet-valves, through a chamber heated by steam coming directly from the boilers. The system ensured that steam was maintained in a superheated condition throughout.) Chief Engineer Collins was kept busy checking and report writing. Tom Reed says, 'Fortunately, the Second and Third Engineers, both South Shields men, were knowledgeable and experienced types, not new like me, so all went well. She was a fine ship.'

Dorington Court's first commander was Captain John Harmann Korn. He was born at South Shields in 1885. His father, a German master mariner, had also sailed in command of British ships. The ship's, and young Tom Reed's, maiden voyage was from the Tyne to San Nicolas in the Argentine with coal, and then up the Paraguay-Parana river to load grain at Rosario, topping off at Buenos Aires before sailing for Rotterdam. The voyage passed off without incident, with ship and engines performing admirably. The second voyage was to Iquique on the west coast of South America to load a cargo of phosphate for Hamburg, and it was while the ship was on her way back to Europe and passing through the Panama Canal that war was declared. The phosphate cargo was eventually discharged at Tilbury, no doubt after it had been officially seized as enemy property. Tom Reed left the ship at that Essex port. Like

---

3. From correspondence and telephone interviews with Thomas Reed (b.1918) during 1999.

Embassage, the *Dorington Court* also met her end during the war. Captain John Korn was still in command when she was bombed and damaged by a German aircraft three miles east of Buchan Ness on the north-east coast of Scotland on 6 September 1940 when making for Hull with a cargo of wheat from Bahia Blanca. On 6 November 1941, Korn was relieved by Captain Ernest D. A. Gibbs. In the following year, on 24 November, she was torpedoed in the Indian Ocean when en route from Madras to Lourenco Marques. She was struck in way of the engine- and boiler-rooms, and as his ship began to settle, Captain Gibbs ordered abandon ship. The submarine then surfaced and finished *Dorington Court* off with shellfire. Four members of the crew were lost but the others eventually reached safety.

The last of the prototypes was the *Empire Liberty* even though her keel was not laid until *after* those of some of her direct progeny in the United States, an apparent contradiction that will be explained later. The construction of *Empire Liberty* began in early 1941 and she was launched in August of that year, a fairly rapid building time for those days in Britain, especially as little work could be carried out after dark due to the blackout. It took three months on the fitting-out berth to complete *Empire Liberty* after her launch and for her trials to be run, and she sailed on her maiden voyage in November. It is in this ship with her beam of 57ft, 2½ft less than that of *Dorington Court,* and with a length overall of 441ft, a gross tonnage of 7157, and a carrying capacity of 10,170 tons, that we see the final stage in the paternity of the Liberty ship, quite apart from the name she enjoyed. Thompson's were to build ten more ships to the same design.

The clock must now be turned back to September 1940. Early in that month Cyril Thompson was summoned to the British Admiralty in London. According to his wife Doreen's diary, that first trip was made on Monday 2nd. The relevant entry reads, 'Cyril up to London to see about this American idea. Two [air] raids and Cyril did not get back until about 2 [the following morning].' Cyril had been recommended by the Admiralty's own North-Eastern District Shipyard Controller, Rear-Admiral Sir Wellwood G.C. Maxwell, for a special task, a task that could mean the difference between life and death for Britain at a crucial stage of the war. The meeting at the Admiralty was a high-powered one held under the aegis of the Fourth Sea Lord, Rear-Admiral (later Sir) Geoffrey Arbuthnot. It was chaired by Sir James Lithgow, the Controller of Merchant Shipbuilding and Repairs, a most experienced man for he had held down a similar appointment during the last war. Cyril was told that a man of his background and experience was needed to proceed to the United States and there to persuade that still-neutral country to build merchant ships to British order. He was briefed on the current critical shipping situation and was told that unless a new source for new ships was found, Britain might not survive. The new source was needed as soon as possible, for, given the lead-time for building merchant ships, even should building contracts be signed right away it was unlikely that the first of the new vessels would be available until the end of the following year. As a shipbuilder, Cyril Thompson would have been aware that the shipping situation was critical. He had many contacts with shipowners, government and naval officials and, on top of that and despite the best efforts of the official censors, no one could live near a major British port without hearing horrendous stories about ship sinkings from merchant seamen who had survived one. Nevertheless, even he had not realised that Britain was sitting on the very edge of a precipice.

Cyril was asked to head a British Shipbuilding Mission to the United States and, still only thirty-three, he accepted the job on the spot, as is confirmed in his wife's diary entry for the following day. He was asked to choose a marine engineering expert to accompany him and the choice fell on Harry Hunter of the North-Eastern Marine Engineering Company's branch at Wallsend-on-Tyne, the firm which had designed the new-style engines for *Embassage* and *Dorington Court*. Six feet tall and well-built, Harry Hunter was almost of a size with Cyril. They got on well despite, size apart, being contrasting types of men. At that time Cyril liked to wear light-coloured clothes except at weekends when he favoured dressing the part of a 'tweedy' country gentleman, and he tended to laugh and joke a lot. Harry, born in August 1891 and therefore sixteen years Cyril's senior, was of a more serious demeanour and was rather conservative in dress with but one quirk in his apparel; around the works (where, naturally, he was known as 'Mr. Harry'), he would as likely as not be seen walking about in a rather experienced mackintosh. As an Engineer-Lieutenant on HMS *Barham* at the Battle of Jutland, Harry had earned special promotion for his services, and had later been awarded the OBE. He was the inventor of the 'Hunter governor', an improvement on the hydraulic system for 15in guns which increased their rate of fire. He had joined North-Eastern, a firm with which he had several family connections, after leaving the Navy with the rank of Lieutenant Commander in 1919. By 1940 Harry was considered to be one of the leading figures in the marine engineering industry and he possessed the rare knack of being able to describe complex engineering matters succinctly and in a way most laymen could understand.

Cyril Thompson's letter of appointment from the Admiralty was dated 11 September 1940. Although addressed to a civilian it was couched in the style that that august body had developed over many, many years of writing to the captains of its ships. In line with that tradition it used capital letters to highlight words considered to be of particular significance and, also in line with that tradition, was very precise in telling Cyril exactly what money he could spend in the way of day-to-day expenses. It read:

Sir,

I am commanded by My Lords Commissioners of the Admiralty to inform you that they understand you are willing to accept an invitation to be the leader of a Technical Merchant Shipbuilding Mission to Proceed immediately to the United States of America to carry out the objects indicated in the attached memorandum. I am accordingly to confirm hereby your formal appointment to undertake the duties involved in these and such further Instructions as may be communicated by the Admiralty.

Arrangements are being made as regards your passage to the United States, and passage tickets and an advance to cover your initial travelling expenses will be provided; as regards further funds necessary to meet your expenses in the United States your claims will be dealt with by the British Purchasing Commission, 15 Broad Street, New York, who will be Authorised to pay at the rate of 12 dollars 50 per day for food and accommodation where this is not included in the travelling expenses. Apart from the payment of your expenses, the question of the financial terms of your appointment, in particular that of insurance against risks, is under Consideration and will form the subject of a further letter.

My Lords cannot at this stage indicate with any precision the probable duration of your services which will to a very large extent depend upon the time that has to be taken in travelling from place to place examining shipyards and works and undertaking preliminary negotiations, but as indicated in the enclosed memorandum your duties will Terminate on your return to this country.

I am, Sir,
Your obedient Servant,
(Signed I. Fry)[4]

Harry Hunter's letter was similar in construction, the only difference being that he was to serve as a 'member' of the mission, while Cyril was its nominated leader.

All previous written accounts of the Thompson Mission have stated that Cyril carried with him to the States either the plans for *Dorington Court* or those for *Empire Liberty*. Both these statements are incorrect. The Mission's objectives as outlined in the secret Admiralty memorandum dated 11 September 1940, which accompanied Cyril's letter of appointment, in fact made no reference to building the required ships to any *British* design.[5] (This document is reproduced in full in Appendix 1; only a precis being given here.) The main objective of the mission was to endeavour to obtain as quickly as possible sixty tramp-type ships averaging 10,000 tons deadweight and capable of 10.5kts service speed. The

---

4. File AVIA 38/117, PRO, London.
5. Secret document entitled 'Merchant Shipping Mission to U.S.A.' in ADM/10278, PRO.

Mission had authority to substitute two faster and larger cargo ships and two tankers for four of the tramps. Amongst Cyril Thompson's principal duties listed in the document was that he was to approve the types and sizes of the ships and all technical details concerning the design and construction of them. It was recognised that the types of ships and propelling machinery which ordinarily would be built at Britain, were not available to any extent in the USA . . . 'and we must take what we can get'. The document shows that by the autumn of 1940, so desperate had the shipping position become, that the British were by then prepared to take ships with geared turbine engines, this being in complete contrast to the attitude held earlier in the year during the purchase negotiations for second-hand American tonnage. The document went on to state that the Mission might be faced with proposals to include in the price of the ships the capital expenditure of new or extended yards and plant, and that any such proposal 'must be carefully handled'.

Nowhere in the document was there any mention that the ships were to be built to a British design. Nevertheless, Cyril Thompson was to take with him to the States a number of drawings of one of his company's ships as a guide to the type of ship required, and, one supposes, just in case no suitable American plans were available. It was general practice for each shipyard to give its ships consecutive hull numbers, sometimes called yard numbers, and throughout the building process a ship was usually, though not invariably, known by this number rather than by its eventual name; all drawings pertaining to an individual ship being 'marked up' with its particular hull number. The drawings Cyril carried with him were not those for *Dorington Court* (hull No. 592), nor were they for *Empire Liberty* (hull No. 611). Instead, as is evidenced by several official British documents dating from October/November 1940, documents emanating from British officials based in the States, he took with him drawings of a vessel on which construction had just begun at Thompson's yard. She was hull No. 607, which when launched on 28 March 1941, was to become the *Empire Wave*. She was similar to *Empire Liberty*, but being 2ft shorter but wider in the beam, had a larger gross tonnage. Had the plans for *Empire Liberty* been available in September 1940 instead of still being on the drawing board, it is likely that Cyril would have taken those drawings instead, for he had a most intimate knowledge of that ship. In the next chapter we shall see just when the *Empire Liberty* plans did enter the picture.

Cyril made another visit to London on 16 September to clear up some loose ends and to receive his final instructions. He met again with Sir James Lithgow, and with Sir Amos Ayre, who held the title Director of Merchant Shipbuilding at the Admiralty. In his other life, Ayre, a man from South Shields on the Tyne, was a director of the shipyard at Burntisland, Scotland. It is likely that Sir Amos had a role in the initial selection of Cyril Thompson and Harry Hunter for the mission, for he knew both men well. It may have been Ayre's involvement at this stage that became the source of one of the two Scottish myths that have developed over the prototype for the Liberty ship. One source has it that the true prototype was an 'economy' ship built by Ayre's firm at Burntisland. The other myth has it that the true prototype was the *Scottish Monarch* built by Caledon Shipbuilding, at Dundee, a ship that in fact bears no resemblance, either in size or motive power, to the true prototype, quite apart from the fact she was not built until March 1943.

Armed with the wide discretionary powers the critical shipping situation demanded, ten days after receiving their letters of appointment, Cyril Thomson and Harry Hunter were on the high seas. They sailed from Liverpool for New York aboard the Cunarder *Scythia* on 21 September 1940. The ship sailed at night during an air raid and the two men stood on deck and watched as bombs fell, anti-aircraft guns blasted away, and the blacked-out docks became silhouetted under the beams of searchlights. The pair had embarked upon what was arguably the most important technical mission ever to leave British shores for, without a new source of ships, the nation was lost, a fact being graphically underlined by the mayhem they watched as the ship crept silently seaward.

The 16kt *Scythia* made what was called an independent voyage across the North Atlantic. This was in line with the Admiralty policy, based on the maximum surface speed of U-boats, that any ship capable of 15kts should not sail in convoy. That is not to say *Scythia* was entirely on her own, as for parts of the crossing she sailed in company with other 'fast' ships, and there was sometimes a British destroyer lurking in the vicinity. Cyril got a taste of the war at sea on 26 September when depth charges were heard going off in the distance and when later the ship sailed through a patch of oil and wreckage. On the following day the ship passed an eastbound convoy. Following that, the weather became so bad the ship had to heave to for a spell. The ship finally arrived at New York on 3 October 1940.[6]

---

6. See letter from Cyril Thompson to the Admiralty in MT9/3533, PRO.

CHAPTER 2

The British Shipbuilding Mission to the United States

It was mid-December, it was bitterly cold, and the sea was rough. Four lifeboats, each with a sea-anchor streamed to help keep its bow heading into the weather, were striving to keep in sight of each other. In No.2 boat some of the survivors were pulling at the oars whilst others went about the business of bailing out the water that kept slopping in over the gunwales. One of the rowers, a youngish man of large build, was not a sailor although he had once briefly served as a ship's engineer. It was Cyril Thompson, who had been on his way back to England from the United States in the ship that had just been torpedoed and sunk. He kept glancing down, for between his feet and for the most part under the water in the bilge, was his black briefcase. As he pulled at his oar, two thoughts of somewhat conflicting nature kept running through his mind. If the U-boat that had been sighted on the surface a short while ago came back, the briefcase would have to go overboard. On the other hand, he prayed that the case was watertight for there was no way he could keep it dry. He was only too aware of the importance of the documents in the case, documents that might in the long run mean the saving of Britain. In the knowledge that the nearest land lay over 200 miles away, Cyril pulled even harder.

Cyril Thompson and Harry Hunter had scarcely set foot ashore in New York when they were plunged into a flurry of activity. They were whisked away to the headquarters of the British Purchasing Commission (BPC), an arm of Britain's Ministry of Supply (MoS). There, at 15 Broad Street, they met with Sir (later Lord) Walter Layton, Director-General of Programmes, MoS, who was on a visit to the United States, and Arthur Purvis (later to be knighted), the Canadian head of BPC. Cyril and Harry were given advice and briefing notes on the best way to handle the Americans they were soon to meet. The most important of the briefing notes concerned Admiral Land, Head of the United States Maritime Commission, and his deputy, Commander Vickery. Cyril was told that despite preparatory lobbying on Britain's behalf carried out with the Commission by the American Ambassador in London, Joseph Kennedy, and Harvey Klemmer, Kennedy's Special Attaché, both of whom had previ-

ously been associated with the Commission, it was of paramount importance that he make a good first impression.

After that Thompson and Hunter got their heads together with three
Britons already in the United States who were to make up the numbers
of the British Shipbuilding Mission. They were Richard Powell, William
Bennett and John Heck. Richard (now Sir Richard) Powell was to provide the main continuity in the Mission's staff, from its inception right
through to the end of its remit in late 1943. Whilst the others left the Mission at various times and for various reasons, he stayed on. If it can be
said that the other members provided the technical know-how and drive,
it was Richard Powell who provided the vitally important administrative
and advisory functions. He was also the main link with British officialdom. A small, slim man, he was born in 1909 and was therefore two years
younger even than Cyril Thompson. He had entered the British Civil
Service in 1931 after gaining a degree at Cambridge. By 1934 he was Private Secretary to the First Lord of the Admiralty, a post he was to hold
for three years. Soon after the war began in September 1939, he worked
under Sir James Lithgow, the man behind Cyril Thompson's appointment. In July 1940 he was sent to Ottawa as secretary to the Admiralty
Technical Mission stationed there. On the arrival of Cyril Thompson in
North America, Powell was given the additional responsibility of acting
as permanent secretary to the British Shipbuilding Mission.[1] The only
surviving member of the team, he confirms that the Admiralty could not
have chosen a better man than Cyril Thompson to lead the Mission. He
regards Cyril as the father of the Liberty ship and says 'he was a man of
considerable energy and drive.' Sir Richard has but one criticism of him.
'Cyril was', he says, ' typical of the North-east shipbuilders of the day,
with old-fashioned views on the master/man relationship. He was the
boss and he made sure everyone knew it.' Richard also got on very well
with Harry Hunter despite the difference in their ages. Hunter, who was
to spend much longer in America on Mission business than Cyril
Thompson, was something of an art fancier, and so was Richard. The pair
often spent the odd spare hour or so at the Institute of Modern Art in
New York, the city that housed the Mission's base. 'Harry', says Richard,
'was a very nice man indeed.'

William Bennett, fifty-two years old at the time, was the Principal
Surveyor for Lloyd's Register in the United States and Canada, and John

---

1. Sir Richard Royle Powell (b.1909). In 1944 he made a brief return to Britain. Because of
his American experience he was then appointed Civil Advisor to the Commander-in-Chief,
British Pacific Fleet which was operating alongside, but very much a junior partner to, the
US Pacific Fleet. Back in Britain after the war he took up several senior Civil Service
appointments. He was knighted in 1961 and rose to be Permanent Secretary of the Board of
Trade. He retired from the Civil Service in 1968, thereafter holding several directorships in
commercial companies.

Heck, sixty-one, was Principal Engineer Surveyor for Lloyd's at New York. Richard Powell describes both of them as being 'very technical men'. They were available for consultation on technical matters when called upon but for the most part carried on with their functions for Lloyd's.[2]

The basic groundwork completed, on the day after his arrival in the States Cyril Thompson and his team flew to Washington and that night he and Powell dined with Lord Lothian at the British Embassy. Then, on Saturday 5 October, came the vital first meeting with Admiral Land. As head of the United States Maritime Commission, Land could make or break the British venture; without his blessing the project would at best be a lame duck, and probably a dead one. Amongst those present on the American side at that first meeting was the Commission's vice-chairman, Commander Howard Vickery USN.

The United States Maritime Commission had been created by the Merchant Marine Act enacted by President Roosevelt in 1936 as part of his New Deal. The Act itself was born out of the necessity to upgrade the American Merchant Marine of which, by 1936, over 90 per cent of its ships were twenty years old or more. In the national interest the Commission was given regulatory powers over the shipping industry with the authority to either award grants for new ships, or to contract for new ships itself and thereafter charter them out to U.S. shipping interests. Its first chairman was Joseph P. Kennedy, father of the future president, but he had left in 1937 to become, in the following year, ambassador to the United Kingdom. Kennedy's place was taken by an old friend of President Roosevelt's from his Secretary of the Navy days (between 1913 and 1921), the then Rear-Admiral Emory Scott Land. In fact Land was a very good friend; it was said that if you had been 'for' Roosevelt before 1932 when he made his successful bid for the Presidency, you were in, and Land went back a lot earlier than that.

Land was not a tall man, and in the early 1940s wore his light-coloured hair in a brushed-back quiff. After gaining considerable distinction both academically and on the sports fields at Annapolis, the US Navy's equivalent to the Royal Navy's Dartmouth College, he had spent most of his career in naval shipbuilding. Unlike certain of his contemporaries in the US Navy, Land was not an anglophobe; in fact, he had got to quite like the British during a spell as Naval Attaché in London in the rank of commander during the early 1920s. In 1937, in order to take up the post with the Commission, he took early retirement from the navy. By that time he

---

2. William Bennett OBE (1888-*c*1970). Naval architect. In 1944 Bennett received a special grant of $2,500 from the Admiralty for his work with the British Mission. Awarded OBE in New Year's Honours List 1950. He retired from Lloyd's Register in 1953. John Shaw Heck (1879-1952). Served as a ship's engineer during the early part of his career and gained 1st Class Certificate. In 1944 awarded $1,000 for his work with the British Mission. He retired from Lloyd's in 1945.

was an old Washington hand, having over the years built up many contacts in both the executive and legislative branches of government. If anyone knew his way around the corridors of power – perhaps 'channels' of
power would be a more appropriate phrase for someone who dealt
almost solely in marine matters – then that man was Jerry Land as he was
called by his friends. The Commission's official historian, Frederic Lane,
has recorded that Land made several impressive performances as a witness before congressional committees, 'where his footwork was just as
agile as it had been on the football field'. Lane also wrote that the
Admiral was prone to utter rather salty phrases.[3]

Admiral Land certainly had the gift of the gab and knew how to hold
an audience. Sometimes he came up with an apposite ditty, as in an
address he gave at San Francisco on the occasion of National Maritime
Day on 22 May 1943.

> God gave us two ends to use.
> One to think with!
> One to sit with!
> The war depends on which we choose.
> Heads we win!
> Tails we lose!

That piece may not have scanned properly but it certainly went down
well with his hugely patriotic audience. On a later occasion, when on the
receiving end of criticism over the prices being paid for ships, he replied,
'If you want fast ships, fast shipbuilding, fast women or fast horses, you
pay through the nose for them'.

Commander (later Rear-Admiral) Howard Vickery, was a tough-
looking, pipe-smoking man of average height, stockily built with a neck
that gave the impression of being too short for his height. He looked a bit
like the depiction of John Bull as a bulldog, an attribute he shared with
Winston Churchill. Like his chief, Vickery had risen through the Construction and Repair Bureau of the US Navy. Also like his chief, he was
a veritable glutton for work, so much so that it was eventually to under-
mine his health and he was to die an early death in 1946. As the months
passed and Land became more and more occupied with policy making
and lobbying in Washington, it was Vickery who took on most of the
practical tasks of the Commission. Land was an excellent negotiator
whilst Vickery was at his best as a motivator if of the rather hard-nut
variety. After dispensing compliments for work well done, Vickery
would as likely as not add a rider indicating that he would make
considerable trouble for the recipients of the compliments should the

---

3. Frederic Lane, *Ships for Victory: a History of Shipbuilding under the U.S. Maritime
Commission* (Baltimore 1951).

good work not be maintained. So frequent were riders of this sort that they gained a name, being called 'Vickery needles'. The Land-Vickery combination can be likened to the 'good-cop, bad-cop' act, and was one which served America and the Allied cause very well indeed.[4] Sir Richard Powell, who attended meetings with both admirals on several occasions, says they were great friends to Britain. He holds especially good memories of Vickery, who was 'always most helpful'. (It is of interest to note, for it indicates President Roosevelt's close interest in shipping matters, that Harry Hopkins, special advisor to the President, attended some of these meetings, but Powell cannot now recall the exact dates.)

These then were the two men who Cyril Thompson and his team had most to impress if Britain was to get the new ships it needed. But the Mission had not arrived at a good time. Most American shipyards were working flat-out on new naval tonnage, with the remaining capacity being taken up by orders for commercial ships from Admiral Land's Commission. Furthermore, Land was under fire from certain quarters for not having yet done enough to improve the American shipping situation. These attacks on Land's policies were well summed up in a *Shipping World* article dated 21 August 1940. Under the sub-heading 'Admiral Land's Task', the author of the piece said,

> . . . It has been the chief weakness of all the activities of the Maritime Commission that it has shown insufficient appreciation of the fact that the capacity of the shipyards was the principal problem confronting it from the very beginning. Some firms, such as the Bethlehem Steel Company [Baltimore], have extended their yards or reconditioned old building ways, but present needs call for very much more than this.
>
> Owing to the cycle created by the vast building programme of the last war, every section of the American mercantile marine is suddenly

---

4. That is not to say that Admiral Land could not be a hard man himself on occasion. His close relationship with President Roosevelt is evidenced by the fact that he was one of the American representatives at the Quebec Conference held between Roosevelt and Churchill in September 1944, and one of the stances Land took at that conference illustrates the tougher side of his character. During that conference, the long-serving (since 1934) US Treasury Secretary Henry Morgenthau Jnr. outlined his proposal to 'pastoralize' post-war Germany by totally obliterating its industrial base; in effect turning Germany into one huge agricultural community. Cordell Hull, US Secretary of State, was opposed to the plan, later writing that it 'would wipe out everything in Germany except land . . . and 40 percent [of the German population] would die [as a result]'. Churchill was at first opposed to the Morgenthau Plan, calling it 'unnatural, unchristian and unnecessary'. According to Harry Dexter White, Morgenthau's assistant, Admiral Land was all for the plan, and thumped the conference table with his fist whilst making his supporting remarks. Churchill, despite the resistance of Foreign Secretary Anthony Eden, was eventually talked round to initialling a document in support of the scheme. (Churchill may have been influenced by the proposal, also placed on the table by Morgenthau at that conference, that a total of $6.5 billion of American aid be made available to Britain.) A few days later, however, details of the pastoralization plan leaked out, and so widespread was American public condemnation of it, that it was consigned to the rubbish bin.

in desperate need of replacement, at a time when a 70 per cent increase in the Navy is demanded. In the new world situation the Americans are being forced to look to their defence rather than their bank balances, with the result that part of the plans for the mercantile marine may have to be abandoned.

It was against that background that the British Shipbuilding Mission's first meeting with Land took place. Cyril was impressed with Land's attitude, noting in his report that, 'Admiral Land said that the Maritime Commission was anxious to be as helpful as possible'. However, talking positively and being able act positively are two very different things. Land went on to point out that most of the present shipbuilding capacity in the United States was already taken up with orders for naval ships and by others from his own commission, exactly as the author of that *Shipping World* article had indicated. According to Cyril, Admiral Land then went on to say that 'The Mission would be completely free to conduct negotiations with U.S. shipbuilding firms, but that when definite proposals had been formulated, they would need to be submitted to the U.S. Government through the usual channels, and U.S. Government clearance obtained', which was a diplomatic way of saying that British orders would not receive preference over American orders.

Land went on to give some typical costs of building merchant ships in the States and then added ominously, 'If capital expenditure [he meant the construction of new yards] is required to carry out the British Mission's shipbuilding programme, the British Government would probably have to meet it'. To the British party those words were bad news indeed. A paragraph in the mission's terms of reference had covered this possibility, but it had been hoped that the Americans would take the view that any such new yards would be considered part of their own defence measures and that the US Reconstruction Finance Corporation would foot that part of the overall bill.

Unbeknownst to Admiral Land, the entire project to purchase sixty ships in the States had already been subjected to severe scrutiny and strong criticism from Britain's Chancellor of the Exchequer. The views of the Chancellor, Sir Kingsley Wood, were summed up in an official memo he signed on 7 September 1940, two weeks prior to Cyril Thompson sailing from England.

> . . . though I do not wish to contest the necessity of increasing our mercantile shipping resources on the scale proposed, I am not satisfied that it is necessary to place so large a contract as this in America at once.

He went on,

> This is for me a serious addition to the burden of $ expenditure. . . . [the ships] if built in the U.S. will cost at least twice as much as ships built

here, even allowing for the cost of American steel in both cases. [My department is] not satisfied that it is not possible to obtain a substantial part of the increased tonnage now in question by additional building at home.[5]

The Admiralty, being more practical than the Treasury and not quite so interested in either the bottom line or in the depletion of British dollar reserves, had pointed out that building more merchant ships in British yards would only be possible at the expense of part of the naval building programme. (Which, of course, was exactly the same problem under which the Americans were labouring.) At a meeting of a sub-committee of the British Cabinet, the Admiralty view prevailed, with the result that on arrival at New York, Cyril Thompson delivered a letter dated 16 September from the Admiralty to Sir Walter Layton in which the following appeared:

> ... the Chancellor of the Exchequer has agreed with the First Lord that our efforts to obtain the construction of new ships in the U.S.A. can proceed to the extent of ten million Pounds expenditure, the sum to be expended in the next six months limited to five million Pounds.

Cyril came away from that first meeting with Admiral Land in the knowledge that it was extremely unlikely he would be able to keep within the Chancellor's financial parameters especially if Britain was going to have to pay the cost for constructing new shipyards. Although some of the signs emanating from that first meeting did not auger well, Cyril was not about to be put off by them for he was made of sterner stuff than that. He concluded that the only way to find out for himself whether it would be possible to make any kind of deal in the States would be to travel around and find out.

Accordingly, after several preparatory meetings with top executives in the US shipbuilding community, and a meeting with Treasury officials, he set out on 8 October with Harry Hunter and Richard Powell on what was to be an extraordinary three weeks' tour of every American shipyard, one that for good measure took in visits to all the yards over the Canadian border as well. On top of that the team visited many of the North American marine engineering works and, as if all that was not enough, visited a number of possible sites for new shipbuilding yards. By the end of that period the Mission had travelled some 17,000 miles, mainly in a chartered Dakota aircraft, had visited thirty-five shipyards and a large number of engineering works and, in Cyril's own words, 'had also surveyed innumerable mud-fields and stretches of coast where shipyards might be built'. As leader of the party, a fact which he tended

---

5. MT9/3368, PRO, Kew.

not to let the others forget, he kept up a phenomenally fast pace. When asked during a post-war interview how he and his team had managed to fit in so much in such short a time, Cyril replied, 'Our method was to work away by day, interviewing shipbuilders and engineers and surveying sites in one particular area. Then we would fly by night to the next stop, sleeping on the journey. We never lost any odd hours that way.'

During their time in Canada Cyril and his companions met with C.D. Howe, the Canadian Minister of Munitions and Supply, and his Director of Shipbuilding, D.B. Carswell. The possibility of building ships, over and above those already being built in that country, were explored, for there was some spare capacity in Canadian yards though far from enough to satisfy the present British needs. The Dominion laboured under some special difficulties; there was concern over the country's ability to manufacture ship engines and there was a general shortage of materials. The main problem, however, was a geographical one; the shipyards were so far north that those in Eastern Canada had to contend with severe ice conditions in winter. Compared with the States however, the signals coming out of Canada were positive and encouraging. To Cyril it was clear that his Mission must concentrate its persuasive efforts in the United States. By that time it had also become clear that there were no American ship designs suitable for Britain's requirements; the designs that did exist were for much more sophisticated ships.

On 29 October Cyril sent a message to London summing up the results of his travels. He added,

> . . . no large existing yards in United States can undertake work for us. [But] Todd Shipyard Corporation has been practically allocated to us by Maritime Commission . . . provided we act quickly.

During his many meetings with American shipbuilders Cyril found himself confronted with what he later described as a 'psychological barrier'. Britain and its Empire was at that time fighting the Axis alone, for Germany's attack on Russia was still several months off. Night after night British cities were being subjected to heavy air raids. Many survivors from British ships were being landed in the Americas, some with horrific stories to tell. In consequence, American newspapers and wireless broadcasts were filled with stories of German bombs raining down on a beleaguered country, and of ship after ship being sunk. 'The general opinion in the States among all classes, even among very high officials and officers' Cyril said, 'was that Britain was on her last legs.' It was therefore hardly surprising that American businessmen in general were none too anxious to have much to do with the Mission and were also writing Britain off. 'We got the impression that they thought they were being invited to back a losing cause', Cyril added.

At first the only positive reactions he received in the States were from people out to make a fast buck and from companies not considered capable of producing the goods. On 4 November he received a memo from Arthur Purvis, Head of BPC, passing on a warning received from Gordon Rentschler, chairman of the First National Bank, a man who had assisted BPC on several other occasions. It warned that 'we might find ourselves receiving offers from people unable to carry out their proposals'.[6] Then, suddenly, the negative nature of the environment in which the Mission members found themselves working changed for the better. According to Cyril Thompson the catalyst for that change came in the person of Henry J. Kaiser, head of a group of West Coast companies working in conjunction with the Bath Iron Works at Maine and with the Todd Corporation, the latter an established shipbuilding firm and the one that Admiral Land had 'practically allocated' to the British. 'It was clear from the start,' stated Cyril, 'that Kaiser was ready and anxious to get our orders.' Cyril's words conflict somewhat with the rather brief description of the negotiations with the British presented by Bradford Mitchell in his official history of the Todd Shipyard Corporation. Mitchell states that the American trio of companies took the strong line that they wanted the entire British order or nothing. That statement does not fit comfortably with Admiral Land's 'allocation' of Todd to the British. It also seems strange that the Todd history makes no mention of Cyril Thompson by name yet suggests that it was Todd executive Joseph Haag Jnr who was the prime negotiator with the British over the contract. There is no doubt that Haag, who in 1953 was to become President of the Todd Corporation, was involved in some of the negotiations, but there is also no doubt about who Cyril Thompson thought was the main man. Kaiser is mentioned several times in Cyril's diary, and was mentioned several times by him in interviews concerning his Mission after the war; in comparison, Joseph Haag got no mention at all.[7]

Cyril's first meeting with Kaiser had been on 23 October at Portland, Oregon when Kaiser escorted him around various sites and works. However, it was not until he met the man again, this time at the Kaiser head office in Oakland, California, when matters really began to take off. In 1940 Henry John Kaiser was fifty-eight years old. Although now plump and bald-headed he was still very much the ball of fire he had always been. He had started out owning a photographer's shop but then had gone into the 'sand and gravel business', as he called it. Later he headed a highway construction company, building roads in Cuba and British Columbia as well as in various parts of the United States. In 1931 he directed the consortium known as Six Companies Incorporated which

6. AVIA38/117, PRO, Kew.
7. C. Bradford Mitchell, *Every Kind of Shipwork* (New York 1981).

had successfully bid to build the Boulder Dam in Colorado, and after that, two more giant dams; in the process he had constructed the longest conveyor belt ever built. Over the years Six Companies had developed a bidding procedure by which one of the participant companies would take the lead position, the others coming in for smaller shares of the work. In 1936 Kaiser's was the lead company in the contract to construct the San Francisco-Oakland Bay Bridge. Kaiser was not a skilled engineer nor was he an expert on finance, but he possessed a combination of talents that made him an out-of-the-ordinary innovator, and what he did not know about production line techniques and pre-fabrication methods was not worth knowing. He thrived on solving problems which, as he once famously said, were 'only opportunities in work clothes'. His motto was reputed to be, 'never be afraid to do things in a new way'. To sum up, Henry Kaiser was a man with the ability to make things happen; he typified the American can-do spirit and held the strong belief that anything was possible providing enough men were put to the task. Perhaps Kaiser's character is best summed up by a story, probably apocryphal, but one attributed to his son. It goes something like this. A few weeks before one of his boyhood Christmases, the son was asked by his mother what he wanted as a present, to which he replied, 'a little sister'. 'Sorry, son', said Mrs. Henry Kaiser, 'little sisters take a lot longer than a few weeks to make.' 'But Mom', replied the lad, 'I know you can do it. Pop says if you put enough men on the job, anything is possible.'[8]

Although it took place nearly sixty years ago, Sir Richard Powell still vividly recalls that second meeting with Henry Kaiser, held at the Kaiser offices in Oakland. 'It was broad daylight outside but when we were ushered into the great man's office, it was pitch dark in there except for a small spot-light illuminating the white blotter on his desk. He didn't have an eye-complaint. It was all done for effect. Pure theatre.'[9] In the opinion of many of those who worked with Henry Kaiser or had dealings of any sort with him, the man's principal fault was an exceptionally strong predilection for publicity and self-aggrandisement. In his autobiography Admiral Land had this to say about Kaiser:

> I would be the last one to sell Henry Kaiser short. He built more [ships] than any other constructor and if his public relations department worked overtime, so did the boss. His telephone calls were

8. Henry John Kaiser (1882-1967). b. Canajoharie, New York. A man with fingers in many pies. He had once, before the United States entered the Second World War, unsuccessfully tried to combine with Howard Hughes in the production of warplanes. After the war he joined with Joseph Frazer in automobile manufacturing, the Kaiser-Frazer Corporation becoming for a time one of the largest concerns in that industry. He founded Kaiser Steel and the Kaiser Aluminium & Chemical Company.
9. Information from Sir Richard Powell during an interview with the author in November 1999, and in telephone conversations.

legion, his trips to Washington so numerous that it was easy to believe he slept only four hours out of every 24. However, I was not one of those who subscribed to the myth that Kaiser could work miracles, and I know at first hand that, thanks to good press relations, he received credit that was not due to him.[10]

But all that was in the future. Cyril's main concern at the time was over Kaiser's shipbuilding experience, which was not much. Kaiser, together with the group of civil engineering contractors known collectively as Six Services Incorporated, had recently entered into an association with Todd Shipyards to build and operate the Seattle-Tacoma Shipyard, a small operation with, at that time, limited berthage and which was already fully engaged in building American ships. Although Todd was an established shipbuilding firm, it was small compared with some of the others in the industry, and his association with them at Tacoma was the sum total of Kaiser's shipbuilding experience.

Nevertheless, Cyril was struck by Kaiser's enthusiasm and drive. 'Give me the backing,' Kaiser proclaimed, 'and I'll build you 200 ships during 1942.' It was an attitude that greatly impressed. 'On top of that,' Harry Hunter said after the war, 'Lend-Lease had not yet started and we had to pay spot-cash for everything. Even for only sixty ships, that represented a very large sum of money indeed. Also, as there were no shipyards available, we would have to pay for the construction of those, too.' And civil engineering works were of course, right up Kaiser's street. An important additional consideration was of course, that the Todd Shipyard Corporation would be involved.

Cyril Thompson and his team had visited the Kaiser-Todd facility at Seattle during their journeying and had been impressed with what they had seen. Now they sought confirmation from the Maritime Commission that the two ships so far built at the yard had been well-constructed. The Commission's reply indicated that the ships had been constructed satisfactorily, and reported that Kaiser and his associates had built part of the yard *and* the two ships in under eleven months. It was that which swung it; Britain needed the sixty ships as soon as possible and if it was going to have to pay for constructing the facilities required to build them, then obviously it would be a good thing to award the contract to someone with a track record for doing that quickly. Subject to United States Government approval, which in effect meant getting Admiral Land's blessing, and also subject to getting Land's agreement over where the new yards would be constructed, a provisional agreement was struck with the Kaiser-Todd-Bath Iron Works consortium on the basis of the plans of Hull No. 607 which Cyril had brought with him. Throughout early

---

10. Emory Scott Land, *Winning the War with Ships* (New York 1958).

November Cyril worked on those plans with people from the Todd organisation, making the changes necessary to fit in with American ship-building practice. On 7 November, Gibbs & Cox, a firm of New York naval architects, were engaged to assist in this despite Cyril's initial reservations over the move, reservations the reason for which he apparently never fully explained.

A decision of great importance had to be made about the method of constructing the ships. Cyril asked London whether there was any objection to the sixty ships being welded and not riveted as in the original specifications of the British ship. Welding was already being used on a fairly wide scale in American yards, not only because it produced faster results, but also because there was a shortage of trained riveters in the country. The problem with welded ships from the British standpoint was that there was not much in the way of experience with ships constructed that way. Furthermore, if there were weaknesses with such ships as some experts thought, then those weaknesses might be aggravated under wartime conditions when ships were sometimes called upon to carry unusually heavy deck loads. Even in Britain welded ships were not new. The first all-welded British ship, the *Fullagar*, had been built by Cammell Laird in 1920, and there had been no problems with her. On the other hand, the all-welded *Joseph Medill* built by Swan Hunter on the Tyne had disappeared with all hands on her maiden voyage in August 1937. A subsequent Official Inquiry held that she had probably struck an iceberg, though some authorities, including the Admiralty, tended to associate her loss with the method of construction. The loss of that ship had turned most British shipbuilders away from the 'new-fangled' technique of welding. Notwithstanding that, Cyril Thompson was convinced that to get the ships fast, and from America where there was a shortage of skilled riveters, welding was the only option, for welders could be trained much more quickly. Furthermore, the technique saved on total steel weight, a not unimportant detail; for each ship of the size of those being planned, the weight-saving was of the order of 200 tons.

London's reply came back to the effect that provided Cyril was convinced that the contractor would carry out good work, then there was no objection to welding. That, however, was not an indication that British concern over welding had diminished. On 13 November 1940, J.P. Mackay of the Ministry of Shipping, told the Chairman of Lloyd's in London, Sir Vernon Thomson, that the organisation's surveyors in America must exercise strict supervision over the welding practices to be used. Cyril had got his way, but it was not to be too long before the practice of welding was to come under the gravest scrutiny and suspicion. (The sixty ships were not in fact to be entirely welded. The ships' side frames – 'ribs' to the layman – were riveted to the shell plating; this involved comparatively few rivets and the ships were always referred to as being welded.)

Another decision taken was over the type of engine to be used. Because a British design of ship was now to be followed, it was natural that given the availability of coal in Britain and that the experience of most British marine engineers lay with steam engines associated with Scotch boilers, that the engine type should follow a British design as well. Despite the fact that such propulsion units were considered very old-hat in America, it was decided to fit the ships with a 'traditional' type of triple expansion engine manufactured to a design of Harry Hunter's company, North-Eastern Marine Engineering. The General Machinery Corporation of Hamilton, Ohio, was brought into the deal as the main contractor to build them. As it had been some years since engines anywhere resembling this type had been constructed in America, the eighty original British working plans for the various engine parts had to be amplified into about 350 for General Machinery. (A contributory factor behind the decision to go for this style of engine was the slow production of turbine engines in America.) These 'old-hat' engines, each weighing 118 tons, were to be built in awesome numbers, for as we shall see they were used not only to power the sixty ships of the British order, but also all the American-built Liberty ships and the Canadian-built Fort and Park boats yet to come. One writer has estimated that 3259 of these massive engines were manufactured in North America during the war, and he made no attempt to estimate the numbers of the same engines manufactured in Britain which would have raised the figure even higher. The largest of all the engine producers turned out to be the Joshua Hendy Iron works at Sunnyvale, California. (The founder of that company was to have a Liberty ship named after him.) The company built almost 700 of them including those built under a contract it took over from the Iron Fireman Manufacturing Company when that company's factory at Portland, Oregon was burnt down in a huge fire in early February 1944.

In order to obtain official approval for the ships, the engines, and for the construction of the yards, the ball was started rolling with the submission by the British Purchasing Commission of what was called an RPN, or 'Report On Preliminary Purchase Negotiation'. (An RPN was required for anything purchased in the States whose total value exceeded $150,000.) On 13 November an RPN was presented in the usual way to the President's Liaison Committee of the U.S. Treasury Department, accompanied by a covering letter stating that, 'Admiral Land's principal assistant . . . Commander Vickery, is fully aware of the proposals . . . and fully approves of the general scheme. We understand that Admiral Land . . . is also of the same opinion.'[11]

When one considers the magnitude of the purchase, far and away the largest Britain ever made in the United States under the system, the infor-

---

11. AVIA 38/117, PRO, Kew.

mation contained in the RPN was exceedingly brief; but it was to the point. It identified the intended purchase as sixty cargo vessels of approximately 10,000 tons deadweight each. It gave as the estimated total value of the deal, the sum of $96m (£24m at 1940 exchange rates), a figure that included $9m for two 'new shipyards to be built in localities to be approved by the U.S. Maritime Commission'. The named supplier was given as the Todd Shipyard Corporation, in conformity with the convention that with only one supplier being named, all official correspondence, permissions, etc., could be channelled through them.

Suddenly, and completely out of the blue as far as Cyril was concerned, the Admiralty decided to change all the specifications of the ships being ordered. Cyril's diary entry for 16 November reads, 'Cable from London changing size of all ships. Oh Hell.' This was the point at which the *Empire Liberty* plans entered the story, for the changes were in fact to those of the specifications of Thompson's Hull No. 611, the ship that some months later was to be called *Empire Liberty*. Cyril's diary gives no explanation for these late changes, nor has any explanation been found in official British files. Perhaps the Admiralty was impressed with the plans for Hull No. 611, newly completed at the Thompson drawing office, and the ship being slightly larger than Hull No. 607 could carry more cargo at a time when every ton getting through to Britain was of vital importance. Whatever the reason, Cyril had to spend all of the following day, and parts of several days afterwards, in as he says, 'correcting Plans and Specifications to new size ship'. Those entries in Cyril's diary, a document written contemporaneously and which has not previously been made available outside the family, are quite clear on this point. He had to spend several days upgrading all the specifications to those of this new vessel. It was Cyril himself who was later responsible for confusing the issue. In a lecture called *The British Merchant Shipbuilding Programme in North America 1940-1942* which he and Harry Hunter presented post-war before the North East Coast Institution of Engineeers and Shipbuilders in Newcastle, no mention was made of Hull 607 or of *Empire Wave*, only of the *Empire Liberty*. This omission is completely understandable. Lectures have usually to be kept within certain prescribed lengths and so many 'minor' details have to be left out. Furthermore, both Cyril and Harry were involved in that presentation, but Harry had not been directly involved in the days of specification changes in 1941, so in deference to his friend perhaps Cyril decided that this detail was not worth the mention. And anyway, was not the most important thing that it was indeed the plans of the *Empire Liberty* that came to be used as the basis of the largest shipbuilding programme the world has ever seen? However, in consequence of that Eleventh Andrew Laing Lecture, all previous writers on the subject of the birth of the Liberty ship have included a phrase such as 'the plans Cyril Thompson took with him to the States, were those of the *Empire Liberty*'. That has been shown here to be incorrect.

The changes in ship specification did not, of course, affect the permission required for building the yards. The original Kaiser-Todd-Bath plan called for building three new shipyards, one each at Portland (Maine), Richmond (California) and at Mobile (Texas). Despite the length of the US coast line, the choice of sites was restricted, for they had to be within short travelling distance of large conurbations with a potential workforce to tap into, be adjacent to deep-water channels, and have good inland transport connections.

When outline permission was received at the end of November, only the building of the first two yards had been approved. On 1 December, Richard Powell cabled London with the news that the US Government had given its blessing to the construction of two new facilities, each of which would build thirty ships. Powell added that the payment terms for the combined construction of the yards and ships was 'for an initial payment of $2,800,000, and further payments of the same amount each month for the first three months, thereafter increasing to a maximum of $5,200,000 between the tenth and fifteenth months of the contact, and thereafter falling'. That meant that the cost of each ship, including a proportion of the capital cost of the yards, worked out at $1.6m (£400,000). Powell asked for an immediate reply to his cable but had little hope of getting it because of the size of the sums of money involved. He ended the cable with, 'Thompson leaves for England in the middle of the month'. The message was considered of such importance that it was sent by secret RAF cipher.

Cyril Thompson's primary task was over; a provisional deal had been struck with potential suppliers and it had received the approval of the United States Government. But the proposed deal made mockery of the Chancellor of the Exchequer's directive regarding overall expenditure for he had instructed that a maximum of £10m or $40m was to be spent, and the draft contract, still unsigned, called for considerably more than twice that sum. Furthermore, about ten per cent of the overall figure was for the construction costs of the yards, a contingency the British had hoped to avoid. Although London had been kept in the picture throughout, there was a lot of explaining to do back in Britain, and Cyril was the best one to do it.

Cyril did not wait for the middle of the month. On 6 December, the draft contract documents and the background material that he would need to argue his case with safely packed in his briefcase, he boarded the passenger cargo liner *Western Prince* at New York. This Prince Line vessel, with a crew of 108 commanded by Captain Reid, sailed that evening, and as a 'fast' ship, travelled independently. There were sixty-one passengers on board including several women and children. Cyril was not the only VIP amongst them, nor was he the only one on urgent shipping business. A fellow passenger was C.D. Howe, the Canadian Minister of Supply who Cyril had met during his marathon travels, and who was making the dangerous trip to Britain to finalise details for building additional ships in Canada.

The ship was on a zigzag course and some 250 miles south of Iceland when at 0640 hours on the 14th she was struck by a torpedo. In his subsequent report Chief Officer E.P. Ellis said that the missile hit the ship forward of the bridge on the port side. He went on, 'There was a terrific explosion more like that of a bomb, but no fire. An immense column of water shot up almost drowning us on the bridge. The ship shuddered violently and started to go down by the head.'[12] Captain Reid ordered everyone to muster at lifeboat stations and for the boats to be swung out and lowered to deck level to await his order to abandon ship. Ellis says, 'Then the Captain called me to clear the ship and to wait [close alongside] for him, but he was now of the opinion she would not sink; I did not agree with him.' By the time Ellis got back to his boat, No. 2, it was already in the water so instead he boarded No. 3 which was under the charge of the Fourth Officer. He says that the boat was about 250ft from the ship, and had stopped to await the captain, when the submarine surfaced about 60ft away. The U-boat (it was *U-96*, commanded by Kovettenkapitan Lehmann-Willenbrock who was going through a purple patch, *Western Prince* being one of his five victims around that time totalling more than 37,000 tons) made no attempt to communicate. But, reported Ellis, 'some people in my boat said that the submarine had taken flash-light photographs'. He went on, 'forty-nine minutes after the first torpedo struck, there was a second terrific explosion, and within 30 seconds, the ship had disappeared.'

After the lifeboats cleared the ship two of the crew were still on board in addition to Captain Reid. They were Second Officer R.F. White and Steward Thomas Franks. The latter, according to C.D. Howe, had suddenly remembered that the ship's Spitfire Fund collection was in the ship's safe and had gone looking for it. Franks was never seen again. White reported later that 'up to within a few minutes of the second explosion, the Captain did quite confidently believe that she would not sink'. He went on to say that he had gone to the chartroom to fetch his sextant and,

> was half way down the bridge ladder when the second explosion came. It appeared to be in the engine-room. There was a sheet of flame. The whistle started to blow and continued to do so, for it was jammed. The ship heeled to 45 – 50 degrees and within 30 seconds sank by the head.

12. ADM199/2135, PRO, Kew

I was taken down with the ship and seemed to be under a very long time. When I came to the surface I found myself amongst wreckage. I picked out a heavy plank and hung on. I saw the U-boat only 30 feet away, then she steamed off. I think the Captain must have been killed by the second explosion . . .

Cyril Thompson was asleep in his cabin when the torpedo struck. This is how he described his experiences.

The vessel shuddered and seemed to stop. I threw on more clothes, grabbed my dispatch-case in which were the Mission's documents, and rushed up on deck. I found the lifeboats were being cleared. The ship was already dangerously low in the water but I thought she would stay afloat for a few more minutes. I scrambled into one of the lifeboats. [It was No 2, the one Chief Officer Ellis had missed.] As the vessel slid beneath the heaving swell, there came two blasts from her whistle. We were alone in a waste of sea that was dark grey and menacing. Most of the passengers and crew were saved, but the prospects did not look too bright for us.

A heavy sea was running and there was a cutting Arctic wind. The temperature was below freezing. Next to me on the thwart was a Manchester banker. Others among the survivors was the [Lieutenant] Governor of British Columbia [Eric Hambler], James Bone a well-known Fleet Street journalist, and next to me on the thwart, C. D. Howe. Up to another thirty people were huddled in the bottom, and the spray froze as it hit them.

For nine hours Cyril kept pulling at his oar and, at the same time, according to reports of other survivors, doing his best to keep up the confidence of the others. Here is Cyril again.

It was now growing darker, and the other boats were hardly distinguishable as they pitched in the troughs. Actually, things might have been worse, for we found out later that we were in the relative calm centre of a storm zone – it would have been worse a few miles away.

Suddenly, just as the survivors in the boats were resigning themselves to spending a dreadful night in the boat, a freighter was sighted and flares were sent up. The ship turned out to be the British *Baron Kinnaird* (H. Hogarth & Sons). Chief Officer Ellis in No. 3 boat, who described the weather as 'rather bad with a very heavy swell which necessitated the use of a sea anchor', was infinitely relieved to see the ship, but unfortunately, the horrors of that day were not yet over for him and the other survivors.

She made a lee for us and poured oil to calm the sea. We managed to get alongside and I got my passengers on board. Then the motor boat came alongside but she caught the discharge from the steamer, and everyone was thrown over to one side and the boat overturned throwing everybody into the water. I managed to pull two of them out and most of the others were pulled aboard. [One lady passenger was lost at that juncture, together with a male passenger – the Hon. Gordon Scott, a member of C.D. Howe's staff, who was crushed between the boat and the ship's side – and one of the ship's radio officers.] The ship's carpenter called McGranagan climbed on to the keel of the boat and while trying to hold up a passenger who could not swim, had his arm crushed between the ship's side and the boat. He drifted away . . . The other boats came up and the occupants got on board *Baron Kinnaird* without incident, the women, children and older men being pulled up the side in baskets.

After nearly eight hours in the water Second Officer White was rescued 'when practically all in' by the destroyer HMS *Active* who also found and picked up the injured McGranagan from the upturned motor boat. Both men were exceedingly fortunate to have survived for so long in those waters in mid-winter. Including Captain Reid, nine crew members and six passengers had been lost, either during the sinking or in its aftermath.

Before the rescue, *Baron Kinnaird* had been westbound. She was a trampship of vintage 1927 with a maximum speed of under 9kts. All vessels unable to make 9kts were considered too slow for convoys so they voyaged on their own, just like ships with speeds of over 15kts but for diametrically opposite reasons. (Every day at sea for one of these slow ships was one of the gravest peril, and service on such ships was not for the faint-hearted. Statistics show that 71 per cent of the ships sunk by U-boats prior to December 1941 when America entered the war, were sailing unescorted, and a large proportion of those losses were in the slow ship category.) After the rescue with so many extra people on board, the captain turned his ship and made back for the Clyde, arriving at Gourock at 1000 hours on the 18th. Within the hour Second Officer White and the injured carpenter were also landed at that port by HMS *Active* which had been ordered to escort the merchantman in.[13]

It seems that the U-boat commander had been able to identify *Western Prince* as his victim. That would not have been difficult as the ship was one of only four sister-ships of rather distinctive appearance and which had been sailing since 1928/1929. (The others were all named *Prince* preceded by the other cardinal points of the compass.) On the evening of the day of the sinking, Cyril Thompson's wife Doreen happened to have her radio tuned in to a German propaganda station and heard an announcement of the sinking. She knew her husband was on his way back across the Atlantic, and feared the worst. The sinking also caused consternation at the Admiralty because of the importance to the war effort of some of

13. *Baron Kinnaird*, under the command of Captain L. Anderson, was torpedoed and sunk in the North Atlantic by *U-653* on 12 March 1943. There were no survivors.

the men on board, especially the one carrying documents of immense import. When news of the rescue came in, it brought great relief, a relief that probably accounts for *Baron Kinnaird*'s naval escort back home.

On board the rescue ship Cyril opened his briefcase to find its contents sodden. He was able to dry them out and fortunately only a few were left unreadable. On landing he had them all re-typed before heading for London and the Admiralty. Over the years several myths have developed about Cyril's hours in the lifeboat and the days that followed. One of them had him in the lifeboat clad only in his underclothes, but that is disproved by his own account. Another story is that when he entered the office of Sir James Lithgow at the Admiralty, he apologised profusely for arriving two days late and for not being able to present the original paperwork. That story may or may not be true, but it fits in with his character.

Cyril put his case to the Admiralty and won its backing. Behind the scenes much pressure was put on the Chancellor who finally agreed to the required dollar expenditure. One can speculate that Cyril's own adventures as a victim of a torpedo attack might have brought the critical situation facing British merchantmen more forcibly home to Chancellor Kingsley Wood. Anyway, the upshot was that on 20 December 1940, a British representative in the United States signed the necessary contracts with the Kaiser-Todd-Bath consortium, whereupon two new companies were formed to build and manage the yards. The Todd-Bath Iron Shipbuilding Corporation was established at Portland, Maine, with 35 per cent of the stock going each to Todd and to Kaiser's group, and 30 per cent going to Bath Iron Works. Todd-California Shipbuilding Corporation was formed to build and operate the Richmond facility, with Todd taking 35 per cent of the stock, all of the balance going to Kaiser and his consortium.

In the United States the deal was not kept secret. It was splashed on the front page of the 6 December issue of New York *Herald Tribune* for instance, under the headline 'British to Build Own Shipyards In U.S. to Get Mass Production'. The reporter went on to say that the 'British Government has decided to build its own ship assembly yards and construct pre-fabricated freighters on a mass production basis'. Furthermore, the lucrative nature of the deal was not lost on Kaiser-Todd competitors and others in the shipping industry. Within days of the deal, British Naval Intelligence intercepted a cable from Chairman E.A. Roberts of the Waterman Steamship Corporation of Mobile, Alabama, one of the men who had previously shown little interest in the project, but who now wanted in. The cable was addressed to shipowner Lord Runciman in Britain with whom Waterman had a business relationship. Roberts requested Runciman's intervention on his company's behalf. The relevant file in the Public Record Office at Kew does not record whether Lord Runciman did attempt to intervene; indeed, it does not record whether Runciman ever actually received a copy of the intercepted cable.

CHAPTER 3

Birth of the Liberty Ship

Within a month of the signing of the Kaiser-Todd-Bath contract and as a direct consequence of the Thompson Mission's visit to Canada, British representatives in that country signed deals with three existing Canadian shipyards for the building of another twenty-six ships. The ships were called the 'North Sands' type after the name of the Thompson yard at Sunderland, and were to be even closer to the *Empire Liberty* design than the ships about to be constructed in the States for they were to be mostly riveted throughout. (At about the same time the Canadian Government itself placed orders for ships to the same design and specifications.)

Back in the United States the immediate challenge for the newly formed companies was the construction of the two shipyards required to build the ships for Britain. Because British money was involved this was not a matter left entirely to the discretion of the Americans, and neither was the subsequent building of the ships. Richard Powell, who was to make many visits to both yards over the period of the contract, says, 'We had to ensure that all the work was carried out without waste of British taxpayers' funds'. Writing after the war Cyril Thompson who, as we shall see, returned to the States in the Spring of 1941, said, 'We got on very well with Kaiser and his vast organisation of engineers. They never resented our advice or suggestions'.

One of the two chosen sites, at Richmond in the Bay to the north of San Francisco (a yard that later came to be called Permanente Metals Yard No.1 by which time the Todd Corporation had little to do with its management) was described before the civil engineering work began as 'a place of scattered houses, with just mud-flats along the water-front'. Due to the nature of the terrain this facility was built wholly on concrete piles, Cyril Thompson reporting that the 100-acre site with a water-frontage of nearly 4000ft, required no less than 25,000 of them. These piles, 70ft long monsters, were at one time being driven in at the remarkable rate of 700 a day. Seven slipways were constructed, each with a large pre-assembly area at its head where ship sections could be prefabricated before being lifted into position with giant cranes. The civil engineering works were carried out by Kaiser's own work force, many of the senior men being drafted in from other Kaiser projects.

The site at Portland, Maine, was different. The chosen place for it was at Casco Bay, South Portland which had a rock foundation and a wide tidal range. Said Cyril Thompson, 'we decided to make this a series of shallow dry-docks or basins.' Behind a 1500ft long cofferdam, three basins were blasted out and dock-gates fitted. No. 1 and 2 basins could accommodate two ships at a time, and No. 3, three ships. The modus operandi being that on completion of the ships, the basin would be flooded and the ships floated out. Adjacent to each basin a pre-assembly area was constructed, much the same as at Richmond. This yard later became the New England Shipbuilding Yard East, run by the Todd Corporation and Bath-Iron, with Henry Kaiser having no part in the management of it.

Kaiser, however, was later to build and operate several more yards as part of America's own shipbuilding programme and Cyril Thompson had this to say about the man's overall efforts:

> Kaiser went about the task in a big way. First he hired a vast flood of workers.Unlike in Britain there was no shortage of labour; there were 12,000,000 unemployed in America in the early days. Many of the newcomers not only had a high degree of intelligence, but had mechanical aptitude as well. That explains why the Americans were able to build up a vast shipbuilding industry in such a short time, practically from nothing . . . By 1943, two of Kaiser's yards alone employed more workers than the whole of Britain's shipbuilding industry.

At another point Cyril said of the Richmond operation particularly,

> Progress in California was astonishing. Workers were drafted in from all over the country and special arrangements were made with trade unions for newcomers to be taught various trades.
>
> British representatives were continually on the job during this vital period - advising, criticising, explaining.

At both Richmond and Portland there were other geophysical factors to contend with apart from terrain difficulties and, in the case of Portland, the tidal range. During the winter of 1940/1, heavy frosts in Maine at times held up construction work, and in California early Spring rains had a similar effect. Nevertheless, both yards were completed in a remarkably short space of time. Perhaps the achievement is best gauged by the fact that the keel of the first Richmond ship was laid on 14 April 1941, less than four months after the signing of the contract; at Portland, Maine where the terrain conditions were more difficult, the first keel was laid only six weeks later on 24 May. It was altogether a fantastic achievement and one which completely vindicated Cyril Thompson's original recommendation.

According to Cyril the many drawings required for the ships, including those for the engines, were prepared in Britain and then flown across the Atlantic. Some blue-prints of specially urgent nature were radioed 6000 miles from Britain to the US Pacific Coast. Cyril reported that 'design details, often left out in Britain where they were taken for granted, had to be incorporated in the blue-prints in the US.'

It was at this point and with British approval that the involvement of Gibbs & Cox, the firm of New York naval architects, really took off. The firm had been employed initially to fill the gap caused by the absence of much in the way of drawing and design office staffs at the two new yards, but its involvement now became very much more than that, the earlier British reservations over the company's role having by this time been laid to rest. Gibbs & Cox was led by William Francis Gibbs, yet another of the remarkable men to be thrown into greater prominence by the Allied ship-building programme. Gibbs was a rather cadaverous-looking, dour-visaged man and, in contrast to Henry Kaiser, was one who preferred to keep a relatively low profile. He did not boast much about his work, pre-ferring results to speak for themselves. *Fortune* magazine of July 1941 described him thus:

> Gibbs, who looks as though he had just stepped out of a coffin, is a *faux-naif*: he pretends to have no social graces, he insists that he is a rank amateur, and if you ask him about his business he will answer, 'You never heard a waiter say the fish was poor'.

William Gibbs was a trained lawyer as well as an engineer and naval architect. He and his partner had created the firm in 1929 and one of their most publicised early achievements was when Gibbs designed *Savarona III* in 1931 which, at 4677 tons, was then the largest yacht in the world after Britain's Royal Yacht *Victoria & Albert*. (*Savarona III* was built for Emily Cadwalader, whose grandfather had built the Brooklyn Bridge.) However, the firm did far more than design private ocean cruisers, and only four years later, such was the reputation it had built up, it was appointed General Design Agent for a total of sixteen destroyers ordered from US Naval Yards and from shipyards in the private sector. The destroyers were all of the same class and it soon became evident that to achieve the best possible economies of scale the selection of the major equipment for these ships should be centralised within the design agency. Not only that, the company was also given the responsibility for prelim-inary negotiations with all the subsidiary suppliers involved. The ex-perience gained in the destroyer contract was such that, not long after Gibbs had gained the contract for producing the working drawings for the sixty British ships, the company was also given the task of purchas-ing all materials required for building the ships and their engines. 'Their function,' recorded Cyril Thompson, 'was to produce a new set of plans, based upon those provided by us, but modified as regards to the substitution of welding for riveting, and to suit American practice . . . Gibbs were to purchase all the major items . . . and arrange for everything to be delivered at the shipyard at the right time.'

It was the Gibbs' practice to make scale models of every part of the ship, models that were complete down to the smallest detail. So detailed was the engine-room model, for example, that it showed the best lead for each one of the myriad number of pipes and electric cables involved. This information was then incorporated in the drawings. 'In other words,' reported Cyril Thompson, 'nothing whatever was left to be arranged on the ship. This practice [saved] endless time and argument in the shipyards where local surveyors were responsible only for seeing that all plans were exactly followed.'

After the war, Cyril attributed much of the credit for the overall success of the British project to Gibbs & Cox, and made no mention of the initial reservations he and other members of his Commission had held over the company's involvement. However, in April 1942 Harry Hunter had penned an apologia to the firm. He wrote:

> I feel that Mr. Thompson and myself owe an apology to Gibbs & Cox because 18 months ago when we contemplated that [the firm] would undertake to produce working plans and do all procurement in New York together with many other things that would normally be done by a shipyard we felt very sceptical and agreed this was impossible. I say we want to apologise because Gibbs & Cox have been able to do it and have accomplished the result magnificently

There is little doubt that the company achieved its excellent results largely due to the perfectionist attitude and strength of will of William Gibbs. Frank Braynard, the author of one of the Gibbs' company histories has pointed out that Gibbs 'always knew he was right, and probably was 99 percent of the time'.[1] Gibbs' desire for perfection is attested to by Tom Holt who worked in the great man's office at 21 West Street, New York, installing a special telephone system that facilitated Gibbs being able to hold a telephone conference with half a dozen of his variously situated staff at the same time. Holt spent several days 'splicing about 300 wires for the system' under the desk in Gibbs' personal office, and had a chance to listen in to a great deal of talk and was duly impressed.[2]

We have seen that the Kaiser facility at Richmond laid the first keel in the British programme. It was Henry Kaiser, with the assistance of Gibbs

---

1. Frank Braynard, *By Their Works Ye Shall Know Them* (New York 1968).
2. Quoted in *The Ugly Duckling* magazine, Fall 1998.

& Cox, who was at the forefront of adapting the techniques of mass production, previously used on any large scale only with much smaller fabricated units than a 10,000-ton ship, to the shipbuilding industry. (Some naval architects prefer the term multiple production to mass production when applied to ships, but it amounts to the same thing.) Professor Frank Bull says that central to Kaiser's 'secret, was prefabrication . . . he may not have invented the technique but was certainly the first to apply it on such a large scale to shipbuilding'. A necessary adjunct to prefabrication was that, on top of the necessity for materials and parts to arrive at the yard at the right time, all work processes and materials handling within the yards had to be co-ordinated and controlled to an extent never before achieved in the industry. And it was Kaiser who showed the way. Everything was planned ahead, nothing was left to chance. The storage, handling, and movement of heavy materials within the yards, the order of precedence for lifting pre-assembled parts into position, welding sequences, and just about everything else, was planned down to the smallest detail. Human nature being what it is there were occasional hiccups, even cockups, but they were comparatively rare. Throughout the British project something of a race developed between the two yards. Materials and parts were sometimes in short supply and it was reported that rivalry between the yards resulted in underhand methods being used on at least on one occasion. The story has it that Henry Kaiser's hand was behind the diversion to his own yard of an entire freight train of supplies originally intended for Todd at Portland, Maine.

Back in England, the first three months of 1941 were extremely busy ones for Cyril Thompson. He oversaw the production of copies of the plans and blueprints for the still unnamed ship (that was to become the *Empire Liberty*) for remitting to the States, and also arranged for that ship's keel to be laid at North Sands. Busy as he was he still found time to visit his rescue ship *Baron Kinnaird* when he heard on 11 March that she had berthed at the riverine port of Billingham not far away on the River Tees. A week later he travelled down to London to meet again with Sir James Lithgow and Sir Amos Ayre at the Admiralty. At that meeting it was decided that he should visit the United States again. He left England on 4 April 1941 and no doubt with the trauma of his last transatlantic crossing in mind, this time he took a plane. He recorded, 'I decided to fly back to the States . . . speed was essential anyway. I flew on a Dutch KLM plane via Lisbon, Portuguese West Africa, Brazil, Trinidad, and Bermuda.' It took four days to reach New York. (The very aircraft he travelled in was to be shot down by the Germans in the Bay of Biscay in 1943. Amongst the passengers on that fatal flight was British actor Leslie Howard, one of the stars of the film *Gone With The Wind*. It is said that Howard was returning from a mission for British Intelligence. There were no survivors.)

In New York Cyril met with Harry Hunter and Richard Powell and received their reports on the progress of the British shipbuilding programme. After that he embarked upon another marathon of yard visits and talks with top people in the American and Canadian shipbuilding industries. In several visits to Canada he discussed additional British orders for ships. In Washington he met with Vickery of the Maritime Commission. On 9 May he flew to Portland, Maine and inspected the yard which was still under construction. Eleven days later after visits to Victoria, British Columbia, and Seattle, he arrived at Richmond, California. That place, he said, 'had changed beyond recognition'. It was now 'a compact mass of slipways, plater's, welder's and machine shops. A working shipyard had been conjured up on what had once been a mud-flat. Already ships were under construction. The vast system of prefabrication of parts was in full swing, with powerful cranes lifting the parts into position. Thus, a complete ship's bow or stern would be added in one operation.' He might have added that in comparison with blacked-out Britain, every night the yard was ablaze with light emanating from dozens of strategically placed light towers, under which, like a non-stop display of fireworks, all in shades of yellow and gold, streams of sparks and flames were to be seen as teams of welders and burners went about their tasks; all this activity carried on against the background of emergent vessels, each surrounded by its cocoon of scaffolding.

Cyril stayed for three days in the Bay area, two of them spent touring the Richmond yard. He was very impressed with Clay Bedford, the manager at Richmond. In Oakland he met with Henry Kaiser, before flying back east. Later he went on to visit yards at Los Angeles, Houston, New Orleans and Baltimore. On 6 June he was back at Portland, Maine to inspect the first fortnight's work on that yard's first ship. On the following day, according to his diary entry, he spent the afternoon 'examining weld specimens and looking into expediting procedures'. He added, 'management not very impressive'.

Then came more meetings with officials of the US Maritime Commission, and on 11 June he accompanied Vickery on a visit to the new Bethlehem-Fairfield yard at Baltimore. There Cyril would have seen, six weeks into its construction, the first of a vast series of Liberty ships all to be largely built to the plans produced at his own yard. The sight must have given him a great kick, but strangely, although he made mention of the visit in his diary he gives no extra details. Further days of meetings in Washington were followed by another visit to Portland. On 4 June he flew to Gander, Newfoundland, and whilst waiting for a berth on a plane to take him home, spent some days inspecting the yards at St. Johns. On 10 June he flew out of Gander on a Liberator aircraft which landed him safely at Prestwick, Scotland on the following day. That journey brought an end to Cyril Thompson's physical involvement with the British Shipbuilding Mission, though he continued to be kept updated with progress in America. His diary entry for Sunday 13 June read, 'Lazy day at last'. The speed of construction of the British ships, a foretaste of greater things to come, was quite remarkable. The first ship was launched at Richmond on 16 August 1941, only four months after its keel had been laid.

Most wartime merchant ships built in Britain, or built elsewhere in the world to British order, were given names beginning with the word *Empire*. For the sixty ships built in the States however, London considered that the prefix might offend American sensibilities. The British Ambassador in Washington also advised against the *Empire* prefix.[3] So, after considerable deliberation – the prefix *Atlantic* being among those mooted but thought inappropriate for those ships being built on the Pacific coast – *Ocean* was settled upon. (At around the same time another exception to the general ship-naming rule was made. It was decided that the twenty-six ships ordered from Canadian yards would enjoy the prefix *Fort*. This prefix was also used for those ships ordered directly by the Canadian Government, and when the Canadians ran out of forts after which to name the ships, they used the suffix *Park*.)

Ocean Vanguard was the name selected for the first of the Richmond-built ships. According to an official British document it was at the suggestion of Henry Kaiser, that master of publicity, that the ship's name began with 'V' to link up with the British 'V for Victory' campaign which 'has caught on strongly over here'. In view of this one wonders why the name *Ocean Victory* was not used for this first ship instead of being saved for the last of the Richmond-built Oceans launched in July 1942. All thirty Richmond Oceans were given names beginning with 'V', but not those built at Portland. One suggested 'V' name thrown out was *Vulture*, 'regarded as being too Axis'.

That first launching and naming ceremony, called 'sponsoring' in the United States, was conducted by Admiral Land's wife. All the members of Cyril Thompson's team were in attendance except, of course, Cyril himself who was back in England. The chief British delegate at the ceremony was Sir (later Lord) Arthur Salter, head of the British Shipping Mission in North America (not to be confused with Cyril's British *Shipbuilding* Mission). Again using his unerring eye for publicity, for the ceremony attracted an estimated audience of 20,000, Kaiser arranged for

---

3. MT9/3550, PRO. This file also contains a letter on the naming of these ships from G.C. Duggan, a senior British civil servant at the time attached to the Ministry of War Transport in London. It was dated 9 October 1941 and addressed to Richard Powell in New York. It is quoted from here as it tends to epitomise the general attitude of officialdom towards the men of the Merchant Navy, both then and ever since. It is especially reprehensible coming from someone like George Duggan, a civil servant since 1908 who worked in the government departments dealing with shipping in both World Wars. On the naming of the Oceans, he wrote, 'Our only anxiety is not to tax our seamen too heavily by asking them, whether sober or otherwise, to pronounce too unfamiliar words'.

the youngest worker at the yard, sixteen year-old Howard S. Doolittle Jnr, to present flowers to Mrs. Land, and for a representative member of the work force, a burner with works number 3121, William E. Carson, to be in attendance on the podium, he having won the honour in a lottery. As it turned out, the large crowd was well entertained. As Mrs Land stood by to wield the champagne bottle, Sir Arthur gave a short preparatory speech. After commenting on the speed at which the ship had been constructed he had just begun the next sentence with the words, 'She is ahead of her time . . .', when, as if in acknowledgement of that sentiment, *Ocean Vanguard* decided not to wait for the champagne and began sliding down the slipway of her own volition.

Only fifteen days later, on 31 August, the second ship, *Ocean Vigil,* slid down another of the Richmond ways. She was sponsored by Mrs Henry Kaiser. (The author of the official history of the Todd Corporation states that the *Ocean Vanguard* was the only ship of the British order to be launched before America came into the war on 7 December 1941. In fact there were two others, the *Vigil,* and the *Voice.*)

On the other side of the Atlantic the British were not far behind. The *Empire Liberty* herself was launched on 23 August 1941, exactly a week after *Ocean Vanguard.* Her keel had been laid prior to *Ocean Vanguard*'s, but being riveted rather than welded and because the blackout reduced the opportunities for nightwork, her construction period was longer. (It is of interest to note that the average time measured in man-hours taken to build a ship in Britain during the war was of the order of 25 per cent *less* than the average in America, American shipbuilding being far more labour-intensive.) Completed in late October, *Empire Liberty* was placed under the management of Chapman's of Newcastle and sailed on her maiden voyage on 5 November under the command of Captain Alexander Laidlaw. She was the first of nine of the type to be built at Thompson's North Sands yard. Unlike the other two prototypes, *Embassage* and *Dorington Court,* the *Empire Liberty* was to survive the war. In 1943 she was handed over to the Greek Government-in-exile in London and renamed *Kyklades* and thereafter sailed under the Greek flag with an all-Greek crew. After the war she was purchased by H.C. Dracoulis of Piraeus and renamed *Mentor.* Dracoulis kept the ship busy until October 1960 when she arrived at Osaka, Japan, for breaking up.[4]

---

4. During 1960 this author was in command of a ship which spent three months having a new engine-shaft fitted in one of the Hitachi dry-docks at Osaka port. During that time he was taken on a tour of the nearby breaker's yard, and *Mentor* was one of the ships there awaiting the blowtorch. The ship was specially pointed out as having once been a British vessel. The end of any ship is a sad sight for a sailor but that scene would have been even more poignant had the author then possessed the knowledge to appreciate the historical significance of that particular one.

Although *Ocean Vanguard* was in the water by mid-August there was still work to be done on her and sea trials to be carried out. The ship was finally handed over to a British crew in late October 1941, the Ministry of War Transport placing her under the management of W.H. Seager & Company, a firm of Cardiff trampship owners.

It was not until 20 December 1941 that the first pair of Portland ships were floated from their double building basin. Even so, given that the yard had to be built from scratch and carved out of rock, and that most shipyard operatives had to be trained on the job, it was still an impressive achievement. The first ship to emerge was named *Ocean Liberty* and she was sponsored by Mrs. Sumner Sewall. (Mrs. Sewall got in on the launching act twice, for a year later and at the same yard she sponsored the Liberty ship *Timothy Dwight*.) *Ocean Liberty* was completed and handed over to the British in March 1942. The second of the pair was *Ocean Freedom,* and she was sponsored by Lady Margaret Campbell, wife of the Director-General of the British Information Service in America. (The BIS was a propaganda organisation with close links to the so-called British Security Co-ordination office in Washington, which was itself an off-shoot of MI6.) This ship was handed over to a British crew in April 1942.

In October 1942, the wife of John Heck, one of the two Lloyd's Register members of the British Shipbuilding Mission, sponsored the *Ocean Angel* at Portland, and one month later, *Ocean Glory,* the last of the sixty Oceans was sponsored by the wife of the other Lloyd's representative, William Bennett. At least one other British lady was involved in an Ocean ship launching at Portland. In September 1942, Mrs. Doris 'Dodo' Symon, sponsored *Ocean Seaman*. Dodo was the wife of Mr. (later Sir) Alexander Symon, Secretary to the Indian Supply Mission based in New York.

The degree of rivalry that had developed between the two Ocean yards has already been commented upon. Over the coming months this type of mainly friendly but often strong rivalry, was to be fostered by American authorities in the interests of speedy production. As a sort of precursor to all that, something of a race developed between *Ocean Vanguard* and the first of the British-ordered ships built in Canada. The Canadians wanted very badly to deliver at least one ship in 1941, for it would be good for morale. Their first ship was the *Fort Ville Marie* constructed by Canadian Vickers at Montreal, a company whose facilities were of long-standing so no new yard had to be built. As December arrived it became obvious that if the ship remained at Montreal to be completed she would be there until the following Spring for the St. Lawrence River was about to freeze up. So the ship was towed, shipyard workers and all, down to Quebec. Stevedores then joined in the race and a full cargo was loaded in double-quick time after which *Fort Ville Marie* made for Halifax, the starting point for most east-bound Atlantic convoys. It was reported that she was still carrying a handful of

Montreal shipyard workers who were finishing off their tasks. (Another source has it that some work was not completed until the ship arrived in Britain.) The upshot was that she and *Ocean Vanguard* sailed in the same convoy. The American-built ship, after loading on the US Pacific coast, had traversed the Panama Canal and sailed up the eastern seaboard of America to reach the convoy gathering point. The joint sailing made for good propaganda, for with the attack on Pearl Harbor on 7 December, America was now in the war. Throughout North America the Press made much of the sailing (hopefully without revealing the date, which would have benefited Axis spies). One newspaper headlined it as a case of the 'New World Succouring the Old'.

Ocean Vanguard suffered a collision during that first Atlantic crossing, a not infrequent occurrence with ships sailing in close company during the war, but was not seriously damaged. When Cyril Thompson heard about this he jumped to a rather hasty conclusion. 'The welded hull', he said, 'withstood the test and set our fears to rest'. He was being premature, for as we shall see, problems over welded ships, far from being put to rest, were in the not too distant future to become a matter of grave concern to the Allies. In fact an inkling of things to come was to present itself with another of the Oceans. Early in the morning of 3 February 1942 at Portland, Maine, when *Ocean Justice* was still being worked on in her building basin, and as a welder 'struck his arc' to complete a part-finished job, fractures suddenly appeared in the vicinity. Parts of the main deck, 'tween deck, and the starboard shell plating being affected. However, for the time being all seemed well, and by the time *Ocean Vanguard* reached Britain the Richmond yard had delivered five more ships. But *Ocean Vanguard* was not destined to survive the war. The ship was torpedoed and sunk by *U-515*, Lieutenant Commander Henke, on 13 September 1942 in a position 70 miles east of Trinidad. Ten seamen and one gunner went down with her. *Fort Ville Marie* did survive the war and ended her days at a ship-breaker's yard at Ghent in 1963. *Ocean Liberty* also survived and was still trading well into the 1960s.

When Cyril Thompson flew back to England he left Harry Hunter behind to nurse the remainder of the project. Hunter, Richard Powell, occasionally Lloyd's Register men Bennett and Heck, and, more often, other Britons seconded to the Mission, one of whom was John Robson of the Admiralty Department of Merchant Shipping, kept up regular visits to the two American yards, to the yards in Canada, and to the engine and accessory works involved. It seems these visits were never resented. Richard Powell has specially good memories of Clay Bedford, the general manager of Kaiser's Richmond facility, the man Cyril Thompson had also admired. 'We got on well', Richard recalls. That this was indeed so is backed by a fulsome compliment to the Britishers which appeared in a 1942 edition of the Kaiser in-house magazine called *Fore 'n' Aft*.

These tight-lipped British, men who say little but act with the swift-sureness of the truly skilled, more than shared the responsibility for the shipyard's achievements. When they did speak it was with an authority of shipbuilding never questioned. For they were trained in the arts and crafts of shipbuilding, schooled in the practical yards and technical plants of Great Britain. They came quietly, saw the job they had to do, set about doing it, and as time sped on no one in the yard could deny they knew their job and did it well. Their counsel was helpful, their patience kind, their judgement unerring. These men of Britain have done perhaps more than any other group to aid the cause of their mother country in guiding American industry to productive heights in the help that has gone, and is going, to Britain.

Making due allowance for a certain degree of hyperbole in that article, an extravagance perhaps generated by the even closer collaboration between the two nations that had come with America's entry into the war in December 1941, it nevertheless indicates that the relationship between the American operatives and the visiting Brits was a good one, and it acknowledges the parts they played in the operation.

We must now return to the end of 1940 and to America's own merchant shipbuilding programme. Those American shipyards not engaged in turning out naval ships were building merchant ships to the order of the Maritime Commission. These were either standard design tankers called T2s, or cargo ships of one of three classes known as C1, C2 and C3 (C for cargo, with the numbers indicating ships of under 400ft in length, ships between 400 and 450ft, and over 450ft respectively). All the ships were of sophisticated design, turbine-driven, and built to last. In modern-day parlance, they were top of the range. At this time Admiral Land was being strongly criticised over the slow production of these ships, the main bottle-neck being the production of the turbine engines, for American engine-works just could not produce them fast enough.

Although American entry into the war was still a year away, the rapidity with which the war was spreading caused the Maritime Commission and its political masters to think again about the policy of building only quality ships. The question was being asked whether quantity rather than quality was the way ahead at least in the short term. Furthermore, if quantity was the principal requirement, was the hull design on which the British Oceans were based, the one to use? It would be costly and time-consuming to come up with a new design, so why not opt for one for which all the preparatory work had already been carried out? American firms with vested interests argued against the idea and, according to Cyril Thompson, a strong objection was lodged by the US Navy Department on the basis of the difficulties involved in 'convoying ships of such low speed if the United States was to enter the war'. (This American objection seems rather strange in view of the fact that upon the country's entry into the war in December 1941, the US naval authorities and more particularly, the anglophobe Admiral E.J. King, refused to follow British Admiralty advice to place ships traversing the US eastern seaboard into convoys. Until King saw the light, after an extraordinary personal intervention by President Roosevelt based on criticism of the naval lack of action by General George C. Marshall, King's reluctance had led to the loss of many American merchant ships and seamen, most of them in sight of their own shores.)

Admiral Land was out on a limb and, what is more, one he had climbed out on at his own volition. For in a memo dated 18 November 1940 he wrote. 'In my judgement we are not interested in the type of ships proposed by the British, which type is for emergency use only. If it is decided to augment our own program, we should build ships for 29-year's life and have an eye on the future. Therefore build ships to our standard designs.'[5] Eleven days later he minuted the view that it would be a mistake for the Americans to build emergency type ships and then lease or charter them to the British. Let the British purchase the vessels he said, and then 'we . . . would be entirely clear of this design of vessel, which are suitable for their purpose, but would not be suitable for ours.' He concluded that memo, 'Furthermore, if our emergency becomes equal or greater than that of the British, we can always commandeer the vessels.' Admiral Land was pro-British, but was an American first and foremost!

In the following month, after yet more criticism that America's own merchant ship building programme was not producing the goods fast enough, Admiral Land began to change his mind, not an easy thing to do after being so adamantly inclined the other way. But as each day passed it was becoming clearer that to maintain the policy of building only ships for longevity would mean that the necessary enlargement of the American Merchant Marine would be a long time coming. The first contrary move came when the Commission drew up line drawings of an emergency ship of its own. Many American experts favoured it over the British design and the Bethlehem Yard at Baltimore agreed to prepare a plating model for the ship. The design was more box-like than the British one for, to facilitate prefabrication, some of the double-turns and twists in the shell plating that always pose problems at the extreme ends of a ship where it narrows had been eliminated. William Gibbs of Gibbs & Cox then stuck an oar in, pointing out that if the Commission's own designs were used then the commencement of construction of the ships would be considerably delayed. The principal argument used against Gibbs' view was that any initial delay could be made up by the speeding up of later deliveries.

---

5. Quoted by Frederic C. Lane in *Ships for Victory* (Baltimore 1951).

After further deliberation, Gibbs' view prevailed and Admiral Land did a U-turn and opted decisively for the British design. In January 1941 he presented a case to a Congressional Committee for the production of an 'Emergency' type vessel (over and above the classes already in production), based on the British design though with some modifications. The Committee agreed with him and supported a special appropriation of funds for the purpose. By doing so the Committee had set in progress what was to turn out to be the largest shipbuilding programme the world has ever seen, the production of the Liberty ship. The Committee, however, did not use the word Liberty in its report, for that name for the class was yet to come, and instead they termed it a 'five-year vessel' to distinguish it from other American ships designed for much longer lives. Of the proposed new class the Congressional Committee said;

> It is slow and seaworthy and has the longevity of a modern steel ship, but for the demands of normal commerce in foreign trade it could not compete in speed, equipment and general serviceability with up-to-date cargo vessels. The design is the best that can be devised for an emergency product to be quickly, cheaply and simply built. They will be constructed for the emergency and whether they have any utility afterward will have to be determined then. The coastal trade may offer some possibilities in that direction.[6]

By that time the full specifications and plans for the British prototype vessel had been handed over to the Maritime Commission. This is confirmed by a cable sent to the British Admiralty dated 24 January 1941, by the British Consul-General in New York. It read:

> U.S. Maritime Commission has asked for and been given all plans and specifications of British cargo vessels being built here also circulars for defence measures. Plans and specifications here also sent to Bethlehem Newport News in connexion with U.S. programme of 200 cargo ships. This may indicate adoption of our hull design for US ships which we understand will be oil burning and have water-tube boilers.[7]

The content of that message serves to highlight the principal difference between the Ocean ships and those that came to be called Liberty ships. The American versions were to be oil-burning instead of coal-burning and be fitted with water-tube boilers instead of the Scotch type. There were other internal differences too, coal bunkers for example not being needed, but fuel oil tanks were. From the external aspect the most obvious difference was that the Americans placed all the accommodation

---

6. US Congressional Committee Report, January 1941.
7. MT59/2209, PRO.

in one block amidships above the engine-room, in contrast to the British (and Canadian) ships that had the original 'two-island' layout, with bridge and machinery spaces being separated by No. 3 hold.

The ships were to be welded, but that statement needs some elaboration. Although Liberty ships are usually talked about as being all-welded, there were in fact three variations, each of the shipyards involved keeping to one them. Some were literally *all*-welded with not a rivet anywhere in the structure. In others, rivets were used to connect the ship's side frames to the shell plating (the system used with the Oceans), all other connections being welded. The third variation, used only by the Bethlehem-Fairfield yard at Baltimore, was one where all shell plate seams were riveted. (Seams, or edge laps, are those joints which run fore and aft between plates, that is, along their longer edges. The vertical joints in shell plating are called butts, and in all Liberty ships these were welded.)

The American public learned of the planned building of the emergency type ships when, in a Presidential broadcast in February 1941, Roosevelt announced that 200 of the ships had been ordered. Subsequently Admiral Land's Commission gave the class a special classification of its own, EC2-S-C1, the 'E' being for emergency, 'C2' indicating its length (as described earlier), and the 'S' standing for steam. The last sub-group, 'C1', indicated that the ship concerned was built to a standard design with no modifications. In time, so versatile was the hull form found to be, that some ships were modified to carry specific cargoes, with that last sub-group being changed accordingly. ('C2' indicated tank carriers, 'C3' oil tankers, 'C4' troop carriers, and 'C5' were those modified to carry crated aircraft. A more significant modification came with those vessels built to carry coal for they were slightly increased in length and had the machinery placed aft. They were given the special designation group, AW1.)

The adoption of a British ship design by the Americans for what was to turn out to be the major part of their emergency shipbuilding programme had the effect of making Britain partners with the United States instead of just mere customers, according to Cyril Thompson. To that statement he added, 'the quick start which the British had made with their shipbuilding programme in the States, was the foundation for the mighty shipbuilding effort which the USA herself launched'. He went on, 'The Kaiser organisation which had gained such rich experience with British guidance, now became the spearhead of the U.S. construction plan.' This British influence on the American wartime shipbuilding scene – quite apart from the fact that the basic ship design involved was British – has hitherto been largely overlooked by historians. Cyril Thompson could have gone on to say that after the contracts for the British Ocean ships had been completed, the Americans, at British taxpayer's expense and with not an inconsiderable amount of British expertise and guidance, ended up with two splendid, modern, and fully operational shipyards at Richmond and Portland. He could have gone even further and added that those two yards, after being substantially extended at American taxpayer's expense, went on to produce between them no less than 725 Liberty ships, Richmond also producing 110 Victory-type vessels.

The ordering of the emergency ships called for the construction of additional new yards, and contracts for building them and for the first batch of the 200 ships went to two companies, a Kaiser offshoot called the Oregon Shipbuilding Corporation at Portland, Oregon, and a subsidiary of the Bethlehem Steel Company at Baltimore, called Bethlehem-Fairfield. By the fall of 1941 work began on the construction of another seven yards to build Liberty ships, and in the following year with America now in the war, orders for many more of the ships were placed with those new yards and with several established ones. The peak of Liberty ship construction came in early 1943 by which time no less than eighteen yards were engaged in the work; nine on the Atlantic coast, five on the Pacific, and four in the Gulf. Six of the yards were controlled by Henry Kaiser's organisation which built more of the 2710 Liberty ships than anyone else; to be precise, 1168 of all types, or 43 per cent of the total.

Kaiser did not, however, lay the first keel. That honour went to the new facility called Bethlehem-Fairfield at Baltimore which laid it on 30 April 1941, a measure of the speed at which that facility had been constructed. Kaiser's Oregon Shipbuilding Company at Portland, Oregon (not to be confused with Portland, Maine on the opposite coast) was not far behind, two keels being laid there during the third week of May. Bethlehem also won the race to the first launching which took place on the 27 September 1941, only six months after the initial contract had been awarded. The ship was named *Patrick Henry* and was sponsored by Mrs Henry Wallace, the wife of the Vice President of the United States. The day of the launching was termed Liberty Fleet Day, although *Patrick Henry* was the only Liberty ship among the fourteen merchant ships launched from American yards on that particular date.

We have seen that in the early months of 1941 when the new emergency ships were being discussed, the designation Liberty ship for the class was not used; that term was to come into use a few months later. It is sometimes said, especially in Britain, that the class name stems from the prototype *Empire Liberty*, Thompson's Hull No. 611. Brian Tebbutt, who began a successful career in the British shipbuilding industry at the Thompson drawing office in 1943, says that he always understood that it was indeed the *Empire Liberty* that gave the class its name. Professor Frank Bull, who was to become very involved with certain aspects of the Allied emergency ship programme, says that the story at the time was that the ship plans carried to the States by Cyril Thompson happened to be marked up for *Empire Liberty*, hence the class name. But as we have seen, the ship plans Cyril carried to the States were for Hull No. 607 and were not marked up for any named ship.

A letter written by Thompson's company secretary to the Secretary of the Admiralty and dated 19 July 1941 clears the matter up conclusively. It reads:

Dear Sir,
Ship No. 611 – A/MS 223

We should be obliged if you would let us have the name for the above vessel at your earliest convenience.

Yours faithfully

P.S. In view of the fact that this vessel is the parent type for those building in Canada and the U.S.A. we think that special consideration be given to its name.
As ships building in America are known as the Liberty fleet we suggest that an appropriate name would be *Empire Liberty*.[8]

The Secretary of the Admiralty replied on 20 August 1941 advising the yard that the name *Empire Liberty* for Hull No. 611 had been agreed.

Patrick Henry, after whom the first Liberty was named, was a lawyer, who at the time of the American War of Independence gained immortality by enunciating the words, 'Give me liberty or give me death!' (He also wrote the bravely seditious, 'Caesar had his Brutus, Charles I his Cromwell, and George III – may profit by their example!'.) Had the selection of a famous name from the American War of Independence been the sole criteria, without any liberty phrase connotation, then a name even better known than Henry's could have been selected. Amongst those that come to mind are several that were in fact used for later Liberty ships; *Thomas Jefferson,* launched February 1942, *Benjamin Franklin,* launched March 1942, even, arguably, *Paul Revere,* launched April 1942. So Henry's name, not so well known as some of the others, was probably chosen because his words linked in nicely with a class name that had been in use for some months prior to the ship's launching. (It is of interest to note that had the British not changed the name of the first *Patrick Henry* to *Empire Steelhead* when they bought the ship from Lykes Lines in 1940, that first Liberty might have been called something else, if only to avoid confusion.) *Patrick Henry* was to survive the war virtually unscathed. Her first master was Captain Richard G. Ellis, and her first Chief Engineer was Leonard Whaley. Whaley was to stay with the ship until April 1946. He said of her,

8. Thompson company letter ref. DMB. GGH/LF, dated 19 July 1941. Copy courtesy of Patrick Thompson.

'She ran like a charm. She was a great ship – the greatest!' But three months after Whaley left her, she struck a reef off Florida. The ship was eventually refloated and finally laid up in the Reserve Fleet at Mobile, Texas. Twelve years later she was towed to Baltimore to be broken up by a sister company of the one that had built her.[9]

The launching of Kaiser's first Liberty ship at Portland, Oregon, called *Star of Oregon*, took place very shortly after the Bethlehem launching and by the time the ships were fitted out and handed over to their respective operators, the time gap had narrowed to only a day. Henry Kaiser had lost the race to build the first Liberty, but had the satisfaction of knowing that his ship had been built, fitted out, and handed over in a shorter total time than *Patrick Henry*.

In early 1942, under President Roosevelt's Lend-Lease Act which had become law in October of the previous year, America took over the responsibility for the duration of the war of footing the bill for most war materials and supplies ordered in the United States by Britain and other Allied nations. This was not back-dated to apply to the already con-tracted-for Ocean ships, the cost of those remaining the responsibility of the British Exchequer, although it did cover all but two of the twenty-six Fort boats originally ordered by Britain from Canada. (The two excep-tions, *Fort Ville Marie* and *Fort St. James*, had by early 1942, already been delivered.) In April 1942, under what was called the Hyde Park Agree-ment concluded between Canada and the USA, America ordered and purchased more Fort-type ships based on the British design. This Agree-ment, which for political reasons was never committed to paper, must rank as the most costly unwritten undertaking ever, for under its terms the United States agreed to purchase $300 million of Canadian products, including the ships, to help the Dominion with its US dollar exchange. In the case of the ships, as they were completed they were transferred to Britain under Lend-Lease arrangements along with the balance of twenty-four from the original British order. It should be noted that although Fort ships differed in layout from the Liberty ships, the differ-ences between the two types were largely superficial. Many ship parts were interchangeable between the two types, a fact that was to help with repairs in many parts of the world. Engines and boilers whether manu-factured in Canada or the States were exactly the same, so that on one occasion when the Dominion Engineering Works in Quebec got ahead of themselves, they were able to supply twenty-three engines to the United States Maritime Commission for fitting in Liberty ships.

In conformity with shipping law and practice and under the umbrella of what was called the Anglo-American Demise Charter Plan, the

---

9. Leonard Whaley's remarks as quoted by Bunker in *Liberty Ships; the Ugly Ducklings of World War II* (Annapolis 1972).

transfers of the Fort ships were made under bare-boat charterparties. (A bare-boat charter is one under which the Owner supplies the ship and the Charterer is responsible for supplying everything else including the crew.) The charterparty conditions were not onerous. Article 7, for example, calling for the charterer (HM Government) to pay the owner (the US Government) 'from the time of delivery until that of redelivery or, if the vessel is lost, until and including the time of loss . . . $1.00 as monthly charter hire, payable to the Owner in cash in Washington, D.C.' About ninety Fort boats, as British mariners called the ships, were involved in these transaction, and one cannot help wondering who it was who was given the task of taking $90 in cash around to the appointed recipient each month. There was some argument over a clause dealing with fair wear and tear and about who was to foot the bill for it, but in general the British found the terms agreeable. Another condition was that 'the vessel during the currency of this Charter shall be at the absolute disposal and under the complete control of the Charterer', a condition both commonsensical and in line with usual shipping practice.

The arrival into its merchant fleet of the Ocean and Fort boats throughout 1941-2 brought some relief to a hard-pressed Britain, but they were not enough. In the year 1942 alone British shipping losses totalled 3.8 million gross tons, and British gains from new construction in the same period including the Oceans, and including the Forts which strictly speaking were not British gains because they were American-owned, amounted to only 2.2 million, an overall loss of considerable size. In contrast, American losses during 1942 amounted to 2.0 million tons and gains from new building (not including the Forts) totalled 4.9 million, a net gain of little short of twice the size of Britain's net loss.

A large proportion of the food supplies required to feed the British people had still to be imported, despite the strict food rationing in operation. In order to pay for those supplies and for important raw materials required directly for the war effort, it was necessary for Britain to maintain many of the trade links that had existed before the war. For example, coal from Britain was still being traded to the Argentine in return for grain and meat. Simply in order to exist and carry on its war effort Britain needed these 'ordinary' shipping links on top of the need to import and move around the more obvious war requirements, such as oil, tanks, planes, guns and men. Britain did not have enough ships for all these purposes, so throughout 1942 and as the new Liberty and other types of ships began pouring off the stocks in America, Britain repeatedly requested the allocation of some of the new tonnage for British purposes on a voyage-to-voyage basis. The Americans were very accommodating, but like Oliver Twist, Britain kept asking for more. (One Liberty ship in this category was *Benjamin Contee,* launched in August 1942. In November 1942 this American-flagged and American-crewed ship was allocated to the British for carrying Italian prisoners-of-war away from North Africa.) The British requests were made through the medium of what was called the American-British Combined Shipping Adjustment Board.

In February 1942 President Roosevelt had issued an Executive Order creating the War Shipping Administration (WSA). This body was given complete control over United States ocean shipping for the duration of the war (much the same as British shipping was controlled by the Ministry of War Transport in London). The new agency was placed under the charge of Admiral Emory Land as an addition to his responsibilities with the Maritime Commission. In effect this meant that Land now controlled every facet of the American Merchant Marine, from the placing of orders for ships, to overviewing their construction, allocating them to shipping lines for manning and day-to-day management, and regulating their cargoes and routing. Not only that, Land also had control over the training of officers and seamen for the rapidly expanding American merchant fleet, and even over a total of seven convalescent and rest centres scattered around the American seaboard for these men.

Soon after the establishment of the WSA, it partnered Sir Arthur Salter's British Merchant Shipping Mission in the USA in establishing the American-British Combined Shipping Adjustment Board which, with offices in Washington and London, had, according to an official British file, the set purpose to 'adjust and concert in one harmonious policy', the shipping of both countries. (Sir Arthur had plenty of experience in this direction, having been Chairman of the Allied Marine Transport Executive during the First World War. He got on well with Americans, so well that in 1940 he married one, the widowed Mrs Arthur Ballard.) For that purpose, the British document went on, 'the resources of the two countries will be deemed to be pooled and the fullest information will be interchanged'. It should be noted that the Board was Anglo-American and not an 'Allied' organisation, though it did confer with representatives of 'Russia, China and others as necessary'.[10] In practice, such was the dominant shipping position of the two prime movers, that the Board held strategic sway over most Allied shipping, and in general it worked well and ensured the most economic usage of Allied shipping.

All the new American-built vessels (excepting, of course, the Oceans) were American-manned and by early 1943 this had led to a growing manpower crisis in the American Merchant Marine. Britain, on the other hand, had a surplus of seamen because of the number of ship losses she had sustained. The problem and the way it was decided to overcome it, is described in a letter written by President Roosevelt to Prime Minister Churchill on 28 May 1943. He wrote:

---

10. MT59/2209, PRO.

Our merchant fleet has become larger and will continue to grow at a rapid rate. To man its ever increasing number of vessels will, we foresee, present difficulties of no mean proportion. On your side, the British merchant fleet has been steadily dwindling . . . and you have in your pool as a consequence about 10,000 trained seamen and licensed personnel. Clearly it would be extravagant were this body of experienced men of the sea not to be used as promptly as possible. To fail to use them would result in a wastage of man-power on your side, a wastage of man-power on our side, and what is of equal importance, a wastage of shipping facilities. We cannot afford this waste.

Then, after commenting on the current system of allocating American-controlled ships to Britain on an ad hoc basis, the President said:

What I am now suggesting to you, and what I am directing the WSA to carry out, will be in the nature of a substitution . . . for the American tonnage that has been usually employed in your war program.

Details of this new arrangement were presented to the American public in a WSA Press Release dated 27 July 1943. It was carefully worded in an attempt to reduce opposition to the scheme from vested interests, an endeavour that was not to prove very successful. Admiral Land began by describing the system as a charter programme for operations 'during the war only', under which American-built ships would be bare-boated to 'members of the United Nations with excess pools of maritime personnel due to severe ship losses during the war and who are in need of tonnage'. Land went on to describe how the expanding US merchant fleet was stretching the resources of his maritime training programme. In the certain knowledge that one of the questions raised by opponents of the scheme would be why Britain, for instance, could not build more ships for itself, he described the reasons behind the understanding reached between Churchill and Roosevelt after Pearl Harbor that Britain should devote the bulk of her shipbuilding facilities to naval vessels, whilst the US would become the main merchant shipbuilder for the duration.

Firstly, we had the raw materials; second, we had the manpower; third, we had developed a technique which enabled us to produce in mass and with unbelievable speed a vast tonnage of merchant ships; fourth, the cargo was here in the United States to be moved to the various theatres of war.

Land went on to say that any other arrangement would have resulted in a costly wastage of ship time for it would have otherwise been necessary to ship raw materials to Britain for shipbuilding and then to sail the completed vessels back to the States in ballast to pick up waiting cargo. He added that the new scheme would also provide 'insurance' against an excessive burden on American manpower. For the benefit of the critics waiting in the wings he pointed out that the ships concerned, although flying foreign flags and manned by foreign crews, remained American property and their usage would be controlled by the Combined Shipping Adjustment Board.

In that Press Release Admiral Land named Britain, Norway, Greece and the Netherlands as recipients of ships, but later, Russia, China and Belgium were added to the list. Not all the transfers were Liberty ships, but the great majority were. In the case of Britain, Land stated that between fifteen and twenty Liberty ships a month would be transferred 'over the next ten months'. Apart from the manpower implications, the American authorities hoped that this large allocation of tonnage would end once and for all Britain's Oliver Twist act. This was another endeavour that was not very successful, for Oliver's bowl continued to be tendered over the coming months especially on those occasions when some of the allocated ships were not handed over exactly to the planned schedule.

Admiral Land and his superiors were expecting trouble from American vested interests over the transfer arrangements and they did not have to wait long to get it. In fact the first blast came on the day following the Press Release. In the Introduction it was shown how Frederick Myers of the National Maritime Union of America had reacted to the earlier sale of old American ships to Britain. Now it was the turn of Joseph Curra, the president of that Union. Various newspapers in America on 28 July 1943 carried reports of a 'sharply worded letter' from Curra to Land in which he denounced 'the transfer of 200 Liberty ships to the British merchant marine, and called for an explanation.' He said there was no need for any such transfer on the grounds of shortage of US seamen.

Trade Union representatives were not alone in throwing brickbats at the scheme, not a few politicians joining in the act. Some of the attacks were very virulent indeed and sometimes were based on erroneous and inadequate information. For example, most critics were not aware of the fact that from early on in the war, well before the Americans had even entered it, the British had themselves been transferring ships to other Allied nations who had spare crews based in Britain. Because this transfer of British ships has never received much in the way of publicity, certainly not as much as the transfer of American ships has, it is worthwhile giving a brief survey of it here. Although these transfers were nowhere near on the same scale as the American ones, it must be remembered they were made by a nation which was itself suffering from an acute shortage of shipping.

When Belgium was invaded in May 1940 the 100 ships making up her merchant fleet were ordered to British ports, and all had made it by the summer except for thirteen which had been detained either in France or in French colonies. The remainder, still under the Belgian flag and manned by Belgian crews, were chartered to the British Government. By the end of 1942, no less than forty-six of those ships had been sunk. In consequence, from 1941 through to 1943, Britain handed over ten Empires, the *Ocean Veteran,* and three others ships to Belgium. The Dutch, with a pre-war fleet of over 900 ships, lost 278 of them during the war amounting to approximately 1,200,000 gross tons. They received twenty-six Empires and three Oceans from Britain. In the years 1941-2 Norway gained nineteen Empires, and Poland received three and later an Ocean, plus another ship, the *Baltyk,* built in Newcastle to the order of the Polish Government in exile. Some new Oceans were also transferred to Yugoslavia and to Greece, and in 1943 the *Empire Liberty* itself was handed over to the Hellenic authorities based in London. The Russians were not left out. They received *Empire Nigel, Empire Carpenter,* and *Empire Starlight,* the latter ship after it had been salvaged at Murmansk where it had been sunk by German bombers.

In America, as a consequence of the political furore, Admiral Land, the man in the direct firing line, set members of his team to devise ways to protect him, and of course his superiors, from any similar attacks in the future. To ensure that other Allied nations, and Britain in particular, did not keep making demands for more tonnage it was decided to make the charterparty terms more onerous, it being considered that by the middle of 1943 it was no longer necessary to maintain quite the same high level of Anglo-American shipping harmony as that developed from 1940 on the back of fear of Axis world domination. (The title of a book about the war-time working relationship between Britain and America well sums up the relationship between the two nations. It is called *Allies of a Kind* and the book shows there were faults on both sides.)

The backdrop to this diminution in shipping harmony between the two major Allies was that by mid-1943 there had been considerable improvements in the Allied strategic position worldwide. The Germans had been driven out of North Africa and the Allies had landed in Sicily on 10 July; the Russians were pushing the Germans back on the Eastern Front; in the South-west Pacific General MacArthur had commenced the campaign that was to culminate in his reconquest of the Philippines, and the Japanese had suffered some severe naval defeats further north. Of more direct importance to Admiral Land was the improved position on the Atlantic convoy routes brought about by better naval and air protection and by the influx of the new American tonnage; the attrition gap had closed and the Allied merchant fleet was now in an overall increase mode. There was still a long way to go, but it was clear that the Allies were now winning the war.

These changes of circumstance were not lost upon people working within Allied shipping circles on both sides of the Atlantic. The improvement in the Allied military position caused some eyes to turn to a post-war future, and some of those eyes carried more than a glint of concern. As the American merchant fleet grew apace, the British faced the worrying prospect that they might never again be in a position to dominate the world's sea routes. On the American side they had no intention of allowing Britain to do so. The likely effect on the post-war trading situation caused by the influx of American ships was well summed up in an article by Arthur Kroek that appeared in the *New York Times* edition of 25 July 1943, just two days prior to that Press Release of Admiral Land's mentioned above. Under the headline 'Our Ships and Planes pose a Big Peace Issue', Kroek wrote:

> The pooling of operations and facilities by Allied nations during a war is one thing, but the post-war division of the pool is quite another, as U.S. and British shipping and aviation administrations are beginning to find out. Although no decisions have been reached, investigations have gone far enough to persuade Washington and London that in the peace settlements none will be more delicate and difficult than those affecting merchant marine and commercial flying. The basic British concern is over whether, as a consequence of our vast production and the time of our entrance into the war, Great Britain will start the peace time trade era a poor second in the air and on the surface of the sea. The fundamental U.S. anxiety is how to make a fair division of the pool – not forgetting other nations and the Axis countries – and yet not sacrifice more national advantages than the American people will be willing to approve. The need of maintaining good diplomatic relations with the British and Russians especially, is at the heart of the delicate and many-sided problem.

Kroek went on to quote Lord Rotherwick, chairman of Britain's Clan Line Shipping Company, saying that his lordship probably spoke for British officialdom. Rotherwick had commented on the great losses suffered by Britain's merchant fleet and on the growth of the American merchant marine, noting that these would bring considerable disparity at the end of the war. He had gone on to say that 'Great Britain exists as a world power largely in consequence of the great proportion of the world's shipping that has been under the British flag'. He then made the suggestion that there should be an agreed arrangement to restore Britain's position soon after the war, using such mechanisms as pooling all Axis ships and new building, and throwing the US war-time built tonnage into the pot. This rather extraordinary suggestion did not go down well with Kroek, who commented:

> This is all very well from Lord Rotherwick's point of view. But it has not the same aspect of reasonableness when viewed from Washington or even from the average American fireside.
>   It all adds up to the most difficult problem in post-war settlement.

Confirmation that Lord Rotherwick was indeed reflecting the views of British officialdom is to be found in a secret memorandum issued by F.H. Kerryman, a senior official of Britain's Ministry of War Transport, on 27 March 1943 under the heading *Merchant Shipping Under the British Flag*.

> On present indications the bulk of the world's carrying-trade is bound to fall to the Americans in the immediate post-war years, Their fleet will be the largest in the world and only a relatively small part is likely to be needed for trade to and from the United States. British maritime leadership is of the highest value to this country not only directly but indirectly. The loss of this leadership would be quickly interpreted in many quarters, Imperial as well as foreign, as a sign of exhaustion and decline.
>
> It follows, therefore, that we should do all we can now to equip ourselves with ships provided that the war effort does not suffer thereby.

The man at the centre of Admiral Land's strategy to adopt a tougher stance over ship charters was Franz Schneider, an Associate Administrator of Shipping Control, who Land placed in charge of 'negotiating' the new arrangements with the British. That the British thought that the WSA's tougher stance was at least in part caused by a desire to protect Land's backside is made abundantly clear in a 'Most Secret' communication sent by the British Merchant Shipping Mission in Washington to London dated 12 November 1943.

> As you realise, politics are much to the fore with the result that watchdog Franz is more diligent than ever in his efforts to protect his Master [Land] from any attack or criticism . . . when the political storm broke over the bare-boat deal Franz was frightened for his Master's safety and has therefore in my opinion tried to make the conditions of such nature as to discourage any further application for bare-boats.[11]

The new charterparty conditions put forward by the Americans were not imposed all at once. The first handing-over of Liberty ships to the British took place in July 1943 – six ships being involved – and the charter conditions for those, although more stringent than for the earlier Fort boats, were not too onerous. But the draft documents became progressively tougher so that by March 1944 A.K. Ogilvy-Webb of Britain's Ministry of War Transport was complaining that the situation was then very different from the early days. He commented that Article 11 of a newly submitted draft charterparty which dealt with the employment of the vessels, a matter that is normally always left to the discretion of the Charterers, 'suggests that the Owner does not trust the Charterer to

---

11. MT59/27, PRO. Most Secret cable No. 1845/11, 12 November 1943.

employ these vessels in the best interests of the war effort', and added that acceptance of that article would indicate the Charterers acquiescence to that implication. He went on to list the main objections to the WSA draft document, these being prejudice to fundamental British interests, financial sacrifices, inequitable principles, administrative inconvenience (which Webb described as being 'often intolerable in degree'), obscurity, admission of new principles which might be taken as precedents, provisions contrary to English law, and inconsistency.[12]

The British Treasury weighed in, its representative stating that the draft document had 'no resemblance to a document of agreement between willing and equal partners', and calling it 'intolerably dictatorial' and 'bad mannered'. Mr. Proctor of the Treasury pointed out that the draft document called for any dollar revenues earned by the vessels to be paid over to the owners, and that Article 1 of it gave the President of the United States the unilateral right to terminate the charterparty at any time before the termination of the war. (We shall see below that there was also concern that the new conditions might effect such matters as salvage claims.)

The correspondence on these matters between the British representatives and Franz Schneider's department, was voluminous and went on for months, the upshot being that for a long time no charter documents were signed at all. Fortunately this did not stop delivery of the vessels, one British official noting that 'apparently the operation of these vessels is proceeding satisfactorily, and the absence of a charterparty is no handicap'. In effect, chartered ships were plying the world's oceans without any of the usual legal and commercial paperwork.

A search of the British records dealing with the stiffening-up of the charterparty conditions has revealed an interesting consequence with one of the earlier Liberty ships handed over. The *Frank D. Phinney* was renamed the *Samovar* when handed over to her British crew on 4 August 1943. She was managed by Brocklebanks. After loading at San Francisco for the Middle East, she set sail later that month across the Pacific making for her first bunkering port which was to have been Hobart, Tasmania. On 8 September in a position some 1300 miles east of New Zealand, the ship's radio operator picked up distress signals coming from the Anglo-Saxon tanker *Trocas*. There had been a major fire in the tanker's engine-room and she was lying totally disabled. *Samovar* altered course, and coming up with the tanker on the following day, took her in tow. After what must rank as one of the epic towing operations of the war, the two ships arrived off Auckland eighteen days later. In an official British file there is an exchange of letters between officials at the Ministry of War Transport dated 24 September, three days before the two ships

---

12. MT59/26, PRO.

arrived in port. The writer of the first letter enquired whether 'there is anything in the proposed charterparty of the *Samovar* which may effect a claim for salvage services rendered'. He received a reply from the legal department to the effect that 'as *Trocas* is a British ship [we] can see no reason that crew of *Samovar* should not be entitled to salvage'.

A total of 182 standard Liberty ships were eventually handed over to Britain. Five others which were specially converted into naval fleet-train repair vessels were also allocated although only two of them had been completed before war's end. Those two became HMS *Assistance* (F173) and HMS *Diligence* (F174). The other three were retained by the United State Navy. Thirteen vessels called Landing Ship Infantry (Large) or LCI(L), a hybrid type, were also transferred to the British Merchant Navy and were named after various forms of ancient weaponry such as *Battleaxe* and *Cutlass,* each preceded by the prefix *Empire.* In this case this form of nomenclature did not appear to concern the Americans after all. (It should be emphasised that these thirteen LCL(L)s were transferred to the Merchant Navy, not to the Royal Navy, and they were manned by merchant seamen. This emphasise is necessary because a well-known painting entitled *D-Day The Normandy Landings 6th June 1944,* apparently depicts one of these ships flying the White Ensign of the Royal Navy instead of the Red Ensign of the Merchant Navy.) Details of the transfer of Liberties to other Allied countries will be presented in a later chapter. Suffice it to say here that the combined total of these other transfers amounted to less than half the number handed over to Britain.

What happened to Cyril Thompson, the man who began it all? In the summer of 1941, after his final return to England, he was made a Commander of the British Empire (CBE) which in retrospect seems a rather measly award for one who had done so much for his country and for the Allied cause. However, his son Patrick says Cyril always let it be known that he would never accept a knighthood – the KBE – until his father had been so honoured. Whether that meant that Cyril had been offered a knighthood and turned it down, accepting the lesser award instead, is not known. Cyril's father (Robert) Norman, the chairman of the company, was knighted later in the war. During Cyril's absences in America his younger brother John Victor had taken over the position of Managing Director at North Sands, and on his return the two held that position conjointly. Cyril was at the yard in 1943 on the occasion of a visit paid to it by King George and Queen Elizabeth. Later that year he must have decided he was not doing enough for the war effort, or perhaps everything was now an anti-climax after those heady days in America. In the knowledge that the yard was in the safe hands of his father and brother he applied to join the Royal Navy. That service turned him down on the basis that he was too valuable where he was. Nothing daunted, this remarkable man then applied to join the RAF, and that service did accept him. He signed up in the lowest rank of all, Aircraftsman, Second Class, and trained as a flight-mechanic. He quickly rose to flight-sergeant and saw service in Italy. He was commissioned before the end of the war. He then rejoined the company, again sharing the day-to-day control of it with his brother. In 1951, after the death of his father he took over the chairmanship. By the end of that decade the British shipbuilding industry was entering upon a very difficult period, one that resulted in the demise of many famous parts of it. Early in 1967 he and Ken Douglas, who was himself in a senior position in the industry, reached an agreement that they would become Chairman and Managing Director respectively of a proposed grouping of the remaining Wearside yards. Ken recalls, 'But within a week of that agreement, Cyril was dead'. Cyril had just returned home after a day in the office on 10 March 1967 when he suffered a massive heart attack. He died instantly, not yet having reached his sixtieth birthday. On the following day British newspapers carried many glowing obituaries, London's *Daily Mail* beginning its with the words,

> The man who played a big part in stopping Hitler's U-boats from starving out Britain in the last war, died from a heart attack yesterday.

That, as we have seen, was but the half of it. It was a sad and sudden end to the life of a man who among all the unsung Allied heroes of the Second World War, probably did more than most to win it.

It is the normal practice for the designer of a ship to receive a royalty fee, which is set at a percentage of the total cost of the ship, whenever the design is taken up by another yard. The firm of J.L. Thompson & Sons, however, received not one penny in royalties for the Ocean ships, the Fort and Park boats, nor for the 2710 Liberty ships, all largely built to the company's design. The same applies to the many engines built in North America to the design of Harry Hunter's company, North-Eastern Marine Engineering. Britain was in a state of total war, and all was thrown in the kitty as part of the war effort.

And what of Harry Hunter, Cyril Thompson's able lieutenant? Arriving back in England from the States in late 1942 he was appointed Managing Director of an Admiralty-sponsored naval ship fitting-out yard at Hendon Dock, Sunderland. At the end of the war he became Technical Director of North-Eastern Marine Engineering at Wallsend, becoming Managing Director in 1955, a position that had been passed down in the Hunter family since 1900. Still active in retirement, he enjoyed grouse-shooting and sailing his own boat. He died on 15 April 1970, in his 78th year.

CHAPTER 4

The Shipyards and their Workers

From keel laying to launching the very first Liberty ship, *Patrick Henry*, was constructed in 150 days by Bethlehem-Fairfield at Baltimore. Another ninety-five days were needed to complete the ship at the outfitting berth and to carry out sea trials, a total of 245 days. It was a remarkable achievement but one that was almost immediately eclipsed by Henry Kaiser's yard at Portland, Oregon. His first Liberty, *Star of Oregon,* was handed over on the day following that of *Patrick Henry* even though its keel had been laid a fortnight later. As time went on Liberty ships were built and completed in ever shorter times until by 1945 when the last one was constructed, the overall average building time was something less than forty days according to the official statistics of the US Maritime Commission.

It was Henry Kaiser, the man who controlled one third of the yards involved and who built more of the ships than anyone else, who led the way. Being Kaiser he made sure everyone knew it and it was he who grabbed most of the headlines. 'I'll do even better', he was quoted as saying after building a ship in only 100 days. 'Kaiser versus the U-boats', headlined a newspaper when he got the time down still further. A piece of film footage exists which depicts Kaiser, his face gleaming with pride, as he slots together the pieces of a Liberty ship model to show just how the ship was built up in sections on the slipways. That three-dimensional jig-saw probably took him about ten minutes to complete. He did not, of course, ever get to build an actual ship in such a short space of time, but on one memorable occasion he got closer to it than anyone would have imagined possible.

In October 1942 the Kaiser yard at Portland, Oregon launched the *Joseph E. Teal* only ten days after laying its keel, a seemingly miraculous and unbeatable time. However, in the following month. between 8 and 12 November, at the second of his two yards at Richmond, Kaiser achieved a time that can still astonish after the passage of nearly sixty years. As the *Robert E. Peary* slid down its way, a large placard on her bow proclaimed the incredible fact that it had taken only 4 days 15 hours and 29 seconds from keel laying to launching; the paint must have still been wet on some of those figures. That record, one that will never be surpassed, was achieved as part of a propaganda exercise and in order to do it workers and machines had been taken off other ships in the yard so putting back their construction times. That, however, in no way detracts from Kaiser's achievement. (It is worth mentioning here that *Robert E. Peary* not only survived the war, but American records also show that this ship suffered none of the structural problems experienced by many other Liberties, of which more later.)

As the feat was part of a propaganda exercise it was given press and radio headlines all over North America. It became the subject of a famous cartoon by Markow in Collier's Magazine in which, with a Liberty being waved to and cheered as it slid down the way in the background, one yard worker turns round to another and says, 'We got an hour before we knock off. Let's build another boat.'

News of Kaiser's record-breaking building of the *Robert E. Peary*, and of that ship's subsequent fitting out in only another three days, must very soon have reached Berlin and it would have raised all kinds of concerns in the mind of Admiral Karl Doenitz, the commander of Germany's U-boat arm, when he heard about it. The Germans were well informed about all aspects of the American shipbuilding programme which was, of course, a matter of supreme importance to them. As early as May 1942, six months after the launching of *Patrick Henry*, it is clear from a brief he presented at Hitler's Headquarters, that Admiral Doenitz was receiving accurate and up-to-date intelligence concerning the American shipbuilding effort. After commenting in that brief of 14 May, that 'the Americans are the largest enemy shipbuilder' and, after reporting on the success of his submarine operations especially off America's eastern seaboard since 15 January, he stated, 'I do not believe that the race between the U-boats and the enemy new ship constructions is hopeless'. He then went on to present a summary of the predicted output of Allied merchant ship production up to the end of 1943.[1] Further indications of the depth of information on Allied shipbuilding being picked up by German intelligence are to be found in a handbook issued by the Intelligence Division of the German Naval High Command on 1 November 1942. It lists by name many of the Liberty, Ocean and Fort vessels that had been launched by that date.[2] The

1. Briefing by Commander of U-boat forces, Admiral Karl Doenitz on 14 May 1942 at the Fuhrer's Headquarters. Anlage zu O.K.M. 1375/42. Copies of this original German document and an English translation of it kindly supplied by Kapitanleutnant Dirk Steffen of the Militargeschichtliches Forschungsamt, Potsdam. (Dirk Steffen is also responsible for the translations of other German documents mentioned in this book.)
2. Die Handelsflotten der Welt 1942. OKM 3/Skl. 1 November 1942. U-boat commanders did not as a matter of course differentiate the one type of emergency-built vessel from the other in their reports. It also seems that, unlike the fictional U-boat commander in one of the propaganda pot-boilers produced by Hollywood during the war, they did not expressly use the term 'Liberty ship'. The particular film referred to is Warner Brothers *Action in the North Atlantic*, made in 1943 and starring Humphrey Bogart and Raymond Massey. (This film is credited with influencing many young Americans to volunteer for the Merchant Marine.)

War Diary of the German Naval High Command for the first half of 1943 is yet another source that indicates receipt of continuous and high grade intelligence updates about the Allied shipping situation from German agents in the United States. Moreover, in that same year the semi-official German publication *Nauticus*, presented many details of the US Maritime Commission's building programme, its standard ships, even giving profile drawings and full specifications of the Liberties. *Nauticus* for the following year, 1944, elaborated even further. It contained reproductions of original Liberty ship drawings and plans, and much else besides.

Lieutenant Commander Dirk Steffen has this to say about German intelligence sources in the United States during the war.

> Generally [speaking] the Germans were reasonably in the picture about American activities that were not subject to excessive secrecy. The reason is very straightforward: the large number of German immigrants and anglophobe elements – which had opposed Roosevelt's policy towards Britain all along – provided the German Abwehr (military intelligence) with a vast amount of information. Until December 1941 sensitive information flowed practically unchecked from the U.S. to Germany via the German diplomatic representatives in the U.S.. By the time the U.S. entered the war the Abwehr network in American industry and civilian administrations was firmly in place, although information now had to take a more clandestine route to Germany, often via embassies of 'friendly neutral' countries.

The existence of these 'more clandestine' neutral routes is confirmed by Professor John W. Chapman in his *Price of Admiralty*, in which he states that Swedish, Spanish and Portuguese embassies and ships provided conduits for much information.

Dirk Steffen goes on to say that as the U-boat war neared its climax in May 1943, German naval commanders became increasingly concerned about the prospect of the Americans outbuilding the losses inflicted on the Allied merchant fleets, and points out that 'most high-level German documents touch on this issue although they do not explicitly mention the Liberty ships by name'.[3] The Germans had every reason to be concerned. From the moment in early 1941 when the contracts for the first two batches of the initial order for 200 Liberty ships went out to Kaiser's Oregon Shipbuilding Corporation and to Bethlehem-Fairfield at Baltimore, American shipbuilding took off in a fashion that no heavy industry in the world had done before or has done since. Peter Stanford, president of the American National Maritime Historical Society, says

---

3. a. Professor J.W. Chapman, *The Price of Admiralty* (Ripe, 1989). b. Letters to author from Kapitanleutnant D. Steffen dated 19 November and 6 December 1999.

that the greatest accomplishment of the industrial era was the building of these ships. On top of the ever-growing size of the undertaking as the US Maritime Commission increased its number of orders, the other outstanding feature of it was the rapidity with which it was carried out at every level. So fast were developments that by the peak of Liberty ship production in 1943, no less than eighteen yards, most of them new and including the two yards originally constructed to build the British Oceans (which were expanded and transferred over to the new work once the British programme had been completed) were engaged in the work. (For a list of the yards see Appendix 2.) All this was on top of the production of naval vessels and other types of merchant ships including T-2 tankers, which were also rapidly increased.

A measure of the American shipbuilding achievement is that 41 per cent of all ocean-going ships built in the US in the thirty years between 1915 and 1945 were built in one year alone. In that year, 1943, American shipyards responded to a Presidential decree which asked for 16 million deadweight tons of shipping to be constructed, by actually building 19.2 million tons. When that is compared with the 1.1 million of 1941 and the 8 million of 1942, one can begin to appreciate the rate of growth.

We have seen how it was that Britain financed the building of the Ocean yards as well as the ships themselves. For its expanded shipbuilding programme the US Maritime Commission adopted more-or-less the same pattern. For accounting purposes the major difference was that with the American contracts the yard building costs were separated out from the costs of building the ships; in the British contract they were taken together.

It was the West Coast of America which witnessed the most dramatic effects of the Commission's enhanced programme. Most of America's old established shipyards were situated on the East Coast and were mainly concentrated on building naval vessels. During the war well over half of all naval shipbuilding contracts went to eastern yards, less than a fifth going to Pacific yards with the balance going to the Great Lakes and the Gulf. With the merchant shipbuilding programme it was the other way round, well over half going to the West Coast and less than one third going to the East.[4] The main reason for the West Coast's predominance in the building of emergency type ships was the existence of a largely untapped labour supply on that coast and the area's attractiveness to workers from other parts of the United States. A move to California would not be considered too much of a hardship for an unemployed man from Oklahoma, for instance.

One of the new yards on the West Coast was called Marinship at Sausalito. It was among the smallest, but its experiences and problems

---

4. Frederic Lane, *Ships for Victory* (Baltimore 1951).

can be taken to be fairly representative of all the others except in scale. Sausalito lies in the Bay to the north-west of San Francisco, in approximately the same latitude as Richmond where Kaiser's facility lay, but on the opposite shore. The township lies in Marin County, just round the corner from the northern end of the Golden Gate Bridge. The choice of Sausalito as a site for one of the new yards was approved by the Maritime Commission in early 1942 by which time Sausalito was one of the few suitable Bay sites with good road and rail access still available. The contract for the yard was awarded on 12 March and it went to the W.A. Bechtel Corporation, the lead company of a joint venture, and it was among the last such contracts awarded by the Commission. Bechtel was one of the firms which together with Henry Kaiser had earlier formed Six Companies Incorporated, and although Kaiser was not involved in the Sausalito operation, some of the other Six Companies partners were. Bechtel, through the Six conglomerate, was a junior partner in the Kaiser facility at Richmond and in the Kaiser-Todd yard at Seattle-Tacoma. This intricate interaction and co-operation between the constituent members of Six Companies (and those between some other operators), was later to cause difficulties for American Treasury officials and Senate Committee investigators when they were looking into charges of excessive profit-making by some shipbuilders.

The guiding force behind the Sausalito operation, which came to be called Marinship, was thirty-eight year old Kenneth Bechtel, one of the sons of the late 'Dad' Bechtel, the founder of the firm, who had been very much a self-made, hands-on sort of man. Robert Ingram, the author of the Bechtel company history, describes Kenneth as a financial and administrative man, the implication being that he was an altogether different sort of fellow from his father.[5] However, Kenneth was to show, rather unusually for man trained to look closely at the bottom line of balance sheets, that he also possessed considerable entrepreneurial skills.

Bechtel's first task was to construct a six-slipway yard on a waterfront that was mainly marshland. To provide fill for the marshes and to create a safer medium for the piles that were to be driven, a local beauty spot called Pine Hill which overlooked the waterfront, was blasted away, changing forever the town's aspect. In order to do this the residents of the thirty houses on the hill received government eviction orders instructing them to vacate within a fortnight. Although the residents received adequate compensation, life for the families involved was never to be the same again. The oldest resident, eighty-year old Mrs Frances Jackson, whose tree-planting efforts before the turn of the century had led to Pine Hill getting its name, is on record as saying that it would be hard to find

---

5. Robert Ingram, *The Bechtel Story.*

another place to live like the one she was being forced to leave. Mrs Jackson and her fellow residents were, in effect, as much victims of the war as any bombed-out family in London or Coventry, except, of course, that for the Pine Hill folk there was no danger to life or limb.

Pine Hill began to disappear in April and over the coming weeks 25,000 piles were driven along the foreshore, a similar number to those used earlier at Richmond across the Bay. The road leading from the town to the main highway was widened and improvements made to the railroad link. Out in the Bay itself a deep channel was dredged. No sooner had sections of the foundations been completed when work began on the slipways, outfitting docks, prefabrication yards, an administration block and various other buildings, and the laying of tracks for heavy cranes. So rapid were the construction works and so well planned and organised, that the keel of the yard's first ship was laid on 27 June, less than four months after the contract had been awarded and even while other sections of the yard were still under construction. The facility was complete by the end of the year by which time the yard had already built four Liberty ships. It was then employing 19,000 workers, a figure that was later to rise to 22,000.

As with all similarly contracted companies, Marinship was directly reimbursed by the Maritime Commission for the actual building costs of the yard and for the cost of equipment. Profits were earned only on the shipbuilding contracts which were designed around a variant of the cost-plus agreements that had been in force in America during the First World War. The variant was known as 'cost-plus variable fee', it being deemed that its use would be an improvement on the method used during the previous conflict which had encouraged contractors to over-spend and had provided little incentive for fast performance. For the Liberty ship contracts all of a yard's provable expenses were paid, but fees and profits were adjusted up or down based on performance. The standard performance was rated as 500,000 man-hours per ship, and initially a yard was paid $100,000 for each ship built to that standard. A less than standard performance could drag the fee down to $60,000, and a superior performance raise it to $140,000. As the average time for building the ships diminished throughout the Liberty programme, the Commission adjusted its fees accordingly, but the basic principle remained. The average overall cost of a Liberty ship to the American taxpayer works out at a little under $2 million.

The work techniques at Marinship, as with all the other Maritime Commission yards, were based on the practices developed with the aid of Gibbs & Cox by the Kaiser-Todd yards engaged on the British Ocean contracts. In point of fact the firm of Gibbs & Cox was as intimately involved in all aspects of the Liberty programme as it had been with the Ocean ships, although with Maritime Commission representatives always hovering in the background to keep an eye on costs, yard practices and quality, Gibbs did not have quite so free a hand with the Liberties.

When Admiral Land said of his shipyard operations in 1942 that 'we are more nearly approximating the automobile industry than anything else', he was right. Prefabrication and pre-assembly were the twin techniques around which all yard functions revolved, and the operations bore a considerable resemblance to a car production line, though one of giant size. One of the Marinship chroniclers, Charles Wollenberg, has written that at the Sausalito yard 'the application of mass production techniques to ship construction may have reached its highest stage of development'. This can be partly accounted for by Marinship's late entry into the game which enabled it to take full advantage of the experience gained at other yards through the control and information service maintained by the Commission. Another factor was the comparative compactness of the Marinship operation, for it was relatively easy for management to keep a purview over the entire undertaking.[6]

Let us construct a mental picture of the Marinship 'production line'. It ran north to south and was about a mile in length. Steel plate and girders, engines and boilers, and a host of other requisites arrived in almost continuous procession by road and rail at the northern end, and at the other end the final product slid down the ways at intervals. Close to the 'front end' was a traditional Mold Loft Building where design staff produced wooden templates, patterns to which plates and girders were shaped and cut. The shaped and cut sections were then carried down the 'line' to a pre-assembly area where they were welded together into larger sections. These large sections were then lifted into position on the slipway by giant cranes and then welded to other sections already there. Some large items such as engines and boilers which were manufactured under Maritime Commission contracts at plants sometimes many miles away from the yards, were brought in by rail in completed form and lifted into position on built-up beds and foundations at the requisite time. The major difference between this operation and line production in an automobile plant, was that in the latter operation the product itself moves along the line by converyor belt; ship parts were far too large and heavy for that, so instead they were moved to the next position either by crane or by specially designed low-bed trucks. In some yards these special turcks were run by the yard's own transportation staff; in others (as at the Todd facility at Houston, Texas) this internal transportation job was leased out to a specialist company.

It has been estimated that something like a quarter of a million items went into the construction of a single Liberty ship, almost all of which

6. Charles Wollenberg, *Marinship at War* (Berkeley Ca., 1990).

were joined together in the pre-assembly areas to form about 120 large units that had to be lifted into position on the slipway. Some of these pre-fabrications weighed well over 100 tons and were lifted by cranes working in tandem. Comparatively few units, mainly smaller items such as windlasses, winches, derricks (called booms in the United States), lifeboats, davits, anchors, and guns, maybe 200 pieces in all, were left to be fitted at the outfitting dock after the ship had been launched. It was also at the outfitting dock where the interior of the accommodation block was finished off, where the cabins were furnished and where the many items required for navigation, ship maintenance and crew sustenance were placed aboard, and where the ship's first crew boarded.

The techniques of line production allowed assembly workers to work on parts of several ships at the same time, and the lifting of huge prefab-rications into position on the slipway ensured that each way was occu-pied by any one ship for a relatively short period compared with traditional shipyard practice. Like the automobile manufacturing indus-try, inexperienced workers could quickly be trained to carry out one, or perhaps two, specialised tasks. Also as in the automobile industry, all was dependant upon precision timing of the various tasks and on ultra-reliability of deliveries of parts and materials. Timing was so critical that a breakdown at any point could, and sometimes did, especially in the early days, cause the entire system to grind to a halt. Sometimes the solv-ing of line production problems led to a bottleneck developing on the outfitting berths. Ray Hamilton, Marinship's production manager, said that whenever problems occurred, tension ran high and there were frayed nerves everywhere. Management at all levels had to be on the ball all of the time, for if it was not, the firm would as likely as not be on the receiv-ing end of one of Admiral Vickery's barbed 'needles'. On top of that, any delay could adversely effect the size of the fee received from the Maritime Commission. With Commission offices and officials at every yard, any shortcomings were soon notified to Vickery at central headquarters.

The outline operation described above gives no indication of the problems involved on the slipway in precisely fitting and welding together huge prefabricated parts. The first section to be laid was the keel, on top of which went the prefabricated double-bottom and tank top sections, and so on and so on, as the ship took shape. Some of the sections lifted into place, such as the complete bow and stern sections, were very large indeed, but no matter what section was being fitted and what its size, it had to fit precisely the gap between two or more adjacent sections, a requirement that became progressively more difficult to achieve as the structure grew. There was no occasion for even the tiny bit of give-and-take allowed by the overlap joints as used in riveted construction. Precise fitment was crucial, for any 'unfairness' as a misalignment is called, would be an area of potential weakness.

87

Even that description does not tell of half the construction difficulties involved, for the welding process itself created 'fitting' problems. When a weld cools it contracts and this causes distortion which makes it more difficult to fit subsequent parts into the structure. Rear-Admiral R.W. King USN has recorded that at one of the yards engaged in naval ship-building, the bow of a cruiser under construction was raised over a foot above the slipway after completion of the welds on the top deck and after the cooling – and consequent contraction – of those welds.[7] (Similar discernible deflections, albeit smaller ones, can take place due to the heating effect of the sun.) This raising of the extreme ends of a vessel, and the concomitant drop in the centre is called sagging, and in Liberty ships was of the order of one or two inches. It was counteracted by raising the centre blocks on the slipway by a similar amount and it was of extreme importance to get the adjustment just right, otherwise the stern tube running from the engine amidships to the propeller right aft, could be out of alignment with the most serious results on engine performance even amounting to engine failure. That the ship prefabrication process was made to work at all in those early formative days of ship welding can be regarded, as Professor Frank Bull has said, as something of a miracle.

Speedy construction techniques generated several other problems, mainly in the health and safety field. Acetylene gas explosions and fires were fairly common occurrences despite the rigid safety practice codes in force which included the wearing of protective clothing and hard hats. Despite the codes, a total of twenty-eight Marinship employees were to die on the job. But that was not the end of it, for there was another, more insidious health hazard, one which at the time was largely unsuspected. One of the 'cleanest' and therefore most desirable jobs in the yard, was that of lagging pipes and some parts of a ship's engines. This work was often carried out in confined spaces, and the medium used was asbestos. The workers involved, many of them women because it was light work, were supplied with white overalls but apparently not with masks. Marinship Yard Superintendent Ed Vacha has recorded that when the insulation was being installed in the engine-room, it looked as if snow was falling. We now know that asbestosis and forms of cancer linked with the inhalation of asbestos fibres, a link first demonstrated by South African pathologist Christopher Wagner (1923-2000) in the late 1950s, have a long, twenty to forty years, incubation period. It was estimated by American authorities in 1978 that several million workers from the war years might have been exposed to contamination; so, in the long run, the most desirable jobs in the yards turned out to be the most dangerous.

---

7. Rear-Admiral R.W. King *et al, Naval Engineering and American Seapower* (Baltimore, nd).

As in all labour-intensive operations, especially one in which the working environment is built around the carrying out of repetitive tasks, absenteeism and loafing on the job were continuous problems. Kenneth Bechtel once said, 'There will be a job for everyone who will work and take an interest, but there will be no jobs for loafers'. On another occasion it was 'work or else'. Incentives for faster and better production were devised, and various forms of morale boosting techniques employed. Among the latter was the publication of *The Marin-er*, Marinship's in-house weekly magazine, professionally produced and jammed full of patriotic news, personnel profiles, records attained, letters of appreciation from merchant mariners and servicemen, and the like.

Who were the Marinship workers employed on these vitally important tasks and how were they trained and accommodated in a town that pre-war had a population of only about 4000? Throughout Marinship's four-year existence – it was decommissioned in March 1946 – the majority of the workforce commuted from the San Francisco area. Most came by car, others by Greyhound bus in a forty-minute journey via the Golden Gate Bridge, or by ferryboat. The bus and ferry operations were both subsidised, the former directly by the yard management, the latter by the Maritime Commission. Marinship management encouraged carpooling as did the Bridge toll authority which offered reduced rates to car poolers. The system must have been effective, for statistics show that Marinship commuters averaged over four persons per car. Other workers came in from surrounding towns. Private builders built extra houses in Sausalito town, until it accommodated nearly twice its pre-war total.

These measures, however, were not enough to bring in all the workers required and so in mid-1942 work began on constructing what came to be called Marin City, a housing complex constructed a little away from the main town but within walking distance of the yard. The funds for building the complex came from the Maritime Commission which throughout the United States as a whole spent $40 million on a total of 36,000 dwelling units for shipyard workers during the war.[8] At its height

---

8. The provision of accommodation for war workers was not a new concept, nor was it confined to the United States. In 1916, for example, whole 'villages' were constructed along the road leading from Eltham in south-east London down to Woolwich on the River Thames to house workers employed at the giant Royal Arsenal at the latter place. A total of 1500 bungalow-type homes were provided, all constructed from timber. They were called huts, each group of them, a hutment. For the times, they were quite spacious, and their usage was not confined to only the lowest grades of workers. Future British Foreign Secretary Denis Healey lived in one for the first five years of his life, his father being a qualified engineer.

If the residents of those hutments ever needed reminding of why their homes had been constructed, they needed only to look at the names of some of the roads. There was a Howitzer Street, a Rifle Road, an Amatol Avenue, a Lyddite Lane, and a Torpedo Terrace. Maybe Grenade and Mortar Gardens were more peaceful havens than the names suggested.

Marin City rivalled Sausalito itself in size and eventually provided, in the form of detached and semi-detached houses and apartment blocks, accommodation for 1500 families. In addition, dormitories were provided for about 1000 single workers. This accommodation, most of it built on a hillside with Bay views, attracted workers from far and wide. It was considered a model project and unlike most others of its kind elsewhere in the States, it operated a non-racial discrimination policy, which once gained it plaudits from a visiting member of a Congressional Sub-committee.

Many of the residents of Marin City migrated there from considerable distances. Marinship employed a number of recruiting agents who travelled to many parts of the nation in a search for workers. The territory of one agent, Guy MacVicar, was the mid-West, and he began his quest with serious doubts about whether people in that neck of the woods could be persuaded to move west. He had apparently forgotten his country's history. When he told the very first applicant that the shipyard was 'just across the Golden Gate from San Francisco', the man's eyes lit up with all the fervour of one of those covered wagon pioneers of yesteryear. From that moment, 'just across the Golden Gate Bridge' became the firm's recruiting catchphrase. By the end of the war, Marinship had employed workers from just about every state in the union, especially large contingents coming from Minnesota, Missouri, Oklahoma and Arkansas.

One Marinship worker came from even further afield. A young British seamen had arrived at New York aboard a rescue ship after his own vessel had been torpedoed; it was the second time this had happened to him and he decided enough was enough. So he absconded, or 'jumped ship' as it is called, and made his way across country. He was employed as a welder at the yard and quite how he got the job remains a mystery, for every young man of draft age had to get an official deferment from the local draft board or end up in the armed services. (Sixty years on and now an American citizen living in Washington State, the one-time seaman wishes to remain anonymous and has been prepared to supply only the bare bones of his story.)

After being taken on by the yard the next step for a new employee was to pass through a training course. Not only had most workers never worked in a shipyard before, most had never worked on a job that remotely resembled the one they were about to embark upon. Training was made easier, of course, by the production line concept under which most jobs were broken down into easily-taught components. Marinship, like all the other yards, set up its own training procedures under general guidelines issued by the Maritime Commission. Welders, by far the largest requirement, were expected to reach competence in under four months and their training began in the classroom and ended up 'on the job'. Trainees received significantly lower wages than their trained colleagues so the incentive to reach competence level as soon as possible was very strong. Those rare birds with previous welding experience soon found themselves raised to supervisory or trainer level.

The expansion of America's industrial might during the war caused many social changes, but perhaps none was as dramatic and as lasting as the influx on a large scale of women into the workforce, and nowhere was this more evident than in the shipbuilding industry. In the country as a whole, from a few dozen women operatives in the industry in early 1940, the figure had grown to 13 per cent of the workforce in 1943, the peak year of ship construction, and it was 18 per cent by the end of 1944. Most women were recruited as a result of the US Government's famous 'Rosie the Riveter' poster campaign. At Marinship itself, women were at first taken on only as clerks, canteen and cleaning workers, but all that was to change quickly. The first woman production worker at the yard was a welder called Dorothy Gimblett and her arrival on the work floor was a major event. According to Marinship's women's counsellor, Marcia Patterson, 'production slowed down and men turned from their tasks in astonishment'. Dorothy was but the first of a long line, most of them employed as welders, a job at which women seemed to excel. In view of the fact that in most yards there was hardly a rivet in sight, perhaps 'Wendy the Welder' would have been a more apposite name for use in that national poster campaign. On the other hand, one authority has it that 'Rosie the Riveter' did not originate in the shipbuilding industry at all, but instead, in the aircraft industry where a large number of aluminium rivets were used in aeroplane frame construction. Anyway, by December 1943, nearly a quarter of Marinship's operatives were women, a higher proportion than the national average. Employment of women at Marinship (and in the industry generally) did not come without some initial difficulties, most of them union-inspired. When the local office of the Boilermaker's Union was asked for clearance for Marinship's first five women workers it was at first refused. Clearance was finally given from the union's headquarters. Those difficulties over women, however, were as nothing compared with the union's attitude over the employment of black people, even though the numbers involved were fewer.

During the war the number of black citizens in the Bay area trebled, and nearly three-quarters of the black newcomers came to work in the area's shipyards. Many of them were women, one of whom, an ex-maid, made the notable remark that it had been Hitler that got her, and others, out of the kitchen. At Marinship by the middle of 1943 black workers comprised nearly 10 per cent of the work force, close to 2000 workers and many of them with families. It has already been noted that Marin City operated a non-discrimination policy for accommodation which was strictly allocated on a first-come, first-in basis. But there was not enough accommodation there to house all, and most blacks had to live in the Bay's private sector, most parts of which were highly segregated. Accommodation was not the only problem. Within the yard itself black and white workers got on reasonably well together even if at times the relationship was an uneasy one. Several black people commented after the war on the generally good race relations within the yard although that harmony did not always spread into Sausalito town itself. Some restaurants refused to countenance black customers and when contralto Marian Anderson gave a concert at the yard, the Bechtel management had to make a careful choice about the luncheon venue for her.

The Boilermaker's Union were not nearly so diplomatic. The union had begun life as a whites-only organisation, though in 1937 it had altered its constitution so that all-black local auxiliary units could be formed. Members of these auxiliaries did not have all the rights that white union members had, and received smaller insurance benefits. Under a closed-shop master agreement with all Pacific coast shipbuilders, the union controlled entry into the industry. As blacks arrived during the first two years of the 1940s, instead of rethinking its policy, the union put off making a decision by issuing clearances so that blacks could work in the industry without joining the union and without paying dues. But by 1943, so large was the influx of blacks, that some local union officials created new auxiliaries and tried to force blacks to join them and pay dues at the same level as whites. The result was trouble. The auxiliary covering Marinship was called A-41, and many black workers refused to join it. In consequence, and under the provisions of the closed shop agreement, the union 'instructed' Marinship to fire over 400 workers unless they paid their dues within 24 hours. Mayhap in private the Marinship management was opposed to this, but it had little option but to comply, and two days later the firm began barring some black staff from the yard. As a result on 27 November 1943 a protest demonstration was held outside one of the yard gates, a demonstration described by the local newspaper as the area's 'greatest labor demonstration and most critical situation to arise since the San Francisco general strike of 1934'.

That led to repercussions elsewhere, not least in the office of Admiral Land in Washington, who asked Marinship to suspend the layoffs. Marinship replied to the effect that they could not do so under the terms of the closed shop agreement they had signed with the union. Federal and State courts became involved, and temporary restraining orders issued. President Roosevelt's Fair Employment Practices Commission (FEPC) entered the fray in mid-December and came out on the side of black workers, ordering Bechtel and other west coast employers (including Kaiser) not to enforce closed shop provisions that contributed to discrimination. The employers appealed the decision and while the appeal was being considered, FEPC suspended its order. At the Boilermaker's

Union convention held at Kansas City in January 1944, the union liber-
alised some of its rules, but it was not enough. In February a judge of the
Marin Superior Court ruled that the Boilermaker's auxiliary policy was
contrary to California public policy, and so prohibited the practice. Both
union and employers appealed and it was not until January 1945 that the
California Supreme Court came down in favour of black workers. While
the courts were deliberating, black employees continued working
without having to pay union dues.

By the time this matter was finally sorted out Marinship had long since
completed the last of its fifteen Liberty ships. For in mid-1943 the yard
was transferred to T-2 tanker production, a move that required extra facilities to be constructed. The first of the yard's Liberties, launched on 26
September 1942, was named *William A. Richardson,* and she was sponsored by the wife of one of the company's carpenters, Edward H. Winkler,
who had won the honour in a lottery. Making nine separate wartime voyages the *William A. Richardson* covered a total of 102,000 miles. After the
war, the ship was fitted out as a trooper to bring soldiers home. One of the
returning soldiers happened to be looking at a framed photograph of the
ship's launching hanging on the bulkhead of the ship's saloon, and was
surprised to see his cousin featured in it. It was Mrs. Winkler, the ship's
sponsor. The yard's last Liberty, launched on 16 July 1943, two months
after the launch of the yard's first tanker, was named *Jack London* after the
novelist, and was sponsored by Mrs Ann Pendleton Doud. One of the
yard's Liberties was handed over to China. She was named *Sun Yat-sen*
and was sponsored by Madame Wei Tao Ming.

Thirteen of Marinship's Liberties survived the war, but two did not.
Sebastian Cermeno was returning from its maiden voyage when it was
sunk in the Indian Ocean by *U-511* on 27 June 1943. There is still something of a mystery surrounding the loss of the other ship, the *Francis
Preston Blair.* She went ashore on Saumarez Reef, an outlying crop off
the southern end of the Great Barrier Reef, Queensland, on 15 July 1945
whilst on a voyage in ballast from Manila to Sydney. The Royal Australian Navy, which later used the wreck as a target ship, maintains that
the vessel went ashore due to an error of navigation. Other authorities
have it that the ship grounded whilst taking evasive action from a
Japanese submarine. The hulk, then still virtually intact, was still being
used as a target into the 1980s.

Marinship Production Manager Ray Hamilton observed after the war
that no vessel built by his yard had suffered major structural failure. He
should have left it at that, but instead went on to boast that there had
been 'never so much as a bulkhead leak'. In fact by the end of the war
four of Marinship's Liberty ships, *William T. Coleman, Peter Donahue,
Philip Kearney* and *Mark Hopkins*, had suffered structural cracks, the
first one on three separate occasions and the second one, twice. On top

of that, during the same period two of the yard's T-2 tankers had similarly suffered. Two years after the war, on 9 December 1947 and well after Ray Hamilton's remarks, another of the yard's T-2s, *Ponganset,* was to break in two in calm weather.

Another six-slipway yard like Marinship was constructed at the Gulf port of Panama City, Florida. The contract for this one went to the J.A. Jones Construction Company, another civil engineering firm that had never before built a ship. The original contract was for the building of the yard and thirty-three Liberty ships, but the company proved so successful that the ship order was eventually increased to twice that number. The yard was named in honour of General Jonathan M. Wainwright (1883-1953) who succeeded General MacArthur as C-in-C Philippines and who then became the defender of Bataan and Corregidor until forced to surrender to the Japanese. When the yard was named for him, Wainwright was a prisoner-of-war of the Japanese. As at Sausalito, Wainwright was built on a reclaimed swamp, called a palmetto flat in that part of the world. The first pile was driven on 27 April 1942 and the first ship keel plate laid on 9 July, yet another phenomenal achievement. The first ship, the *E. Kirby Smith* was launched on the penultimate day of that year, and the second one was not far behind. The two main problems confronting Jones at Wainwright were similar to those experienced at Marinship, namely accommodation for the workers, and how quickly those workers who had previously been clerks, filling station attendants, farm hands, and the like, could be turned into skilled shipyard operatives. Both problems were solved in similar fashion to Sausalito. An accommodation complex was built and the company set up technical schools to train the workers. These schools never closed because the armed forces draft never stopped; staff turnover therefore being a continual problem. A newly trained male welder, for example, could be a great acquisition for a US Army construction battalion.

The speed and quality of work, carried out at Wainwright under the management of Raymond Jones, must have greatly impressed Admiral Land at the Maritime Commission, for in January 1943 he asked the Jones Corporation to take over another six-way yard already in operation at Brunswick, Georgia, a yard which had not been productive enough under its original operator. At Brunswick the problem facing Jones was somewhat different than at Wainwright in that the company was taking over an existing workforce. The yard, which was eventually to produce a total of eighty-five Liberties, became part of Raymond Jones' responsibility though he delegated the day-to-day operation of it to Emil Kratt, a man famous for his motivational skills and devices. At Brunswick motivation was the prime problem, so Emil Kratt was in his element. His very first walk around the yard convinced him that 10 per cent of the employees were idling, and subsequent perambulations showed that it was always the same 10 per cent. He ordered his super-visors to fire the malingerers, and despite many protests, not least from the unions, the order was carried out. He did this three times, reducing total manpower by nearly a third, and it was found that after each round of sackings, production actually went up!

But firing people was only one weapon in Kratt's management armoury. Lenore del Valle, the first lady estimator to be employed at the Jones headquarters, saw another part of the man's *modus operandi* and has recorded her impressions. Apparently Kratt would go down to one of the slipways and spend time watching a particular operation. Then he would call the men together and say that he had just come from another of the ways where the men there had discovered a new method of doing the job, a method that 'seemed to work real well'. Whilst the first group was still in the process of changing over to the new method, Kratt would walk over to the slipway he had named as the originator of the idea, and introduced the changes there in similar fashion. Says Lenore, 'If they ever figured out that the improvement originated with Mr Kratt, they forgave him, for their work improved'.

Kratt had the entire Brunswick yard rigged for sound and once a week he would use the loudspeaker system to talk to everyone, and he did it for each shift. Employees had a name for these talks, calling them 'Kratt's preachin's [*sic*]'. During them he would remind 'the ladies and gentlemen of the shipyard' of their brothers, sons, and husbands who were 'over there' fighting the enemy, adding that those fighting men needed the sup-plies that only the product of the shipyard could carry to them. Ted Kratt, Emil's son, says that his father would 'whip those people up, and after he'd got through with that preachin', then they'd build like crazy'.

So profound were the production changes wrought by Kratt at Brunswick, that in December 1943 the Maritime Commission awarded the yard various honours including the right to fly its Maritime Merit Pennant. Wainwright yard at Panama City had to wait a further two months before it received the same honour. Honours and prizes for effi-ciency and for coming up with cost-saving ideas were a feature of all the Maritime Commission's yards, and all the in-house magazines featured them prominently. Steel was in short supply throughout the programme and any person who came up with an idea for saving in steel usage was appropriately rewarded. Scrap saving was another area highlighted in the company publications, each yard having a department whose sole job was collect scrap metal for re-processing. A call went out from the Maritime Commission in November 1944 for each of the nine six-slipway yards around the country to deliver six ships in the following month, despite the Christmas holiday. At Brunswick, such was the moti-vation Kratt had instilled in the workforce, that the employees them-selves decided instead to aim for seven ships. In order to accomplish this it was decided that the yard must work on Christmas Day itself. The eighty-strong ship-fitting team then decided to go one better; they would work Christmas Day for free as a donation to the war effort. Emil Kratt broadcast this all over the yard, and many other workers joined in the scheme. As it was illegal to permit workers to work without pay, Admiral Land's permission was sought and a separate payroll set up for the work done on that day, the workers then endorsing the sums they would have earned, at time-and-a-half rates, over to the US Treasury. About 1300 workers turned up on Christmas Day and their wages, totalling $16,080, a goodly sum in those days, went to the Treasury along with a matching donation from the company itself. One of the workers who cheerfully gave up Christmas Day, was Geraldine Bennett Dees, just sixteen in 1944. In 1997 she told *The Brunswick News* that she could not remember many of the details surrounding the event, and could not recall the spirit of Christmas being involved. 'The older I got, the more I realised why we did it,' she said. 'We wanted to do something to help our country.' Both Geraldine's mother and brother also worked at the yard, and she herself dropped out of high school to work for the war effort. She was a welder and says , 'It was very hard work'. Another Brunswick 'Rosie' was Annie Cottingham Jones, twenty-one at the time. 'I just remember that we worked and we were real proud of ourselves.' Ralph Blackwell, a yard foreman at the time and the man credited with originating the idea of working Christmas for free, says, 'It was a great time. I have a lot of fond memories about that time and the people that worked in the yard. You just don't see that spirit of patriotism today.'

The patriotic spirit did not end there. Suppliers in the area donated the materials used that day, and transportation companies ran workers to the yard at no charge from up to ninety miles away. A group of musicians bowled up and played music all day over Kratt's sound system. And Carley Zell, who ran the shipyard cafeteria, provided a free Christmas dinner for all, with members of the yard's management team helping to prepare and serve it. It was a day Brunswickians are proud of to this day, and quite rightly so.

Admiral Land sent the following 'permissions' message to the yard.

Your splendid telegram has conveyed news of the finest Christmas gift from Brunswick, Georgia, that can be given to your government and its fighting men. You ask for approval by return of wire. Approval is too weak a word to endorse this unselfish and spontaneous outbreak of the old American spirit that has made this country what it is. Even to extend congratulations on this splendid contribution seems inadequate. This is the spirit that will win this global war at the earliest date. Let me join with Tiny Tim in saying, 'God bless you every one', and let me sign this wire as I do to my closest friends.
Jerry Land.

The Jones office at Brunswick was swamped with congratulatory messages as the story was taken up by the Associated and United Press Agencies and by the nation's top radio commentators. One message came from Admiral W.F. 'Bull' Halsey, Commander of the Third Pacific Fleet. Ordinary servicemen sent thank-you letters from overseas. The crew of the US submarine *Pompon,* joined in by signing a round-robin. (One imagines that over in his Oakland offices, Henry J. Kaiser must have given his Public Relations Department a tough time for not having thought up something similar for his own yards.) The best of the congratulatory messages came at the end of December when Admiral Land congratulated the yard on delivering seven Liberty ships during the month, 'a performance unequalled by any of the six-slipway yards . . . you have made an extra contribution for hastening the day of victory'.

At the other Jones yard, Wainwright, as with all the yards in the programme, the principal problems were absenteeism, loafing on the job, arriving at work late and quitting early. Editorials in the yard's in-house magazine *Wainwright Liberator* nearly always concentrated on these problems. The edition for 25 March 1944 noted that 'we lose a frightful number of man-hours by those who feel that one day off each week is not enough'. It also remarked upon the 'astounding' number of days lost through safety rules being ignored.

But these problems were only one side of the coin. Most workers did more than their bit. Welding records, for instance, in the form of total number of feet completed in a day were continually being broken. At Wainwright on 16 March 1944, the total welded footage for the day was 57,544, or nearly 10 miles. A month earlier, welder A.J. Lee, Jr., set a new national record by completing over 344ft of welding in a day within the restricted confines of a ship's double bottom. At about the same time the *Liberator* noted that a record 880 tons of steel had been delivered to and handled by the Fabrication Shop in one day. The slipways and other work places within a yard vied with each other to get operations completed more quickly. On top of that yards competed nationally for the various trophies, merit flags and badges issued by the Maritime Commission.

Another six-way shipyard was situated at Jacksonville, Florida, and run by the St. Johns River Shipbuilding Company. This one was different from the yards mentioned earlier in that it was operated by a firm, the Merrill-Stevens Dry Dock & Repair Company, which was experienced in the shipyard business. In early 1942 the Maritime Commission contracted with the Merrill brothers, Jim and Kenneth, to build a new yard at a cost of $7 million, with an initial order for thirty Liberties, eventually increased to eighty-two. The first of 40,000 piles was driven on 28 April 1942, and the keel of the first ship, the *Ponce de Leon,* laid just seventy-seven days later. Apart from the number of piles used in the construction, other measures of the size of the task were that over half a million cubic yards of sand and rock were used as fill, 46,000 tons of concrete poured, and 16 million board feet of timber utilised.

Ponce de Leon was launched on Sunday 14 March 1943, having taken 211 days to build. The ship's sponsor was Mrs Jim Merrill and the event was watched by an estimated 30,000 people. Some of the yard's later ships were sponsored by even more prominent persons, the ceremony for its eighteenth for example, the *Harvey Cushing,* which had taken only 56 days to build and which was launched on 31 October 1943, being conducted by Mrs John Hay Whitney the former wife of President Roosevelt's son James. One of the ships launched at the yard in July 1943 was the *Richard Montgomery* a ship that to this day has a certain notoriety in Britain and which will feature in a chapter of its own later in this book.

The Maritime Administration, as already noted, kept a watchful eye over the costs involved in the merchant shipbuilding programme and on the rate of ship completion. It was, of course, also concerned with the quality of the end product. However, most of the direct overseeing of the work, quality control if you like, was undertaken by the American Bureau of Shipping (the American equivalent of Britain's Lloyd's Register), an organisation that classified ships built to its standards, for insurance purposes. In so far as safety at sea was concerned, the United States Coast Guard was also involved in the overseeing function. The Coast Guard had inspectors at each yard, with briefs to watch over the ship from keel laying to sea trials. One of the inspectors at Jacksonville, was Captain Jefferson Carey, a one-time ship's captain who in 1943 at the age of thirty-seven, was taken on by the Coast Guard for this purpose. He oversaw Jacksonville's first Liberty and at least five others. They were 'his babies' until the times of acceptance by the Maritime Administration.

By the middle of 1943 many new welding trainees at the Jacksonville yard were being trained by a lady who may well have been the best looking 'Rosie' in the country. She was Wynona P. Ely, said to be pretty enough to be a GI pinup girl in spite of the fact that she, like all lady welders, was denied the use of make-up on the job and had to wear ungainly overalls and low-heeled shoes. Wynona was indeed a rare lady, for she was one of the few woman holders of the welding instructor's certificate issued by the American Bureau of Shipping. Instruction in welding never stopped because of the draft and because there was a continuous turnover for other reasons. It is recorded that there could be as many as 600 welding vacancies at any one time.

One man who worked intermittently as a rigger in the launching and sea-trial crew at Jacksonville, was John Simms who had begun his sea career as a deck boy in 1937. He says,

Some merchant seamen found employment in the shipyards during their time off between ships. Usually 4 to 5 weeks in the shipyards and you went to sea again. I came home three times during the war . . . and was employed as a trial crew member. During the [actual] construction [of the ship] there wasn't much to do except to keep the lines and gangways secure at the wet dock and keep bilges and deep tanks sounded.[9]

John had been aboard Lykes Line's *Cranford* when she was sunk by a submarine with the loss of eleven lives in July 1942 and so knew at first hand what the war at sea was all about. In the later war years he sailed as Bosun on three Liberty ships and then as Second Officer on another. (After the war he gained his master's licence and sailed in command.) He looks back upon the periods spent as a shipyard rigger as furloughs from a more dangerous sort of occupation. But that is not to say that the 'furloughs' lacked excitement. John says that the Jacksonville Liberties were launched bow first, a rather unusual procedure for most were launched stern first or, as at New Orleans, sideways. He says that whenever a ship was launched at Jacksonville, bearing in mind that at those times there was no steam supply to the deck machinery, the anchor with its cable attached was lashed to the ship's bulwark with heavy manila rope, the anchor itself hanging down at about the vicinity of the bridge. As the ship slid down the way into the river at an ever growing rate, riggers stood by the rope lashings ready to cut them when the order came to let go the anchor. The system worked successfully every time, the ship being brought up in mid-stream where tugs took over.

The launching of any ship is exciting, high-adrenaline stuff, especially for the men of the rigging gang as 10,000 tons of steel under their feet moves down the slipway to strike the water at around 15kts. However, at the Delta yard at New Orleans, Louisiana, such events were perhaps more exciting than anywhere else, for due to the narrowness of the waterway there, the sideways method of launching was adopted. Such a launching was an awesome show as the ship, leaning over towards the river at an angle, slid downwards to strike the water with such force that the wave created rose to deck height before racing off to swamp the other side of the waterway. Delta built a total of 132 standard Liberties, thirty-two Liberty tankers and twenty-four Liberty colliers. In outward appearance Liberty tankers looked in almost all respects just like standard Liberties. This was a subterfuge to disguise the oil carriers as ordinary cargo ships, since tankers were the preferred targets for U-boats. One of this yard's standard Liberties was the *Benjamin Contee*, already mentioned as being loaned, fully crewed, to Britain soon after its launching for the carriage of

---

9. Letters to author, dated between August 1999 and January 2000, from Captain John E. Simms.

Italian prisoners-of-war from North Africa. It is of interest to note that the ship carried up to 1800 prisoners at a time, a figure far in excess of the maximum number of Allied personnel carried when the ships were used as troop carriers.

From the very beginning of the Liberty ship programme, cost-controls were put in place by the Maritime Commission, but at first those controls were rather loosely imposed for it was a question of getting the ships built in a hurry whatever the cost. In the last chapter we saw how by 1943 with final Allied victory in sight, albeit still a long way off, the Maritime Commission began tightening up the conditions under which it allocated ships to Britain. For the same reason, towards the end of 1943 at a time when it was clear that the American shipbuilding programme had more than filled the attrition gap caused by U-boat sinkings, American authorities began looking more closely at the costs of building ships, and particularly into the profits being made by shipbuilders. It was around this time that Admiral Land made his memorable remark to a Congressional committee that 'if you want fast ships, fast shipbuilding, fast women or fast horses, you pay through the nose for them'. In 1944, when again up in front of Congress, and this time referring not only to the high costs of the project but also to the suspect nature of the quality of some of its products, some of which were cracking up, he said, 'I would be a stupid ass to come up here and tell you that we are running this with any degree of perfection. We are not. We are just doing the very best we can with the tools we have'.

There was much for the Government investigators to look at. The range of per ship cost between the various yards engaged in building Liberties, was vast. At the end of the programme in 1945 when the average cost of a ship from each of the yards was worked out, it was found to vary from between $1.5 million per ship at the yard in Wilmington, North Carolina, to $2.1 million at Jacksonville. Although in general it appeared that the costs per ship coming from the smaller-output yards was, as to be expected, higher than the larger-output yards, that was not always the case. The yard at Wilmington built approximately the same number of Liberties, 126 against 138, as Kaiser's Number 1 yard at Richmond, yet the average cost per ship at Richmond exceeded Wilmington's by over 21 per cent. There were many contributory reasons for such disparities of course, but what concerned American Treasury investigators the most, was the astronomically high level of earnings of shipbuilders when set against the original capital they had invested. Henry Kaiser was accused of earning something of the order of 11,600 per cent on the original capital he had invested in one of his companies. Even Bethlehem-Fairfield, the offshoot of an old established shipbuilder, made 1200 per cent. The record however seems to have belonged to St. John's River Shipbuilding at Jacksonville, the yard which produced the highest cost Liberties. It was accused of making 50,000 per cent 'after taxes on an initial investment of only $400'.

Probably because Henry Kaiser built more Liberties than anyone else, he received more than a fair proportion of the charges of profiteering flying around, charges that were still under investigation well after the war had been won. In fact, says the Maritime Commission chronicler, the 'attacks on Kaiser were interlarded in attacks on the Maritime Commission [itself] for showing him favouritism'.[10] Kaiser's lawyer, Oscar Cox, did his best to help his client's case during a House of Representatives' hearing in 1946, when he came out with the following brilliant piece of obfuscation, a piece well worthy of any of the politicians to whom it was directed. He said;

> ... theoretical earnings on shipbuilding, without regard to actual losses on other operations, and after theoretical Federal income taxes, would have been about $40,000,000. Of that theoretical amount, the theoretical share of the Kaiser interests, based on their stockholding in those companies, would have been around $16,000,000.

That passage, if it is clear about anything, highlights the fact that projects run by consortia, whatever the original merits of such joint undertakings, can later cause problems if financial investigators have to be brought in.

Profiteering on Maritime Commission contracts were not the only shipbuilding contracts placed under investigation. A 'Special Committee to Investigate National Defense Programs' headed by Senator Harry S. Truman, one day to become President, looked into the cost of naval work including ship conversions. At one hearing, representatives of Todd Shipbuilding Corporation testified that the Navy's ship conversion contracts gave them such a profit that, 'if it hadn't been for taxes, we couldn't have handled our profit with a steam shovel'.[11]

---

10. Lane, ibid.
11. Harry S. Truman, *Memoirs* (New York 1955).

CHAPTER 5

The Naming Game

The naming of a ship has never been simply a matter of picking one out of a hat. Navies have their Ship Naming Committees and most of the world's shipping companies have standard nomenclature practices. British examples of the latter are Shell Tankers with their use of the Latin names for sea shells, Blue Funnel which uses characters from Greek mythology, Harrison of Liverpool who called their ships after trades and professions, and the other Harrison, based in London, whose ship names invariably began with the first three letters of the company's name. Similar conventions are in use on the other side of the Atlantic, American President Lines for example always calling their ships after presidents, and Moore-McCormack Lines who use the prefix 'Mormac'. The principal problem in naming the wartime Liberty ships was the sheer number of ships that were built.

Soon after the orders went out for the construction of the first 200 Liberties in early 1941, the US Maritime Commission established a Ship Naming Committee as part of its Public Relations Division, the head of it eventually being Eleanor Kunitz. Very early on the decision was taken to name the ships after persons who had made significant contributions to American life and history, with the proviso that the person concerned had to be dead. As time went on and the number of ships requiring names rapidly increased, naming sub-committees were formed at each of the eighteen yards engaged in the construction of Liberties, it being their task to decide on names and submit them to Mrs. Kunitz's department for approval. The authors of the standard catalogue of Liberty ships, Sawyer and Mitchell, record the story that one man, a prominent politician, complained when his name was allocated for the purpose, stating that 'I am not dead, not in dry dock and do not need my bottom scraped'. He asked for his name to be cancelled. It is not known whether the gentleman concerned felt any chagrin when he was advised that the ship in question had been named for another person with the same name and who had long been dead.[1]

---

1. L.A. Sawyer and W.H. Mitchell, *The Liberty Ships* (2nd ed., London 1985).

The convention to call the ships after prominent historical Americans was broken almost from the very beginning. We have already seen that the second of the long line of Liberty ships was named *Star of Oregon*. She was named after the very first deep-sea sailing craft built in Oregon in 1841, exactly 100 years before her successor. Only a few commercially operated Liberty ships were given such impersonal names, however. Another in that category was *Stage Door Canteen* (Baltimore, October 1943), named after the famous New York entertainment venue visited by many thousands of servicemen during the war and at which they could expect to bump into, and even dance with, idols of the stage and screen who were out doing their bit for the war effort. Other exceptions to the standard naming convention were those Liberties operated by the US Navy, for they were usually named for stars and constellations, though even some of those were launched under names in keeping with the convention.

But in the majority of cases the American-name-of-note convention was adhered to, although as time went on the names of a few foreigners with historical connections to the American continent were allowed to creep in. In some cases the connection was rather tenuous. For example, one assumes that *Antonin Dvorak* (Richmond, December 1943) was so named because the Czech composer had spent some time in America imbibing inspiration for his New World Symphony. The American connections of some other foreigners so honoured were less vague. *Amerigo Vespucci* (Richmond, March 1944) was named after the Spanish explorer who gave the continent its name, and *George Vancouver* (Portland, July 1942) after the British mariner who explored and charted the north-west coast of the continent.

American citizens so honoured came from across the board. Male names predominated, but a total of 118 Liberties carried those of ladies. One of the ladies was *Virginia Dare* (Wilmington, N.C., March 1942), named for the first child of English parents born at the settlement on Roanoke Island in 1587. (The grapes from which the wine used at the ship's launching was made were grown on the island.) Film stars, trade union leaders, authors, newspaper editors, inventors, and, need one say it, politicians, were all represented. One ship named after an inventor was the *Hiram P. Maxim*, son of an even more famous inventor, the Anglo-American Sir Hiram Stevens Maxim, after whom the famous gun was named. The original inhabitants of North America were not neglected, such names as *Pocohontas* (Wilmington, December 1942), *Black Hawk* (New Orleans, February 1943) and *Chief Osceola* (Brunswick, October 1944) being utilised. Some names of note came from the Civil War. Examples are *George A. Custer*, the famous Union general (Los Angeles, October 1942) and from the Confederate side, *Samuel G. French* (Panama City, April 1944) a ship which was sponsored by the General's granddaughter, Miss Ada French. Other names came from the 'Wild West', *Wyatt Earp* (Los

Angeles, August 1943) and *Annie Oakley* (Los Angeles, September 1943) being two of them. Some names such as *James Bowie* (Houston, November 1942) and *Davy Crockett* (Houston, June 1942) were connected with the Alamo; the hand of the local naming committee in that Texas shipyard is obvious. Black Americans were not left out, eighteen ships being named after prominent members of that community, and, as an early exercise in what is now called positive racial discrimination, at least two of those ships were to be manned by all-black crews. Another family connection similar to the *Samuel G. French* occurred at Panama City and in the very same month, when Wave (the equivalent of Britain's Wrens) Lieutenant Frances Jay sponsored the *Josephine Shaw Lowell* named for her great-grandmother. Possibly as much as a sort of side-swipe at the Japanese as it was to the memory of the man himself, one Liberty was named *Townsend Harris* (Baltimore, July 1943). Harris (1804-78) was America's first plenipotentiary to Japan, his presence having being imposed on that country as a result of the Treaty of Kanagawa, itself a direct imposition which came as a consequence of Commodore Matthew Perry's two voyages of gunboat diplomacy to Japan in 1853/4.

In addition to *Patrick Henry,* other names from the American War of Independence were honoured. *Francis Marion* (Wilmington, NC, April 1942) was one of them. The 2000 film *The Patriot* is based on the exploits of Marion (*c*1732-95) although his name is changed to Benjamin Martin, a role played by Mel Gibson, for the purposes of the film. Marion earned the nickname 'Swamp Fox' during his guerrilla war againt the British. He eventually became a senator for South Carolina.

Not counting three Wills, one of which was *Will Rogers* (Baltimore, November 1942) named for the actor, no less than 202 of the ships were given names beginning with William. One cannot help wondering what effect this had on port captains and their signalling staffs at times when identical-looking ships with nearly the same, and often very long names, were anchored in close proximity to each other, especially when one remembers that for security reasons each ship had its name painted out before its maiden voyage. The longest name of all was *Brigadier General Clinton W. Russell* given to a Liberty, launched as *Robert W. Bingham* (New Orleans, July 1944) which was renamed after conversion into an aircraft repair ship for the US Army. The shortest name was one of the impersonal ones, *Ammla* (Baltimore, December 1943) named after the American Municipal Library Association which sponsored her. The last hundred or so Liberty ships constructed were mostly named after American merchant seamen killed earlier in the war, and *Am-Mer-Mar* (New Orleans, 1944) was named after the American Merchant Marine as a whole.[2] It was in this category that the second part of the standard

---

2. From US Maritime Administration Fact Sheet issued 22 May 1945.

naming convention, namely that the person concerned had to be dead, was broken for the one and only time and as a result of a mistake. (The circumstances which brought about that mistake will be found in a later chapter of this book.) One seaman who did not get a ship named after him was Captain M.E. Respess of Baltimore who had twice had a ship torpedoed from under him before losing his life during a third torpedo incident on 24 July 1942. However, in September of the following year his memory was honoured when his widow sponsored the *John Russell Pope* built at her husband's home port. (That ship was handed over to the British on 6 October, and renamed *Samdak* and made her maiden voyage to the Middle East later that month.)

Sponsoring ceremonies, or launchings, of the ships were always treated as exercises in morale-boosting and publicity. Sponsors, mostly women, were either themselves national or local figures of note or were married to someone who was, or were chosen from the ranks of those who built the ships, or from those with connections with the person for whom the ship was being named. Sponsoring was quite rightly considered a great honour. Members of the shipbuilding families, new firms and old, were involved. At least five members of the Bechtel family sponsored ships on the west coast, and on the east coast at Jacksonville, it was Mrs Jim Merrill who swung the champagne bottle at the bow of the yard's first Liberty, the *Ponce de Leon*, on 14 March 1943. It seems that no one wanted to be left out and several Hollywood film stars got in on this new act. Dorothy Lamour sponsored the *Willis Van Devanter* in July 1942, Bette Davis the *Hinton R. Helper* in the following month, and Carol Landis the *Vernon L. Kellogg* in July 1943, all at nearby Los Angeles. At the same yard in January 1944 the *Carole Lombard*, named for the actress who had died in a plane crash two years earlier, was sponsored by her friend and Hollywood colleague Irene Dunne. One Liberty, the *John F. Steffen*, was sponsored by Lady Beveridge at Portland, Oregon in June 1943; quite what the wife of the architect of Britain's National Insurance Scheme was doing in America at this time is not known, nor how she got to sponsor a ship that had no direct British connection.

One rather strange sponsor, strange because nothing has been discovered about her background or about exactly from whence she hailed, was a lady called Queen Shirley II of Rosario, who launched the *Ephraim W. Baughman* at Portland, Oregon, in June 1943. The ship was named for the first licensed pilot on the Columbia River. One ship, the *Mary Pickersgill*, was named for the lady who gained undying fame by stitching together the giant-sized American flag flown over Fort McHenry during the British bombardment of that fort in 1814. That event is commemorated in The Star Spangled Banner Flag House Museum at Baltimore, and the person chosen to sponsor the ship on 24 June 1944 at Baltimore was, appropriately, Mrs Elizabeth Sewell, the wife of the Curator of that

Museum. The ship's first master was Captain Henry Fritz and he kept up a regular correspondence with the Museum after the launching. The ship's first voyage was to the Normandy beaches with a full cargo of bombs loaded at Philadelphia. After the war she passed through several changes of ownership and changes of name until she was scrapped in Taiwan in 1971, by which time this ugly duckling was a venerable twenty-seven years of age.

The handing over of Liberty ships to Britain and other Allied nations brought new twists to the naming game, for most of the original American names for these ships then disappeared for the duration of the war. (Sometimes when this happened the old name was used again for a subsequent Liberty.) The ships that went to Britain received names beginning with 'Sam', and over the years various authors have come up with differing derivations for that prefix. Some said it was a direct reference to Uncle Sam, the owner of the ships, whilst others said it was either an abbreviation for 'superstructure all amidships' or for 'standard American merchantship'. Nothing has been found in the relevant British official files to conclusively support any of these theories. However, one document does show that the prefix was chosen by British authorities. The document concerned is a copy of a message marked 'secret' sent from London to the British Merchant Shipping Mission in Washington on 10 July 1943, the second, and relevant, paragraph of which reads,

> We think there would be some advantage in change of name and in order to preserve identity of ships as a group we suggest a series of names beginning with 'Sam'. If this is agreed by WSA [War Shipping Administration] we will send list of names . . .[3]

The words 'preserve identity' seem to support the 'Uncle Sam' theory more than it does the others, for Liberty ships were not the only wartime-built ships with superstructure all amidships.

To add yet another twist, a few 'Samboats' as British sailors called the ships, were launched under their British names, never having had an American one. One of these, *Samnid,* launched at Baltimore in January 1944 was sponsored by Hollywood superstar Mary Pickford. Seven out of the total of 182 standard Liberty ships handed over to Britain had their original American names quickly reinstated, in six cases after objections from the families involved, and in the case of *Ammla,* named for the American Municipal Library Association, after that association objected. The other six were *John J. McGraw, Adolph S. Ochs, Edward Bruce, Frank A. Vanderlip, Ben H. Miller,* and *Frederick Banting.* The complainant in the case of *Frank A. Vanderlip,* named for a journalist, banker

---

3. MT59/27 Message No. Bilge 3202, 10.7.1943. PRO, London.

and one-time US Treasury official who had died in 1937, was Mr. Vanderlip's widow.

The very first Liberty to be handed over to the British was called *Samholt* (ex-*Jacob Riis*) built by Henry Kaiser's Calship yard at Los Angeles. She was boarded by a British crew on 17 July 1943 and, under the management of Cunard, made her maiden voyage to India. The very last one was *Samlamu* built by Bethlehem-Fairfield and managed by Reardon Smith of Cardiff. Her maiden voyage was also to India, beginning on 2 July 1944.

The names of the twelve Liberty ships transferred to the Norwegian flag were changed to those of deceased Norwegians, *Liev Eiriksson*, *Fridtjof Nansen* and *Edvard Grieg*, being the prominent ones. The others were less well known, amongst them *Viggo Hansteen*. Viggo Harald Hansteen was born in Oslo in 1900, the son of a doctor. He became a lawyer in 1923, and being politically left inclined, joined the Norwegian Communist Party. When the Germans invaded Norway in 1940 he became a leader of the anti-German movement. He was arrested in September 1941 and on the 10th of that month he and a companion were tried, found guilty, and immediately taken outside and shot. Four more of the Norwegian Liberties were named after other patriots executed by the Germans. They were *Carl Oftedal*, *Harald Torsvik*, *Lektor Garbo* and *Sverre Helmersen*.

The Belgian Liberty ships all had their names changed to *Belgian* something or other, including *Belgian Liberty*. When the *Bert Williams* became *Belgian Unity* in November 1944, another Liberty was given the original name that same month.

The Liberties handed over to the Russians had their American names changed to either those of famous dead Soviet citizens or to those of Russian cities, except for two. Stalin was not dead but being all-powerful, managed to get the family name commemorated, not once but twice, in the city names of *Stalingrad* and *Stalinbad*. One of the Russian Liberties, built at Portland, Oregon as the *Louis Agassiz*, was handed over as *Emilian Pugachev*. The anglicisation of the Russian name apparently did not suit the Russians for they first changed the spelling to *Emelyan Pugachev* then stepped into the realm of unpronounceability for most Westerners by changing the spelling to *Yemelyan Pugachyov*. Although all forty-three Russian Liberties were transferred under Lend Lease terms, only three were returned after the end of the war, and none of the others were paid for. (More will be said about this in a later chapter.) The three returned were the Liberty tankers *Apsherson* (ex-*Charlotte P. Gilman*), *Byelgorod* (ex-*Paul Dunbar*) and *Maikop* (ex-*Thomas H. Gallaudet*). They were handed back on 15 April 1948. Just why the Russians made exceptions of this trio is not known, but one can hazard a guess that it might have been because they were tankers and that America was a large oil-exporting nation; had the ships called at an American oil port they might have been seized. Anyway, for operational reasons it was better for tankers in peacetime to be built with the bridge and accommodation all aft, and these ships had it amidships.

The naming game continued after the war ended when many Liberties became essential components of world-wide merchant fleets. Those that were not sold to commercial interests and which ended up being mothballed in the American Reserve Fleets retained, or regained, their original names whilst in the reserve. At least one ship sold to an American shipping company in 1946 and afterwards to Greek interests, retained its original name, *Richard D. Lyons* for its entire commercial life which ended under the breaker's torch in Japan in 1968. Despite the superstitious belief held by sailors generally, that it is unlucky to change the name of a ship, most of the Liberties sold off to commercial interests underwent at least one name change, and five, six and seven changes in a ship's lifetime were not at all uncommon. Some ships experienced eight, but the record goes to the eight ships that each enjoyed nine name changes; with one or two of these the last name was given only for the purpose of the final voyage to the breaker's yard. (Full official records for those Liberties which ended up in Chinese hands are not available so it is possible that one of those might hold the record for name changes.) One of the 'niners' was the *Matthew Brush* (Baltimore, August 1943) which successively became *Samoa, Eurymedon, Glenlogan, Eurymedon* again, *Angelos, Mimosa, Alplata,* and *Anka* before being scrapped at Bilbao in 1971.

Even that is not the end of the story. A few months after the end of the war and when mines were still a danger, the American Liberty *Nathaniel Bacon* ran into a minefield off Civitavecchia, Italy on 19 December 1945. She caught fire, was beached and there she broke in two. In 1950 the stern part was salved and towed to Genoa. In the following year the fore part of another Liberty also arrived at Genoa, the half of what had once been *Bert Williams* (the second of the two Liberties to hold that name). This ship had broken in two after drifting ashore near Mersa Matruh in 1948. Although the first ship had been built at Baltimore and the second at Portland, Maine, they were, of course, identical twins, and the two halves were capable of being joined together relatively easily. The resulting ship was called *Boccadasse*. This cloned ship ended up being 30ft longer than a standard Liberty with a consequent higher gross tonnage. *Boccadasse* traded successfully for Italian owners Porto Figari for twelve years until the ship was broken up at La Spezia in 1963.

Porto Figari and the Genoa shipyard turned out to be something of Liberty clone specialists. The *Josephine Shaw Lowell*, already mentioned above, was sold to the Italian company in 1946, becoming the *Albaro*. The line also purchased in 1958 the third-hand Liberty *Samdaring*

(Portland, Maine 1944), renaming her *Priaruggia*. In 1960 the line needed a larger ship, so the fore part of *Priaruggia* was joined to the after part of *Albaro* the discarded halves being scrapped, and the new ship being given the latter name. She ended up 70ft longer than a standard Liberty with a gross tonnage of nearly 8500 tons. She was sold on in 1963 and ended up at the Hitachi breaker's yard in Osaka in 1968.

The keel of the very last Liberty to be built was laid on 11 July 1945. She was launched as the *Albert M. Boe* just over two months later on 26 September by the New England Shipbuilding Corporation at Portland, Maine. She was one of the four-hatch variants specially constructed to carry boxed aircraft, and operated first with the Army Transportation Service then with the Military Sea Transportation Service, until being mothballed as part of the reserve fleet in 1954. Ten years later she became a floating fish cannery plant at Kodiak, Alaska with the name *Star of Kodiak*. She is still there although no longer afloat, having been surrounded by landfill. She no longer has masts, the accommodation has been reduced, and holes have been cut in her hull to facilitate the cannery operations. But well maintained, she remains recognisable as a Liberty. It was appropriate that the last Liberty ship ever to be constructed came from the Portland, Maine, yard, for that was one of the two yards where the story all began with the construction of the British Ocean vessels.

CHAPTER 6

The Wartime Liberty Crews

The American Merchant Marine

A shortage of trained merchant seamen in the United States was the principal reason behind the American decision to transfer Liberty ships to other Allied merchant fleets during the war. This manpower shortfall grew larger by the day as the country's shipyards kept churning out merchant ships at an ever-increasing rate. At one stage, when an average of four ships a day were being added to the American Merchant Marine, there was a daily requirement for around 200 additional men to man them and, despite the best recruiting efforts of the US Maritime Commission, there were just not enough qualified men for the job even when experienced former seafarers like seventy-six year-old Ship's Cook James Logan were dragged out of retirement, in his case to serve on the Liberty *Joshua Hendy* (Richmond, July 1943). Even when standard training programmes were short-circuited in various ways, a shortfall still remained, and this despite a huge four-fold increase in personnel that took the Merchant Marine from 55,000 strong at the time of Pearl Harbor to 215,000 by March 1945.[1] The Merchant Marine lost 6700 officers and men killed in the war, a higher proportion of the total who served, than any of the American armed services.

The US Merchant Marine Cadet Corps was established in 1938 to train young men as ships' officers, and the Merchant Marine Academy at Kings Point on Long Island was built for the purpose on an estate previously owned by automobile tycoon Walter Chrysler. By the end of the war it had produced 6000 new officers. Upon the United States entry into the war, and for the duration of it, four additional academies, three on the east coast and one in California, were created. In comparing American and British merchant officer training, two differences stand out. Firstly, in America where the importance of the mercantile marine as a constituent of national defence was enshrined by statute, there was greater involvement by government agencies than in Britain where there was no such formal enactment. The Kings Point Academy, for example, was

---

1. US Maritime Administration Fact Sheet, 22 May 1945.

staffed principally by US navy personnel and was very much run along the lines of its naval counterpart at Annapolis. Secondly, American deck and engine-room cadets were trained in the same establishments. The situation was different in Britain where most officer training remained as it had always been, in the hands of individual shipping companies. In the case of British deck officers, most began their careers as apprentices, cadets, or midshipmen attached to a particular shipping line, and were sent to sea from day one, the adequacy or otherwise of their shipboard training being largely dependant upon the masters under whom they served. The formal, academic, side of the British method of training usually came at the end of the qualifying sea time period required by the Merchant Shipping Acts, and was carried out in nautical schools and colleges situated in most major ports and which were largely financed by the municipality concerned. In Britain, deck and engine-room training establishments were kept quite separate.

Training of non-commissioned personnel in the US came under the guidance of a government department called the US Maritime Service, also established in 1938. As well as training new recruits, it looked after upgrading matters, including examinations. The Service operated three training stations, at Sheepshead Bay close to New York, at Treasure Island near San Francisco, and in the middle of the nation, at Waukegan on Lake Michigan, just north of Chicago. One man, whose string of upgradings took him from deck boy through to master, 'coming up through the hawsepipe' as he calls it, was John Simms. (Coming up through the hawsepipe, a colloquial way of describing a rise through the ranks as opposed to being a cadet officer first, has never been an uncommon practice in the world's merchant fleets. Uninformed commentators sometimes use the phrase in a derogatory sense, which is quite wrong. One thing is for sure; any 'hawespipe' officer certainly knew his seamanship.) The five ships John sailed in consecutively between mid-1943 and 1946 were Liberty ships. He joined *John N. Maffitt* as an Able Seaman at Charleston in August 1943 for her maiden voyage to what he calls 'Russia's backdoor', Khorramshar, in Iran. His next two Liberties were the *Andrew Turnbull* and *William Crane Gray,* on both of which he served as Bosun. By the time he arrived back in the States in the fall of 1944, John had five years sea time to his credit, so he took a three weeks' course at a navigation school before successfully sitting for his Second Mate's Licence.

In the following month he signed on the Liberty *Frederic W. Galbraith*. John says, 'As I actually shipped as Second Mate, it was hard'. It was his first experience as an officer, not even having had the benefit of a breaking-in period as Third Mate. As Second Mate, in keeping with standard sea-going practice, John was the ship's navigating officer and, again in line with practice, he kept the two 12 to 4 watches each day. The outcome was that it was rarely possible for him to get more than three consecutive hours in his bunk. Not only that, during his brief time at navigation school there had only been time for him to learn the Time Sight Method of finding the ship's position at sea, the calculations for which are rather laborious especially after being hauled out of one's bunk only minutes, it seemed, after having laid one's head down. After about a year of this John says he 'got smart and changed to H.O. 214'. (H.O. 214 were pre-computed tables produced by the US Hydrographic Office which enabled navigators to do away with long calculations. At that time, and for many years afterwards, the use of such 'new-fangled' methods was very much frowned upon by nautical school tutors and by many ship captains. The main criticism levelled at them was that their use often meant that the theory behind the longer calculation methods went unlearned.) John's fifth and last Liberty was the *Thomas J. Rusk* in which he sailed as Chief Officer after the war. The influence that the convoy system had on American officer training has been largely over-looked by post-war commentators. The fact that the majority of merchant ships, especially in the Atlantic, sailed in convoy, must have been one of the factors taken into consideration when the American authorities decided to reduce the periods of sea-going experience required before an officer could sit for his examinations. For, providing a ship did not straggle from the convoy, no great navigational expertise was required when sailing in consort with others. As long as the commodore ship knew where it was, then so, within a ship's length or two, did everyone else.

Two Kings Point graduates were Deck Cadet Romuald Holubowicz and Engineer Cadet John Brewster. Romuald arrived at Kings Point on his eighteenth birthday, 24 January 1942, as a cadet midshipman. Born in Wisconsin within sight of Lake Michigan, he had never seen the sea before arriving at Long Island. By that time, because of the United States' entrance into the war on 7 December 1941 and the consequent growing shortage of trained merchant marine officers, the original length of an individual cadet training programme had already been considerably foreshortened. Cadets were now required to spend only six months at the academy to receive basic training in the sea-going arts and sciences, to be followed by six months training 'on the job' at sea, then a further twelve months at the Academy for additional academic work and officer-licence examinations. Under that system a certificated officer could be produced in only two years. But even that foreshortened period was not sustainable throughout the war, and it was reduced even further as the number of ships increased and as some officers lost their lives in the line of duty. Fast advancement is one of the few sweeteners of war, and it sometimes led to ships having very young captains indeed. Captain William Travers of the Liberty *James Ford Rhodes* (Los Angeles, August 1942) for example, was only twenty-two; not only that, his brother who was a year his junior, was the ship's First Mate! (It is good to know that the *Rhodes* and both brothers survived the war.)

Due to the emergency Romuald Holubowicz ended up joining his first ship, Lykes Line's *Syros,* as Deck Cadet on 7 March 1942, having managed over the preceding six weeks to imbibe only the very basics of his adopted profession. Along with him went fellow Kings Pointer, Engineer Cadet John Brewster. *Syros* was not a Liberty ship – she was an old freighter of 1919 vintage – but Romuald's experiences aboard her are relevant to our story as being representative of the sort of on-the-job and under fire training that most of the intake of new American sea officers received, although perhaps Romuald's experiences turned out to be a little more hair-raising than most. The wartime exigencies that resulted in further reductions to the time many cadets spent at the Academy meant that Romuald, as we shall see, was to spend a total of only a little over three months there instead of the prescribed eighteen.

Romuald's recorded insights on the political leanings of some members of the crews he sailed with are also of interest as many of the type of men he described served on Liberty ships. He points out that, in the United States, the Great Depression of the 1930s brought about not only President Roosevelt's New Deal, but also, within certain elements of the American working class and intelligentsia, a sympathy for the type of socialism being developed in the Soviet Union. Romuald says that the invasion of the USSR by Germany cleared the way for this built-in sympathy to find expression. He says,

> As a result, there was no lack of willing hands to man ships bound for Murmansk in the early days of USA involvement [in the war], who saw their participation, very sotto voce of course, as a mission or crusade to assist 'comrades' facing the threat of conquest by Nazi Germany which was seen as being even worse and infinitely more evil than raw capitalism. One met, in the crews of some of the early convoys, veterans of the International Brigade and others who were part of the bitter strikes of the mid-1930s, eager to give active support to the USSR's war effort. Putting aside political orientation, it must be said that these veteran crewmen were, overall, excellent and experienced seamen. By volunteering to man the ships bound for Murmansk, they contributed significantly in the initial stages of the War in the North.

He goes on,

> As the US merchant fleet expanded, rapidly and prodigiously, the composition of US ships' crews changed very quickly into the mainstream of American youth with many thousands of fresh recruits from the farmlands of the Midwest to the bayous of the south and the metropolitan centres of the coastal areas – in short, a cross section of the population . . .

> . . . I was part of this 'new breed' and benefited greatly from the experience, patience, and tolerance of the 'veterans' I encountered on board who taught me seamanship and helped me make my own contribution to what was to follow.[2]

We shall see that there was a great deal 'to follow' for young Romuald whose first four months on shipboard were not only to provide him with a 'University of the Sea' education, but also a baptism of fire.

Romuald and his friend John Brewster joined *Syros* at Philadelphia where she was loading a cargo for Murmansk. Loading completed, she headed for Halifax, Nova Scotia, the starting point for most eastbound convoys. There she joined a thirty-ship convoy, and under British naval protection made it safely to the River Clyde. During that passage Romuald received his first taste of war at arms-length, it coming with the sound of depth charges going off in the distance. Like most American freighters in early 1942, *Syros* had not yet been fitted with guns for self-protection, so at Greenock on the Clyde she was fitted with four twin-.30 calibre machine guns dating from the previous World War, together with a pair of special devices designed to bring down low-flying aircraft. These were PAC rocket-launchers, the letters standing for 'parachute and cable-carrying', and their placement on board was indicative of the general shortage of proper armaments for ships at that time of the war. The theory behind this contraption was that when the rocket, which trailed about forty feet of piano wire to each end of which was attached a small parachute to delay final descent, was fired ahead of a *very* low-flying plane, the wire would become entangled in some part of the aircraft's fuselage, or better still its propeller, or perhaps even slice a wing off.[3] Romuald and other crew member volunteers received some rather basic training on these armaments. The armament training over, *Syros* joined convoy PQ-16 for Murmansk in May, the commodore ship being the almost brand-new *Ocean Voice,* launched at Richmond, California, just five months earlier. It was a slow convoy; it had to be for *Syros* was only capable of 8kts flat out, a characteristic she shared with several of the other ships there.

Air attacks began on 25 May and carried on until the surviving twenty-seven of the original thirty-five ships reached the Kola Inlet five days later. But *Syros* was not one of those who made it, for early in the morning of the 26th, when west of Bear Island and in waters of minus 2° centigrade, and whilst she was straggling behind the convoy, she was struck amidships

---

2. From Romuald Holubowicz papers entitled *War in the North* at the Imperial War Museum, London, with additional material from correspondence and telephone interviews with the author.
3. Captain S.F. Nicolson papers at Imperial War Museum, London, and additional material in correspondence with the author.

by a torpedo from *U-703* (Lieutenant Commander Bielfeld). Romuald was standing watch at that time with the ship's Third Mate, an octogenarian seaman 'who had come out of retirement to play his part in the war'. The sea was dead calm and Romuald saw the track of the torpedo just seconds before it struck. There was a giant explosion as the missile tore into the engine-room killing all five men on duty there including Cadet John Brewster on only his eightieth day at sea. The ship stopped dead in the water and began settling fast. As the order came to abandon ship Romuald decided to make for his cabin to rescue some papers, a decision that almost cost him his life. Although he quickly gave up that quest, the ship went down taking him with it. He certainly owes his life to the lifejacket he was wearing but to this day does not really know how he managed to get back to the surface. He does recall 'what seemed to be an enormous silence' as he looked around in the water, and also a great sense of abandonment as he saw the shapes of the convoy disappearing into the darkness.

In addition to the five men lost in the engine-room, the ship's captain and chief officer did not make it, but the remainder of the crew were pulled from the water by the minesweeper HMS *Hazard* and the armed trawler HMS *Lady Madeline*. All the survivors except one were lucky to have survived the experience of spending about thirty minutes in freezing waters. The exception was an able seaman known as 'Boston Blackie' who never even got his feet wet. The story goes that as he stood on the rail of the sinking ship, an emergency life-raft broke loose and conveniently floated by. Boston stepped upon it and a little later was picked up by *Hazard*'s crew who spotted him with his thumb in the air as if hitching a ride. Landed at Murmansk the *Syros* survivors were there placed aboard the equally old Lykes Line sister-ship *Hybert* which had been in the same northbound convoy. That ship sailed as part of southbound convoy QP-13 on 28 June and it suffered no air attacks at all because the Germans were more interested in the loaded one then heading northwards, the famously ill-fated PQ-17 which suffered devastating losses because the British Admiralty withdrew its escort ships, mistakenly believing that the *Tirpitz* and other German capital ships were about to break out from their lairs.

Not being on the receiving end of air attacks did not mean that Cadet Holubowicz's baptism of fire was over, not by a long chalk. At 2100 hours on the evening of 5 July, when close to Iceland, all hell let loose as a result of what at first was assumed to be a submarine attack on the convoy. Merchant ships fired their guns and escorts dropped depth-charges, as here and there ships began blowing up. *Hybert* herself was 'wracked by an immense explosion at the stern, bringing the ship to a standstill'. Once again Romuald had lost his ship, but this time as it went down, the entire crew got away in boats. Convoy QP-13 had not run into a U-boat pack. Commander A.J. Cubison aboard the convoy's senior escort, the minesweeper HMS *Niger*, had mistaken an iceberg for land and altered course, only to run into a 'friendly' minefield. *Niger* blew up with heavy loss of life and, including *Hybert*, five merchantmen were also lost. Another merchant vessel, the Liberty ship *John Randolph* (Baltimore, February 1942), was badly damaged. It was a tragic incident that has been rather overshadowed by the blaze of notoriety over the fate of the contemporary but northbound PQ-17.

An hour or so after the sinking a British escort trawler came alongside the boat Romuald was in and began taking the occupants off. But the fates had not yet finished with the young cadet. Halfway through the operation the trawler skipper received a report of a submarine contact, and raced off. That was bad enough, but to the horror of those left in the boat, Romuald amongst them, it was found that those who had been manning the oars before the rescue operation, had simply dropped them overboard. 'The next three hours,' reported Romuald, 'drifting around in mountainous and confused seas in a lifeboat without oars was yet another experience.' They were finally picked up by the Free French corvette *Roselys* under the command of Lieutenant de Vaisseau A. Bergeret who, with two British trawlers, spent over six hours criss-crossing in darkness an area by then known to be a minefield. The gallant Bergeret and his crew saved 179 men that night. Romuald and his shipmates were put ashore at Reykjavik. There he joined the Honduras-flagged passenger ship *Toltec*, 'whose Captain agreed to my signing Articles for a penny a month, which I had requested, to ensure I would be credited with sea time for the passage to satisfy the Merchant Marine Academy's procedural requirements'. The ship reached Boston towards the end of July.

Still only eighteen but now a veteran, by that time Romuald had four of the required six months sea time under his belt, and after a brief leave taken at home rather than at one of the seven rest and recreation centres set up nationwide by the US Maritime Commission, he reported back to Kings Point for a posting to another ship. One would have thought that, on balance, considering the hair-raising incidents he had passed through during his maiden voyage, that the chances were that Romuald's next voyage would be somewhat less adventurous. However, that was not to be. His next ship was a Liberty, but the story of his experiences as she sank under him must wait until the next chapter where it will fit very nicely into the story about the structural cracking problems in welded ships.

Romuald Holubowicz points out that wartime entrants into the American Merchant Marine came from all parts of the country. They came in answer to repeated calls made by the US Maritime Commission that began 'Uncle Sam needs you . . .'. They came from all walks of life and were of all colours and creeds. Some had been rejected by the military on health grounds and came even though they could have remained in safe jobs ashore. Conversely, some able-bodied men joined to escape the draft and sometimes when these individuals discovered that life on a merchant ship could be more dangerous than being in the army, they left to join the armed services. There was little in the way of racial bias on board American merchant ships. The background to that was the avant-garde attitude of the National Maritime Union on this matter, an attitude that ensured no colour barrier and resulted in a very large number of black seamen being employed. The Union's attitude would not have counted for much, however, had not merchant seamen themselves been a tolerant lot. During their voyaging sailors came into contact with people of all races – very, very close contact sometimes – and over the years that had bred a degree of racial tolerance. Klene Wilson, a black ship's steward, encountered no racial problems in his time at sea and says 'all that counted was that you did your job'. He added that because culinary matters were important on board ship, being a steward he was often blamed when things were not quite right, 'but not because of my colour'. Black merchant seamen were not confined to the steward's department, however, and held positions ranging from captain to deck boy. That should be compared to the attitude in the United States Navy. American historian Gerhard Weinberg has written that on this issue the Navy top-brass was unmoving, and that 'even President Roosevelt, the Commander-in-Chief, found that he could hardly budge the Navy's insistence that blacks were to be used only for mess duty'.

As noted above with the Travers brothers, close relatives sometimes served aboard the same ship. In 1945 a father and son served in the Liberty *Webb Miller* (Portland, Maine, December 1943). Lloyd Kinsinger, then forty-one years of age and his son Allen, nineteen, were on that ship as firemen/water tenders. One can only wonder what Mrs. Kinsinger's thoughts must have been about that.

Treated as part of the US Navy Reserve for the duration of their training, new entrants, officers and men, received instruction along military lines and the wearing of uniform was a requirement. As often as not a new rating joining a ship would be told to forget the military training and put his uniform away. Then he would start to learn the trade from the veterans on board. Seaman Bill Bailey said he was helped by many old-timers who did not appear to be too put out by these unpaid coaching jobs.

The important contribution made by foreign seamen in the manning of American merchant ships during the war has been largely forgotten. According to Kalevi Olkio who was one of them, the story has 'never been chronicled'. He was then a Finnish national, and when he joined his second Liberty ship at the age of twenty-three, he already had seven years sea-experience under his belt. He and many others like him must have been welcomed with open arms. He says that on that Liberty, it was the *Tristram Dalton* (Baltimore, September 1942), he had the pleasure of teaching practical seamanship to several teenage seamen who had boarded straight from the training school. He says, 'in two weeks their teamwork was better than a Scandinavian crew'.[4]

Kalevi goes on,

> Many of the foreign seamen who served on Liberty ships in the war came from Denmark and Sweden, and in lesser numbers from Finland and Estonia; also Latvians and Lithuanians in small numbers. There were others like Dutch and Polish and even Swiss seamen that I ran into during the war. Norwegians were very few due to the fact that they were committed to sailing on Norwegian ships, just like the British were committed to sailing on British ones.

Before his service in American ships Kalevi served aboard Swedish and Norwegian vessels. Taken ill, he signed off the Norwegian tanker *Ole Jacob* at Singapore on 5 November 1940. Although hospitalised, he did not then know how lucky he was. Five days later, after that ship had cleared the northern end of the Malacca Straits, she was captured by the German raider *Atlantis*. On the following day *Atlantis* sank the British ship *Automedon*, but not before taking aboard the many important and highly secret British documents she was couriering to Singapore. With a German prize crew on board, the *Ole Jacob* was used to convey those documents to Kobe, Japan, from whence they were carried via the trans-Siberian railway – Russia not then being at war with Germany – to Berlin. Because Japan was not then at war (except with China), and helped by the intervention of Hubert Graves, the British Consul-General in Kobe (who also headed the British MI6 intelligence organisation in Japan), some of the *Ole Jacob* crew were repatriated home by the Siberian route, while others were repatriated via Shanghai and Singapore. Kalevi was still at the latter place when some of the *Ole Jacob* crew passed through. One can only guess at what might have happened to Kalevi had he still been on board at the time. (The Russo-Finnish war had ended by treaty on 13 March 1940, but the Finns were still none too popular in Russia even before Finland joined the Axis assault on that country in July 1941.)[5]

As a Finnish national, life at sea was not always straightforward for Kalevi. He signed aboard the Norwegian tanker *Minister Wedel* as an ordinary seaman in January 1941 and stayed in that ship until she was

---

4. Correspondence with Kalevi O. Olkio, July/August 2000. Born at Viipuri, Finland in 1920 Mr. Olkio went to sea at 16. He became a US citizen in 1947, and set up his own business supplying equipment direct to ships and to shipchandlers. In Baltimore he founded the All Nations Foundation, an umbrella organisation dedicated to ethnic minority matters. He is a board member of Project Liberty Ship the organisation behind the preservation of the *John W. Brown*.

5. See this author's books *Far Eastern File* (London 1997) and *Life-Line* (London 1999) for the fullest descriptions yet published about the *Atlantis/Automedon/Ole Jacob* saga.

torpedoed in January 1943. During that period the *Wedel* called at a port in New Zealand where the authorities tried to arrest and intern him. This must have been sometime after 5 December 1941 on which date Britain – followed by New Zealand – declared war on Finland (and Rumania and Hungary) as that country had allied itself with Germany in the war against Russia. Only the intervention of the Norwegian captain, who told the New Zealanders that Kalevi was a vital member of the ship's gun crew, kept him out of internment for the remainder of the war. His brother was not so lucky, being interned for several years in Britain.

In July 1943 Kalevi attended a Navigation School in New York and, over a total period of six months, was sent on two assignments as junior Third Officer aboard US Army Transport vessels. But then,

> Being a Finnish national and the US declaring war on Finland, I went back to school and then signed on as Bosun aboard the Liberty *Joseph N. Nicollet* [New Orleans, June 1943].

A week later he had to sign off again. The ship was sailing to Murmansk, and being a Finnish citizen that would have meant imprisonment in Russia. For the remainder of the war Kalevi sailed as Third Mate aboard neutral Swedish ships, although in one of them he still entered the war zone around Britain.

When America first entered the war many ships sailed unarmed. This situation was soon corrected but in the interim false guns that could be mistaken for real ones from a distance were sometimes fitted. Once a ship had been fitted with proper armaments the ship's complement was increased on average by between 30 and 50 per cent by the arrival on board of men to man the guns. These men were not merchant seamen, but members of a division of the United States Navy called the Naval Armed Guard. (By the end of the war some 145,000 men had served in Armed Guard units, nearly 2000 of them losing their lives.) A Liberty ship's Armed Guard contingent usually consisted of an Ensign or Lieutenant (jg), four petty officers and about twenty seamen. Typically, Liberty ships were fitted with two dual-purpose 3in guns and eight 20mm anti-aircraft guns. Sometimes in place of one of the 3in, either a 4in or 5in gun was fitted. At sea the Guard divided into three watches, or two when in hostile waters, enough men being on duty at any one time to man both heavy guns, half the smaller ones, and to keep a lookout. At anchor and when alongside in port, they stood anti-sabotage watches. The officer in charge of the unit was not directly responsible to the captain of the ship, and as a result there was a certain dichotomy of command on board. 'Two commands ran each merchant ship during World War II, a merchant marine crew and a Navy crew', state the authors of a book on Liberty ships published by the Texas Historical Commission. In another reference to this problem, Lieutenant A.A. Hoehling of the Armed Guard was later to write in a memoir of his war years some highly critical remarks about an unnamed captain of an unnamed Liberty, which included the passage,

> . . . warwise, he believed gun crews to be a useless luxury. This attitude did not distinguish him from the average merchant skipper who could not adjust or be comfortable with two distinct commands on *his* ship.[6]

A divided command is rarely a good thing and possibly never more so than in the restricted confines of a ship. In those cases where the shipmaster and Armed Guard officer got on well and developed a good working relationship, this dual command had few if any bad effects. But in many instances the pair just did not get on.

By law the master is responsible for the safety of the ship, and that was supported by the content of a US Navy Department document issued to the masters of all American ships. After stating that it was US Government policy that no ship must fall into enemy hands, it went on,

> The ship shall be defended by her armament, by maneuver [US spelling], and by every available means as long as possible. When, *in the judgement* of the Master [author's italics], capture is inevitable, he shall scuttle the ship . . . [7]

That confirms that it was the shipmaster who was the final arbiter of the ship's fate. That notwithstanding, some of the clauses in another Navy Department document entitled 'Instructions to Armed Guards', a document marked 'RESTRICTED' and therefore not to be viewed, officially anyway, by anyone outside the Armed Guard itself, tended to support the stance taken by some Guard officers and men that they were completely outside the master's jurisdiction. One especially contentious aspect of the relationship was whether it was the master or the Armed Guard Officer who had the right to order 'open fire'. Armed Guardman Carl Winder summed up the entire situation very well with his remark that 'we took no crap from anybody'.[8]

The working relationship between Armed Guard and merchant crews on some ships certainly left much to be desired, a situation not helped by the fact that, apart from training crew members in the use of the guns, there was little if any fraternisation between the two groups. 'Only

---

6. (a) J. Barto Arnold and others, *Texas Liberty Ships* (Austin 1998). (b) A.A. Hoehling, *The Fighting Liberty Ships* (Kent, Ohio 1990).
7. US Navy Department document, marked confidential, OP-23L-JH, March 30 1942.
8. US Navy Department document, Instructions to Armed Guards, marked restricted, and dated 1943.

U.S.N. personnel are permitted in your quarters', proclaimed the Navy Department Rules, and, 'Ship's crew quarters are off limits at all times'. This segregation was facilitated by the Armed Guard living aft in the poop, right under one of their main guns, whilst everyone else was accommodated amidships. On top of that, Armed Guard officers who were largely 'hostilities only' reserve officers and rather young with limited experience – merchant seamen called them '90-day wonders' – were required to write voyage reports for the Navy, and often these were used as vehicles for criticising individual crew members, especially captains. Sometimes these criticisms were justified, and sometimes not. When the Liberty *Park Holland* went aground off Scotland on 24 March 1944 after the master, Captain Enar Lindholm, had decided to deviate from the prescribed routing instructions because of prevailing weather conditions, the ship's Armed Guard officer was very critical. In his voyage report submitted to the US Naval Port Officer at Gourock, Scotland, Ensign Pete Drakulich USNR, reported the incident as he was required to do, but ended his report thus:

> Captain Lindholm admittedly violated his routing instructions, although he stated that to do so was necessary for the safety of his vessel. Obviously the steps taken to insure that safety were not effective and it is felt first, that those steps i.e. deviation from routing instructions – were not necessary, and second that proceeding for the length of time that Captain Lindholm did on the course adopted was an error.

Two comments on Ensign Drakulich's report come to mind. One is that it is easy to be wise after the event. The second is more in the way of a query. Was an ensign in the naval reserve qualified to question the judgement of a qualified shipmaster?

One Armed Guard officer took offence because the captain did not ask him along to the convoy Commodore's Conference held prior to sailing. These conferences, especially when run by the British and Canadians, were nearly always for masters only and invariably were very crowded affairs anyway, so the navy man was being unreasonable. On the other hand, Ensign Leo Koons on board the Liberty *Charles A. Dana* in January 1944 seems to have had a point when in his report he strongly criticised both Captain Viktor Peterson and the ship's Steward when, only eight weeks into the voyage, food had to be rationed when sufficient stores should have been aboard for six months. But that pales into insignificance when compared with the dire relationship that developed between Lieutenant (jg) Marion Vickery and the captain of the Liberty *Rachel Jackson*. Their relationship fell apart completely, and the report filed by Vickery in November 1943 later led to accusations that the captain was pro-Nazi. In his report Vickery listed several occasions when the captain's actions had 'placed the ship and her personnel in serious danger'. He reported that the captain had refused to move cargo booms and other impedimenta from the gunners' arc of fire, and had refused to share with Vickery radioed reports about submarine sightings in the ship's immediate area. When these allegations were investigated by naval authorities at San Pedro, it was concluded that Vickery's complaints were probably justified; not only that, the Port Director of the Sea Transportation Service noted that the captain 'has a distinct foreign accent that appears to be Germanic', and said that the master's name had been 'added to the Merchant Marine Suspect List as of September 1st 1943'. There is little doubt that the captain's actions on board ship were reprehensible, but there was no proof to support the pro-Nazi allegations. Nevertheless, apparently the end result was that the captain was relieved of his command.

During the war the shipping companies running ships for the US Maritime Commission were expected operate them on a commercial basis, and that included making a profit. On at least one occasion the profit motive led to a dispute between a ship's captain and the Armed Guard officer on board. The dispute on the Liberty *Dwight L. Moody* arose over the deployment of the ships anti-torpedo nets, clumsy devices designed to prevent torpedoes ever reaching a vessel's hull. On a voyage to Canada the *Moody*'s nets were rigged by the ship's crew only to be taken in on the following day when the sea became rough, perhaps because the captain decided the weather conditions were not conducive to submarine operations. After the sea moderated, Lieutenant (jg) David Marx importuned the captain to re-stream the nets on several occasions but this was refused, apparently on the grounds that the extra work would entail overtime payments to the civilian crew, an expense the company would have to foot. On a few occasions, this dichotomy of command led to the breaking of one of the unwritten, but nevertheless golden, traditions of the sea, that the captain should always be the last to leave a sinking ship.

In case the impression has been given that this Navy/Merchant Marine relationship was all bad news, an incident involving the Liberty *John Bascom* in December 1943 will be related later in this book which proves that an excellent relationship could develop between the two 'sides'. In general it seems that in cases where the ship's captain was a mature, well experienced man with years of man-management behind him, and the Armed Guard officer who sailed with him acted with common sense and gave the captain's experience and his own comparative inexperience their proper due, the relationship could develop into a positive one.

It should not be assumed that antagonism between the two sides was confined solely to the two senior officers involved. Often it went all down the line. Naval men sometimes levelled draft-dodging accusations at merchant sailors and accused them of being 'red'. Furthermore, wages and conditions of employment of merchant crews remained under the umbrella of union contracts that were in effect despite the war, and an appointed union delegate was on every ship to ensure the contracts were not broken. American merchant seamen were therefore generally thought to better paid than the naval men on the same ship, and it is certainly true that merchant seamen were paid overtime, a concept unheard of in the navy. Without mentioning overtime, former Armed Guardsman Edward Haake remembers that in mid-1942 a merchant ship Able Seaman was paid '$100 a month, 100% bonus, war zone $15 per day, and an air raid allowance of $150 for each port'. He compared that with a Navy Seaman First Class who 'received $56 a month and 10% sea pay'. Purser Bob Gifford, who on board ship had payroll responsibilities, says that merchant ship seamen's base pay was supplemented with bonuses for being in 'certain so-called dangerous waters'. He goes on, 'we also got port pay in certain waters and once, a bonus for undergoing an air raid'. That was on board the *Edwin M. Stanton* (Portland, Oregon, September 1942) at Naples in early 1944. That payment was made, says Gifford, because 'we had all that ammunition on board, naturally'.

Edward Haake has made a study of the comparative wage situation, and although not all bonuses were received on a regular basis, he records several instances in which, over certain periods and under certain conditions, war zone and air raid bonuses could raise a merchant marine Able Seaman's average emoluments to over ten times that of an Armed Guard seaman serving in the same ship. One example he cites concerned the Liberty *Morrison R. Waite* (Richmond, November 1942), serving in the Pacific between May 1944 and January 1945. That ship was in the thick of things, and during that period, war zone and air raid payments for an A.B. aboard her amounted to $4050 (equating to about $80,000 nowadays) which the Navy men did not receive. (This American system of war bonuses should be compared to the more modest, and more simple, British system outlined below.) According to an official War Shipping Administration report, wages for equivalent positions in the Navy and the Merchant Marine, were about the same or perhaps higher for Navy personnel, when their other benefits including paid leave, paid uniforms, generous retirement benefit, and free medical care for themselves and their families was taken into consideration. That report made no mention of the merchant marine special bonuses, although it had been the WSA that had agreed the bonus structure with the maritime unions. Neither side during the original negotiations could, of course, have had any idea of the anomalies that were to result.

Some misconception over this issue, possibly based on not having the full facts, rubbed off on commentators ashore who added fuel to the fire. Merchant seamen were accused of taking advantage of the war to get rich. Westbrook Pegler a columnist with the New York *World Telegram*, a man known for his caustic remarks about public figures, took the matter even further when on several occasions he concentrated his venom on merchant mariners. He variously called them 'riffraff and bums', 'draft dodgers', and 'scum of the earth'. Walter Winchell of the New York *Daily Mirror* and of radio broadcasting fame, once zeroed in on the marine unions, and went as far as to announce that merchant seamen were sabotaging US ships. Deck-hand Vito Verzi says of these writers, 'we were out there fighting for their right to sit behind their typewriters to type those things'.

During the war over 140 Distinguished Service Medals were awarded to American Merchant Marine personnel for 'service beyond the call of duty'. In addition, 362 Meritorious Service Medals, a slightly lower grade, were presented. The Mariner's Medal, the equivalent of the American Armed Service's Purple Heart, was awarded to over 5000 individuals or to their next of kin. The Americans also instituted a Gallant Ship Award, of which a total of ten were awarded. The first of these went to the Liberty *Samuel Parker* (Portland, Oregon, November 1942) for months of service in the Mediterranean during which she frequently landed cargoes at ports close to the front line. She survived frequent air attacks and also incidents with mines and torpedoes. When she eventually returned to the States her hull and superstructure bore witness to her war service, for she was had been holed in hundreds of places. Another Liberty recipient of the Gallant Ship Award was the *Stephen Hopkins,* and her story will be found in Chapter 9. The Philippines Government issued another type of ship award in the form of a Liberation Ribbon. Two Liberty ship recipients of this ribbon were the *William H. Allen* (Richmond, August 1943) and *Jim Bridger* (Portland, Oregon, December 1942) named after the famous frontiersman and army scout.

Towards the end of the war when a Bill of Rights for returning servicemen was first mooted, President Roosevelt intended it to include merchant mariners, but that fell through after he died. Senior armed service chiefs lobbied against the idea, and the end result was that merchant seamen were excluded from veteran's benefits. That remained the situation until 1986, when by order of the Supreme Court no less, and much too late for many, the US Government granted Second World War merchant seamen the coveted veterans' status. At the same time campaign medals were struck for them, but they were not handed out free. Herk Esibill says, 'in effect we had to pay for them twice, first to earn them, then to attain them!! What an insult!'[9]

The British Merchant Navy

According to official government figures issued in 1946 the British Merchant Navy suffered 30,248 known fatalities during the war with another

9. Herk Esibill of Project Liberty Ship, letter to author dated 8 November 1999.

4654 reported as missing. This enormous combined total of 34,902 deaths (some authorities place the figure even higher than that) was a far higher proportion of its total strength than that of any of the Allied armed services except possibly the Russian Army. A further 4707 British seamen were wounded, and 5720 became prisoners of war. The first of the deaths came within hours of war being declared on 3 September 1939 when the liner *Athenia* was sunk with the loss of 128 passengers and crew. Despite these huge losses and the call-up of merchant seamen, especially officers, into the Royal Navy Reserve during the war, the Merchant Navy did not suffer many manpower shortages except during the early days of the naval call-up and during particularly bad periods. If it can be said that from 1942 onwards America had a surfeit of ships but a dearth of seamen to man them, then it can be said that with the British it was the other way round.

There were several reasons for this positive manpower situation. To start with, when war was declared in 1939 the British Merchant Navy was by far the largest in the world and so started off from a much higher base of ships and men than any other fleet. Although many ships were soon lost, most of the crews concerned were saved either by being picked up by other merchant vessels including neutral ships, or by the Navy, or by reaching safety as a result of their own efforts. So, despite devastating losses among British seamen during the first three years of the war, those losses were never directly proportional to the even more devastating loss of ships (even more devastating that is, from the strategic and not the humanitarian point of view). The content of an official British Ministry of Shipping memorandum dated 18 June 1941 shows this quite clearly.

> As a very rough guide it can be assumed that one third of the Mercantile Marine [ships] is lost each year, and figures given to us by the Admiralty recently indicated that of the ships torpedoed in the last three months, 75% of the crews have been saved.

(A follow-up memo from the same source dated 3 July 1941 shows that merchant seamen deaths reported up to that date amounted to 6737, of which 3261 had occurred up to the end of 1940. The memo went on to list the reported deaths for the first five months of 1941 as, January 624, February 664, March 495, April 431, and May 1262. The writer of that memo ended it with a note to the effect that there could be a five- to six-month delay in reporting some losses.)

Another helpful factor was that many veteran seamen who had earlier retired from the sea were brought back to serve again under the Red Ensign at the outbreak of war, thanks largely to a register of such men that was kept pre-war by the shipping authorities in London. At the other end of the age spectrum, many youngsters of sixteen went to sea as cadets and deck, cabin and galley boys. Not a few fourteen and fifteen year-olds who lied about their ages also went down to the sea in ships. It is worthwhile remembering that both these age groups, the very old and the very young, lay well outside the recruiting age for the armed services. Some men too, who could not get into the armed services for medical reasons were accepted into the Merchant Navy; a pair of flat feet, for instance, not being considered too much of a hindrance to a man heaving coal as a member of the so-called 'black gang' in a ship's stokehold. The strictest part of the medical test concerned eyesight, especially colour-blindness; for not being able to distinguish red from green, port from starboard, could have led to disaster. (In both the American and British merchant fleets the physical standards required of new entrants had always been considerably lower than those required by military and naval authorities. Captain Elwin Knowles of the American Liberty ship *John Harvey,* for example, had a club-foot and would never have passed a medical for the US Navy. Captain Knowles will feature again in this book.)

As far as officer training was concerned, Britain did not reduce the necessary sea time requirement for examinations for certificates on anywhere near the same scale as did the Americans. Cadets, apprentices, and midshipmen with only three years sea service to their credit instead of the four required under pre-war legislation, were allowed to sit the Second Mate's examination and, provided they passed, were granted what was called a Temporary Second Mate's Certificate. This remained valid until the officer passed his First Mate's examination. There was a catch. The regulations called for eighteen months sea service between sitting for Second and First Mate's examinations, but the year 'allowance' permitted for the temporary certificate was added to this period so that overall the officer put in the same amount of sea time as pre-war. The pool of officers was further increased by allowing uncertificated but experienced men to take jobs as Fourth and Third Mates. Similar procedures were adopted but on an even larger scale with junior Engineer Officers. This use of uncertificated officers was not a new departure, for uncertificated junior officers had been around for a long time in tramp ships, but the incidence was greatly increased during the war.

In 1941 the headmaster of the famous Gordonstoun School in Scotland, Kurt Hahn, and Lawrence Holt, of Blue Funnel Line, got together, the end result being the founding of the Outward Bound Sea School at Aberdovey. This school began by providing month-long pre-sea nautical courses for cadets, but was so successful that it soon widened its horizons. Prior to joining his first ship, Blue Funnel's *Maron* as an apprentice on 1 September 1942, Sandy Mackenzie spent his month there having had no previous nautical experience. He was to go on and serve in *Samsette,* built as the *Augustus Herman* at Baltimore in November 1943.

All over Britain established nautical schools and colleges expanded their courses, and new schools were formed to train even more men. The

Shipping Federation, a shipowner's organisation, developed additional training schemes for ratings. In 1942 the government created the Merchant Navy Training Board with the stated task of co-ordinating these training programmes. On top of all that, Britain was able to draw upon seamen from the Commonwealth and Empire countries. Canada built a Merchant Navy training camp and some of the men trained there came from across the United States border before that country entered the war, much like the American citizens who volunteered for the British armed services. One such American was Richard Maury, a descendant of Matthew Fontaine Maury, the great oceanographer. Maury joined the Merchant Navy in 1940 and, being an experienced seaman, was appointed as instructor at the Canadian camp and stayed there right up to the time his own country entered the war. Seamen from other neutral countries also served in the British Merchant Navy, perhaps the largest contingent coming from Sweden. At least one anti-Fascist Spanish sea captain served on a British ship. He had made his home in Britain prior to 1939. In 1941 the British ship on which he was serving as a supernumerary, was blown from under him but he managed to survive.

In general it can be said that there was never a dearth of new applicants for the Merchant Navy. Some of the applicants no doubt mistakenly thought that service in the Merchant Navy was rather safer than being in the armed services; others would have been attracted by the comparatively high wages paid to merchant seamen, especially when the so-called War Risk Payment was taken into account. The War Risk money was paid at a flat rate of £10 per month to every seaman irrespective of rank, the only exception being those under eighteen years of age who received only £5. (A rather strange arrangement, for from an actuarial point of view, the youngsters had more to lose.) This extra payment was reasonably cast for the times, but it was not large. There were no air-raid bonuses and no extra bonuses for serving in particular war zones, except on very rare occasions. (The blockade run to Sweden to bring back much needed ball-bearings was one of the exceptions.) So, to suggest as some people in authority did immediately after the war, and as some writers have maintained since, that a large proportion of new entrants joined the Merchant Navy because it was better paid and safer than the alternatives, is not true and is an unjustified slur on the great majority.

As in the US, accusations of draft-dodging and cowardice were sometimes levelled at merchant seamen during the war, usually by self-appointed members of what can be called the 'White Feather Brigade'. This situation was aggravated by the fact that, except for officers, few merchant seamen wore uniforms. Britain was in a state of almost total mobilisation, and any young or youngish man found walking around in civvies could find himself the butt of derogatory remarks. This kind of thing probably did not happen as often as some old salts from those days like to say it did; for in the nation's ports, where most seamen on shore leave would have stayed because they lived nearby, the presence of civilian-dressed seamen was common. (It certainly never happened as often as some television documentary producers, out for the telling phrase rather than historical accuracy, would have us believe.) Nevertheless it happened sometimes and, in view of the percentage of casualties the service sustained, it was totally unjustified. To cover this situation the British authorities decided to issue the small distinguishing silver-coloured lapel 'MN' badges, emblems that many sailors proudly display to this day.

On reaching British shores survivors from British ships rarely received much in the way of rest and recreation leaves, and this had the effect of increasing the total pool of men available at any one time. Such was the number and world-wide spread of British merchant ships, that even survivors in far-flung places were soon returned to the fold, either by being placed on a visiting ship as a permanent member of its crew or as a 'passenger' for the voyage home. In the case of 'company' men, mostly officers but sometimes including senior ratings, most were permitted to rejoin their shipping company at the first available opportunity.

The case of Blue Funnel Midshipman Mike Curtis, who was eventually to crew one of the Liberties handed over to Britain, provides a good example of the reallocation of a company man, even if it is one that contains more than a fair share of adventure. Mike, who rose to command several Blue Funnel ships after the war, was the senior midshipman of four aboard the company's *Talthybius* at Singapore just before that so-called fortress fell to the Japanese in February 1942. The ship was badly damaged by Japanese bombs and despite several days of heroic efforts by the crew and a local diver to save her, the ship, which by then was sitting on the bottom of Empire Dock, had to be abandoned only four days before Singapore surrendered. Most of the Chinese members of the crew disappeared to lose themselves amongst the majority of that city's residents, whilst the British crew members, mostly officers, were ordered to escape on other ships still in the doomed port. Most were taken aboard HMS *Ping Wo,* a small, flat-bottomed, requisitioned ship that in a previous life had been a Yangtze river boat. *Ping Wo's* commander was very pleased to see the group because most of his own Chinese seamen and stokers had acted similarly to the Blue Funnel Chinese. The result was that when the little steamer made good her escape from the port, which by then was under shellfire as well as being continually bombed, and with over 200 evacuees on board, she sailed with probably the best qualified deck and engine-room crew of any vessel ever to have sailed from the port. The steamer made it safely to Batavia on the island of Java, where the spirits of Mike and his companions were mightily uplifted at the sight of the distinctive funnel shapes of four Blue Funnel ships in the harbour. After the ordeals of *Talthybius,* to say nothing of the perils of *Ping Wo,* they looked forward to rejoining the fleet. It was not to turn out that way.[10] The disabled Australian destroyer HMAS *Vendetta* was in port and required a tow to Fremantle, and the only ship available for the task was HMS *Ping Wo* despite being highly unsuited for the job. Deep-sea tugs, any tugs, have comparatively deep drafts for their size in order for their propellers to bite deep in the water. *Ping Wo,* on the contrary, had been designed with a minimal draft to operate in shallow waters. Perhaps it was the unsuitability of the craft that made the naval authorities at Batavia decide to keep the highly-qualified crew on board; a good crew had a better chance of succeeding. So, on 15 February, the ungainly duo left Batavia on the 2000-mile journey to Fremantle. They passed through the Sunda Strait twenty-four hours later having made a bare 100 miles in that time. Then, says Mike, 'both ships started to roll steadily to varying degrees, and continued to roll for the next sixteen days'. Suffice it to say that both ships arrived safely at Fremantle on 4 March and there, in order of seniority, the Talthybians were placed on other ships for home. Being at the bottom of the pecking order the four midshipmen were last, and when, after enjoying six weeks of the very best kind of Australian hospitality they were placed aboard a ship for home, one suspects they were not anywhere near as keen to rejoin the fleet as they had been at Batavia.

Mike arrived home in the late summer of 1942 and served on other Blue Funnel ships. By the autumn of 1943 he had risen in rank to Fourth Mate despite not yet having sat for his Second Mate's ticket. He then travelled on the troopship *Queen Elizabeth* to New York as a member of a crew sent over to man a Liberty ship. By that time he was on a salary of £28 per month, plus £5 a month War Risk Payment, riches beyond imagination compared with the lowly sums paid to officer cadets. After two months of what Mike calls 'easy living' in New York, the crew was sent to Baltimore to collect their Liberty. Launched as the *Martha C. Thomas* she became the *Samharle* and was handed over to the British on 23 December. On the previous day at that same shipyard a ship called *Samtampa* was handed over to a Houlder Brothers crew, whilst on the day after *Samharle,* another Liberty called *Samkey* was delivered to a crew of the New Zealand Shipping Company. Of this consecutive British trio, only *Samharle* was to avoid a tragic end. The stories of the other two will be found later in this book.

Mike Curtis was an observant chronicler, and it is worthwhile noting his comments on the Bethlehem-Fairfield yard at Baltimore (remembering that this was the only Liberty shipyard to use rivets to fasten the ships' seams).

---

10. Captain Michael J. Curtis, correspondence and telephone interviews with author, 1999-2000.

Just to be in an American shipyard in those days was an education. The hooter blew for the start of a shift and almost immediately several hundred pneumatic rivet hammers commenced operation on various stages of construction embracing, I suppose, about fifteen slipways.When the whistle blew at the end of the shift the silence was deafening. Each ship to be handed over to the British was completed to the US standard. After running sea trials and having had the final details adjusted . . . everything was signed for by departmental heads.

After the actual handing over had taken place he says,

The ship was then moved to a bunkering port and thence to a final fitting out berth where certain equipment and parts of the structure were brought up to U.K. specifications, armaments fitted, torpedo net defence booms fitted together with paravanes which were then tested.

Eighteen years old at the time, Arthur Harvey was another seamen sent to the States to take over a Liberty ship. He travelled with other members of two Union Castle crews on the trooper *Île de France,* embarking at Greenock in June 1943 for the voyage to New York. He and his shipmates spent eight weeks in that city before being sent across country. In common with many other British seamen with time on their hands in New York and little money with which to enjoy it, he got himself a temporary job to earn some beer money. He was employed as a greaser in Knickerbockers Ice Plant on West 67th Street. Others in the crew 'got positions as store detectives in large department stores'. The two crews then went by train to San Francisco and spent a further two weeks waiting there, where Arthur, again short of drinking money, got himself a job at the main railroad station hefting mailbags for $1 an hour. Then it was on to Los Angeles where the crews joined the *Samsteel* (ex-*James H. Robinson*) and *Sampan* (ex-*William I. Kip*) on 15 and 17 August respectively, Arthur's ship being the latter.[11]

Another seaman to travel to join a Liberty in the comparative luxury of the *Queen Elizabeth* was Tom Flack. He was a member of a Prince Line crew sent to pick up the *Samdaring* at Portland, Maine, the ship which as the *Priaruggia* at Genoa in 1960 was to supply the after part of the lengthened clone ship *Albaro,* as described in the previous chapter. Tom Flack does not report having taken a temporary job during his several week's wait at New York; but does say that he enjoyed the Broadway shows and films he saw by courtesy of free tickets issued by the United Services Organisation. Third Radio Officer Ian Malcolm also

---

11. Captain Arthur Harvey, correspondence with author, 1999-2000.

travelled on the luxury liner. He says that all but a handful of the passengers on board were either Merchant Navy personnel travelling to join new ships, or Royal Air Force recruits being sent to Canada for training as air crew.[12]

One young British officer who enjoyed his period of waiting in New York more than most was Welshman Richard Humphreys; after experiencing three years of unlimited war at sea, who can blame him? At the latter end of 1943 with a two months' wait on his hands before the *Samboston* (ex-*Willis J. Abbott*) at Baltimore was ready, and having family connections on Long Island, he applied for a Green Card and a social security number which gave him the legal right to look for employment in the States, a nicety that most of the other Brits seem to have avoided. He went along to Macy's Department Store where the Personnel Manager apparently thought that anyone from Britain must know all there was to know about English china. Richard had heard of the names Royal Doulton and Wedgwood, but that was about the sum total of his knowledge. Nevertheless it was enough for him to be taken on as supervisor in the store's china department, a job that provided him money enough to splash around a bit. At one of the night spots he visited he became friendly with the fabulously pretty Hollywood starlet Joanne Dru, so proving that war is not all hell. The United States and its people must have left lasting impressions on Richard, for he later married an American lady.[13]

Although many British Liberty ship crews were sent to the States as complete units, on occasion captains were sent ahead on their own to watch over the final stages of construction. One of those was Captain T. Davies who crossed the Atlantic to New York aboard the trooper *Aquitania* and then made the long rail journey to Portland, Oregon. He arrived there in time to see his ship launched as *Charles A. Broadwater* on 29 August 1943. That name was changed to *Samthar* before the ship was handed over and placed under the management of Captain Davies' company, Royal Mail Lines. (After the war the ship was purchased by the company, becoming the *Barranca*.)

Another of the seven Liberties managed by Royal Mail was the *Samakron* launched at Portland, Maine in November 1943 as the *Jeremiah L. Chaplin*. She was sponsored by Mrs Mary T. Bixler, who after the launching ceremony presented Captain H.A. Wright and Chief Engineer S.H. Shorto with framed pictures and biographical details of the man after whom the ship had been originally named. This proffering of presentation pieces was a common feature at launching ceremonies, and sometimes the

12. (a) Captain Tom Flack, correspondence and telephone interview with author, 1999-2000.
(b) Ian M. Malcolm, 'Voyage 1 of the *Samite'*, *Nautical Magazine* (September 1994 to February 1995).
13. Lansdale Humphreys, *Merlin's Man* (Gwent 1995) and correspondence with author.

gifts were books containing official photographs depicting the various stages of building a Liberty ship.

One other Royal Mail master to stand by at Portland, Maine, during the final building stages of what was to be his ship, was Captain J.M. Duncan. Together with some of his officers he arrived at the yard some days before the launching date and reported that he 'was much impressed by the hustle and bustle of the American workmen'. He wrote that 'each person had his or her job to do and this never varied', and gave as an example the case of a farmer's wife from Ohio whose job it was to fit all the bell pushes aboard. 'She had a plan on which to work and went ahead on her own without any further instructions.' He went on to say that although he had a watching brief over the ship, he was not allowed to make any suggestions. He was told by the Yard Manager that he would be able do exactly what he pleased once the ship had been handed over, but until then, nothing could be altered. 'The whole operation depended upon one person doing exactly the same job on every vessel.'

Captain Duncan's ship was launched on 5 December 1943 as the *Charles A. Young,* and the sponsoring was carried out by twelve year-old Alexandra Sewell, the daughter of the Governor of Maine. Amongst the exchange of gifts was a State of Maine flag. After fitting out and trials the ship sailed on her maiden voyage on 17 December having had her name changed to *Samspring* the day before. 'As a gesture of goodwill,' said Captain Duncan, 'I sailed with the Stars and Stripes where the Red Ensign should have been and the flag of the State of Maine to the fore.' Only when the ship was out of sight of the shipyard was the British flag hoisted. After loading at various American ports the ship then sailed in convoy for the Central Mediterranean, Captain Duncan noting that of the 106 ships in that convoy, no less than eighty-nine were Liberties. (This ship too, was purchased by Royal Mail after the war, becoming the *Beresina.*)

Because it was not possible to name in advance the ships to which men were being sent to join in America, instead of signing the usual Articles of Agreement before sailing from Britain the seamen involved signed a Special Pool Contract 'which provided that they shall proceed to America and there join ships to which they may be nominated by representatives of the Ministry [of War Transport].' Radio Officer Ian Malcolm says his ship was referred to in documents as Liberty Ship 'D'; which when he finally joined her turned out to be the *Samite.* The contract required that officers be paid 75 cents, and men 50 cents, per day, plus a daily subsistence allowance, from the time of disembarkation in the States or Canada until the day they joined their ship.[14]

Not all British Liberty crew members were given the opportunity to enjoy prolonged stays in American ports. Some were sent instead to a

14. MT9/3537, PRO, London.

British Seaman's Pool based at Montreal, Canada, and run by Cunard Line. Maybe news of the good life that some of their compatriots were enjoying in the States filtered through to these men, for some of them apparently ended up in trouble. An official British memorandum dated 30 June 1943 stated that, 'It has recently been decided by the Canadian Authorities that in order to maintain discipline in the Montreal Manning Pool, a system of fines shall be operated for offences committed by seamen while in that Pool.' The Canadians also demanded an amendment to the Pool Contract 'to cover the withholding of pocket [*sic*] money for minor disciplinary offences'.

In early 1943 an able seaman's wage on American ships lay somewhere between $200 and $225 a month, cast sufficiently high to compete with wages ashore, and a wage very, very much higher than that paid to the same rank in British and other Allied vessels. (In 1945, Colin Mackinnon, a third mate with a second mate's certificate aboard the Glen Line Liberty ship *Samsette*, was earning £20-5-0d a month plus £10 War Risk Payment, which added together and converted at the then rate of exchange of $4 to the pound, equated to only $121.) Because of the high wage differentials, some British seamen who joined Liberty ships in the States attempted to jump on the American bandwagon. Through their union, the National Union of Seamen (NUS), they claimed that as the ships were American and to a large extent employed in sailing between US ports and other areas, the crews should be entitled to the American scale of wages. They were encouraged in the idea that they were manning American ships by references in the US Press to the renaming of the 'Samboats', references which emphasised that the ships remained American-owned. According to an official British report the authorities got round this problem by arranging to bring the ships back to the United Kingdom 'as far as possible on their first outward or their first homeward voyage, to enable crews to be changed and so dispel the idea that the ships are based in the U.S.'.

Linked to the wage comparison matter was another major problem involving merchant seamen of many nations when visiting United States ports. That problem was desertion. By the end of September 1941, two months prior to America's entry into the war, Admiral Land of the US Maritime Commission informed the British that a total of 3402 seamen of several nations were known to have absconded in US ports. Admiral Land described the situation as a serious one, 'aggravated by a real shortage of labor in US war industries and on American ships'. He listed the following deserter numbers: Belgians 143, British 664, Chinese 160, Greek 437, Norwegians 847, French 31, Dutch 268, and Danish 88. Not even neutral seamen were immune to the attractions of life in America, for Admiral Land included 168 Swedes, 61 Spaniards, and 97 Finns in the total. On top of that, about 200 Poles whose ships had been lost at sea were refusing to join other Polish vessels. Some members of the largest contingent, the

Norwegians, were known to have joined Panama-registered ships on which the pay levels were twice those on their own vessels.

The deserter problem never fully disappeared. In a letter to Sir Arthur Salter dated 2 December 1942, Admiral Land remarked upon 'the problems of Chinese deserters from British and Dutch ships, which as you know is now critical'.[15] At that time there were around 8000 Chinese serving on British ships and about 5000 on Dutch vessels. A year later in January 1943, it was reported that seventy-five Chinese had deserted from the *Empress of Scotland* at New York, and a total of sixty-eight from four other British vessels. At that same time the Dutch *Nijkerk* lost nineteen. These desertions went on despite a proclamation made to all Chinese seamen by the Chiang Kai-shek government in Chungking, urging them to stay with their ships.

There is nothing in British records which suggests that there were deserters from the crews sent to America to man Liberties, and certainly no British seaman would have done so because of the living conditions he found on board these ships. Almost without exception, officers and men were pretty pleased with their new floating homes. Although in the background rumours circulated about the safety of welded ships, crew members were more impressed with the standard of accommodation aboard. With all the crew accommodated amidships in cabins, gone as far as these ships were concerned, were the dreadful and fetid conditions of the fo'c'sle, the home of deck-hands on most pre-war built ships. The cabins on Liberties had running water, and luxury upon luxury, and the one feature that every seaman from those days still recalls, there was an ice-fountain in the mess room. 'That was a real treat', recalls Bosun Mike Baker. Len Farnham, a sixteen year-old deck-boy at the time of joining the *Samfairy* in February 1945, says, 'there were rumours that welded Liberty ships were subject to breaking up in heavy weather. Personally, I could not have cared less, for the ship had ice cold drinking fountains, well-located comfortable mess rooms, a refrigerator in the mess *and* a coffee urn, all luxuries unheard of in any British tramp of the era.' Even officers of Blue Funnel, a shipping line which knew how to look after its people and on whose own ships the accommodation had always been a cut above the average, were impressed by their new American-built homes. Midshipman Ronald Farquhar who eventually went to live in New South Wales, says that when he joined *Samgara* at Baltimore in 1943 after spending a week in the luxury of the Biltmore Hotel, he was impressed with the accommodation on board. He recalls that each table in the officer's saloon was equipped with a toaster, something unknown even in Blue Funnel ships! These anecdotes, typical of many, serve to

---

15. MT59/2209, PRO, London.

illustrate war's capacity to enhance the importance of the trivial and, concomitantly and mercifully, to dwarf danger and major crises.[16]

In contrast to all American-flagged Liberty ships, some British Liberties were not handed over to their crews in the usual wartime camouflage livery of all-grey paint. Some British Liberties had their funnels and the upper parts of masts and derricks painted white – the *Samvannah* built at Savannah and handed over in December 1943 being one example. This was an exercise in detection avoidance that nowadays falls within the wide-ranging phrase 'signature reduction'. In wartime most ships carried deck cargo (which was included in the overall camouflage scheme by paint or by being covered in appropriately coloured tarpaulins) and in consequence often sailed with the derricks secured in a raised position instead of the usual – and more seamanlike – lowered position, hence the reason for *Samvannah*'s derricks being included in the white work. This special white painting of the upperworks was used by many British merchant ships during a period of the war and was based on the theories of countershading and tonal balance first put forward by the American artist Abbott Henderson Thayer (1849-1921) in the First World War. David Williams, an authority on camouflage at sea, says the 'idea was to help conceal the ship when hull down, i.e. just over the horizon, which would have been a lot nearer, of course, when viewed from the low position of a U-boat's periscope'. With a periscope height of, say, 3ft, the visible horizon would be only 2.1 miles away. David goes on, 'Thus all the higher extremities . . . were painted white, a colour proved by Sir Peter Scott's Western Approaches Scheme to blend in well with skylight on clear days as well as the hazy, grey skies more typical of the North Atlantic'. The white paint practice is reported to have been effective, and quite why and when it was stopped is not known. David Williams surmises that the reason it was discontinued was likely to have concerned maintenance for it would have been easier to maintain an all-over grey colour, and white paint camouflage would have required constant attention as any rust streaks would have defeated the object.[17] Another factor would have been that this form of camouflage was deemed only suitable for the light conditions usually prevalent in the North Atlantic in winter, and merchant ships were not normally confined too long to any particular theatre of war. *Samvannah*'s maiden voyage which commenced in January 1944 was to the Middle East, so it is likely that her white guise was soon painted over.

The Liberty ships transferred to the British flag were extremely important and timely additions to the badly depleted Merchant Navy fleet. It

---

16. Mike Baker, correspondence with author, 1999; Len Farnham, interview and correspondence with author, 1999; Richard P. Farquhar, correspondence with author through the good offices of Blue Funnel Association, 1999.
17. Letter to author from David L. Williams dated 8 May 2000.

has passed almost completely unnoticed that as well as providing great strategic value, the arrival of those ships into the fleet brought about the beginnings of several significant social changes on board British ships.

Since the advent of the first engineer officers on board ships in the first half of the nineteenth century, a climate of unarmed hostility had grown up between them and the deck officers, and between the 'other ranks' on both sides. This hostility is best summed up by the phrase 'oil and water do not mix', which was still in popular usage on board ships to this author's direct knowledge into the 1950s. This separatism in part stemmed from the conservative nature of sailing ship seamen, and in part from the fact that from the very early days the First Engineer was paid more than the First Mate, and a coal-trimmer more than an able seamen. Nothing gets a sailor more riled than when he experiences a wage differential of which he is not the beneficiary. This separatism was encouraged by the pre-war design of British cargo ships in which the engineers lived in accommodation under the funnel and over the engine-room, whilst the deck officers lived in accommodation under the bridge, the two sets of living quarters being separated by one of the ship's holds. The separatism was further enhanced by the deck-hands living in the fo'c'sle, and the trimmers and oilers sometimes being housed right aft. In general it can be said that the only occasions when both sets of officers got together in ships constructed in that way, were mealtimes, when the two sides conjoined together in the saloon. However, even there they nearly always sat at different tables. For the other ranks it was even worse for there was no conjoining at mealtimes; junior men (or rather boys) called 'peggies' being used to carry meals in metal containers, fore or aft as the case might be, to the men who then ate them on tables set up adjacent to their bunks. Constructed with all accommodation in one block amidships, the Liberty ship began the process that put a stop to all that. On those ships deck-hands were accommodated at main deck level on the starboard side, and oilers and wipers on the port side, both sides of the accommodation being joined by cross alleyways and both 'sides' of the crew eating in the same centralised mess-room. On the deck level above that, deck officers were housed to starboard and engineer officers to port, with the ship's saloon joining the two branches. (The captain, and radio officers, lived a further deck up, still in somewhat splendid isolation.) That layout ensured that oil and water began to mix, and although certain aspects of the original antagonism carried on into the 1960s, the social divide on board had been breached, and the credit for that can be directly attributed to the Liberty ship.

Another social aspect needs to be mentioned. Many of the transferred Liberty ships were managed by British shipping companies whose fleets had previously been manned, apart from the officers, by Asian or African crews. Now aboard Liberties, those officers had to deal with mainly all-white crews. Different man-management techniques were required and these crews were usually not nearly so deferential as the ones those officers had been accustomed to handle. The learning curve for many was both steep and rather painful, not least for some of the captains.

As on American merchant ships, the guns of British ships were manned by professionals, but there were some major differences between the two systems. The British gunners came from the Royal Navy, the Royal Marines, and from the Maritime Regiment, Royal Artillery (MRA). There were six specially raised and trained MRA regiments with headquarters strategically sited at Glasgow, Edinburgh, North Shields, Southport, Shoeburyness and Bristol. (The guns of some troopships were manned by men from the Royal Air Force Regiment, but this seems to have happened only when the ships concerned were conveying RAF personnel.) The gunners from the Navy and Marines were collectively known as DEMS – short for Defensively Equipped Merchant Ships; strictly speaking MRA gunners were not DEMS, but the two sets of men are usually combined together under that abbreviation. Except on some larger vessels, the senior man was never a commissioned officer but instead was a sergeant or corporal or the naval equivalent of those ranks. Often the senior men had been called back to the flag from retirement. The most important difference between DEMS and the American Armed Guard, however, was that DEMS gunners signed ships' Articles of Agreement as supernumerary deckhands which made them legally members of the crew and as such directly responsible to the ship's captain. In consequence there was no dichotomy of command on British merchant ships. Another difference between the British and American systems, was in the size of the gunnery unit. There were rarely more than fifteen DEMS gunners on board a cargo ship, and often less. This reduced number was possible because many merchant seaman passed through gunnery courses – in London these took place aboard HMS *President* – and such men augmented the professional gunners. One of the ship's officers, usually but not always the Second Mate, was designated Gunnery Officer. If he had any sense, and most of those concerned had, such an officer left the main business to the professionals, confining his own role to relaying telephoned orders and information from the bridge and to ensuring that crew members of the team kept the flow of ammunition coming up from the lockers. In general the system worked well, and there seems to have been few signs of the inter-service antagonism that characterised the American system. Arthur Barnes of the Maritime Artillery says he never saw any sign of antagonism, and neither did Lance Sergeant Don Lyford who served aboard the Liberty *Samsip* during the D-Day landings.[18]

---

18. Arthur Barnes and Don Lyford, interviews and correspondence with the author 1999-2000.

As supernumeraries DEMS gunners were 'signed on' at a nominal wage of a shilling a month – 'which we never got', comments Arthur Barnes. Their actual wages were paid by the Army or by the Navy as the case maybe. General administration however, resided in the Royal Navy. For instance, a document given to all DEMS personnel entitled 'Rules for Abandoning Ship', was issued by Captain Aylward RN at Bombay in November 1944. It stated,

> No opportunity should be lost in inflicting damage on the enemy even after a ship has been hit. Unless the Master or other officer represent-ing him has ordered 'abandon ship' or unless it is plainly evident that the ship is about to sink, guns' crews must stand by their guns as long as there is a chance of being able to use them effectively. Enemy sub-marines frequently surface after torpedoing a merchant ship, and if the armament is kept manned as long as possible, an opportunity may well occur of damaging or even destroying the attacker.[19]

Arthur Barnes says that Maritime Artillery gunners carried more gear around with them than any other branch of the British Army. 'When we joined a ship no one would know where she was going. So we carried civvies for use in neutral ports, tropical and winter kit, Bren guns, rifles; you name it, we had it.' In port, DEMS gunners operated sabotage watches. Whilst alongside in port they might be paid a fleeting visit by a military officer on an inspection trip, but officer contacts were otherwise rare. The senior gunner was required to make a report concerning any action the ship had taken part in – the Royal Army Ordnance Corps always required an ammunition expenditure chit – but that was usually as far as reports went. There was no attempt to ban fraternisation with crew members and very often gunners volunteered to work alongside merchant seamen at ordinary shipboard tasks in return for what they called 'grog money'. A total of 3935 British gunners lost their lives dur-ing the war, 2713 from the Navy and Marines, and 1222 from the MRA.

It has already been noted that nearly 35,000 British merchant seamen lost their lives during the war, another 4700 being wounded. On top of that, over 4600 became prisoners-of-war in the Western theatres of war and 1100 more to the Japanese in the Far East. Those in Japanese camps received much the same sort of horrific treatment as was meted out to armed services prisoners. However, it seems that the Japanese were not alone in inflicting harsh treatment on British merchant seamen prisoners. It is a little known fact that around 400 merchant navy personnel were taken into custody by the Vichy-French in North Africa. Eighty of them

---

19. Extract from AMDI 35/44. Issued as document DEMS/6/9497/44 by Captain G.H. Aylward R.N. DEMS Administration, Bombay, 25 November 1944.

ended up in a camp at Timbuctou. They were the survivors from *Criton*, a French prize being sailed back to England but which was intercepted and sunk off the West African coast on 20 June 1941 by Vichy-French warships, and the surviving members of the crew of the freighter *Allende* after she was sunk on 17 March 1942 by *U-68*. The treatment these Timbuctou prisoners received was atrocious, their captors even withholding medicines and Red Cross parcels sent out to them. Two *Allende* crew members died in captivity and lie buried in the European Cemetery at Timbuctou. After the war the French Government made an *ex gratia* compensation payment to the British Government, but the prisoners received not a penny of it.

The trials, tribulations and bravery of men and women serving on British merchant ships during the war brought in excess of 8300 individual awards for bravery. That total includes awards made to military and naval gunners and to other service personnel who happened to be serving on merchant ships. The awards ranged from the George Cross (the civilian equivalent of the Victoria Cross), through Knighthoods, Orders of the British Empire etc, to Mentions in Despatches and Commendations. Some merchant seamen whose ships were on special missions and under direct naval orders, received naval medals instead of the more usual civilian ones. Britain did not have an equivalent of the American Gallant Ship Award. A similar system was mooted in mid-1942 by a committee headed by Sir Horace Wilson, a senior civil servant. On the table was a proposal to award a deserving ship the George Cross, much as earlier in that year, on 16 April, that medal had been awarded to the island of Malta. Mainly because it was considered that the most deserving ships, 'the noblest' as the committee's report put it, were often lost, it was decided instead to carry on with the usual system of presenting awards to representative individuals who had shown special gallantry on a ship.

There was another, non-National award system in operation in Britain from December 1940. This was Lloyd's War Medal For Bravery At Sea, instituted by the Corporation of Lloyd's. A total of 530 were presented, some posthumously, and often these were awarded to persons who had also received a national award for the same deed. Five of these medals were awarded to women, and twelve went to DEMS gunners. One of the DEMS awardees was double-medalist Bombadier Henry Herbert Reed of the 2nd Maritime A.A. Regiment, and although he did not serve on Liberty ships his story is worthy of note here as an example of heroism that was outstanding even amongst that band of brave men, and because the main award he was given was an incorrect one. Bombadier Reed was serving on *Cormount* (Cory Bros.) in the English Channel on 20 June 1941 when the ship was attacked by a German aircraft using bombs, machine-guns, and finally a torpedo. Reed was stationed on the bridge, and whilst returning fire was badly wounded but remained for a time at his post. In the words of the official citation he 'behaved with the utmost gallantry', when, with the bridge still under fire, he then carried Chief Officer C.W. Davies, who had also been badly wounded, from the bridge and down two ladders to a sheltered position near a lifeboat, thereby saving the officer's life. There Bombadier Reed died, and only then was it discovered that he had carried out the rescue operation with his stomach ripped open by machine gun bullets. Chief Officer Davies was subsequently awarded the OBE for bravery, a civil award because he was Merchant Navy, together with the Lloyd's medal. On 23 September 1941 Bombadier Reed was posthumously awarded the George Cross, the highest British *civilian* award for gallantry. On the medal itself he was described as being in the Merchant Navy, which of course was incorrect. As an army gunner the award should have been the Victoria Cross. This brave man is buried in Bishopwearmouth Cemetery in his home town of Sunderland.

On 30 October 1945, the House of Commons and the House of Lords passed identical Resolutions which read:

> That the thanks of this House be accorded to the Officers and Men of the Merchant Navy for the steadfastness with which they maintained our stocks of food and materials; for their services in transporting men and munitions to all the battles over all the seas; and for the gallantry with which, though a civilian service, they met and fought the constant attacks of the enemy.
>
> That this House doth acknowledge with humble gratitude the service of all those who, on land or sea or in the air, have given their lives that others today may live as free men, and its heartfelt sympathy with their relatives in their proud sorrow.

Fine words. But fine words are not worth very much and certainly do not compensate for the official neglect British merchant seamen suffered at the hands of officialdom during certain stages of the war. Seamen signed Articles of Agreement when they joined a ship, and from that moment were 'on pay'. At the termination of the voyage, on their return to a British port, they signed off and were then off pay. During the first eighteen months of the war there was one other circumstance which terminated the Articles and so brought pay to an end, and that was when a ship was sunk for whatever reason, including enemy action. To put it another way, a seaman could have his ship blown from under him and then spend days, weeks, even months in a lifeboat in the knowledge that he was off pay from the time of the sinking. That was not the end of it, for there was an equally objectionable corollary. At the time of signing on a seaman could allot part of his salary to his next-of-kin, the money being remitted regularly by the shipping company involved. Those allotments, too, came to an end at the time of the sinking. It was not a system designed to ease the mind of a seaman struggling for his life in a lifeboat, not to mention the effect the allotment cessation must have had on his next-of-kin back home who often would have no firm knowledge of what had happened to the husband or son involved. That system carried on until the Essential Work Order for the Merchant Navy (EWOMN) was promulgated in May 1941. That Order made it illegal for anyone to leave the service but balanced that by guaranteeing wages between voyages. The EWOMN was a move in the right direction, but iniquities remained. The authorities, for instance, would not grant a wife a war widow's pension if her Merchant Navy husband was posted merely as 'missing presumed lost'.

Other Allied merchant fleets also suffered grievously during the war. Norway lost a large part of its pre-war fleet and a total of 3588 officers and men killed, 377 of them before 9 April 1940 up to which date the country was officially still neutral. Those ship losses resulted in a total of twenty-four ships being lend-leased to the Norwegian Government in exile by the Americans, half of them Liberties. Kornelius Korneliussen, who began his career at sea in 1938, signed off a ship at New York in 1943 and then volunteered for the Royal Norwegian Navy. He was sent to the port of Lunenberg, Nova Scotia, where the Norwegian Navy had set up a training camp. There he was trained in gunnery before being sent with five other gunners under Gunnery Officer Anker Kristiansen to join the Liberty *Viggo Hansteen* (ex-*George M. Shriver*) at Baltimore in October of that year. He says that, 'because there were more guns than gunners, we were paid as an Able Seaman with an additional £3 a month for training the crew as gunners, but we could also be used for ordinary shipwork in harbour or in neutral waters'. Kornelius, who after the war sailed as Second Mate before becoming a coastal pilot based at Narvik, says that the Norwegians had three other wartime training camps in addition to the one at Lunenburg. They were situated at Dumbarton, Scotland, Travers Island, New York, and Sydney, Australia.[20]

In Belgium's case, seven Liberties were handed over under lend-lease terms. By the end of the war Belgium had lost sixty-four of the 100 ships she had started it with and had lost 800 men killed or missing, 294 of them from one shipping company alone, the Compagnie Maritime Belge. From mid-1942 onwards the Belgians had considerable difficulty manning those of their ships that remained in the service of the Allies – thirteen of their ships had been detained by the French earlier in the war – so much difficulty in fact, that between March 1942 and July 1944, between a quarter and a third of crew members were foreigners. This shortage was not caused solely by personnel losses at sea. Professor Greta Devos has written that 'there were numerous reasons for this shortage . . . the more attractive conditions on ships under American and Panamanian flags'

---

20. Kornelius Korneliussen, correspondence with the author.

being one. She goes on, 'Some Belgian seamen . . . had themselves recruited. Seamen who jumped ship in American ports, sometimes encouraged by German agents . . . were quite the norm . . . the phenomenon degenerated into a real scourge'.[21] On Belgian merchant ships certain tensions did develop between ordinary crew members and gunners. The gunners, averaging about six per ship, were trained, appointed and paid directly by the Belgian Government in exile, and the wages were slightly higher than those of the merchant seaman ranks from whence most of them had originally come. A gunner's work was also generally less strenuous than an ordinary sailor's. On some ships this friction between the groups became so bad that the sailor-gunners had to be replaced by soldiers. Perhaps it was the desertion and dissent factors that caused the Belgian Government after the war to give but sparing acknowledgement to their merchant navy's contribution to the war effort. In the words of Belgian officialdom, as volunteers the merchant seamen had 'done their duty and their job', an off-hand and empty phrase which aroused considerable resentment at the time. It was not until January 1968 that the survivors were granted national recognition with the title *combattant en mer*, or sea fighter, a recognition somewhat analogous to veteran status in the United States

The lend-leasing of four Liberty ships to China had nothing to do with crew availability. It was a political decision, no doubt designed to appease the Chinese leader Chiang Kai-shek. However, the input into the war effort by seamen of Chinese descent was a large and important one and many of them lost their lives in the process. Most of those who served on British ships had been recruited in the British colonies of Hong Kong and Singapore, others in pre-war Shanghai,. Many sailors of Chinese extraction also served and died on Dutch ships.

---

21. (a) Information received from Riet De Block, CMB Archivist. (b) Professor Dr. Greta Devos and Guy Elewaut, *CMB 100: a Century of Commitment to Shipping* (Antwerp 1995).

CHAPTER 7

Close to Calamity: the Structural Failure Problem

The Spring of 1944 was a critical time in the Second World War for the Allies. The D-Day landings were only a few months away and, in preparation for them, ships were being directed towards British ports to form the greatest armada the world has ever seen. Yet, even as those ships gathered, hundreds of other recently constructed Allied merchant vessels were laid up for repairs in ports all over the world, the repair work needed on them having nothing whatsoever to do with the consequences of enemy action. A British Security report of May 1944 referred to the fact that two months earlier in the Port of Glasgow alone, there had been ten Liberty ships awaiting the rectification of non-enemy inflicted defects.[1] The ships concerned had all suffered some degree of structural failure. In some cases the failures were of a comparatively minor nature. In others they were serious enough to make the ships unseaworthy. As a consequence, orders had gone out that most merchant ships built in the United States since 1942 were to undergo certain modifications as soon as possible in order to prevent yet more cases of failure. With already 'failed' ships and the many more needing these modifications, queuing up outside repair yards all over the place, the possible impact of this on Allied logistics looked exceedingly grim. Rear-Admiral W. King USN has written to the effect that the structural failure problem, whilst not producing the same order of losses as that from U-boat attacks, seriously affected the Allied supply position.[2] The problem was not confined to Liberty ships, but by 1944 the incidence of structural failure was greater in that class of vessel than in any other because more of that type had been built. The problem was, however, almost entirely confined to welded ships, scarcely a riveted ship being affected. As a result, when the phenomenon first reared its ugly head the immediate reaction was to

---

1. British Security Report dated 11 May 1944, MT9/3882, PRO, London.
2. Rear-Admiral W. King and others, *Naval Engineering and American Seapower* (Baltimore nd).

place the entire blame on the comparatively new technique of welding ships' structures. However, there was another wrinkle to the problem. Although some British-built ships were then being welded – Cyril Thompson's yard at Sunderland was in the van of those British yards starting to change over to the newer technology – only three British-built welded ships had up to that time suffered structural failure and those incidents had been of a relatively minor nature. This was in sharp contrast to the American experience where a number of their ships suffered severe failures which in some cases led to the loss of the ships involved.

Without getting too technical, it should be noted here that a welded ship, in which each edge of every one of the ship's plates is welded in the same plane to the edge of the adjacent plate, once it is completed, has effectively become a single piece of steel. This means that any crack that develops will continue to propagate as long as sufficient stress is available, and in the process may well travel across any weld it meets in its path. A riveted ship on the other hand, where at every seam and butt (both these shipbuilding terms have been defined in a previous chapter) between ship's plates, the edge of one plate is laid over the edge of another before the two are riveted together, does not end up being the same form of continuous structure. Therefore, when a crack starts in a riveted ship it usually progresses only to the first break in the continuity of the plating, that is to the nearest riveted connection, where the joint acts as sort of natural crack arrester.

An official British report produced late in 1944 provides an indication of the scale the structural failure problem had reached by 1 September that year. By that date, less than three months after the D-Day landings and with the task of supplying the Allied forces in Europe then in full swing, no less than 407 Liberties, nine Ocean ships, seventy-six T-2 tankers, and sixty-six miscellaneous types of vessels, a total of 558 ships altogether, had suffered some form of structural failure. Some of those ships had suffered failure on more than one occasion, so necessitating more than one visit to the repair yard, and raising the total number of reported failure incidents to 785.[3] That report and other official ones produced on both sides of the Atlantic, emphasised that there had almost certainly been more incidences than those actually reported; some minor failures, for instance, may have been repaired by the ship's own engineers or by shore-based military engineers, particularly in some of the more remote parts of the world, and it was suspected that those involved might not have bothered to send in reports. Unreported cases may also have occurred with ships subsequently lost to enemy

---

3. FE4/146, British Admiralty Preliminary Report on Analysis of Casualty Reports.

action. On top of that it was possible that some cases of structural failure might have gone unreported because the required remedial work was carried out at the same time as repairs necessitated by other causes. One case, which was reported, shows how such remedial work was carried out at the same time as other repair work. The ship involved was the British Liberty *Sampep* (built as *Victor F. Lawson* at Los Angeles at August 1943). Arthur Harvey was on that ship's maiden voyage to Karachi via Hobart, Tasmania, when, whilst crossing the Great Australian Bight in November in bad weather, a crack suddenly appeared in the deck forward of the bridge. At about the same time a locomotive being carried as deck cargo broke free and did considerable damage in more or less the same place. After Karachi the ship proceeded to Bombay where repair work and a 'strengthening butt was fitted for about three-quarters of the length of the hull'. (*Sampep* was later available to take part in the D-Day operations.)[4]

The most comprehensive of all the general official reports on these failures (as opposed to the many scientific reports produced on specific aspects of them) was that produced under the auspices of the US Secretary of the Navy and dated 15 July 1946. It was a 'Final Report' following two earlier ones of 3 June 1944 and 1 May 1945. The statistics included in the Final Report were based on data collected up to 1 April 1946, seven and a half months after the surrender of Japan. It covered only those ships constructed under the US Maritime Commission's programme and so did not include the Ocean ships built in the States to British order, or any other British or Commonwealth-built welded or part-welded ships. (It did include eighteen British-operated Liberties that had suffered failures.) The overall Allied shipping problem from this cause during the war had therefore been worse even than indicated in the report.[5]

That report shows that of the nearly 5000 Maritime Commission ships constructed by 1 April 1946, no less than 970, in other words about one in five, had sustained a 'casualty' in the form of a structural failure. In fact the total number of casualty incidents was 1442, for some vessels had sustained fractures more than once. Top of the list for the record number of such incidents was the tanker *Conastoga* and the non-Liberty freighters *Lightning* and *Shooting Star*, all built by Sun Shipbuilding at Chester, Pennsylvania, each of which sustained a casualty on no less than eight occasions. (That same company built the tanker *Ohio* which, manned by Britons, gained fame and glory in the Operation Pedestal convoy to Malta in April 1942.) As far as Liberty ships were concerned, the record

4. Letter to author dated 19 October 1999 from Captain Arthur Harvey.
5. 'The Design and Method of Construction of Welded Steel Merchant Ships', Final Report of Board of Investigation. 15 July 1946.

for the highest number of casualties, six each, went to *Carl Schurz* (Portland, Oregon, December 1942) and *Schuyler Colfax* (Los Angeles, November 1943), both ships having been constructed at yards owned by the Kaiser organisation.[6] It is of interest to note that the *Robert E. Peary*, the ship built at Richmond by Henry Kaiser in the world record time of well under five days, suffered no cracking incidents at all.

The above summary indicates the scale of the problem at various dates and the extreme seriousness of its effect on the Allied cause. It was a problem first hinted at by an incident on a ship not listed in the American report because she had been built to British order. The ship was the *Ocean Justice* and the incident took place as the ship was nearing completion at Portland, Maine on 3 February 1942. At 0630 hours that morning after a particularly cold night during which the ambient temperature had dropped to 14° Fahrenheit, well below freezing point, a welder 'struck his arc' to complete the welding of a heavy ash-shoot insert plate. Immediately he did so, and undoubtedly much to his consternation, fractures appeared in the structures in the vicinity, with parts of the main deck, 'tween deck, machinery casing, and starboard shell plating all being affected. The faults, which the British classified as serious, were subsequently rectified and the ship was launched and delivered two months later. (The sea-going career of *Ocean Justice* did not last long. Managed by Hain of St. Ives she was on a voyage between Durban and Trinidad when she was torpedoed and sunk by *U-505*, Lieutenant Commander Zschech, on 6 November 1942. Her crew were saved.) That ship was the first of nine Oceans out of the grand total of sixty which, up to the autumn of 1944, suffered fractures of varying severity. Three of the others occurred during heavy weather in the North Atlantic, the remainder during 'normal' operations. Two of the weather-damage incidents were classified as serious. One of those concerned *Ocean Angel* which suffered a 6ft long split in the main deck, with the adjacent hatch coaming also being affected. The other serious incident took place in November 1943 aboard *Jan Leivens,* built as *Ocean Merchant* but renamed after Britain handed her over to the Dutch. The ship's hull fractured at bilge level during a storm. All nine Ocean ships affected had come from the yard at Portland, Maine, no cracks having been reported in any of the thirty Richmond-built Oceans. The significance of that fact will become clear later. (No mention was made in the British report of the damage sustained to *Ocean Vanguard* in a collision in convoy during

---

6. The *Carl Schurz* was scrapped at Tacoma in 1961, but the *Schuyler Colfax* had a rather more fiery end. Built as a Liberty tanker, she was transporting a cargo of molasses between Hawaiian ports in August 1946 when she took the ground and was badly damaged. She lay derelict at Honolulu for about a year before being transferred to the US Navy as a target ship. She was towed out to sea, caught fire after air attacks, and was then torpedoed and sunk by a submarine.

its maiden voyage because the damage was caused by external rather than internal factors. As the ship's hull withstood this 'test', the incident led Cyril Thompson to say that 'it set our fears [over welded hulls] to rest', which was a rather premature judgement.)

On 10 November 1942, in chronologically the next incident after *Ocean Justice,* and potentially a much more serious one because it took place at sea, the American all-welded bulk freighter *Enders M. Voorhees* suffered a complete fracture of the main deck. The very next day brought the first such incident with a Liberty ship when, in 'normal' weather at sea, cracks suddenly appeared in part of the shell plating of the *Jeremiah Wadsworth.* That ship, launched at Houston in the previous month, fell victim to *U-178,* Commander Ibbeken, off the South African coast only sixteen days after the cracking was reported, and whether the crack acted as a sort of 'assist' to the effects of the torpedoing is a matter for conjecture only. Between mid-November 1942 and 12 January 1943, nine more Liberties and one other welded freighter suffered potentially serious structural failures. All these cases were classified by the American authorities as Class 1, which was defined as a casualty which involved weakening the main hull structure so that the vessel is lost or is in a dangerous condition. During the same period a further eighteen vessels sustained cracking not considered to endanger the safety of the ship and which were recorded, according to their extent, as either Class 2 or 3. Class 2 fractures were those in the main structures with the potential to spread and become Class 1. The Class 3 designation gathered in all the others.

At first, and for reasons at least partly to do with the morale of the seamen who had to sail these ships, both the American and British authorities attempted to keep the extent of the problem under wraps. The attempts at secrecy were not very successful – how could they be with so many people both ashore and afloat in the know? – and rumours about the nature and extent of the problem began to spread amongst the seagoing fraternity. Sailors' scuttlebutt tends towards the outer limits of exaggeration, and with the failure of so many welded ships – the rumours always accentuated the welding aspect – the rumour-mongers had a field-day and presented the problem as being even worse than it actually was. There were other, more sinister, aspects of this rumour-mongering. Professor Frank Bull, who was subsequently the leader of the group set up by the British Admiralty to investigate the structural aspects of the problem, sums up the overall situation thus:

> In the early days of the programme there were odd rumours from sailors whose brothers had a friend who was on one of these Liberty ships when one of these prefabricated units split along the welds and the ship just disappeared. It was always an indirect story and one which

was difficult to track down. If it was an enemy-inspired rumour to disturb the morale of seamen, it was certainly successful. [7]

It is more than likely that some of these rumours were indeed inspired and spread by German agents in America, for, as has been already noted, the Germans were singularly well informed about all aspects of the American shipbuilding programme, and that included the negative aspects of it. An article in the 1944 edition of the German publication *Nauticus* (based on intelligence received during the previous twelve months) made several mentions of the structural deficiencies of Liberty ships and other vessels of the American shipbuilding programme. At one point the authors stated,

> With all due respect for the American achievement in the field of mass production of ships, it has to be said that several shipyards are producing sub-standard work. . . . a considerable number of ships have developed defects, particularly fractures . . . [8]

By 1944, the year of that German publication, the Americans had in fact given up any attempt to keep the problem secret. The *New York Sun* edition of 25 April 1944 carried a major article on the subject by Phelps Adams in which he revealed something of the extent of the problem and actually named one of the ships involved.

It was not, of course, only the seamen who had to sail these ships who had worries over the safety of these vessels. By Christmas 1942 the danger bells were ringing regularly inside the offices of the United States Maritime Commission in Washington. Frederic Lane, author of the Commission's official history, colourfully summed up the situation thus: 'Small wonder if at that time those responsible for the program had nightmares about the sailing of schizophrenic ships likely to burst at any moment to relieve their split personalities'.[9] Then, early in the New Year, the decibel level of the danger bells and the frequency of the nightmares, suddenly increased.

The new 15,000-ton T-2 tanker *Schenectady* had been completed at Henry Kaiser's Swan Island Yard at Portland, Oregon on the last day of 1942, and on the 16 January 1943 she was lying alongside a fitting-out berth having successfully completed her trials on the Columbia River. The crew were on board, the ship was fully provisioned, and water ballast had been pumped into some of the bow and stern tanks in preparation for the maiden voyage due to start the following day. The night was very cold with

7. Frank B. Bull, *Stresses in Ships* (St Lucia, Queensland 1962).
8. *Nauticus* (1944), pp317-18.
9. Frederic Lane, *Ships for Victory* (Baltimore 1951).

an air temperature below freezing at 26° Fahrenheit. A light breeze was producing ripples on the surface of the river, for there was no ice because the water temperature was well above that of the air. As midnight approached all seemed well to the duty watchmen on board. Then, without any warning, there came a loud roar like an explosion, said to have been audible more than a mile away

In fact there had been no explosion. The noise had come as *Schenectady* split in two amidships just abaft the bridge structure, the fracture cutting right across the main deck and down both sides from top to bottom, with only the bottom plating holding. The vessel jack-knifed upwards amidships, with the bow and stern, weighed down by ballast and by the ship's engines at the after end of the ship, settling on to the river bed. When daylight came, such was the magnitude of the hogging configuration, that the bottom of the ship in the vicinity of the crack was well clear of the surface of the river, observers on shore being able to see right under the vessel amidships. On both port and starboard sides the crack had opened to a giant-sized 'V', the gap at the top being some 10ft across. It had all happened so quickly that the jack-knifing upward had prevented any significant quantity of water entering the ship through the fracture.

Again the immediate reaction was to place the entire blame on the welding processes, perhaps including bad workmanship, but, as Frank Bull has written:

> a glance at the wreck immediately dispelled any delusions on this score; for it was obvious that the fatal crack did not follow the welds, and, in general, was feet clear of the welds, running right through parent metal. Naturally in a ship with both longitudinal and transverse welded joints, any crack which ran round three-quarters of the entire girth was bound to cross some welds in its track. A close examination of the detail welding did show some defects, but the obstinate fact remained that the crack itself passed almost entirely through parent plate.[10]

If it was not the welding, what could have caused the failure? It could not be excessive loading for the ship was in 'light' condition. Calculation of the stresses at the point of fracture showed them to be only one-sixth of the breaking strength of the steel, so it also could not be an error in design. Was there something wrong with the metal itself then?

Metallurgists cut specimens from the vicinity of the *Schenectady* fracture and sent them off for all the standard tests. It was noted that the fractured steel appeared to have acted as if it was cast-iron, that it was quite brittle – as if the bits that had broken apart would fit neatlyback in place if brought together, like pieces of a jigsaw puzzle. (This had also been

---

10. Frank B. Bull, *Gravitas*.

noticed in the *Ocean Justice* incident.) It was most puzzling, for the steel was supposed to be ductile and should therefore have shown considerable stretching and general distortion in the vicinity before the metal fractured, which would have meant that the parts could not then have fitted neatly back into place.

The metallurgy test reports came back to the effect that the steel was in accordance with specifications and had passed every test set by the American Bureau of National Standards. Bull writes:

> In summary, the welds were not involved, the steel was O.K, and the theoretical stresses were only a small fraction of those needed to cause failure. It followed that the ship could not possibly have failed. Unfortunately a glance out of the office window suggested otherwise.

Something unexpected and most unusual had taken place. Some of the basic tenets of naval architecture, and indeed of structural engineering, seem to have been overturned. Furthermore, wrote Professor Bull, 'if every ship built by the Maritime Commission was subject to these "new rules" – whatever they were – it cast grave doubts on the viability of the whole program. Could these ships be used with any great degree of confidence. If not, then final Allied victory in the war could be set back by years, perhaps for ever.'

Not very wisely, for none of those involved could come up with a rational explanation for the *Schenectady* failure, some old-established shipbuilders were not unhappy to see this product of a yard belonging to Henry Kaiser, a man considered by many in the industry to be an upstart, come to such grief. This gloating was perhaps accentuated by the fact that of the total of ten Liberty ships that had suffered Class 1 failures prior to the *Schenectady* incident, seven had come from Kaiser yards. However, the gloating was short-lived, for of the next eleven Class 1 failures, all but one of them Liberty ships, only three came from Kaiser yards.

Amongst that next batch of failures two were very serious indeed, both resulting in the total loss at sea of the ship concerned. Neither of the shipyards involved were Kaiser facilities. The first was the *Thomas Hooker* completed at Portland, Maine in August 1942. Managed by the American-West African Line, the ship was on a voyage in ballast from the North African port of Bona to New York, and on 5 November 1943 was within two days of the Newfoundland coast when the convoy she was part of ran into heavy weather. The evening was cold with an air temperature well below zero. At a little after 2000 hours a loud cracking was heard and it was found that the ship had opened up abreast of No. 3 hatch, the crack extending across the deck and down both port and starboard sides to about the level of the 'tween-deck. The ship was hoved to, and at first it was thought that she could be saved. The cracked section was examined as closely as possible and it was later reported that the cracks ran through parent metal and not along the welds. By the following morning it was clear that with the complete failure of the strength deck the ship could not be saved, and at 0900 hours on the 6th she was abandoned, her crew being picked up by another Allied vessel. By that time the *Hooker* had a large list to port, and she later foundered.

The second of the serious incidents involved the *J.L.M. Curry*, the first Liberty to come off the stocks of the yard at Mobile, Alabama. She was launched in May 1942 and after completion and trials and under the management of Lykes Lines, sailed for more northerly ports for loading. On 21 August she was berthed at Jersey City, just across the North River from Lower Manhattan and was due to sail on her maiden voyage that very day. An excellent account exists of the *Curry*'s first and, as it turned out, last voyage, because on the day of sailing she was boarded by an intrepid young mariner we have met before in these pages. Deck Cadet Romuald Holubowicz had arrived home at the end of July after the most traumatic of first voyages, and now, only three weeks later, had been ordered to report on board the *Curry*. Romuald says that as the ship pulled away from the dock that afternoon he casually inquired of the chief officer where the ship was bound. 'With great enthusiasm he advised: Murmansk. I was stunned. After my previous experience, I had not expected to be again sent so soon on the North Russia run. There was absolutely nothing I could do about it . . .'[11]

Despite a few submarine scares, *Curry*'s convoy reached Hvalfjord in Iceland safely, and there the ships lay for three months. For security reasons no shore leave was permitted and to amuse themselves the crews exchanged ship visits and organised lifeboat sailing races, otherwise having to rely on what was on board for entertainment. *Curry* carried an extensive library and Romuald spent much of the time reading, and he looks back on those three months as the equivalent of a university course in the liberal arts. Something Romuald did not learn until very much later was that the three-month stopover was caused by a severe difference of opinion between Russia and her Western Allies. The United States and Britain were to launch Operation 'Torch', the landings in North Africa, in November and about 500 merchant ships were to be used. To escort them meant withdrawing many ships of the British Home Fleet used previously to guard northern waters. The upshot was that all convoys to North Russia were temporarily suspended, much to the anger of the Russians. (A series of single ship sailings, alternately British and American, did sail north between 20 October and 2 November, in what was called Operation 'FB'. Half the ships involved did not reach their destination.) At the

11. Romuald Holubowicz, *The War in the North*.

end of three months the suspension was lifted, but first Romuald's convoy sailed for Britain where all the ships had their bow sections strengthened with heavy wooden beams, stiffeners made to withstand voyaging through ice. Then, on 15 December, sixteen ships including *Curry* sailed from Loch Ewe in Scotland as Convoy JW-51A, the first convoy to sail north since September. This time, unlike his previous voyage, Romuald had the comfort of knowing his ship was fitted with proper defensive armament and carried a detachment of professional Armed Guards to man the guns. He says that probably because it was the first convoy to sail north after a long break and because it was routed close to the Norwegian coast in what was the continuous darkness of the Arctic winter, the convoy arrived at Murmansk unscathed. At Murmansk *Curry* and her consorts suffered continuous air attacks, but at last the cargoes were discharged. *Curry* then loaded 2000 tons of fertiliser as ballast and sailed from that port on 1 March 1943 as one of thirty ships comprising Convoy RA-53. On 5 March the convoy was attacked by *U-255* (Lieutenant Commander Reche), and the American freighter *Executive* was sunk with the loss of nine lives. A second torpedo struck the Liberty ship *Richard Bland* (Captain L. Dodd), penetrating the ship's No. 1 hold but failing to explode. Reche was in position to have another go at the *Bland* on the 10th, and this time the ship broke in two. Four lifeboats were launched and everyone on board the ship got away. Two of the boats were severely overloaded and one of them was never seen again. A number of men clinging to the side of the other overloaded boat perished from exposure. When the remaining survivors were rescued later in the day by the destroyer HMS *Impulsive,* thirty-six men were missing. The after end of the ship sank, but the forward part was later taken in tow by the rescue tug HMS *Horsa.* However, six days later both tug and tow ended up ashore on the east coast of Iceland.

Meanwhile, on the 7th, the weather had turned foul and two more Liberties were in trouble. The *John H.B. Latrobe* suffered a complete engine breakdown but despite the appalling conditions was taken in tow by the destroyer HMS *Opportune* (Commander J. Lee-Barber). In an astonishing feat of seamanship the Liberty was towed into Seidisfiord on Iceland's east coast, an episode later described by Admiral Sir John Tovey as 'an excellent piece of work'. (The *Latrobe* – Baltimore, July 1942 – was repaired, survived the war, and was eventually scrapped in 1969.)

The second Liberty in trouble was the *J.L.M. Curry,* and she was not nearly so lucky. Let Romuald Holubowicz take up the story.

Up to this point, the *Curry* struggled on into gale force westerlies, pounding and slamming ferociously but maintaining reasonable position in convoy . . . On the 7th on the mid-day 12 to 4 watch, the ship experienced an extraordinary sea, rose bow up precipitously, and instead of the usual slam and shuddering when coming down to meet the sea, 'exploded'. [The incident occurred at 1320 hours.]

I was off watch in my cabin at the time, and because of my previous experience, immediately concluded we had been torpedoed.

Romuald hurriedly donned a lifejacket and raced up to the bridge where he was told that the ship had not been torpedoed but that the hull had cracked in two places, immediately forward and abaft of the amidships accommodation. The cracks extended across the deck and down each side. The ship was almost in three parts, and, 'each time a head-on sea was encountered, the three segments of the hull articulated vertically, opening wide gaps fore and aft each time'. The official US Coast Guard Report, no doubt based on information supplied by the ship's master and/or the Armed Guard officer, states that the ship cracked in four places, not just two. However, whether the ship was articulating in three segments or five, it was in a highly dangerous condition and the captain issued the order to fall off into a trough of the sea to relieve some of the strain on the hull structure.

The captain's next order was to have all but a volunteer skeleton crew abandon ship and transfer to the escort trawler HMS *Northern Wave* which was standing-by for the purpose. Romuald says that because he was a cadet he was automatically 'volunteered' by the captain, a not infrequent experience for such junior officers in most merchant navies. Despite the danger, attempts were made by the volunteers to save the ship. The captain tried heading into the weather again but as the hours passed it became apparent that the *Curry* was doomed unless she steamed on a southerly course with the sea on the beam, a course that would take her ever nearer the coast of Enemy Occupied Norway. So, at 1115 hours on the following morning, Romuald found himself once again leaving a sinking ship. Despite the heavy seas, lifeboats were launched and all hands were accounted for. They left behind what from the distance looked like a 'whole ship', reports Romuald. From the deck of *Northern Wave* he then watched as the trawler's gunners pumped round after round into the derelict *Curry*, but although fires broke out on board, the ship refused to sink. The trawler then made a close-in pass of the ship and lobbed a depth-charge with a short fuse at it. 'That succeeded,' says Romuald. 'The ship began to settle slowly in the water, turned over gracefully, and finally sank'. The *Northern Wave* landed Romuald, and the other survivors, in Iceland. From there he was sent home and he served on other ships until the end of the war. One of his later ships was another Liberty, the *Tarleton Brown*. By then the fates must have decided enough was enough, for no more ships were sunk under this remarkable young man. In March 1944 he found himself awarded the Soviet military medal 'For Gallant Service', and until the Cold War set in, each year he received the equivalent in dollars of five Russian roubles, the pension that went with the medal. By that time he had left his temporary calling.[12] The official Coast Guard report on the *Curry* structural failure, states that 'the cracks did not occur along the welds, but were clean breaks in the plating', yet another indication that something other than the welding must have been involved.

Even as the reports on the loss of the *Curry* were reaching the States there came another catastrophic incident, this time with a T-2 tanker, a twin of the *Schenectady*. The ship was the *Esso Manhattan*, and the incident silenced the Kaiser critics once and for all for the ship had nothing whatsoever to do with him, having been constructed by the long-established Sun Shipbuilding Company of Chester, Pennsylvania. The incident took place on 29 March 1943, and like the *Schenectady* ten weeks earlier, the ship was in ballast. But unlike the former ship, the *Esso Manhattan* incident took place at sea. The tanker was making for the approaches of New York at a speed of 14kts, there was a low swell running and the sea was slight under a gentle Force 2 breeze, with the air temperature hovering just above freezing point. Two anti-submarine patrol blimps (airships) were flying overhead, and their crews were to get a grandstand view of what was about to happen; not only that, they were able to take pictures of it. Just after mid-day, 'with a sound described variously as a thump, thud, bang, crash or explosion, fractures ran across the deck in way of No. 6 tank, and down both sides to the bilge port and starboard', says the US Coast Guard Report, which then goes on,

> The vessel jack-knifed and the bow dug under an incoming wave. The crew abandoned and were picked up by the USCG *Kimball*. The bottom fractured later and the two parts drifted apart.

As with many tankers during the war the *Manhattan* had been fitted with a raised platform over the main deck for almost its entire length for the carriage of aircraft, and it seems that this acted as a sort of hydrofoil, driving the fore part of the vessel even deeper under the water, so ensuring a complete break. On this occasion the exact point where the fracture started was identified as a butt weld between two main deck plates at the centreline of the ship. Furthermore the report said that the weld at that point 'contained oxide, slag and porous areas', seemingly indicating that this time the welding definitely was involved. (The two parts of the ship were eventually salved and rejoined. That ship, like the repaired *Schenectady*, went on to play its part, albeit a delayed one, in the Allied

12. In September 1991, on the 50th anniversary of the first Murmansk convoy, Romuald Holubowicz together with over a hundred other British and American veterans of the 'northern run', visited that port and the port of Archangel. He now resides in England.

cause. One cannot help wondering however, about the states of mind of crew members aboard both those vessels, especially as *Schenectady* suffered two further, though minor, cracking incidents in the summer of 1943, and the *Esso Manhattan* one more in September 1944.)

Within three weeks of the *Esso Manhattan* incident on 20 April 1943, Frank Knox, the US Secretary of the Navy, set up as a matter of the utmost urgency a Board of Investigation to inquire into the causes behind the structural failures in welded ships. (Knox was to die in 1944, two years before the Board made its final report.) The Board was an extremely high-powered one with no less than three admirals serving on it including the by then promoted Vice-Admiral Howard Vickery of the US Maritime Commission. Another Board member was the vice chairman and chief surveyor of the American Bureau of Shipping, the American equivalent of Lloyd's Register. There was a Sub-Board consisting of naval officers, naval architects, metallurgists and other scientists, and Research Advisory and Welding Advisory committees were constituted. No stone was to be left unturned, and research programmes were to be implemented immediately.

At about the same time, similar intensive research programmes were implemented on the other side of the Atlantic under the aegis of the Admiralty. In Britain the research into the metallurgical aspects of the problem were carried out principally at the Engineering Laboratory, Cambridge University. The purely structural aspects were undertaken by a special group set up under the leadership of Frank Bull. Over the coming months and years there was considerable co-operation between the American and British engineers and scientists involved, including regular exchanges of information and occasional visits to one side by liaison officials representing the other.

John Vasta was a member of the American Research Advisory Committee and later wrote,

> These structural casualties played no favourites. They struck the tankers, the ore carriers, and the Liberty ship. The outlook was very serious indeed. [We were] swamped with such ominous [sounding] terms as welding residual stresses, locked-in stresses, strain concentrations, discontinuities, and notch-sensitive materials.
>
> The predominance of structural failures during the winter period pointed to low temperature as a contributory factor.
>
> Our complacency about the construction program was . . . seriously disturbed.[13]

---

13. John Vasta, unpublished report on *Structural Tests on the Liberty Ship Schulyer*.

John Vasta's remarks indicate that theories about what might be causing the failures were legion and were being thrown about thick and fast. In truth, in 1943 there was a great paucity of scientifically validated information about the brittle failure of mild steel and about how the comparatively new technique of welding might impinge upon the problem. The factors which might cause a normally ductile material like the mild steel being used to behave in a brittle manner were not understood at all. One indication of the poor state of knowledge existing at the outset of the inquiry was that, despite intensive efforts, it took well over a year for research workers to reproduce in the laboratory the conditions that led to brittle fractures of similar nature to those being found in the ships. The lack of scientific knowledge had over the years led naval architects, Ship Registration Societies such as Lloyd's and the American Bureau of Shipping, government departments involved in shipping matters, and others, to adopt empirical rules for the structural design of ships based on experience and the so-called trial and error method. This, on the whole, had resulted in the satisfactory design of ships' structures, allowing an adequate factor of safety against unforeseen eventualities – that is until the phenomenon of brittle failure suddenly manifested itself.

Writing in 1946, Sir Amos Ayre, Director of Merchant Shipbuilding at the Admiralty during the war, made mention of the reported characteristics of the structural failures and confirmed that at the time the incidents took place, some of those characteristics were not understood.

> A number of the reports drew attention to the suddenness with which the fractures occurred, while photographs and samples taken from fractured ships indicated that most of the fractures were sharp and accompanied by very little deformation or reduction in thickness at the fractured edges. The importance of these observations was not realised until fairly recently . . .[14]

Ayre also pointed out that there was a tendency for fractures to occur more frequently at low temperatures, both external and internal, 'the latter arising in some refrigerated ships'. In the temperature context he could also have mentioned that a welded ship built at a cold place seemed more susceptible to fracturing than a similar ship built at a warmer place, as was indicated by the experiences of Ocean vessels built in the comparatively cold climate of Portland, Maine, compared with those built in the warmer clime of Richmond, California.

Until the establishment of the American Board of Investigation there had been little official attempt to correlate details of the ship failures that had taken place. The first step therefore was to ascertain the extent of the

---

14. Sir Amos Ayre, *The Work of the Admiralty Ship Welding Committee.*

problem, so data sheets were sent out to shipmasters asking for details of any structural cracks which their ships suffered. (The receipt of official requests for such information could not have done much for the morale of the recipients, even if their ship had not so far cracked.) At this stage the data sheets were circulated only to American shipmasters for it was to be a few months yet before the first American Liberty was handed over to the British ally, and the Ocean ships were not within the American Board's remit. At a later date similar data sheets were circulated among the British shipmasters concerned. This data collection was to be continued on a regular basis for the remainder of the war and for some time after, but some defects still managed to slip through the reporting net. During the Summer of 1944, for instance, the *Samalness* (Brunswick, March 1944) on her maiden voyage reported structural defects at Capetown, but this vessel does not feature in the Official US Reports.

The first batch of returns covered the period to the end of April 1943 and they showed that by that date there had been well over 100 casualties, twenty-eight of them classified as serious (Class 1), and no less than twenty-three of that twenty-eight involved Liberty ships. Whether Class 1 failures or not, all the failures sooner or later resulted in ships being out of commission for days, weeks, even months at a time, until repairs could be effected. Merchant seamen whose lives were in danger enough as it was, were now often obliged to sail damaged ships, in other words unseaworthy ones, from a port which had no repair facilities to another that did. Not only was that dangerous, it added to the total time the ship was out of commission.

An examination of the overall statistics shows that the worst month of all for casualties was March 1944 during which 138 cases were reported, ten of them being Class 1. The worst month for Class 1 casualties, with a total of twenty, had been January 1944; in fact the northern winter of 1943-4 proved to be the worst period of all for cracking incidents, thus highlighting the fact that temperature was likely to be a contributory factor. By the end of the war the number of Class 1 failures had risen to 114, and by 17 March 1946, the end of the period covered by the American Final Report, to 132. That was, however, far from being the end of the matter. By December 1949 the number of reported Class 1 casualties had risen to 197, one of the later ones being the British-flagged Liberty *Samaritan* in February 1947, and by 1967 to over 260. No doubt there were further failures as the wartime built ships aged, but systematic recording of such incidents appears to have been discontinued in the late 1960s.

Even as the data was coming in and being analysed, the research teams set about their tasks, and if the Americans involved in the investigations needed any extra push it came on 23 November 1943 when a structural failure occurred which resulted in the loss of American lives. The

Liberty *John P. Gaines* (completed at Portland, Oregon, in July 1943 and placed under the management of the Northland Transportation Company) was sailing between Dutch Harbor in the Aleutian Islands and Seattle, when at 2200 hours loud noises were heard, the source of which could not be located in the dark. At about 0240 hours the following morning, when the ship was some 40 miles off Chirkoff Island, an exceptional sea struck the port bow and a fracture, believed to have started earlier when the noises had been heard, 'immediately propagated' at the forward end of No. 3 hatch. As the vessel rode between swells she broke partially in two, and when riding the next swell, the fore part of the vessel broke away completely and was presumed to have sunk. Fortunately, because of the noises heard earlier, all crew members, and the Armed Guard and the military passengers on the ship, were aboard the still floating after part. The captain ordered abandon ship and everyone got away in lifeboats. The survivors were picked up by other ships in the area except for eleven men in one boat which was never seen again, the eleven comprising five crew members and six soldiers. The stern of the vessel was later washed ashore on Big Koniuji Island where it eventually broke up.

With that incident the cracking problem had brought its first known fatalities. It may be that other structural failures, failures of the sort not triggered by torpedoes, bombs and mines, had been a contributory factor in the loss without trace of other welded ships, but no one knows. The eleven *John P. Gaines* deaths are therefore the only *wartime* ones that can be directly attributed to the cracking problem. Furthermore, it can be said that those fatalities should not have occurred once the men were in lifeboats. The wind at the time was Force 6 and although there was something of a swell running, the conditions were not so bad that a well-found lifeboat should be lost. Such boats had survived far worse conditions. Therefore this small, though regrettable loss of life, debunks the myth put about over the years to the effect that many Liberty seamen lost their lives during the war because their ships broke up under their feet when no enemy was in the vicinity. That having been said, what cannot be gauged is whether some Liberty ships and their crews lost to direct enemy action might have survived had the ships been constructed differently. In other words, did the propensity to crack contribute in some other sinkings? We shall never know.

That the 'directly attributable' loss of life in the war years was indeed small is confirmed by the contents of a secret memorandum by John Scott Maclay (later a Member of Parliament and Secretary of State for Scotland) of the British Shipping Mission in the States, sent to the Ministry of War Transport in London on 17 February 1944. Maclay was commenting on the background to the American questionnaire on cracking which at that time was being circulated to British masters of Liberty ships, and he stated that by that date five Liberties had broken in two at sea but 'the loss of life has been very small'.[15]

Three of the five Liberties referred to by Maclay have already been mentioned here. The other incidents took place in January 1944, when both the *Joseph Smith* and the *Samuel Dexter* were abandoned after cracking-up at sea. The former ship was later shelled and sunk by an escort ship in the North Atlantic, and the latter ended up ashore in two pieces on Barra Island in the Hebrides off the Scottish coast. One breaking-in-two incident not included in Maclay's report was that in which the Russian-flagged Liberty *Valeri Chkalov* (*Alexander Baronof,* Richmond, April 1943) was involved on 11 December 1943 in the North Pacific. When she cracked right across the deck and down both sides, the Russian crew, including four women, took refuge in the stern half. The ship was taken in tow by the Russian tug *Josef Stalin,* but after she broke completely in two, both halves were salved by US Navy tugs and towed to Vancouver, Washington, where they were rejoined. The repaired ship then reverted to its original name and sailed under the American flag. She survived the rest of war and was eventually scrapped at Philadelphia in 1965.

A Liberty once thought to have been a victim of structural failure after she 'exploded', broke in two, and sank in Alaskan waters on 19 April 1944, was the *John Straub,* Captain A.W. Westerholm, with seventy men on board. However, none of the American Official Reports on structural failures ever attributed this ship's loss to any such failure. We saw with the *J.L.M. Curry* how the 'explosion' accompanying a major structural failure was likened to a torpedo striking. With the *John Straub* it seems it was the other way round, an explosion that was in fact due to a torpedo strike, or a mine, being likened in an early report on the sinking, to one caused by a major structural failure. However, the Coast Guard report made soon after the event, attributed the sinking to enemy action, to a mine in fact, on the assumption that no Japanese submarine was operating so far east at that time. That assumption is no longer necessarily valid because recent research has shown that the Japanese *I-180* was operating in that same general area and was itself sunk a week later by the destroyer USS *Gilmore.* Whether the casualty was caused by torpedo or mine, fifty-five of the men on board perished. It seems likely that the incorrect attribution made by some authorities to the effect that this vessel was lost as a result of structural failure was due to two earlier reports of deck fractures on this vessel, the first on 12 January 1944, the second on 22 March only four weeks prior to the ship's loss, although on both occasions the cracking was classified as minor.

---

15. MT59/1871, PRO, London.

The data collected as a result of the American questionnaire showed that almost all the cracks reported had the brittle appearance first noted on the *Ocean Justice,* then more obviously on *Schenectady,* and moreover, that the fractured surfaces bore characteristic chevron-shaped markings which always pointed back to the trigger point, whence the crack had emanated. In most cases this initiating point was found to be at a place where higher-than-average stresses could be expected, for instance, where there was a discontinuity in the ship structure such as at the square corners of a hatch opening – hence the large number of breaks reported as having occurred in the vicinity of No. 3 hatch which is situated longitudinally near the middle of the ship where the effect of bending stresses can be expected to be greatest. Other initiating points were associated with imperfections in the structure, such as faulty welds. Engineers termed these trigger points, whether they were caused by a structural discontinuity in the design of the ship or by a faulty weld, a 'notch'. From that they developed the term 'notch sensitivity', which they defined as that property of steel which reflects its reluctance to absorb energy in the presence of notches particularly at low temperatures and at high rates of strain.

Although in the worst cases once they had been triggered, huge cracks could develop almost instantaneously with an explosive-like roar or a noise like a gunshot (one shipmaster reporting that 'you can hear them crack like gunshots, and the cracks, once started, run like ladders in a woman's stocking'), it was found that other cracks were creepers, proceeding in a kind of stop-go fashion; yet other cracks did not develop very much at all. A crack in brittle material can sometimes be halted by drilling a hole immediately in front of it, the stress concentrated at such a circular hole being much less than that at the sharp leading edge of the crack itself. There is one case on record where the ship's chief engineer attempted to halt a crack on a Liberty ship by taking just such action. The crack continued to spread because the chief engineer did not realise that the front point of the crack was deep under the surface of the plate and so could not be seen. He was drilling holes in places which the front of the crack had already passed.

As a result of the preliminary investigations into the structural failures and well before full scientific knowledge had been gained, and because the situation was so serious that action just could not wait for such new knowledge, orders went out that certain design features on all ships still under construction were to be changed and that preventative measures must be taken on all existing ships as soon as practicable. Because so many fractures were found to begin near hatch corners, the corners of hatch coamings in new ships were now to be rounded instead of square, rounded corners causing smaller stress concentrations than square ones, whilst in existing ships the square corners were to be strengthened with makeshift inserts. Another major change introduced in new ships and, as soon as possible, retro-fitted to existing ones, was the provision of so-called crack arresters.

The fitting of these on new ships was relatively easy and cheap, but on existing ones it was neither, and it also entailed ships being taken out of service for some days, or even weeks, whilst the work was carried out. In existing ships longitudinal slots were first cut in the ship's plating in the places where the crack arresters were it be fitted. Each slot ran longitudinally for over 300ft, which was about two-thirds of the ship's length. The slot was then covered by a 16in wide strap, which was increased to 18ins in the midships section. This was then riveted to the ship's plate, on either side of the slot, using a double row of rivets on each side, increased to triple rows amidships. On Liberty ships, four such arresters were fitted, one each, port and starboard, close to the edge of the main deck plating, and a further pair, again one to port and the other to starboard, on the sheer strake, the highest line of plating of the ship's hull. In new construction, the arresters often took the form of a heavy angle iron riveted to both deck plating and sheer strake. The idea behind the crack arresters was that they would act as a barrier to any crack from the deck into the hull plating, and vice versa. Additional design changes were made to new ships and other alterations made to existing ones, but the main modifications were those described above. It must be said that the decision to fit the arresters alone could not have been taken lightly. To fit each one required the drilling of about 7000 holes followed by the driving of 3500 rivets. As four arresters were fitted, those figures must be multiplied by four for each ship. About 1000 existing Liberties were eventually fitted with these devices, so that the programme required the drilling of millions of holes and the driving of millions of rivets, and remember, that was only for the Liberty ships already constructed. The extra cost to the American taxpayer was estimated at a colossal $50m, or at today's prices, about $1 billion.

Whilst all this rectifying work was taking place, research scientists and engineers were still hard at work behind the scenes. Welding practices were examined and new welding sequences devised in the hope that so-called locked-in stresses could be reduced. The value of reducing such locked-up stresses was subsequently brought into question, when later research led to the conclusion that locked-up stresses had little influence on structural cracking, providing that the steel remained ductile. At a more mundane level, the practice of paying welders piecework rates which might produce scrimped work was looked into by Maritime Commission officials, and a system of day payments for welders was instituted. As Welding Inspectors and Ship Surveyors began tightening up weld inspection processes, they often found evidence of working malpractices. An official British report dated 7 March 1944 stated:

At Portland, Maine, faulty welding had been found to be caused by workmen breaking away the flux covering before the metal had cooled sufficiently. The uncovering of the hot metal resulted in the atmospheric oxygen and nitrogen entering into chemical combination with the metal, thus weakening the weld.[16]

Another example of welding malpractice was noted by Captain S. Theophilatos while he was standing by to take over the Greek Liberty *Ameriki* (built as *William H. Todd*, September 1943) at Portland, Maine in November 1943. He noticed as many as three loose welding rods being stuffed into the 'V' between deck plates to reduce the size of the gap, 'the surface then being very lightly covered by melted metal so as to give the appearance of a satisfactory joint'. Captain Theophilatos reported the incident on arrival at the Scottish port of Stranraer on 1 May 1944 to the Security Officer there, Major W. Dyer. The captain described the incident as 'attempted murder' and went on to say that two welders had been sentenced to long terms of imprisonment for sabotage, 'a decision which had given him and other seamen great pleasure'. He added that 'he considered it important that the distinction between good design and bad workmanship should be made clear'. Similar incidents took place at the Bethlehem-Fairfield yard at Baltimore. James W. Wilson, a Maritime Commission surveyor, was a witness at the trials of nine of that yard's workers who had been arrested 'on charges of placing unfused electrodes, and slugs of iron and steel, in the plate grooves, and then covering them with a weld'. It must have been a widespread practice because yard workers had invented a word for it, calling it 'slugging'. One of the defendants, a minor, was convicted and sentenced to eighteen months in a reformatory.[17] There was a rather strange aftermath to those stories in that when engineers later carried out strength tests on 'slugged' welds, as compared with properly executed ones, they found only a marginal difference in strength between the two and, moreover, the slightly stronger one was the improper one.

An analysis of the returned questionnaires from shipmasters indicated the probability that low temperature was somehow involved in some cases of structural failure, and so the step was taken to route welded ships away from cold areas whenever possible. (The unknown American official who produced the original questionnaire is worthy of our admiration, for right from the start the form seems to have covered most pertinent factors.) Such re-routing was not possible of course, with ships engaged on the Murmansk and Vladivostok runs. Strict routing rules were however

---

16. Letter from J.L. Adam, Chief Surveyor of the British Corporation Register of Shipping, to Sir Amos Ayre at the Admiralty, dated 7 March 1944. File MT9/3882, PRO, London.
17. Lane, op.cit.

maintained with those Liberties engaged in the carriage of troops. By January 1944 it had been found that a few Liberty ships which had oper-ated in extremely heavy weather conditions had developed buckling in both the bottom shell plating and in the inner bottom plating. As not many ships were involved, the problem had not occasioned too much concern. However, in the case of Liberty troop carriers and hospital ships, where so many lives were at stake, the extra precaution was taken of fitting four extra longitudinal bottom girders to each such ship.[18]

The combined effort of scientists and engineers on both sides of the Atlantic to get to the bottom of the structural failure problem, not only during the war but for several years after it, proved to be a landmark in the study of brittle failure of mild steel and also of the way in which ship structures (both welded and riveted) responded to actual conditions at sea. It was a very expensive business, for during the programme both the Americans and the British actually took ships out of commission to run tests on them. Eight American ships were used in a series of static tests in order to ascertain what happened to them under stress conditions. The British used half a dozen ships for the purpose, and their tests were more wide-ranging than the American ones and they certainly went on for longer. None of the American tests were conducted on a ship actually at sea, whilst the British did conduct sea tests, one in the winter 1944/45, and another which began at Christmas 1945 and went on until May 1947. The American Final Report of 1946 states:

> The British are at present engaged in a long range, full scale study of the loads imposed upon vessels at sea, together with the strains experienced in service. The need for such a study was also recognised in this country and the findings of the Board's investigation have served to accentuate this need.
>
> A number of American observers, including representatives of the member agencies of this Board, have been afforded access to these studies and have, in several cases, made voyages in the experimental vessels.
>
> It is hoped that the United States may also find it possible to initiate long range instrumental studies of loads and strains in ships at sea.

Despite the hope expressed in that official document, there is no evidence that such American sea trials ever did take place.

One of the ships used in the American static tests was the Liberty *Philip Schuyler* (Portland, Oregon, April 1942). Those particular tests took place in the summer of 1944. (That ship itself suffered a Class 2 casualty on 12 June that year.) Scientists set up a host of electric strain

---

18. E. M. MacCutcheon in letters and other material sent to the author, March/May 2000.

gauges on the ship and then, by moving heavy weights around and by altering the quantities and distribution of water ballast, simulated some of the stress conditions that the ship might experience in actual operations.

The following description concentrates on the British programme because of the uniqueness of the British sea tests. In Britain three separate projects were undertaken, though in the interest of flexibility they were not closely defined says Professor Frank Bull, who describes them thus:

1) In what way do riveted and welded ships differ in their structural behaviour?
2) What influence do the stresses locked into a ship by welding have on the onset of fracture?
3) What is the fundamental nature of the breakdown of steel which causes fracture, and, in particular, what are the circumstances which cause an apparently ductile material like mild steel to break in a brittle manner?

Frank Bull was chosen to head the group of British engineers and scientists working on the first of these projects. At the time he was very young and rather inexperienced and was chosen, he says, because he knew nothing at all about ship design and was therefore considered not to be handicapped by preconceived notions. The second project was undertaken by the British Welding Research Association in conjunction with engineers at Cambridge University. That same University worked on the third project, the leader of that particular team being Dr. Constance F. Tipper.

Bull says that as a new boy he received much advice from shipbuilders and naval architects, many of whom did suffer from preconceived notions. The most popular thesis proffered by these 'experts' to explain away the mystery of why the failures were occurring mainly in welded as opposed to riveted ships, concerned the notion of 'rivet slip' and its effect on the rigidity of the ship structure. They told him that when a wave strikes a riveted ship and high stresses are set up, the rivets slip or give a little and this takes the edge off the blow. In the case of a welded ship, the same 'experts' explained, welding effectively converted the ship into one rigid girder, that there was then nothing to give and therefore no relaxation of peak stress under storm conditions. As an adjunct to the rivet slip theory, the riveted ship was supposed to be much more flexible and so bend more to fit the waves than the welded ship which suffered from relative inflexibility.

The first British experiments took place on the newly-built and all-riveted freighter *Empire Duke* during the last two months of 1943 immediately after that ship's completion at the J.L. Thompson yard at

Sunderland. It may have been at this stage that Frank Bull had his one and only meeting with Cyril Thompson; he cannot now recall the exact date of that meeting or the circumstances of it. These preliminary investigations, held whilst the ship was berthed alongside, did not produce much in the way of results, but did help with the development of methodology and instrumentation for the later experiments. The next tests, again static ones carried out in still water, were held in July and August 1944 aboard the all-welded Anglo-Saxon tanker *Neverita*. For direct comparison purposes a similar range of tests was then conducted on a sister-ship, but mostly riveted, tanker *Newcombia*. Much as in the American *Philip Schuyler* experiments, the working of a ship in a seaway was simulated by filling various combinations of tanks with seawater, but as each of these ships was a tanker and not just a freighter with comparatively limited tank capacity, the 'weights' being moved around were considerably larger.

Then, in the winter of 1944/45, a preliminary sea trial was conducted aboard another tanker, the *Niso*, identical to *Newcombia* right down to the fact that she was mostly all-riveted. That tanker sailed on its maiden east-west transatlantic voyage with some of the experimental party on board, their main task on this crossing being to test newly developed instrumentation and to familiarise the party with conditions aboard a ship when actually at sea. Amongst the group were Frank Bull and, to represent the American Board of Investigation, Lieutenant-Commander Edward MacCutcheon of the United States Coast Guard. That voyage forged a friendship between the two men that survives to this day.[19]

The very extensive British trials in still water had established beyond all reasonable doubt that so-called rivet slip simply did not exist. Stresses and deflections on the welded and riveted tankers were measured at a large number of places and it was found that the stresses in the welded ship were for all practical purposes the same as in the corresponding riveted ship, and that there was no evidence to support the rivet slip theory. Indeed, so far as overall rigidity was concerned, the evidence was slightly the other way, the welded ship was, if anything, slightly the less rigid. The British had decided that measurements should be made in every possible stress condition to which ships were subjected, so in October 1944 strain and deflection measurements were carried out on two vessels, one mainly riveted and the other mainly welded, during their actual launching processes. The ships involved were the *Empire Haig* and the *Empire Allenby* respectively, the latter another ship from the J.L. Thompson yard. Once again the riveted and welded ships behaved in much the same way, so far as structural stresses and deflection were concerned.

---

19. MacCutcheon, ibid.

Around August 1945 MacCutcheon came over to England again to further the liaison between the research workers on both sides of the Atlantic. He was particularly interested in going to have a look at a 'graveyard' of damaged ships at the River Blackwater in the County of Essex, the entrance of which lies some 30 miles north of the Thames Estuary. A stretch of the river near the entrance was considered remote enough from German attack to be used as a temporary anchorage for war-damaged ships whilst decisions were reached about their future. At the time Bull and his American colleague visited the anchorage, it held about a dozen ships, perhaps four of them being Liberties. All had suffered major damage by bombs, mines, or torpedoes, rather than simple structural failure. However, even though the damage they saw had come about as a result of direct war operations, they were able to see just how efficient the crack arresters could be no matter what the prime cause of damage.

> The magnitude of the damage on some of the ships was horrific. Great holes had been torn in their sides ... Although the damage had in most cases been caused by explosions of one sort or another, the fractured plates frequently showed the characteristic forms of brittle failure. Of particular interest was a study of how effective the riveted crack-arresters had been in stopping the spread of cracks. In many cases it looked as if the ship had survived only because the crack-arresters had worked. One of the ships examined in detail was the Liberty *Colin P. Kelly Jnr* which had suffered a major crack across the full width of the upper deck, besides a number of other cracks in the deck plating. The major crack over twenty millimetres wide had not passed the riveted crack-arrester fitted at the intersection of the deck with the ship's side. This was a magnificent example of how effective the crack-arresters could be. It was arranged to have the relevant pieces burned off and shipped to the States to show the authorities there just how effective crack-arresters could be.

The damage to the *Colin P. Kelly Jnr* (Baltimore, January 1943) had come on 4 June 1945 when she struck a mine off the Belgian port of Ostend. The explosion, which had blown a hole in the ship's side causing the engine-room and the adjacent cargo holds to flood, had also fractured the main deck both forward and aft of the bridge, the most serious cracks being on both sides of the forward end of No. 4 hatch. Later the ship was towed to Sunderland where surveyors decided that repairing her would be uneconomic. (Early in 1948 she again came under tow, this time to Rotterdam where she was scrapped.) Another of the Liberties laying in the Blackwater at that time, or rather, half of another one because only the forepart was there, was the *James Harrod* (Portland, Oregon, March 1943). She had caught fire in the English Channel after colliding with another Liberty on 16 January 1945. After being beached she broke in two and the forepart was then towed to the Essex haven. Perhaps the American authorities became a mite too optimistic about the efficiency of the crack arresters as a result of this incident and others. The Final Report of the Board of Investigation (issued in July 1946) stated that no case was known of a crack having crossed a crack-arrester. This may have been true at the time the statement was made, but subsequent events showed that although crack-arresters were on the whole very effective, they did not provide 100 per cent protection.

When the Second World War was reaching its climax in 1945, every available merchant ship was needed to supply the invading Allied armies and later to carry food to the starving populations in Europe. At this time it was not found possible to release ships for testing purposes. Nevertheless it was during this period that Bull and his colleagues planned for the definitive series of trials which would settle, once and for all, the nature and extent of any differences in structural response between otherwise similar riveted and welded hulls. The trials were planned to include the conditions actually experienced in stormy weather at sea, for there were still some die-hards who held the view that 'scientific' testing in still water was unable to reveal the truth. They firmly believed in the old expression, 'worse things happen at sea', although they were not prepared to define the nature of those 'worse things'. These critics of still-water testing conveniently turned a blind eye to the failure of the *Schenectady* and several other ships which had fractured in still waters. The plan, as subsequently approved by the Admiralty, was in two parts. First, it was proposed to fit out one ship with instruments to measure all the forces experienced by the ship in a seaway, and to sail this vessel back and forth across the North Atlantic for at least one year, so as to experience at least one annual cycle of weather. The second part of the trials involved the still water testing of two ships, one riveted and the other welded, when subjected to maximum forces as measured at sea. The two ships chosen for the trials were the welded American-built *Ocean Vulcan* and the riveted *Clan Alpine*. The *Clan Alpine* was a product of the Thompson yard at Sunderland, and built in 1942, was typical of the standard riveted British wartime-built ship.

In 1946, while the experiments with *Ocean Vulcan* were in process, Sir Amos Ayre wrote:

> The ship has been fitted with instruments that will simultaneously record the distribution of water pressure on the hull; the accelerations at several points in the ship from which the inertia forces at all parts of the structure can be deduced; the stresses . . . at a few important points; the wind forces on the ship; the angles of roll and pitch; speed of the vessel relative to the water; and the profile of the wave surface on the hull.

167

The master of the *Ocean Vulcan* was instructed that within the bounds of safe navigation, he was not to go out of his way to avoid any storms he might run into, with the result that Bull cheerfully refers to the time aboard the ship as a period of sailing the North Atlantic looking for storms.

Bull says of the overall project:

It could be said that despite all our efforts, our conclusions were largely negative. We had set out to find what differences of structural behaviour might exist between ships of riveted construction, and otherwise similar ships of welded construction. Although we had indeed found that there were differences, they were not of such magnitude as would by themselves, account for the fact that the casualty rate for welded ships far exceeded the corresponding rate for riveted ships.

In a way it was disappointing that our own side of the overall investigations into the failure of Liberty ships finished up with such negative answers. Negative results, however, can be important and we had, on the way, gained a great deal of information on how ships' structures really did behave, and what the forces of the sea can do to a ship.

He goes on:

The final static testing on the measurement of strains in otherwise idencal riveted and welded ships which were carried out was the most intense and comprehensive series of testing on ship structures that had ever been undertaken, and remains so to this day, more than fifty years on.

The sea trials were unique in measuring over a period of seventeen months, the actual forces experienced by a ship in a seaway . . . Nothing on the same scale as the sea trials on the *Ocean Vulcan* has been attempted since the end of WWII. This does not mean that there is no longer any need to carry out further research. The findings of the *Ocean Vulcan* trials . . . may not be applicable to other ships, particularly very large ships, and more needs to be found out about the behaviour of ships in gales exceeding the Force 9 encountered on the *Ocean Vulcan* trials.

Mariners and others familiar with the statistics that show the number of giant bulk carriers that have been lost at sea in recent years, will heartily agree with Frank Bull's remarks. In the period 1975 to 1990 alone, no less than 279 such vessels were lost totalling nearly 6 million gross tons, amongst them the British *Derbyshire* off Okinawa in September 1980 with all hands

Negative results they might have been, but the Admiralty set much store by the nine separate reports produced by Bull's group which were subsequently published by the Government Stationery Office. Naval architects consider them to be definitive in the field which they cover. In fact, by the time Bull and his associates dealing with stresses, and the experts on both sides of the Atlantic who were investigating all aspects of welding technology, had reached their separate conclusions, the prime cause of the structural failures was identified as lying in the field of metallurgy. From the time of the *Schenectady* incident onward, steel samples had been taken from fractured ships and subjected to all the standard tests and, according to Sir Amos Ayre, 'it was found . . . that with very rare exceptions the steel complied in all respects with the pertinent specifications'. However, perhaps the Americans had not relayed to Sir Amos all the information they had on this particular subject, for the exceptions could not have been all that rare as is indicated by some of the deliberations of the Special Committee Investigating the National Defense Program headed by the then Senator Harry S. Truman.

At one stage, according to President Truman's memoirs, his Committee served notice on the Carnegie-Illinois Steel Corporation, a principal subsidiary of the United States Steel Corporation, that the steel plate manufactured at its Irvin Works for the United States Navy and for the Maritime Commission and for Lend-Lease, 'was defective and that the physical tests to which the finished steel plate was subjected to determine its tensile strength were faked and falsified'. Truman went on to add that the steel company men in charge of the testing operations had testified that about 5 per cent or more of tests were deliberately faked and the steel plate falsely reported to be in accordance with specifications. 'To do this they instructed the testers under them to cheat.' In defence of the United States Steel Corporation, Dr. Rufus Zimmerman produced a letter sent by the American Bureau of Shipping in 1942, authorising their inspectors to waive tests of specimens when in their opinion 'steel delivery can be expedited and the serviceability of the ships for the present emergency will not be adversely affected'.[20] The letter certainly did not give the right for tests to be falsified, but its existence may have been what caused Truman to let the Corporation off the hook. He said, 'The Committee served notice on all such companies that the only excuse it would accept was an early and complete correction'. Perhaps the word 'all' in that sentence is the most illuminating.[21] According to Frederic Lane, the US Maritime Commission historian, Admiral Vickery of the Commission did not crack down too hard on the steel companies, 'lest worry over high specifications slow down the production of steel plate and so delay ship construction'.

Because the 385 Liberty ships built at the Bethlehem-Fairfield yard at Baltimore produced comparatively few major structural failures, an

---

20. Lane, op cit.
21. Harry S. Truman, *Memoirs* (New York 1955), pp184-5.

investigation was made during the war into the shipyard practices at this yard in order to compare them with the practices at other yards where the failure rate was higher. The Baltimore yard, it must be remembered, was the only Liberty yard to use riveting to any great extent; all their Liberties having riveted plate seams, and according to Bull, die-hard supporters of the rivet-slip theory used this fact to support their views even though tests had shown that rivet slip was non-existent. However, the riveted seams on Baltimore ships did make excellent *in situ* crack arresters, and yet despite the probability that this yard's comparatively good record could be largely attributed to this in-built crack arrester effect, there was a suspicion in American circles, a suspicion never proven, that the yard's parent company, Bethlehem Steel, might have been supplying its own shipyard with better-quality steel than to its competitors.

It will no doubt have registered with any merchant sailors from those days who are reading this, that little if any note was taken of what their feelings might have been over this matter. Perhaps officialdom's almost callous disregard for the feelings of seamen is best summed up by the contents of a memorandum which emanated from the British side of the Atlantic. The document was dated 17 January 1944 and was sent by the Ministry of War Transport to the British Admiralty. It began by saying there was concern over the number of Liberties which had broken in half or had suffered other serious splitting problems. It then went on,

> We would like to feel that if anything which, *without serious expenditure* of materials and labour, could make the crews feel fully assured of the seaworthiness of these new vessels, it should be given effect to.

(The italics are this author's, but neither the tenor of that passage nor its bad grammatical structure are his responsibility!)[22]

Dr. Constance Tipper's researches at Cambridge and the metallurgical research programmes conducted on the other side of the Atlantic threw up the concept of what was called 'notch brittleness', that being defined as the property by which mild steel may fracture in a brittle manner if a notch is present and provided the temperature is sufficiently low. She and the Americans found that most mild steels in use in shipbuilding usually give a ductile fracture at normal temperatures, even when notched, and in order to produce a brittle fracture the temperature had to be lowered to values only rarely encountered in the service life of a ship. On the other hand some steels actually used on Liberty ships were so notch-sensitive that brittle failures were encountered even in ships operating in the warm waters of the Central Pacific. Dr. Tipper found that the usual tensile and

---

22. MT9/3882 PRO, London.

bend tests to which shipbuilding steel is subjected for acceptance purposes did not disclose whether the steel was or was not notch brittle at
low temperatures, which was the reason why the steel samples taken
from fractured ships gave satisfactory test results for strength and duct-
ility even though the sample had been taken from close to where a brittle fracture had taken place. This notch brittleness at service temperatures
was relatively rare in ship-quality mild steel manufactured in Britain,
particularly when compared to the corresponding ship steels produced in
America. Dr. Tipper discovered that steels in which the proportion of
manganese to that of carbon was low, as with some American steels, were
significantly more notch sensitive than British steels which tended to
have a higher manganese/carbon ratio. (Dr. Tipper was a remarkable lady
in several ways. She was among the first top-class female engineers. She
lived to the grand age of 101, dying in 1995.)

To sum up the eventual overall findings of the scientists and engineers
engaged in the metallurgy and welding investigations, we return to Sir
Amos Ayre. He said that the possibility of the effect of welding on the
steel plate being a factor was precluded by the fact that very few of the
fractures followed the welds. That, even when a fracture commenced at a
faulty weld, it seemed to run away from the weld as soon as possible and
progress across virgin plate; the majority of the fractures, in fact, progressed as if the welds were not there at all. In the few cases where there
was evidence of cracking due to welding, the cracks were sometimes confined to the close vicinity of the welds, and could be explained by incorrect welding methods. American and British scientists investigated all
aspects of welding including the possible effects of locked-up or residual
stresses caused by welding. (This was the area of investigation where
American research was considerably more extensive than the British.)
They were able to confirm that provided both the steel plate and the
welding material, can behave in a normal ductile manner, such locked-up
stresses did not impair the strength of the ship structure.

Let Professor Bull have the last word.

> The problem was not riveting versus welding, but ductile steel versus
> notch sensitive steel. Presumably the Americans would have got into as
> much trouble if they had used rivets (although there is an additional
> saving grace in a riveted joint, in that cracks tend to stop at a plate edge,
> and rarely continue on through a riveted joint). Similarly, the British
> steels should have shown a superior performance even when used on
> welded ships, and this was indeed the case, as the few welded ships pro-
> duced in the United Kingdom had a much better record than those
> built in the USA.

Structural steel failures were not the only problems suffered by Liberty
ships. More than a few suffered propeller shaft problems due to

misalignment of the shaft created during the ship construction processes, a problem already touched upon in an earlier chapter. Several ships had their propellers fall off at sea. Others experienced difficulties with the steering gear, which on at least two occasions resulted in a collision. Some ships had problems with the main engines. However, taken overall, the incidence of these other problems was in no way comparable to the incidence of structural failure, and certainly not so bad as was implied in a letter dated 25 May 1944 from a sailor identified only as 'Ron', written to a Mrs. E. Melville living in Chicago. Ron was serving aboard *Samlea* (Baltimore, March 1944) on her maiden voyage from New York to Indian ports, and his letter was intercepted by the official censors at Colombo. This is the relevant extract, word for word:

> I have just had to leave this letter for a moment for I felt the engines stopping, so I went up on the bridge to see what it was about, its the jolly old engines giving out, good ship, what, we will be home in no time at this rate . . . Bloody good ships these are, every day we have found something wrong with them, one don't feel safe on them, never know whats going to happen next, gives one a feeling that its likely to fall apart any minute, give me a stout old tramp, at least it goes without stopping every other day and you feel safe on it knowing its well built.
>
> We have just started again but I doubt if it will be for long for this stopping is getting a daily affair with the ship.[23]

One matter which may on occasion have contributed to the structural stresses on a ship and so cause a crack to propagate in the first place, or which may have contributed to the severity of a structural failure after a crack had started, was not directly mentioned in any of the Allied official reports. It was, however, hinted at in an official British memorandum, dated 7 March 1944, sent to Sir Amos Ayre at the British Admiralty by the chief surveyor of the British Corporation Register of Shipping, J.L Adam, who at that time was visiting the Stares. (In those days there were two British Ship Registration Societies, Lloyd's Register and the British Corporation.) Mr. Adam was privy to most official shipping information during the war. In the memo he wrote:

> We have not had any reports of any major trouble on any of the 'Sam' ships with which we have so far dealt. Minor cracks in bulwarks, etc., yes, but not any of the order which has been so disturbing in other Liberty ships. This is all the more peculiar in that, during the same period, the number of cases of American Liberty ships in which there has been major trouble has been very large indeed.[24]

---

23. MT9/3882. Extract marked 1101/44 from Ceylon Censorship Report dated June 1944.
24. MT9/3882 Memo dated 7 March 1944.

Mr. Adam did not volunteer a reason for this 'peculiarity'.

The statistics contained in the Final American Report of 1946 confirm Mr. Adam's report. Of the 132 Class 1 structural failures listed as having occurred up to March 1946, ninety-nine were Liberty ships. As Britain during that period had been allocated 187 Liberties, or about 7 per cent of the total number constructed, statistically one would have expected that six or seven of those Class 1 failures would have involved British-flagged Liberties. In fact, not one did. (We have to wait until February 1947, by which time another six Liberties had become Class 1 casualties, before the first British ship, the *Samaritan,* finds a place in the lists.) Furthermore, in the case of the Class 2 and 3 casualties that occurred during the same period, of the approximate total of 660 Liberties involved, only seventeen were British-flagged, or about 2.6 per cent of the total. It is easy to make misleading comparisons from the raw data presented in the American report, nevertheless, it does indeed seem peculiar that not one British-flagged Liberty suffered a Class 1 failure in those early years.

What possible reasons could there be for this? The British Liberties came from a range of yards; Portland (Maine), Richmond, Brunswick, Savannah, Los Angeles, Portland (Oregon), Wilmington, and Baltimore. It has been previously noted that because Baltimore Liberties were constructed with riveted seams, that yard's output produced a smaller proportion of casualties than any of the others. (In fact, only two of the Class 1 casualties listed in the American final report were Baltimore-built Liberties.) As 105 of the British contingent of 187 Liberties were products of that shipyard, it follows that the statistical chance of a British casualty was significantly reduced. However, that fact would not have reduced the chance to zero, and so does not provide an entirely satisfactory explanation.

Is it possible that part of the explanation lay in the relative skill and experience of the seamen sailing these ships? We saw in the previous chapter how the Americans were compelled by circumstances to reduce the sea time requirements for officers to a much greater extent than the British. It follows that many of the newly recruited officers in the American Merchant Marine during the war were relatively inexperienced and unskilled. Many of the tasks of deck officers can be learned by rote; the simple mechanics of working out the ship's position at sea, for example, perhaps using 'short-cut', pre-computed astronomical tables and using a pattern as a guide, can be quickly taught in a school ashore. The officer concerned may end up knowing nothing at all of the mathematical theories behind his calculations, as would be required in normal circumstances, but providing he follows step-by-step instructions, he will come up with the right answer. (Many of today's yachtsmen-navigators use those same quick-fix methods.) That the Americans did cater for the possibility that new officers would not know much about basic navigation is indicated by the nature of some of the 'aids to navigation' supplied to Liberty ships. This author recalls a magnificently, and one suspects, expensively, made metal instrument, complete in its mahogany box, that he discovered hidden away in the back of a drawer of the chartroom of the *Harpagon* (ex-*Samderry*) in about 1950. The instrument had three movable circular scales and was designed to help the user convert compass bearings and courses, to their magnetic and 'true' equivalents, a procedure that any experienced navigator can do in his head. (This author has seen a plastic modern day version of this instrument designed for yachtsmen.)

The American system of creating officers did produce the necessary results; their ships were manned. But the experience of some of the men concerned was severely limited, and not every part of the mariner's art can be taught at school. Some of the arts are only learnt by experience, and this applies especially to the wide-ranging subject called seamanship. Two aspects of that subject will be discussed here as they may have had relevance in some of the cases of structural failure. They are the efficient ballasting of ships, taught to ship's officers as part of the subject known as 'ship stability', and the proper handling of a ship in a seaway. In practice these two aspects sometimes impinge upon each other. Most merchant ships during the war, including Liberties, made the return westward voyages across the North Atlantic in an unloaded, or 'light', condition, because most cargoes at that time were being carried one-way from the 'arsenal of democracy', the United States. For these empty return voyage the ships had to be ballasted. All ships are fitted with an arrangement of double-bottom tanks which can be used for the carriage of water ballast. These tanks are integral parts of the ship and are situated at the bottom of the structure, which means that when these tanks are filled with water, the ship's centre of gravity is lowered thereby increasing its positive stability. Ships are also fitted with so-called deep tanks, which are not so low down, but which can also be used to carry water ballast. Filling all these tanks when a ship is voyaging in an unloaded condition will, under normal circumstances, ensure sufficient immersion of the hull to make the ship navigable and seaworthy and also ensure that the ship's propeller is sufficiently immersed to prevent it coming out of the water in the seaway. Should the propeller emerge even partly from the sea, it results in a condition called 'racing', for the propeller revolves much faster in air than it does in water. This places considerable strain on the engine and propeller shaft and to some extent on the ship structure itself. Every professional seaman will have experienced such a condition on occasion, and will recall that it makes the ship shudder and rattle as if it was being shaken by some giant hand. Professor Bull says that his team measured the effect of racing whilst aboard the *Ocean Vulcan*, and found that the effect on the hull structure was minimal. This author has discussed this particular matter with several experienced masters from both sides of the Atlantic, and has yet to find one who agrees with Professor Bull's findings! No doubt the measurements taken were correct, but all would depend, one supposes, on the degree of racing that Bull and his associates experienced; or perhaps, what they were allowed to experience. Maybe the captain of the *Ocean Vulcan* in the interests of the safety of the ship reduced the engine revolutions or altered course, either or both of which would reduce the racing effect, without informing the team. (In this author's direct experience, he knows of a chief engineer who once himself took the responsibility to reduce revolutions in order to save his beloved engines!) Anyway, Professor Bull does not say that racing had no effect at all on the hull, only that it was minimal.

When bad weather is expected, as in the North Atlantic in winter, filling the double-bottoms and deep tanks with water ballast may be insufficient to immerse the ship to a safe draft, and it is then advisable, even necessary, to supplement the water ballast with ballast of a more solid nature carried in the holds. This was especially important with the Liberty ship, for in its unloaded state and when carrying only water ballast in its tanks, the Liberty was what seamen and naval architects call a 'stiff' ship, a technical term that has nothing whatsoever to do with structural rigidity. In the simplest terms, and without digressing into a discussion of the technicalities of ship stability, a stiff ship is one which in the unloaded condition has a relatively low centre of gravity. Such a ship is therefore inherently stable, but one however, with a very short period of roll with a tendency to right itself violently when rolling in a seaway. This made her an uncomfortable ship at sea as any Liberty seaman will confirm. Radio Officer Ian Malcolm who served on *Samite* (built as *Holland Thompson*, Baltimore, August 1943) on her maiden voyage, has written that Liberty ships in ballast 'rolled frighteningly in bad weather . . . They rolled slowly to port before drawing up at an angle of 40 degrees . . . Then, at an accelerating and alarming speed, they swung over to starboard'.[25] This angle of roll was almost certainly exaggerated for as Professor Bull has pointed out, the simple pendulum gauge used on most ships to register the angle of roll is notoriously unreliable. The movement in a seaway to which Liberty ships in the light condition were especially prone and the concomitant, irregular and fluctuating wave pressures inflicted on sections of the ship, in that seaway, would have set up stresses in the ship and, as we have seen, stress was a requirement in triggering a crack in the structure. The US Maritime Commission acted upon this and issued special instructions on the ballasting of Liberties in late 1943. The British followed suit early in 1944.

The American instructions called for a total of 1500 tons of solid ballast to be carried, usually in the form of sand, and specified exactly how

---

25. Ian M. Malcom, 'Voyage 1 of the Samite', *Nautical Magazine* (1994-5).

it was to be loaded in the ship; 1050 tons were to be divided between Nos. 2, 3, and 4 lower holds, and, in order not to lower the centre of gravity too much and so aggravate the ship's tendency to stiffness, the remaining 450 tons was to be loaded in the 'tween decks. The British rules were different, and called for a total of 1650 tons spread over four holds not three, and with 400 tons of it stowed in the 'tween decks. The memorandum from the Director of Merchant Shipping at the Admiralty to the Ministry of War Transport, suggesting that particular ballast configuration, began with the words:

> Following allocations would give the most kindly distribution from the strength point of view, having in mind the conditions that are to be endured in an all-welded ship.

It is perhaps as well that paragraph was not promulgated to seamen along with the ballast instructions.

An analysis of the circumstances surrounding the 132 casualties listed as Class 1 in the Final American Report on structural failures, shows that sixty-one of the ships involved were in ballast at the time of the incident. (It is possible that a further thirteen, for which the reports were incomplete, were also in a light condition.) So, something like one half of all the Class 1 casualties occurred when the ships were in ballast. A proportion of those casualties occurred after the issuance of the official instructions on ballasting, and this leads us to the second of the two aspects of seamanship mentioned above, the art of handling a ship in a seaway.

Movements of a ship in a seaway can contribute to the overall stress situation in a ship's structure. These movements are more prevalent in bad weather and experienced sea officers have learnt how best to handle a ship in such conditions. The required knowledge comes from experience, and begins by observing an old salt doing it. It cannot effectively be learned from a book. Some storm conditions demand that in order to keep the ship's head into the wind – when to get beam-on might court disaster – full engine revolutions be maintained. Other conditions call for a reduction in engine revolutions perhaps together with a change in course, a change perhaps amounting to turning the ship about and using oil to calm the sea in the process. Timing is of the essence, and that too comes with experience. It cannot, therefore, be expected that inexperienced sea officers would have had time to learn these things, and it follows that some cases of structural failure might have come about, or have been made worse, by the inexperience of those in charge.

In this context it is interesting to note that not one of the twelve Liberties (or of the six similarly all-welded T-2 tankers) lend-leased to the Norwegians during the war features in the list of 132 Class 1 failures in the American report, although two of their Liberties, the *Liev Eiriksson* and the *Harald Torsvik* did report having either Class 2 or 3 failures. On the other hand, of the total of forty-three Liberties handed over to Russia, six feature in that list, including the *Valeri Chkalov* mentioned earlier. (The T-2 tanker *Donbass III* leased to the Russians is also featured in that list. When she broke in two at sea after the war on 17 February 1946, fifteen lives were lost.) With regard to these Russian casualties it should be noted that the ships concerned would have operated mainly in the cold conditions of the North Pacific, and therefore, under worse than average weather conditions and often in unusually low temperatures.

That the handling of a Liberty ship in ballast in bad weather called for a high degree of professional skill is confirmed by Captain Kenneth Cummins. He joined the P&O managed *Samettrick* (Baltimore, January 1944) as master at the port of Middlesbrough in March 1946. (At that time P&O used the title Commander rather than Captain, but that is no longer company practice.) By that time he was already a very experienced seaman. After leaving the training ship *Worcester* in 1918 he became a Midshipman RNR and served aboard the armed merchant cruiser HMS *Morea*. Then, in 1919, he joined P&O as a Cadet and in 1929 obtained his Master's certificate. On one occasion, a cargo ship he served in had to leave Hong Kong harbour in a hurry because of a typhoon warning. In the event the typhoon did not hit Hong Kong at all, but it did pass over Kenneth's ship which makes him one of the comparatively few mariners to have passed through the eye of a tropical revolving storm. When the Second World War came along Kenneth was serving as Chief Officer aboard the passenger liner *Viceroy of India* which soon became a troopship. He was aboard her when in 1940 she was involved in the rescue of over 200 people from two other troopships, the *Ceramic* and *Atlas,* when they were in collision in the South Atlantic west of Cape Town. 'You don't normally get ships colliding out at sea but, of course, there was a war on and they were travelling without lights during a hazy, drizzling night', he says. He was still aboard the *Viceroy* when she was torpedoed and sunk in the Mediterranean on 11 November 1942 by *U-407* (Lieutenant Commander Bruller). Fortunately the trooper was on the return voyage from Oran having recently disembarked her contingent of troops at that port. Four men lost their lives in the incident, the survivors being rescued by the destroyer HMS *Boadicea*.

The *Samettrick* was Kenneth's second command, and in her he sailed to the Caribbean in ballast where he was to load a cargo of sugar. He says that despite the Liberty's reputation for structural failure;

> My Liberty held together, no leaks, in one of the worst Atlantic storms
> I have encountered. Whilst steaming full ahead I could just keep her
> head on, most uncomfortable, but the only damage was a broken pipe
> to the boiler which necessitated a call into the Azores for repairs.

After *Samettrick* Kenneth went on to command larger and more illustrious P&O ships, the last two before he retired in 1960 being the splendid passenger liners *Carthage* and *Stratheden*. At this point the reader may well find himself – or herself- engaged in an exercise in mental arithmetic, and with very good reason. For Kenneth was born on 6 March 1900, and so became a centenarian in 2000. This almost certainly makes him the oldest surviving ex-Liberty ship captain in the world.[26]

Another anecdote about Liberty ship seaworthiness comes from Bill Ellis, who now lives in Ottawa, Canada. He served as Third Mate aboard Furness Withy's *Pacific Ranger* (*Samdaring*, Portland, Maine, March 1944) during 1950/1951. Bound for Britain from North Africa that winter, he was standing watch in moderate to rough weather when, he says;

> I observed, some distance ahead one of those waves that is very obviously different from the others – I think some call it the Seventh Wave. Anyhow I drew it to the attention of the helmsman, so ensuring he took extra care, and we both watched as it came nearer and nearer. Finally the ship dipped into the preceding trough and the whole foredeck disappeared under a mass of water. I had heard about Liberty ships breaking in half amidships so I just watched, and waited, until the bow emerged again and the water poured out of the scuppers. A fascinating experience because it took a long, long time for that wave to arrive – I suppose it was like being mesmerised by a cobra.[27]

Returning to the Americans, an early indication that United States authorities were being obliged to issue orders on rather basic seamanship matters, was Operations Regulation No. 52 issued by the War Shipping Administration on 22 April 1943. The regulation was headed 'Shaft Alley Doors'. It stated that the practice of leaving the vertical sliding door between the [propeller] shaft alley and the engine room open at all times had been a contributory factor in the loss of several ships after explosions caused by torpedoes had caused the doors to jam in the open position. The regulation required that the door be closed at all times except when maintenance work on the propeller shaft was being carried out. Experienced seamen, and that includes ship's engineers, would have needed no official reminder of the very basic safety rule that watertight doors must be kept secured.

---

26. Correspondence and talks with Kenneth Cummins, June-July 2000. During this author's visit to meet with him, Kenneth proudly produced his 100th Birthday letter from Queen Elizabeth together with the splendid accompanying coloured photographic portrait of Her Majesty.
27. Correspondence between Bill Ellis and the author, May/July 2000. Like Kenneth Cummins, Bill was a one-time *Worcester* cadet. In fact so many Old Worcesters served on Liberty ships that one is left with the impression they were as ubiquitous as the ships themselves.

PART II: THE LIBERTY AT WAR

CHAPTER 8

Ubiquity

In one of his wartime speeches President Roosevelt described Liberty ships as forming a 'bridge across the Atlantic' and there can be no doubt that the ships performed their most doughty service across that ocean. The building of that bridge began with the maiden voyage of the first Liberty, the *Patrick Henry*, in January 1942, just two months after America entered the war. As their numbers increased and the war wore on, Liberty ships were not confined to that route and they soon became the maritime workhorses of the Allies on every sea and ocean. From the time of Operation 'Torch' in North Africa in November 1942, whenever and wherever Allied armies made landings, the Liberty ship was there, sometimes involved in the very landing operations themselves, but always there in support. They carried every type of equipment needed by armies in the field, from tanks, lorries, jeeps, landing craft, guns, ammunition, and fuel, and in the South-east Asia Command Area, even mules. Very often, they carried the fighting men themselves.

Control of sea-routes was the key aspect of the Second World War, and the most crucial part of that battle took place in the North Atlantic for, as President Roosevelt realised even before America came into the war, if the Allies were to have any chance of final victory, the supply lines to Britain from America had to be kept open. The Battle of the Atlantic went on for the better part of six years, and the winning of it must rank even higher in the grand strategy of the war than those much shorter turning points, the Battle of Britain, Midway, Stalingrad and El Alamein. No less a person than Winston Churchill once wrote;

> The Battle of the Atlantic was the dominating factor all through the war. Never for one moment could we forget that everything happening elsewhere, on land, at sea, or in the air, depended ultimately on its outcome.

For the first three years of the war, control in the North Atlantic was very largely in the hands of the Germans primarily through the success of their

U-boat campaign. So great was this success during the latter part of 1940 for instance, that it became known as the 'happy time' by U-boat crews. The devastating losses suffered by two British convoys in October 1940 provide indication enough of the success of the submarine wolf-packs at that time, when attacks upon convoys SC-7 and HX-79 resulted in the loss of over thirty ships and damage to others.

Another happy time for a comparatively small number of U-boats oper-ating along the Eastern and Caribbean seaboards of the United States, began early in 1942 and lasted into the summer. Germany (and Italy) had declared war on the United States on 11 December 1941, but for a month no attacks were made on Allied shipping within the so-called Pan-American Neutrality Zone that President Roosevelt had declared in 1939, a zone which extended from the American coast out to approximately longitude 60° West. That month's delay enabled boom-defences and mine-fields to be laid off the principal ports; it should also have allowed time for a system of convoys to be implemented along that coast. That it was not was almost entirely due to Admiral Ernest J. King's refusal to adopt the lessons learned at very high cost earlier in the war by the British. It is unfortunate that the Admiral's well-known antipathy towards anything British may have influenced his decision, a decision only reversed in the spring after the personal intervention of his Commander-in-Chief, Presi-dent Roosevelt. It must have hit Admiral King very hard when the British transferred ten 'Flower' class corvettes to the United States Navy, and loaned twenty-four anti-submarine trawlers, to assist in this task, a 'reverse' transfer of ships that is now little remembered.[1]

Notwithstanding that aid, by the end of August, German submarines had managed to sink no less than 485 ships off the eastern seaboard of the United States and the coasts of Central America. An American historian has written that this 'must be regarded as the most disastrous defeat ever suffered by American naval power'.[2] Although most victims of that onslaught, which began on 12 January 1942, were American, the first ship to be sunk within the Neutrality Zone was the British Blue Funnel Line *Cyclops*, torpedoed on that day in a position about 300 miles east of Cape Cod by *U-123*, Lieutenant Commander Hardegen. That sinking signalled the opening of an operation that Admiral Doenitz called *Paukenschlag* or 'Roll of Drums'. The climax of the Battle of the Atlantic can be said to have begun in November 1942, the month during which the Allies suffered their highest shipping losses of the war, amounting to approximately 860,000 tons, on all oceans, of which over 700,000 tons was a result of submarine actions. Of that total figure, 474,000 tons, or well over half, was British.

---

1. In this transfer the British ships gained more warlike names. For example, HMS *Candytuft* became the USS *Tenacity*, and HMS *Periwinkle*, the USS *Restless*.
2. Gerhard L. Weinberg, *A World At Arms* (Cambridge 1994).

War histories written prior to the mid-1970s credited the final Allied victory in the Battle of the Atlantic against the U-boats to a combination of factors. Amongst the most important of them were the convoy system itself and improvements in naval convoy protection tactics; improvements in submarine detection technology; vast increases in the numbers of naval escorts and new forms of them, including escort carriers which helped to cover the area known as the Mid-Atlantic Gap which could not be reached by shore-based aircraft; longer ranged shore-based aircraft which also reduced that Gap; improved anti-submarine weaponry; and additional bases for aircraft in Iceland and the Azores. These developments took place over months and years, the Portuguese only permitting Allied bases in the Azores, for example, in October 1943.

Histories written after the mid-1970s, when some of the secrets of Britain's wartime codebreaking centre at Bletchley Park were revealed for the first time, added to the above mentioned factors the British ability to read German naval coded signals from May 1941 onwards. The German signals were encoded automatically by the 'Enigma' machine at the point of transmission and then decoded by a similar machine aboard each submarine, and throughout the war the Germans thought the machines to be inviolate. The British ability to decipher these messages meant that not only could convoys be re-routed around the known positions of submarine wolf-packs, but that those wolf-packs could themselves be attacked. This code-breaking facility was however, far from being of a continuous nature, and furthermore it was to some extent negated by the Germans being able to break the British convoy codes in 1941 and 1942. This meant that when the British sent signals diverting convoys around danger areas that had been revealed by their own code-breaking efforts, these signals were read by the Germans who then sent new orders to their submarines.

The fact that the British ability to read the German naval codes was not continuous needs some explanation. To do so it is necessary to describe briefly the sequence of events that created the British Enigma codebreaking ability, and in particular, its effect on the war at sea. It began with Polish intelligence officers supplying materials, including an actual Enigma machine, to the British very early in the war. Then, on 9 May 1941, Lieutenant David Balme from HMS *Bulldog* boarded the sinking submarine *U-100* and was able to recover its Enigma machine along with the requisite daily keys, additional rotors, an array of documents that described its operation, together with code-books; enough material in fact to fill two large packing cases.[3] This was despite the efforts of the German crew under Lieutenant-Commander Julius Lempe to scuttle the boat. In a recent interview the U-boat's radio operator, George Hogel, defended the failure to keep the material from falling into British hands

3. David Balme, telephone conversations, July 2000.

by stating that the crew believed the submarine would sink fast and that anyway, no one believed Enigma could be cracked. A young radioman on board called Heinz Wilde said much the same sort of thing, adding that none of his three superiors in the boat's radio section had taken any steps to throw the machine and its associated paperwork overboard. It was a grave mistake, for once in the hands of the boffins at Bletchley Park, the captured material led to the British being able to read signals sent to its submarines by German Naval Headquarters. The intelligence reports based on Enigma material were codenamed 'Ultra', and the existence of Ultra was one of the best-kept secrets of the war.

The *Bulldog* incident took place seven months before America's entry into the war. It is necessary to point this out because of Hollywood's propensity to rewrite history for the sake of box-office receipts. The film '*U-571*' released in 2000, gives the credit for capturing that first Enigma machine to Americans. This is unfortunate, and not only because many moviegoers learn their 'history' from such films. In this case it is particularly unfortunate because that early British success with Enigma might well have resulted in the saving of American lives and ships even *prior* to 7 December 1941, the day America entered the war. On 10 November 1941 an wholly American convoy called WE-12X consisting of nineteen ships, sailed from Halifax, Nova Scotia. The convoy was led by the carrier USS *Ranger*, which, along with two cruisers and ten other warships, were protecting six troopships, the largest of them the crack liner *America* now renamed *West Point*. Extraordinarily, and a sign of President Roosevelt's deep desire to aid Britain in every way possible even before his country was at war, unbeknownst to the American public the troopships were carrying the men and light equipment of the British 18th Division being sent to the Middle East. The convoy was guided safely down to the Caribbean and then across the South Atlantic using submarine avoidance information supplied by Bletchley Park although the Americans were given no inkling of the Ultra source. It was not until that convoy reached South African waters that news came of the attack on Pearl Harbor. (The 18th Division then found itself diverted to the so-called impregnable fortress of Singapore, and to disaster, but that is another story.)

In the latter half of 1941 and for the first month of 1942, this codebreaking effort seemed to give Britain the edge, for shipping losses fell during that period. Leaving aside the anomalous month of December 1941 during which the figures shot up as a result of Japanese seizure or sinking of numerous ships in the month they entered the war, the average monthly number of British ships lost, on all oceans, fell during that time to thirty-five, compared to an average of seventy-one for the preceding six months. The credit for that fall cannot wholly be attributed to Bletchley Park, for during that period Admiral Doenitz decided to divert some submarines from the North Atlantic to the Central Atlantic and to the Mediterranean where the pickings were not quite so good. Not only that, American assistance to the Royal Navy in the North Atlantic rose during that period despite the fact that for most of it that country was still officially neutral. Nevertheless, Ultra played a large part in it.

Then, on 1 February 1942, the German Navy made improvements and changes to the Enigma machines of submarines operating in the Atlantic, incorporating an additional rotor. (These changes were not introduced to submarines operating in the Baltic and in more northern waters, the signals to and from which the British continued to be able to read. This is proof that the 1 February changes were not brought about by any German fear that Enigma might have been compromised.) Despite the best efforts of Bletchley Park, for most of the remainder of 1942 the British were unable to read all the German naval codes. In consequence, between February and the last month of that year, the average number of British ships lost, again on all oceans, rose to fifty-one a month, with of course, a concomitant increase in losses amongst other Allied merchant fleets.[4]

In December 1942, thanks again to the Royal Navy and in particular to the bravery of two members of it and a civilian, additional Enigma material fell into British hands enabling Bletchley Park once again to read all the German naval codes. This fact, linked to a change in the Royal Navy's own machine encoding in 1943 which the Germans were unable to break, helped again to bring about a fall in the number of Allied ships being sunk, a situation that was maintained for the remainder of the war. This came with the sinking of *U-559* in the eastern Mediterranean in late October 1942. Earlier, when the destroyer HMS *Petard* was on its way out from England (it reached that part of the Mediterranean via the Cape and Suez), her captain, Lieutenant Commander Mark Thornton, summoned his radar technician, Petty Officer Reg Crang, to the bridge. 'I need a U-boat', Thornton told Crang, which the petty officer took to mean that one must be captured rather than sunk. If Crang's view is correct, and subsequent events seem to bear it out, it is likely that Thornton had received special orders to that effect from the Admiralty under whose wing Bletchley Park operated.[5] Thornton was to get his wish on 30 October when, together with three other Royal Navy destroyers, *Hero*, *Dulverton*, and *Hurworth* and with the aid of a Sunderland flying boat from RAF 47 Squadron, he found and attacked *U-559* off Haifa. After some seventeen hours underwater trying to evade the destroyers, the submarine surfaced, with says, Reg Crang, 'a great whoosh, and a smell of diesel oil', to come under a hail of small-arms fire. By then it was already 2200 hours, so what was about to happen took place under the glare of the

---

4. David Syrett, *The Battle of the Atlantic & Signals Intelligence* (Aldershot 1998).
5. Petty Officer Reg Crang, video recording *Enigma*.

destroyer's searchlights. The U-boat had been holed by depth charges and the engineers had opened the sea-cocks, so to the crew it seemed the craft was about to sink and they abandoned ship. Commander Thornton immediately ordered cease-fire, and as a boarding party began lowering a boat, Lieutenant Tony Fasson and Able Seamen Colin Grazier stripped off, dove in, and swam to the submarine, almost immediately followed by a civilian NAAFI canteen assistant on *Petard* called Tony Brown. Brown was only fifteen, for he had lied about his age when he applied for the post. The three reached the submarine, clambered aboard, and climbed down into the control room. Whilst this was going on the other Royal Navy ships were busy picking up survivors, at the same time listening for other U-boats. Down in the bowels of the sinking submarine Fasson and Grazier were busy collecting documents and codebooks, which Brown then carried up on deck to waiting members of the boarding party that had arrived. The greatest care was taken in handling the material as the ink used was water-soluble. Three times Brown carried great armfuls of material up to the deck as the submarine sank ever lower in the water. He was then told by the officer in charge of the boat not to go below again and to call Fasson and Grazier up on deck. The two were just about to come up when the submarine sank, taking them down with it. For their bravery both Fasson and Grazier were awarded a posthumous George Cross. Tony Brown who stepped off the U-boat just as it went under, was awarded the George Medal, although he did not live to actually receive it before he died in a house-fire in 1945. The captured material was flown to England, and no news of the sinking of *U-559* was ever published. The material was enough to permit Bletchley Park to break all German naval codes by 13 December 1942.

All the factors mentioned above were important in changing the balance of the war at sea, but there were two more factors so far not mentioned in this analysis. Both of them – in fact the one impinges upon the other – were crucial, and yet they have been largely overlooked by historians and given but cursory attention by nearly all of those who have bothered to mention them at all. One of these was the rate of construction of new Allied ship tonnage, especially that of the American shipyards, and even more specifically, those yards engaged in the construction of the Liberty ship. From December 1941 when the first Liberty ship of all, the *Patrick Henry,* was launched, the flow of new ships grew and grew as construction times fell. By the end of 1942 no less than 511 Liberties had come off the stocks, 319 of them from yards controlled by Henry Kaiser. So great was the output of ships that by February 1943 newly constructed tonnage exceeded that sunk by submarines for the first time. One of the few historians to give more than cursory attention to this pertinent factor in the battle of the oceans, and even he did not dwell on it too long, was Gerhard L. Weinberg, who wrote that after February 1943, 'the [vessel] construction curve continued to rise dramatically even as losses levelled off'.[6] So massive was the output of new ships that it can be argued that even had the benefit of Ultra intelligence, and perhaps some of the other factors mentioned above, not been available, the time would have eventually arrived when the US shipyard output would have surpassed U-boat sinkings. The second of these largely neglected factors was that, contrary to German expectations, and in one way or another, the Americans and their Allies were able to find crews for all the new ships. In the last analysis it was, of course, the bravery, endurance and skill of these men, aided by their navy comrades, that brought victory at sea. And without that, victory in the land battles would have been impossible.

By the end of 1942 Liberty ships, together with their half-sisters the Oceans and the Forts, were already on the way to becoming ubiquitous. By D-Day in 1944, they were exactly that, despite the structural cracking problems and intervening losses due to enemy operations. By the end of the war in August 1945 a total of 215 Liberties had been lost – from all causes – and many more had been damaged. The first Liberty to be lost to enemy action in the North Atlantic was the *George Calvert* (Baltimore, April 1942). She was on her maiden voyage from Baltimore to Bandar Shapur in the Persian Gulf, one of the ports that provided a 'back-door' for military cargoes to Russia. On 20 May she was torpedoed by *U-753*, Commander von Mannstein, and soon broke in three and sank. Around this time von Mannstein sank another freighter and damaged two others whilst other U-boat commanders in the area achieved even greater successes. This was around the middle of the period during which Admiral King refused to consider placing ships in convoys.

But it had been the Japanese and not the Germans who sank the first Liberty ship in the war. This took place at the southern end of what the Allies called the South Pacific Islands Supply Route. This route ran from San Francisco and Hawaii down to Brisbane in Queensland. The northeast coast of Australia and the sea area between Fiji and Samoa were dangerous parts of it, the comparatively constricted waters there providing a possible killing ground for submarines. Maintaining the integrity of the route was vital to the build-up of American military strength in Australia. In the air heavy bombers staged through the islands, and on the ocean beneath, cargo ships ploughed the route carrying fighter aircraft, fuel, and all the other necessities of war. One would have therefore expected the Allies to operate a convoy system on the southern sections of the route, but that rarely happened because escort ships were in short supply and were needed elsewhere. One would also have expected that those same areas would have come under sustained attack from Japanese submarines. However, whenever Japanese submarines did strike in the area, the attacks

---

6. Weinberg, op.cit.

were neither heavy nor sustained. This was a marked feature of all Japanese submarine operations throughout the war, and was caused by the belief among senior officers of the Imperial Japanese Navy that submarines should be used in support of surface warships, rather than against enemy merchant shipping. A subsidiary reason might have been that Japanese submarines had to operate on very long lines of communications.

Nevertheless, submarines of what was called the Eastern Advance Detachment of the 8th Japanese Flotilla based in the Marshall Islands, met with some success against merchant ships on the southern end of the Allied route in May 1942, and one of the ships that met its end then was the *John Adams* (Richmond, March 1942), which like the *Calvert* mentioned above was on her maiden voyage. She was sailing from San Francisco to Brisbane with a cargo of aviation spirit in drums, amongst the most dangerous of all cargoes. She sailed from the port of Noumea, New Caledonia, on 5 May on the last leg of the voyage to Brisbane, and had reached a point about 120 miles south-west of that island when a torpedo struck in the way of No. 4 hold. The ship caught fire and blew up on the following day. Only twenty-four of those on board survived to get back to Noumea in a lifeboat; amongst those who lost their lives were five members of the ship's Armed Guard. On 9 November 1942 the Japanese submarine *I-21*, Commander Matsumura, torpedoed another Liberty, the *Edgar Allen Poe* (Portland, Oregon, April 1942), also off Noumea. The torpedo wrecked the ship's engine room but did not sink her. The Liberty was later towed to Noumea and beached there. In August 1943 she was taken over by the US Navy. The ship's hull was repaired but not the engines, and she became a non-propelled naval store ship which did sterling work travelling around the Pacific theatre of war under tow of her very own private tugboat. The *Poe* never returned to the United States, ending her days at a Hong Kong breaker's yard in 1950.[7]

The first British-flagged Liberty ship to be lost to enemy action was *Sambo*, which, handed over on 12 August 1943, was also on her maiden voyage. She too, was lost to a Japanese submarine. *Sambo* had been constructed at Los Angeles as the *Edwin Joseph O'Hara*, a name whose derivation we shall hear about in the next chapter. *Sambo*, under the management of Cunard and with Captain John Smith in command, sailed from Los Angeles late in August bound for Iquique, Chile, where she loaded 8850 tons of nitrates for the Middle East. (The first British-flagged Liberty had been handed over in the previous month, and of the total of twenty-five such handovers in July and August, four were

---

7. Submarine *I-21* disappeared with all hands some time after sending a final signal on 27 November 1943 when off the Gilbert Islands. After that date, a Commander Matsumara Midori is reported to have been Staff Operations Officer, 6th Japanese Imperial Fleet, but the author has no confirmation that this was the same man.

ordered to Iquique to load nitrates.) On the way across the Pacific to Wellington, New Zealand for bunkers, one of her lifeboats was lost overboard in a storm. By 10 November she had reached the Gulf of Aden and was on a zigzag course when she had the misfortune to enter the patrol zone of the Japanese submarine *I-27*, commanded by the veteran skipper Commander Fukumura Toshiaki, who was responsible for sinking 30,000 tons of Allied shipping around that time.

It was mid-afternoon when *Sambo* was struck aft by a torpedo which caused a violent explosion, almost immediately followed by an even more severe one as the stern magazine blew up. A second torpedo tore into the starboard side of No. 4 hold. Hatch covers and beams, and every sort of debris, were thrown in the air. Captain Smith later reported that the whole of the ship from the bulkhead that separated the engine-room from No. 4 hold, had 'shattered and blown off'. Ten men including eight gunners who had been on that stern half were never seen again. As what remained of the ship lurched to starboard and began settling, Captain Smith ordered abandon ship, and the survivors made for the only two remaining serviceable boats. In the water and before the master's motor-boat could pull the second one clear, it was struck by a davit as the ship began to capsize. The men in that boat were thrown into the sea but all save two managed to reach the rafts that had been released and were floating nearby. Everything had happened so quickly there had been no time to send an SOS, but fortunately help was close to hand. The Norwegian *Helgoy*, bound for Aden, was four miles away and had seen the explosion. Despite great risk to his own vessel the Norwegian master did not hesitate, and turned back to pick up the survivors. After that he carried out a search of the immediate vicinity for the missing men, but no one was found. The survivors were eventually landed at Aden.

It is not known whether Commander Fukumura deliberately refrained from firing at the Norwegian ship during this humanitarian act, but it seems likely that was so. Even had he already expended his last torpedo, he could have engaged the Norwegian with his gun had he been so inclined. We shall see in a later chapter that some Japanese submarine commanders were noted for inhuman conduct towards survivors, but Fukumura did not have that sort of reputation. Within three months Commander Fukumura was not around to answer any questions anyway, for on 12 February 1944 whilst operating further south in the Indian Ocean, *I-27* was lost with all hands. By coincidence, one of the warships involved in her loss was HMS *Petard,* the destroyer involved in the Mediterranean Enigma capture in October 1942, though she was now under the command of Commander R.C. Egan.

On that date *Petard*, together with another destroyer HMS *Paladin*, was fussing around Convoy KR-8 which was *en route* from Mombassa to Colombo. The convoy, an important one consisting of five troopships between them carrying over 9000 British and Commonwealth soldiers, was led by the rather antiquated cruiser HMS *Hawkins*. In the interests of speed Captain J.W. Josselyn DSC RN aboard the cruiser had decided not to zigzag, a decision that was later to cause him to receive a severe reprimand from the Admiralty. With light airs just enough to ruffle the sunlit water, it was a fine day to be at sea even if there was a war on; at least it seemed like that until mid-afternoon when two torpedoes from *I-27* struck the trooper *Khedive Ismail* on her starboard side. The ship sank in under two minutes and of the 183 crew members and 1300 troops on board, including eighty-five women from the ATS, Wrens, and a Field Hospital, only 214 were saved, six women amongst them. It was one of the most tragic troopship sinkings of the war.

Petard and *Paladin* raced into to attack with depth charges, and this went on for well over an hour before the damaged *I-27* suddenly rose between them. Both destroyers turned to ram with all guns blazing, but realising how badly damaged the submarine was, Commander Egan aboard *Petard* hauled off and signalled *Paladin* to do the same. But it was too late, for as *Paladin* turned, the submarine's hydroplane guard caught the destroyer and opened her up like a can-opener, causing her to take no further part in the engagement. *Petard* carried on the fight, but Fukumura refused to surrender. Commander Egan later wrote, 'A running battle now ensued for nearly an hour during which time the enemy circled blindly, having lost her periscope'. He went on to praise his adversary's 'amazing tenacity in battle'. Finally *Petard* finished off the submarine with a torpedo, not a trace being left but an oil slick. Fukumura did not know it, of course, but he went down without adding a British destroyer to his list of sinkings, for with the greatest of difficulty and with all hands to the pumps, *Paladin* managed to reach Addu Atoll in the Maldives.

In the remaining chapters of this section of the book the stories of outstanding episodes in the wartime history of Liberty ships will be presented. These stories will not only highlight the vital roles the ships played in the war, but also the outstanding bravery of the majority of the men who sailed in them. The author recognises the fact that in largely concentrating on ships that were lost, or ones involved in what can euphemistically be called 'incidents', that this is at the expense of the many thousands of Liberty ship voyages that were completed successfully. However, it is mainly the stories of lost ships that are found in preserved records; the records of 'ordinary' voyages have not been deemed worthy of preservation, probably because there were so many of them. On top of that, a description of most ordinary voyages would make singularly dull reading.

Furthermore, some of the stories related under a particular chapter heading could have been just as reasonably included under another. The author has exercised his judgement on where to record the story.

CHAPTER 9

A Liberty versus a German Raider

On the morning of Sunday, 27 September 1942, an epic sea battle took place in the South Atlantic. It involved three vessels, two German and one American. The American ship was a Liberty fitted with only those armaments needed for self-defence. The Germans were also merchant ships, although one was now fitted out as a heavily-armed commerce raider, and the other was a blockade-runner under naval orders. Before relating the run of the battle, something must be said about the three ships and how it was they came to meet in that mid-ocean clash.

With the German ships the story can be said to have begun on 30 January 1941 as Hansa Line's *Tannenfels* lay in the harbour of Kismayu, Italian Somaliland. No one who saw the rust-stained, barnacle-encrusted ship as she lay at anchor there would have believed that she was about to embark upon a career that would make her, with two 'home-runs' to her credit, one of the most successful Axis blockade-runners of the war. One of a class of eight ships of the same design, *Tannenfels* was constructed in 1938 at Wesermunde for use on Hansa's East African service. Registered at the port of Bremen, she had a gross tonnage of 7840 (slightly more than that of a Liberty) and was capable of 16kts, an above-average speed for a merchantman of those days. She had been at anchor in Kismayu harbour since late August 1939, when all German ships had been ordered either to make back to the Fatherland with all despatch or, if unable to do so, to make for the nearest port likely to remain neutral in the looming war. Captain Steuer on *Tannenfels* had elected to head for Kismayu, in the knowledge that although the port was controlled by Germany's Axis partner, it was likely that Italy would remain neutral until Benito Mussolini decided which way the wind was blowing. Ever since, for over seventeen months, she had lain there idly rusting away, as the war passed her by. Italy had come into the war in June 1940, and by the beginning of 1941 a British Army was pressing up from Kenya, and the port of Kismayu was the first major Somalian conurbation in its sights. It was time for *Tannenfels* to risk sailing or stay in port and face the certainty of falling into British hands. German Naval Headquarters sent a secret signal ordering the ship to sail and to make for a remote spot in the Arabian

Sea code-named 'Nelke', where she was to rendezvous with the German raider *Atlantis* then operating in the Indian Ocean. Before he sailed, Captain Steuer set about disguising his ship as the *Atlantis*, the plan being that if he was intercepted by a British warship he would scuttle his ship and hope the British would be fooled into thinking that it was the raider that had gone to the bottom. The disguise was not difficult to assume, for the *Atlantis,* officially called *Schiff 16* by the Germans and *Raider C* by the British, had been built as the *Goldenfels,* and was one of the seven sisters of *Tannenfels.* All Steuer had to do was to have some dummy guns fitted, as at that time the ship carried none of her own. That done, she slipped away from the port during the night of 31 January.

Captain Steuer did not meet up with any British warships and so did not have to scuttle, and nine days later after taking a circuitous route, safely rendezvoused with *Atlantis,* commanded by Captain Bernhard Rogge. Both ships then turned south and on the following day fell in with two vessels previously captured by Rogge, the British freighter *Speybank,* soon to be renamed *Doggerbank* by the Germans and to become a blockade-runner, and the Norwegian tanker *Ketty Brovig,* both with prize crews aboard. *Tannenfels* was acutely short of fuel and so topped up from the tanker. She also took on board most of the Merchant Navy prisoners captured during Rogge's recent run of successes against Allied shipping. The traffic in men was not all one way, for Rogge 'commandeered' several members of the *Tannenfels's* crew to augment his own numbers. Rogge and his small flotilla of ships then headed south, and on 15 February rendezvoused in mid-ocean about 1000 miles east of Madagascar, with the pocket-battleship *Admiral Scheer.* For the Germans aboard those five ships it must have been an uplifting experience to meet thus in an ocean supposedly a fiefdom of the Royal Navy. Two days later Rogge despatched *Tannenfels* on the hazardous run to German-occupied France. The ship sailed far south of the Cape of Good Hope before turning north to sail up the least frequented parts of the Atlantic Ocean. After running the British blockade of the Bay of Biscay she eventually arrived at Bordeaux to a hero's welcome. It was 19 April 1941, which just happened to be Hitler's birthday.

Beginning in the autumn of 1941 the Germans sent a series of blockade-runners to Japan, and by August 1942, five had successfully made it, carrying between them 32,850 tons of cargo, principally engines and engine parts, chemical products and potash, but also mines and torpedoes. Some of the ships also carried Germans specialists as passengers.[1]

---

1. The five ships in chronological order were the *Rio Grande, Dresden* (which was to arrive at Yokohama on the same day as *Tannenfels*), *Tannenfels, Regensburg,* and, arriving at Yokohama on 19 August 1942, *Doggerbank* ex-*Speybank.* This latter ship had arrived at Bordeaux on 19 May 1941 under the command of Paul Schneidewinde, who until the time of that rendezvous in the Arabian Sea with *Atlantis* had been Second Mate aboard *Tannenfels.* The *Doggerbank,* known to its German crew members as *ein Nimmerweiderkehr-Damfer* or

Amongst the five was the newly fitted-out *Tannenfels* now under the command of Captain Haase. By now she had been armed not only with machine guns on either side of the bridge, but also with one 6in gun mounted aft.[2] It was no easy matter running the British blockade out of, or for that matter in to, the Bay of Biscay. A cable sent from Berlin to Admiral Wenneker, the German Naval Attaché in Tokyo, on 16 December 1941, reported that *Tannenfels* would be despatched some time towards the end of January 1942, but in the event she did not manage to slip through the British net until 16 March. She arrived at Yokohama on 23 June. A follow-up cable informed Wenneker that for the run, the ship would be adopting the disguise of either the Norwegian *Talabot* or *Torrens*, both of which she resembled.[3] After discharging her inward cargo *Tannenfels* lay alongside in Yokohama throughout July and the first week of August 1942, loading a badly-needed consignment of rubber for Germany. (Japan, having overrun Malaya earlier in the year, had some of that commodity to spare.) Because blockade-runners doubled as supply vessels for German warships at sea, she also loaded stores for three raiders, *Thor, Michel* and *Stier.* It seems she also loaded a small spotter seaplane for delivery to the *Stier.*[4]

As was his wont, Admiral Wenneker visited the ship before it sailed to hand Captain Haase his sealed orders. No doubt Wenneker also took the opportunity to raise the morale of the crew. To all intents and purposes German blockade-runners, although manned by merchant seamen, were treated as naval auxiliaries and the seamen were considered to be 'military' personnel as regarded discipline. As with all merchant navies, such regimentation did not go down well, and Admiral Wenneker's diary shows that he was having considerable problems with the crews of ships in Japan. In this context it is interesting to note that he had asked Berlin to send out to him via *Tannenfels* a copy of the new disciplinary code for the armed forces 'for urgent reasons'. In January that year when he made that request he reported seven serious charges involving theft of cargo aboard the blockade-runner *Portland,* and traced the problem 'back to a reduction in pay [of merchant seamen] not understood here'. In that same month he also informed Berlin that he was sending an engine-room

'never-come-back-ship', because of her typically British appearance which they thought would make her a tempting target for their own submarines, was torpedoed and sunk on 5 March 1943 in the Atlantic on her way home from Japan. The crew's epithet had been justified, for the submarine that sank her in error was the *U-43.* Only one man from the ship was saved.

2. Information received from Lieutenant Commander Dirk Steffen of Militargeschichtliches Forschungsamt, Potsdam. The gun referred to is clearly visible on a line drawing of *Tannenfels* dating from 1942 which is in German records.

3. John W.M. Chapman, *The Price of Admiralty* (Ripe 1989).

4. See R.J. Witt & P.M. Heaton in *The Gallant Ship, 'Stephen Hopkins'.*

artificer home under arrest on the blockade-runner *Rio Grande* when she sailed from Kobe.[5]

Tannenfels sailed for Europe on 8 August, but Captain Haase and his crew had much work to do before they reached the North Atlantic, some of it not envisaged by the naval planners in Germany. After sailing down the South China Sea and out into the Indian Ocean, the freighter made a fast passage and met up with the raider *Thor* on 28 August somewhere deep in the South Atlantic. Despite bad weather, stores were transferred in one direction and merchant marine prisoners in the other. On the following day *Tannenfels* headed north, but the weather deteriorated so much that it was not until 20 September when she managed at last to meet up with *Michel*, the second of her raider customers. In the prevailing conditions it took three days to transfer stores to the raider, after which *Michel* made off to meet with a supply tanker, leaving the freighter to wait in that position for its next customer.

Tannenfels's third customer was the commerce raider *Stier,* so named by its commander, Captain Horst Gerlach. It means 'Bull'. Originally the *Cairo,* in German official circles she was *Schiff 23,* and was known as *Raider J* by the British. Built in 1936 at Kiel for the Atlas-Levante Line of Bremen, at 14kts she was the slowest of the ten raiders used by the Germans during the war; according to one of her officers, Lieutenant Petersen, who had earlier sailed on another raider and so knew what he was talking about, she was much too slow for the purpose. *Stier* was armed with six 5.9in, two 37mm and four 20mm guns, a pair of torpedo tubes and an Arado Ar-231 reconnaissance aircraft which could be catapulted off and recovered by crane. With a crew numbering well in excess of 300, she was, like the other German raiders, considered to be more than a match for any warship smaller than a cruiser she might fall in with. The purpose of these raiders was two-fold, to sink or capture and generally play havoc with Allied merchant shipping, and to provide over as wide an area of the oceans as possible, such a threat that it would stretch Allied naval resources to the limit. Taken all in all, the raiders did an admirable job for the Fatherland.

Escorted by the 5th Torpedo Boat Flotilla and sixteen minesweepers, *Stier* had broken through the English Channel from Rotterdam in mid-May 1942 despite the loss of two of her escorts and being shelled by British shore batteries in the Straits of Dover. She reached the Gironde Estuary in the Bay of Biscay on the 19 May and two days later successfully broke out from there. Her first success as a raider came on 4 June when, off the coast of Brazil, she sank the British freighter *Gemstone,* Captain E.J. Griffiths, carrying a cargo of iron ore to Baltimore. (Ships

---

5. Chapman, op. cit.

carrying iron ore usually went down very fast.) Gerlach took the survivors on board. *Stier*'s next victim came two days later but was not nearly so easy meat. The Panamanian tanker *Stanvac Calcutta* returned the raider's fire and the *Stier* had expended nearly 150 shells and a torpedo, before the tanker sank with the loss of fourteen men including the master, Captain Gustaf Karlsson. Thirty-seven survivors including some wounded were taken aboard the raider. Between 10 and 15 June she rendezvoused with the blockade-running tanker *Charlotte Schliemann*, taking on board fuel and stores and transferring all her prisoners except Captain Griffiths of the *Gemstone* and one crew member from the *Stanvac Calcutta*, both of whom ended up at Milag prisoner of war camp in Germany. (The retention on board of certain prisoners was probably for purposes of interrogation.) The *Charlotte Schliemann* was on the outward part of a run to Japan, so the transferred prisoners had the misfortune to end up in Japanese hands.

July turned out to be a barren period for the *Stier* even though Gerlach tried using his seaplane for spotting purposes. The aircraft proved faulty, and this may have been the reason why another aircraft for *Stier* was loaded aboard *Tannenfels* in the following month. In mid-July another rendezvous was made with the *Charlotte Schliemann* when again the raider refuelled. On 28 July *Stier* met up with the raider *Michel*, commanded by Captain Helmut von Ruckteschell, a veteran who earlier in the war had commanded another raider called *Widder*, and the two commanders exchanged reports. *Michel* had been about her business longer than *Stier,* and von Ruckteschell had met with more success. He correctly counted amongst his successes the American Liberty *George Clymer* (Portland, Oregon, April 1942), despite not having stayed around to see that vessel actually sink. The *Clymer,* Captain Edward Ackerman, was on her maiden voyage which was to have taken her to Cape Town with a cargo of timber and aircraft. By 30 June she reached a point about 600 miles south-west of Ascension Island when her propeller shaft fractured. She radioed for assistance and then drifted helplessly for six days before being struck by two torpedoes from the torpedo boat *Esan* launched from *Michel.* The Liberty crew abandoned, apparently so quickly that the Armed Guard and some seamen on the after end of the ship were left on board. But on the following day the master and crew reboarded. Meanwhile, Captain von Ruckteschell had picked up his torpedo boat and left the scene. Had he not done so he might have added the scalp of a British armed merchant cruiser to his haul. For on the following day the AMC HMS *Alcantara* arrived on the scene in answer to *Clymer*'s original call for assistance. *Alcantara* took off the crew and was about to commence taking the Liberty in tow when orders were received to sink it instead. *Alcantara* set the *Clymer* ablaze with gunfire and depth charges and eventually the ship capsized. But all that did not sink the ship – possibly it was the buoyancy of her timber cargo that kept her afloat – and the hulk was still floating when *Alcantara* left the scene. Another ship later reported that the *Clymer* had sunk.

Five days prior to the meeting with *Stier*, the *Michel* had rendezvoused with the tanker *Charlotte Schliemann* which was having a rather busy time. Also taking on fuel from the tanker at that time was the *Dogger-bank* (ex-*Speybank*), the British ship captured by *Atlantis*. Captain von Rucktescell transferred prisoners to *Doggerbank*, it being unfortunate for that batch of prisoners that that ship, like the *Schliemann*, was on her way out east, so those prisoners, too, ended up in the hands of the Japanese. At that meeting between *Stier* and *Michel* on 28 July, the two captains decided to conduct a joint patrol, but nothing was seen until 9 August when *Stier* sighted the British freighter *Dalhousie* which was in ballast from Cape Town to Trinidad. After a four-hour chase *Stier* scored a direct hit on the freighter which then stopped. After taking off the crew, *Stier* sank the ship with a torpedo. The British ship had managed to get off a signal, so for safety's sake the two raiders decided to separate.

Captain Gerlach then received orders from Berlin to reconnoitre remote Gough Island as a possible raider base, and after doing so, rendezvoused again with the *Schliemann* for refuelling and for yet another transfer of prisoners. On 4 September the Free French ship *Pasteur* managed to evade Gerlach's clutches, and a fortnight later a day-long pursuit of another ship led to another failure. Then, on 25 September *Stier* arrived at the point about 650 miles north-west of Tristan da Cunha where *Tannenfels* was waiting. Transfer of stores and the seaplane were effected by the end of the day, but it was decided that the two ships would stay in company until the expected return of the *Michel* which had yet more prisoners to transfer to the freighter. The two ships were still waiting as Sunday 27 September dawned.

The *Stephen Hopkins* was built at Henry Kaiser's first yard at Richmond, California, a yard which came to be called Permanente No. 1. The yard was only halfway through its part of the British Ocean ship contract when Liberty ships began to be launched from the adjacent yard called Permanente No. 2. The seventh among the long line of 351 Liberties to be launched from that yard was the *Stephen Hopkins*. Named after a colonial governor of Rhode Island who became one of the signatories of the Declaration of Independence, she slid down the ways on 14 April 1942. After completion and trials, the Maritime Commission placed the ship under the management of the long-established Luckenbach Steamship Company of New York. The company appointed thirty-nine year-old Paul Buck as master. He had been at sea since he was sixteen and this was his second command. Married for ten years, his home was in Merrimacport, Massachusetts. Whilst the ship was being loaded at San

Francisco with a military cargo for Australia, the other forty members of the crew signed on. They were a cosmopolitan bunch and included four Greeks, and one national each from Spain, Ireland, Sweden and Denmark. At sixty, the oldest crewman was the Greek-born but American naturalised Able Seaman George Papas. The two youngest crew members were in the engineering department, Cadet Edwin Joseph O'Hara and Wiper Henry Eagle, who were both eighteen. A fifteen-man Armed Guard unit also arrived on board. The party was led by 23 year-old Ensign Kenneth M. Willett, the other members all being Seamen 2nd Class Gunners. No member of the unit had seen any action so far. They were there to man the ship's single 4in gun mounted aft on the poop, the dual-purpose 37mm gun at the bow, and two .30 calibre and four .50 calibre machine guns mounted at various places around the bridge and superstructure. During the coming voyage Ensign Willet was to train members of the ship's crew in the use the guns, and no one took more interest than Engineer Cadet O'Hara. In the process he became firm friends with Willet.

The ship sailed from San Francisco on 25 May and made for Los Angeles for topping off with more cargo. She sailed from that port three days later and had an incident-free voyage across the Pacific to reach Wellington, New Zealand on 5 July. After a short stay for bunkers she made for Melbourne. The military cargo was discharged there, and the ship then made for Port Lincoln in the Spencer Gulf to load bagged wheat for Durban. Sailing from Port Lincoln on 2 August she had a very rough passage across the Indian Ocean and on the 20th reported by radio that cracks had appeared in her deck plating forward. (*Stephen Hopkins* appears in the official list of structural failures produced by the US Navy, but an incorrect date, 20 May 1943, is given for the incident.) After discharging the wheat at Durban the deck damage was repaired and she sailed from that port in ballast on 13 September. After a short call at Cape Town for bunkers, the ship set out across the South Atlantic for Paramaribo where she was booked to load a cargo of bauxite for the States. However, that final leg of *Stephen Hopkins*'s maiden voyage was never to be completed.

The weather on the morning of Sunday, 27 September at the point in the South Atlantic some 650 miles north of Tristan da Cunha where the three ships were destined to meet, was the sort that deep-sea fishermen often describe as 'dirty'. The sky was overcast and gloomy, and a fresh wind was whipping up a rough sea. Frequent rain squalls affected visibility. It was a part of the ocean where it was unlikely that another ship would be met with, which was of course, precisely why all three ships were there. But suddenly, as a squall ahead began to clear, Third Mate Walter Nyberg, a thirty-four year-old from Hoquiam, Washington State, on the bridge of *Stephen Hopkins*, sighted first one, and then another ship. Both appeared to be merchantmen, but Nyberg was taking no chances and, ordering the helm hard over, rang down for his captain to come to the bridge. Even as Captain Buck arrived and ordered the US flag raised and the crew to action stations, the two strange vessels hoisted the swastika-emblazoned ensigns of the Kriegsmarine. Radio Operator Hudson Hewey attempted to send an RRR signal indicating that his ship was under attack from an enemy raider, but *Stier* jammed the transmission.

The *Stier* gave chase, and even a speed of only 14kts was more than a match for the Liberty's 11kts. As *Tannenfels* also joined in the pursuit, Captain Gerlach ordered his gunners to open fire with the 5.9in guns. One of the first shells to strike the Liberty severely wounded Chief Mate Richard Moczkowski, who hailed from Richmond where the ship had been built. Shrapnel also severely wounded Ensign Willet in the stomach as he made for the after gun. Despite his wounds, Willet took charge of the gun and to excellent effect. German sources report that the *Stier* was hit no less than thirty-two times; 'the two most critical hits which doomed the *Stier* were the one – the first hit – in the steering flat, and shortly thereafter, the round which penetrated the engine-room bulkhead and came to a stop against the main engine's No. 7 cylinder'.[6] That first American shot, fired at a range of only 1000 yards, jammed *Stier*'s helm, leaving her unable to bring her torpedo tubes to bear. But it did not prevent her firing her guns, and shells and machine gun fire rained down on the Liberty causing devastation everywhere. Then *Tannenfels* came up, and not only joined in with her machine guns but also fired her 6in, the largest gun aboard any of the ships. It is not known whether this gun scored any hits, but German records indicate it was definitely fired during the battle, a fact that seems to have been missed in all previous American and British accounts of the engagement, and one that makes the achievement of the *Stephen Hopkins* even more remarkable.[7]

Aboard *Stephen Hopkins*, as Armed Guardsmen were cut down, crewmen took their places at the guns. One German shell hit the radio shack and it is likely that Radio Operator Hewey was killed at that moment. Second Mate Joseph Layman, who had taken charge of the 37mm in the bows, was cut down along with the men manning that gun. In the wheelhouse Captain Buck fought to keep his ship's stern to the enemy vessels to reduce her size as a target, taking guidance from shouted instructions on the relative positions of the ships from the badly wounded Chief Mate Moczkowski, who with the help of Ordinary Seaman Roger Piercy and the first aid ministrations of Chief Steward Ford Stilson, had propped himself up in the wing of the bridge. A shell struck in the boiler room, putting the engines out of action. Another struck the main magazine aft,

---

6. Information from Dirk Steffen, 25 January 2000.
7. Ibid.

and the 4in gun fell silent. By that time the ship was listing and on fire, so Captain Buck ordered abandon ship.

It was at that point that Cadet Edwin O'Hara made his way to the after gun. He found his wounded friend Ensign Willet on the gun platform and helped him down to the deck. Returning to the gun he found it largely undamaged and discovered five shells for it in a locker close-by. Entirely unaided he fired all five shells at the *Stier*, and so close was the range, all were hits. No one knows exactly what happened to O'Hara after that, for he was never seen again. At 0918 hours Captain Gerlach ordered his ship to cease fire after an engagement that had lasted only twenty-two minutes. By then it was obvious that the American vessel was sinking, and Gerlach had other things to worry about. His ship could not steer and was on fire in many places, one fire burning close to the torpedo store. Three of his men had been killed and twenty-eight wounded. At about 1030 hours lookouts reported that the *Stephen Hopkins* had sunk, but the information brought little comfort to Gerlach. About half an hour later with the fires raging out of control, he signalled *Tannenfels* to assist in the evacuation of his ship by sending over boats. He ordered demolition charges set, and later watched with his crew from the deck of the blockade-runner as they went off, sending the burning vessel down to join the Liberty ship.

Before *Stephen Hopkins* sank, and under a hail of shrapnel, her one still serviceable lifeboat was launched. Life-rafts were also released and the last anyone ever saw of Ensign Willet was as he organised that task. Second Engineer George Cronk was helping to lower the lifeboat when he saw Captain Buck on the bridge throwing the ship's codebooks over the side. Cronk tried to make it to the bridge but was cut off by fire; he then threw himself into the sea. His sighting of the captain was the last one reported. Chief Steward Ford Stilson had helped Chief Mate Moczkowski from the bridge to the boat deck, and was preparing to lower him down into the water when the Mate violently objected and ordered Stilson to 'look to himself'. It seemed to Stilson that Moczkowski with his open chest wounds was unlikely to survive exposure in the water, so he left him there and slid down a rope into the sea.

After some twenty minutes in the water Second Engineer Cronk found the lifeboat and clambered in. It already contained several survivors including two wounded men and two dead bodies. The bodies were consigned to the sea. Seven more men were picked up from the water or from rafts, the rafts also being relieved of stores and a water breaker. Stilson and Ordinary Seamen Roger Piercy were amongst those pulled aboard. In the end there were nineteen souls on board, fourteen crewmen and five Armed Guardsmen. Five of the survivors were suffering from injuries of one form or another. Another group of survivors was sighted on a raft some way off but high seas and poor visibility made it impossible to get to them. Unbeknownst to the men in the lifeboat, after taking aboard the crew of the *Stier,* Captain Haase on *Tannenfels* ordered several passes of the area in a search for American survivors but found none.

As the senior officer aboard – the only other man of officer rank was Chief Steward Ford Stilson – Second Engineer George Cronk took command. He was no navigator but after raising sail, knew that if he sailed north-west the boat must eventually fetch the coast of South America and that was a big target for which to aim. Stilson acted as doctor, treating the wounded as best he could from the boat's first aid kit. Food and water were rationed from day one. In fact there were sufficient provisions on board that food never became much of a problem, and although the water supply got short on occasion, the survivors were fortunate in that several times they ran into rain to replenish the supply. Cronk kept a rough log of events from which the following has been extracted. Over the succeeding days the boat passed through a succession of strong winds alternated with days of calms. Two of the wounded, Second Cook Eugene McDaniel and Leonardo Romero, a Filipino, died of gangrene during the second week. Rain at about that time permitted the water ration to be increased. Early one morning in the third week a flare was sighted a short way off, apparently coming from a submarine. Although Cronk ordered a Very pistol fired, no contact was made. On the day after that Fireman George Gelogotes died, for 'no apparent reason' noted Cronk, for the man was not one of the wounded. Four days later, on 16 October, one of the Greek members of the crew, Wiper Athenosies Demetrades, died of wounds. By then most of those on board were suffering from salt sores that would not heal. 'Seems as if we should have sighted land', Cronk noted in his log. A week later he wrote that 'everyone very weak', but spirits must have picked up later that day when someone sighted a butterfly and moths. 'All think we are near land.' On 26 October, the sea changed to a dark green, and early on the following morning land was sighted.

Later that day, thirty-one days after the sinking, fifteen survivors, ten from the crew and five from the Armed Guard, landed near the small Brazilian town of Barra do Itabapoana, from where the police notified their arrival to the American Consulate in Rio de Janeiro. The men from the *Stephen Hopkins* were taken to Rio and hospitalised, and after that were sent back to the States. Led by George Cronk, a thirty-two year old from Bessemer, Alabama, who must have been quite a character, the men had survived in better than fair condition. Lieutenant Joseph Rich USNR was one of the men sent from Rio to fetch them. He wrote:

The survivors were in wonderful condition, considering what they'd been through. One could not help but feel the deepest admiration for these men who had faced such odds and were never for one moment beaten. After thirty days of being battered together on a cramped lifeboat, they were still lavishing praise on one another, and best of all, wanting to go back again.[8]

Lieutenant Rich was commenting only on the marathon boat journey, for, as ship losses were subject to secrecy rules, the news of the battle with the *Stier* was not made public until 10 December 1942 when the *New York Times* published an exclusive story of the engagement and the subsequent boat voyage. The paper quoted a Navy report which commented on George Cronk's 'alert and cool-headed actions' and the fact that he was 'credited by other survivors as having been the major factor in their successful voyage of thirty-one days . . .'. In all such stressful situations, there are always some whose conduct does not quite live up to that of the majority, and so it was on that boat journey. Cronk and Stilson reported two of the survivors, an able seaman and an oiler, for reprehensible conduct, but that in no way diminishes their overall achievement.

The *Stephen Hopkins* was awarded the US Maritime Administration's Gallant Ship Award. Ensign Kenneth Willet was awarded a posthumous Navy Cross and had a destroyer escort named after him. Liberty ships were named after Captain Paul Buck and Chief Officer Richard Moczkowski, the captain also receiving a posthumous Distinguished Service Medal. Cadet Edwin Joseph O'Hara also received that medal and a Liberty was named for him too. But a more lasting honour was bestowed on the memory of that brave young man when a hall at Kings Point, the Merchant Marine Academy, was named O'Hara. The sinking of the *Stier* was the only occasion in both World Wars when a *lone* merchantman engaged and sank an enemy raider. The distinguished British naval historian, Captain Stephen Roskill, was to write of the event, 'the crew of the *Stephen Hopkins* fought an action of which all the Allied Navies and merchant marines would be proud'.

On his way back to Europe aboard *Tannenfels,* Captain Gerlach, still unaware of his adversary's identity, wrote a report of the battle in which he vastly overestimated the Liberty's firepower. He reported that she had a 5.9in gun at the stern and six guns, three on each side, of between 10.2 and 12.7cms 'as well as a few 2cm and 4cm anti-aircraft guns'. In fact each of the *Stier's* six 5.9in guns could throw a shot three times as heavy as the Liberty's single 4in gun. In any comparison of overall firepower between

---

8. Quoted in Witt & Heaton, op.cit.

the two sides, the *Tannenfels*'s 6in gun must also be taken into considera-tion. Captain Horst Gerlach cannot be accused of lying in his report; to him the Liberty's firepower must just have seemed to be considerably in excess of what it actually was. *Tannenfels* was once again to successfully run the British blockade, and she arrived at Bordeaux on 2 November. Her log book describing the engagement with *Stephen Hopkins* has not been traced in the German archives, and no other clues have been found indi-cating whether or not she scored any hits on the Liberty. *Tannenfels* was scuttled by the Germans in the River Gironde on 26 August 1944 in the face of advancing Allied armies. Let a German have the last word on that epic engagement in the South Atlantic, for it seems to provide a perfect epitaph. In his book *Der Seekrieg*, a history of the Second World War at sea written from the German point of view, Admiral Friedrich Ruge described how the *Stier* met her end, thus: 'She encountered the U.S. Lib-erty ship *Stephen Hopkins* which used her guns bravely and to good effect.'

The thirty-one day voyage of George Cronk and the other survivors from *Stephen Hopkins* was far from being the longest open boat voyage of the Second World War. Another epic boat voyage came with the sink-ing of the *Roger B. Taney* (Baltimore, 9 February 1942), and like the *Hopkins* event, it took place in the South Atlantic. The *Taney* was the fourth Liberty ship to be launched from the Bethlehem-Fairfield yard. She was managed by Waterman Steamship Corporation of Mobile and had already completed one transatlantic voyage when in August 1942, twenty-nine year-old Captain Thomas James Potter was placed in com-mand. Tom Potter had first gone to sea, very much against the wishes of his mother, at the age of seventeen, and apart from a brief period sailing with the United Fruit Company, had worked his way up through the ranks with Watermans. The *Taney* sailed from New York for Port Said in September with a cargo of steel mesh mats used in the construction of temporary air strips. To avoid U-boats, the ship took the long route. She sailed south to the Caribbean, through the Panama Canal, down the west coat of South America, rounded the Horn, and crossed the South Atlantic to call at Cape Town for bunkers. The ship than voyaged up the Indian Ocean and arrived in the Suez Canal just before Christmas. The ship was quickly unloaded – the British forces in North Africa urgently required the steel mesh – and sailed on the return voyage in ballast on the last day of the year. The ship bunkered again at Cape Town and then sailed for Bahia, Brazil, where she was to load a cargo of bauxite, for Mobile, Tom Potter's home town. For the first three days the *Taney* voy-aged in a small convoy escorted by British warships, but soon the escorts left, leaving the merchant ships to disperse and make their separate ways to their destinations.

By 7 February 1943 the *Taney* was traversing a remote area of the South Atlantic about 900 miles south of St. Helena Island. The area was not part of a usual trade route and so was outside the normal operational zone of U-boats. However, that very remoteness made it a perfect place for U-boats to refuel from those submarine tankers the Germans called 'milch cows'. *U-160*, commanded by Lieutenant Commander Georg Lassen, had recently refuelled from one and was now on the surface and making south prior to entering and operating in the Indian Ocean. At noon Lassen was called to the conning tower by a report that a ship had been sighted on the horizon, and crossing the U-boat's track. The ship was the *Taney* which was on a zigzag course. Not knowing whether he had been spotted from the ship or not, Lassen dived and shadowed the ship for the remaining hours of daylight and well into the night. At 2200 hours he surfaced and fired his first torpedo at the ship. The torpedo passed ahead of the *Taney*, but its wake was sighted by the bow lookout. As general quarters was sounded on the ship, Captain Potter arrived on the bridge and began ordering evasive action. At 2220 hours, just as he ordered a wide alteration of course, Lassen's second torpedo slammed into the starboard side in way of the engine-room. The explosion killed the three men on duty there, destroyed the engines, wrecked two lifeboats, put the ship's radio out of commission and started a fire. The ship's Armed Guard fired at the U-boat which rapidly dived.

Aboard the *Taney*, some confusion reigned among the merchant crew. Speaking last year (2000), Captain Potter recalled that 'there was no way to train the people the way they come and go in the Merchant Marine. It's not like the Navy'. The crew abandoned ship in the two remaining lifeboats, the Armed Guardsmen staying on board. Tom Potter was the last crewman to leave, sliding down a handline into the water to be picked up by one of the boats. At 2320 hours another torpedo slammed into the ship, this time at No. 4 hold, upon which the Armed Guard launched life-rafts and also abandoned, to be taken aboard the lifeboats at dawn. Shortly after the second explosion the *Taney* sank. Commander Lassen closed with the lifeboats and asked for and received the name of his victim. He then left the scene. By March 1943 he and his craft were causing not a little havoc in the Mozambique Channel, as we shall see in Chapter 19.

Tom Potter decided that the two boats should make with the prevailing wind for South America, the nearest point of which was over 2000 miles away. He was confident that the coast would be reached. 'How the hell you gonna miss South America?' he asks. However, the two boats soon became separated in heavy weather. The one commanded by the Chief Officer was sighted by the British *Penrith Castle* twenty-two days later, all twenty-eight men on board being rescued. Although food had to be rationed aboard Captain Potter's boat, frequent rain squalls ensured that drinking water was never much of a problem. However, everyone lost weight. Potter, who began the voyage weighing 150lbs, lost nearly three stone. The men kept their spirits up by talking about every topic under the sun, except women, Potter recalls. The favourite topic was, of course, food. It never entered the Captain's head that he and his crew would not make it, although he says that by the 38th day 'everybody got religion'. He had marked each passing day with a notch cut in into the boat's compass box, and there were forty-two notches when, within ten miles of the Brazilian coast and after crossing 2300 miles of ocean, the boat was sighted by the Brazilian merchantman *Bage* which rescued all twenty-six men on board.

When asked recently by his friend Dean Bruch about some of the grimmer details of his forty-two day ordeal, eighty-seven year-old Tom Potter replied, 'Gosh, Dean, it wasn't too bad. The crew got to swim every day'.[9]

---

9. Information from Captain Thomas Potter through Dean Bruch, January 2001.

CHAPTER 10

The North Atlantic

By far the greater proportion of Allied wartime voyages were made across the North Atlantic and in the waters adjacent to it, and Liberty voyages were no exception to the rule. It was in these waters that Admiral Doenitz ordered his greatest concentration of U-boats in the knowledge that Britain, the main recipient of the cargoes carried across 'the bridge of ships', was the key to final victory of one side or the other. It follows that more Allied ship losses were sustained in that ocean than in any other, and that includes Liberty ships. The total number of Liberties lost during the war, from all causes including those not involving enemy action and on all oceans, was 215. Of those ninety-seven were lost in North Atlantic waters including the Caribbean, the Arctic route to North Russia, and in the waters around the British Isles and northern France. In comparison, forty-one Liberties were lost in the Mediterranean, thirty-six in the Pacific, twenty-four in the Indian Ocean, and seventeen in the South Atlantic. Overall, something of the order of one in four of the Liberty ships that were lost were on their maiden voyages. Liberty ship operations to North Russia and in European waters, are deserving of special chapters to themselves. This chapter concentrates on the North Atlantic convoy routes and the Caribbean.

Among the earliest of the Liberties to be sunk in these waters was the *Sam Houston* (Houston, May 1942). She was on her maiden voyage when on 26 June 1942 in West Indian waters and en route to Bombay via Cape Town, she fell in with *U-203*, Lieutenant Commander Mutzelburg. A torpedo struck the ship between the engine-room and No. 4 hold and both of those compartments flooded rapidly. The explosion also started fires in the ship's cargo of Army supplies. With his ship settling until the deck was only a foot or two above the water, Captain Robert Perry ordered abandon ship. Three men had been killed in the attack, but everyone else got off in three lifeboats. According to Mutzelburg's log the attack was made from as close as 500 metres, and when the torpedo struck there was a violent explosion on board. After the crew had abandoned it took Mutzelburg's craft half an hour and forty-three 88mm shells to finish the Liberty off. Captain Perry was temporarily taken aboard the submarine for questioning, and was surprised to learn that

Mutzelburg already knew the name of the ship and his own despite the fact that Perry had been a last-minute replacement. The German intelligence system in the United States at that time was very good indeed. The survivors were picked up two days later by the minesweeper USS *Courier*, but not before four more men had died from burns received during the attack. Yet another man was to die of burns in the hospital on St. Thomas Island where the survivors were landed.

Captain Mellin E. Respess must be rated as one of the unluckiest shipmasters of the war. A Baltimore man, in early 1942 he had been Chief Officer of a freighter sunk by a submarine and had been severely injured in the incident. After he recovered it was back to sea again, this time in command of a brand-new Liberty launched at his home port in May 1942. The ship was the *Thomas McKean*. Loaded with planes, military supplies and food, her maiden voyage was to have been to the Persian Gulf via Cape Town. On 29 June she was off the West Indies and on a zigzag course when a torpedo from *U-505*, Lieutenant Commander Loewe, hit aft in No. 5 hold, killing three Armed Guardsmen and a crew member. The damage was extensive and Captain Respess ordered everyone to abandon ship. The U-boat then surfaced, and according to the survivors in the four lifeboats, fired a total of fifty-seven shells at the ship before she caught fire and sank. Commander Loewe then approached the lifeboats and sent some of his men aboard them to administer first-aid to the injured. By the time he left the area he had shown that the true traditions of the sea can rise even above the horrors of war. Over the next two weeks the four lifeboats arrived one by one at various West Indian Islands. All the survivors eventually boarded ships for home. Four weeks after the sinking Captain Respess boarded the small American freighter *Onondaga* as a repatriated passenger. On 27 July, when heading for Havana, the ship was torpedoed by *U-129*, Lieutenant Commander Wirt. Only fourteen of the thirty-four men aboard the freighter survived, and Captain Respess was not amongst them. On 27 September 1943, the second anniversary of the Liberty Fleet Day proclaimed by President Roosevelt, Captain Respess's widow sponsored the Liberty *John Russell Pope*. But it was a ship name that did not last long, for on 6 October the ship was handed over to a British crew under the management of the Moss Hutchinson Shipping Company and renamed *Samdak*. She survived the war, and also many years of post-war trading under various other names and national flags, and was finally scrapped in 1973.

Also amongst the earliest of the Liberties to be lost in the North Atlantic was Henry J. Kaiser's pride and joy, the *Star of Oregon*, the ship built at Portland that had almost pipped the *Patrick Henry* to the post as first in the long line of such ships. Managed by the States Steamship Company and under the command of Captain Ellis Thomas, she was voyaging home independently from Durban with a cargo of manganese ore. She had reached a position to the north-east of Trinidad on 30 August 1942 when sighted by *U-162*, Commander Wattenberg. The Liberty was on a zigzag course but that did not save her, a torpedo striking her in the vicinity of No. 4 hold. The explosion blew the hatches off that hold and from No. 5, and a seamen in the vicinity was blown overboard and never seen again. As the ship began to settle, Captain Thomas ordered abandon ship. Before the Armed Guard unit left they fired five rounds from the 3in gun aft; it was a gesture of defiance for the submarine had not by then been sighted. The U-boat surfaced later, and having ascertained from the men in the boats that no one was still aboard the Liberty, Wattenberg expended eighteen rounds from his deck gun at it. Within half-an-hour the ship sank by the stern and the submarine then left the scene. The survivors were picked up by an American patrol craft on the following day.

In that same general area another early victim was the *John Carter Rose* (Baltimore, August 1942). The circumstances of her loss are worth recording because they include a marathon sea chase and some atypical confusion between the two German submarine commanders involved, a confusion that has led to at least one authority crediting the wrong submarine with the final kill. The *John Carter Rose,* managed by Barber West African Lines and commanded by Captain Magnus Leknes, was en route from New York to Accra on her maiden voyage with a cargo that included aircraft, gasoline, bombs and machinery. On 6 October 1942 she had reached a position about 850 miles east of Trinidad in an area where two German submarines were operating, *U-201* commanded by Lieutenant Commander Rosenberg, and *U-202* under Lieutenant Commander Poser. Although the German commanders were aware of each other's presence in the area, their attacks on the *John Carter Rose* were entirely unco-ordinated.[1]

U-201 was the first of the two to sight the *John Carter Rose,* sometime before midday local time, but was unable to close because of trouble with the port engine clutch caused by damage sustained during an earlier American air attack. Then, halfway through the afternoon *John Carter Rose* was also sighted by *U-202* at a distance of about fourteen miles, Commander Poser noting in his log that the ship was of 7000 tons, which was almost spot on. Because the Liberty was zigzagging, Poser waited for it to close his position as he prepared to use his stern torpedo tube. Meanwhile Rosenberg's *U-201* had at last managed to get close enough to the ship to fire a torpedo, but it proved a dud. At that time the men on the bridge of the *John Carter Rose* must have sighted the *U-202* ahead and so slowed down, causing a second missile from *U-201* to miss as well. The Liberty opened fire on *U-202* which in turn fired three

---

1. From RM98/405 and RM98/406, the log books of *U-201* and *U-202* respectively, Bundesarchiv, Potsdam. Translated by Dirk Steffen.

torpedoes at it, only one of which detonated and that with little visible effect. So good was the gunnery from the Liberty – Poser reporting 'accurate fire from the ship's two guns and several machine guns' – *U-202* was forced to dive.

After firing her torpedoes, *U-201* had also dived and on resurfacing some twenty minutes later was unable to locate the *John Carter Rose* though some distant gunfire was heard. Apparently, whilst underwater, men aboard that submarine had heard explosions and what was taken to be the sound of bulkheads collapsing, and a report to that effect was radioed to Berlin. *U-202* picked up that broadcast but when she investigated the given position, did not sight anything. On the following morning Rosenberg's *U-201* relocated the Liberty, but again due to the defective clutch was not in a position to fire at it until much later. Meanwhile the *John Carter Rose* was sighted again by *U-202* which fired a bow torpedo at her, which missed. The torpedo's track must have been seen on the Liberty, for with *U-202* in hot pursuit on the surface, the ship began taking evasive action. By then *U-201* was in position to fire two torpedoes, but they also missed although some on board thought they heard the sound of a dud striking the ship's hull. Visibility was now decreasing, and with *U-201* hobbling up astern, *U-202* got ahead of the Liberty and fired his last torpedo at it. Commander Poser was of the opinion that the torpedo's wake had been seen from the ship and that it took evasive action, for again no hit was scored. Having now expended all his torpedoes, Poser withdrew from the action, leaving Rosenberg's craft to finish the job, if he could.

On 8 October, after a search and chase that had lasted for over thirty-six hours, a torpedo from *U-201* struck the *John Carter Rose* immediately before the bridge. The Liberty was soon ablaze and the crew abandoned ship, but despite a series of explosions on board, she refused to sink. Four hours later Rosenberg closed the range again and fired another torpedo. 'Impact amidships . . . ship settles slightly, no further visible effect', Rosenberg wrote up in his log. For five hours the by-then rather despairing Rosenberg watched as the ship remained afloat. He then made another approach and began pumping shells at the ship with his deck gun. After the expenditure of fifty-one shells the gun malfunctioned, but by then ship was definitely on her way down; an hour later she disappeared bow first beneath the waves. Rosenberg closed the three lifeboats in the water and gleaned from the survivors the ship's details. He handed over cigarettes, first aid supplies and some food and then left the scene, no doubt a very relieved man having at last conquered one very stubborn foe. Eight men had died during the attacks on the Liberty, but the remainder of the crew survived. The three boats became separated on the first night but the men in one of them were picked up after three days by the *West Humhaw* and were finally landed at Freetown. The others were picked up by the Argentinean tanker *Santa Cruz* which was going in the opposite direction, so they ended up in Recife, Brazil.[2]

Winston Churchill once wrote, 'the only thing that ever really frightened me during the war was the U-boat peril'. It is likely that he was referring particularly to the critical period of the Battle of the Atlantic which began in November 1942, the month in which the Allies suffered their heaviest shipping losses of the war, and which can be said to have ended in May 1943. By the latter date, not only had German U-boat losses, both of boats and men, risen above the rate at which they could be replaced, but the output of merchant ships from American yards meant that more and more vessels and their cargoes were reaching Britain and other North Atlantic destinations safely.

During this critical period there were many tragedies, some of them involving Liberty ships. On 8 November 1942 the *Nathaniel Hawthorne* (Portland, Oregon, May 1942) was making the run in convoy from Paramaribo to New York with a cargo of bauxite when she was struck by two torpedoes from *U-508*, Lieutenant Commander Staats. Captain Richard Brannan had somehow allowed his ship to run ahead and to port of the convoy and so was not within escort cover. The Liberty sank in about a minute and as she did so, her acetylene store blew up. Of the fifty-two men on board, only fourteen survived to swim to life-rafts that had been released. Lieutenant Kenneth Muir of the Armed Guard played a prominent role in directing survivors to these rafts and was awarded the Navy Cross for his bravery. The destroyer USS *Biddle* picked up the survivors thirty-nine hours later and landed them in Trinidad.

Stragglers from convoys, those ships which for one reason or another fell out of the main body, were always in special danger. Tragedy was to strike two such ships, both of them Liberties in mid-Atlantic in late January 1943. They had been part of Convoy UGS-4 en route from New York to North Africa, when on the 21st of that month in heavy weather both had separately straggled from the convoy. They were the *Charles C. Pinckney* (Wilmington, May 1942) and *Julia Ward Howe* (Portland, Maine, December 1942). Due to conflicting reports, something of a mystery surrounds the loss of the first of them. On the 27th, six days after straggling and still on her own, lookouts aboard *Pinckney* sighted a surfaced submarine. As Captain Frank Woolverton changed course and made away at top speed, the Armed Guard fired on the submarine. Later that day the track of a torpedo was spotted by lookouts, and although the helm was put hard over, the torpedo struck the ship near the bow, blowing off the fore end of

2. After landing the 'passengers' at Freetown, *West Humhaw*, commanded by Captain T.S Selness, sailed from that port on 8 November making for Takoradi on the Gold Coast. Three days later she was torpedoed by *U-161* (Lieutenant Commander Achilles), but all hands were soon picked up by the British motor launch ML *281*.

the vessel in a pillar of flame. Six men were killed by the explosion. Captain Woolverton ordered 'stop engines' and 'abandon ship' and everyone got away in the lifeboats except for the Armed Guard officer and some of his men. As the U-boat surfaced nearby, the gunners opened fire and hit the submarine several times, driving it away. Early on the following morning Captain Woolverton and the men in the boats reboarded the ship, but failed to get steam up, and half an hour later as a submarine surfaced nearby, the ship was abandoned again, this time by everyone. German officers on the submarine questioned some of the survivors in the boats about the ship's name and cargo, before sinking *Pinckney* with gunfire. The U-boat then submerged. The four lifeboats kept together for the remainder of the day but became separated that night. Ten days later one of the boats with an officer, two crew members and nine Armed Guards on board, was sighted by the Swiss ship *Caritasi* and rescued and later landed in the Azores. The other three boats and the men in them were never seen again.

Now for the mystery. In one of the standard books on American merchant ship casualties, its author, Robert Browning, has recorded that the U-boat concerned in both the torpedoing and gunfire incidents was *U-514*, Lieutenant Commander Auffermann. Although the earlier sighting was mentioned by him, he made no comment on the identity of the submarine involved in that incident and did not say that it had fired a torpedo at the ship. In their book on Liberty ships, Sawyer and Mitchell presented a different version of events, stating that the ship was first damaged by a torpedo from an unknown submarine, and then on the following day, torpedoed, shelled and finally sunk by *U-514*. They also said that when this submarine surfaced among the survivors, it was ascertained that this submarine had *not* been the one involved in the initial attack. Those authors went on to state that as no other U-boat subsequently claimed that first torpedo attack, it is likely that the first submarine had been sunk by the Armed Guard's shellfire. They even specified that four hits had been made on that submarine. (Another twist to the mystery is that US sources once claimed that it was the *U-514* itself that had been sunk by the Liberty ship's gunfire, but in fact that submarine was sunk later in the year on 8 July 1943 in the Bay of Biscay by British planes from 224 Squadron RAF.) These rather conflicting records were based on survivor's reports which can sometimes be very misleading. Many such reports were not written up directly by survivors themselves but by debriefing officers ashore. Some are composite reports, based on the descriptions given by several survivors, with the interviewer, one supposes, deciding what to include and what to leave out when he heard differing versions of the same events. In the case of the *Pinckney,* neither the ship's captain nor the Armed Guard officer were among the survivors, so the reports must have come from more junior members of the ship's complement who may not have been fully aware of all the details involved.

If it can be assumed that the 'initial attack' mentioned by Sawyer and Mitchell was not that first distant sighting of a submarine mentioned by Browning, is it possible that another U-boat was involved and that there were actually two separate attacks on *Pinckney* and that her gunners actually did sink one? Of the total number of U-boats lost during the war, only the sketchiest details exist of the fates of around two dozen of them, some of those having disappeared without trace on dates unknown. Was there such an event in the North Atlantic around the time of the *Pinckney* incidents? The answer is yes. In the chronological list of U-boat losses kept by the German Navy, copies of which are available in both British and American official archives, after noting the demise on 21 January 1943 of a submarine of which the full details were shown, the following entry appears:

— January. *U-553* [Commander] Thurmann. [Cause of Sinking] Unknown

So neither the exact date nor the cause of *U-553*'s sinking is known, although the date was assumed to have fallen sometime after 21 January and before the next fully detailed loss on 3 February. The first *Pinckney* incident took place on 27 January, so the dates fit. But there is another problem. The German source notes that the assumed position of *U-553*'s loss was 55° north, 33° west. The *Pinckney* incident took place in about 36° north, 31° west, about 780 nautical miles to the south. However, the position of the submarine is noted as approximate in the German list, and was probably a guesstimate based on the boat's last reported position. As the intervening distance could have been covered by *U-553* in about three days at surface speed, on the details as listed here we can say that there is at least a possibility that the *Pinckney* was the only Liberty ship in the war to sink a U-boat.

The second Liberty ship straggler from UGS-4 was the *Julia Ward Howe* on her very first voyage. She was carrying 8000 tons of military supplies and sixty tanks for the American forces in North Africa, and was under the command of Captain Andrew Anthony Hammond. In broad daylight on 28 January 1943, a torpedo from *U-442*, Lieutenant Commander Hesse, blew a hole in the ship's side at the point where a bulkhead separated No. 3 hold from the machinery spaces. The explosion killed Captain Hammond and two others, wrecked two lifeboats, and destroyed the radio room. The ship immediately took a 15° list, but as she settled came upright again. The survivors took to the remaining two boats and to life-rafts. Forty minutes later *U-442* finished the job with a second torpedo after which Hesse surfaced. He took the second mate on board for questioning, and then returned him to a boat. Early the following morning the survivors were picked up by the Portuguese destroyer *Lima* which landed them at Port Delgado in the Azores. The chief engineer of the Liberty unfortunately died aboard the rescue ship.

During February and March 1943, German U-boats massed along the usual North Atlantic convoy routes and met with many successes. However, already there were small signs that the tide was beginning to turn. Due to previous losses many U-boat crews were relatively inexperienced, some being on their first, or at best, second patrols. Of the twelve U-boats lost in February, half were commanded by inexperienced commanders, and this pattern carried on into March. The experienced crews, at sea for many weeks, were growing tired. On the other side, the Allies were continually improving their convoy techniques and longer-range aircraft were coming into service.

None of that prevented the tragedy of the *James Sprunt* (Wilmington, February 1943). Carrying 4000 tons of explosives for Karachi from Charleston, and in a convoy making for the Panama Canal, before dawn on 19 March 1943 the ship had reached a position south of Cuba. For some reason the *Sprunt*, commanded by Captain Elie Constantine Carr and managed by the Black Diamond Steamship Company, had fallen out of position. A torpedo from *U-185*, Lieutenant Commander Maus, struck the ship, no one knows where. The ship blew up and disintegrated, in a blast so vast that it was witnessed by a ship forty miles away. Debris from the explosion fell on every other ship in the convoy. All sixty-seven men on board perished. That rounded off a good night's work for Maus, for only two hours before he had torpedoed the non-Liberty freighter *Virginia Sinclair.*

Because of known U-boat concentrations to the north, the sixty-ship convoy HX-228 was ordered to take a more southerly route when it sailed from New York in early March 1943. (Earlier in the war all eastbound trans-Atlantic convoys had foregathered at Halifax, Nova Scotia, hence the HX. In September 1942 New York replaced Halifax as the main ocean assembly point but the original prefix was kept. In March 1943 some convoys, those made up of slower ships reverted to using Halifax to assemble, because of congestion at New York.) On 10 March the convoy had reached the halfway mark across the North Atlantic when the *William C. Gorgas* was hit amidships by a torpedo from *U-444* commanded by new boy Lieutenant Albert Langfield on his first operational patrol. The resulting explosion ripped through the engine-room of the Liberty, killing everyone on watch there. That was but the beginning of what turned out to be a multi-faceted tragedy.

The sea was rough and it was snowing as Captain James C. Ellis on the *Gorgas* ordered his men to abandon ship. The British destroyer HMS *Harvester,* a veteran of the Dunkirk evacuation commanded by Commander A.A. Tait, picked up sixty survivors out of the original seventy men on board. On the following day the Liberty was still afloat but blew up and sank after *U-757*, Lieutenant Commander Deetz, put a another torpedo into her. On that day *U-444* attempted another attack on the convoy but was spotted by *Harvester* which rammed at full speed, passing right over the submarine which fouled on her stern and, jamming under a propeller shaft, hung there for several minutes before being shaken free. *U-444* was then finished off by being rammed again, this time by the Free French corvette *Aconit*, commanded by Lieutenant de Vaisseau J.M.L.M. Levasseur. A third submarine, *U-432*, Lieutenant Commander Eckhardt, then entered the fray, torpedoing the crippled *Harvester* despite the best efforts of the *Aconit* to prevent it. *Harvester* broke in two and sank almost immediately, and many of those on board did not live to see their assailant being first forced to the surface by depth charges from *Aconit* and then meet its end as the Frenchman rammed again. Commander Tait and 144 of his men went down with the ship, along with most of the survivors from *Gorgas*. A few survivors of the *Harvester* crew and only twelve men of the Liberty crew were pulled from the sea by the gallant *Aconit*, which also picked up survivors from its two U-boat victims.

There is an interesting aftermath to those incidents. The Liberty *Henry Wynkoop* (New Orleans, December 1942), had been straggling behind Convoy HX-228 for two days but managed to catch up on the day the *Aconit* did her excellent work. As she did so, she struck a submerged object. The ship lifted in the water and rolled as the object passed right under it, leaving behind a great patch of oil. According to Sawyer and Mitchell, 'it is assumed the ship hit, and sank, a U-boat', which gives the impression the Liberty had scored her own kill.[3] However, official records show that only two U-boats were sunk that day and they were *Aconit*'s two victims, so it seems that the Liberty must have struck the submerged and abandoned hull of one of them. As the *Henry Wynkoop* slowed down to inspect the collision damage she had sustained, thirty-three seamen decided to abandon ship without orders. The *Wynkoop* later recovered eight of them before proceeding on its way short-handed. Most of the others were picked up by other ships in the convoy.

Only six days later, on 16 March 1943, as part of Convoy UGS-6 to North Africa, the Liberty *Benjamin Harrison* (Baltimore, March 1942) met her end. The convoy had just been ordered by the commodore ship to take evasive action, when the Liberty was struck by a torpedo from *U-172*, Lieutenant Commander Emmermam. Captain George Sterne did not order abandon ship, but someone shouted out the order and the crew began leaving in the most chaotic way. One lifeboat had been damaged in the blast and as confusion reigned, two others were upended in

---

3. Sawyer and Mitchell, *The Liberty Ships* (London 1998).

the launching process, their occupants falling into the sea. A fourth boat was then properly launched together with some life-rafts. Before hastening the ship to the bottom with shellfire, the escort destroyer USS *Rowan* picked up three men from the sea, the other survivors being rescued by the American freighter *Alan A. Dale*.

In that same month of March 1943 an incident occurred with a Liberty ship that did not result in her sinking, although later she was declared a 'constructive total loss', an insurance term meaning that the ship was so badly damaged as to make repairing her uneconomic. It was on 8 March when the *James K. Polk* (Wilmington, August 1942), managed by the American South Africa Line and under the command of Captain Herbert Olson, whilst making for the port of Paramaribo in Dutch Guiana, was struck on the port side by a torpedo from *U-510*. With his ship well down by the stern, Captain Olson radioed for assistance and a British naval tug arrived to tow her to Port-of-Spain, Trinidad, which was reached safely nine days later. The ship was in such a dangerous state during the towing operation, that only Captain Olson and seven volunteers stayed aboard. Captain Olson's conduct during that tow did not save him from some severe criticism. Prior to making for Paramaribo, his ship had been in convoy from Suez to Bahia, Brazil, and according to the reports subsequently submitted to the 7th US Naval District Headquarters at Miami, the commodore of the convoy, Captain T.B. Robinson, reported that Olson was incapable of command and that he, Robinson, 'had been carrying the ship along'. The report said that Olson 'could not navigate, failed to carry out routing orders, and continually bickered with the ship's officers and Lieutenant John M. Gregory, the gunnery officer'. One crewmember said of the captain, 'I'll be damned if I'll ship out again with him and they can't make me do it even if they throw me in jail or in the army, for he's just no good'.

It seems as if reports were being made that were designed to condemn the captain to a future life ashore for, as if all the other criticisms were not enough, the document ended:

> Olson is said to have associated in Bahia almost constantly with a red-haired woman of the street known as Torpedo Annie who resided at the Palace Hotel. This is mentioned in this report because both informants stated that this woman was known for her associations withonly captains of merchant vessels and that she knew them all 'from New York to Australia'. Informants said it was believed Torpedo Annie had Nazi connections.[4]

In December 1945 *James K. Polk* was towed to Mobile and was scrapped the following year. The fate of Torpedo Annie is unknown.

---

4. Summary of the relevant American documents found in ADM199/2135, PRO.

One of the pivotal convoys of the Battle of the Atlantic, pivotal because it sailed at the time which turned out to be the climax of that battle, was Convoy HX-229. A total of seventy-eight merchant ships were involved, nine of them Liberties. The convoy sailed in two sections. One part left New York under the original designation on 8 March 1943, and consisted of forty ships including seven Liberties. The second was designated 229A and sailed from New York on the following day, and after some leavings and joinings off Canada, consisted of thirty-eight ships including two Liberties for the voyage across the Atlantic. On 5 March an earlier and slower convoy of over sixty ships, designated SC-122, had also set out, so that by the second week of that month there were three Allied convoys comprising some 140 merchant ships and a total of twenty-eight escorts in the Western Atlantic and heading eastward. Lying in wait for them to the south and east of Greenland were about fifty U-boats in three main wolf-packs, and with others acting independently.

The original Allied plan had been for SC-122 to take the most southerly course of the three, HX-229A the most northerly, with HX-229 between the other two. The background to the coming events was that both the Germans and the Allies were receiving and acting on intelligence from their respective naval commands. On 15 March HX-229 swung east so putting it to the south of SC-122 but well to the westward of it. At about the same time HX-229A swung northwards, and all but nine of its ships eventually arrived safely at their destinations. Eight of the nine which failed, including the Liberty *Pierre Soule* (New Orleans, February 1943), straggled from the convoy but got back safely to North American ports. The ninth straggler, the British-manned tanker *Svend Foyn*, struck an iceberg and sank. So the Germans met with no successes against that convoy. However, SC-122 was not so lucky, losing nine ships, eight of them in convoy and the ninth while straggling. But it is HX-229 with its seven Liberties with which we are mainly concerned here.

Thirteen out of the original forty ships fell victims to U-boats, three of them Liberties, two being torpedoed on the same day. The first was *James Oglethorpe* (Savannah, February 1943). She was on her maiden voyage under the command of Captain Albert W. Long. A very bad storm blew up on 14 March but had blown itself out by the night of the 16th which was clear with a bright moon, perfect weather for submarine operations. Two other ships in the convoy had already been lost, and the Liberty was steaming a zigzag pattern when a torpedo from *U-758*, Lieutenant Commander Manseck, struck her on the starboard side in way of No. 2 hold. A consignment of cotton in that hold caught fire and the ship listed to starboard. However, Captain Long must have decided his ship could be saved for he did not order abandon ship. Nevertheless, and it will never be known who started it, many crew members and all the Armed Guard did abandon ship even though the ship was still under way. The falls of one boat were cut too soon, spilling its occupants into the sea and drowning thirteen of them. Other lifeboats under the charge of the Chief and Third Officers got away safely. Thirty men from those boats were picked up by the corvette HMS *Pennywort.*

On board the *Oglethorpe* Captain Long and his remaining mate, Second Officer Joseph Duke who came from the ship's home port, and the balance of his crew, fought the fire and eventually put it out. For some reason – it is possible that the helm was left untended whilst the fire-fighting went on – the ship kept turning in wide circles to port and in doing so nearly ran down lifeboats from one of the previously torpedoed ships. Eventually Captain Long got his ship back under control. After picking up the survivors Lieutenant O.G. Stuart RCNVR, in command of *Pennywort,* got close enough to *Oglethorpe* to hail the master. Captain Long told Stuart that he intended to turn back and attempt to make a Canadian port independently. Stuart then tried to persuade the *Oglethorpe* men on board his ship to return, but no one was willing to go. With no time to argue the point, Stuart wished Captain Long, God-speed, and raced back to the convoy. The *Oglethorpe* men aboard *Pennywort* were eventually landed at Londonderry. It is not known exactly what happened to the *James Oglethorpe* after that. One authority records her as having perished on the day after the first attack when *U-91,* Lieutenant Commander Walkerling, administered the *coup de grace.* Another authority hazards the guess that the ship finally succumbed to the effects of the first torpedo, perhaps in a storm. What is known is that no signal was ever received from the ship and that she and the men who stayed on board never did make port.

The *William Eustis* was the second of the Liberties to be torpedoed that night. She had come off the stocks at Houston, Texas, in January 1943 immediately following the *Stephen C. Foster.* The *Foster* had also been part of HX-229 but had earlier developed cracks and returned to the States. Managed by the United Fruit Company, and commanded by Captain Cecil Desmond, the *Eustis* was carrying a much needed cargo of sugar and foodstuffs for Britain. *U-435,* Lieutenant Commander Strelow, fired two torpedoes at her, one of which missed. But the other hit the ship in the vicinity of No. 2 hold, the explosion causing a 20ft split in the starboard shell plating. No. 2 hold began flooding rapidly and with his ship slightly settling by the stern, about thirty minutes after the explosion Captain Desmond ordered abandon ship. The crew had time to don special rubber survival suits before lowering rafts and the one serviceable lifeboat that had remained undamaged after the previous storm. Everyone got away. After about four hours the survivors were picked up by the destroyer HMS *Volunteer.* Sub-Lieutenant R.G. Goody serving on that ship described the rescue thus:

They were all wearing safety lights . . . these were red and, in the darkness, they looked like fairy lights bobbing up and down above the water as you could not see the boats or the men at any distance in the dark. . . . We stopped and put our scrambling nets over the side. . . . The sea was not rough at the time and I doubt very much whether more than a few got their feet wet.

Lieutenant Commander G.J. Luther of the *Volunteer*, the senior escort ship, who had stopped his ship at great risk to pick up the survivors very much against Admiralty standing instructions, was somewhat annoyed to find that most of the *Eustis* men had brought full suitcases with them. But that was trivial in comparison to his other objections. In his opinion the *Eustis* had been abandoned too soon and he discovered from Captain Desmond himself that the ship's codebooks and confidential papers had not been dumped overboard. To add insult to injury, the ship's chief engineer then suggested that if the *Volunteer* could hang around until daylight, which was clearly out of the question in submarine-infested waters, he might be able to get the *Eustis*'s engines going again. Luther dared not leave the ship afloat with its codebooks on board, so he went past the ship close-in and at speed, and lobbed four depth charges at her. 'They all exploded underneath her and lifted her about five feet out of the water – it was quite a dramatic sight', wrote Lieutenant G.C. Leslie of the *Volunteer*. He added, 'Later we worked out how many cups of tea that [cargo of] sugar would have made and were horrified to think we had just sunk about three weeks sugar ration for Britain'.

Another three weeks of that sugar ration was lost two days later when the third Liberty ship from that convoy met her end. It was just after midday on 18 March when a torpedo from *U-221*, Lieutenant Commander Trojer, struck the *Walter Q. Gresham* (New Orleans, February 1943) right aft. It blew a hole about 30ft wide in the ship and probably blew off the ship's propeller in the process. The explosion destroyed the Armed Guard's accommodation aft and it is a wonder that only five members of that unit perished. As the ship came to a stop. Captain Byron Miller ordered abandon ship. Two boats were successfully lowered but a third capsized during the process. Other men got away on rafts. About an hour later the *Gresham* went under stern first. A total of twenty-eight men were lost, but the other survivors were picked up by the British corvettes *Pennywort* and *Anemone*. Another Liberty in convoy HX-229 must have had a charmed life. The *Hugh Williamson* (Wilmington, July 1942) had straggled from the convoy during that earlier storm on 15 March but pressed on for Britain on her own. It seems she must have passed right through the U-boat packs without being sighted.

Although HX-229 and SC-122 between them lost twenty-two ships from enemy action, it could have been much worse considering the number of U-boats laying in wait for them. Nevertheless, that part of the Battle of the Atlantic must be considered a definite win for the Germans. They lost only one submarine in action against the convoys, and that was not to an escort ship but to a Flying Fortress out from Britain and at the extremity of its range. Nine other U-boats were damaged either by escort ships or by aircraft, and when on its way home later in the month in the Bay of Biscay, another of the submarines involved was sunk by a Wellington bomber. It was through the successes of these aircraft that the Allies could see the chink of light at the end of the tunnel.

Like the *John Carter Rose*, mentioned earlier, the *Frederick Douglass* (Baltimore, May 1943), was another Liberty which required the ministrations of two submarines before she sank. Under the command of Captain Adrian Richardson she was in ballast as part of Convoy ON-202 from Avonmouth to New York. The convoy was in mid-ocean on 20 September 1943 and the *Douglass* not only had her torpedo nets out, but also her 'Mark 29' gear which consisted of a hydrophone towed alongside designed to give early warning of a torpedo's approach. But neither the nets nor any hydrophone warning that may have been received stopped the torpedo from *U-238*, Lieutenant Commander Hepp, striking her on the port side aft. The torpedo blew a small hole in the ship, and she began to settle slowly. All the crew got away in boats, but according to Captain Richardson some of his men abandoned ship before being ordered to do so. In this respect he singled out for special mention No. 1 boat which was ordered lowered by Chief Engineer Donald Redman before any order came from the bridge. A few hours after the abandonment, the *U-645* arrived on the scene and supplied the *coup de grace* with another torpedo. The crew of forty and the larger than normal contingent of thirty-six Armed Guard were picked up by the British convoy rescue ship *Rathlin* and landed at Halifax, Nova Scotia. So was a stowaway from the ship, a very pretty young lady of twenty-three years, named as Miss Domillie James, of 23 Oxford Street, Bristol, England. The author of a Royal Canadian Navy report noted that she was 'coloured'. The report went on:

> She said she boarded the ship on Sunday 12 September whilst the [gangway] watch 'was seeking shelter from the rain'. Alleged that the ship's bosun, Jerome Davis, had aided and abetted her hiding on board. Taken into custody by Canadian Immigration Officials.
>
> It may be of interest to note that the majority of the ship's crew including the master, are coloured.[5]

On that very same day *Rathlin* was also involved in saving men from another torpedoed Liberty in the same convoy. Again *U-238* was

5. ADM199/440, PRO.

involved, her torpedo striking the *Theodore Dwight Weld* (Los Angeles, March 1943) in way of No. 3 hold. The engine-room exploded and the ship broke in two. The after part sank almost immediately, taking many men down with it. There was no opportunity to launch lifeboats or life-rafts, although three 'doughnut' rafts floated clear and were boarded by survivors who had either jumped or been washed overboard. One of the Armed Guard contingent was plucked directly from the bow of the ship by *Rathlin* which eventually picked up forty-one of the ninety men who had been on board. One of those who did not survive was the ship's master, Captain Michael Formanack.

This seems to be a good place to make special mention of the official rescue ships, like *Rathlin,* attached to many but not all North Atlantic and Arctic convoys from about the beginning of 1941. Twenty-nine of these specially selected ships operated during the war, out of which six were lost to enemy action. They were manned by RNR crews and carried medical teams. In all they saved some 4000 Allied seamen from near certain death, and their very presence as 'tail-end Charlies' in convoys made a world of difference to a merchant seaman's state of mind.

Unfortunately there was no *Rathlin* around on 16 January 1944 in the tragic incident involving the *Sumner I. Kimball* (Portland, Maine, September 1943). This Liberty, returning to New York from Britain in Convoy ON-219, had straggled from the convoy in bad weather. The story of the ship's demise comes from German sources for not one of the total complement of sixty-nine men under Captain Harry Atkins aboard the ship lived to tell the tale. Lieutenant Commander Heinrich on *U-960* sighted the zigzagging *Kimball* through a rainstorm and fired a torpedo from about 800 yards. Heinrich was not able to see where it struck, although he knew it had. The Liberty made off at an estimated 7kts with the submarine in hot pursuit. Half an hour later Heinrich missed with two more torpedoes and then briefly lost his prey. Sighting her again, two more torpedoes were fired from 2000 yards, both of them being seen to hit. The Liberty stopped, and the radio operator aboard the submarine heard a distress message being sent from the ship. From much closer in, two more torpedoes were fired which were also hits. Heinrich then dived to reload, and when he resurfaced his victim was seen to be in two parts, each half moving away from the other. Heinrich noted in his log that no survivors were sighted as he left the scene. None were ever found.

Not all Liberty ship losses in the North Atlantic were caused by enemy action. The 'normal' peacetime hazards of storms and strandings and collisions did not stop during the war years. Indeed the switching-off of lighthouses for security purposes increased the risk of stranding, and the fact that ships now travelled in close convoy, increased the risk of collision. On top of that of course, were those casualties caused by structural failure. On 19 December 1943 the *James Withycombe* (Portland,

Oregon, July 1943) ran aground off Margarita Point at the Atlantic end of the Panama Canal. Fully loaded with a cargo of military supplies for Melbourne, she broke in two. After most of her cargo had been salvaged, she was ruled to be a constructive total loss. Almost a year later, on 31 October 1944, the Baltimore-built *John Banvard,* carrying supplies for the Allied bases in the Azores, was driven ashore near Terceira in those islands. She was refloated two months later but was also declared a constructive total loss. Eventually towed to the United States she was broken up at Jacksonville. Another storm victim was *James Longstreet.* Named for a general in the Confederate Army who was one of Robert E. Lee's top commanders, she was launched at Houston in October 1942. Early in her existence the Liberty *James Longstreet* developed a reputation for bad luck that had nothing whatsoever to do with contact with the enemy. And as any seaman will tell you, once a ship gains a reputation for being unlucky, it tends to follow in the ship's wake or lurk ahead like an ominous black cloud. The ship made her maiden voyage to India, after which its Armed Guard lieutenant made a highly critical report about the ship and its performance, and about the poor relations between the merchant seamen and his men for which he blamed the ship's officers. (In complete contrast, he had nothing but praise for his own men.) The *Longstreet*'s next round trip was to Liverpool and back to Boston, Massachusetts. She struck an unidentified underwater obstruction on the outward leg, cracking three propeller blades. There was a fire aboard at Liverpool, and another one during the return trip when a box of rockets broke adrift in the wheelhouse. To cap all that off, she suffered stevedore damage at Boston which necessitated some time at a repair yard. In August 1943, she is recorded as having suffered a minor structural failure. Her next and last voyage began on 20 August, and that was also to England. Off Halifax, Nova Scotia on 7 September whilst joining a convoy in foggy weather, she was in collision with a British ship. Neither vessel was seriously damaged, but the incident eventually led to a law suit. The return voyage across the Atlantic was without incident, that is, until the very last day of it, 26 October.

A north-east gale was blowing as Captain Thomas Nelson was ordered to lay off the Ambrose light vessel outside New York Harbour to await a pilot. It was a severe gale, one of the worst on record, and so *Longstreet*'s confrontation with it was well in keeping with her unlucky reputation. That night the gale blew four ships ashore and of course, the *Longstreet* was one of them. She ended up on the beach at Sandy Hook, New Jersey, on a stretch of coast forming part of the Fort Hancock military reservation, an area banned to civilians unless they had special passes. The military received many unauthorised and unannounced visitors that night, for two of the other grounded ships also ended up on the reservation. The men aboard *Longstreet* spent a very rough night aboard the ship as gusts reaching 70 miles per hour, pushed her ever farther up the beach. 'It was the biggest storm I've ever seen', Armed Guard officer Ensign George Clayton later told reporters. He went on,

> We went aground at 2100 and then we put on lifejackets. We took a severe beating from the sea and there was a crack seven or eight inches wide just forward of the wheelhouse. . . . At 0200 I asked the captain if we should leave the ship and he told us to use our own judgement. We were all ready to go ashore when the coast guards standing by advised us not to.
>
> The waves ran 35 to 40 feet high and came over the wheelhouse. The men had to hang on to the rails to stay aboard.[6]

Ensign Clayton went on to add 'that when the time came to leave the ship, we climbed down a Jacob's ladder and walked ashore'.

Even as a wreck onshore the ship's bad luck continued. The *Washington Evening Star* of 28 October carried the story that the ship's Armed Guard had been taken off by breeches buoy, a much more dramatic form of exiting a ship than climbing down a rope ladder to the beach. But the *New York Herald Tribune* gave the game away in its account, stating that Coast Guards in hip-length boots had waded out to the ship when the wind died down, and carried all seventy-one men on board up the beach. That newspaper account ended, 'For the benefit of newsreel and newspaper camera men, some of the men returned to the ship later and came ashore in a breeches buoy', a report that rather destroyed the dramatic effect. A newspaper man only likes a scoop when it is his own, and one can hazard a guess that the Washington newspaper had been involved in the rescue 'reconstruction', and the New York one had not. Captain Nelson was the last person to leave the *Longstreet* and he reported that she had split in the vicinity of No. 3 hatch and that the crack was widening all the time. 'She is buckling pretty badly on sides and deck.'

It seemed that the *Longstreet*'s useful life was over and along with it her reputation for bad luck. But that proved not to be the case. Although declared a constructive total loss the ship was patched up on the beach and refloated late in November and towed to New York. In June 1944 she was taken over by the US Navy and used in the undignified role of target ship for early forms of air-to-surface guided missiles. In September the missile damage was repaired to make her reasonably seaworthy again, but in the process of being towed back to the target area, the tow-line parted and she grounded on a sand bank in the Ambrose Channel. Again refloated and repaired, in November 1944 she was towed out to the target area and

---

6. *Asbury Park Evening Press*, 28 October 1943, quoted by Noel Beyle, *The Target Ship in Cape Cod Bay*.

moored to a buoy. Towards the end of that month a gale blew up, another severe one that lashed the entire north-east coast of America, and during it – what else? – the *Longstreet* drifted away carrying the mooring buoy with her. A sea and air search failed to find her until 5 December when she was sighted some eighty miles out in the Atlantic. Two tugs then towed her into Norfolk, Virginia. In April 1945 she was under tow again, this time to her last resting place in Cape Cod Bay, Massachusetts. She was scuttled there in 20ft of water, and for the next quarter of a century was used by the Air Force and Navy for target practice. She ended up in two pieces and peppered by thousands of shell holes.

Collisions with other ships resulted in the loss of two Liberty ships in the North Atlantic. On 1 June 1943, the *John Morgan* (Baltimore, May 1943) on her maiden voyage and carrying a cargo of ammunition for Russia via the Persian Gulf, collided off Cape Henry with the American tanker *Montana*. The tanker survived, but the *John Morgan* blew up and sank. On the other side of the Atlantic on 24 March 1944, *Artemas Ward* (Wilmington, June 1942) was severely damaged in a collision with the tanker *Manassas* in the Irish Sea. The Liberty was towed to Milford Haven, beached there and later declared a constructive total loss. But she had one more valuable part to play in the war when, three months later, she was towed to Normandy and used as part of an artificial breakwater to protect the Allied landing zones.

The three Liberty ships lost because of major structural failures in the waters covered by this chapter, have already been mentioned in Chapter 7. The first was the *Thomas Hooker* on 5 March 1943, and the other two, the *Joseph Smith* on 11 January 1944 and ten days after that, the *Samuel Dexter.*

So far we have discussed only Liberty ships that were either sunk or which were declared constructive total losses. Some Liberties damaged by U-boat attacks managed to survive to fight another day. Two such ships were in the same convoy and torpedoed within minutes of each other. The convoy was BT-6 en route from Bahia, Brazil to Paramaribo. The two ships, both of them in ballast, were *Mark Hanna* (Portland, Oregon, October 1942) and the *James Smith* (Richmond, July 1942). The *Mark Hanna* was the first to be hit, just after two o'clock in the morning, when a torpedo from *U-510* commanded by Lieutenant Commander Nietzel, struck the ship port side aft. The explosion ripped a great hole in the hull, buckling the deck, shearing the propeller shaft and jamming the rudder. Two minutes later, another torpedo fired from the same submarine struck the *James Smith* in more or less the same place and resulting in the same kind of damage. Aboard the now unmanageable *Hanna* it seemed to Captain Henry Hoeppner that his ship was about to collide with the stricken *Smith* and he ordered those men consigned to the port lifeboats to abandon ship but to standby for a possible return later. Somehow the collision was avoided, but by then the lifeboats had drifted away in the dark, the men in them later being picked up by the patrol boat *PC-592.*

Aboard the *Smith,* on which eleven men had been killed in the explosion, Captain William Aguilar also thought that his ship was about to sink, so he ordered abandon ship and it was carried out in an orderly fashion. As dawn broke, Captain Aguilar and the men in two lifeboats reboarded the ship which was by then so well down by the stern that the after gun platform was almost under water. The men in the other two boats were picked up by *PC-592.* Three days later British naval tugs arrived on the scene. One of them took the *Hanna* in tow and reached Trinidad safely on the 17th. At first it was thought that the *Smith* was beyond salving, and so the master and the rest of the crew were taken off. But the ship refused to sink and Captain Aguilar, the Armed guard officer, and three crew members, reboarded as the ship was taken in tow by the tug HMS *Zwarte Zee.* She too, eventually arrived safely at Trinidad. Both ships were soon back in service and both survived the war. *Mark Hanna* was finally scrapped in 1961 and the *James Smith* two years later. One authority has it that the *James Smith* was involved along with HMS *Itchen* and HMCS *Morden* in the sinking of *U-260* on 29 September 1943. However, that appears to be erroneous, for that submarine met its fate when it struck a mine south of Ireland on 12 March 1945.[7] In fact there is no record of any German U-boat being sunk on 29 September 1943.

7. Sawyer and Mitchell, op.cit.

CHAPTER 11

Liberty Ships and the Northern Route to Russia

There were three Allied sea supply routes to the Soviet Union during the war. One of them was through Persian Gulf ports and then overland by rail to the Caspian sea, sometimes called the 'back door' route. Although overall losses along this route from enemy action was kept to a comparatively low 8 per cent, there were several major problems with it. The gravest one was the enormous sea distances involved from America, for whether ships voyaged west and so traversed the Pacific and Indian Oceans in order to reach the Gulf, or came the other way and traversed the Atlantic, rounded the Cape of Good Hope, and then sailed north up the full extent of the Indian Ocean, it was a long, long way. (Later in the war, after the Allied landings in Sicily in July 1943, the Suez Canal could be used, and this, of course, considerably reduced the distance they had to travel.) Distance was not the only drawback however, for the use of Gulf ports necessitated the building of additional port and rail facilities in Persia and, to top it all off, the back door route placed a well-nigh intolerable burden on the Russian internal transportation system.

Another route was across the Pacific from America to Vladivostok and other Siberian ports. The Americans began to develop this route before they themselves were even in the war. To service it the USA lend-leased many old freighters to the Soviets, the ships then flying the Russian flag and being manned by Russian crews. After Pearl Harbor these ships remained free from Japanese attack because Japan and Russia were not at war with each other. The two nations even got together to lay down certain designated routes for these ships to travel along as, for part of the way, they had necessarily to sail within a few miles of one or other of the Japanese home islands. This situation, one among several strange strategic anomalies that came with the global war, created a continuous stream of protests from Germany to the Japanese government. However, they were to little avail. Throughout the war the Japanese largely turned aside German demands for action against these ships using the arguments that the cargoes being carried were not as great as indeed they were, and that they did not include war materials, which in fact they did; by the end of the war about one half of all American aid to Russia had passed along this route.

On the rare occasions that Japan temporarily arrested one of these re-flagged ships as a sop to its Axis partner, Russian protests were immediate and strongly worded to the effect that such actions were a violation of the 1941 Soviet-Japanese Neutrality Pact. The ship concerned was soon released, for the Japanese were only too aware that any permanent seizure of, or any attack upon, these ships, would likely result in a declaration of war by the Soviet Union and the possibility of American air bases then being constructed on Soviet Far Eastern territory, bases that would be well within range of Japanese cities. The possibility of outright war with the Soviets had coloured Japanese military planning and political thinking for many years, a situation often aggravated by skirmishes between the two countries along the Manchurian border, and now, having taken on the United States and Britain, Japan was not about to take on Russia as well just because of complaints from Berlin, however strident those complaints may have been. That route, however, had one severe drawback. After reaching Siberian ports the cargoes concerned had then to be transported thousands of miles overland across the length and breadth of the USSR to get to where it was needed. (An air route to Russia from Alaska was also developed in conjunction with the newly constructed Alaskan Highway, but as with all air shipments, the tonnages concerned were small compared with those carried by ships. Anyway, the Russians were never happy for American planes to over-fly their territory.)

The third route to Russia was via Arctic waters to the ports of Murmansk and Archangel. It was the route most favoured by the Russians because it was the shortest; once they had been landed, it brought weapons and supplies closer to the front line than did either of the other routes. But it had to pass through some of the most bleak and inhospitable waters in the world, and not only that, parts of it were through relatively confined waters that were well within reach of German submarines and the northern part also lay within reach of German surface warships and of dive- and torpedo-bombers based in Norway. This route was by far the most dangerous of the three and approximately one fifth of all the cargoes shipped along it ended up at the bottom of the sea. Throughout the period of these convoys, their protection was a major commitment for the British Home Fleet.

Britain began shipments along this route within weeks of the German attack on Russia despite the fact that Winston Churchill and most members of his government had little love for the new ally, an attitude not solely to do with the fact that the country was Communist. In mid-September 1939 Russia had attacked Poland from the east, the earlier German invasion of that country from the west having been the event which started the World War. Later, Russia had extended not an inconsiderable amount of aid to the Germans. They permitted the use of the Trans-Siberian railway for the carriage of certain strategic commodities, including rubber and wolfram, from the Far East to Germany, and they assisted with ice-breakers the voyage through the North-east Passage of the raider *Komet* in July and August 1940; which ship, after breaking out through the Bering Strait, played no little havoc with British shipping interests in the Pacific. Nevertheless, when Germany attacked the Soviet Union in Operation 'Barbarossa' on 22 June 1941, Britain was no longer standing alone against the Axis partners. Churchill immediately broadcast a promise of all possible aid to the Russians.

The first of the aid voyages was made by the cruiser HMS *Adventure* which arrived at Archangel at the beginning of August 1941 with a cargo of mines and other war materials. The first convoy of merchantmen consisting of five British freighters and a Dutch one together with a British fleet oiler and escorted by no less than nine Royal Navy ships, arrived safely at Archangel on the last day of August. That convoy was code-named Operation 'Dervish', but later convoys were given a number after the prefix PQ, the letters being reversed for the return voyages. (According to Captain Harry Denham, the British Naval Attaché in wartime Sweden, the 'PQ' designation stemmed from the initials of Commander P.Q. Roberts, an Admiralty planning officer, who 'was delighted to have got away with it'.) By the end of 1941 nine north-eastbound convoys comprising a total of sixty-three ships had reached North Russia. The largest port there was Archangel, but being situated on the shores of the White Sea, it became ice-bound during much of the Arctic winter. Murmansk on the Kola Inlet to the west could be kept open by ice-breakers, and the majority of convoys ended up there. Other smaller ports in the vicinity were also used. This route to Russia ran north between Iceland and Greenland then passed just south of Jan Mayen Island before passing between Spitsbergen and lonely Bear Island, which lies about 300 miles from Norway's North Cape. It was after reaching this point and entering the Barents Sea when the convoys were most likely to be attacked by German aircraft based at one or other of three airfields in North Norway.

The conditions faced by Allied seamen, both merchant and naval, who took part in those Arctic convoys, were by far the worst experienced by seamen anywhere. Not only did the men (and more than a few women on Russian ships) have to contend with attacks from submarines, surface ships and aircraft, they had to fight the weather and the cold. Gales and high seas, snow, fog and ice, were standard hazards most of the time. Ice which formed on deck fittings and superstructures was sometimes a particular hazard, the extra weight making ships roll sickeningly. The probability of meeting up with sea-ice required that ships' bows be strengthened with timbers, and it was so cold that special lubricating oils had to be supplied to the ships. Temperatures could fall so low that to touch metal with the bare hand could lead to the loss of fingers. The Arctic summer with its permanent daylight much increased the chance of a convoy being spotted and attacked, so sailings were reduced during that season although political necessity ensured they were not completely curtailed. Conversely, the long Arctic winter nights might have made the task of U-boats and aircraft more difficult, but they also made travelling in convoy more dangerous than usual.

In the prevailing conditions it was difficult for men to sleep during off-watch periods and, anyway, as often as not those periods were truncated by calls to action stations. And when, after braving bombs, mines and torpedoes on top of ice, storm and tempest, the seamen reached their northern destinations, they often found themselves treated with contempt and discourtesy by Russian officials and there was little in the way of shore comforts laid on for them. American seaman Alfonsas Urbelis who sailed to Murmansk aboard the Liberty *James Monroe* (Los Angeles, June 1942) says that the Russians provided an International Seaman's Club inside the docks to discourage foreign seaman from going into the town. Not only were the Club amenities rather sparse, something sinister went on there. Alfonsas says that when he and a shipmate got on friendly terms with two hostesses at the Club by presenting them with silk stockings, they were quietly told by the ladies themselves to be careful what they said, as the ladies were under strict instructions to report back any conversations to the KGB.[1] Even when the British themselves improved the shore conditions for visiting Royal Navy personnel, the force which held the prime responsibility for the protection of the Russian convoys throughout the war, little was done for merchant seamen even though their periods in port were nearly always much longer than those of their naval counterparts. The little that was done in the way of amenities for merchant seamen had to be wrung out of officials in London. It seemed to the sailors involved that each concession was made, with the most remarkable nicety, just when it no longer could be deferred.

And as if all that was not enough, sea navigation in those high latitudes was problematical, to say the least. Magnetic compasses were of little use in high latitudes (some, but not all of the participating merchant ships were specially fitted with gyro compasses), and the high proportion of overcast days meant that opportunities to take sun and star sights were few and far between. Navigation in Arctic waters is an art all of its own, and the only seamen any good at it were the comparative few who had previous experience of it, for example some of the Russian captains involved and some of the skippers of the trawlers that were now being used as escorts. Inexperienced shipmasters had sometimes to rely on the commodore ship or the naval escorts for navigation, which not only went against the grain, but was of no use to stragglers who for one reason or

---

1. Alfonsas Urbelis, letter of September 2000.

another lost contact with the convoy. Life on the Murmansk run was not one to be envied.

It is little wonder that the route was known, amongst other things, as the 'Gateway to Hell' by seamen of all the nations concerned. American Armed Guardsman George Hurley sailed to Murmansk in early 1944 aboard the Liberty ship *Henry Lomb* (Baltimore, September 1943). He writes;

> I served on four Liberty ships during the war. In them I went to the Persian Gulf, Normandy and the Philippines, but nothing compared with the suffering and storm of winter cold, 103 air raids, and no sleep . . . on the Murmansk run.

Armed Guard regulations required that no diaries be kept, so George resorted to keeping his in poetic form, 'so that no one would know'. His record of the Murmansk run is eighty stanzas long and in them he describes standing to his gun covered in snow and ice and with feet so cold he could not feel them. He uses the phrase 'Gateway to Hell' several times in his description of the voyage north, and describes 'Hell', also known as the Kola Inlet on which Murmansk stands, as 'bleak and bare' and 'no haven from German bombers'. He noted that the town itself was pock-marked with craters with scarcely a building standing, and with no electric light, no water and no food for the local inhabitants, many of whom were driven to begging for crusts at the ship's side. After Hell itself, it was back through the gateway until 'we got back to good old friendly Scotland where we were treated great'.[2]

Canadian-born seaman George Evans knew the Murmansk convoy route as 'the suicide run'. When at the age of sixteen he joined the Dutch freighter *Pieter de Hoogh* which was about to make the run as fireman/trimmer, he had already had a ship sunk under him. A year earlier when only fifteen, he had joined the Norwegian *Einvik* at St. Johns, Newfoundland and four days after sailing the ship was torpedoed and he spent the next nine days in a lifeboat before the craft made it to the coast of Iceland. Young as he was he knew what it was all about. He says the Russian convoys were a nightmare and that 'to say that we were scared to death would be putting it mildly'. Yet, like many other brave men from many nations, that fear did not stop him going.[3] George Hurley and George Evans both survived the run, but many others did not.

During the war a total of forty convoys sailed north to Russia and over 800 merchant ships took part. The cargoes carried by those that arrived safely, cargoes that included planes, tanks, and munitions, played a

---

2. George Hurley, letter dated March 2000 and copy of his 'Saga of the Murmansk Run (1943)'.
3. George Evans, as quoted in an article in *Northern Light*, No. 60 (March 2000).

significant part in Russia's war although that fact was never properly acknowledged by the Eastern ally. Of the merchant ships that took part, eighty-seven were lost, fifty-eight of them whilst on the outward voyage and the rest on the way back, except for five lost to air attacks in Russian ports. Of the total lost, twenty-one were Liberties including the *J.L.M. Curry*, which sank after suffering a structural failure as we saw in an earlier chapter.

An interesting feature of the Murmansk convoys was that most of the ships used on the run were comparatively modern. Due to the prevailing weather and sea conditions in the Arctic, this may not have resulted in the average speed of the Murmansk convoys being all that much higher than that of convoys across the North Atlantic, but it did mean that older coal-burning vessels were largely kept away from the run. Coal-burning ships had a nasty habit of belching out black smoke especially during the necessary and regular process known as 'cleaning the tubes'. This was a dead giveaway to any lurking submarine and the cause of many frantic 'cease making smoke' signals from commodore ships to members of their flocks on the North Atlantic run. Another fact of interest is that even after engineers and scientists concluded that cold conditions were a contributory factor to structural failures in welded ships, Liberty ships were kept on the run; they had to be, for they formed the bulk of the ships available. Liberty ships predominated in the make-up of more than a few of the convoys.

The first American freighter to make the run, as part of Convoy PQ-8 in early January 1942, was the *Larranga*, while the first Liberty ship was the *Francis Scott Key* (Baltimore, January 1942). She was one of ten American-flagged vessels in the twenty-five ship Convoy PQ-14 which sailed from Iceland on 8 April 1942. Two days later the convoy ran into heavy ice and ships began separating. Six ships including the *Key* carried on independently until, one by one they joined up with the southbound QP-10 with which they then returned to Iceland. On 26 April the *Key* sailed north once more as part of PQ-15, and this time there was another ship with the same silhouette in the convoy, the *Zebulon B. Vance* (Wilmington, February 1942). Both these Liberties survived the run (and the rest of the war). The other merchant ships in this convoy also reached Russia safely, though the voyage was not without incident. On 2 May the Norwegian destroyer *St. Albans* (ex-USS *Thomas* and transferred from the Royal Navy to the Royal Norwegian Navy) and the minesweeper HMS *Seagull*, of the convoy escort, picked up an Asdic contact and made a depth-charge attack. The submarine was in fact the Polish *Jastrzab* (ex-USS *S-25*), and, damaged by the depth-charges, she surfaced between the two escort ships. They raked her with machine-gun fire before the mistake was discovered, but five of the submarine's crew had been killed and six wounded including her captain and his British liaison officer. The survivors were rescued and the damaged submarine then sunk by gunfire from *Seagull.* At the subsequent inquiry all three commanding officers were exonerated from any blame, *Jastrzab* being well outside her patrol area because bad weather had prevented any position-finding sights from being made for the previous five days.

Having begun mainly with British ships, by early 1943 American merchant ships predominated in the Russian convoys. The reasons behind this change was that the US Merchant Marine was growing apace, and that most of the cargoes carried to Russia originated in the United States. It would have been a waste of scarce shipping resources to send empty British ships across the Atlantic when American ships were already available there. (Britain's own direct contribution of aid to Russia was not insignificant. For instance, of the 12,700 Allied tanks shipped to Russia, nearly 3900 came from Britain and a further 1300 from Canada, the balance coming from America.[4]) The summer of 1942 was a crucial period for the Russians. A German army, held up during the previous winter before the gates of Moscow, was expected to renew its attempt to take the city; another German army, pushing south, had captured Sevastopol. The Russians were being hard pressed everywhere and they needed all the supplies they could get. It was against this background that the Allied convoy designated PQ-17 set sail north-eastward in late June 1942. For the Allies it was to prove the most disastrous of all the Russian convoys, and for the Germans it was their most famous victory in the Arctic seas.

Convoy PQ-17 sailed from Iceland on 27 June 1942 and consisted of thirty-six merchantman, twenty of them American, the rest being British, Russian, Dutch and Panamanian. Seven of the American ships were Liberties, all on their maiden voyages. Five had been launched at Baltimore during the previous March and April. They were *Samuel Chase, Benjamin Harrison, Christopher Newport, John Witherspoon* and *Richard Bland.* The other two were *Daniel Morgan* and *William Hooper,* both built at Wilmington and launched in March. *Richard Bland* ran aground off Iceland and was left behind, so leaving six Liberties to take part in the convoy.

The convoy's close escort comprised three minesweepers and four anti-submarine trawlers. One of the British merchantmen, the *Empire Tide,* was a CAM ship carrying a single Hurricane fighter plane which could be catapulted off. Two former British merchantmen, the *Palomares* and *Pozarica,* now converted into anti-aircraft cruisers, and three rescue ships were also included in the formation. Because Liberty ships were considered comparatively well-armed they were strategically deployed in the most vulnerable positions in the convoy. On 30 June the ocean escort of destroyers and corvettes, led by Commander J.E. Broome aboard HMS

---

4. Figures interpolated from Richard Woodman, *Arctic Convoys* (London 1984).

Keppel joined the formation. Distant cover was provided by an Anglo-American cruiser squadron under Rear-Admiral Louis Hamilton, so it seemed that PQ-17 was unusually well protected, especially as the British Home Fleet under Admiral Sir John Tovey was also at sea. But there was a special reason for all this naval activity. The Admiralty in London believed that the German battleship *Tirpitz* together with major support ships had sailed from her Norwegian lair with the intention of attacking PQ-17 and the returning southbound QP-13 convoy which was also at sea. In point of fact, until she was sunk in November 1944 by British Lancasters fitted with specially designed 12,000lb bombs, the very existence of the *Tirpitz,* whether at sea or not, was to colour British Admiralty strategy and hold down large elements of the British Home Fleet which could have been used elsewhere.

PQ-17 encountered heavy loose ice in the Denmark Strait, and the American freighter *Exford* was damaged enough to have to turn back. On 1 July the first sighting of U-boats was made but they were driven off by the escorts. By 3 July, after several other alarms, the convoy had reached the Barents Sea, sailing a course that would take it about 200 miles north of Bear Island. Early the following morning the convoy lost its first ship, and it was a Liberty, not a good beginning for a day which happened to be American Independence Day. A torpedo from a Heinkel bomber narrowly missed the Liberty *Samuel Chase* before striking the *Christopher Newport*'s starboard side amidships, exploding in the engine room and killing three of the men on watch there. The gunners on board the stricken ship had sighted the low-flying aircraft but had been unable to fire at it because another ship was in the way. The explosion stopped the engines and jammed the steering gear, the ship narrowly missing other vessels in the adjacent column as she careered to port before coming to a stop. Captain Charles Nash ordered abandon ship and the forty-seven survivors got away in the two port lifeboats, and within fifteen minutes were taken aboard the rescue ship *Zamalak*. The master of that rescue ship, Captain Owen Morris, made a note in his logbook regarding the surprising cheerfulness of the Liberty's mainly black crew, although he was not too happy that more than a few of them brought baggage with them. He reported that he 'discouraged this vigorously', which was just as well, for the *Zamalak* was to become a very crowded ship before the voyage was over. As the *Christopher Newport* was still afloat, consideration was given to taking her in tow, but Commander Broome aboard HMS *Keppel* decided this would have placed the towing vessel in extreme jeopardy. He ordered a British submarine in the vicinity to sink the *Newport* but the attempt failed, and depth-charges lobbed at the ship by HMS *Dianella* similarly failed to sink her. A few hours later she was finished off by *U-457*, Lieutenant Commander Brandenburg. So now there were five Liberties left.

As the convoy continued its way eastward other U-boats closed in, but the next kills went to torpedoes from attacking aircraft. The Liberty *William Hooper* and the British freighter *Naverino* were struck at about the same time. Aboard the Liberty, the resulting explosion blew parts of the engine up through the ship's funnel and the engine-room skylight, and the ship caught fire as she began to settle. Without waiting for any order from Captain Edward Graves or for the ship to lose way, some of the crew began to abandon ship, even as the Armed Guard manning the main gun managed to score a hit on one of the attacking planes. Seven men, including four Armed Guardsmen, jumped overboard without orders, and Captain Graves had personally to stop lifeboats being lowered before the ship had stopped. Three men had been killed in the explosion, but all the others were picked up by *Zamalak* and its sister rescue ship, *Rathlin.* Although she had settled well down in the water, *William Hooper* did not sink despite some extra 'help' from two of the escort ships, which did however, manage to finish off the *Naverino.* Again it was a submarine, this time the *U-334,* Lieutenant Commander Siemon, that administered the *coup de grace* to a Liberty.

It was about this time that Admiral Sir Dudley Pound, Britain's First Sea Lord, made a decision that was to turn out to be a major naval blunder, one which resulted in two-thirds of the ships of PQ-17 ending up at the bottom of the Barents Sea, including two of the remaining four Liberties. The Admiralty knew that the *Tirpitz* had left her base at Trondheim, but on 4 July the British had no idea exactly where she was. Bletchley Park, the British cryptographic centre, had only 'negative' information; the Admiral was told that had the *Tirpitz* been at sea, Bletchley would have intercepted certain signal traffic which would have confirmed the fact. Unfortunately Pound chose to ignore that advice, relying instead on information he had received from Captain Henry Denham, the British Naval Attaché in Stockholm, that German surface task forces were about to sail to strike at the convoy. Denham (who had in the previous year supplied the intelligence that was eventually to lead to the destruction of the *Bismarck*) had obtained this information from Swedish sources, and it was excellent as far as it went. However, no one could have suspected that after the German task force had sailed Hitler would impose such restrictions on it that the ships very soon returned to base. The upshot was that Admiral Pound ordered Hamilton's cruiser squadron to withdraw westward at speed, and for the ships of PQ-17 to disperse and proceed to the nearest Russian haven. Soon after those first signals were sent, Commander Broome on *Keppel* received a second signal, directing the convoy to scatter, a signal he took to indicate that an attack from the *Tirpitz* was imminent. In fact, the brief foray to sea of *Tirpitz* and her consorts took place *after* PQ-17 had scattered. By that time U-boats and German aircraft were taking such a toll on the convoy that the intervention of surface craft was not required anyway.

The convoy began to scatter as Commander Broome relayed the Admiralty order to his flock, but the scattering was not comprehensive. This was not the wide North Atlantic ocean, but instead the ice-bound Barents Sea, with the Russian coast not far away to the south and the islands of Novaya Zemlya ahead. So, as all the ships continued to head in the general direction of Archangel or other havens, some tended to stick together in small groups.

The following day, the 5th, was the day that the mayhem really began as ship after ship succumbed to attacks. Four American vessels were gathered around the protection offered by HMS *Palomares,* one of the anti-aircraft ships. Three of them were the Liberties *Daniel Morgan, John Witherspoon,* and *Benjamin Harrison,* the fourth being the freighter *Fairfield City.* That protection did not last long for the *Palomares* had her own orders to make for the nearest Russian port and she soon detached herself. German bombers spotted the group and roared in, first attacking and sinking the *Fairfield City* and then setting about the *Daniel Morgan.* For over an hour that ship's Armed Guard unit under Lieutenant Morton Wolfson fought off the bombers, later reporting that they had shot down two planes and damaged another. The bombers dropped over eighty bombs at the zigzagging Liberty, thirty of which were near misses. It was one of these near misses that split open the ship's side in the vicinity of Nos. 4 and 5 holds, and the ship listed over. Some of the crew panicked and in trying to launch a lifeboat prematurely, capsized it killing two men. As Captain George Sullivan tried to avoid the planes, the *U-88,* Lieutenant Commander Heino Bohmann, put a torpedo into the ship's port side. Sullivan then ordered abandon ship and as the survivors pulled away in the three remaining lifeboats, Bohmann finished the job with a second torpedo. A few hours later the survivors were picked up by the Russian tanker *Donbass,* and although Lieutenant Wolfson and his Armed Guardsman were by that time almost dead on their feet, they volunteered to man the Russian ship's guns. In fighting off a later air attack they damaged a German bomber and when the tanker later arrived safely in port, the American gunners received plaudits from the officials there, a rather unusual event.

The mayhem continued amongst the largely dispersed ships, but it was not until the 7 July when another Liberty met its end. The *John Witherspoon,* Captain John Clark, had previously been successful in avoiding several air attacks, but coming out of a fog bank on that day her luck ran out. Lookouts reported a submarine on a parallel course and the ship opened fire, forcing the submarine to dive. But a little later, two out of a fan of four torpedoes fired at the ship from *U-255,* Lieutenant Commander Reche, struck amidships, and Captain Clark ordered abandon ship. One man lost his life in this operation. As the boats pulled away,

Reche fired another torpedo and the ship broke in two and sank. Two days later the men in one of the lifeboats were rescued by the Panamanian freighter *El Capitan* which was then itself sunk by German bombers, all on board then being rescued by the trawler HMS *Lord Austin*. On that same day the corvette HMS *La Malouine* rescued the remaining *Witherspoon* survivors.

Of the merchant ships still afloat, two were Liberties, the *Benjamin Harrison* and the *Samuel Chase*. Both were among the few ships that made for and safely reached an anchorage in the narrow Matochkin Strait between the two main islands of Novaya Zemlya. *Samuel Chase* had 'enjoyed' an adventure getting there. On 5 July the ship's lookouts sighted a surfaced U-boat astern, and in contravention of the US Maritime Commission's orders to masters and the US Navy's orders to the Armed Guard, that no American ship was to be allowed to fall into the hands of the enemy, the ship was stopped and all hands took to the boats. Fortunately no attack was forthcoming – which may indicate that the sighting of the submarine had been false – and after two hours the crew reboarded, raised steam, and made east. According to F. Gleichief's book about the Armed Guard, Lieutenant John Sexton of that ship later made a report that was not only disparaging about the British Navy, but also highly critical of the guns under his own charge.[5] The latter criticism seems likely to have been designed to excuse the uncalled-for abandonment.

On 7 July the merchant ships in the Matochkin Strait left the anchorage with an escort of British warships to make the south-westward run to Archangel. They soon ran into fog, and the master of the *Benjamin Harrison* turned his ship about and went back. In the White Sea on the 11th, the other ships came under air attack and some near misses apparently brought the *Samuel Chase* to a standstill, although the standard book on American ship casualties does not list the ship as having suffered any damage.[6] That notwithstanding, she was taken in tow by the minesweeper HMS *Halcyon,* and reached Archangel later that day. Together with a few more stragglers, *Benjamin Harrison* eventually reached Archangel on 24 July. She was not to survive the war, being sunk on 16 March 1943. The *Samuel Chase* did survive the war but her later service was not without incident. In May 1944 she suffered some small-scale structural cracking, and again in both March and April of 1945. Then on 4 June 1945 she suffered a Class 1 failure when part of her side plating cracked.[7] She was scrapped at Philadelphia in 1967.

No less than twenty-four of the merchant ships of PQ-17 had been sent to the bottom, eight by U-boats, eight by aircraft, and the others by

---

5. F. Gleichief, *Unsung Heroes* (Annapolis 1990).
6. Robert Browning, *US Merchant Vessel War Casualties* (Annapolis 1996).
7. US Navy Final Report on Structural Failures, July 1946.

a combination of both. German losses amounted to about half-a-dozen aircraft. Along with the ships, a quarter of a million tons of urgently needed supplies had gone down. The disaster led to strains between the Allies. The Russians were not exactly pleased to lose all those supplies and what they had to say about the Royal Navy was extremely abusive. The Americans were also highly critical.

But perhaps the worst effect of the PQ-17 disaster was the immediate deterioration it brought in the relations between merchant seamen and their Royal Navy protectors. The merchant mariners involved were not told why they had been ordered to flee the comparative safety of the convoy formation, and even had they been, they probably would not have appreciated the reasons for the decision. Merchant seaman, of whatever nation, have always been somewhat antagonistic towards their naval counterparts. In Britain the origins of the antagonism probably lay in the actions of the Press Gang in the Age of Sail, for trained seamen were always the Press's favourite prey. More generally and latterly, the antagonism stemmed from the comparatively free and easy life and attitudes aboard merchantmen, one of the most obvious signs of which was the lack of uniforms. Merchant seamen were independent of mind and character and inclined to be a bit 'bolshie'. The rules and regulations within national navies were not for them, and indeed many men dead set on a life at sea deliberately chose the merchant side to get away from what they considered the bullshit of the other side, a side moreover which anyway tended to look down rather disparagingly on the other. But all that notwithstanding, from the early part of the Second World War and especially after the gallant sacrifice made in November 1940 by HMS *Jervis Bay* and its crew in trying to save the ships of Convoy HX-84, merchant seamen had slowly developed a trust for their naval protectors; and that despite the many criticisms emanating from escort commanders over such matters as standards of signalling and station-keeping in convoy. But that trust was fragile, and could be taken back much more quickly than the time it had taken to build it up. PQ-17 had just that effect.

The loss of life on PQ-17 – a total of 153 merchant seamen were killed – seems small in the context of total war, but it did not seem small to surviving merchant seamen many of whom owed their lives only to the valiant efforts of the rescue ships, themselves largely manned by merchant seamen. Whatever their nationality, the seamen who got through either on their own ships or aboard rescue craft, felt themselves to have been let down by the Royal Navy, which had not suffered a single casualty during the voyage. And when news of the disaster got around, which it did very quickly indeed, it badly effected the morale of merchant seamen everywhere. When the survivors from the British ships sunk in PQ-17 eventually arrived in Glasgow, they were assembled in that city's St. Andrew's Hall and addressed by the Parliamentary Secretary to the

Ministry of War Transport, Labour Member of Parliament Philip Noel-Baker. Sent north by the Government to bolster morale, he was the wrong man for the job. The politician told the men that he knew what the convoy had cost. Then he added that 'whatever the cost, it was worth it'. He was howled down, and probably spent the remainder of his ministerial career wondering why. The sort of unfeeling foolishness indicated by that remark, certainly did nothing to assuage the fall in morale.

It was now the season of continuous daylight in the Arctic and that fact on top of what had happened to PQ-17 caused the Admiralty to suspend the sailing of the next convoy until September. PQ-18, which sailed from Loch Ewe on 2 September, consisted of forty merchant ships, of which twenty-one were American, ten British and the remainder either Panamanian or Russian. Of the American contingent, eight were Liberty ships, amongst them two of particular interest. The *Patrick Henry*, the first of all the Liberty ships, was there, and so was the *St. Olaf*. Launched at Baltimore in May 1942, *St. Olaf* had originally been earmarked for conversion into an hospital ship for the US Navy, hence its special name. That conversion did not to take place until November 1943 and then for the US Army and not the Navy, but in the meantime she was used as a freighter.

This time, not only was the convoy heavily protected, the escorts stayed with it all the way. Nevertheless, thirteen ships were lost, among them two Liberties. The first ship to be sunk was the Russian *Stalingrad* on 13 September, its loss leaving the door open for giving that name to one of the Liberties later lend-leased to Russia. She was sunk by one of two torpedoes from *U-589*, Lieutenant Commander Horrer. The Liberty *Oliver Ellsworth* (Baltimore, June 1942), was in position immediately astern of the *Stalingrad*, and as Captain Otto Buford ordered the helm hard over to avoid hitting the sinking Russian, the second torpedo struck the Liberty between holds 4 and 5. The ship's engines were stopped, but the ship still had plenty of way on it as the four lifeboats were launched and in consequence the two starboard boats were swamped. Then one of the port boats struck a raft and sank, so there were men in the water everywhere. But except for one Armed Guardsman, all were picked up by the rescue ship *Copeland* and the trawler HMS *St. Kenan*. An hour later the trawler finished off the *Ellsworth* with gunfire. The convoy suffered massive air attacks later that day, which led to the loss of the Liberty *John Penn* (Wilmington, June 1942) but not before the planes had achieved several other successes. Two British ships were sunk, one of them the munitions-carrying ship *Empire Stevenson* which blew up after being enveloped in a huge pillar of smoke and flame, the explosion leaving only an oil-slick on the water. The American freighter *Wacosta*, positioned just astern of the British ship, took the full blast from the explosion which pushed her main engine from its seatings and ruptured valves and pipe-lines. As *Wacosta* lay helpless in the water, she was struck by an aerial torpedo and sank, bow first. Miraculously everyone on board that ship was saved.

In the space of thirteen minutes, eight Allied vessels had either gone down due to direct enemy action, or were so crippled that they had to be sunk by escorts. One of the latter was the *John Penn,* which like the *Ellsworth* was on her maiden voyage. An aerial torpedo struck her bow, and a second one hit in the way of the engine-room, killing those on duty there. As the ship began to settle there was some confusion as the survivors abandoned ship, and initially twelve men, amongst them some wounded, were left aboard until one of the boats went back for them. The survivors were picked up by British warships which then sank the *Penn* with gunfire. Perhaps here is a good place to note that very often when only a handful of men lost their lives on any particular ship, they were the engineers on watch at the time. Engine-room staff were amongst the bravest of merchant seamen, for should a torpedo strike anywhere near the engine spaces, there was little chance for the men on duty to escape; in order to do so they had to negotiate many feet of metal walkways and ladders, and often there was no time for that even in cases where those structures had not been destroyed in the blast.

On the following day there was almost a re-run of the *Empire Stevenson/Wacosta* affair when the American freighter *Mary Luckenbach* was attacked by German torpedo-bombers. The ship blew up, fire and debris rising a thousand feet into the air. Several differing stories exist about the circumstances of that attack. One version has it that one of the attacking planes dropped its entire load of torpedoes on to the ship's foredeck as if they were bombs. Another story is that a German plane actually crashed on to the foredeck. Chief Radio Operator Horace Bell aboard the rescue ship *Copeland* had yet another version. He said that the plane dropped its torpedoes when about 300 yards from the ship and then raked the ship fore and aft with its guns, and when the *Mary Luckenbach* blew up, she took the aircraft with it. As with the *Empire Stevenson* there were no survivors from the ship. Only a cable's length away from that explosion, the Liberty *Nathaniel Greene* was showered with wreckage, the blast injuring eleven on board and damaging bulkheads. Lieutenant Billings of the ship's Armed Guard said in his report, 'It is impossible to put into words the force of the explosion or the amount of debris to hit the ship'. Captain George Vickers apparently thought his ship had been torpedoed and abandon ship stations were ordered but very soon cancelled when the damage was found not to be critical. Five of the most injured men were taken off by the destroyer HMS *Onslaught* which had a doctor on board, and the *Greene* eventually reached port safely. Lieutenant Billing's gunners were credited with shooting down no less than five of the attacking aircraft.

On 17 and 18 September, four Russian destroyers joined the convoy, raising the total number of escort ships to nearly forty. Nevertheless, air attacks continued, and the losses among the merchant ships would almost certainly have been much higher than thirteen had not many of the German torpedoes proved to be duds. The British *Empire Tristram* was struck by one of those and her master ordered abandon ship and dumped his confidential books before he realised his ship was intact. Wild gunnery from some merchant ships also wreaked some havoc. A gunner aboard the *Patrick Henry* was wounded, and some of the aircraft carried on its deck damaged, when she was struck by 'friendly fire' from another, unnamed, merchantman. So violent and persistent were the air attacks, that the captain of the Liberty ship *William Moutrie* (Wilmington, June 1942) which was carrying 4000 tons of explosives, requested the convoy commodore for a safer station. Commodore E.K. Boddam-Whetham signalled *Moutrie* to exchange positions with the British ship *Goolistan* which was also carrying explosives, adding as a postscript to his message that the only difference he could see between 4000 tons of TNT and 2000 tons, was a fractional part of a second should she be hit. There was not much humour in the Murmansk convoys and what there was, tended to be of the rough variety.

The Germans lost a total of forty-four aircraft and the submarine *U-589* in battles against the convoy. That, together with the fact that a much higher proportion of Allied merchant ships reached the destination than in PQ-17, and that four Russian warships and some Russian shore-based planes had been involved in the escort operations, caused the Russians to claim a great victory for themselves. However, it is to the Royal Navy that most of the credit for the diminished loss ratio must go, and after PQ-18, merchant sailors' trust in the Navy began slowly to rise again.

The Western Allies now called a temporary halt to the Russian convoys, much against the wishes of the Russians. The Allied decision was partly caused by the combined loss of thirty-five merchant ships from that convoy and its predecessor, but mainly because Operation 'Torch', the landings in North Africa, were imminent. Escort ships were needed to cover the landings and there were not enough available to do that and also to provide the massive naval cover that was given to PQ-18. In fact that convoy was to be the last to sail under the PQ prefix. The next Allied convoy to sail north was JW-51A in December, the convoy to which the Liberty *J.L.M. Curry* was attached as already related in Chapter 7.

Meanwhile, as a sop to Russian feelings, a series of unescorted individual ship sailings were sent north in what was called Operation 'FB'. One British seaman who took part in the operation thought that 'FB' must have stood for 'Foolish Bastards'. Over the five days between 29 October and 2 November, a series of ten ships sailed north at intervals, five British, four Americans and a Russian. Another three ships, two British and the American Liberty *John H.B. Latrobe* were recalled soon after sailing because of what was happening to the ships ahead of them. (The later adventures of the *Latrobe* were related in Chapter 7.) All four of the American ships were Liberties, the *William Clark* (Portland, Oregon, February 1942), *Richard H. Alvey* and *John Walker* (both Baltimore, July 1942) and *Hugh Williamson* (Wilmington, July 1942). The last three ships and two of the British ones arrived safely in Russia. But three British ships, the Russian, and the *William Clark* did not make it. The only naval protection afforded these ships was a sparse line of armed trawlers along the route and even sparser submarine patrols.

Captain Walter Elian aboard the *William Clark* had been informed to expect contact with one of the trawlers every five hours, but in fact his lookouts spotted nary a one. On 4 November a torpedo from *U-354*, Lieutenant Commander Herbschleb, struck the ship amidships near the engine-room, which immediately began to flood. Captain Elian ordered abandon ship, and sixty-six men got away in three lifeboats, the motor-boat towing the other two. Later, as the sea got up, the towing lines had to be cast off and the boats then lost contact. After three terrible days of bad weather and numbing cold, twenty-six men in one boat were rescued by the trawler HMS *St. Elston*, and fifteen more from a second boat were picked up by HMS *Cape Palliser*; that second boat also had two dead and frozen bodies on board. No. 1 boat carrying Captain Elian and twenty-two men was never seen again.

The horror of that almost pales into insignificance compared with the experiences of the crew of the British ship *Chumleigh*, which also attempted the 'FB' run. In trying to evade German bombers, Captain Williams took his ship too far north and it ended up on a reef off Spitzbergen. The crew took to two boats just before the stranded ship was sighted and bombed by German aircraft. In bitterly cold weather the two boats made eastwards, making for the settlement of Barentsburg. Some time later the boats became separated, one never to be seen again. After a week the other boat under Captain Williams and with twenty-seven others on board, was driven ashore in a storm. The survivors found an abandoned sealer's hut and set up residence in it. Over the next four days a third of the men died from gangrene caused by frostbite, and more were to die from cold and hunger over the weeks that followed. Captain Williams and nine remaining survivors were found on 3 January 1943 by a party of Norwegian soldiers out of Barentsburg. Yet another man was to die before the party eventually got home to Britain six months later. Volunteers had been called for to man the British ships of Operation 'FB', and British shipowner Jack Billmier offered a bonus to every man that did. The bonus was a substantial one for the times, but it is doubtful that Captain Williams and his men thought the earning of it had been worthwhile.

There was a heavy loss of life when the *Penelope Barker* (Wilmington, December 1942) met her end as part of JW-56A on 24 January 1944. Two torpedoes from *U-278*, Lieutenant Commander Franze, struck the ship, Franze having sighted the Liberty coming out of a snow squall. One hit aft, blowing off the No. 5 hatch covers and beams and killing the Armed Guards stationed at the machine guns there. The other hit under the bridge, toppling the funnel and filling the engine-room with a mass of hissing, scalding steam. The ship, which was carrying 8000 tons of steel, planes and tanks, sank stern first in under ten minutes. Fifteen men died in the explosions but the remainder got off in two lifeboats or by jumping into the icy waters and then being hauled into the boats. The survivors were soon picked up by the destroyer HMS *Savage*.

The *Andrew G. Curtin* (Baltimore, February 1943) was another ship lost from that convoy, and the details of her end smacked of being a torpedo-assisted structural failure. On 26 January a torpedo from *U-716*, Lieutenant Commander Dunkelburg, slammed into the starboard side of the ship between Holds 2 and 3. The ship began to settle by the head and list to starboard as the duty men in the engine-room were ordered by Captain Jacob Jacobson to shut down the engines. A crack extending right across the deck developed forward of No. 3 hatch, and as the bow settled the crack widened until the hull had hogged amidships to an angle of about 25°. Abaft the crack the crew and Armed Guard abandoned ship, but three men were lost in the process. One book about the Arctic convoys records there were no survivors from this ship. In fact, apart from the three mentioned above, all other members of her crew of seventy-one were picked up within the hour by the destroyer HMS *Inconstant* and later landed at Murmansk. From his lifeboat Captain Jacobson observed his ship breaking in two before she sank.

When Convoy JW-58 sailed from Loch Ewe on 27 March 1944, it was unusual in several respects. It was large, consisting of no less than forty-eight merchantmen, thirty-nine of them American, nine British, and one Norwegian. Every one of the American ships was a Liberty, and five of the British ships were Forts. The convoy was one of the best protected ever to sail north. The main ocean escort comprised the cruiser HMS *Diadem* and two escort carriers, together with the cruiser USS *Milwaukee*. The convoy's close screen consisted of no less than twelve British destroyers, with two support groups close by made up of four more destroyers and five sloops. The aircraft-carriers HMS *Victorious* and *Furious* accompanied by three further escort carriers provided fighter cover, that task force being led by the battleship HMS *Anson*. The battleship HMS *Duke of York* with cruisers and destroyers in support, was also at sea.

The naval protection afforded the merchant ships of JW-58 was almost in the ratio of one to one, and although the *Tirpitz* threat still existed, an additional possible reason for this unique situation was the presence of the *Milwaukee*. Ever since Italy had changed sides in September 1943, Stalin had been agitating for major units of the Italian fleet to be transferred to the Russian navy in reparation for the actions of the Italian soldiers who had fought alongside German troops on Soviet territory. Agreement was finally reached to transfer the *Milwaukee* instead, and politics demanded that this ship must get through. She did, and on arrival became the *Murmansk*. Two months later, and as part of the same deal, the battleship HMS *Royal Sovereign* also joined the Russian fleet, becoming the *Archangelsk*.

Despite heavy air attacks against the convoy, every ship in it arrived safely apart from one straggler, the *Gilbert Stuart* (Portland, Oregon, April 1943) which had turned back to Iceland. However, one of the JW-58 Liberties was to be lost on its return voyage to Britain. The ship was the *William S. Thayer* (Baltimore, August 1943). Commanded by Captain Daniel A. Sperbeck, she had a crew of forty and an Armed Guard unit of twenty-eight men. She was carrying 930 tons of sand ballast and a contingent of 165 Russian navy personnel, who were proceeding to Britain to join the crew of HMS *Royal Sovereign* mentioned above. Just north of Bear Island on 30 April, the *Thayer* was struck by two torpedoes from *U-711*, Lieutenant Commander Lange. One of the torpedoes struck forward and the other aft, causing the ship to break into three. The bow section sank within seconds and the midships section within two minutes. There was no time to launch lifeboats, but six small rafts floated free. Most of the Russians were plucked from the after section by the destroyer HMS *Whitehall.* Other survivors were picked up by the Liberty *Robert Eden* (Baltimore, July 1943). Thirty members of the crew and Armed Guard and twenty Russian seamen died as a result of the attack. The *Thayer*'s stern section was subsequently sunk by escort ships.

Only about a dozen British-flagged Liberties ever took part in the Murmansk convoys, and only one of those was lost. The thirty ships making up the return convoy RA-69 sailed from Murmansk during the night of 26/27 September 1944, and the *Samsuva* (Portland, Maine, July 1944) and the American Liberty *Edward H. Crockett* (from the same yard, but January 1944), were parts of it. Only two days out from Murmansk both were hit, one immediately after the other, by torpedoes from *U-310*, Lieutenant Ley. Three members of the engine-room staff on *Samsuva* were assumed to have died in the explosion, and one engineer aboard the *Crockett,* but the remaining members of both crews were picked up by that indomitable and ubiquitous pair of rescue ships, *Zamalak* and *Rathlin.* In his official report, Captain C.H. Churchill of the *Samsuva* said that the explosion caused by the torpedo which had struck near the engine-room on the starboard side and torn a hole in the side, had also opened up an 18in wide split on the port side, the crack stretching from the main deck to below the water-line. He added, 'both ends of the ship were working as if they were hinged together amidships'. Before he left the ship he 'looked into the engine-room for the missing men but all four entrances were blocked with debris, and it looked a mass of twisted steel with all ladders and platforms destroyed'. The explosion had burst the boilers, 'and dense smoke and fumes made it difficult to see. I gave up all hope of finding the missing men'. Both the *Crockett* and the *Samsuva* were finished off by gunfire from escort ships. Captain Churchill reported that his ship 'had taken a lot of sinking'.[8]

There were more Liberty losses on the Murmansk run during the final year of the war. The *Horace Gray* (Baltimore, February 1943) was sailing in convoy between the North Russian ports of Molotovsk and Murmansk on 14 February when the Norwegian tanker *Nofjell* ahead of her in the column was struck by a torpedo from *U-711*, Lieutenant Commander Lange. Within minutes a second torpedo from the same submarine struck the Liberty, blasting a great hole first in the port side and then a smaller one to starboard. The ship settled by the stern but Captain Charles Fox Brown waited until the sea reached after deck level before ordering abandon ship. All the crew got off in four lifeboats, and two boatloads were soon picked up by a Russian submarine chaser. An hour later, with his ship still afloat, Captain Brown and the men from the other boats reboarded the ship and managed to raise steam. A small Russian tug appeared and passed a tow-line, but as the ship neared Tyuva Bay in the Kola Inlet on the following day, a large crack began to propagate down the starboard side. Captain Brown beached the ship which was later declared a constructive total loss.

That is the story as based on official American files, but British records provide a few additional details. In this context it should be remembered that as the prime responsibility for the protection of ships on the Murmansk run fell to the British, it was British naval officers based in Russia who initially recorded crew reports from any ships lost or damaged. Lieutenant F. Holder RNR (the RNR designation indicates that he had previously been a serving Merchant Navy officer) was a reporting officer in Murmansk at this time, and it was he who took down the reports of some of the *Horace Gray* survivors. Holder stated that the ship's Chief Officer thought the ship should never have been abandoned in the first place, and that Captain Brown 'had given the order to abandon ship because of engine trouble but afterwards when *Horace Gray* was boarded again by half the crew, she was beached with her engines'. The report also stated that before the crew members reboarded, sailors from a Russian escort ship had boarded the *Gray*. The Chief Officer had not been amongst those who reboarded, and Lieutenant Holder noted that 'there appeared to be much dissatisfaction amongst the crew in the two lifeboats who were taken by the Russian

---

8. ADM199/2149, PRO, Kew.

submarine-chaser to Murmansk as the Chief Officer stated that the other half of the crew who reboarded had pilfered their personal belongings and ship's equipment'. Holder then made a note that a question mark remained whether the master had done 'all in his power' to save his ship. On the cover of that particular report there is a notation to the effect that a copy had been sent to COMNAVEU, the Anglo-American joint Naval Bureau in London 'for information and such action as is considered necessary'.[9] We shall see in a later chapter that *Gray*'s Chief Officer may have been right to conclude that the ship had been abandoned too precipitously.

On the same day as the *Gray* incident the *Thomas Scott* (New Orleans, October 1942) commanded by Captain Jack Teston, left her anchorage in the Kola Inlet to take up position in the southbound convoy RA-64. The ship entered the sights of Lieutenant Commander Westphalen on *U-968* at 1150 hours, only a little over an hour after a torpedo from Westphalen's boat had blown the stern off the sloop HMS *Lark,* causing her to be beached. Somehow Westphalen had avoided detection, and now he fired again, hitting *Scott* starboard side amidships, causing her to career out of control and take a list to starboard. The explosion had blown the ship almost in two, the parts being held together only by the deck plating. As the stricken ship came upright again, from a distance it seemed that there was not much wrong with her, and this caused Rear-Admiral Roderick McGrigor, who was flying his flag on the escort carrier HMS *Campania,* to criticise Captain Teston unfairly for ordering abandon ship. The crew, together with forty Norwegian refugees on board, were picked up by the escort carrier HMS *Fencer.* The crew members were then transferred to the Russian destroyer *Zhestkij* and the tug *M-12,* those two vessels then making an attempt to save the *Scott* by towing her shorewards stern first. An hour or so later the ship broke completely in two, the after part sinking immediately and the fore part following it shortly afterwards.

The *Henry Bacon* (Wilmington, November 1942) was also in that southbound convoy. Two days after sailing the convoy encountered heavy weather and the *Bacon* straggled from the convoy as did another Liberty, the *Crosby S. Noyes* (Baltimore, July 1943). The *Noyes* was to make it back, but the *Bacon* did not, and in the manner of her passing gained the dubious distinction of being the last ship to be sunk by German aircraft in the war. On the 23rd she was attacked by no less than twenty-three torpedo-bombers which were out looking for the convoy but found only her. It was later reported that each of the aircraft launched its two torpedoes at the ship, which smacks somewhat of overkill.

---

9. ADM199/524, PRO, Kew.

Whatever the actual number of torpedoes used, Captain Alfred Carini managed to avoid all except one as the Armed Guard put up a barrage of covering fire. The one that struck the ship hit aft, blowing a hole in the hull, damaging the propeller and rudder, and rupturing steam lines. One lifeboat was damaged in the attack and another capsized while being lowered, leaving only two. The ship was carrying several dozen Norwegian refugees, and Captain Carini placed these and some crew members in No. 1 boat. Other members of the crew and Armed Guard got away in the last one. A doughnut raft floated free of the ship and some of the men remaining on the Liberty jumped into the sea to climb aboard it as behind them the ship sank stern first. Because both boats were overcrowded, some crew members transferred to the raft. Before the ship was abandoned a plain-language distress radio message had been sent, and two planes flown off the escort carrier HMS *Nairana* flew along the radio bearing and managed to locate the survivors. Three British warships were soon on the scene to pick them up. Six of the eight *Scott* officers, seven of the twenty-six Armed Guard unit, and nine of the ship's thirty-two crewmen lost their lives in the incident but all of the Norwegian passengers survived. In the true tradition of the sea, some crewmen had voluntarily given up their places in the lifeboats in order that passengers could be disembarked from the sinking vessel.

As with the *Horace Gray* and *Thomas Scott*, attempts were made to save both the Liberties that were torpedoed within a few hours of each other when sailing north-eastward as parts of JW-65 on 20 March 1945. One of these attempts was partially successful but the other met with defeat. The *Horace Bushnell* (Baltimore, October 1943) was the first, a torpedo from *U-995*, Lieutenant Commander Hess, blowing a hole measuring 33ft by 26ft in her hull in way of the engine-room. The explosion, which killed four men, completely destroyed the engines and cracked the deck plating. The ship developed a small list and settled about 6ft by the stern, but then seemed to steady. Captain William Lacey must have been quite a man for there was no panic as he ordered the crew and Armed Guard to stand by to abandon at a moments notice, but in the meantime to take on board a tow-line from the destroyer HMS *Orwell* that had raced up to the rescue. It was hoped that the ship could be towed and beached on the nearby Russian coast, but heavy seas prevented any headway being made. Two hours later the captain of the *Orwell* advised Captain Lacey to abandon and so all hands were taken aboard the destroyer. Soon afterwards the hulk was taken in tow by two Russian tugs and finally beached near Toroborski. The Americans declared the ship a constructive total loss.

Three hours after the *Bushnell* was torpedoed, the *Thomas Donaldson* (Baltimore, February 1944), then within twenty miles of the comparative safety of the Kola Inlet, suffered a hit from *U-968*, Lieutenant

Commander Westphalen, who was going through a busy period. The blast destroyed the engine-room, killing all three men on watch there. Because his ship was carrying munitions, Captain Robert Headden ordered most of his crew and all the Armed Guard to abandon, and they were soon picked up by British warships. Captain Headden and eight of his crew stayed aboard long enough to haul aboard a towrope from the corvette HMS *Honeysuckle* before being taken off by the towing vessel. A little later a Russian tug took over the tow, but the ship sank stern first when within half a mile of the beach. *U-968* was to survive the war.

A Liberty veteran of the run which also survived the war was the *Joshua Thomas* (Baltimore, August 1943), a ship of which it can be said she was something of a Russia specialist. She made her first run north loaded with explosives, guns and aircraft as part of the JW-58/*Milwaukee* convoy mentioned earlier, and a second one a year later in April 1945. A year before that first Murmansk run, the ship's maiden voyage had taken her to the Persian Gulf ports which were Russia's back door. She made a third voyage to North Russia in September 1945, four months after the end of the war in Europe. The *Thomas* now lies some ten fathoms under the sea off South Padre Island, Texas, still doing a valuable job as one of the several ships that form the so-called Texas Artificial Reef.[10]

---

10. J. Barto Arnold, *Texas Liberty Ships* (Austin, Texas 1998).

CHAPTER 12

Liberties and Operation 'Torch'

At talks held in London in July 1942 the two main Western Allies discussed the existing global strategic situation and laid plans for future operations. The Americans seemed set on a landing in North-west Europe, a move that would have been applauded by Stalin who was pressing for much the same thing. The British on the other hand, who were busy reinforcing the 8th Army in North Africa which had recently managed to hold the Germans outside the gates of Alexandria but which had not yet been able to push them back from there, were far more cautious. Churchill and his Chiefs of Staff, no doubt with the military debacle of Singapore's surrender of only five months before in mind, were not willing to risk another such disastrous defeat by making an attack that year on 'Fortress Europe'. The many victories of Japan in the Far East had resulted in the United States allocating more forces to the Pacific area, despite the overall Germany-first policy, and that meant that if such a landing in Europe was to be made that year, the main burden of it would have to be carried by Britain. British unwillingness therefore killed the idea stone dead.

For military reasons Stalin wanted the so-called second front opened in Europe as soon as possible; from his viewpoint this would amount to an attack in the enemy's rear and would relieve some of the pressure on his front. Conversely, President Roosevelt's view that some move against Germany must be made during 1942 was mainly political. From his point of view any delay in a major move against German forces until the following year was unacceptable. No one knew better than he that many of his countrymen had not wanted to engage in a war against Germany in the first place and he understood that if the hearts, souls and energies of his people were to be taken up with that side of the war in the same way that the Japanese had managed by themselves to take them up in the East, then something must be done to catch the public's imagination, and soon. The end result of the talks was a sort of compromise. It was agreed to launch Operation 'Torch', a combined American and British landing in North-west Africa. If successful, and associated with a renewed thrust west by the British forces on the other side of North Africa, this would eventually throw open the Mediterranean to the Allies and re-open the Suez Canal, which would hugely relieve the overall Allied shipping situation by taking thousands of miles off many voyages.

Churchill went himself to Moscow to inform Stalin of the decision to launch 'Torch' instead of an attack on mainland Europe. Stalin was none too pleased, and later that year was even more put out when the decision led to the temporary suspension of the Murmansk voyages as many escort ships were withdrawn from the Arctic to protect the 'Torch' armadas. Gerhard Weinberg has pointed out that, 'having helped the Germans [over Poland] drive the Allies out of the European continent in the first place, he [Stalin] was not in a very good position to complain about their difficulty in returning to it'.[1] But Josef Stalin had a rather short memory over some matters. The decision reached in July 1942 was implemented on 8 November, a fantastic planning and operational achievement in view of the shortness of the intervening time. (It was based on an earlier British plan called 'Gymnast', which somewhat eased the 'Torch' planners' burden.) The logistical problems involved were enormous, and overcoming them provided the best possible training for other landings still to come. The Anglo-American planning staffs from the various departments concerned, met twice daily and, more often than not, worked sixteen-hour shifts. Military commanders had first to decide precisely what was wanted and where, then ships were selected after which they were loaded 'tactically', so that tanks, guns and stores would come out in the correct order on the landing beaches. This is where the officers and men aboard the ships came into their own with their cargo-work knowledge and expertise in ship stability. Tanks and vehicles had to be securely lashed down, and many were loaded with steel lifting slings that were left in place for swiftness of handling at the other end. It probably appalled some ships' officers that all vehicles were loaded with their petrol tanks full, but there was a war on and safety measures dating from more peaceful days had to be ignored.

The American and British landings at various places on both the Atlantic and Mediterranean coasts of North-west Africa on 8 November came as a complete surprise to the Germans and to their Vichy-French partners. German minds had been concentrated on the other side of the continent where, during the last week of October 1942, the British 8th Army under General Montgomery had launched the attack at El Alamein and having broken through, had the Germans fleeing in some disorder by the first days of November. As far as land battles were concerned, November 1942 can be looked upon as one of the critical turning points of the war. The push on from El Alamein combined with the 'Torch' landings on the 8th began the process of destroying Rommel's Afrika Korps.

---

1. Gerhard L. Weinberg, *A World At Arms* (Cambridge 1994).

On the 19th, Soviet armies broke through the German 6th Army at Stalingrad. In between those dates and on the other side of the world, on the 13th it can be said that the tide turned against the Japanese at Guadalcanal.

Operation 'Torch' involved what was up to then the largest armada in history. Large convoys sailed from Britain and others came direct from the States, with Liberty ships playing significant roles in both. During the first phase over 240 merchant ships sailed from Britain escorted by nearly 100 naval ships, whilst from the States 112 merchant ships sailed under the protection of about 75 warships. One wonders whether Stalin, who kicked up a considerable fuss about the concomitant cessation of his Murmansk life-line, would have much cared had he known that the use of that number of merchant ships in Operation 'Torch', for a time seriously impeded the importation of supplies into Britain including food. Even after the first phases of 'Torch' had been successfully implemented, the invading forces needed the services of over 100 merchant ships a month to sustain them at a time when the Allies were not yet dominant on the sea. The initial 'Torch' convoys from Britain included no less than forty-five Liberty ships (all under the American flag because it was to be July 1943 before some began to sail under the Red Ensign), and forty-two Oceans and forty-six Forts. Perhaps no one in those vast convoys would have then had the knowledge to recognise amongst their ranks the 'mother' of all Liberties, Oceans and Forts. For the *Empire Liberty* had not yet been handed over to Greece (as the *Kyklades*), and for 'Torch' she carried military stores with aircraft on deck.[2]

During the six months following the landings, ships from Britain alone transported 63,784 vehicles, 900 tanks, nearly 4000 guns and close to 400 aircraft to North African ports. A quarter of a million tons of cased petrol and thousands of tons of ammunition, bombs and explosives were also carried, often in a potentially lethal mix aboard the same ship. As the Allied troops moved eastward, the merchantmen kept pace with them. There was little sleep for anyone, and one captain of a British ship who sailed to Algiers and back in April 1943, said that for the duration of the voyage he had slept for only three hours a day and even that was split into two halves, and that he never took his clothes off except in Algiers.[3]

On 8 November American forces landed at three places on the Atlantic coast of North Africa near Casablanca, and Anglo-American forces at Oran and Algiers inside the Mediterranean, and then further east at Bougie and Bona. Merchant ships were in the front line throughout. One Liberty, the *Thomas Stone* (Baltimore, May 1942), was damaged by a torpedo from *U-205* on 7 November on its way across the Atlantic in one of the first 'Torch' convoys. The first merchantman to be lost in the

2. Files MT59/585 and MT59/604, PRO, London.
3. Quoted in *Merchantmen at War* (London 1944).

operations was not a Liberty but the British trooper *Cathay,* sunk after air attacks off Bougie on 11 November, fortunately after having already disembarked its troops. Before the end of that first month, twenty-two Allied merchant ships had been lost in 'Torch' actions, and two, including the *Thomas Stone,* damaged.

The first Liberty ship to be sunk in the operations was *Arthur Middleton* (Mobile, Alabama, July 1942). Managed by Lykes Lines and under the command of Captain John Smith, this ship had been part of a convoy from New York to Casablanca. After reaching the North African coast she was detached with ten other ships with orders to proceed to Oran. On New Year's Day 1943 when about three miles off Oran, the ships began forming in line to enter the port. It was then that the *Middleton* was struck near the bow by one, possibly two, torpedoes from *U-73*, Lieutenant Commander Deckert. The ship was carrying 6412 tons of cargo, much of it explosives. The first explosion lifted the bow out of the water and ignited the cargo, and the ship then blew up. Apart from the very sternmost section, the ship disintegrated with debris joining the flames and smoke that shot 1000ft into the air. Of the total of eighty-three men on board, only three survived. They were Armed Guardsmen, and they jumped overboard from the still-floating after section to be picked up by the destroyer HMS *Boreas,* no doubt thinking with good reason, that they were the luckiest men alive.

Six days later, another Liberty came under attack, and the mantle of being the luckiest men on the face of the earth must have passed to the ninety-seven crew and passengers aboard it. The ship was the *William Wirt* (Baltimore, July 1942), commanded by Captain Cameron Simmons. Her cargo consisted of the lethal mix of 16,000 cased drums of high octane gasoline and cases of TNT. On 7 January the convoy of which she was part was off the port of Bougie when it was attacked by German torpedo and dive-bombers. The Armed Guard unit on board *Wirt* opened fire and later claimed to have shot down four planes. As one of the planes flew towards the ships port side, machine gun fire from the ship struck its wing, and its engine burst into flames. The plane banked and dropped its bombs, one of them striking the ship's side at No. 1 hold, about 4ft above the waterline. The bomb penetrated the ship, but, ending up amidst cases of gasoline and under cases of TNT in the 'tween-decks, it failed to explode. Water flooded into the hold but the ship managed to reach the port of Phillipsville two days later where her cargo, together with the unexploded bomb, was discharged. (One cannot help wondering whether some Axis prisoners-of-war might have been persuaded in some way to act as stevedores.) After repairs, the ship sailed on the return voyage and off Gibraltar on 7 February suffered more damage from bombing. This ship with a charmed life survived the war to be scrapped in New Jersey in 1966.

Off Bougie on 20 January the *Walt Whitman,* launched at Portland, Oregon in July 1942 and one of a series of ships from that yard named for American men of letters, was badly damaged by an aerial torpedo. The explosion blew overboard four members of the ship's Armed Guard but quick-thinking crewmen launched rafts and the four men were soon picked up by an escort vessel. Repaired at Algiers, that Liberty made many more wartime voyages and managed to survive them all. Old Walt would have been proud of his namesake, which to paraphrase half a line from his *In Cabin'd Ships at Sea,* had fulfilled her destiny.

It took a brace of submarines to sink the brand new *Molly Pitcher* (Baltimore, February 1943). The ship was sailing as part of Convoy UGS-6 making for Casablanca from New York. Her cargo consisted mainly of sugar, coffee, tanks, and military vehicles. But she also carried a consignment of TNT, and no doubt it was that which created the panic when the ship was torpedoed by *U-167,* Lieutenant Commander Sturm, during the evening of 17 March 1943. The missile blew a hole in the side of the ship between Nos. 2 and 3 holds, causing both those holds to flood. The helmsman hurriedly left the wheel, which caused the ship to career among the ships at the centre of the convoy. Captain David Bailie and fifty-two of the men on board abandoned ship in great confusion whilst it still had way on and was still turning in circles. Seventeen men were left behind, and they not only managed to get the ship back under control, but were also able to avoid the survivors in the water and get clear of the other ships in the convoy. As the convoy disappeared in the gathering darkness ahead, those still aboard made a gallant attempt to catch up with it, but the attempt failed. On the following day using the one raft still available to them and two improvised ones, the seventeen left-behinds also abandoned ship. The destroyers USS *Champlin* and USS *Rowan,* and the Liberty ship *William Johnson* between them picked up all the survivors apart from two ship's officers and two Armed Guards who had drowned in that initial rush for the boats. Captain Bailie might later have wished that he had been one of the lost men, for at a subsequent inquiry into the incident he had his master's licence suspended for misconduct. The USS *Champlin* fired a torpedo at the ship on that second day in an attempt to sink her. But *Molly Pitcher* proved a tough old bird and it took a torpedo from a second submarine, the *U-521* commanded by Lieutenant Commander Bargsten, to finally send her to the bottom.

The *Matt W. Ransom* (Wilmington, February 1943) was either struck by a torpedo from *U-117* or hit a mine laid by her (the authorities differ on the exact cause) on 11 March 1943 off Casablanca. In view of the kind of keel damage the vessel sustained, it seems likely that a mine caused the damage. Two of the forward holds soon flooded and Captain John Metsall ordered all the crew to standby lifeboat stations, but did not give the order to abandon ship. But that is exactly what most of the crew did, and in the process one boat was lost. Captain Metsall eventually abandoned ship himself, but later together with six volunteers, reboarded and managed to raise steam and get the ship into Casablanca. Patched up, the *Ransom* then made for Gibraltar for more repairs and afterwards made it safely back to the States. She made one further voyage across the Atlantic, but maybe the repairs carried out on her did not prove effective in the long run, for in June 1944 she was one of the ships selected to be used for the Gooseberry breakwater around the Mulberry Harbour at Normandy.

The sinking of a Liberty ship on 11 April 1944 resulted in three of the longest lifeboat voyages undergone by American merchant seamen in the war. The *James W. Denver*, launched at Baltimore only the month before, was under the command Captain William Staley and making for Casablanca from New York. She was carrying about 6000 tons of cargo including some aircraft. Due to overheated engine bearings she soon straggled from the convoy, and in conformity with standard rules then took a more southerly 'straggler's route', one that in theory should have kept the lone ship out of trouble. The theory did not work this time. The ship's bosun spotted the wake of a torpedo when it was only 40 yards away and so there was no chance for any evasive action. It came from *U-195*, Lieutenant Commander Buchholz, and it struck the ship forward below the waterline. The general quarters alarm was sounded and the duty staff in the engine-room ordered to secure engines. The ship took a severe list and began to settle by the head, and the propeller was already out of the water when Captain Staley ordered abandon ship. Six boats were launched, but one of them capsized although all the men in it were picked up by other boats. Captain Staley was the last to leave the ship, indeed he stayed aboard for an hour after the others had abandoned. That night four of the boats set sail for the African coast, the nearest point of which was 600 miles away. Staley's boat stayed in the vicinity of the sinking until the following morning, and then he followed suit. Of the first four boats, one was found by the Spanish *Cabo Huertas* after seven days, a second by the steamship *Campana* after thirteen days, and a third by a Portuguese fishing boat twenty-three days after the sinking. Captain Staley and his men reached the African coast north of Port Etienne after twenty-five days. The last boat had drifted northward and after thirty-five days it was sighted by the crew of the Spanish sailing vessel *Juan*, and the men in it picked up and taken to Lisbon. Miraculously only one man died during those boat trips, although an oiler was to die later in hospital at Gibraltar.

The *Pat Harrison* (New Orleans, January 1943) had discharged her cargo at Oran and on 8 May 1943 was among other ships at anchor in Gibraltar Bay waiting for a return convoy to the United States. On that date she had the misfortune to be one of three ships selected by an

Italian diver, possibly from a midget submarine, as his victims. The mine attached to the *Harrison* exploded in the early hours of the morning almost breaking the ship in two, and lifting the boilers from their seatings. The engine-room and No. 3 hold flooded, and fuel oil, spouting up through the ship's funnel, coated the entire midships section. One man on duty in the engine-room was killed. Tugs were soon on the scene and the Liberty was taken under tow and beached. On inspection it was found that only the top three strakes of plating on either side of the ship were holding it together. Divers discovered the clamps which the saboteur had used to clamp the mine to the bilge keel. The ship was declared a constructive total loss and after the war she was cut completely in two, both parts then being towed to Cadiz for scrapping.

Another Liberty to be severely damaged in port during the North African campaign was the *Daniel Huger* (New Orleans, September 1942). On 9 May 1943 she was at anchor in the port of Bona and was discharging a cargo of 7000 tons of petrol in drums into barges when the port came under attack from German aircraft. As the port's air raid warning siren sounded, the ship's Armed Guard ran to their stations. A near miss from a bomb sent hot shrapnel through the ship's plating into No. 5 hold, igniting the cargo there. Captain James Adams was determined to save his ship and set about organising fire-fighting parties. Cadet Midshipmen Phil Vannais and Elmer Donnelly and a seaman volunteered to enter the burning hold with hoses and stayed down there for an hour and a half before being driven out by a series of small explosions and smoke fumes. The fire then burned out of control, flames from it shooting up mast-high. Except for a few volunteers the crew then abandoned ship as a British Army fire-fighting crew boarded with chemical gear and water pumps. For five hours they fought the blaze, flooding the after two holds in the process until the fire was extinguished, and leaving the ship with its after end sitting on the bottom of the harbour. The crew then reboarded and it took the ship's pumps two days to remove the water and refloat the vessel. The Third Mate and an Armed Guard had died during the air attack. After temporary repairs the ship returned to the States where the work was carried out properly. The *Huger* survived the war, and in 1974 she was scuttled off the coast of Alabama as part of an artificial fish reef. Cadets Vannais and Donelly were each awarded the Distinguished Service Medal for their bravery at Bona and in 1975 the builder's nameplate from the *Daniel Huger* was presented to them. In turn they handed it over for permanent display at the US Merchant Marine Academy at Kings Point.

One of the big problems throughout the 'Torch' operations was the ballasting of ships for their return voyages. By the end of 1942 it was already known that Liberty ships required special ballasting arrangements, but all merchant ships required some such attention, and in North

Africa there were no return cargoes. There was, of course, plenty of sand, but to get it down to ports and loaded aboard ships was a logistical headache in its own right. Part of the ballasting problem on at least one ship was solved in a rather novel way. Bosun Kalevi Olkio says that the ballast used in No. 3 hold of his Liberty at Oran, was a huge spare gun barrel that the French had kept in store there for the battleship *Richelieu*. He and another sailor spent a full day in securing the barrel for the sea voyage after Army stevedores had done a most inadequate job. He says it is just as well he did, for on the voyage to Norfolk, Virginia, the ship struck bad weather and rolled like mad.[4]

It seems that British authorities may have learned a lesson from the Murmansk convoys. In a contemporary pencilled note appended to a document in the official Operation 'Torch' files, someone wrote under the heading 'Welfare of Merchant Seamen', that they must share the 'shore amenities of the Services', in North African ports and that the responsibility for seeing to this lay with the Naval Sea Transport Officer at each port. Although it seems it may have been something of an after-thought, at least it was a step in the right direction.[5]

---

4. Correspondence with Kalevi A. Olkio, 2000.
5. MT59/604, PRO, Kew.

CHAPTER 13

Liberties as Troopships and Animal Transports

Early in the Liberty construction programme it was planned that some of these ships would be purpose-built for troop carrying and the proposed sub-type was even given its own designation, Z-EC2-S-C4. However, none of that sub-type were ever built. Instead, about 250 standard Liberty ships were specially converted to carry troops; it was considered that making the necessary internal alterations to the standard ship at the fitting-out stage would be faster than changing the arrangements during the initial construction. As we have seen, speed was the very essence of the American shipbuilding programme. Thirty-four Liberties were 'fully' converted to this purpose and throughout the war these ships were run by the military services. The 'tween-decks of these ships were altered to accommodate troops, the holds being used to transport the unit's equipment. Such ships sometimes became a sort of semi-permanent floating base for outfits such as the Seabees, the US Naval Construction Battalion. ('CB', hence 'Seabees', a unit immortalised by John Wayne in the film *The Fighting Seabees*.) The majority of these Liberty conversions however, over 200, were partial, with only some parts of the ships' 'tween-decks being converted to carry troops and their equipment, the remaining spaces being utilised for cargo-carrying purposes. Many such ships were used as troopers for only a portion of the time and reverted to ordinary use when not needed to carry soldiers. As early as 11 December 1943, Brigadier General John R. Kilpatrick of the US Army Transportation Corps told a group of masters and chief stewards from some of these partially converted ships that, 'The use of Liberty Ships as troop transports has been one of the deciding factors of the war'.[1]

There is little doubt that the General was right. But the real object of his talk with those senior merchant mariners – it was at a convoy conference – was to impress upon them the need to do their utmost to cater for the physical comfort of the troops under their overall care. For these troop carriers were not at all like the British *Queen Mary* or the American *West*

---

1. Quoted in William R. Wheeler (ed), *The Road to Victory* (Newport News 1946).

Point (ex-SS *America*), which, despite the war, had comparatively good accommodation and other facilities on board for troops. Perhaps the best one can say about these Liberty troopers is that conditions on board them rather resembled those for steerage-class emigrants in early passenger ships. In reference to the many US servicemen who crossed the Pacific, the longest voyage of all, in these ships, John Costello has recorded that the crowded conditions resembled those on slave ships, which is rather overstating it. However, conditions were certainly not comfortable. 'You wouldn't even treat sardines that way', recollected an officer of the Army Transportation Service. One fighting General recorded that, 'Passage on a Liberty ship serves well in preparation for the hardships ahead'. Some of the troops concerned described their trans-Pacific passage less euphemistically. 'You spend a couple of weeks in the troop compartment of a Liberty ship and you'll fight anyone to get ashore.'[2] One of the other maritime anecdotes collected by Costello and taken at face value by him, concerned the fact that American merchant ships like their naval counter-parts, were dry. No liquor was allowed on board. Someone told Costello that the bosuns of Liberty ships were always the most popular men on board – a doubtful statement in its own right, for most bosuns were hard-cases who stood no truck from anyone and had few friends – because they had access to the 100% alcohol used to top up the liquid in magnetic compass bowls. Costello stated that thirst and not the fierce tropical heat accounted for the rate at which compass bowls dried out at sea. That is nonsense. The bottles of alcohol supplied to top up compass bowls on the rare occasions, even in tropical conditions, that an air bubble appeared in them, were tiny; phials would be a better word to describe them. Fur-thermore, the one or two phials supplied to each ship would have been kept handy in the chartroom, and not in the bosun's locker Anyhow, they certainly did not contain enough alcohol to make the hard-case bosun himself very merry, let alone any of his unlikely mates!

The policy of using partially-converted Liberties for troop conveyance was first put forward in early 1943, and, dependant upon the facilities placed aboard, after conversion the ships could carry between 350 and 550 troops together with their equipment. Such ships were fitted with extra life-rafts and life-jackets, and a small Post Exchange (colloquially 'PX' and the equivalent of a British NAAFI) was supplied, but that was about as far as the 'good' things went. The main conversions took place in Nos. 2 and 3 'tween-decks. No. 3 was usually reserved for officers' quarters, an hospital and an operating room, a mess room, and a deten-tion centre. Most importantly, proper toilet facilities were installed there. An overhead blower ventilation system was fitted. That last fitment was

2. John Costello, *The Pacific War* (London 1981).

also a feature of the much larger No. 2 'tween-deck where the enlisted men found themselves housed, and it was just as well. For it was there that men were packed into five-high tiers of bunks, tiers that were not just one-wide, but two and even three-wide. In order to get out, those on the inner bunks not only had to clamber over persons using the outer ones, but unless they were on the bottom level, had then to climb down to reach the deck. Latrines and washing facilities for the enlisted men were situated in a toilet block constructed between hatches 2 and 3 on the main deck above, although primitive 'caught-short' facilities were also provided below in the 'tween-decks, sometimes unofficially by the men themselves. The tendency for Liberty ships to roll heavily in a seaway has been mentioned elsewhere in this book and, as many of the soldiers had never been to sea before, it is little wonder that the troop deck often smelt dreadfully; not just of vomit and urine, but also of food, for cooking facilities had to be provided below because the ship's galley was only able to cope for the requirements of the crew and Armed Guard.

Although troops were warned beforehand about the conditions they could expect on board, few could have expected them to be as bad as they were. In some cases the conditions were even worse than indicated above. Officially listed as one of the advantages of using some partially-converted Liberties as transports for American troops was that some of this class of ship 'had been used for the purpose of bringing prisoners of war to this country', and therefore, 'those particular ships were immediately available as transports'. The authors of those words had the grace to add, 'to the probable disgust of those shipped on them'.[3] These POW ships had been even less adequately converted than the others, and needed to be cleaned and fumigated thoroughly before they could be used for American troops.

Each of the converted ships carried an Army Transportation Officer who was obliged to produce a report at the end of each voyage. The earlier reports complained of lack of adequate sanitation, insufficient ventilation, and poor messing arrangements. But another main cause of complaint was the black market that grew up on board many ships in which crew members sold items of food to the soldiers at exorbitant prices. It probably made matters worse that the market operators were housed in accommodation infinitely better than their customers had to put up with. None of this, of course, did much for the morale of the prospective fighting men. But gradually these matters were sorted out, though a journey aboard one of these ships for a soldier was never a pleasure cruise even after a Special Service Officer was appointed to each ship to organise morale-lifting activities, and after No. 4 'tween-deck was converted into a recreation centre of sorts. Even then, the Liberty's

---

3. Wheeler, op.cit.

penchant for rolling was scarcely conducive to a good game of table-tennis or pool. Towards the end of the war the numbers embarked on each ship were severely reduced, and that did make for greater comfort.

On some Liberties fitted to carry troops on an *ad hoc* basis only, the facilities were even more primitive than those indicated above. The British *Samkansa* (launched as the *Nikola Tesla* at Baltimore, October 1943) had its No. 2 'tween-deck fitted with accommodation for troops at Algiers towards the end of 1944. The 'conversions' were rudimentary according to then seventeen year-old deck-hand J.C. Bellaby, and included the 'dreaded Port Said Ensigns' erected over the stern as latrines. (These contraptions, otherwise known as thunderboxes, were once a feature of ships that carried their own stevedoring gangs around with them on some East of Suez coasts.) The *Samkansa* made several troop-carrying trips between Algiers and Italian and French ports. 'What joy we had when we eventually received the order to cut them [the thunderboxes] loose and see them float merrily, if loathsomely, away'.[4]

Captain John Hughes who now lives in Bradenton, Florida, joined the newly constructed *Samouse* at Baltimore as Chief Officer in November 1943. The ship sailed for the Mediterranean and spent about a year in those waters transporting supplies and small units of troops around. Then, one morning in late 1944 when the ship was loading at Alexandria, he received an urgent message from his Captain who was ashore, to ready the ship for sailing at 1600 hours that day and in the meantime to do what he could to prepare the 'tween-decks for 450 troops of the British 8th Army who were coming aboard for passage to Naples. Let John Hughes take up the story himself:

> Although there was cargo in the 'tween-decks we did our best to sweep up what spaces were left for the troops . . . an almost impossible job! Carpenters then came aboard to rig accommodation-ladders from the 'tween decks to the main deck. Bear in mind that our cooking and sanitary facilities were designed for only forty men – the normal ship's company. The toilet arrangements constructed by the carpenters were quite unique. They brought aboard a trough about 15 feet in length. 55 gallon drums (with ends knocked out) had been welded together and then cut in half lengthwise. This was secured to the ship's rail alongside No. 4 hatch. A fire-hose was secured to one end and a drain at the other, The whole contraption was secured at an angle to allow for the flow. On top of it there was a plank for a seat. It was screened off with burlap.
>
> The troops had nowhere to sleep except on the steel main and 'tween-decks. I offered my cabin to the CO (who was a Captain) and his two Lieutenants. I had intended to double up with the

---

4. J. C. Bellaby, 'A Year in a Liberty Ship', *Ships Monthly*.

2nd. Engineer . . . however, the officers refused this accommodation and slept on deck with their men.

What little cooking they could do, they did for themselves, and I cannot recall even one incident where these appalling conditions affected the morale of the men at all. They were infantry, from the Liverpool and Manchester areas . . . butchers, bakers, and candlestick makers . . . but in all my lifetime, I have never been more impressed by the toughness and complete indifference to the conditions they endured. Have in mind the weather conditions in the Mediterranean were not too bad, and that they were with us for only six days. Imagine . . . in the Pacific where Liberty ships were used as troop carriers and the men were forced to live with these conditions for weeks!

They certainly made them tough in those days.

An idea of the numbers of troops conveyed by Liberty ships across the Atlantic comes from the Chesapeake Bay area. The first such convoy was UGS-11 which left Hampton Roads on 26 June 1943. Eight Liberties were involved between them carrying 1542 men. Apart from those aboard the *John W. Brown* (Baltimore, September 1942) which had picked up its contingent of troops at New York before sailing south to join up with the convoy in the Chesapeake, all the other troops had passed through nearby Camp Patrick Henry. Because of this the *John W. Brown* is often referred to as being the first Liberty to load troops, but as will be shown below, that statement needs something of a proviso.

The second Liberty ship troop convoy sailed from the Chesapeake in mid-July, this time carrying 3400 men, to be followed about twelve days later by another 4600. The two convoys that sailed in August carried 6300 and 8000 troops respectively, a total of forty-two Liberty ships being involved. By the end of 1943 over 77,000 soldiers had passed through Camp Patrick Henry to sail out aboard Liberties. The peak sailings came in April 1944, two months before D-Day, when in three separate convoys of Liberties, 12,889, 14,349 and 14,446 troops sailed, each convoy of men being the equivalent of about a full division. Including those April sailings, no less than 103,000 men had sailed out since 1 January that year. During the twelve month period from June 1943 to May 1944, 454,360 men and women had embarked on ships at Hampton Roads and of those, 44 per cent were carried on a total of 562 Liberty ship sailings. It should be noted that the number of American soldiers to pass through Hampton Roads made up only about 10 per cent of the total to be embarked for Europe and Africa. Four million others were embarked at other ports and many of those also travelled on Liberty ships.

On 11 November 1942, Sir Arthur Salter of the British Shipping Mission in the United States sent a 'Most Secret' memorandum to Admiral Emory Land of the US Maritime Commission. It read:

Embassage, launched by J. L. Thompson of Sunderland in 1935, was the first of the trio of designs which were to evolve into the Liberty ship. (Courtesy Patrick Thompson)

Dorrington Court, the second prototype, launched in 1939. (Newcastle Museum)

A model of *Empire Liberty*, launched in 1941 and the third design from which the Liberty ship evolved. (Sunderland Museum)

The visit of King George VI and Queen Elizabeth to J. L. Thompson's North Sands Yard in Sunderland in 1943. Cyril Thompson is on Her Majesty's right. (Copyright *Northern Echo*)

Harry Hunter in Lieutenant-Commander's uniform, 1938. (Copyright Harry Hunter Jnr)

Sir Richard Powell of the British Shipbuilding Mission. (Copyright Godfrey Argent)

Admiral Emory Scott Land, Chairman of the US Maritime Commission, from a portrait by Jay Wesley Jacobs, 1947. (US Naval Historical Center: NH85579)

William Francis Gibbs of Gibbs & Cox, Naval Architects. (Gibbs & Cox)

Right: Henry Kaiser (right) explaining a technical point to President Roosevelt at the launching of a Liberty ship at Portland, Oregon in 1942. (US Naval Historical Center: NH46486)

Liberty ship construction at the Todd-Houston Yard, February 1942. Section of double bottom including floors, interbottom, longitudinal girders and frames 124.5 to 140.5 being swung into place. Total weight 34.18 tons. (Hull Museum)

Fitting the supporting column for the main engine block. (Hull Museum)

Structural failure: the tanker *Schenectady* at Portland, Oregon 16 January 1943.
(US Navy Archives)

The tanker *Esso Manhattan* entering New York Harbor, 29 March 1943. (US Navy Archives)

Above: Stern section of ss *John P. Gaines* after breaking in two in the North Pacific, 23 November 1943.

Left: Termination of fracture at gunwhale, starboard side of ss *Colin P. Kelly Jr.* (US Navy Archives)

A burning Liberty ship under tow. Salvage vessels saved many damaged ships and their cargoes during the Second World War. (Imperial War Museum: AX44A)

A Liberty ship on fire after being torpedoed.

THE PRE-FABRICATED SHIP
A NEW METHOD OF CONSTRUCTION IN SEPARATE UNITS

COMPLETE MAST UNITS

PRE-FABRICATED BULKHEADS

MAIN DECK PLATING & HATCH OPENINGS

MAIN FRAMES AND OUTER SHELL PLATING

BREAKWATER

WINCH

COMPLETE BOW UNIT

PRE-FABRICATED DOUBLE BOTTOM AND TANK TOPS

BETWEEN DECK PLATING

KEEL PLATES

L. ASHWELL WOOD

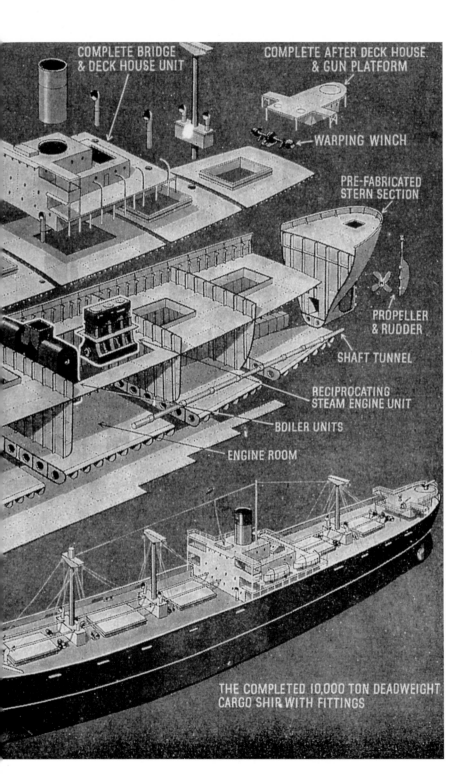

COMPLETE BRIDGE & DECK HOUSE UNIT

COMPLETE AFTER DECK HOUSE & GUN PLATFORM

WARPING WINCH

PRE-FABRICATED STERN SECTION

PROPELLER & RUDDER

SHAFT TUNNEL

RECIPROCATING STEAM ENGINE UNIT

BOILER UNITS

ENGINE ROOM

THE COMPLETED 10,000 TON DEADWEIGHT CARGO SHIP WITH FITTINGS

Above left: Troop deck on a Liberty ship. 'You spend a couple of weeks in the troop compartment of a Liberty ship and you'll fight anyone to get ashore!' (Courtesy Project Liberty Ship)

Left: The animal transport *Jose Navarro*, sunk on 27 December 1943. Note the mule sheds on deck. (Courtesy John Hill)

Above: The commissioning ceremony of the ss *Belgian Amity*, Portland, Maine 7 April 1945, one of seven Liberties Lend-Leased to Belgium during the War. (Courtesy CMB, Antwerp)

Above: Liberty ships in reserve in Tomkins Cove on the Hudson, some 35 miles upstream from New York City, c1965. By 1971 all had been scrapped.

Left: Looking aft from the foremast of *Park Holland* undergoing grounding repairs at Hull in April 1944. Note the anti-torpedo net booms on the after mast, similar to those on Liberty ships. (Albert Faulkner)

Above: The officers of the *Samkey* in a photograph taken before the ship sailed on her final voyage on 24 January 1948.
Standing, left to right: D.M. Gee (4th Officer), K.D. Simpson (3rd Officer), E. Harradine (Chief Radio Officer), W. Bouchard (SIC), H.C. Laing (3rd Engineer), R.N. Cleland (4th Engineer).
Seated, left to right: G.B. Chambers (2nd Officer), L.E. Ambrose (Chief Officer), C.A. Cremin (Captain), T.C. Barry (Chief Engineer), E.P. McKenzie (2nd Engineer)
(Courtesy Marjory Bain and the NZ Shipping Company)

Right: Window in the Church of All Hallows by the Tower. The lower centre section is all that remains of the *Samkey* window from the Mariners' Chapel to St Andrew, Victoria Dock Road, London.

Samtampa on the rocks at Porthcawl, April 1947. (Courtesy Jason Winstanley)

The *Universal Trader* on Little Basses Rocks, Sri Lanka, 9 March 1963. The fore part of the vessel is at right-angles to the rest.

Above: The steering platform on the bridge of the *Jeremiah O'Brien*, San Francisco August 2000. (G.V. Monk)

Right: The oldest surviving Liberty ship captain? Captain Kenneth Cummins at age 100 in 2000.

The *John W. Brown* at Halifax, summer 2000, alongside at the Canadian National Memorial Trust. The other ships are HMCS *Sackville* (left) and HMCS *Acadia* (right). (Canadian National Memorial Trust)

The meeting of the two surviving Liberty ships, *Jeremiah O'Brien* (left) and *John W. Brown* (right) off Cape Cod on 16 August 1994.

I confirm having been asked urgently to seek your approval for two special operations for the use of *Agwimonte* and *Alcoa Prospector* and the *Benjamin Contee* respectively. I have explained orally the purpose for which they are required at the instance of the Chiefs of Staff. You have been good enough to agree to the use of these vessels . . .[5]

The first two named vessels were non-standard freighters built in the States in 1941. The *Benjamin Contee* (New Orleans, August 1942) was a Liberty. The purpose for which these vessels was required, though this was not mentioned in the Salter memorandum, was the transport of prisoners of war, German and Italian, away from behind British lines at El Alamein. In November 1942 all three ships were in the vicinity of Egypt, having previously voyaged out to Suez via Cape Town. It follows that in November 1942, well before the American Liberty ship conversion scheme had begun, the *Benjamin Contee* was engaged in moving troops, albeit that the troops concerned were enemy ones. Some form of conversion must have been carried out on board, perhaps at Suez, Port Said, or Alexandria. Thus, the first Liberty engaged in this kind of work was the *Contee* and not the *John W. Brown.*

There is no record in British files of how long the *Agwimonte* and the *Alcoa Prospector* were engaged in this traffic, but it could not have been for long. The first of those ships was sunk off South Africa on 27 May 1943, and the second was damaged by the Japanese submarine *I-27,* Commander Fukumura, on 5 July 1943. The ships were not carrying POWs on those dates. The *Contee* on the other hand was still moving prisoners in August 1943. On the 16th of that month she was making the short voyage from Bona to Oran where she was to link up with a convoy. In addition to the crew and the Armed Guard unit on board, Captain Even Evensen's ship was carrying 1800 Italian POWs, twenty-six British guards, and seven US Army security personnel. A German dive-bomber attacked the ship at about 2300 hours. It was a moonlit night and to avoid being detected by the British corvette escorting the *Contee,* the plane came in with its engines switched off. It released a torpedo which struck the ship between Holds 1 and 2, blowing a hole some 50ft by 20ft in the side. The explosion blew several POWs over the side.

As the ship began to settle steeply by the head, the prisoners in the forward holds panicked, and brushing aside their guards, rushed the boat deck. With the aid of two Italian-speaking crewmen, Captain Evensen managed to calm things down, informing the POWs that the ship was in no immediate danger. By flooding No. 5 hold Evensen managed to bring the ship back to something like its proper trim. A tug soon arrived on the scene and the *Contee* was towed to Gibraltar. Sources differ on the exact

---

5. File MT59/2209, PRO, Kew.

number, but somewhere between 270 and 320 POWs had been killed in the explosion and another 140 injured. There were no Allied casualties. The Liberty received temporary repairs at Gibraltar and then made the voyage to Britain. In June 1944 she was one of the ships deliberately scuttled off the Normandy coast in Operation 'Gooseberry' to protect the Mulberry Harbour.

Those 1800 Italians must have been crammed into the *Contee*, and that was only for a short coastal voyage. James Stevenson from Oakland Park, Florida, was a Fireman aboard the *William Floyd* (Los Angeles, May 1942) when in mid-1943 she carried general military cargo from New York to Casablanca and Oran. With no special troop-carrying facilities on board, she made the return voyage across the Atlantic to Norfolk, Virginia, carrying no less than 2000 German prisoners.

American records show that of the total number of troops embarked for Europe and Africa, about 3600 were lost at sea. Two thirds of those occurred in three separate incidents. Listed in the order of severity, one involved a British troopship, one a Belgian, the other an American Liberty ship. The heaviest loss occurred on 25 November 1943, the day after the British liner *Rohna* (British India Steam Navigation Company) left Oran with a crew of 195 under Captain Murphy, and carrying 1995 American troops. She joined up with fourteen other merchantmen and ten escort vessels as part of Convoy KMF-26. On the 25th the convoy was attacked by thirty German bombers. A glider bomb released by one of them struck *Rohna* on the waterline in way of the engine-room and the resulting explosion was immense, the after end of the ship soon becoming an inferno. All the port lifeboats were destroyed by the explosion but the starboard ones were lowered, although some of those were soon swamped by the troops who jumped overboard into a rough sea. An hour and a half after the explosion, the ship had settled so far by the stern that the engines and boilers broke loose from their seatings and fell through the hull. Survivors were picked up by American and British warships and by the merchantman *Clan Campbell*. In that single worst incident involving US troops at sea in the war, 1015 American soldiers and 120 crewmen lost their lives. Captain Murphy was amongst the survivors.

After Germany invaded Belgium in May 1940, the *Leopoldville* (Cie. Maritime Belge) became an Allied troopship and continued to be manned by Belgians. On Christmas Eve 1944 she was conveying 2200 troops of the US 66th Division from Southampton to Cherbourg when there was an explosion caused by a mine or torpedo. The ship was then only about five miles from her destination. The explosion caused two decks to collapse aft, trapping many soldiers below. It seems that the ship's captain did not fully appreciate the seriousness of the situation, disembarkation into the lifeboats taking place at an almost leisurely pace. As the destroyer HMS *Brilliant* stood by taking on survivors, the other escorts went off to search the area for submarines. Under the impression that the *Leopoldville* was in no immediate danger, *Brilliant* made for Cherbourg with the first detachment of rescued troops. But an hour later the trooper's bulkheads suddenly collapsed and she sank in less than ten minutes. Due to a mistaken order, part of the crew abandoned ship leaving soldiers on board to lower the remaining boats as best they could. Small craft from Cherbourg hurried to the rescue but arrived too late to save 802 soldiers. Only six members of the crew lost their lives, amongst them the captain.

The third worst incident measured in terms of American troops lost involved one of the Liberty ships which sailed from Hampton Roads. The *Paul Hamilton* was launched in October 1942 at Wilmington and placed under the management of the Black Diamond Steamship Company. Until the ship joined Convoy UGS-38 on 3 April 1944 her war service had been largely uneventful. Now, and under the command of Captain Robert Winans, the ship was loaded with a cargo of ammunition and explosives. In addition to forty-seven crew members and twenty-seven Armed Guards, the ship carried 504 troops. The soldiers were members of a Demolition Unit so it is possible though unlikely, that they were not too concerned about the explosives carried in the holds under their sleeping accommodation. (This mixture of troops and explosives aboard ships was not unusual, though there is some evidence that after convoy UGS-38, the Allies tried to avoid it whenever possible, which was not very often.) Another troop carrying Liberty in the convoy was the *Stephen F. Austin* (Houston, July 1942), but she carried only seventy-two and is not listed as ever having been converted for troop carrying purposes. The *Josiah Bartlett* (Portland, Maine, October 1942) was also in the convoy; she carried no troops but with ammunition and high octane gasoline on deck, she was another example of the floating time-bombs which abounded on the seas at that time.

The convoy which gathered off Cape Henry in Chesapeake Bay comprised eighty-five merchant ships, most of them Liberties, and eighteen US warships. The convoy commodore was Captain Thomas Symington USN who sailed aboard the American freighter *Carrillo*. Commander R.L. Lovejoy USN was vice-commodore, and he was aboard the British tanker *Athelchief*. The merchant ships were drawn up in eight columns of ten or eleven ships, around which the warships fussed. The British Liberty *Samite* (built as *Holland Thompson*, Baltimore, August 1943) had drawn one of the short straws. She headed the port wing column, one of four positions in any convoy that sailors dubbed 'coffin corner' – as previously indicated in this book, the wartime sense of humour of merchant seamen tended towards the macabre. Another British Liberty in the convoy was the *Samaffric* (Baltimore, March 1944) which was on her maiden voyage.

Routed well south of the usual U-boat haunts, the voyage across the Atlantic towards Gibraltar was largely uneventful. The eye-aching boredom of those on watch was relieved only by the many signals emanating from the commodore ship regarding bad station-keeping and straggling. Seven days out, and obviously in answer to received radioed intelligence, the Commodore ordered all ships to stream their torpedo nets, then bawled-out the masters of two American ships that failed to do so. A British tanker which fell behind with engine trouble later managed to rejoin, but fell out again and was ordered to proceed to Gibraltar at her own best speed and with her very own escort ship. Two ships with cargo for the Azores detached, followed by five more including two Free-French ships, all heading for Casablanca. Two merchant ships sailing up from that port joined on 17 April, the day before the convoy passed Gibraltar. It was all very routine. But that was soon to change.

The usual system was for Royal Navy escorts to take over from the US Navy ocean escorts off Gibraltar, but this time that did not happen, and the convoy continued to be escorted by the Americans. Off Melilla, Spanish Morocco, the escorts were joined by four additional American destroyers and the cruiser *Van Heemskeerck* of the Royal Netherlands Navy. Off Oran on the 19th, about a third of the convoy detached to enter that port.

Radio Officer Ian Malcolm aboard *Samite,* one of the fifty ships still remaining in the convoy which was now heading for the Anzio beaches, had seen it all before. As part of USG-18 in the previous September, *Samite* had been badly damaged in the first Mediterranean convoy to be attacked by radio-controlled glider bombs.[6] He has written:

> The coast of Algeria was in sight to starboard and the weather continued fine, but we, on the *Samite*, were no longer seduced by these seemingly comforting factors and became more apprehensive as we headed eastward.[7]

It was dusk on 20 April when the attack on USG-38 came. A message had earlier been received from the Commodore warning the ships that they could expect aircraft attacks that night and, as there would be no moon, they should not open fire except in self-defence to avoid giving away the position of the convoy. The *Samite* was still in her coffin corner leading the port column when at about 2100 hours there came a sudden violent explosion followed by a blinding flash over on the ship's starboard beam. Within seconds the *Samite* itself was struck by an aerial torpedo. Captain L. Eccles immediately hauled out of the convoy and stopped ship so that the damage could be inspected.

6. Stephen Roskill, *A Merchant Fleet at War* (London 1962). See also File ADM199/2146, PRO, Kew.
7. Ian Malcolm, *Voyage 1 of the Samite.*

That first explosion had come from the *Paul Hamilton*. Captain Ernest Ban on the nearby *Stephen F. Austin* was later to report that he saw the *Paul Hamilton*, which was two columns over from his own ship, open fire with her guns and then immediately explode. The blast as the *Hamilton* blew up was felt by several ships in the vicinity, and flames and debris rose high in the air. As the smoke cleared and the disturbed sea settled down, the only signs left of what had once been a ship were floating scraps of timber There was not a single survivor from among the nearly 600 men on board. Paul Salvo who was serving aboard the *Josiah Bartlett* was another witness to the tragedy. He says' 'Coming down our column was the German plane that hit and sank the *Paul Hamilton*. Our ship made direct hits on the plane with the assistance of a gunboat astern . . . we brought the plane down'.[8]

Up on the bridge of the *Stephen F. Austin*, Captain Ban did not have much time to ponder on the tragedy he had just witnessed. Lookouts spotted a torpedo plane making a run for the ship and Ban ordered 'hard right rudder', and a torpedo passed 20ft astern. There were two more near misses before one torpedo struck on the starboard side in way of No. 2 hold, the explosion tearing a great hole in the hull below the water-line. As the ship listed and seemed about to go down by the head, Captain Ban ordered abandon ship, and everyone got away in four lifeboats, including all seventy-two troops on board. But it soon became evident that the ship was not about to sink after all, and the crew reboarded. On the following day the rescue tug HMS *Hengist* arrived on the scene, and she stood by as the *Austin* managed to reach Algiers safely under her own steam. No one had been killed in the attack on the ship. The *Austin* was repaired and survived the war, suffering no more great adventures on the way. Engineer Steve Antos served in her during 1945/1946 and she showed no signs of ever having suffered major damage. The *Austin* went to a breaker's yard in New Orleans in 1967.[9]

The torpedo that hit *Samite* had, as with the *Austin*, struck in the vicinity of No. 2 hold, in *Samite*'s case, towards the fore end of that compartment. There was no fire and no one was hurt, but the ship was soon down over 9ft by the head and the rudder refused to function. HM tug *Vagrant* arrived and, a tow-line was passed, and *Samite* was towed stern first towards Algiers, arriving there on the following day.[10] The *Samite* crew knew the port well for it was there the ship had eventually ended up for repairs after the glider bomb incident of the previous year. This time as the *Samite*, down by the head and obviously sorely stricken, was once again towed slowly past the end of the harbour mole, she was spotted by

---

8. Correspondence with Peter Salvo, 2000.
9. Correspondence with Steve Antos, 1999.
10. ADM199/2147, PRO, Kew. This file contains Captain Eccles's official report.

three British soldiers standing there. Then took place one of those small never-to-be-forgotten incidents that go partly towards compensating for the horrors of war. One of the soldiers must have been associated in some way with the ship's previous visit, for Ian Malcolm who was standing on the ship's boat deck heard one shout out, 'It's the *Samite*!' Then, 'Three cheers for the *Samite*!' The hearty cheers then came over the water. 'Those three squaddies would never know how much we appreciated their spontaneous gesture and how I have remembered it down the years', wrote Ian Malcolm in 1995.

The great loss of life caused by the sinking of the *Paul Hamilton* resulted in an Official Inquiry by American authorities, but this author has not been able to view the records of it. Because of the pre-warning of air attacks issued to all ships in the convoy by the commodore, Captain Thomas Symington USN, one of the questions that must have been raised at that Inquiry was why torpedo nets had not been streamed. On arrival at Algiers, Captain Eccles of the *Samite* made the usual report to the Naval Reporting Officer there, and when asked why his nets had not been streamed, he replied that no such order had been received from the commodore. He went on to say, however:

> I am of the opinion that nets reduce speed and manoeuvrability and that most vessels could not have maintained convoy speed with their nets streamed.

He added;

> Also, as we carried deck cargo, it would have been impossible to slip the nets in the event of having to launch the life-rafts. This was known to the crew, whose morale would have been seriously affected if the nets had been streamed in these circumstances.

At the end of his report Eccles said he was of the opinion that in the case of his own vessel, the torpedo would have struck even had the nets been in position. He did not, of course, offer an opinion on whether or not nets might have saved the *Paul Hamilton*.

The concept of rigging nets from booms on merchant ships so that they hung clear of the ship's sides to prevent a torpedo striking was developed by the Admiralty in the First World War. In the Second World War various experiments were made with progressively improved designs on a number of British ships until the final design was fitted on a trial basis to the freighter *Empire Rhodes* and the tanker *Empire Celt*. (The nets did not prevent the latter ship from being torpedoed and sunk on 24 February 1942.) After that more British-built ships were fitted with the device, but by no means all of them. In America, Gibbs & Cox the firm of naval architects involved in the construction of the Liberties, had a department working on their own design which was known as

T.N.D. for Torpedo Net Defense. One of the Gibbs' people working on this project was Robert Herbert who, with a US Navy commission, later worked in this field with the Admiralty.

Only about a fifth of all Liberty ships were fitted with T.N.D., and one way to recognise from a distance whether a Liberty had the gear or not was to look at its fore and after masts, for the fitting of net lifting booms required extended lattice crosstrees on those masts. (Such booms were not fitted to the main mast, the middle of the three, so the crosstree there was of normal size.) The booms were fitted on either side of the masts, with their topping-lifts attached to the ends of the crosstrees. When lowered into the horizontal position the booms projected some forty feet away from the ship's side, with the nets hanging from them going down a few feet under the water. They worked on the principle that a torpedo would get tangled in them without coming any closer to the ship than the length of the outstretched boom.

There were several problems with this 'passive' form of protection, however, and two of them were mentioned in Captain Eccles's report as given above. There was, however, another fault with the gear. Hanging as they did from booms attached to the fore and after masts, the nets only stretched over the middle section of the ship. Captain John Simms who sailed as a deck hand aboard the Liberty *John S. Maffitt* (Wilmington, August 1943) on its maiden voyage, says the ship was fitted with 'a new experimental torpedo net to be used in the passage through the Mediterranean . . . we tried them out in the Atlantic, but streamed them in the Med'. He confirms that 'they covered the area from the foremast to the mizzen [after] mast'.[11] That coverage would certainly have eased the minds of the men working down in the vulnerable engine-room amidships, but offered no protection to the extreme ends of the ship, which is probably why Captain Eccles was of the opinion that nets would not have protected the *Samite* even had the nets been streamed, because the torpedo struck at the fore end of No. 2 hold. As there were no survivors from the *Paul Hamilton,* and because it was dark when that ship was struck and blew up, it is not known where that particular torpedo hit. But there must remain at least the possibility that nets might have saved that ship. In an article Robert Herbert wrote for *Liberty Log* in 1985, he said the T.N.D. programme could be considered a success since for an expenditure of around $31 million there were confirmed attack saves amounting to $60 million in ships and cargoes, to say nothing of seamen's lives saved. He also mentioned that the device saved two troop carriers although he did not mention their names.

Another anti-torpedo device was an 'active' rather than a passive one. It was called either the Anti-torpedo explosive device or Mark 29. It con-

---

11. Correspondence with John E. Simms, 1999-2000.

sisted of 50ft sections of rubberoid hose packed with explosives and detonators. Sections were joined together and linked by electrical wires that
ran to a console on the ship's bridge. The 'hoses' were towed on each side
of the ship attached to a sort of paravane device which kept the hose clear
of the ship, the hose itself floating at a depth of about 10ft. The theory
was that when a torpedo track was spotted and reported by a lookout,
the console operator would use his judgement about where and when the
missile was to strike, and by pressing the right buttons, blow the appropriate section of the hose up, together with the torpedo. There were several negative aspects to this device, not the least important one being that
because it needed the assistance of a visual sighting, it was not much good
at night. It was later improved by fitting a sound-monitoring device.
When a torpedo was heard on the monitor, the system would be armed
from the bridge and the appropriate hose section would then be set off
automatically by the noise of the torpedo. The arming had still to be carried out from the bridge, and the standing instruction was that the system should only be armed after a torpedo had been heard. The danger
with even the improved system was that once it was armed, the ship
could not manoeuvre properly for fear that the hose might become
entangled in the propeller with potentially disastrous consequences.

One Liberty fitted with this device was the *John A. Poor* (Portland,
Maine, June 1943). Two days out from Halifax, Nova Scotia, on 28 July
1943, the ship ran into a series of mines laid by *U-199*, Lieutenant Commander Kameke. One explosion damaged the boilers, steam lines and generators. The *Poor* was towed back to Halifax by the tug *North Star* and
Captain W.J. Uppit made a report there, which the Canadian naval reporting officer noted as being 'highly imaginative'. Captain Uppit reported
that at one point he thought he had seen a U-boat, and other crew members reported sighting torpedo tracks. The Canadian officer added a note
to the report that, 'tracking evidence shows that it is *most* unlikely that a
U-boat was in fact present' (a fact confirmed after the war by German
records). The Canadian report went on to note that it was probable that
detonations from the Mark 29 gear streamed from the ship were the cause
of the crew assuming torpedoes had been involved. It went on, 'the system should be carried *unarmed* at all times except when a torpedo is heard
over the monitoring system'. (The *Poor* was to meet its end in the Indian
Ocean on 19 March 1944, by which time Captain Francis Dulac was in
command. The ship was sunk by *U-510*. Almost half of the ship's complement went down with her, the only officers among the group of survivors picked up three days later by the British *Fort Walsh* being Chief
Officer Louis Moreto and Purser Russell Corbin.)[12]

---

12. ADM199/526 and 440, PRO, Kew.

It may seem strange that in a 'modern' conflict such as the Second World War, it was still necessary to transport pack animals around the globe for use in some campaigns. Most of the animals concerned were mules, and their numbers ran into many thousands. An official British document dating from October 1944 summarises the animal requirements for the British and Indian Armies as 'Horses 10,924 – Mules, 63,204 – Camels, 6,657'. During 1942/43, sixty-four Husky sledge dogs were purchased in the United States by the British Army Veterinary Service for training purposes at the Snow and Mountain Warfare Training Centre in Scotland. Some dogs, called 'War Dogs', were also used in the detection of mines.

Between July 1941 and April 1945, ten British ships were specially fitted to carry a total of 4179 mules from the United States to India for use by British and Indian troops operating in Burma, and later on for American and Chinese forces operating in that country. From late 1943 a total of thirteen American-flagged Liberty ships were also converted to this purpose.[13] Such was the importance of these animals in jungle warfare that their well-being during long sea voyages was a major concern. The British shipments from the States were at first accompanied by British Army veterinary officers and later by officers and men from the American Quartermaster and Veterinary Corps, and when that source dried up, Canadian officers were used. Amongst the British ships concerned in this traffic were the Richmond-built *Ocean Vista* and the Canadian-built *Fort Crevier.* None of the British ships were lost whilst carrying mules, although the *Edgefield,* an old American freighter purchased by Britain in 1941 was sunk after her mule-carrying days were over. On 1 July 1943, and by then called the *Empire Ibex,* she sank after a collision in convoy with the British *Empire MacAlpine.*

At mule dealing centres in the USA, British and American purchasing officers often attended the sales together. There was no international rivalry between the two purchasing groups as they required different size animals. The Americans bought only animals over 13.3 hands, whilst the British requirement was for animals between 12.2 and 13.3 hands. 'Animals which were too big for the British were often acceptable to the Americans, and conversely, animals too small according to the American specifications could be accepted by the British.'[14] The main reason for

---

13. The ten British ships used to transport mules from the United States (others would have been used to carry mules from other sources) in order of date of sailing were, *Antemis, Edgefield, Fort Crevier, Theseus, Manchester Commerce, Empire Welfare, Empire Trail, Empire Symbol, Ocean Vista,* and *Empire Mauritius.* (After discharging her mules the *Fort Crevier* was badly damaged in the Great Bombay Port Explosion when the ammunition ship *Fort Stikine* blew up on 14 April 1944.) The thirteen Liberties used were *William S. Halstead, Santiago Iglesias, Peter Sylvester, Zona Gale, Charles W. Wooster, Alcee Fortier, Henry Dearborn, Joshua Hendy, William J. Palmer, Cyrus W. Field, John J. Crittenden, Samuel H. Walker,* and *Jose Navarro.*

14. *Army Veterinary & Remount Services,* p88.

this different requirement seems simply to have been one of tradition. Many mules used by the British Indian Army in pre-war years, for example, were locally bred and were smaller than American Missouri mules, the largest in the world.

The United States was far from being the only source of mules. One of the British ships first used to carry American mules to India was subsequently used on three mule-carrying voyages between Durban and Indian ports with South African animals. The ship concerned was the old Blue Funnel freighter *Theseus* dating from 1907. An excellent account of those voyages has been written by Radio Officer Bill Bond. Although the *Theseus* experience was somewhat extreme, some of Bond's remarks are worth mentioning here as they probably applied in some degree to all other ships engaged in this work including the Liberty ships.[15] On her first mule voyage from the United States in the Spring of 1944, *Theseus* transported 415 mules to Karachi. They were destined for General Joe Stilwell's operations in Burma and were accompanied on board by a contingent of American troops including vets and muleteers. Stalls for the animals were erected on deck and in some of the 'tween-deck spaces, the remainder of the 'tween-decks being available for troop accommodation. Fodder, bedding straw, and water for the mules had to be carried in vast quantities, the ship's deep tanks being used to carry the extra water required. For some reason the British crew dubbed the muleteers the 'Fort Knox Cavalry', and apparently they were not a very happy group of men due to having to sleep in close proximity to their charges.

The convoy of which *Theseus* was part crossed the Atlantic without incident but came under air attack when passing through the Mediterranean. The mules did not take kindly to the sound of the ship's guns and had to be placated. While waiting to transit the Suez Canal, the OC Troops ordered that all mules must be sheared before reaching the heat of the Red Sea. That task, with the dirt and stench involved, brought the muleteers close to mutiny, a situation only defused by some hard, straight talking from the Military Police contingent on board.

After discharging her charges at Karachi *Theseus* was ordered to sail for Durban. After two days of fumigation there 'designed to destroy all vermin still lurking in the ship', the ship underwent a refit to increase her mule-carrying capacity. Then 'hundreds' of South African mules were loaded, a smaller breed than the Missouri but even more fractious. The ship sailed for India independently, zigzagging its way up the length of the Indian Ocean. 'We had constantly to muck out the ship by removing manure and straw overboard. This had to be done after dark, under the illusion that it would avoid giving our position away to the enemy.' Sent

15. Brian Bond, 'The Theseus Experience', *Defence Quarterly Journal* Vol 124, No 4 (October 1995).

back twice again to Durban, on one of those trips the mules carried by *Theseus* were supplemented with a number of donkeys and zebras. Said Bond, 'those who have grappled with the traditional stubbornness of mules have seen nothing until they try to domesticate zebras'. On the third trip the ship carried no less than 1150 mules and donkeys and in addition, sheep, goats, pigs and rabbits to be used as food for the troops of the British 14th Army. The *Theseus* had by then become a sort of floating zoo, and 'the crew became a stinking, muck-sodden gang whose state is best left to the imagination'.

Two of the thirteen American Liberty ships engaged in carrying mules were lost to enemy action. Because the inherent behaviour of mules under stress seems to have influenced the actions of one of the masters of those ships, it will be useful at this point to relate a couple of anecdotes concerning what happened to mules after they reached north-eastern Indian ports such as Calcutta. One of the anecdotes confirms that they were not easy animals to deal with in confined spaces. After being landed at the port the mules were transported by rail or road to airfields in Assam, the Indian state that lies to the north and west of Burma. From those airfields they were flown into Burma over a range of mountains known as 'The Hump', by American pilots flying Dakota aircraft. Some mules were even carried in glider aircraft; maybe they got to recognise gliders from powered aircraft for at least one authority says that it was much more difficult to get mules to walk aboard gliders. Mules were used on a large scale in both of the British Chindit Expeditions organised and led by Major General Orde Wingate behind Japanese lines in Burma, and by the American unit known as Merrill's Marauders after its commander, Brigadier General Frank Merrill, as well as by other more conventional units who fought in that campaign. An indication of the importance of mules in the Burma scheme of things is given by Lieutenant Dominic Neill of the 3/2nd Gurkha Regiment. He once wrote 'Wingate is more interested in the mules than the muleteers'. Again, 'He [Wingate] was very interested in the mules but he ignored my Gurkha muleteers completely'. The importance of the mule is clear from figures concerning the first Chindit Expedition in which 2000 men were supported by 1000 mules. And, in an example of how the indispensable can suddenly become dispensable, on that expedition's return from the jungle all the surviving mules were released to their own devices because they would have hindered the march out.

Most of the mule-carrying flights over the Hump were filled with incident, for the animals did not take to the experience. They were usually flown in groups of four and Lieutenant N. Durrant once wrote,

When the engines started the mules made frantic efforts to force themselves through the sides of the aircraft. As the plane rushed forward, the most truculent of the mules leant to the side, his hooves got off the floor matting and on to the aluminium. He slipped and was on the floor thrashing about before we could do anything. This naturally upset the other three and they began lashing out until the place was a bedlam. By superhuman efforts we got the mule to its feet, soothed the others with soft words and tightened the lashings, and peace was restored.[16]

The first mule-carrying Liberty to be sunk was the *Jose Navarro* (Houston, October 1943), and thanks to the excellent interviewing technique of H.G. Fletcher, the official Port Officer at Cochin, India where the survivors from the ship were landed, we have been left with a detailed account of the incident and the background to it.[17]

For what was her maiden voyage the ship loaded 3000 tons of military cargo at New Orleans including 357 mules. Of the 166 men on board, eighty comprised an American Army unit there to look after the animals. Unlike the *Theseus* which carried some mules below decks, all the stalls on *Navarro* were on the main deck. In order to provide enough life-saving capacity for all the men on board, the ship was fitted with an additional lifeboat at every davit; in other words the boats were double-banked with the ropes for the upper tiers being led to deck winches for lowering and raising purposes. However, because of the stalls on deck, the run of the ropes to these winches was not straight and they tended to foul on the stalls. For this reason the master, Captain Ernest MacLellan, did not, indeed could not, adopt the usual practice of having the boats swung out at sea in good weather. In his report MacLellan added that from his previous experience aboard another torpedoed ship, lifeboats already swung out were liable to be lowered 'by excitable persons' before being ordered to do so. The mule stalls were also in the way of some of the rafts carried on board.

The ship made it safely across the Atlantic, through the Mediterranean and Suez Canal to Aden, and then set out independently for Calcutta. In fine weather on 27 December 1943 the ship had reached a position north of the Maldives. The *Navarro* had her torpedo nets streamed even before receiving instructions from Colombo to do so, instructions that must indicate that the British naval authorities had information that an enemy submarine was in the vicinity. Those nets, stretching as they did aft from No. 2 hold, did not prevent a torpedo striking forward of the net at the after end of No. 1 hold at about 0400 hours. The explosion blew a hole in the side and destroyed bulkheads, and as the sea rushed in the ship began to settle by the head. Chief Officer Samuel Condrey on watch on

---

16. Quoted in Lowell Thomas, *Road to Mandalay* (London 1952).
17. ADM199/1405, PRO, Kew contains the reports made before Port Officer H.G. Fletcher at Cochin, India.

the bridge immediately rang 'stop engines' and blew the siren signal ordering all hands to their lifeboat stations. Captain MacLellan rushed to the bridge, took charge and sent Condrey forward to inspect the damage.

> ... informed that Nos. 1 and 2 holds were almost full of water and the vessel settling fast by the head. I ordered all top lifeboats to be manned and lowered with army personnel on board. As the vessel continued to sink by the head I ordered all remaining persons to abandon ship.

Before the Armed Guard under Lieutenant Fan left the ship they fired two rounds in the dark at a floating object which later turned out to be a raft. Before he abandoned ship, Chief Radio Officer John Kardell sent off the signal indicating that the ship had been torpedoed and had it acknowledged by the Colombo radio station. He and the Captain then set about dumping all the ship's papers and codebooks.

Everyone got away safely although Third Engineer Holford was injured when he was caught between a boat and the ship's side. The boats stayed in the vicinity and when daylight came the vessel was still afloat. Calling for volunteers Captain MacLellan reboarded with a number of the crew, Armed Guard, and Army personnel, to attempt to save the vessel. Radio Officer Kardell was amongst those who reboarded and, using emergency battery power, repeated the distress message which was again acknowledged by Colombo which then sent a message in an Admiralty code which could no longer be deciphered on board. With the Armed Guard manning the ship's guns, the ship's engineers managed to start the pumps. However, by now the water in No. 3 hold had almost reached the 'tween-decks and the pumps had no effect. In mid-morning a seaplane flew overhead and signalled that help was on the way. By noon the deck forward was awash and as it was clear the pumps could not save the ship, MacLellan ordered everyone off again. Late in the afternoon the seaplane returned and signalled for the boats to keep together and that a rescue ship would arrive on the scene the following day. But there was still more drama to be played out. About two hours after dark, a flash was seen and concussion felt coming from the direction of the ship. Captain MacLellan assumed another torpedo had struck his ship and when the sun came up there was no sign of the *Navarro*. Just after noon the minesweeper HMIS *Rajputana* hove into view and took everyone on board. The minesweeper then made a sweep of the area and a large amount of wreckage was seen, and some floating mules. On 29 December all the crew were landed safely at Cochin where the injured engineer was hospitalised. After the war German records showed that the attacking submarine on both occasions was *U-178* commanded by Lieutenant Commander Spahr. This submarine was scuttled off Bordeaux on 25 August 1944.

'As regards the Master's orders to abandon ship on each occasion,' wrote Port Officer Fletcher in his summing up of the incident, 'apart from the precarious position of those on board, he was influenced by the presence of mules which had they broken loose and jumped overboard would have made for the lifeboats and rafts, thus presenting a grave danger to their crews.' There can be little doubt that Captain MacLellan was right. Sad as the fate of the mules was, no human lives had been lost in the incident.

That was not to be the case with the sinking of another mule-carrying ship, the *Peter Sylvester* (Los Angeles, June 1942). She was travelling the other way round the world having passed through the Panama Canal and across the Pacific. On 28 January 1945 she called at Melbourne for bunkers and then sailed for Colombo. With Captain Bernard Dennis in command she was loaded with military stores and 317 mules. Her crew and Armed Guard contingent had been augmented by 107 American troops, bringing the total number of men on board to 175. On 6 February she had reached a position about 700 miles west of Fremantle when she had the misfortune to fall in with *U-862*, Lieutenant Commander Timm. Two torpedoes struck *Sylvester* on the starboard side amidships. One of them was seen entering No. 3 hold and exiting on the other side, but the other exploded in the hold, rupturing the deck just forward of the bridge. Thirty minutes later two more torpedoes struck the ship in No. 2 hold and the ship began rapidly to settle by the bow. Captain Dennis ordered abandon ship and the survivors got off in four lifeboats and six rafts. As the boats cleared the ship, Commander Timm sent two more torpedoes into the fore end, causing the ship to break in two, the forward end sinking immediately. Why Timm thought it necessary to expend a total of six of his precious stock of torpedoes is not known; perhaps it was simply because he was on his way home.

Two days after the sinking fifteen survivors in one boat were picked up by the freighter *Cape Edmont*. On 13 February the USS *Corpus Christi* rescued ninety men from the six rafts including Captain Dennis, and on the following day another twelve from a lifeboat. Between the 13th and 18th HM escort carriers *Slinger* and *Speaker* on passage from Colombo to Sydney searched the area unsuccessfully, but on the 28th, twenty-one days after the sinking, the escort carrier HMS *Alacrity*, also on passage to Sydney, picked up twenty men from another lifeboat. Aircraft from the carrier HMS *Formidable* carried out another unsuccessful search, but thirty-one days after the sinking and over 1000 miles from where it had taken place, the submarine USS *Rock* rescued fifteen men from the last boat. Of the original complement of 175, thirty-three men had been lost.

One of the successful mule-carrying Liberties was the *William S. Halsted* (Baltimore, March 1943). James Stevenson, by then graded Oiler, served on that ship from July 1944 to May 1945. He says that while he was aboard, the ship carried mules from Westwego, Louisiana, to Calcutta, then horses from Townsville, Queensland, to that same Indian port.[18] At least 500 of the mules sent to Burma had a further military use after the war. In April 1947 the *Fort Bourbon* arrived at Rangoon and loaded mules and fifty-two accompanying British troops. The ship arrived at Volos, Greece on 10 May where half the mules were discharged, the remainder being on-carried to Salonika. The mules were for use of the Greek Army in its local war against the Communists.

Some of the mule-carrying Liberties were used after the war for the commercial carriage of animals. The *William J. Palmer* (Richmond, October 1943) was carrying horses from New York to Trieste and Yugoslavia. On 4 August 1945 she sailed from Trieste and was a few miles off the coast when she struck a mine. The ship began to sink by the stern as the after engine-room bulkhead collapsed, leaving Captain Joseph Moody no alternative but to order abandon ship. A British cutter arrived on the scene and Moody boarded it and circled the ship in the hope that some horses could be saved. But only the six that had been tethered separately on deck were rescued, being towed ashore by local fishermen. The remainder perished when a bare fifteen minutes after striking the mine, the *Palmer* rolled over and sank.

The *Webb Miller* (Portland, Maine, December 1943, named for an American War Correspondent who was killed whilst covering the London Blitz), had an animal-carrying adventure just after the war that had nothing to do with mules. Towards the end of 1945 the ship loaded a part-general cargo at Calcutta and then proceeded to Colombo to top up with more cargo for the States. The war being over and supplies being more readily available, the crew had spruced the ship up inside and out. A lick of paint in the crew's quarters made it seem 'more homey' writes Allen Kinsinger, who was one of the oilers on board. They need not have bothered. Having completed loading and battened down the hatches ready for the voyage home, the ship was at anchor within the Colombo breakwater awaiting a pilot when a barge approached the ship. It was carrying some large canvas-covered crates which were lifted and positioned on Nos. 4 and 5 hatches. After securing the crates with ropes the canvas covers were removed and says Allen Kinsinger, three hundred monkeys 'screamed at us all at the same time'. The consignment was for a firm of animal traders in the States called Meens Brothers and were to be used in infantile paralysis experiments; during the coming voyage the animals were to prove they were not yet suffering from that disease. 'They were wild, noisy, and smelly', reports Kinsinger. Although the cages had been placed on battens to facilitate the hosing away of droppings underneath, it did nothing much to dissipate the smell.[19]

---

18. James Stevenson correspondence, June-August 1999.
19. Allen J. Kinsinger correspondence, 2000.

The cages had come aboard secured by crude locks, and a few days into the voyage, someone picked them. Three rather nasty-looking customers had boarded the ship at Calcutta for the journey home. They were Office of Strategic Services men who had been working in Burma. (The OSS was the precursor of the CIA.) The three, accompanied by a vicious Alsatian dog called Duke, kept themselves to themselves and were extremely unfriendly, and the crew were pretty certain it was they who had let the monkeys out. From that moment onwards there were monkeys everywhere. They were up masts, booms, and stays, and down in the engine-room. No place was inviolate. Whenever they got hungry, which was often, they made forays into the galley, messrooms and cabins, leaving a trail of havoc and nasties behind them. Captain Walter Townley posted a bounty for each monkey recaptured, but they were 'real smart', says Kinsinger. Some were recaptured, but not all. The Ugly Threesome developed a game which had nothing to do with capturing the monkeys alive. They used to climb the mast and shake the radio aerial, a favourite swinging place for the animals, until they fell. Duke was then encouraged to chase the fallen monkeys forward to the bow where, with no other place to go, they would jump overboard. During the cold weather of the Atlantic many of those still free died in inaccessible places, and the 'stench was unbelievable'. It may have been the smell that drove the health authorities in New York to ban the ship from berthing there, so she was sent to Providence, Rhode Island, instead. Providence indeed, for according to the local *Journal* edition of 11 January 1946, it was likely that some of the simians managed to take up temporary residence in the town's Washington Park.

Raymond D. Molony was serving aboard the *Joshua Hendy* (Richmond, July 1943), which had been a mule-carrier in the war, in November 1946 when she hauled horses from Savannah to Gdansk in Poland. He writes;

> We had wooden stalls on deck and carried our own veterinarians and cowboys to take care of the horses. We lost 40%-50% of the horses in a rough trip across the Atlantic. Then we ran out of water and feed and had to put into Rotterdam to re-supply.[20]

Animal-carrying at sea is no fun for anyone, especially the animals.

---

20. Raymond D. Molony in *Liberty Log*, August 2000.

CHAPTER 14

Liberties in the Mediterranean

By May 1943 all surviving Axis forces had been driven from North Africa. At the Casablanca Conference held in mid-January 1943, with the prospect of that feat of arms in mind, President Roosevelt and Prime Minister Churchill and their staffs once more discussed the general war strategy and laid down plans for the future. However, those January discussions were not straightforward and there were many disagreements. At first the only subject on which the Americans and British could agree upon was that the war at sea must continue to receive the highest priority. The Allies were still suffering a high level of ship losses, and whatever plans were agreed for the future, they would come to naught unless the U-boat menace was defeated. With the American merchant shipbuilding programme by that time showing every sign of shifting into top gear, if extra effort was put into building more and better escort ships, it could be assumed that it would not be long before new shipbuilding would come to exceed the number of sinkings.

On future military strategy there was a major divergence of opinion between the Americans and the British. The Americans wanted to hold the position in North Africa and concentrate the next large effort on a landing in North-west Europe. Churchill did not agree. His views are perhaps best summed up by an expression he used in his history of the Second World War, 'I never meant the Anglo-American Army to be stuck in North Africa. It is a springboard, and not a sofa . . .'[1] Churchill and his Chiefs of Staff pressed for a vigorous follow up to 'Torch' with a view to knocking Italy out of the war. They argued that this would not only make the Mediterranean lines of communication more secure, but give the Germans no respite for recuperation and reforming. Moreover, by sucking in German troops that might otherwise be used on the Russian front, a follow-up attack in the Mediterranean area would aid Marshal Zhukov's army which was already on the offensive. President Roosevelt came round to the same point of view, and an attack on Sicily was decided upon. It was to be called Operation 'Husky' and take place

---

1. Winston Churchill, *The Second World War* Vol. IV.

in July. In the meanwhile the build-up of American forces in Britain would continue in preparation for a future landing in western Europe.

Compared with the 'Husky' landings in Sicily on 10 July 1943, the earlier 'Torch' landings almost pale into insignificance. The majority of the ships involved, both warships and merchantmen, were once again British, and Britain also supplied about two-thirds of the nearly 250,000 soldiers landed. For the first time landing ship tanks (LSTs) were used on a large scale, together with that new phenomena, the DUKW amphibious vehicle. Over 2600 warships, merchant ships, and landing craft took part. The naval side of the operation was planned and conducted under the direction of Admiral Sir Andrew Cunningham who remarked that it seemed 'almost magical that great fleets of ships could remain anchored on the enemy's coast . . . with only such slight losses from air attack as were incurred'. In view of the size of the fleets involved losses were indeed small, but it was far from all plain sailing for the merchant fleets including the many Liberty ships that took part.

The first Liberty to be lost in those operations was the *Robert Rowan* (Wilmington, April 1943). With a cargo of ammunition and army vehicles she arrived at the port of Gela, Sicily, on the day after the initial landings. She was also carrying 348 American troops. No sooner had she arrived than the port was attacked by German bombers. Three bombs struck the ship but only two of them exploded, the third one penetrating the main deck and passing out through the ship's side without going off. The explosions started fires which soon spread to the ammunition in the cargo. Captain Ivar Rosenquist ordered abandon ship and everyone got away in boats and rafts, though many of the troops elected to jump into the water. The *Rowan* finally settled on the bottom with most of her superstructure remaining above the surface. No lives were lost in the incident.

A little later that same night the *Joseph G. Cannon* (Richmond, January 1943) was lying off Avola Harbour along the coast. So was the British hospital ship *Talamba,* fully marked and illuminated in accordance with the Geneva Convention. German bombers sank the *Talamba* but fortunately there was no loss of life despite the fact she was carrying 400 wounded. The bombers missed the *Cannon* that night but not when they came back on the following morning. A bomb struck her No. 5 hold, killing several British soldiers on board. The *Cannon* settled until her stern was on the bottom, but was not abandoned. She was subsequently raised and towed to Malta for repairs. Two months later she returned to the United States carrying Italian POWs.

On the following day, the 13th, and again off Avola, a tragedy occurred that involved British troops being carried on the Liberty *Timothy Pickering* (Richmond, April 1942). The ship was hit either by an aerial torpedo or by a bomb, the authorities differ, which struck No. 4 hold before penetrating the engine-room and exploding there. The explosion set off a chain reaction in the ship's cargo of ammunition, and soon the entire midships section was engulfed in flames. Most of the 128 British troops on board were trapped below. There was no time to launch boats or rafts and those members of the crew and Armed Guard that could, jumped overboard or slid down ropes into the water. Only twenty-nine men survived the tragedy and of those only one was a British soldier. Two hours later the still-burning *Pickering* was finished off by a British destroyer.

The *Samuel Parker* (Portland, Oregon, November 1942) was anchored off the beachhead at Avola for ten days whilst discharging her consignment of troops and her cargo. Every night there were air attacks. On the 19th the ship was straddled by twelve bombs, one damaging the port bow, other near misses peppering the hull with shrapnel. On the 22nd, more near-misses damaged the ship again. She was then strafed, machine-gun fire killing two Armed Guardsmen on board. When the ship eventually arrived at Tripoli, something of the order of 200 holes were found in her hull plating and superstructure. For his actions during Operation 'Husky', the *Palmer*'s master, Captain Elmer John Stull was given a British 'mention in despatches'. So was Lieutenant Stanley Williams RNR, who was serving aboard the ship during the operation. For six months the *Palmer* shuttled troops and stores around the Mediterranean theatre of war, and was frequently in the front line of battle and often under attack. She epitomised the Liberty as both a war- and work-horse. When she finally arrived back in the States for repairs, those original 200 holes had multiplied several times. She richly deserved the hero's welcome she received, and she became the first recipient of the 'Gallant Ship' award. Before she was scrapped in Florida in 1968, the plaque that went with the award was removed and it is now on display at the offices of the US Maritime Administration.

Ships on their way to Sicilian ports with supplies and reinforcements and others leaving those ports in ballast after being discharged did not escape the attention of the Germans. One of the latter was the Liberty *Pierre Soule* (New Orleans, February 1943). She sailed from Palermo, Sicily for Bizerte, Tunisia, together with three destroyers and a naval tug. The escorts could not prevent Lieutenant Commander Rother in *U-380* from firing a torpedo at the merchantman on the evening of 23 August 1943. It struck right aft, blowing off the ship's rudder and propeller and damaging the propeller shaft and engines. Water pouring through the shaft tunnel (which runs from the stern through Holds 4 and 5 to the engine-room) partially flooded the after holds and engine spaces. The ship was carrying fifty passengers in addition to the crew and Armed Guard, but no one was injured. Captain Patrick Driscoll and his men stayed aboard the immobilised ship and took on board a tow-rope from the tug USS *Nauset*. The ship was successfully towed to Bizerte and eventually to Taranto for repairs, and lived to fight another day.

The Allied successes in North Africa followed by the taking of Sicily, opened up the Mediterranean and the Suez Canal to 'passing through' traffic. The much shorter voyages now possible from the USA and Britain to the Middle East via the Mediterranean (and vice versa of course) had a significant effect on overall ship availability. Although the Allies were not slow in taking advantage of the route, the Mediterranean remained the haunt of some German submarines, and the Luftwaffe continued to make many sorties against ports and ships.

Two Liberties were lost, one immediately after the other, from torpedoes fired from a single U-boat on 26 August 1943. Convoy USG-14 was making for the Middle East and on that date was passing between Sardinia and the North African coast. Lieutenant Commander Fenski on *U-410* caught the convoy when at its most vulnerable, just as the ships were forming into fewer columns to pass through a swept channel through a minefield. Fenski's first torpedo struck *John Bell* (Houston, March 1943), his second, the *Richard Henderson* (Richmond, February 1943). The *Bell* was hit aft where a cargo of aviation spirit was stowed and soon that part of the ship was a mass of flames. Five Armed Guardsmen stationed on the poop had no option but to save themselves by leaping into the sea. As the flames began to creep forward, Captain David Higbee ordered abandon ship. Not long afterwards, the ship was ablaze from stem to stern although she did not sink until the following morning. Apart from one man who had been working in the shaft tunnel when the torpedo struck, all the crew were saved. Some of them were picked by the *Southern Maid*, a whaler in the service of the Royal South African Navy. *Southern Maid* was also involved in picking up some of the survivors from the *Robert Henderson*. A torpedo had struck that ship right aft, blowing away both the rudder and propeller and flooding the engine-room. No one was killed, and the crew got away in six lifeboats. The men aboard three of them were picked up by rescue ships, but under the overall charge of Captain Lawrence Silk, the other three boats made it safely to La Calle on the Algerian coast on the following day.

After gaining control of Sicily, the Allies launched thrusts against mainland Italy in early September 1943. On the 3rd of that month the British 8th Army crossed the Straits of Messina in Operation 'Baytown'. In Operation 'Avalanche' on the 9th the American 5th Army landed at Salerno. The *James W. Marshall* (Los Angeles, December 1942) was lying about a mile and a half off the beachhead at Salerno on 13 September. Most of her cargo of tanks, guns and amphibious vehicles had already been discharged when, in mid-afternoon, the anchorage was attacked by German bombers. One 250lb bomb struck the ship's bridge, glanced off and then exploded in the cabin of Captain Ragnar Roggenbihl who fortunately was not in it at the time. There were no casualties and a small fire on board was soon put out. Two days later the anchorage was again attacked by planes and this time the *Marshall* was not so fortunate. A glider bomb penetrated the boat deck and then exploded in the engine-room, destroying much of the crew accommodation on the way. Fire broke out, on the ship and on two landing craft tanks (LCTs, vessels much smaller than the sea-going LSTs) loaded with cased gasoline which were lying alongside the ship. The midships section of the *Marshall* was soon an inferno, and many of the crew and the 100 Army stevedores on board were only able to save themselves by jumping over the side or clambering down it via cargo nets. Thirteen crew members and fifty stevedores did not make it. The British freighter *Empire Perdita* later towed the *Marshall* to Bizerte for temporary repairs. In February 1944 she was towed to Britain. Two days after D-Day she was scuttled off Normandy as part of the Gooseberry breakwater.

During that same spate of air attacks on the Salerno anchorage the *Bushrod Washington* (Baltimore, April 1943) met a fiery end. For three days she had been discharging her cargo including ammunition and aviation spirit, under almost continuous air attacks. Then, on the afternoon of 14 August her luck ran out. An aircraft coming out of the sun dropped two 500lb bombs. One missed but the other hit the boat deck and exploded above the engine-room. The force of the explosion was so violent that the entire engine was lifted from its seatings and moved over to starboard. Then the aviation spirit in No. 4 hold ignited. Valiant attempts were made to put the fire out but the ship's pumps were unable to cope and soon flames were shooting mast high. Captain Jonathan Wainwright then had no option but to order the crew and the 200 Army stevedores on board to abandon ship. Two lifeboats were launched, but many men decided to jump overboard or clamber down cargo nets to await the arrival of LCTs to pluck them off. Four crewmen and ten stevedores lost their lives. A fire-boat arrived on the scene but her attempts to douse the fire also failed. The *Washington* burned into the next day and then exploded as the fire reached a consignment of bombs.

Two Liberties became casualties on their way to Salerno during September 1943. Carrying a cargo of guns, gasoline and ammunition, and with 191 soldiers on board, the *William W. Gerhard* (Baltimore, May 1943) was part of a convoy making for the beachhead from Oran. In mid-morning on 21 September a torpedo from *U-593*, Lieutenant Commander Kelbling, hit the ship on the port side of No. 1 hold. The explosion lifted the ship's bow from the water and the deck buckled just forward of the bridge. As the vessel began to shake as if by some giant hand, Captain Olaf Anderson ordered the engines stopped. The forward holds filled with water and suddenly large cracks appeared on both sides of the hull.

Captain Anderson ordered abandon ship and soon the surrounding sea was crowded with men aboard four lifeboats, four life-rafts and fifteen floats. The escort commander was not satisfied that the ship was beyond saving and ordered the Liberty crew back aboard whilst the troops were taken aboard other ships. The salvage tug USS *Moreno* took the ship in tow, but three hours later fire broke out in the Liberty's foremost hold. Two more tugs, the USS *Narrangansett* and HMT *Weazel,* went close alongside to fight the fire with their hoses, but the attempts failed. The crew abandoned ship for the second time and were taken aboard *Moreno.* As the ship blazed through the night there came a series of explosions on board after which she broke in two. The forward end sank immediately and in the morning the after part was sunk by gunfire from the tugs. One Armed Guardsman died in the initial explosion, and later another died aboard the British Hospital Ship *Vita.* Everyone else survived.

On 22 September the *Richard Olney* (New Orleans, February 1943) was making for Salerno from Malta in a small convoy comprising two other Liberties, two British corvettes and an armed trawler. The *Olney* was carrying trucks, ammunition and 143 troops. The convoy was off Bizerte when the ship struck a mine which holed her on both sides close to the engine-room, killing two men. Although well down by the stern, the ship showed little sign of sinking immediately and Captain Erich Richter did not order abandon ship. HMS *Landguard* (ex-American cutter USS *Shoshone*) arrived on the scene and took the Liberty in tow. On arrival at Bizerte the damage to the ship's bottom was found to be so extensive that she was declared a constructive total loss. In danger of sinking and blocking the harbour she was beached. In 1948 the wreck was dismantled by Italian ship breakers.

Just over a month before the Italian capitulation on 8 September 1943, a Liberty was involved in one of the last acts of war by the Italian Navy against the Allies. On 4 August the *Harrison Grey Otis* (Los Angeles, January 1943) was lying in the Bay of Gibraltar awaiting a convoy for home. About 4 o'clock in the morning a sharp-eyed lookout spotted a man in the water. The swimmer seemed to be exhausted and a cadet engineer from *Otis* dived in and rescued him. On board the ship the man identified himself as belonging to the Italian Navy. Suspecting that the swimmer may have 'fitted' his ship with a limpet mine, Captain Roy Moyes called for aid from ashore and then carried out the standard practice of turning over the ship's engines in the hope that the wash would dislodge the mine. A British naval officer boarded and took the prisoner ashore, promising to return with a diver. The diver had not arrived when three hours later a violent explosion tore a great hole in the side of No. 3 hold. As water flooded that hold and the engine-room, Moyes ordered the anchor cable slipped and then beached his vessel. One man was killed and eight injured in the explosion. The *Otis* was subsequently declared a constructive total loss.

The Allied advance up the spine of Italy turned out to be disappointingly slow. The German Army dug in its heels and managed to slow the advance at several places. One of those was the Gustav Line, sometimes called the Hitler Line, which stretched right across the leg of that country from a point about halfway between Naples and Anzio on the west coast. On 22 January 1944 a combined British and American force landed behind the Gustav at Anzio. This was another beachhead off which Allied ships suffered heavy air attacks. A Liberty lost there was the *Elihu Yale* (Portland, Oregon, June 1942). Under the command of Captain Thure Ekstrom she anchored off the beachhead on 13 February 1944 with a cargo that included ammunition and gasoline. By the evening of the second day about one third of the cargo had been discharged. An air raid alert then sounded as eight enemy planes appeared overhead. A glider bomb from one of them passed straight through the *Yale's* deck aft into the by now empty No. 4 hold and blew great holes in both sides of the ship. The after mast came down in a tangled mass of wreckage and wires, and pipes were bursting all over the place. All was pandemonium. Fire broke out, spreading to an LCT alongside. Soon the ship's stern was resting on the bottom. Despite the fire-fighting attempts of the crew and the nearly 200 stevedores on board, and the help provided by the USS *Hopi*, the fire spread forward to the superstructure. It also spread aft into No. 5 hold which still held ammunition. Everyone abandoned ship although later Captain Ekstrom and some of his men reboarded as the *Hopi's* hoses gradually had an effect. The fires were out by the following morning and some of the cargo in the forward holds was able to be salvaged. The ship itself was declared a constructive total loss. Twelve men including seven Army stevedores lost their lives during the incident.

Italy's capitulation was soon followed by that country's declaration of war on Germany. One of the effects of that was that units of the Italian Navy now came to be used to escort Allied merchant vessels. On 10 March 1944 the Liberty *William B. Woods* (Brunswick, June 1943) sailed from Palermo bound for Naples carrying 407 American troops, together with ammunition and stores. Her escort was the Italian destroyer *Aretusa*. About fifty miles off the coast the *Woods* was hit aft by a torpedo from *U-952*, Lieutenant Commander Curio. The explosion blew a hole in the ships side at No. 5 hold and fractured the propeller shaft. Fortunately a consignment of bombs in that hold did not blow. At first Captain Edward Ames thought his ship could be saved, but had to order abandon ship as the *Woods* began to settle. Most of the members of the ship's crew and Armed Guard, and most of the troops got away on four lifeboats and fourteen rafts. However, seventy men including Captain Ames were left on board. Ames started those on constructing temporary rafts but as the ship began sinking by the stern, he ordered everyone over the side, He was the last to leave. For reasons best known to himself the commanding officer of *Aretusa* made no attempt either to launch rescue boats or to pick up men from the water. The work of rescue was left to two small British vessels which later arrived on the scene. Fifty-one troops and one Armed Guardsmen were lost.

An important feature of all the campaigns in the Mediterranean, important in that it resulted in a reduction in Allied ship availability, was the high incidence of stevedore damage sustained by merchant ships at ports all around that sea. Every such incident meant that sooner or later the ship had to be taken out of service for repairs. In fact the nature of most of the damage, bent and broken derrick booms for example, meant that the repairs had to be carried out before the ship could effectively be used again. As most ports in the area had no repair facilities, the necessary voyage to a port which had, increased the unavailability time. At most of the ports along the North African coast and on the east coast of Italy, the responsibility for unloading ships lay with the Ports Section of Britain's Royal Engineers. At other ports, including those on the west coast of Italy, that responsibility lay with American forces. Many of these military stevedores were experienced in the work, but a number were not. Even when experienced stevedores were being used, the necessity for fast turnaround times in order to get cargoes to the front line as soon as possible and to reduce the time a ship lay in port or at an anchorage and therefore vulnerable to air attack, meant that slow and careful cargo handling was very often not an option. British records indicate that masters of ships in British-operated ports spent much of their time making reports to the military port authorities about such damages. There might be a war on, but shipmasters were still responsible to the managing shipping company for making requisite claims for damages. On Liberty ships the most frequent cause for complaint seems to have concerned dropped and damaged derricks. Some of these cases were attributed to winch mechanical failure, but most seem to be have been caused by careless or too-rapid cargo handling. Damage caused to the ships' structures down in the holds was often sustained when lifting heavy items such as tanks and guns.[2]

At the port of Valetta, Malta, the Liberty *John Morton* (Richmond, August 1942) suffered from a different sort of problem when she arrived there on 22 October 1943. She was carrying a consignment of anchors and cables in one of her holds which the derricks at that hold could not lift. The consignment had been loaded in the States by a giant shore-based crane, but no one had bothered to inform Valetta of this. In consequence time was lost until the Naval Dockyard Crane Berth became available.

Other events resulting in ship delays in ports were damages caused by striking dock walls whilst berthing, or by collisions with other ships. At

---

2. File MT59/34 at the PRO Kew, contains details of many such claims.

Valetta on 29 November 1943, the *Hugh S. Legare* (Los Angeles, January 1943) was damaged whilst 'shifting ship' from one berth to another. In his report Captain F. Skousgard did not state who he thought was to blame. At Catania in Sicily, Captain Charles Bertun of the *David L. Swain* (Wilmington, March 1943) was distinctly annoyed when his ship was rammed and damaged by *LST 33* which was being used as a lighter. Whilst berthing in the harbour at Bone, Algeria on 13 April 1944 the *William W. Campbell* (Richmond, November 1943) rammed and damaged another Liberty the *Theodore Foster* (Baltimore, June 1942) which was already lying alongside. It was, of course, Captain H.G. Foss of the innocent *Foster* who lodged a complaint with the British Port Control Officer.

CHAPTER 15

The Poison Gas Disaster at Bari

One of the best-kept secrets of the Second World War, at least until December 1943, was the fact that the Allies kept stocks of poison gas close to most front lines. They were available for immediate retaliatory purposes should the Axis powers use gas first. In the Far East the Allies knew that Japan had used chemical weaponry including gas during its war with China in the late 1930s. That knowledge, together with intelligence reports that the Japanese had been conducting tests and training men in the use of such weapons for years at Narashino, some eighteen miles east of Tokyo, had led Britain to build up a stock of 12,000 gas shells and 4500 gas bombs in Malaya and Singapore prior to the Japanese capture of those places. During the Malayan campaign itself, Australian troops reported several instances of the use by Japanese troops of chemical weaponry, but the incidents had been of a minor nature and so no retaliatory action was deemed necessary.[1]

The Allies were concerned that Germany, the country that had initiated this type of warfare during the First World War, might do so again. It was thought that Hitler, as his armies were pressed back towards the fatherland, might decide to use gas as a weapon of last resort. Britain in particular amongst the Allies had good reason for assuming that at some point Hitler might well use such weaponry. At the time Britain had 'stood alone' in the desperate year that began with the fall of France in the summer of 1940, General Sir John Dill, Chief of the Imperial General Staff, had put forward the proposal that should the Germans invade Britain, mustard gas should be used against them on the beaches. The proposal met with considerable opposition, it being argued that Britain would lose the moral high ground if this time round it was she who initiated gas warfare. Dill withdrew his proposal, only to find that Winston Churchill had given the idea his support. It was Churchill's view that when a country has its back to the wall, any steps taken to save the day are acceptable however morally reprehensible they might be. As the war progressed and it was Germany with its back against the wall, the Allies attributed the same kind of attitude to the Germans.

Churchill never lost his willingness to authorise the use of gas under

---

1. See this author's *Singapore, the Pregnable Fortress* (London 1995), pp198-206, and *Far Eastern File, the Intelligence War in the Far East 1930-1945* (London 1997).

certain circumstances. In 1941 he said it might suit Allied purposes to use it during a future invasion of Europe, and in 1942 he threatened to 'drench' German cities with gas in the event the Germans used it against the Russians, repeating the sentiment in the following year. 'We must', he wrote in a minute to General Ismay, Secretary to the Imperial General Staff and Churchill's personal link with that body, 'be ready to strike and make good any threat we utter with the utmost promptitude and severity'.[2]

President Roosevelt found the idea of any kind of chemical warfare particularly repellent, but even so, in a statement made in August 1943 which publicly outlined Allied policy on the use of gas, he warned that should 'such desperate and barbarous methods' be used against any one of the United Nation, then:

> We promise to any perpetrators of such crime full and swift retaliation in kind . . . any use of these inhumane methods on their part will be brought down swiftly and surely upon their own heads.

Despite Roosevelt's abhorrence of this type of warfare, with the Chinese experience in mind and from fear that the Japanese might one day unleash gas warfare against the United States or its territories, he very early on authorised a gas production programme. Not only that, from the winter of 1940, twelve months before Pearl Harbor, the United States Chemical Warfare Service began supplying Britain with about 200 tons of phosgene gas every month; it was shipped in foreign bottoms to preserve the image of American neutrality. After the United States came into the war, such shipments were moved around in American ships and for that country's own account.

The United States Army had several elite and highly secret chemical warfare specialist groups. One of these groups, led by Lieutenant Howard Beckstrom of the Army 701 Chemical Maintenance Company based at Baltimore, Maryland, specialised in the transportation of the stuff. In November 1943 Beckstrom and his six-man team received orders to oversee the transportation of 2000 M47AI mustard gas bombs from the Eastern Chemical Warfare Depot at Edgewood in Maryland, down to the port of Baltimore. At that port he was to see the shipment safely loaded aboard the American Liberty ship *John Harvey* (built Wilmington, January 1943 and managed by Agwilines of New York). Furthermore, he and his men were then to voyage with the ship to a destination somewhere in the Mediterranean theatre of operations.

Throughout the war all dealings with Allied gas stocks were very much on a 'need-to-know' basis, with few people anywhere being told of their

---

2. Memo dated 27 February 1943 from Churchill to Ismay in PREM3/88-3, PRO, Kew.

existence. This was in case the enemy discovered that gas was being stockpiled near the front line, which discovery might of itself be used as the excuse to initiate gas warfare, or cause the stockpiles to be deliberately attacked. In consequence, Beckstrom's operation was carried out under conditions of the utmost secrecy associated with the most stringent safety checks. The high level of secrecy involved with all such shipments, in which only the senior commander in theatre was put in the picture, was on this occasion to have horrific consequences.

Mustard gas was produced in the United States by a cheap and speedy method which resulted in an end product containing a high percentage of impurities. These impurities caused instability, which increased with the length of time the gas was kept in storage. In fact, amongst the very few in the know, the American product was notorious for being unstable. The job that Beckstrom and his men had to do during the month-long voyage to Bari in south-eastern Italy, via Oran, and Augusta, Sicily, was not therefore an enviable one. It was their job to see that the 'tween-decks in which the bombs were stowed were kept well ventilated and that the bomb casings (each was some 4ft in length and 8in in diameter) were regularly inspected for signs of leakage and corrosion. Whether any leaky ones were found and if so what happened to them, is not known, but aboard a ship there is always a handy and all-encompassing depository close by.

In command of *John Harvey* was Captain Elvin F. Knowles. He was aged forty-three and came from South Thomaston, Maine. Short and stocky in stature, he walked with a limp because of a club-foot. He had already seen war service, his previous ship being the *Ozark* on which he had served with distinction as First Mate in a convoy to Murmansk. Despite the secrecy surrounding the ship's special cargo it is likely that Knowles knew something about it, for it is scarcely conceivable that he would have permitted soldiers to have free access to the 'tween-decks of his ship without demanding some sort of explanation. It is likely that he was informed of the special nature of part of his cargo by the official representative of the US Army Transportation Corps, Lieutenant Thomas Richardson, who sailed as the ship's cargo officer. There is no place like the cloistered confines of a ship for rumours to get around fast. In an earlier century American sailors had even invented a word for shipborne rumour and gossip; 'scuttlebutt'. So, even if Captain Knowles was the only crew member officially to know about the mustard gas, others, including Deck Cadet Jim Cahill and Seaman Walter Brook who had heard the scuttlebutt, knew that the ship was carrying something highly secret.

The *John Harvey* arrived at Bari on 28 November 1943 only to find the harbour crowded with Allied shipping. The unloading berths were full, and many other ships were awaiting their turn in the unloading queue. Bari was suffering from the same malady that affected all Allied-controlled ports throughout the North African and Italian campaign areas – port congestion. Despite any knowledge he may have possessed about the nature of some of his cargo, Captain Knowles apparently did not demand priority unloading from the authorities in the British-run port. What is more to the point, it is almost certain that neither did Lieutenant Beckstrom, the man with full knowledge of the special shipment, nor Lieutenant Richardson, the cargo officer. The reason behind this reticence must have been the orders both men had received over the need to keep the consignment secret. To have attempted to jump the queue would have set tongues a-wagging, and careless talk could have been picked up by enemy agents in a port which had only recently been liberated from the Germans.

A contrary view has been given by Glen Infield in his book *Disaster at Bari.* Infield states that Lieutenant Richardson reported the nature of the special cargo to the British port authorities and that priority unloading was not granted. Infield presented no evidence to support this claim, and as we shall see, he certainly could not have gained this information from Richardson himself. Infield's statement is not supported by British records. A Prime Ministerial file dated 10 January 1944 stated that 'The American authorities had failed to inform the British Commander-in-Chief of the nature of the cargo'.[3] Infield's statement is not supported either by the subsequent turn of events.

The upshot was that Captain Knowles was ordered to moor his ship stern-on to the outer eastern mole, and there await his turn to unload. *John Harvey* was still moored in that position on 2 December, on which date there were over thirty Allied ships in Bari harbour, twenty-five of them merchantmen. Nine of the ten American merchant ships in port were Liberty ships – Glen Infield lists only seven, missing out both the *Grace Abbott* (Baltimore, October 1942) and the *John M. Scholfield* (Richmond, November 1942). Lying with *John Harvey* on the mole amongst a total of thirteen ships there, were *John L. Motley, Joseph Wheeler,* and *John Bascom.* The other five Liberties, *Samuel J. Tilden, Lyman Abbott, Grace Abbott, John M. Scholfield* and *Louis Hennepin* were moored or berthed alongside at other places within the port complex. The tenth American merchantman was the elderly *Hadley F. Brown* which was alongside and being unloaded. (A Liberty ship with this name was launched six months after the Bari incident.) The *John Harvey* certainly had the most dangerous cargo of any ship in port, but there were many other dangerous cargoes around. All the American ships were carrying ammunition, or explosives, or cased gasoline, some of them all three, a deadly mix if ever there was one. The American naval tankers USS *Aroostook* and USS *Pumper* were also in port, both loaded with high octane gasoline.

---

3. PREM3 88/3, PRO, Kew.

The British *Samaye* (built Baltimore, September 1943 as the *James T. Earle* and on her maiden voyage) had sailed that very morning, so there was now no British Liberty left among the seven ships in the port flying the Red Ensign.[4] But two half-sisters were there, the *Fort Athabaska* and *Fort Lajoie*. Another of the British contingent was Bank Line's *Testbank*, heavily laden with ammunition; she was in the line of ships moored along the eastern mole. *Lars Krus,* a Norwegian ship but sailing under the British flag and a veteran of the Arctic convoys, was at anchor in the harbour with a cargo of aviation spirit in drums, yet another dangerous cargo. The other three British vessels were the *Devon Coast* and *Brittany Coast,* and the *Crista.* The remainder of the merchants ships were Norwegian, Polish, Dutch, and Italian, the Italians having by that date converted to the Allied cause. Several British and American warships were also at anchor in the port.

Moored two ships along from the *John Harvey* on the eastern mole, was the Liberty *John Bascom* (Panama City, April 1943). In command of her was Captain Otto Heitmann, a Moore-McCormack company veteran whose sea service dated from 1922. Heitmann was a consummate seamen and a very brave man. Almost exactly a year before when in command of *West Maximus* he had, at great risk to his own ship, rescued survivors from the British freighter *Teesbank* which had been torpedoed in the Atlantic by *U-128*. At Bari when Heitmann saw the nearby *Testbank* belonging to the same British shipping line, he must have been reminded of that event. Unlike a number of other American shipmasters, Captain Heitmann got on very well with the commander of the thirty-man Armed Guard unit on his ship, Ensign Kay Vesole, USNR. The two men admired each other and had built up a good working relationship, one that managed to bridge the divide caused by the fact that the Armed Guard were subject to naval rules and regulations and were not directly subject to the captain's orders. Vesole was thirty years of age which was somewhat older than most officers in charge of Armed Guard units, and maybe this comparative maturity was at the root of the good relationship.

By 2 December the German army had been pressed back more than 125 miles north of Bari and on that very afternoon Air Marshal Sir Arthur 'Maori' Coningham, Commander Allied Tactical Air Forces in Italy, announced at a press conference that the Allies had total air supremacy over southern Italy and that he would consider it a personal affront if the *Luftwaffe* attempted any significant action in his area. By late evening he must have wished he had eaten those words for by then he had been affronted by the worst Allied port disaster from enemy air action since

---

4. Information from John Hampson, Fourth Engineer aboard *Samaye* at the time.

Pearl Harbor.[5] So complacent were the Allies and so important was the task of getting cargoes unloaded in the fastest possible time, that no special air raid precautions were taken at Bari. The port lay lit by ships' arc lights and by quayside working lights, making it an ideal target for the more than one hundred German Junkers 88 bombers when they roared in from seaward at 1930 hours. So crowded was the harbour, and so well lit, there was little need for the air crews to waste much time taking aim, though to make sure they did drop some parachute flares. When the planes finally departed some twenty minutes later they had sunk seventeen ships and badly damaged another eight, and destroyed quays, warehouses and cranes, and thousands of tons of military equipment and supplies.

The dropping of the parachute flares provided some warning to the crew of *John Bascom*. Rushing to the bridge Captain Heitmann ordered 'battle stations!'. As shore-based anti-aircraft guns opened up, Ensign Vesole's men joined in with the ship's guns, as did other ships in the harbour. The night sky was soon lit with tracer, and everywhere the noise was terrific. Bombs first exploded in the city before the raiders began concentrating on the ships. Sweeping from south to north, some of the German aircraft worked their way along the line of ships on the eastern mole. *Joseph Wheeler* (Mobile, November 1942) took a direct hit and exploded in flames, killing everyone on board. (That ship had been lucky earlier on in the year. In the summer she had sailed from Santos, Brazil, in company with another Liberty. The other ship was attacked by a U-boat and the *Wheeler* returned to port. Peter Salvo, an engine-room hand on board, says that the word spread fast in Santos that an American ship had been sunk. On seeing some of the men from *Wheeler* ashore, the local populace thought they were survivors and feted them with food and liquor. 'But the next day, when the real survivors came ashore, we had a lot of explaining to do', says Salvo. Fortunately for him he had left the ship by the time she sailed for Bari.)

Then it was the turn of *John L. Motley* (Baltimore, May 1943) which was lying next to the *Bascom*. She received a direct hit and burst into flames. Elsewhere in the port the *Samuel J. Tilden* (Portland, Oregon, November 1942) suffered several direct hits and caught fire before sinking. The nearby *Lyman Abbot* (Providence, RI, May 1943) miraculously escaped direct hits although a near miss tore up her decks and started a fire. The American naval tanker USS *Aroostook* blew up, the blast from that explosion causing windows in houses many miles inland to shatter. Somehow the *Grace Abbott* and the *John M. Scholfield* managed to escape serious damage and the *Louis Hennepin* (Richmond, May 1943) suffered none at all. Up to that point so had the gas-carrying *John Harvey*, although the crew were seen

---

5. See Dwight D. Eisenhower, *Crusade in Europe* (London 1948).

busy putting out a small fire which had apparently been caused when burning debris from another ship landed on it.

Of the British contingent *Testbank* caught a direct hit and blew up taking all but a handful of her seventy-five man crew with her. It was a similar story with the *Fort Athabaska* (J & C Harrison Ltd.); when she exploded, forty-six of her complement including Captain W.E. Cook, lost their lives, the only crew members surviving being those who had gone ashore, amongst them Chief Officer Ellis. Ellis later reported that his ship had been loaded with two captured German rocket bombs which were being taken back to England for examination. 'It is possible that . . . [they] . . . may have exploded at some time', he said in his report. He left the port on the following day aboard an undamaged freighter and noted, 'I recognised the remains of our ship as we steamed through the harbour. She was a burnt out wreck resting on the bottom with not even the funnel or masts standing'.[6]

The *Lars Krus* sank after receiving a direct hit after which she began spewing aviation spirit into the harbour, where, with the gasoline from *Aroostook,* it formed a deadly mix on the surface of the water. That mixture was soon to become even more lethal. The *Fort Lajoie* was luckier. There were two giant explosions on board and the ship was peppered with red hot splinters, but she survived, although one man was killed and eight injured. Captain D.M. Sinclair afterwards reported:

> Everyone on board was stunned by the explosion and remained so for about ten minutes . . . In common with everyone else on board my recollection of the whole incident is somewhat blurred. Even the men who saw the beginning of the raid are now hazy as to what actually happened due to the very severe concussion they received as the ammunition ships exploded.[7]

During a brief respite in the bombing, from the bridge of his still-undamaged *John Bascom,* Captain Heitmann looked about him. His main worry was the *John L. Motley* which was ablaze and lying less than 30ft away with its cargo of bombs and high-octane petrol. He thought about cutting his ship's moorings and heading out into the harbour, but ahead of him and less than two ship lengths away, there were two ships at anchor. He had just reached the conclusion that his ship was trapped, when the German aircraft came roaring in again.[8] This time the *Bascom* was hit by at least three bombs. They struck aft, against the fore part of the bridge, and on the fore deck. Heitmann found himself flying through

---

6. ADM199/2146, PRO, Kew.
7. Ibid.
8. From 'Report of Captain Otto Heitmann', War Shipping Administration, Washington, 24 January 1944.

the air as the force of one of the explosions slammed him into the side of the wheelhouse. When he regained his senses he was covered in blood but managed to struggle to his feet. From first one wing of the bridge and then the other, he surveyed the damage to his ship. The fore deck had caved in with every hatch blown open, and half the front of the bridge had disappeared. Fires were burning everywhere. Only one of the ship's four lifeboats seemed still to be serviceable. Heitmann yelled out to Second Mate William Rudolph to prepare the boat for lowering and to place any wounded men in it. Amongst the badly wounded was First Mate Tony Hughes, with head and shoulder injuries. Ensign Vesole came up to report that all the ship's guns were out of action. He too was badly wounded, but refused to get into the boat before his men. Heitmann took a last look around the harbour. Everywhere there were fires and explosions and in places the sea appeared to be alight as the oil on the surface ignited. Along the line of ships on the east mole, or what had been a line of ships a short while ago, every one appeared to be afire. He could make out figures on the deck of *John Harvey,* still not hit by bombs, striving to put fires out. All in all, it was like a scene from Dante's Inferno. His eyes turned again to his own ship. There was no saving her, and so he ordered abandon ship.

The lifeboat built to hold thirty-two men had already been loaded with fifty-four when Heitmann ordered it lowered. It was so overcrowded that the sea came almost up to the gunwales. From *Bascom's* deck the captain ordered the remaining survivors into the water, there to hold on to the boat's life-lines. Heitmann, the last to leave, then lowered himself into the boat by a rope. Aboard the boat there was scarcely room to move and the only unbroken oar available together with the broken half of another, produced no more than a slow crawl through the water as Heitmann ordered the craft headed towards the nearest landing point on the east mole. Only a ship's length away, it took long minutes to reach under the threat of a burning sheet of oil that seemed to be chasing them. Reaching the mole Heitmann ordered everyone up on to it. Flames from burning ships blocked any attempt to walk along it towards the docks and city, so the Captain ordered his men to make for the lighthouse at its seaward end.

Although by that time the German planes had left, the mayhem in the port was a long, long way from over. Not very far away from the group huddled together around the lighthouse, a group that was growing steadily larger as survivors from other ships joined those from *Bascom,* the burning *John L. Motley* had broken her moorings and was drifting in the general direction of the lighthouse. Further along the *John Harvey* was now ablaze from stem to stern.[9] As the *John L. Motley* bore

9. American Official Report entitled *Toxic Gas Burns in the Bari Harbor Catastrophe* by Lt. Colonel Stewart Alexander USAMC dated 27 December 1943.

down relentlessly towards the end of the pier there was nothing the men clustered there could do about it except watch and pray. But suddenly the *Motley* blew up, the blast from it tossing Heitmann and some of the others several feet in the air. The already seriously-injured Ensign Vesole received further head injuries. A tidal wave created by the blast washed over the mole taking several seamen with it. The blast from *Motley* was bad enough, but it was as nothing compared with the one that followed almost immediately as the *John Harvey* blew up. Heitmann later described it as the 'worst detonation' he had ever heard. At the later Official Inquiry it was suggested that aboard *John Harvey*, Captain Knowles, acting perhaps on the advice of Lieutenant Beckstrom, had made an attempt to scuttle his ship. But no one could be sure because Knowles, Cargo Officer Richardson, Lieutenant Beckstrom together with all six men of his gas team, the only ones around who knew exactly what was on board, lost their lives in the explosion along with every other member of the crew apart from a few lucky men who were on shore leave.

When the ship blew up, the explosion vented her deadly cargo over the harbour. Some of the mustard gas burned, whilst some evaporated and rose into the night sky to mix there with the smoke and flames from many fires to eventually end up over the town. The contents of other gas bombs leaked into the sea, there to form a deadly cocktail with the gasoline and aviation spirit already floating and burning there. A garlic-like stench that is a characteristic of mustard gas hung over everything, but there was no one left to recognise it for what it was. All over the harbour survivors from stricken and burning ships had taken to lifeboats, whilst many others were in the water clinging to the life-lines of rafts or hanging on to pieces of floating debris. Over their heads hung a deadly cloud, but many of those in the water were not only breathing in mustard gas fumes, they were swimming in a solution of the stuff.

Back on the end of the mole the situation was becoming desperate for Captain Heitmann and his men as blazing patches of oil were blown in their direction. That was not the only danger heading their way. They did not know about the gas, which was why no one including probably the speaker of the words himself, placed much significance on wounded Ensign Vesole's croak to Second Mate Bill Rudolph that he could smell garlic. It was a boat from the naval tanker USS *Pumper* that eventually picked up Captain Heitmann and the other survivors from the end of the mole, but by that time they had already breathed in gas fumes. *Pumper* itself had been extremely lucky, for the *John Harvey* had swung in her direction before blowing up. The force of the explosion caused the tanker to roll almost on to her beam ends, but she righted herself. Although several crew members were injured by flying debris, it seemed that *Pumper's* very proximity to the *Harvey* saved her from more damage and casualties as the blast from the explosion carried most of the debris and gas clear of her.

All around the harbour rescue teams from the few ships still afloat and others from the shore were hauling men from the water and rushing them to hospital. The British, New Zealand and Indian military hospital units based in what had been the town's Polytechnic, were soon having to cope with hundreds of casualties. So was the civilian hospital in the town. The American 26th General Hospital was also based in the town but was not in operation at the time. All its equipment had been aboard the *Samuel J. Tilden*, which was now lying at the bottom of the harbour. Many of those rescued from the harbour area had in one way or another come in into contact with mustard gas, as had many of the rescuers. The cloud of mustard-impregnated smoke from the harbour which had blown in over the town, had caused gas injuries there too. None of the medics had any knowledge of *John Harvey*'s cargo and they therefore treated all cases of exposure and burns brought before them just as they normally would have done. Survivors were wrapped in warm blankets to await their turn to be examined and treated, and all the while the solution was taking its deadly course beneath the wraps.

Over the next few days nearly eighty out of an estimated total of 617 military and merchant navy gas victims died. (That comes to over 13 per cent and should be compared with the more than 70,000 gas victims of the First World War, only 2 per cent of whom died.) In Bari town similar cases developed among the civilian population and it was later estimated that over 1000 civilians died, mostly from the bombing but many from the effects of gas, though the true number of civilian gas victims was never ascertained. Other gas victims either lost their sight completely or suffered less permanent eye damage. Captain A.T. Masten of the British *Devon Coast* which was also sunk during the raid, but with the loss of only one crew member, was taken aboard the depot ship HMS *Vienna*. He reported that on the day after the raid he remarked on how 'foggy' it was in the wardroom of the ship, 'indeed everything was murky before my eyes'. This blurred vision lasted for five days, and the least light caused him great pain. Other victims suffering from what at first had been taken for first-degree burns, had shed vast areas of skin. Some lost all their body hair. In some victims the worst effect was in the genital region, with penis and scrotum swollen to several times their normal size. All the victims suffered terrible pain.

Some of the few ships that had not been badly damaged in the raid hurriedly left the burning port, some of them picking up survivors from the water on the way. The destroyer USS *Bistera* plucked thirty men from the sea before making south for the port of Taranto. By the time the ship arrived there she was in the gravest peril for, from both direct and indirect contamination, many of her crew, including every one of the navigation officers, were blind and suffering other effects of poison gas. On the following day, the badly-damaged Liberty *Lyman Abbot* was ordered out of the wrecked port. She managed that with the only ten members of its crew who had not been killed or suffered injury.

The smell of garlic that so many patients mentioned after the raid, on top of the unusual 'burn' injuries being treated, raised suspicions among some doctors that they were dealing with something unusual. Rumours along those lines abounded in the port. Two of the seven crew members from *John Harvey* who had been lucky enough to be ashore during the raid, Deck Cadet James Cahill and Seaman Walter Brook, when interviewed by a British Royal Marines officer, reported that as well as ammunition the ship had been carrying something that was a 'big secret'.[10] Two days after the air raid, Major Leonard Gluck of the Ophthalmic Unit of the 98th British General Hospital began to suspect that the eyes of many of his patients had been damaged by some kind of chemical agent.

Some of these suspicions were reported to General Eisenhower's Headquarters at Algiers, and Lieutenant Colonel Stewart Alexander, the United States Army Consultant in Chemical Warfare Medicine on Eisenhower's staff was flown into Bari on 7 December, five days after the raid. Colonel Alexander's first cabled reports to Eisenhower from Bari, indicating that there were gas casualties, reportedly caused near panic at headquarters for Colonel Alexander had not by then discovered where the gas had come from; at first it was thought the Germans had initiated gas warfare. Within a day or two however, Alexander discovered the true source by analysing samples taken from the harbour which indicated an American origin for the gas, a fact confirmed when one of the bomb casings was dredged up from the bottom. It was later still when Alexander received official confirmation that a consignment of gas had been aboard *John Harvey*. This sequence of events, all reported by Colonel Alexander, in no way supports Glen Infield's theory that the British port authorities had known of the shipment from the day the ship arrived in port. Not only that, it also tells us that General Eisenhower's headquarters had not known of it either.[11]

As the number of deaths from gas symptoms rose, scientists from Porton Down, Britain's chemical and biological warfare establishment, and from Edgewood Arsenal, its American equivalent, began flying into Bari. According to Colonel Alexander's report, pathological specimens of forty 'representative cases' were despatched to those centres for microscopic examination and study. The disaster had in fact presented Allied scientists with a never-to-be-repeated opportunity for research.

---

10. James L Cahill, Official Statement ss *John Harvey*, War Shipping Administration, Washington, 10 January 1944.
11. Glen Infield, *Disaster at Bari* (London 1974)

At first Eisenhower's HQ attempted to keep the Bari disaster under the tightest of security wraps in case the Germans got wind of it and used it as an excuse for initiating gas warfare anyway. The order went out that all gas deaths must be attributed 'to burns due to enemy action'. But far too many people knew about it including many civilians over whom the military had little control, and it soon became clear that there was no chance of completely burying the matter even from the Germans. In February 1944 in order to take the heat out of the situation, the Allied Combined Chiefs of Staff issued a communiqué reiterating that it was not Allied policy to use gas unless the Axis did so first.

Mr Churchill had left the 'Big Three' Teheran Conference on his way to Cairo on the very day of the raid on Bari, and it was at Cairo that he must have first learned of the raid for no one would have dared to keep such dire information from him. After two further weeks of travelling and meetings, Churchill arrived back in Britain on 16 December. On the 27th Colonel Alexander submitted his full report to General Eisenhower on the gas deaths at Bari. On 2 January 1944 a 'most immediate and most secret' message signed by Eisenhower himself, and addressed to the War Office, Admiralty, and the Air Ministry in London, as well as to Washington, informed the recipients that an Allied ship carrying chemical gas bombs had exploded during the Bari raid and that there had been casualties. Churchill already knew. A 'most immediate' message dated 29 December from Colonel Ian Jacob to Major General Leslie Hollis, both of them military secretaries to the British War Cabinet, stated:

> Prime Minister has already been informed by General Alexander who shared his astonishment that a ship with such a cargo should have been sent to Bari.[12]

None of that prevented Churchill saying in the New Year in reply to a question asked in the House of Commons, that he 'did not believe there were any mustard gas casualties at Bari on the night of 2 December 1943'. Once upon a time during a House of Commons debate, Mr Churchill had been ordered by the Speaker to withdraw the word 'lie' in reference to something said by another member of that assembly. The great man did so, famously using the words 'terminological inexactitude' instead. Churchill was not the only world leader to use a terminological inexactitude over the Bari incident. In his book *Crusade in Europe,* published some five years after the event, General Eisenhower recorded of the Bari raid:

> The greatest damage came from the fact that a fuel ship was struck and the escaping oil carried fiery catastrophe to many of the neighbouring vessels. One circumstance connected with the affair could have had the

---

12. WO193/712, PRO, Kew.

most unfortunate repercussions. One of the ships was loaded with a quantity of mustard gas. . . . Fortunately the wind was offshore and the escaping gas caused no casualties. Had the wind been in the opposite direction, however, great disaster could well have resulted.[13]

Captain Otto Heitmann of the *John Bascom* was one of many who suffered from inhaling gas fumes, and it took him many weeks to recover. For his actions he was awarded the American Merchant Marine's highest award for gallantry, the Distinguished Service Medal, at a ceremony held in New York on 3 October 1945. Ensign Kay Vesole died at one of the military hospitals at Bari in December 1943 from a combination of gas inhalation and the wounds he had received. Third Officer Alan Collins of the same ship also died at Bari from the effects of gas. The men, most of them Allied merchant seamen, who died from the effects of gas at Bari, left a sort of legacy. An important lesson was learned from the disaster and very soon afterwards the Allied High Command issued a directive that the presence of chemical warfare weapons in his area must be notified to the Chief Military Medical Officer concerned, so that his staff could be immediately informed in the event of another such occurrence.

There is a possibility that the *John Harvey* was not the only Liberty ship carrying mustard gas weaponry at Bari that day. In his preliminary report of 27 December 1944 Colonel Stewart Alexander recorded that 'At some time during the evening [of the attack] someone aboard the *Lyman Abbott* called "Gas" . . . Many of the crew put on their gas masks for about half an hour.' That begs two questions. Who aboard the *Abbot* would have been knowledgeable enough to recognise the smell of gas, and why was that ship carrying a supply of gas masks? Like the *Harvey*, the *Abbott* had loaded at Baltimore, but in itself that does not prove mustard shells were loaded there. But the mystery deepens. George Southern had been a British soldier at Bari and was one of a rescue party that had boarded the *Abbott* that night. He says that although there were fires aboard, the ship was in no danger of sinking yet the crew had abandoned. In later years he became interested in the background to the disaster and wrote to the US Navy Department about it. The reply he received included the extraordinary statement that 'Our records show that only one ship was carrying mustard gas, the *Lyman Abbott*'. That report, added to the facts of the ship's fast abandonment, the warning shout, the supply of gas masks, and the hasty removal of the ship from the harbour the following morning, seem to point to there being a consignment of gas on board.

So important was Bari as one of the main unloading ports for vital equipment and supplies for the Allied armies and air forces in Italy, that

13. Eisenhower, op.cit., pp225-6.

all the stops were pulled out to get it working again. Naval salvage units were sent in and the many sunken wrecks were pulled clear of the wharves and harbour and piled up against the moles. Warehouses were hastily rebuilt by army engineers. Nevertheless, the port was out of commission for some weeks and this had an adverse effect on the Allied campaign in Italy, as did the loss of so many ships and the thousands of tons of equipment, supplies, oil and ammunition. General Freiherr von Richthofen, commanding the *Luftwaffe* in northern Italy, must have been well pleased with the work carried out by his air crews. In fact the attack on Bari turned out to be the *Luftwaffe*'s last great success of the war.

The fates had not yet finished with the port of Bari. A second tragedy involving a Liberty ship took place there on 9 April 1945, some sixteen months after the previous horror. This time however, it was not caused by direct enemy action. On that date the Liberty *Charles Henderson* (New Orleans, May 1943) was one of thirteen Allied ships discharging in the harbour. The *Henderson*'s cargo of around 2000 tons of bombs for the USAAF was being unloaded at Berth 14 by Italian stevedores under the charge of British Army sappers. Around midday flames suddenly shot up from No. 5 hold, followed by a tremendous explosion. The after part of the ship disintegrated in flames, and a cloud of black smoke rose several thousand feet in the air with burning debris from the ship raining down all around. The fore part of the ship, still loaded with about half the ship's cargo of bombs, was blown forward, ending up partly on the quay. As well as destroying the *Charles Henderson* the explosion devastated the berth, the adjoining sheds, and all the port equipment in the vicinity. A large section of the ship's bridge landed in the nearby Navy Yard and everything there went up in flames. Three other ships in port including a tanker caught fire. The tidal wave set up by the explosion damaged every other ship in the port and caused some of the wrecks from the previous disaster to be torn away from the mole and to again block the harbour. It took a month to make the port operational again, a job completed just as the war in Europe was drawing to its close.

In between the two disasters at Bari, a Liberty ship was at the centre of another port catastrophe. On 17 July 1944 the *E.A. Bryan,* a recent launching from the nearby Kaiser yard at Richmond, was loading muni-tions at Port Chicago, a port thirty-five miles north of San Francisco, for what was to have been her maiden voyage. Also in the harbour was the Victory ship *Quinault Victory* built at Portland, Oregon, another of Kaiser's yards, and which had only been handed over to its operators a few days before. The *Bryan* had loaded about 5000 tons of munitions when suddenly there was a tremendous explosion on board. The detona-tion set off the munitions already loaded aboard the *Quinalt Victory* and both ships disintegrated, only the twisted remains of them remaining above water. Parts of the ships were blown many miles inland. The explosion almost completely destroyed Port Chicago, with damage extending up to fifty miles away. The blast from it was felt up to 200 miles from the port. Many hundreds of lives were lost and several thousand naval and military personnel injured. A tanker, several Coast Guard vessels, and fire and patrol boats, were also sunk or damaged. The cost of the damage ran into many millions of dollars.

CHAPTER 16

Liberties and the Allied Salvage Services

In a situation where every ton of merchant shipping space saved, not to mention every ton of cargo, was vital to the Allied cause, the role of tugs and salvage teams during the war was extremely important. It was a role that under the glare of publicity given to more glamorous parts of the Allied naval services has gone largely unrecognised. In the process of carrying out this dangerous work, tugs saved more than few Liberty ships and attempted to save many more.

Pre-war naval tugs fell broadly into two categories, harbour tugs used to assist in mooring, and the so-called fleet tugs whose main peacetime occupation was target towing. During the war the number of fleet tugs were augmented by requisitioned commercial deep-sea tugs and by many newly-built ones. Together they came to be called rescue tugs, their main use then being to tow to safety any ships, naval or merchant, damaged by enemy action. Salvage vessels were also constructed, their main purpose being to salve vessels lost in shallow waters. The new vessels were built either in Britain or the United States and all were capable of ocean voyaging. To an extent they were maids of all work. Their powerful jet hoses and foam installations could be used to fight fires, and their auxiliary machinery to supply steam in emergency situations. After towing the damaged Liberty *Jared Ingersoll* (Baltimore, August 1942) to be beached near Algiers on 1 April 1944, for example, HM tug *Mindful* stood by and supplied steam for *Ingersoll's* winches as her cargo was discharged into another Liberty, the *William Johnson* (launched at the same yard in June 1942).

The work of the tugs was far from easy and could be very dangerous. Some of it was carried out under fire, and a number of tugs became casualties themselves during the war. The first to be lost was the British-built *St. Abbs* dating from 1918 which was sunk by German aircraft off the Dunkirk beaches on 1 June 1940 whilst ferrying troops from the shore. A sister-ship, although in her case built at Hong Kong in 1919, was the *St. Breock*. Under Lieutenant A.G. Clarke RN she sailed from Singapore on 12 February 1942, three days before that 'fortress' fell, only to be sunk by Japanese aircraft on the 14th in the Sebayor Strait off Sumatra. One of the new breed, *Sesame* built in October 1943, was sunk off Normandy by an E-boat five days after D-Day.

It can be taken as a general rule that the British tugs and salvage vessels that worked deep-sea flew the White Ensign, whilst those that worked in coastal waters flew the defaced Blue Ensign of the Royal Fleet Auxiliary. However, there were others which continued throughout the war to be run by commercial organisations and they flew the Red Ensign. The commercial tugs requisitioned by the Navy usually took their crews into the service with them as temporary members of the Naval Reserve. A total of twenty-three American-built tugs were transferred to the Royal Navy during 1942-3 under Lend-Lease arrangements. Most of the tugs in this class were manned by RNR or RNVR officers and men. As with the more modern British sea-going tugs, these craft carried a 3in gun and lighter weapons. 'Some of these [American] tugs earned their laurels even before they arrived in the U.K.', say the authors of *HM Rescue Tugs in WWII*.[1] One of those was the USS *Bat 4*, which became HM tug *Integrity*. Built at Orange, Texas in July 1942 she was immediately commissioned into the Royal Navy, and amongst the Britons who joined her there was twenty-one year-old Bill Stewart, her navigating officer. He says that for a short while the tug worked out of the US Navy Base at Guantanamo Bay but was then sent to Port of Spain, Trinidad. Commanded by Lieutenant Commander J. Kennedy RNR, on 3 November 1942 she was involved in an attempt to save a torpedoed ship. The ship involved was a tanker and not a Liberty ship, but the operation is worth mentioning here as it illustrates some of the dangers intrinsic in attempting to tow a damaged vessel.

The ship concerned was the Panamanian tanker *Leda*, abandoned by her crew after being torpedoed off Grenada by *U-160*, Lieutenant Commander Georg Lassen. Let Bill Stewart, who remembers the incident exceedingly well for it took place on his twenty-second birthday, tell the story in his own words:

> We got hold of a large loaded tanker called *Leda*. Our C.O. laid alongside her and our boarding party made the tow wire fast. They then returned to *Integrity*. That was a smart move, because just after dark she blew up and the forward half made a determined effort to take us down with it – and it was a close run thing. As she went down in about 70 fathoms of water the tow wire on the winch couldn't pay out fast enough, and jammed. It is most frightening to be suddenly enveloped in acrid smoke and fumes and to be skidding astern and pulled over on to your beam ends.

Integrity was saved when the tow wire carried away.[2]

---

1. J.A. Williams & J.B. Guy, *HM Rescue Tugs in WWII* (1992).
2. Correspondence with Captain Bill Stewart, October 1999.

Another American transferee to earn her laurels very early on, was HM tug *Oriana* built as USS *Bat 1*. In late February 1943, in consort with HM tug *Frisky* and the Dutch *Zwarte Zee,* she began the job of towing Admiralty Floating Dock No. 24 from Morgan City, Louisiana to Freetown, Sierra Leone. By the second week in March tugs and tow had reached Trinidad. On the 9th the Dock was left anchored there whilst the trio of tugs, with another based in Trinidad, sailed to the assistance of five Liberties from Convoy BT-6, all badly damaged after being attacked by *U-510,* Lieutenant Commander Neitzel. Four of the ships were the *George G. Meade* (Los Angeles, October 1942), *Mark Hanna* (Portland, Oregon, October 1942), *James Smith* (Richmond, July 1942) and the *Thomas Ruffin* (Baltimore, June 1942). The first was towed to Paramaribo, the other three to Trinidad. The fifth Liberty was the *James K. Polk* whose story has already been told in Chapter 10. The *Ruffin* was later declared a constructive total loss but the others lived to sail again.

No enemy action was involved in an earlier Liberty ship double-incident in which the services of a rescue tug was required. In the Irish Sea and on passage from the Clyde to Swansea, the *William M. Stewart* (Los Angeles, October 1942) and the *John Marshall* (Mobile, Alabama, May 1942), found themselves in trouble in bad weather on 5 January 1943. The *Marshall* was driven ashore on the Isle of Man, whilst the broken down *Stewart* was taken in tow by HM tug *Bustler.* After successfully towing her first charge to Belfast, two days later the *Bustler* returned to the newly refloated *Marshall* and towed her into Kames Bay on the Clyde.

The *Nathaniel Greene* was not a lucky Liberty ship. In Chapter 11 we saw how as a member of Convoy PQ-18 to Murmansk, she suffered damage and casualties when the nearby *Mary Luckenbach* blew up with the loss of all hands. Only five months later, this time off Oran in the Mediterranean, she was in the wars again, and this time it turned out to be terminal. On 24 February 1943 the *Greene* was struck first at the forward end and then in the engine-room, by successive torpedoes from *U-565,* Lieutenant Commander Franken. The explosions disabled the engines, completely destroyed the starboard boiler, and flooded first the forward holds and then the engine-room. Four men on duty in the engine-room were killed. Commander Franken had done a good job, and his victim quickly settled by the head. Then a flight of German planes roared in and, as if the previous damage was not enough, an aerial torpedo from one of them hit *Greene* amidships. Captain George Vickers, who had been in command during the earlier Murmansk incident, ordered abandon ship. The minesweeper HMS *Brixham* came alongside and twenty-six men jumped down on to her deck, and she picked up others who had leapt into the sea. The remainder of the survivors got away in two lifeboats. Until HM tug *Restive* arrived to take over, the *Brixham* took the *Greene* in tow. The Liberty was beached at Salamanda near Oran and declared a constructive total loss, but not before the auxiliary vessel USS *Redwing* had managed to recover about a third of the ship's cargo.

After having successfully taken part in those rescues off Trinidad and completing the tow of Dock 24 to Freetown, the Dutch *Zwarte Zee* was soon in action again. (That redoubtable tug is credited with having rescued 130,000 tons of shipping during the war. In some official British records she is sometimes designated HMS *Zwarte Zee* because she sailed under Royal Navy orders, but throughout the war she was manned by Dutchmen.) The *Flora Macdonald* (Wilmington, February 1942) was on passage from Marshall, Liberia to Freetown on 30 May 1943 when she was struck in the engine-room by a torpedo from *U-126*, Lieutenant Commander Kietz. The explosion killed two men there and the space soon flooded. The blast started a fire in No. 3 hold with flames shooting 40ft into the air. Captain Ernest Jones ordered all the survivors including five badly burned men into the boats. The five injured men were transferred to the sole escort vessel, the trawler HMS *Fandango,* whose captain decided to make with all speed for Freetown where medical help was available. In fact, the five were so badly burned that three died aboard the trawler and the other two later in hospital. On the following day the *Zwarte Zee* arrived on the scene and took the ship, its fire now raging out of control, in tow. Freetown was reached the next day and the ship was beached there. With its combustible mix of cargo consisting of cocoa, rubber and mahogany logs, the ship continued to burn into the middle of July. The ship was yet another to be declared a constructive total loss.

As has been mentioned in several places in this book, not all towing operations were carried out by craft specially built for the purpose. On many occasions when a tug was not available, another sort of craft would take over the crucial role of trying to save Allied tonnage. When the *Francis W. Pettigrove* (Portland, Oregon, April 1943) was badly damaged by German aircraft in the Mediterranean on 13 August 1943, the minesweeper HMS *Hythe* stepped into the breach. Gibraltar was reached after two days but unfortunately this salvage job came to nothing for before the ship could be patched up she had to be beached, for fear she might sink and block the harbour.

In exceptionally bad weather off Newfoundland on 18 August 1943 a collision occurred between two ships in convoy that had horrific consequences. The Liberty *J. Pinckney Henderson,* built at Houston and on her maiden voyage, was loaded with a cargo that included magnesium, glycerine, resin and wax, when she collided with the tanker *J.H. Senior,* loaded with aviation spirit. Both ships were drenched in aviation spirit as it spewed from the tanker, and in a time span measured in seconds rather than minutes, both were raging infernos. Of the seventy-two men aboard the Liberty, only three managed to save themselves by leaping into the sea. Six others survived from the tanker in the same way. The tanker sank but the Liberty remained afloat.

HM tug *Griper* arrived at St. Johns, Newfoundland on 24 August with a westbound convoy, and six days later she was despatched to look for the *Henderson* which had been reported as still afloat. Lieutenant Charles Stamford RNR, officer commanding *Griper,* and his crew, already had experience in towing a Liberty. Crew member Able Seaman Les Rowe says that with that westbound convoy earlier in the month, when four days out from England, the *David J. Brewer* (Richmond, December 1942) suffered an engine breakdown and the *Griper* towed her back to Liverpool.[3] The *Henderson* was located in good time despite the fact that the weather was still bad. She was still burning which must have made the search easier. The weather was due to get worse for a Force 10 storm had been forecast, says Tom Gay, who was a seventeen year-old serving aboard the tug. In a brilliant display of seamanship Charles Stamford managed to place six of his men on board the Liberty to secure the towing wire. The deck plating on the ship was so hot that the men of the boarding party had to wrap sacking around their boots. It had been planned to use the ship's anchor chain as one end of the towing line but the chain was too hot to handle. In consequence the end of the tug's 120-fathom long wire was manhandled aboard and secured.

Tom Gay writes;

> The tow proceeded. As did the Force 10 wind! It was a blessing really, since the constant rain and high seas must have doused the flames to a certain extent. This ball of fire glowing all night was not a sight we enjoyed but it was not a night for submarines either and we were very close to Nova Scotia.

It says a lot for the skill of the tug's crew that despite the weather conditions the towing line held. The port of Sydney was reached the following day, the arrival scene being described as follows by a local newspaper reporter.

> A burning ship, one of two which had figured in a collision at sea . . . was towed into the harbor early today . . . with hundreds of persons gathering at every available spot of vantage along the waterfront to watch the ill-fated craft.
>
> Immense flames broke forth every so often, at one time shooting into the air hundreds of feet.

---

3. Information received from T.L. Rowe, September 1999.

Tom Gay adds the following grisly details.

> In the harbour and tied up alongside the *J. Pinckney Henderson* the crew of the *Griper* were to age at the sight before them. The fire had been so instantaneous that bodies lay on the deck where they fell, all over the place. On the after deck only an arm remained visible of a victim still clutching a bucket. The victims in effect were simply 'kippered' in the inferno. The Canadian search party were supplied with bins into which the remains were placed.

Lieutenant Stamford was incensed by some of the decisions made by the local naval command. He wanted to attempt to put out the fire on the *Henderson* with the *Griper*'s foam equipment, but Sydney's Fire Chief insisted on using water instead, which resulted in the Liberty having to be beached. Stamford also wanted his crew represented at the funerals of some of the thirty-four men found aboard the ship, but that was refused on the grounds of security. The bodies of other crew members were never found, perhaps because they had gone overboard, or perhaps because they had been incinerated. The *Henderson* was declared a constructive total loss and was later salved and towed to Philadelphia to be scrapped. *Griper* recrossed the Atlantic and continued in sea rescue work for the remainder of the war. 'During the six weeks following D-Day, that tug towed no less than 75,000 tons of shipping and invasion material across the English Channel or out of difficulties,' reports Les Rowe.[5] In 1948 the crew of the *Griper* were given a salvage award for their efforts in getting the *Henderson* to port. Tom Gay cannot now remember the amount he received, but believes it was about £80. That was a goodly sum of money in those days but it in no way compensated him for the terrible sights he had witnessed aboard the burnt-out hulk of the Liberty.

On 7 November 1943 the *Thomas Stone* (Baltimore, May 1942) was some 160 miles from its destination, the port of Algiers, when she was struck by a torpedo from *U-205*. The ship was carrying 700 American troops and their equipment, including landing craft on deck. The weather was bad but nevertheless Captain Benehoff decided to lower the landing craft and to disembark the troops and his crew into them. Under escort of the frigate HMS *Spey*, the landing craft then headed for Algiers but on the way, one by one, they either broke up or sank, but all on board were

---

4. Correspondence with Tom Gay, August 1999.
5. After the war *Griper* was sold to what was then the Singapore Harbour Board. In 1960 the author, who worked for the Board at that time, voyaged to Manila in *Griper* to tow back a broken-down Stanvac tanker for repairs. That towing job, the author's only one, was conducted in good weather conditions. Nevertheless, it presented an excellent opportunity to learn about and appreciate, some of the difficulties under which deep-sea tug operators work.

picked up by *Spey* to be eventually landed safely. Meanwhile the destroyer HMS *Wishart* had taken the Liberty in tow with another destroyer HMS *Velox* acting as escort. Little progress was made until HM tug *St. Day* arrived on the scene. She took over the tow but experienced towing difficulties until *Wishart* joined in again, the two then towing in tandem. Algiers was reached safely on 11 November, and after repairs the *Stone* was able to make further contributions to the Allied cause.[6]

In a bad storm on Christmas Morning 1943, the very short working life of *Frederick Bartholdi* (Brunswick, November 1943) came to a dramatic end. Loaded with military cargo she was driven ashore on rocks off Fladdachmain which lies off the north coast of the Isle of Skye. The impact ripped the ship's bottom out. A few hours after the stranding the armed trawler HMS *Polka* under the command of Lieutenant I.A. Thorpe RNVR arrived on the scene to take charge of the situation. Already standing by were three other HM trawlers, two of which soon left, leaving HMS *Mazurka* to assist *Polka*. The first priority was to get the crew off, but a gale blowing from the south-west prevented any attempt to approach the stricken vessel from seaward. Thorpe therefore decided to land a breeches buoy party on the island and to take the crew off that way. After the gear was set up, Thorpe used it himself to board the ship to confer with its master, Captain R. MacAlvanah. It was decided that the Captain and three officers would stay aboard as a skeleton crew, the rest to be taken off. Thorpe obtained full particulars of the damage – by then the engine-room was flooded – and radioed for the assistance of salvage vessels. The Stornoway lifeboat then arrived at the scene and was used to ferry the landed crew members out to *Mazurka*, except for thirteen deckhands who were placed aboard *Polka* to provide assistance when the salvagers arrived. That evening *Mazurka* sailed for Loch Ewe with the balance of the crew. As the Liberty was in danger of breaking up, Thorpe ordered a permanent watch equipped with a radio to be kept on shore, and all the ship's confidential books and codes were taken aboard *Polka* for safe-keeping.

On Boxing Day a further examination of the ship showed that No. 4 hold was making water. Thorpe concluded that any attempt by him to haul the ship off the rocks might result in the ship sinking. Because of the bad weather the salvage vessel *Ranger* and the accompanying trawler HMS *York City* did not arrive until the 28th. The *Ranger*'s Salvage Officer, Mr Thomas, soon decided that in the prevailing conditions nothing could be done for the ship, and on the following day *Ranger* and the two naval ships, having taken the Captain and his skeleton crew off, made for Loch

---

6. ADM199/631, PRO, Kew. This file and others used in compiling this chapter were brought to the attention of the author by Les Reed of the RN Tug Association, whose help is greatly appreciated.

Ewe.[7] For a month there was scarcely any let up in the gales which blew in from every direction. *Ranger* made periodical forays out to inspect the wreck whenever conditions allowed. For a period she was called away on other urgent work and it was ten weeks before a diving survey could be carried out, and by that time the *Bartholdi* had broken almost completely in two. Only the deck plating was holding the bow and stern sections together, with a gap that extended to 10in between the two halves at the turn of the bilge.

Even after the weather improved it was clear that it would be too dangerous to try to salve any of the cargo by placing coasters and barges alongside. So instead it was decided to attempt to refloat the ship as a whole. But in order to do that and to gain sufficient buoyancy by pumping compressed air into the engine-room where the ship was fractured right through to the double bottom, somehow the two parts of the ship had to be sealed together. The use of ordinary welded-on rigid patches was out, it being considered they would fail as soon as the ship regained buoyancy and changed her shape, even ever so slightly, in the process. A unique salvage operation then began. It was decided to use a rubber patch, something never done before, a patch that would move as the ship moved, but stay firmly affixed.

In order to make a start the salvors stretched steel ropes over the 400ft gap between the island and the ship to form a walkway. Then, using heavy jacks, three landing craft which the ship was carrying on the forward hatchways, each weighing 65 tons and which were in the way of the salvage team, were launched over the side. The funnel and ventilators were cut away, the apertures left then being sealed with welded plates. All hatchways were sealed in the same manner. Long rubber strips, their edges gripped between two steel plates were then bolted all around the hull fracture using a Temple-Cox submersible bolt-driving gun. That done and whilst the salvors waited with bated breath, compressed air was pumped into the ship. The rubber strip bulged outward but held. All that had taken until 19 June 1944, and on that day the ship was pulled safely off the rocks. She was then towed to the haven of Uig Bay on the Isle of Skye where the cargo was removed, no doubt to be used in Normandy where great battles were then raging. In September the hulk was towed to the Clyde and scrapped.

The American tug USS *ATR-47* was involved in getting the *Daniel Webster* (Portland, Maine, January 1943) beached near Oran after the Liberty had been badly damaged by an aerial torpedo. The air attack came on 10 January 1944 after which the ship settled until the sea came within 3ft of the main deck, a deck which had cracked across in several

---

7. ADM1/15848, PRO, Kew.

places. Although his ship was in grave danger of sinking, Captain Addison Roebuck decided to make for the North African coast under his own steam. Escorted by the frigate HMS *Barle,* the ship crawled shorewards until the *ATR-47* arrived to help. After the ship was beached some of her 7000 tons of military cargo was discharged into lighters to reduce her draft. She was then refloated and towed into port. On inspection she was declared a constructive total loss and ended her days at a scrap yard in 1948.

The *Samuel Dexter* (launched New Orleans, 29 March 1943) first suffered a deck fracture in November 1943. The damage was considered minor, and was repaired. Two months later on a ballast voyage from Cardiff to New York, the ship was not so lucky. When about 120 miles from the Scottish coast on 21 January 1944 in weather described as heavy with a Force 8 north-westerly, the deck fractured right across at the forward end of No. 3 hatch, the crack continuing down into the hull plating on both sides. Another crack appeared on the forward starboard corner of No. 4 hatch, which meant the ship was in danger of breaking in three. The *Dexter* radioed for assistance and the British commercial tug *Assiduous* raced to assist, sighting the ship on the 22nd. During a heavy squall that night *Assiduous* lost contact, but found the ship again the following day. By then the weather was so bad that all the tug could do was stand by. On the 24th the *Dexter* signalled that conditions aboard were becoming critical and that it was intended to abandon ship as soon as a break in the weather made it possible. That afternoon the crew abandoned, all to be picked up by the armed trawler HMS *Sapper* which was close by. With scarcely an ease in the weather there was no saving this Liberty, and she finally drifted ashore on Barra Island in the Outer Hebrides. There she broke up becoming a total loss.[8]

Lieutenant Commander Korndorfer and his *U-407* had a successful evening off Derna, Libya, on 16 April 1944. Within the space of a minute he torpedoed the two Liberties *Meyer London* (Baltimore, February 1944) and *Thomas G. Masaryk* (Los Angeles, August 1943). The *London* and her 7800 tons of military stores and crated aircraft, sank within the hour but not before almost colliding with the stricken *Masaryk*. The torpedo that hit *Masaryk* exploded in No. 3 hold where drums of acetone were stowed. They immediately caught fire, flames from the hold shooting up the front of the bridge causing the ammunition in the 20mm gun mounts there to explode. The flames drove everyone from the bridge and Captain Robert Sloan had to pass the order to abandon ship by word of mouth. Miraculously no one was killed, and the survivors were picked up by an escort vessel. During their evacuation of Tobruk the Germans had

8. ADM199/768, PRO, Kew.

left behind the scuttled tug *Max Barendt*. The German vessel had been raised and repaired by the Royal Navy after which it was commissioned into the Navy and appropriately renamed HMS *Captive*. It was this tug that now arrived on the scene to take the *Masaryk* in tow, a fact that had he known about it, might have rather spoilt Commander Korndorfer's day. *Captive* towed the still burning *Masaryk* to Maneloa Bay, Libya. To douse the fires, she was then allowed to settle in 28ft of water. With the fire out the Liberty *William M. Meredith* (Portland, Oregon, February 1943) was moored alongside and about half of the *Masaryk's* 5000 tons of cargo was transhipped into her. On 28 August the ship was raised and towed to Alexandria where, after anchoring in the harbour, she was declared a total loss.

On 24 June 1944 a few days after her launching at Baltimore, the *Samsylarna* was handed over to a British crew under Captain W.G.S. Hewison. The ship was managed by Ropners, one of the largest British trampship owners. At New York in early July she loaded general cargo for India. One of the consignments was well out of the ordinary and was loaded in strict secrecy and under special security arrangements. It was a shipment of American silver bullion valued at $4,000,000 in the form of 7600 ingots. It was stowed in No. 3 'tween-deck, the only access to which was through a deckhouse which was right under the noses and watchful eyes of duty officers on the bridge. The silver was consigned to the Bank of Bombay. As part of Convoy UGS-38 the ship made it safely across the Atlantic and halfway through the Mediterranean. Then, on 4 August the convoy was attacked by thirty German aircraft. The planes achieved only one hit, and that was on *Samsylarna*, an aerial torpedo striking aft in way of No. 5 hold. Water flooded into the hold and up the shaft tunnel into the engine-room, and soon the ship's stern was awash. She seemed in such a parlous state that most of the crew were immediately taken off by the destroyer HMS *Petard*, leaving only the Captain and a few volunteer officers on board. *Petard* stood by all night, and in the morning with the ship apparently sinking by the stern, took Captain Hewison and the volunteers off. HM tug *Brigand* was hastily despatched from Alexandria, arriving on the scene on the 27th. The ship was still afloat although by that time so much down by the stern that her after gun platform, including the gun itself, was under water. As the tug circled the wreck it was obvious to her crew that if one of the Liberty's after bulkheads were to collapse, the ship would go down in a rush. It would be a dangerous for men to board to fix the tow, but nevertheless it was a risk that had to be taken. Volunteers were called for, and Gunner J.H. Baldwin, Leading Seaman J.C. Leslie and Able Seaman Case, decided to take a chance. *Brigand* was brought alongside to place the three men aboard. The threesome then hauled the heavy towing wire aboard, made it fast, and hurriedly left the ship. The danger was not over, for if the Liberty suddenly decided enough was enough, the wire would have to be slipped very quickly or the *Brigand* would be dragged down with her. That was not the only problem. No repair facilities were available at Benghazi the nearest port which was only 60 miles away. Tobruk did have such facilities, but was too far away. So the decision was made to beach the ship at the nearest suitable place; the ship might be lost but at least the silver would be saved. The beach selected was as close to Benghazi port as possible, and *Brigand* and her charge managed to reach it safely. From there all 7600 bars of silver were carefully removed and transported to a warehouse in the port. From there it was loaded aboard a ship called *Landrick* which would take it to Alexandria for transhipment to its final destination. The story goes that after the consignment had been checked aboard and a receipt for the full amount issued by the Chief Officer, and just as the ship was about to sail, a shout came from the warehouse to the effect that five more bars had been found in a corner. Patched up by Army engineers as best they could, the *Samsylana* was hauled off the beach by the faithful *Brigand* on 24 August and despite fears that she would founder, was successfully towed to Tobruk. In September she was towed to Alexandria, there to be laid up alongside her sister-ship the *Thomas G. Masaryk*.

There is an interesting post-war sequel to all that. On 31 August 1946 the *Sambrian*, launched as *John Branch*, Wilmington, August 1943, and since then managed by Clan Line, sailed from Port Said in ballast for Naples. Suddenly, without any warning, the ship began to shake and rattle, with everything moving and making one hell of a din. The worst noise was coming from the engine-room and the engines were hastily closed down by the engineer on watch. A look over the stern showed that the ship had shed its propeller. Not only that, an internal examination in the shaft-tunnel, showed that the after end of the propeller shaft, called the tail-end shaft, had sheared and had also disappeared into the sea. The ship was in comparatively shallow waters and so was able to anchor. Four days later the *Saminiver* (Baltimore, February 1944) managed by the Blue Star Shipping Company was ordered to the scene. The towing wires of the two ships were shackled together and *Saminiver* towed the casualty into Alexandria where the damaged *Samsylarna* and *Thomas G. Masaryk* were still lying. *Samsylarna*, as we know, had suffered severe stern damage and so was of no use, but there was nothing wrong with anything in that part of the *Masaryk*. Not only that, the *Masaryk* was obligingly lying down by the head, with its stern in the air. In a neat piece of cannibalisation made possible only by the standardisation of Liberty ship parts, her propeller and tail-end shaft were removed and fitted in *Sambrian*. The ten-day operation was carried out with the aid of a floating crane. The services of a dry-dock were not required for by flooding the *Sambrian's* forward holds, she was put stern-up into the same configuration as the donor vessel.

The *James Eagan Layne* (New Orleans, December 1944) was in convoy from Barry, South Wales, to Ghent on 21 March 1945 when she was hit by a torpedo from *U-1195*, Lieutenant Commander Cordes. Striking in No. 5 hold, the explosion damaged the propeller shaft and, as the engine began to race, the duty engineers closed down the engines. The after two holds soon flooded and the engine-room followed when the intervening bulkhead gave way. Captain William Sleek ordered abandon ship. Everyone got away on boats and rafts, some to be picked up by the British steamship *Monkstone* others by the rescue tug HMS *Flaunt* (ex-USS *ATR-93*). The incident took place within sight of the Plymouth breakwater. An hour later with the Liberty still afloat, and despite its after deck being almost completely awash, Captain Sleek together with fourteen crew members and four Armed Guards, reboarded and took aboard a towline from the tug. Naval Dockyard tugs *Atlas* and *Portic* arrived on the scene and assisted as *Layne* was towed into Whitesand Bay, to the west of Plymouth Harbour. But in the process of beaching the ship, she sank, with only her masts left showing above the water. *Layne* is recorded as carrying 4500 tons of Army Engineers' equipment at the time, all of which went down with the ship. Nothing now remains of the wreck above the surface.[9] But under the water the ship, broken into two sections, is reported to be sitting upright on the bottom, badly corroded and in a dangerous state. The wreck has been the target of amateur salvors over the years who have removed the propeller and other non-ferrous parts. Such people have now been warned away, because some metal discs containing a radium compound have been retrieved from the wreck, and they could be a health hazard.

Tugs were still going about their work in European and Mediterranean waters as the war in the West was ending, and even after it. With the knowledge that his Liberty ship had managed to survive unscathed ever since her launching at Baltimore in August 1942, Captain Cecil Davies of the *Horace Binney* must have considered himself very unlucky indeed when on 8 May 1945, VE-Day itself, his ship struck a mine off Ostend. The explosion, which broke the ship's back, injured twenty men on board. After anchoring, all the crew were taken off by other ships. Two British tugs, one of them HMS *Lincoln Salvor* (previously the USS *Bars-9*) towed the *Binney* stern-first to an anchorage in the Downs off Deal. On the following day the crack in the ship widened, and so she was beached. With the aid of two 'camels' – barges lashed to either side to support her – the ship was subsequently refloated, and with four tugs was towed to the Thames where her cargo of 4000 tons of military cargo was discharged into barges. The tugs and camels used in this operation belonged

---

9. Larn, *Shipwreck Index of the Britiish Isles*, Vol. 1.

to the Port of London Authority Marine Salvage Division. Afterwards the ship was towed to that graveyard of ships, the River Blackwater. She was scrapped at Antwerp in 1948.[10]

The *Pierre Gibault* (Portland, Oregon, March 1943) was even unluckier than the *Binney*, for when she struck a mine in the Mediterranean six weeks after the European war had ended, four men were killed. Sailing between Izmir, Turkey, and Oran, on 22 June 1945 on the edge of a swept channel off the Greek island of Kythera, she struck a mine forward, the explosion spraying fuel oil over the length and breadth of the ship. A fire started which soon spread to the bridge and accommodation. All night the crew, the Armed Guard, and the three woman passengers on board, fought the fire and they had it under control by the following morning. Meanwhile the Greek destroyer *Thermistocles* had arrived to take off the dead, and seven others who had been wounded. Two days later HMSAS *Southern Maid* arrived with a Greek salvage team aboard, followed by HM salvage ship *Prince Salvor*. The Liberty was beached on Kythera where the damaged bow section was cut away. She was then towed to Piraeus. What was left of the *Gibault* was scrapped at Savona in 1949.

---

10. Port of London Authority Monthly, No. 239 September 1945.

CHAPTER 17

Normandy and the Campaign in Europe

The number of ships used in the Operation 'Torch' landings in North Africa had been large, and the number used in Operation 'Husky' in Sicily even larger. But the largest Armada in world history was that used in the Operation 'Overlord' landings on D-Day, 6 June 1944, in the Cherbourg peninsula. The total number of ships employed in the initial operations, merchant and naval, and including the various types of landing craft employed, has variously been estimated being between 6400 and 6900. Even the lower figure is well over twice the number used in Sicily.[1] The maritime part of 'Overlord' was called Operation 'Neptune' and it was commanded by Admiral Sir Bertram Ramsey. The success of 'Neptune' must have given Ramsey a similar sort of satisfaction to that in store later the same year – at Leyte in the Philippines on 20 October – for General Douglas MacArthur. For it had been Ramsey who had organised the evacuation of British and French troops from the Dunkirk beaches in 1940. Now, figuratively speaking, he had returned, and returned in some style.

During the first fortnight up to 20 June, the Allies landed 638,000 troops, nearly 100,000 military vehicles of various types, and 225,000 tons of equipment and supplies. By the end of the first month the number of men landed in France had risen to over one million. Day after day ships sailed to and fro across the Channel in unending streams. During the week ending 8 July a daily average of 10,000 men, 3200 vehicles and 15,000 tons of supplies were ferried across. By 8 August, just over two months from D-Day, the total number of troops transported across was in excess of 1.75 million which, as one author has noted, was more than the then population of New Zealand.[2] Of that Great Armada of ships, 864 were merchantmen including eighty ships specially built or converted to carry troops. Of that grand total no less than 618 flew the Red Ensign, amongst them eleven Oceans and forty Forts, all half-sisters to the twenty-two Liberty 'Sams' that took part. Many other Liberties were in the American contingent. Not included in the overall figure were over fifty Allied ships, including five American Liberties, that were towed to Normandy. The

1. Sydney Waters, *Ordeal By Sea* (London 1949).
2. Ibid.

five were the *James W. Marshal, James Iredell, George S. Wasson, Matt W. Ransom,* and the *Benjamin Contee.* All the towed ships had been damaged earlier in the war and rated as beyond repair, but had been patched up enough to make one final voyage. Getting them to Normandy was a dangerous task, not only because of their doubtful seaworthiness, but also because being towed is a slow operation and provides the enemy with a good target and the enemy was not to know that the ships were mere hulks. In an operation code-named 'Gooseberry', these ships, manned by volunteer crews, were towed to the beachheads there to be scuttled to form sheltering breakwaters. They were positioned whilst under heavy enemy fire. Later, within the shelter afforded by the Gooseberries, the two Mulberry artificial harbours 'A' and 'B' were set up. These were structures consisting of concrete caissons constructed in Britain. (It is said the harbours were based on an idea of Mr Churchill's.) Like the Gooseberries the caissons were towed across the Channel and into position. Mulberry and Gooseberry together entailed the largest mass towing operation in history, no less than 132 Allied tugs being used.

One of the American contingent of Liberty ships used in the Normandy landings was the *Jeremiah O'Brien* (Portland, Maine, June 1943), now preserved at San Francisco. Between June and October 1944, under the command of Captain A.A. De Smeldt, the ship made eleven consecutive crossings from various British ports to the American landing beaches codenamed Omaha and Utah. During roughly the some period the British-flagged Liberty *Samsip* (launched Baltimore, November 1943 as the *Edwin A. Robinson*) fitted in twelve trips to the British/Canadian landing beaches known as Gold, Juno and Sword. Managed by the New Zealand Shipping Company, *Samsip* was commanded by Captain E.A. Quick. On one of those trips she carried troops, motor vehicles and fuel from Scotland to the beaches, transiting the Dover Strait at night because of the long-range German guns positioned on the French coast at Calais. On some of the earlier trips, reported Captain Quick, the ship's cargoes were unloaded into landing craft off the beaches, but once the Mulberry harbour at Arromanches was in operation, she was able to discharge alongside. *Samsip* survived the Normandy operations but was to meet her end on 7 December 1944 when sailing from Antwerp to Barry in ballast. She struck a mine in the River Schelde and caught fire, and despite the best efforts of HM tug *Sea Giant* (ex-USS *Contocook*) to save her, she had later to be sunk by gunfire.[3] Seven of the crew were killed in the explosion, and everyone else on board was injured. Captain Quick's injuries were very serious indeed and as a result he was incapacitated for several months. For his services aboard the ship at the time of the incident, First Radio Officer Lawrence Hadden was officially commended.

---

3. ADM1/17274, PRO, Kew.

The first Liberty ship to be sunk in the Normandy operations, although she did not actually make it to the beaches, was the British *Sambut* (launched at Portland, Oregon, as *C.J. Jones*, August 1943). Under the command of Captain Mark Willis she was carrying 562 troops and their equipment in addition to a crew of sixty-three. She was in convoy from Southend on D-Day itself, and passing through the Dover Strait east of the Goodwin Sands when, at about midday, she was hit by two shells from the big guns at Calais. The first shell landed just abaft the engine-room, the second just forward of the bridge. Inflammable equipment on deck, including lorries loaded with explosives and cases of petrol and diesel, immediately caught fire. The petrol cases had been covered with sandbags but that precaution did not prevent them igniting. Unfortunately the first shell damaged much of the fire-fighting equipment, and in consequence within ten minutes fire had really taken hold. A few minutes later a consignment of gelignite in a lorry stowed on No. 2 hatch exploded, completely wrecking the bridge and all the port side lifeboats. Captain Willis later reported, 'As the fire was spreading rapidly I rang the emergency alarm bell and ordered abandon ship'.

His report went on;

All my crew were clear of the ship in the two remaining starboard lifeboats by 1230. The ship carried some 30 rafts for the troops. These were released and I told the soldiers to jump overboard to them. At first some were rather diffident at the thought of jumping, but they quickly jumped on being told that the ship was liable to blow up at any moment. Everyone should have been wearing lifebelts and I had given specific instructions to the OC troops at 0600 that morning that lifebelts were to be worn from that time onwards.

The pilot, Chief Officer and I were last to leave the ship at approximately 1240. We jumped over the side and swam to a raft. A number of dead bodies were floating in the water, many with lifebelts on. It is possible that many of the missing troops were drowned, but some were undoubtedly killed as they were having dinner in the troop deck which was in the vicinity of the explosion.

Four naval Motor Launches from Dover appeared very quickly but I thought were extremely slow in picking up survivors. MLs are totally unsuitable for rescue work, sides too high and inexperienced crews.

I would like to point out that the convoy did not use a smoke-screen. After my vessel was struck I started my own smoke apparatus and other ships in the convoy followed my example.[4]

Approximately 130 soldiers lost their lives in that incident, together with six crew members including Second Radio Officer G.S. Williams.

---

4. ADM199/524, PRO, Kew.

The *Francis C. Harrington* (Baltimore, November 1943) was the first American-flagged Liberty to be damaged during the landings. On D-Day+1 she ran into two mines when five miles off Omaha Beach. She was carrying 515 American soldiers, five of whom lost their lives in the explosions. The crew under Captain James Hassell were able to make emergency repairs and the troops were disembarked and the cargo unloaded. The ship was towed back to England where she was repaired. Two days later off the same beach the *Ezra Weston* (Portland, Maine, August 1943) was damaged by German shellfire from shore batteries and caught fire. Five of the 600 troops on board were killed. The fire was doused, the troops unloaded, and the ship made it safely back to Belfast under her own steam for repairs. The *Weston* did not, however, survive very long afterwards. In a convoy making back to the beachheads on 8 August, and when about seven miles off the North Devon coast, she was struck forward by a torpedo from *U-667*, Lieutenant Commander Lange. The ship cracked right across the deck forward of the bridge and, as his ship slowly flooded, Captain Joseph Patoka headed for the nearest Devon beach. He did not make it, for within the hour the ship had almost broken in two with the foredeck awash. The Captain ordered abandon ship, and not long afterwards another torpedo from the submarine struck the ship and she sank. All hands survived.

We have seen that the first American Liberty ship casualty off the beachheads was caused by mines, the second by shellfire. The third, as if the Germans were trying to impress with the variety of their attack options, was caused by a bomb. The *Charles Morgan* (Houston, December 1943) had completed discharging off Utah Beach when on 10 June a German dive-bomber dropped a 500lb bomb down No. 5 hatch. The huge explosion buckled the decks and ruptured bulkheads. Eight men were killed, one crewmen and seven Army stevedores. A fire broke out but was soon extinguished, although by that time the stern had settled on to the bottom. An attempt was made on the following day to tow the *Morgan* away to form part of the Gooseberry breakwater, but it failed, and the ship was abandoned to the sea.

An excellent description of what it was like to be lying off those American beachheads aboard an American Liberty ship has been written by a Briton.[5] Born at Newark in England in 1894, George Dale was too old to join the British armed services when war came along in 1939 even though he had fought as a sergeant in the Royal Field Artillery in the First World War. Nevertheless, George was determined to do his bit so joined the Royal Observer Corps, a body of men whose job it was to spot incoming enemy aircraft formations, estimate their numbers, types, speed and height, and report the information to a central command centre. As

5. G.E. Dale. 70/132/1. Imperial War Museum, London.

D-Day approached, members of the Corps were asked to volunteer for service as aircraft identifiers aboard ships. George and his chum Bill Saunders jumped at the chance to see some real action and subsequently found themselves on board the *J.D. Ross* (Portland, Oregon, July 1943), commanded by Captain Phillipsen. The ship was carrying troops, mainly black soldiers, and their equipment. George says that other pairs of British observers served aboard other Liberties, including the *Cyrus H. McCormick* (Richmond, October 1942) and the *John A. Campbell* (Brunswick, August 1943). (Two aircraft identifiers aboard the British Liberty *Samzona* during the Normandy landings, Thomas Bodill and John Reynolds, were both mentioned in despatches for their services.) George says the uniforms worn by aircraft identifiers 'provoked many puzzled enquiries' both ashore and afloat, which is not surprising the way he describes them. He wore an 'RAF battledress, blue beret, 'Seaborne' flashes, and RN brassards', the latter being arm bands with the words RN on them.

On board the *J.D. Ross* they came under the direct command of the Armed Guard officer, in this case, Ensign Wayne Ambler. In view of what has been said elsewhere in this book about the attitudes of some Armed Guard officers, it is worthwhile recording what George Dale thought of Ensign Ambler.

> With his quiet, whimsical manner, friendly smile and easy-going good humour, we should have been odd indeed if we had not liked Mr. Ambler at sight.

George and Bill also got on well with Chief Mate McAndrews who quickly made the only two Limeys on board welcome 'and became one of our best friends on the ship'. A large, tough-looking man, McAndrews had been a film stuntman pre-war, once even acting as bodyguard to Louis B. Mayer of MGM Studios. The two Britons were accommodated in the ship's 'hospital', a four-bunked cabin close to those of the ship's mates. They shared it with Captain Connally, a US Army medical doctor. In fact, George and Bill were treated as officers and took their meals in the officer's saloon. It should be remembered that by then the two men had endured nearly five years of severe rationing in Britain. 'The fare provided on *J.D. Ross*,' wrote George, 'was a revelation to two ration-ridden Englishmen. Whatever lay in store for us, it was not to be malnutrition.' He added, 'We congratulated ourselves on landing on both feet so neatly'. However, he did add later that there was no alcohol on board, so it was not quite heaven.

Armed with pairs of US Navy binoculars, George and Bill took watch and watch about, their place of duty being the monkey island, which is the highest section of the ship's bridge and lies above the wheelhouse. George says, 'the monkey island had railings on all sides and there was no real protection from the elements let alone bomb splinters or gunfire. And up there we were liberally sprinkled with [oil] smuts from the smoke-stack'. At each corner of the monkey island there were concrete emplacements housing Oerlikon guns and ammunition for them. The pair stood watch with three gunners and a petty-officer of the Armed Guard. 'If the Armed Guard was doubtful of aircraft identity', said George, explaining his duties, 'and they always were, that is where we came in. All aircraft looked alike to them'. Before leaving England George was issued with what he called an 'Aircraft presumed to be friendly instruction'. Included in this list of planes not to be shot down were, any plane towing a glider, all four-engined planes, all flying boats, and any plane with fixed undercarriage. He was also given a diagram illustrating the white-stripe invasion markings on Allied aircraft flying in daylight.

Arriving off Utah Beach on 9 June, which was D-Day+3, George noted that the *Ross* was the only ship without a barrage balloon. 'Captain Phillipsen thinks they are more trouble than they are worth. Trouble in getting them in, in stormy weather.' Although he found searching the skies for hours at a time very tiring work, one senses that George was very pleased to be with his American shipmates at a place where history was in the making. He writes of 'amazing sights' with hundreds of merchant ships at anchor with small craft darting to and fro between them. Farther out warships were firing salvoes at the shore, and planes were flying overhead. Here and there a stricken vessel lay, one standing vertically out of the water. Through his binoculars he saw great activity on the beach. 'Bulldozers are levelling and widening tracks. Tanks, DUKWs, jeeps and lorries flow in a constant stream from ships to beach and away inland in swirls of yellow dust.' *J.D. Ross* had to wait its turn to be discharged. 'Unloading done by priority system. A large black ship labelled "Ferry Control" decides all this.'

Everyone's nerves were on edge.

At 9pm without warning a Liberty ship to port begins pumping tracer into the overhead cloud cover. All eyes search the 10/10 cloud cover [completely overcast] in surprise for no aircraft has been seen or heard for some time. Other vessels join in with staccato chatter of Oerlikons and the crashing boom of 3-inchers. Tin hats are clapped on as Bill and I anxiously scan the overhead sky. Soon the misty shapes of two fighters dip out of the cloud and back out of sight, not clear enough to be definitely identified in the gloom.

Gunfire by now widespread with some warships joining in. There are excited appeals from the Armed Guard, now manning their guns with itchy fingers. It is a tense moment for Bill and I as we strive to keep cool-headed amid the racket and concentrate on our job.

Again the fighters are seen, and one of the Oerlikons opens up without orders. Now we see them clearly. All those guns are trained on two Spitfires! Mr Ambler promptly stops our over-eager gunners but many ships are still firing. A shouted report comes of more aircraft ahead. Soon we see them, skimming in and out of the steam-like cloud forward. The glasses reveal bullet-noses, rounded wing-tips and distinctive fins and rudders. Independently we label them 'Messerschmitt 109s'. A curt order comes from Mr Ambler and our guns blaze away briefly ahead. Meanwhile a bomb crashes into the sea with a heavy explosion some 50 yards away. In the general pandemonium several fighter types are seen to crash on sea and shore. After a time, firing dies away and darkness comes early.

Later a small craft comes alongside. A Yankee voice cries out, 'Are you all right?' 'Yes', calls Captain Phillipsen. 'Very well then . . . listen', the disembodied voice shouted back, *'Four Mustangs and one Spitfire have been shot down tonight. Those guys are not all right. You want air cover but you won't get it if you shoot down friendly planes! Remember, four Mustangs and one Spitfire!'*

George Dale says that the American officer conducted the same dialogue with other ships, adding that;

At first we were surprised and upset by this outburst. Had we let them down after all? Our opinion, carefully reconsidered, was that the planes we fired at were hostile. Colleagues later met ashore [in England] all agreed that enemy planes had been present. Some claimed to have seen a Heinkel 177. And there was of course, that little matter of the bomb.

On the ship's next voyage to the beachheads Ensign Ambler was told that the shot-down plane tally over the beach that night had been four German and only one Allied, a Spitfire.

George reported that one of the standing orders for merchant ships at anchor off the beaches was that there was to be no night firing. However, later that same night;

. . . more aircraft heard and gunfire breaks out again on the outskirts of the shipping . . . The drone of aircraft engines gets louder. Soon a ring of flares drifts slowly down to rest on the sea nearby, where they burn for ten minutes. I stand by the smoke-stack with two of the Armed Guard, ears cocked, expecting something to happen. I have not long to wait before an evil-sounding plane approaches low on the port side. Suddenly, above the sound of the engines, comes a harsh droning note which gathers in volume and becomes a whistling shriek. Something crashes into the sea close astern with a great splash.

A dive-bomb or glider-bomb attack? Whatever the answer, the thing was close enough for me. Once again comes the drum-fire of AA guns and the black night is streaked with tracer. Abruptly, a tremendous barrage of red and green tracer squirts up from the Normandy beach in our direction and tin hats are hastily adjusted. There is an angry red glare and a thunder-rock [*sic*] of sound as a load of bombs carpets the opposite beach. More bombs exploded in the sea, and planes shot down descend like fire-balls.

As the racket fades, I join Bill below and we lie in our bunks fully dressed . . . Suddenly a violent explosion rocks the ship. All scramble on deck clutching life-jackets, fully expecting to find that we have suffered a direct hit.

The explosion, however, had come from a near miss.

We try again to sleep . . . and are rudely awakened by another shuddering crack. Again we grab life-jackets and rush above . . . we have again been lucky with a bomb exploding so close alongside that chunks of metal clanged on the ship's plates.

On the 10th George witnessed the sinking of a Liberty he did not know the name of but it must have been the *Charles Morgan* (see above). In mid-afternoon the *Ross* was ordered to move in close to Utah Beach for unloading.

We nose a passage through ranks of laden ships and drop anchor near to where five old ships (gooseberries) have been sunk to form a breakwater . . . Here we lie in the area in which enemy shells have been dropping at intervals all day.

By 7.30 *J.D. Ross* is gradually drawing all those shells like a magnet. For most on board it was a baptism of shell fire [but not for George who had suffered his baptism on the Western Front thirty years earlier] and the chance of a brand new experience is not being appreciated. Shells straddle *Ross* - doing everything but hit us, while splinters whizz and thud on-sides and deck-plates.

His ship was still lying off the beach on the 17th of the month when George Dale witnessed the arrival under tow of the first concrete caissons that were to form the Mulberry Harbours. Altogether he made six round-trips to the beaches in the *J.D. Ross,* the last one ending on 19 July. It was an experience he never forgot.

Captain D.W. Stroud had some good things to say about the construction of Liberty ships after his vessel was torpedoed on 26 July 1944. The *Samneva* (built at Los Angeles in September 1943 as *Henry M. Stanley*) was on its way back to the Thames from its second voyage to Juno Beach, when, only five hours into the passage, she was torpedoed by *U-309*. The explosion was between Nos. 2 and 3 holds, port side, underwater and violent. A column of water shot mast high, hatchboards and beams were blown off, and a lifeboat smashed. As both the damaged holds flooded with water rising to 'tween-deck level, the ship settled by the head. As well as the huge hole blown in the port side, the starboard side had fractured, the crack there being 5ft wide at the bottom and tapering to about an inch or so at the top. Captain Stroud transferred his gunners and most of his crew to an escorting trawler, remaining on board himself with a skeleton crew. Six hours later the American tug *Owl* arrived and took the ship in tow and later the Dutch *Amsterdam* joined in. The ship anchored of Cowes early in the evening of the 25th. In danger of sinking, *Samneva* was beached near Southampton where she finally broke in two to be declared a constructive total loss.

In his report Captain Stroud, a Blue Funnel man and so someone who knew a good ship when he saw one, said:

> She is a welded ship and in my opinion if she had been riveted, the engine-room bulkhead would not have remained tight, owing to the close proximity of that bulkhead to the hole in the ship's side. I think these Liberty welded ships stand up to punishment very well.[6]

The *Charles W. Elliot* (Portland, Maine, May 1943) had discharged her troops and cargo off Juno Beach and had just set out to return to England on 28 June, when she struck first one mine and then another. The first explosion opened up the ship from main deck to the waterline on both sides just forward of the bridge, the second one exploding aft. As his command broke in two, Captain Walter O'Brien ordered everyone to leave the ship. British launches took the injured men ashore, placing the others aboard another Liberty, the *George W. Woodward* (Baltimore, June 1943), for the journey back to England. Salvage tugs pulled both parts of the ship into deeper water, where the after end soon sunk. As if for practice, German bombers later attacked the floating bow half and sent that to the bottom.

As soon as the Normandy landings were known to the Germans, U-boats streamed out of Bay of Biscay ports. Some were soon destroyed by Allied air patrols and surface ships laying in wait for that expected exodus, but more than a few survived to set about inflicting as much damage as they could on the Allies. Until his craft was destroyed by the Canadian warships *Ottawa, Chaudiere* and *Kootenay* on 20 August 1944, Lieutenant Commander Sieder in *U-984* was one of the most successful at this stage

---

6. ADM199/524.

of the war. On a single day, 29 June 1944, and in the space of only ten minutes, he torpedoed four Liberties, three of which became constructive total
losses, and the fourth being put out of action for four months.

The four ships were part of Convoy EMC-17 which formed off the
Isle of Wight on that date to make for the Allied beachheads. The first to
be struck by Sieder's torpedoes was the *Edward M. House* (Jacksonville,
November 1943). The torpedo hit right forward, buckling the ship's bow
section, forward of the collision bulkhead. After a damage inspection
Captain Austin Fithian decided to continue the crossing to Normandy
where the ship safely discharged the 587 troops and cargo on board at
Omaha Beach. The *House* then made it back to Britain under its own
steam and underwent extensive repairs at Newcastle-upon-Tyne. Back in
commission on 31 October, she then sailed for New York.

Situated immediately astern of *Edward M. House* in the convoy was
the *James A. Farrel* (Baltimore, July 1943). Captain Michael Martin saw
the *House* hit and put the helm hard over to avoid colliding with her. But
almost immediately a torpedo struck the *Farrel* aft, blowing a huge hole
in the hull and removing the propeller and tail shaft. The main deck
buckled, and soon holds 3, 4 and 5 were flooding. As the engineers shut
down the engines the ship began to settle by the stern. She was carrying
421 troops of which four died in the explosion, another forty-five being
injured in No. 5 hold when the hatch boards and beams there collapsed
and fell into it. The American LST 50 came alongside and took the troops
and crew off, later landing them at Portland, Dorset. A British tug towed
the ship to Spithead and she was eventually scrapped there.

A third torpedo from *U-984* struck the *John A. Treutlen* (Savannah,
March 1944) on the port side aft, that explosion almost immediately followed by another as the after magazine blew up. Ten men were injured,
but no-one was killed. The double blast sheered the tail shaft, destroyed
the steering gear, and fractured the deck to such an extent that the ship's
stern section was hanging several feet lower than the rest of her. Captain
Gustave Anderson remained on board with a few volunteers, whilst the
remainder of the seventy-three men on board were picked up by an
escort ship and by LST 236. A tug arrived on the scene and towed the
vessel back to be beached near Southampton. Most of her cargo of 6800
tons of equipment was salved, but the ship itself was declared a total loss.

Captain Roman Wank's *H.G. Blasdel* (Richmond, August 1943) was
the last to suffer from Commander Sieder's salvo, and it suffered most
tragically. A torpedo struck in No. 5 hold, the explosion tearing through
the ship's 'tween-decks and killing seventy-six and injuring 180 of the 436
American troops on board. The explosion left the ship's stern sagging, so
much so that the after gun platform was half under water. Water flooding
through the shaft tunnel began filling the engine-room as the engines were
closed down. A British corvette and a buoy tender that were nearby took

off the injured. The American LST 326 which was returning from Omaha Beach with 900 German prisoners of war on board, detached from its convoy to come alongside to take off the remainder of the *Blasdel's* troops. With the ship's stern threatening to break away, two tugs took her in tow and beached her in the Solent. *Blasdel* managed one final voyage under tow in December but it was to be her final one. It was to the ship scrapyard at Briton Ferry, near Swansea.

On the morning of 30 July 1944, *Samwake* (Portland, Maine, April 1944) sailed from Juno Beach having landed Canadian troops and their equipment. She was making for the Thames in company with several other ships and some escorts. Managed by S.& J. Thompson (Silver Line), she was commanded by Captain Owen Llewellyn John who had taken over the ship from the builders in the States a mere ten weeks earlier. Four hours out from the beaches the escorts made contact with a submarine and dropped depth charges, driving it off. But early the following morning the convoy was attacked by three E-boats of the German 6th Flotilla, and a fierce battle ensued. At 0130 hours a torpedo from one of the enemy craft struck *Samwake* on the port side in way of No. 2 hold. The ship immediately took a list to port as that hold flooded, water from it penetrating the bulkheads fore and aft into Nos 1 and 3 holds. The shell plating bulged outwards, and a 'sympathetic' crack opened up in the starboard shell plating opposite the hole on the port side. All available pumps were put to work, but made no impression. Douglas Peel was a junior engineer on board, and was in his bunk at the time of the explosion. He says, 'I knew instinctively what had happened . . . soon the ringing of the ship's alarm bells confirmed it. Grabbing what I could and making it on deck, I observed the whole of the foredeck opened up like a sardine tin'.[7]

Captain John attempted to correct the list by transferring bunkers. 'A destroyer came alongside', he later reported, 'and told me not to leave it too long to abandon ship if situation deteriorated.' It did deteriorate, and soon afterwards he ordered the engineers to make the boilers safe and abandon ship. Everyone got away in the lifeboats, but they remained in the vicinity of the ship. Half an hour later, his ship still afloat, Captain John called for volunteers to return on board with him. Second Engineer Joseph Wells, Third Engineer Cyril Stevens, and Apprentice Charles Telfer who was aged only twenty, from the Captain's own boat, and Bosun Ernest Rawcliffe and two of the engine-room staff, Alexander Patterson and John Orr, from another boat, put their hands up. Back on board Third Engineer Stevens risked his life by going below to attend to the pump that was still transferring oil in an attempt to correct the list. But

---

7. Letter in *The Ugly Duckling*, Spring 1992 edition. Douglas Peel later served on *Edward Bruce* (Baltimore, November 1943), one of a handful of Liberties transferred to the British flag which were not given 'Sam' names.

it was all to no avail, and with the ship showing signs that it was about to capsize, the volunteers left her again and were picked up by the trawler *Wiver*. From *Wiver's* deck Captain John watched his ship 'beginning to tip' and five minutes later she had disappeared.[8] For their efforts in trying to save the ship Captain John and the six volunteers were between them awarded four medals and three official commendations.

With a crew of sixty-one and twenty-one DEMS gunners, the *Samlong* (built as *Elias H. Derby*, Portland, Maine, November 1943) was lying at anchor two miles north of a line of Gooseberry blockships off Juno Beach on 3 August 1944. The sea was rough and there was quite a swell running. At 0300 hours Captain Leslie Cooper was called to the bridge for depth charges were being dropped in the vicinity. At 0530 hours the ship was shaken by a violent underwater explosion, a column of water shooting up as high as the boat deck. The ship listed to starboard before righting herself. An examination showed that a huge hole had been blown in the ship's side close to the boiler room, so close in fact, that the starboard boiler had been blown on top of the port one. The boat deck and several boats had been damaged. Two men who had been on watch in the engine-room were missing and three more injured. As a precautionary measure Captain Cooper ordered everyone into the remaining boats, but stayed on board himself with Chief Officer Melville Storrier, Second Officer Alexander Gilzean and two Able Seamen named White, one George, the other John.

At dawn HM salvage vessel *Salveda* came alongside, bringing with it Commander McKenzie to survey the damage. Captain Cooper later reported;

> I am afraid the main activity of the crew of this salvage vessel was stealing everything they possibly could, including my crew's personal belongings.
>
> *Salveda* went away and was replaced by *Salvage Chieftain* [a British commercial tug]. The crew of this vessel looted what remained of our personal possessions. The main concern of both crews of the salvage vessels was apparently not the safety of the ship, but how much loot they could get away with.[9]

That is the only such criticism of the salvage services that the author has found in British official documents.

The sea off Juno Beach soon cut up even rougher and the *Salvage Chieftain* had to cast off. By that time the heavy swell had caused buckling of the decks. Captain Cooper noted:

8. ADM199/524.
9. ADM199/2147.

The ship's side and deck on the port side had buckled and cracked. Cracks all at right angles to the welding, all cracks stopping where they reached the welding. Not one piece of welding in the ship cracked or broke.

On 6 August *Samlong,* with all her crew back on board, was taken in tow by HM tug *Allegiance.* The ship arrived at Long Reach in the Thames off Greenhithe two days later. There she was found to be beyond economic repair and so was towed to the River Blackwater, remaining there until sold for scrap in 1949.

Captain Cooper produced his official report at Greenhithe. He ended it by saying that he had heard 'that the enemy attacked the ship with human torpedoes', and that afterwards some German seamen had been fished out of the sea and taken aboard the destroyer HMS *Frobisher* off Juno Beach. What he had heard was correct, for on the night of the incident, twenty German Linsen craft, or explosive boats, had attacked ships off the beaches. Captain Cooper was awarded the OBE for trying to save his ship and the volunteers who stayed aboard with him were all officially commended. Later in 1944, when master of the *Samtucky* (launched as *William Blackstone,* Portland, Maine, October 1943), Captain Cooper was himself officially commended for his actions when that ship was attacked and damaged by a U-boat in the North Atlantic

The Normandy beachheads remained dangerous places for Allied shipping throughout that part of the European campaign. Allied ships were still being sunk or damaged there into August 1944. On the 7th the *William L. Marcy* (Los Angeles, January 1943) when anchored off Juno Beach was struck by a torpedo from an E-boat. Only one man was killed. She was towed to Swansea and written off there. The short sea passage between Britain and the landing beaches also remained dangerous. The troop-carrying *Louis Kossuth* (Baltimore, December 1943) was heading for Utah Beach on the 23rd when she was damaged by a torpedo and had to be towed back to Cowes in the Isle of Wight. She survived the war.

Mayhem in the seas off the continent of Europe continued until the end of the war, and because of the danger caused by mines, well beyond it. Amongst the Liberties affected was the *Lee S. Overman* (Wilmington, June 1943). Under the command of Captain Creston C. Jenkins the ship was entering the port of Le Havre on 11 November 1944 when she struck a mine. The ship is reported to have been carrying a full cargo of ammunition and explosives, but apparently these did not blow up, possibly because the initial explosion broke the ship's back and she sank very quickly. So quickly, that for a time the wreck blocked part of the main channel into that harbour. No one was killed.

Twelve days later, on 23 August off Barfleur the *William D. Burnham* (Richmond, August 1943) met the beginning of her end in more tragic circumstances. In mid-afternoon a torpedo from *U-978,* Lieutenant Commander Palst, tore into the stern of the ship and exploded with such force she was lifted almost out of the water. Rudder, propeller, and tail-end shaft were all blown away, and No. 5 hold flooded immediately. Captain Emil Rosen ordered all aboard to stand by lifeboat stations, but as they did so, a second torpedo struck the ship just forward of the bridge. That explosion blew a 40ft hole in the ship's side and destroyed No. 2 lifeboat which was still in the falls, killing eighteen of the men standing in the vicinity. Captain Rosen ordered the remaining three boats lowered, and those still alive got away on them to be picked up later by the auxiliary patrol craft HMS *Fidget.* The US Navy tug *ATR-3* later towed the ship to be beached near Cherbourg. Some of the cargo was salved but the ship itself was a total loss.

December 1944 was another bad month for Allied ships including Liberties, especially those in the vicinity of Antwerp. Whilst proceeding up the River Schelde towards that port on the 3rd, the *Francis Asbury* (Jacksonville, May 1943), struck a mine off Buoy NF 10. Exploding under the engine-room, it broke the ship's back. Parts of the engine tore through the decks, killing fifteen men. The boilers were destroyed, and hot live steam from them inundated the ship to such an extent that most survivors were scalded. The ship's chief engineer and an Armed Guard later died from that cause in hospital. HM salvage vessel *American Salvor* (ex-USS *Bars 5*) and HM tug *Dexterous* hastened to assist and managed to pull *Asbury* clear of the main channel. She was then sunk by deliberate 'friendly fire'. Four days later the British *Samsip,* as related earlier, was lost in similar circumstances and in almost exactly the same place. At around that same time the *Samarina* (built as *James Blair,* Baltimore, September 1943) fired at and destroyed a midget submarine in the Schelde estuary. Gunner John Earnshaw of the Maritime Regiment received a Mention in Despatches for this, and the ship's master, Captain John Blewett, an official Commendation.

Not all of the damage to Liberty ships in the Schelde was due to enemy action. On 23 December the *William Paca* (Baltimore, June 1942) went aground near Terneuzen and had to be refloated with the aid of *American Salvor* and HM tug *Sea Guest.* Repairs were required, which was particularly unfortunate because the ship had just left dry-dock after repairs necessitated by an earlier occurrence. On 30 November, in more or less the same position where later she went ashore, *Paca* had been in collision with the British *Empire Ness.* The *Ness,* built as an ore carrier but at the time carrying a general cargo, sank as a result of the collision when gas bottles in the cargo exploded.[10] Lying at anchor off Antwerp on Christmas Eve, the *Timothy Bloodworth* (New Orleans, June 1943) almost

10. ADM1/17274.

made the record books as being the only Liberty ship to be sunk by a German V-2 rocket. Almost but not quite. A rocket exploded immediately overhead showering the ship with shrapnel, and then another exploded nearby, fragments of it striking the ship's hull. No lives were lost in the incident.

British Admiralty records show that between December 1944 and the middle of April 1945, salvage tugs were called to no less than seventeen incidents involving Liberty ships off the Belgian and Dutch coasts. Some of the incidents were due to mines, but most to strandings and collisions. On 22 February 1945, two Liberties collided with each other, though neither was badly damaged. The ships were the *Jonathan Elmer* (Baltimore, September 1942) and the *Samark* (built as the *John G. North*, Richmond, October 1943). On 14 April HM trawler *Lune* came off second best when the *Samport* (launched as *Israel Wheelan*, Baltimore, December 1943) hit her when she was tied up alongside a berth at Antwerp. *Lune* was out of action for over a month. Almost as fast as Allied minesweepers were clearing areas, the Germans were laying or dropping new mines. Two British 'Sams' were lost to mines on the Schelde between the 18 January and 19 March 1945. On the first date the *Samvern* (built as *Edith Wharton*, Baltimore, November 1943) hit a mine and broke in half. On the second date she was followed to the bottom from the same cause by *Samselbu* (Brunswick, April 1944). Captain John Harper and Second Officer David Heaton of *Samselbu* were specially commended for their actions during the incident, and Petty Officer Jack Critchley RN, in charge of the ship's gunners, was mentioned in despatches.

Liberties and members of their crews continued to be lost in other European waters. The *Dan Beard* (Richmond, February 1943), was torpedoed by *U-1202*, Lieutenant Commander Thomsen, on 10 December 1944. The ship was on passage from Barry to Belfast when the torpedo struck, the explosion breaking the ship in two. Those crew members on the after part abandoned by jumping into the sea, those on the fore part, escaped in four lifeboats. The sea was very rough and two of the boats were swamped. The other two made it to the shore with a total of twenty-five men on board. Thirteen more survivors were picked up by boats that came out from the shore, but twenty-nine men were never seen again.

The *Jonas Lie* (Savannah, September 1944) went down on 14 January 1945, but only after a fight for her life lasting five days. The ship sailed in convoy from Milford Haven on the 9th; she was in ballast making for New York. That same day a torpedo from *U-1055*, commanded by Lieutenant Commander Meyer, struck the ship amidships, ripping open the after engine-room bulkhead and killing two engineers in the process. The ship listed to port as she lost way. Captain Carl Lionel von Schoen ordered his crew into the boats, but remained on board himself with the chief officer, the bosun and an able seaman. The men in the boats were picked up by a British trawler, and so were Captain Von Schoen and his volunteers after they were ordered to leave the ship by the commander of the senior escort ship. All were subsequently landed back at Milford Haven. One man who had been blown into the sea by the explosion was rescued by the Norwegian freighter *Fosna*. He was doubly lucky for he got home far sooner than his shipmates, because the Norwegian was heading for New York. On 10 January, Von Schoen and thirteen of his men boarded HM rescue tug *Stormking* and went in search of the *Lie*. The Liberty had drifted into a minefield, but the crew were able to board on the 11th and they then took aboard a tow-line. On the 12th a storm blew up and in high seas the line parted. By the time HM tug *Sprite* arrived to assist it was obvious there was no saving the sinking ship. Von Schoen and his gallant band were taken off by a lifeboat of the Royal National Lifeboat Institution, the only type of craft that could safely go alongside in the existing sea conditions. The *Lie* sank on the 14th.

A non-enemy inflicted casualty occurred on 16 January 1945 in The Downs off Deal in the English Channel. The incident involved two Liberty ships. The *James Harrod* (Portland, Oregon, March 1943) ran into the anchored *Raymond B. Stevens* (Portland, Maine, April 1944). The *Harrod* and its cargo which included cased gasoline, caught fire and the ship had to be beached at Pegwell Bay. It took six days for the fire to burn itself out and by that time the ship had broken in two, the after part being underwater. The fore part was later salved and towed to that graveyard of ships, the River Blackwater. In 1946 the part-hulk was towed to Bremerhaven, filled with then obsolete chemical weaponry and scuttled at sea.

Even after the war in Europe ended in May 1945, many Allied merchant ships, including several Liberty ships, continued to be damaged or lost to mines. In the last chapter the story of the *Horace Binney* was told, a ship that met its fate on the very day of the German capitulation In Chapter 7 the constructive total loss of the *Colin P. Kelly Jnr* was mentioned, a ship that struck a mine on 4 June 1945. Other Liberties damaged by mines in post-war months included the *John Woolman* (Baltimore, April 1943), *Calvin Coolidge* (Portland, Maine, February 1943), *Cyrus Adler* (New Orleans, July 1944), and *Lord Delaware* (Baltimore, December 1942).

'Let Sleeping Wrecks Lie': The On-going Saga of the Richard Montgomery

On the far side of the Thames estuary from the seaside resort of Southend-on-Sea, and only a little over a mile south of the Yantlet Dredged Channel which is the main route into the Port of London, lies one of the most celebrated wrecks on the British coast. The wreck of the Liberty ship *Richard Montgomery* lies in two sections on the seabed, but her masts and derricks are visible above water at all stages of the tide.

If one knows in which direction to look, the wreck is clearly discernible from the end of the famous Southend Pier just four miles to the north. Much closer to the wreck, over to the south-west, lies the busy Port of Sheerness on the Isle of Sheppey at the entrance to the River Medway. Another mile in roughly the same direction would fetch the proverbial crow over the industrial areas of the Isle of Grain. More importantly perhaps, the wreck lies a bare 200 yards off the northern edge of the channel used by ships passing in and out of Sheerness and the Medway ports. For when in 1944 the ship broke in two and sank, she still had on board over 3000 tons of munitions. That cargo is still there, in a wreck which can be seen by the communities who are threatened by any residual danger it may present. It is scarcely surprising therefore, that the safety of the wreck has exercised the minds of many people living on both sides of the Thames estuary, ever since its existence became generally known. Needless to say, it is Britain's best protected wreck. So famous is the *Richard Montgomery* in the port off which she lies, that, despite the fact that the surrounding waters contain many historic wrecks dating back several centuries, she is simply called 'The Wreck', there being no need to mention a name.

One of the many local people concerned over the safety of the wreck was, until his death in 1997, Southend Councillor David Cotgrove, and his concern did not stem solely from the fact that his home town lay within a few miles of it. He was well qualified to take more than a passing interest in the matter from a professional point of view, for he had once been on the staff of a research establishment dealing with experimental explosives. His active concern over the nature and extent of any residue risk existing in the cargo seems to have been one of the principal reasons why some of the British governmental bodies concerned with the wreck during the years immediately after the war were, after a series of inter-departmental wrangles and buck-passing, at last forced to address the issue properly. The buck-passing, as we shall see, also had an international dimension. Cotgrove's investigations and the letters and reports he produced were important in bringing the matter to the attention of the general public and in ensuring continued public interest in the matter to prevent it sliding back into that comfortable obscurity in which it had been buried between 1944 and 1952.[1] As we shall see, almost from the very beginning of the saga, the ship and what happened to her was subject to controversy, cover-ups, official obfuscation, and misinformation, and as with the buck-passing, not all of that was confined to the British side of the Atlantic.

Richard Montgomery was launched in July 1943 at the St Johns River Shipyard at Jacksonville, Florida, the seventh of the eighty-two Liberties built at that yard. She was named after an Irish soldier born in Dublin in 1738 who settled in America and was elected to Congress; he was killed on the last day of 1775 when fighting against the British during the assault on Quebec. She was managed for the US Maritime Administration by Agwilines Incorporated of New York, and during the twelve months following her launch the ship made three round trips between US ports and Britain, and one to the Mediterranean. Those voyages were largely uneventful although once she came under a bombing attack from German aircraft.

In July 1944, at Hog Island, Philadelphia, a military ordnance establishment, she loaded 6862 tons of TNT, ammunition, and bombs, including many cluster bombs. Spread between Nos. 2, 3, and 4 holds, and on the bottom of those spaces, she also carried 1050 tons of coal slag as ballast and a bed for the bombs. Loading completed, she made north for New York to link up with other ships there. Later, off Halifax, Nova Scotia, she joined Convoy HXM-301 (HX for Halifax, M for Mersey) on 25 July. The ship sailed with a crew of forty-two together with a Naval Armed Guard of twenty-five to man her guns. She was under the command of Captain Wilkie. The convoy was a large one, consisting of no less than ninety-four merchant ships and twelve LSTs (Landing Ship, Tanks), escorted by six warships comprising three corvettes and a minesweeper of the Royal Canadian Navy and two escort vessels of the United States Navy. The convoy was typical of many at that stage of the war, with the merchant ships, twenty-three of them tankers, coming from

---

1. The papers of the late David F. Cotgrove on this subject are in the Essex Record Office, Southend-on-Sea. Copies of some of the Cotgrove papers and additional material on the *Richard Montgomery* can be found in Lloyd's Miscellaneous Files, Research Box No. 2, at the Guildhall Library, London.

The Liberty at War

six Allied countries, the United States, Britain, Norway, Panama, France and Holland. The majority of the ships were American, but both the commodore and vice-commodore vessels were Norwegian, the *Reinholt* and *Samuel Bakke* respectively.[2]

Convoy HXM-301 would have made a memorable, though not at that time a rare sight as it set out to cross the Atlantic. No less than forty-eight of the participant ships had exactly the same silhouette, that of the ubiquitous Liberty ship. The number of Liberties in the convoy would have been greater had not three more missed the sailing for one reason or another. Forty-four of the Liberties flew the Stars and Stripes and one, the *Sun-Yat-Sen* (Sausalito, April 1943), the Chinese flag although she was officered by Americans. The other three flew the Red Ensign. The *Ben H. Miller* (Baltimore, December 1943) was there, being one of only seven Liberties amongst those lend-leased to Britain to retain its original name. The other two British-flagged Liberties were the *Samboston* (handed over at Baltimore, 30 November 1943) and the *Sameden* (Baltimore, 13 March 1944).

The convoy, with a designated speed of 8.5kts, made the ocean crossing without incident and arrived off Loch Ewe, Scotland on 8 August. It then split up, the LSTs and some of the tankers making for Milford Haven, whilst other ships, including the *Richard Montgomery,* made for the Mersey. Off Liverpool Bay the convoy split once more, *Richard Montgomery* and seven other Liberties from the original convoy receiving orders to proceed to the Thames Estuary. The others were *Henry M. Roberts, Henry B. Brown, John Stevenson, George Popham, Harry A. Garfield, John Gibbon,* and *Sidney Lanier.* Arriving there safely on 16 August in company with two more Liberties from another convoy, the *Richard S. Ewell* and *Clyde L. Seavey,* each ship was then ordered to a specific anchorage off Sheerness Middle Sand. There they were to await a convoy for Cherbourg.

All ships entering or leaving the Thames Estuary came under the aegis of the Royal Naval Control Service based at Southend Pier with additional offices at Nos. 7, 8 and 9 Royal Terrace on the Southend sea-front. This shore establishment had been given the name HMS *Leigh,* after a town a little higher up the Thames. Its senior officer was Commodore J.P. Champion DSO RN, who had been called out of retirement at the outbreak of war. The King's Harbourmaster, the officer directly responsible for allocating anchorages, was Lieutenant Commander R.J. Walmsley RNR. His assistant was Lieutenant Roger G.J. Foley RNVR.

Like all RNR officers at that time, Robert James Walmsley came from the Merchant Navy. Born at Middlewich, Cheshire in 1890, he gained

---

2. Convoy information from Document FX-3733, Naval Historical Center, Washington, DC.

328

his master's certificate at Liverpool in 1919. His entire seagoing experience, apart from the short periodic training sessions with the Royal Navy that were a requirement of his Naval Reserve status, was spent with various constituent companies that formed Ellerman Lines, one of the most prestigious of British shipping organisations. He gained his first command, aged thirty-seven, on 16 September 1927 with Hall Line's *Stanley Hall*. Before being called for service with the Royal Navy on 15 July 1940, his last Ellerman ship was the *City of Newcastle*. (He was to rejoin Ellermans in 1946. His very first post-war ship happened to be a Liberty, the *Samshire*. Built at Baltimore as the *Emma Lazarus* she was handed over to the British on 30 August 1943 as the *Samara* and given to Ellerman's to manage. For some now unknown reason she immediately underwent another name-change becoming *Samshire* before she sailed from Baltimore on her maiden voyage – to the Middle East – on 8 September. Ellermans purchased the ship on 16 December 1946, and the ship then became the *City of Doncaster*.) It is clear from Walmsley's career details – for not one of the twenty-three ships he served in as First Mate or Master between 1918 and 1940 ever suffered any recorded casualty – that he was a highly experienced seaman. That makes it very difficult to understand his actions concerning *Richard Montgomery*.

Montgomery had sailed across the Atlantic well trimmed by the stern, her draft aft being 31ft. Commander Walmsley allocated the ship an anchorage just off the northern edge of the Middle Sand where the depth was only 33ft at low water, leaving very little margin for error or for any vagaries of the tide that might result from meteorological conditions. Cotgrove once wrote that the ship's draft was 'nearly three feet more than was usual for a Liberty ship'. But Cotgrove was no seaman, otherwise he would have known that 31ft was not an exceptional draft aft for such a ship. Many loaded Liberties did sail lighter than that because of the nature of many wartime cargoes, military vehicles for example, which could fill a ship without putting her down to her marks. The main point was not that the ship's draft was out of the ordinary, but that given her draft she was consigned to an anchorage position that provided insufficient water under her keel. Not only that, and in the event this was the most important factor, the berth was so close to the Middle Sand that even with only the minimum scope of anchor chain out, should the wind blow from the north and/or should the ship's anchor drag, the ship's stern would swing perilously close to the shoal.

One report has it that after coming to anchor Captain Wilkie, then sixty-four years old and therefore well-experienced in his own right, criticised his ship's location but that he received orders from Southend to remain in that position because of the dangerous nature of his cargo. Unknown to Wilkie was that Walmsley's decision to anchor the ship in that position had also been questioned by Lieutenant Foley, the Assistant King's Harbourmaster, and that his protest had gone unheeded. An article published in 1980 in the House Journal of the Central Electricity Generating Board at Tilbury (just upriver in the Thames and therefore an organisation keenly interested in the welfare of the wreck) states that the pilot involved also objected to the anchorage, but the author of the article did not give a source for that information. Anyway, the pilot duly carried out his instructions.[3]

There is more. When Foley, who was a Volunteer Reserve officer with considerably less experience in these matters than Walmsley, had questioned the suitability of the allocated berth, he was directed to carry out the order. Foley then requested that it be given him in writing, a request that resulted in a heated argument between the two men, a dispute which attracted the attention of Commodore Champion who overheard part of it. Foley suggested that the *Richard Montgomery* swap positions with another ship which was drawing only 24ft of water. Not only was Foley overruled, he was given an ear-bashing for questioning the judgement of a more senior and much more experienced officer. Foley withdrew from the room without the written order he had asked for, and Walmsley's original order was then carried out.[4]

Just before dawn on the morning of Sunday 20 August 1944, the wind fell northerly and *Richard Montgomery*'s stern took the ground, ending up on top of Middle Sand. The incident took place at the height of spring-tide, a tide of maximum amplitude, and as the next such tide was not due until 5 September, the ship in nautical parlance was 'neaped'; until that date she was stuck there and there was no guarantee of getting off even then unless some of the cargo was discharged. But all that soon became hypothetical. For as the tide ebbed the strain on the ship's hull caused by her stern being on the sands and her forepart being still afloat, resulted in deck and hull plates in the vicinity of No. 3 hold cracking with a loud explosive sound reminiscent of a gunshot. So loud was the noise it was heard by the crew of the fishing launch *British Queen* which was about her business over a mile away.

It would seem that it was a report made by *British Queen*'s skipper, Clive Cobb, that became the basis of the story that the *Richard Montgomery* crew rather hastily abandoned ship being 'naturally apprehensive of the noise and of the nature of their cargo'. As Cobb could not have known of the ship's cargo at the time of the incident, that smacks of hindsight. The fishing skipper also noted that the emergency evacuation took place 'via the ship's own lifeboats and rafts'.

3. Peter Hopker in *Til -'B'- ury Tattle*, the in-House Journal of the CEGB 'B' plant at Tilbury.
4. This information was supplied to Cotgrove by Roger Foley during a postwar interview.

In complete contrast, the official report made by the ship's Navy Armed Guard commander on 19 September 1944, stated:

> SS *Richard Montgomery* broke in two forward of the bridge. . . . Ship appeared to be resting on an obstacle underwater. Communications were immediately made with Southend Pier for emergency aid. The British Admiralty ordered the US Naval Armed Guard to abandon ship and also the merchant crew.
>
> . . . other vessels in the anchorage rendered assistance by coming alongside with lifeboats. The Naval Control Service came alongside with tugs to take off the Naval Armed Guard and merchant marine crew.[5]

Whatever the exact facts of the abandonment, the ship now lay aground with some of her plates fractured but with most of her deck and superstructure still above water and laden with nearly 7000 tons of dangerous cargo. Captain Wilkie and his crew were taken to Southend.

Two days later, on 22 August, Master Stevedore T.P. Adams from nearby Rochester, whose firm had been awarded the job of salvaging the cargo, boarded the *Montgomery* to inspect the condition of the ship. He was met there by the ship's Chief Officer specially sent across from Southend, who handed him copies of the ship's cargo manifest and stowage plan. One can hazard a guess that it is at least possible that Mr Adams would have been somewhat alarmed at what the documents revealed, but not so alarmed it seems as some of the stevedores at nearby Sheerness. When interviewed about this matter in 1972, a Sheerness dock worker named Silcock said the local dockers would not work the ship and so stevedores had to be brought in from Gravesend and paid £1 per hour danger money. That was confirmed by another docker from those days, named Dewell. Retired Thames River Pilot Bob Manson, said much the same thing, adding that the 'foreign' stevedores were housed in the Army Garrison building in Sheerness. Towards the end, so dicey did the unloading operation become that even the payment of danger money could not persuade the dockers to carry on. A dispute took place, and as a result the Royal Navy was brought in to do the work according to Stoker First Class Joe Gilhooley who was one of the naval 'volunteers'. All the cargo on board was consigned to the United States Army Air Force, and most of it was very nasty stuff indeed. Amongst it were 13,000 general purpose bombs, about 8000 semi-armour piercing ones, 9000 cluster fragmentation bombs, and nearly 1500 cases each of smoke phosphorescent and 100lb demolition bombs, and fuses. Other consignments of bursters, small arms ammunition, and signal flares, hardly seem worth a mention.

---

5. Armed Guard Officer Voyage Reports, Record Group 38, National Archives, Washington, DC.

In a tricky piece of seamanship Captain J.S. Gardner moored his small British freighter *Empire Nutfield* alongside. The salved cargo was to be transhipped in her to Ipswich (the nearest port to several American air bases in the County of Suffolk). It is possible that this particular ship was chosen for the task because she was considered expendable. Built as the *Bermondsey* in 1919, her name was changed to plain *Nutfield* in 1928. On the River Tyne in December 1942 she collided with another ship and was written off by insurers as a constructive total loss. However, she was subsequently purchased by the Ministry of War Transport and repaired, so becoming the *Empire Nutfield*. The expendable theory is supported by the ship's subsequent short-lived career. In 1946 she was loaded with captured German chemical weaponry and was one of about fifty such ships scuttled in the straits that form the entrances to the Baltic Sea.

With no steam power of her own, the *Montgomery*'s winches were supplied with steam from the tug *Atlantic Cock* also moored alongside, and discharging commenced on the 23rd. In mid-afternoon of the following day, the ship's hull cracked forward of No. 3 hatch, causing holds Nos. 1 and 2 to flood. On 8 September the ship broke its back completely. By the 25th of that month holds 4 and 5 had been cleared of cargo, but by that time the fore end of the ship and what remained of the cargo in holds 1, 2 and 3, had disappeared below the surface where they have remained to the present day. The ship was then abandoned and she was almost completely forgotten, for there was a war on.

Based on the original manifested tonnages and the figures produced by Mr Adams about the quantities he had removed, it has been estimated that just over 3000 tons of bombs of various types, including 2618 cluster fragmentation, and 226 cases of fuses, are still down there somewhere. It was noted at the time that the cluster fragmentation bombs in the now submerged No. 2 hold were likely to have been fused, a statement probably based on the known condition of the 6400 that were actually removed from the ship.

Even as the discharging operation was going on, a Board of Enquiry into the loss of the ship was held. It took place about a week after the stranding. In view of the danger involved to the participants, it seems rather odd that it was held on board the ship, in the officer's saloon to be exact. It was conducted by a team led by a Lieutenant Commander of the United States Navy amidst 'the all-pervading stench of leaking fuel oil'. Lieutenant Commander Walmsley gave evidence on the berth allocation, and the Pilot confirmed that the ship had been anchored in the allocated position. It was established that crew members on other ships anchored nearby had seen the *Montgomery* swinging towards the Middle Sand and had blown warning signals on their sirens. The Chief Officer who had been on anchor watch at the time, when asked why he had not immediately called the Captain to the bridge, replied simply, that he did not know. What can be viewed at best as a disgraceful disservice to Captain Wilkie and at worst a cover-up by a senior Royal Navy officer, was that the Board did not hear evidence from Lieutenant Foley about his objections to the assigned berth. For within two days of the event, Foley had been posted elsewhere, rather conveniently for Commander Walmsley one might feel. The upshot was that both Wilkie and his Chief Officer were found to have been negligent, and each had his certificate suspended for 12 months. (It is reported that Captain Wilkie later lost his life in the Pacific, but in what capacity he was serving and on what ship is not known.) Had Foley's evidence been available to the Board, there might at least have been a chance that the verdict in Captain Wilkie's case would have been rather different.

General Dwight D. Eisenhower, Allied Supreme Commander in Europe, knew all about the loss of the *Richard Montgomery*. This is confirmed in a message from him dated 11 November 1944 and addressed to PEMBARK NY, under the heading, SECRET, PRIORITY. It read:

> PH 241 *Richard Montgomery*
> Due to weather conditions making work impracticable during ensuing period no further discharge will be effected until next Spring. Work originally commenced August 230900 and continued as weather conditions permitted to September 261730 since when due to adverse conditions no further discharge has been effected. Remaining cargo is stowed in Nos. 1 and 2 holds which are under water. Tonnage remaining 3691 WT 3686 MT.
> Eisenhower.[6]

In view of this it is, to say the least, rather surprising that within four years of the original incident, a chain of events began that indicate something had gone very wrong with American official records regarding the *Richard Montgomery*. Pilot Bob Manson, who has been mentioned earlier, when speaking on this subject in 1972, said that he had once seen an official US Naval document 'in which it plainly stated that the *Richard Montgomery* no longer existed, and that the ship and cargo were totally destroyed in the war'. One wonders whether that document might also have been seen by the author of one of the standard books on American merchant ships losses in the war. For in his *A Careless Word – A Needless Sinking*, published as late as 1988, Captain A.R. Moore noted against the name of this ship that she 'was bombed by German aircraft'.

However, the mystery over the American records began even earlier than 1972. In a letter concerning the *Montgomery* sent to David

---

6. Message No. UKX 14256, 11 November 1944.

Cotgrove and dated 12 March 1962, a letter signed by Lieutenant J.S. Cohune USN, Assistant Public Information Officer, at the Naval Historical Center, Washington DC, the following appears; '...declared a marine wreck. She was raised and scrapped in April 1948 and sold to Phillipps, Kraft & Fisher Company on 28 April 1948.'[7] In fact, no such attempt was ever made to raise and scrap the wreck, and Phillipps, an American salvage company, had only surveyed the wreck in 1948 and the proposed sale of it to them by the US Maritime Administration was rescinded in 1951 after the British Government informed the American Government that it was not to be sold. As a consequence, in that same year the Maritime Administration attempted to abandon the wreck to the British Government, which declined to accept it. The wreck therefore legally remains the property of the United States.

For the first few years after the war the British had a lot more to worry about than a sunken ammunition ship in the Thames. For one thing, as bombsites were being cleared in cities and towns, many unexploded bombs were being found within yards of habitations, and at least the *Montgomery* was over a mile offshore. In fact it was not until Dr. R.F. Bennett, the Member for Gosport, asked a three-fold question about it in the House of Commons on 23 April 1952, that the matter was raised from the obscurity in which it had lain for six years. Bennett asked what responsibility the Admiralty held in respect of the wreck, what action was intended with regard to the dangerous cargo in it, and what steps were being taken to ensure it did not blow up. Commander Noble replied on behalf of the Admiralty. 'The answer to all three parts of the question is none. The responsibility lies with the Port of London Authority.' Dr Bennett's 1952 intervention had one beneficial result. It ensured that over subsequent years a series of questions on this subject were asked in the House.

In addition to that, the *Richard Montgomery* became the subject of many articles in the British Press, some of them couched in highly dramatic language, others appearing under melodramatic headlines. Among the first articles were those which appeared in London's *Daily Sketch* in 1962. Then, in its October 1964 edition, *Wide World* magazine ran a feature called 'Doomsday Ship' in which its author quoted Major A.B. 'Bill' Hartley on the subject. Hartley had become known as 'Mr Bomb Disposal' during the war, winning two medals for his work. He was among Britain's foremost bomb disposal experts. He said that the *Montgomery* cargo 'will grow more dangerous year by year'. On another occasion he was quoted as saying that if the cargo went off, it could cause 'the greatest conventional explosion ever in the United Kingdom'. The *Chatham*

---

7. This letter is referenced JSC:mc/5720A.

Observer, the weekly newspaper based at that Medway port just around the corner from Sheerness, weighed in with an article in October 1964 under the headline 'Danger Down Below'. Later articles appeared under such headlines as 'The Town that Lives in Terror', or 'The Island that Could Disappear Overnight'.

Then, on 2 January 1969 it was reported that the Kent County Police were investigating a threat involving the *Richard Montgomery* made by university students who wanted the Government to make a contribution to Oxford University. Twelve days later it was discovered that this was a students' rag-week prank, but nevertheless it had served to give the wreck even more publicity. The London *Times* edition of 20 February 1969 gave the matter its staid attention when it reported that 'Government experts were considering putting a protective barrier around the wreck'. Although of course it made no difference to the status of the wreck, including its safety, it is of interest to note that into 1971 there was still confusion as to the circumstances that led to the loss of the ship in the first place, even in official circles. In a draft document of that year, the Medway Ports Authority stated:

> According to sources she was damaged by enemy aircraft in the Thames Estuary approaches and was towed into her anchorage at Sheerness.[8]

Further on in that same document it is of interest to see the following:

> As regards to accidental and/or spontaneous explosion of the vessel and her cargo, although the USA [*sic*] Maritime Administration accept title to the vessel, it is argued that they would claim 'Sovereign Rights', and this would avoid any claims resulting from explosion.

Until about this time British government departments had continued to fall over each other to disclaim any responsibility for the wreck. But with all this publicity, at last a decision was made, and in 1971 the hot potato ended up in the hands of the Department of Trade and Industry. (The departmental responsibility for the wreck has changed hands several times, but since 1971 it has remained the charge of a single authority.) On 25 July that year a second survey of the wreck was held (the first having been the one carried out by Phillipps in 1948). Boarding a ship called *Felsted* at Dover, an Anglo-American diving team led by Lieutenant Commander J.C. Naquin USN and Salvage Officer D. Bloy, on that date carried out a detailed survey of the wreck site.

---

8. Draft Document entitled '*Richard Montgomery* Investigation', Medway Ports Authority, 1971. MPA files, Sheerness.

In 1973 Britain enacted its Protection of Wrecks Act, and the *Richard Montgomery* was the only designated dangerous wreck mentioned in the document. According to a later Official Report on the ship, a Committee on Hazardous Wrecks was then set up, comprising members of various governmental and official bodies including the Ministry of Defence. Regarding the *Montgomery* the Committee 'sought advice from US experts on the contents of the wreck, the design of the munitions carried, and the nature of the hazards they posed'. (That Committee has since been disbanded.)[9] From the beginning the Committee's consistently firm advice after considering all the options, one of which was to build a coffer-dam around the site, was always 'that no attempt should be made to disturb the site, either by clearing the wreck, or by looking for the remaining munitions on board'. It noted that 'the difficulties of either task would be very considerable, danger apart, given the size of the site of the wreck and almost total lack of visibility in the surrounding water'. Any such action 'would increase the likelihood of the very explosion that must be avoided if at all possible'.[10]

At a meeting of a Working Party on 12 December 1980, it was decided:

(1) Politically it should be seen by those concerned and the general public that something positive was being done by the Department of Transport to establish the stability of the wreck.
(2) An external survey of the wreck to be carried out.
(3) An internal survey of the wreck to be carried out.

Even at that late stage, British ministers were still taking a stance over responsibility. During those discussions a spokesman for the Ministry of Defence declared 'that it was an opportune time to state that the MOD will accept no responsibility for any accidental incident that may possibly occur from the surveying of the wreck'. The Department of Transport took a stance over the costs involved, its spokesman stating that 'the cost of survey would be extremely high . . . and as there was no money allocation for this year, the survey may not be carried out until 1982'.

At least some of the survey work in the 1980s seems to have been delegated to the Port of London Authority. In June 1986 Len Farnham was working as a mate on the Authority's salvage vessel *Hookness,* which together with a sister vessel, *Foulness,* were periodically sent to inspect the wreck. He says;

---

9. 'Report on the Wreck of the *Richard Montgomery*', Maritime and Coastguard Agency, May 1999.
10. The Wreck of the ss *Richard Montgomery*. A Note by Marine General Division, Department of Transport, January 1992.

On arrival our two ex-naval divers would survey the hull. On one occasion I questioned the divers on the state of the cargo and they reported that items were fused together with rust. There was a fear at that time that the IRA would attach limpet mines to the hull in an attempt to sabotage it.

In view of the history of the man after whom the ship was named, any IRA involvement would have been one for the books, as the saying goes. In fact the *Montgomery* had already featured as the objective of the villain in a novel called *Blockbuster* which was published in 1976.[11]

In 1992 an official statement was made about the possible condition of the explosives in the wreck. It was stated that TNT does not react with water, that it will not explode even when a trifle damp. Therefore, if water had got into some of the bomb casings, but it was not certain that it had, then those bombs would be safe. It went on to say that even in its dry state TNT does not remain in good condition for ever, that in the end it decays into a non-explosive state. However, 'experience with mines recovered by fishermen suggests that it can take a very long time for this final stage to be reached . . . but when it starts to decay it first goes through a more sensitive phase in which it could be set off by a sharp knock'. The cluster bombs posed a different problem. 'They have fuses made of brass filled with a lead compound to enhance the detonator shock. Exposed to sea water, the lead compound reacts with brass, forming a highly unstable compound which could explode with the slightest disturbance.'

There can be little argument that to attempt to do anything with the wreck now would be irresponsible and dangerous. The best course is that recommended by the Committee which is to leave the wreck undisturbed and allow nature to take its course. Under the Protection of Wrecks Act it is an offence for anyone to interfere with the site. It is well marked with buoys and notice boards and it is monitored from the Medway Ports Control Centre at Sheerness. Frequent visual inspections are made of those parts of the wreck still above water in order to reduce the risk of parts falling on to the cargo beneath. Early in 2000 the ship's heavy-lift topping blocks were removed, and it says something about their manufacture that after fifty-six years of suffering the elements, the sheaves in those blocks were still in good working order as this author can personally testify. The last three annual surveys of the wreck have been conducted on behalf of the Maritime and Coastguard Agency by Sonar Research and Development Limited, of Beverley, Yorkshire, using the latest techniques in the bathymetric surveying field.

---

11. Stephen Barlay, *Blockbuster* (London 1976). David Cotgrove seems to have acted as some sort of technical adviser to the author of this book.

A special watch is kept by the Medway Ports Control Centre to prevent ships going any nearer than the marked channel into the Medway, the northern edge of which is about 260 yards from the nearest point of the wreck. The May 1999 Official Report on the wreck produced by the Maritime and Coastguard Agency states that, 'There are no records of near misses since the wreck occurred in 1944'.

That all depends, one supposes, on how one defines a near miss. London's *Daily Mail* had no problem in so defining the incident that took place on 22 May 1980, its headline when the news leaked out a week later, being 'Blast Fear Over Thames "Near Miss" '. The incident involved the small Danish tanker *Mare Altum* under the command of Captain Hendrik Helder. She was carrying a cargo of toluene, described as a highly inflammable, low flashpoint liquid. On that date in bad visibility, a then-unidentified vessel was picked up by the control radar as being outside of any designated channel. It was contacted by radio and its master replied that he was inbound for Purfleet on the River Thames and that his position was off No. 5 buoy, Sea Reach, part of the main channel into the Thames. The Medway Duty Officer informed the master that he was not in Sea Reach at all, but in the Medway approach area and that he was nearing the *Richard Montgomery* wreck. He was directed to turn hard-a-starboard and proceed on a northerly course to Sea Reach. Not having any inkling where he was, Captain Helder had in fact come within 600 yards of the wreck. If that is not a near miss in view of the potential dangers involved, then one wonders what is. Captain Helder was arrested on 22 May and subsequently released on a bond of £200,000. The charge was that he 'unlawfully did navigate the said vessel in the River Thames west of Sea Reach No.1 buoy without due care and attention'. There were other charges, one of which was that he was navigating the Medway Approach Area with his vessel on automatic steering, which was against the rules, quite apart from being crazily irresponsible. Later, at the Sheerness Magistrate's Court, Captain Helder was fined £10 on the first charge. The Harbourmaster at Sheerness was quoted by the *Sheppey Gazette* as being 'distressed at the Court's decision in this case'. One sympathises with the Harbourmaster, and one can only assume that the magistrate concerned was no sailor himself and that he lived well away from any possible blast area.

The Harbourmaster's distress was probably compounded by the fact that on the very day before the *Mare Altum* incident, on the 21 May, the British MV *Fletching* also came close to the *Montgomery* site. According to a report in the offices of the Medway Port Authority, the ship's master, Captain David J. Jones, was 'much closer to the wreck of the *Richard Montgomery* than he thought and this was a result of underestimating the prevailing conditions'. Captain Jones' ship had 'narrowly missed No.7 Medway buoy and the East Cardinal lightbuoy marking the wreck . . .

He had passed within 50-100 feet of the wreck buoys at one stage'. Was that not a near miss either? In an official letter to Captain Jones he was 'reminded of his responsibilities', but no further action was taken. (The *Fletching* and *Mare Altum* incidents are the only near misses that have come to the author's attention, but he cannot help wondering whether there were others before 1980, and perhaps more since.)

In reaching the decision not to interfere with the ship or its cargo, the officials concerned took note of what they called the 'unfortunate experience' of the wreck of the *Kielce*, 'a ship of Polish origin' in 1967. Although this incident is cited as an object lesson in what not to do with a sunken ammunition ship by the authors of the 1999 Official Report, in that report they have rather underestimated the effects of the 'unfortunate situation' and also failed to make it clear that there were two explosive mishaps on that ship, not just one. The first occurred almost a year before the one that is mentioned in the report. The *Kielce* met its end on 5 March 1946 off Folkestone. She was flying the Polish flag at the time but in fact was not 'of Polish origin'. Of around 2000 tons she had been launched at the Pennsylvania Shipyard at Beaumont, Texas (a division of Bethlehem Steel) on 11 March 1944. She was named *Edgar Wakeman* but on subsequently being allocated to the Polish Government became the *Kielce* after a Polish town. At the time of the incident she was carrying a cargo of explosives and munitions from Southampton to Bremerhaven for the US Army.

At 2332 hours on 5 March she was in collision with the British *Lombardy*. This ship, belonging to Royal Mail Lines and dating from 1920 was much older than *Kielce* but came off best in the accident. Although badly damaged and down by the head, she survived, but within the hour *Kielce* had gone to the bottom. Immediately after the collision *Lombardy* radioed for urgent assistance and tugs set out from Dover. As the *Kielce* began to sink, *Lombardy* took on board all its crew, including an American Army officer; all that is, save one. For some unrecorded reason the *Kielce*'s Assistant Third Engineer had taken to a raft on his own and was picked up three hours later by the tug *American Salvor*. The *Lombardy* was eventually towed to the Thames. Like the *Richard Montgomery* the wreck of the *Kielce* was forgotten for a number of years. But unlike the Liberty, as no portion of her was above water, no one knew exactly where she had gone down. In the 1950s an unknown wreck was located in the general area, but it was not until ten years later that the wreck was finally identified as the *Kielce*. Local fishermen had known about a wreck being there for some years, one of them reporting that there had 'always been a whelm of white water over the site' on both flood and ebb tides. In the 1960s, with the ever-increasing draft of modern ships, it became necessary to reduce the height of various wrecks lying off the British coast. The Corporation of Trinity House, the Buoyage

Authority for UK waters, required a minimum clearance at low water of 45ft. The *Kielce* was lying on its side on the bottom at a depth of 72ft, but the upper side was only 32ft down. Trinity House awarded the contract of reducing the wreck to the Folkestone Salvage Company. (That company also obtained the contract for dispersing with explosives the wreck of the Liberty *Samida,* which had been torpedoed about 3 miles off Dungeness on 9 April 1945. That operation was duly carried out.)

Part of the *Kielce* contract called for the disposal of the explosives on board. To make a difficult and dangerous task worse, the American authorities could not by that date produce a cargo manifest, which meant that the divers were working in the dark figuratively, as well as to a certain extent literally. The two directors of the Folkestone Salvage Company were Jim Rowland and Captain Dennis Pearce. Rowland is no longer with us, but the formidable figure of Dennis Pearce is very much so. The following description of the *Kielce* affair is based on what he told the *Folkestone, Hythe & District Herald* in 1967, and this author during conversations in August 1999.

Work on the wreck began in 1965, sometimes in freezing conditions and when the underwater visibility was nil. As there was no cargo manifest, 'all we had to go on was what we encountered with our hands', says Pearce. 'To start reducing the height of the wreck it was necessary to remove the uppermost side of the ship, but before we could do that the ammunition in the holds had to be removed.' The firm began bringing 1000lb and 500lb bombs to the surface, using its own method of raising them with air bags. On the surface the bombs were lifted into craft and taken ashore, there to be loaded on to waiting army vehicles. The shore side of the operation was under the charge of Major Styles of the Army Inspectorate of Ordnance, South-east Command, who also gave professional advice on the handling of the bombs. Mrs Marjorie Fuller, the firm's Secretary and a resident of Folkestone, says that sometimes there seems to have been no great hurry in getting the loaded lorries away from the town, for occasionally they were left overnight in car parks. Pearce says he and his divers brought up 'hundreds and hundreds' of bombs. On one occasion he surfaced with an unusual looking object from the wreck, and when he handed it to Major Styles the soldier said, 'Oh-oh! We have a problem', or words to that effect. Pearce cannot now remember what the Major called the device, but does remember it contained fulminate of mercury.

On Thursday 18 August 1966, a cutting charge was blown to get through a steel bulkhead, and it set off a sympathetic explosion among some detonators and small arms ammunition in the cargo. This is how the local weekly *Herald* described the event:

People rushed from shops and homes into the street at lunchtime on Thursday when Folkestone was shaken by a violent explosion. Many people telephoned the police and the council offices to ask if there had been an earth tremor.

. . . A column of water and smoke was thrown 100 feet into the air and a miniature tidal wave swept the beaches. Rumours of an earth tremor started because the noise of the explosion was muffled by the water and only shock waves hit the town.

The *Herald* offices shook for five seconds.

People in the New Metropolitan Arts Centre saw a great plume of water rise from the sea before the blast shook the building.

Mr E.C. Ealey, who during the war was captain of the minesweeper *Fyldea* which operated in the Straits of Dover, said he thought a very big sea mine had exploded.

A spokesman for the . . . salvage company said they knew there would be a big explosion and had warned the police and coastguard.

Apparently the police denied having been informed, for in the following week's edition, the *Herald* took up the story again, adding some more 'human interest'. Under the headline, 'Tell Us Of Blasts, Police Ask', it said the salvage company had been warned to give notice of any future explosions. The newspaper then reported of the previous explosion, that whether warning had been given of it or not, no one had remembered to tell twenty-nine year-old cross-Channel swimmer Philip Kaye who had been only two miles away at the time. Kaye reported that he suffered pain in his ears and had 'the sensation of being beaten with dozens of sticks'.

For the remainder of that year and up to 22 July 1967, the work of bomb removal and breaking down the wreck's hull continued. On that date as bombs were being removed from the forward hold, it was found that some were trapped under a bulkhead that had been damaged at the time of the original collision. 'No matter how we tried, we could not get them out', says Dennis Pearce. So a cutting charge was laid to split the bulkhead. 'But not even we knew what was going to happen when we let off the charge . . . no one could tell.' What was about to happen in fact was another sympathetic explosion. Pearce reported that he fired the charge from a boat about 400 yards away from the wreck, whilst the rubber dinghy containing the divers who had laid the charge was even closer.

No one knows, of course, exactly what happened under water. But it is assumed by Captain Pearce that the approximately 100 tons of bombs trapped by the bulkhead blew up as the charge went off. The sea erupted in a giant mushroom, a huge column of water climbing hundreds of feet in the air. 'Never in my life have I been in a boat that moved as fast as that one did that day', says Pearce. 'As the water poured down on us the sky suddenly grew dark and we lost sight of the dinghy. Fortunately the divers' dinghy survived'.

On the following day the national Sunday newspaper *News of the World* used the alliterative headline 'Bomb Blast Batters Beaches', going on to report on the 'giant bang that shattered windows, cracked walls, and damaged ceilings in coastal resorts'. A worker at the Dungeness nuclear power station was reported to have said that 'cooling towers quivered visibly'. The *Sunday Mirror* reported a 'huge wave surging on to the beach, scattering holiday makers'. Marjorie Fuller's house was situated on a cliff top. When the blast came the house shook. 'I thought I had lost my home,' she said. 'I knew at once it was something Dennis had been up to.' Seismic reports of the explosion came in from at least twenty-five observatories in Europe and America and from as far away as 5000 miles, and it was given a magnitude of 4.5, plus or minus 0.5 on the Richter scale. Although most of the damage was minor in nature and was mainly confined to older and less well-maintained structures, it is estimated that repairs in the area cost in the region of £100,000.

A few days later the *Folkestone Herald* reported that the Town Clerk had received a written assurance from Trinity House that there would be no more blasts in the area. One paragraph of the official letter stated, 'I am pleased to be able to advise that the dispersal of the wreck has been completed', making it seem that the last part of the exercise had been planned. A subsequent survey revealed a crater on the sea-bed measuring 153ft by 63ft, roughly elliptical in shape and 20ft deep. Experts say that the crater, which is still there and which is known by local fishermen as 'the dip', is consistent with sea-bed craters produced in American experiments with explosions with a yield of 2 kilotons.

In view of the *Kielce* affair there can be little doubt that the official policy to leave the wreck of the *Richard Montgomery* well alone is the correct one. When the *Kielce* blew up it contained considerably less munitions than those that remain on the Liberty ship. Not only that, 'The Wreck' lies much closer to the beach than did the Polish vessel, and it is not 72ft down.

CHAPTER 19

Liberties in the Indian Ocean

The task of protecting Allied ships plying the Indian Ocean during the war fell mainly to the Royal Navy, the Allied Chiefs-of-Staff having made that ocean a British responsibility. From February 1942 until August 1944, the commander-in-chief of the British Eastern Fleet in the Indian Ocean was Admiral Sir James Somerville. Until the spring of 1944 Somerville's fleet could be described as being one in name only. Somerville's only aircraft carrier was the antiquated HMS *Hermes*. (HMS *Indomitable* was in the area at the start of his tenure but its principal use then was to ferry aircraft.) *Hermes* and two cruisers, *Cornwall* and *Dorsetshire* were sunk south of Ceylon in April 1942 by planes from Admiral Nagumo's fleet which had entered the Indian Ocean. The operation against the cruisers was brilliant and conducted by Nagumo's carrier-based planes with the same kind of clinical efficiency that commander had evinced at Pearl Harbor four months earlier.

No immediate replacements for lost warships were available. In the summer of 1942 the United States Navy was working to reduce Japan's offensive capability in the Pacific; operations that were to culminate in Operation 'Torch' in the Mediterranean in November of that year were being planned; and on top of all that, there was the continuing Battle of the Atlantic. Most Allied naval resources were therefore needed elsewhere, and so Somerville in the Indian Ocean found himself at the end of the queue. Not only that, what capital ships he had tended to be used as a floating reserve for Royal Navy operations elsewhere. Even when capital ships were available to him, a shortage of destroyers often prevented him taking them to sea. More often than not Somerville's command comprised mainly a hodgepodge of cruisers, destroyers and escort vessels, and he was particularly short of the latter. This shortage resulted in many merchant ships having to sail that ocean unescorted.

After the successes of Admiral Nagumo's foray into the Indian Ocean and the achievements of the Japanese army in Burma, it was deemed advisable to base the British fleet at Kilindini (Mombassa) rather than at Trincomalee and Colombo, then considered to be insecure. At that time and until well into the following year, the Suez Canal was not available to Allied ships, which enhanced the importance of both the Cape route to the Middle East and the trans-Pacific route via Australia into the Indian Ocean. On the western side of the Indian Ocean lay the strategically located Vichy-French island of Madagascar. Between that island and the continent of Africa was the important Mozambique Channel route, a funnel for ships that was to prove a happy hunting ground for Axis submarines. For the Allies there was a perceived danger that the Germans and Japanese, perhaps with the connivance of the French, might join hands in Madagascar. The island's main port of Diego Suarez with its dry-docking facility and air base, would indeed have made an excellent refuelling and repair base for submarines. With that in mind the Allies decided to occupy the island. In a little remembered but important operation codenamed 'Ironclad', the Royal Navy landed British troops on that island on 5 May 1942 and despite French resistance, the port was in British hands two days later. The subsequent occupation of the whole island did not by any means eliminate the danger from submarines but it almost certainly reduced it, although that may not have been evident to many merchant ship victims.

Ever since Japan had come into the war in December 1941, the German Naval Staff had pressed the Japanese to co-operate in a spring offensive against Allied ships using the Cape route to the Middle East. After the capture of Diego Suarez by the British, the Japanese obliged, although their primary intent seems to have been the likelihood of encountering and sinking elements of the British Fleet that were now based at Madagascar.[1] The Japanese sent five submarines to patrol the Mozambique Channel, together with two supply vessels, the converted light cruisers *Aikoku Maru* and *Hokoku Maru* which doubled as commerce raiders. On 30 May midget submarines launched from the Japanese submarines *I-16* and *I-20* managed to damage the battleship HMS *Ramillies* in Diego Suarez harbour and sink the tanker *British Loyalty*. After that the Japanese commenced working the Mozambique Channel itself. They were soon joined by German submarines. Early on, the Axis submarines in the Indian Ocean were serviced by supply vessels or by supply submarines. But after that submarines from both countries used bases at Penang and Singapore, German submariners being frequent and familiar visitors in those Japanese-held ports until the end of the war.

German submarine successes against Liberty ships in the area began with the torpedoing of the *Anne Hutchinson* (Portland, Oregon, June 1942) on 26 October 1942. The ship had arrived in the Middle East on her maiden voyage with a cargo of military supplies and was now on the return leg and heading south for Cape Town. She was in ballast but was

---

1. *War With Japan*, Vol. III.

also carrying 8000 barrels of oil. On a zigzag course, she had reached a point south of the Mozambique Channel when a torpedo from *U-504*, Lieutenant Commander Poske, struck the ship abaft the engine-room on the starboard side, another torpedo having previously passed just 20ft ahead of the ship. The explosion blew a hole in the side and destroyed the main shaft. The blast killed three men who were sitting on No. 4 hatch. Poske then fired at the ship again, that torpedo tearing into the boiler room causing the boilers to explode. Poske surfaced and fired a shell at the ship as if to hasten Captain John Stenlund's decision to abandon. The survivors took to the boats. Ten men in one of them were rescued within hours by the American freighter *Steel Mariner*, and two days later the other boats made it safely to Port Alfred on the South African coast. The *Hutchinson* had remained afloat and was soon boarded by a South African Navy salvage crew. A minesweeper and a small harbour tug tried to tow her into port, but failed, so the salvagers then fired cutting charges to break her in two. The after part sank, but the trawler HMS *David Haigh* managed to tow the forward end into Port Elizabeth. It was subsequently broken up there.

About a month later on 20 November and in the same general area, but when proceeding in the other direction, the fully loaded *Pierce Butler* (Baltimore, August 1942), another ship on its maiden voyage, was struck by two torpedoes from *U-177*, Lieutenant Commander Gysae. The ship's Armed Guard unit fired fifteen rounds in the direction from which the torpedoes had come in an attempt to keep the submarine from surfacing. But struck forward of the engine-room and in No. 5 hold, there was no saving the ship and Captain George Moodie ordered the ship cleared. Five minutes after doing so the ship sank stern first. Called to the scene by the ship's radio distress signals, the destroyer HMS *Fortune* rescued all hands on the following day.

Lieutenant Commander Lassen and his *U-160* had a good week at the beginning of March 1943 whilst operating at the southern end of the Mozambique Channel in conjunction with other submarines. On the 3rd an attack was carried out on a convoy making for Bandar Shapur, Iran, one of the Persian Gulf ports which was being used to supply Russia. This convoy of eleven merchant ships had an escort of sorts, the corvette HMS *Nigella*, the converted whaler *Sondra* and the trawler *Viviana*. A torpedo from the submarine struck the *Harvey W. Scott* (Portland, Oregon, July 1942), in way of No. 2 hold. The crew were fortunate the ship did not blow up, for she was carrying over 8000 tons of cargo including explosives and gasoline. As the ship settled slowly, Captain Axel Uldall ordered everyone to abandon. The escorts had their work cut out in trying to protect the rest of their charges so no attempt was made to pick the *Scott* crew up. In fact over the next twenty-four hours another five ships in the convoy were torpedoed, Lassen also sinking the British *Empire Mahseer.*

Other submarines sank the British *Nirpura* carrying 737 horses, mules and donkeys, and the British *Marietta E.* The *Sheaf Crown*, also British, was badly damaged but managed to reach port. Before setting out for the South African coast with his flotilla of four lifeboats, Captain Uldall saw his ship plunge to the bottom bow first. During the night the lifeboats became separated, the men in one being rescued by the neutral Argentine steamer *Ombu* on the following day. Over the next three days, one by one, the other boats reached Umtata on the Natal coast.

Five days later Lassen and his boat fell in with the south-bound *James B. Stephens* (Portland, Oregon, October 1942). She had set out from Seattle on her maiden voyage in November, on Friday 13th to be precise, a date on which no superstitious sailor likes to set sail. She reached Suez safely and discharged her cargo. But the fates had merely been delayed. Lassen's torpedo tore into the ship late on the night of 8 March, the explosion setting fire to fuel oil. By the time a second torpedo struck, the *Stephens* was already an inferno and the crew were in the process of abandoning as the ship settled by the head. The blast overturned one of the boats, drowning a member of the Armed Guard. Over the succeeding six days the men in the boats were picked up by British and South African naval vessels. Meanwhile the *Stephens* had broken in two, but both parts remained afloat. An abortive attempt was made to tow the fore part to port, but it sank in rough weather. South African warships subsequently sank the stern half with gunfire.

After her successes that month *U-160* returned to Europe only to be ordered out again at the end of June 1943 as one of eleven German submarines known collectively as Group Monsoon, or 'Monsun' to give it its German spelling. Six of the eleven never made it to the Indian Ocean. The RAF sank two and American aircraft four, all in the Atlantic. *U-160* was one of two sunk by aircraft from the USS *Santee* on 14 July. There were no survivors from the submarine, but Commander Lassen was not in command at that date.

On 10 March 1943 the *Richard D. Spaight* (Wilmington, August 1942) was proceeding south through the Mozambique Channel when two torpedoes from *U-182*, Lieutenant Commander Clausen, struck the fore part of the ship. It was a warm evening so two crewmen had decided to sleep on deck. The explosion blew one of them directly over the side and he was never seen again. The other man, who had been lying on a mattress, had what can only be described as a miraculous escape. He was blown mast high, mattress and all, then over the side of the ship landing right-side up still aboard his mattress. Captain Russell Quynn ordered abandon ship, but for some reason the engines were not shut down. One lifeboat was drawn into the still churning propeller and wrecked, but not before the men in it were able to throw themselves clear. They were picked up by the remaining boats, as was the man on the flying mattress.

Clausen then surfaced and finished the *Spaight* off with his gun. Before leaving the scene he approached the boats, questioned some of the men and proffered medical supplies, food and water. Apart from the one missing crewman, all the others made it to the South African coast over the next five days. The story the seaman on the flying mattress had to relate brings to mind that of 'Prince Hussein and the Flying Carpet' in the Arabian Nights, and it is likely that he never had to pay for another drink in his life.

On 21 April 1943 an Italian submarine got in on the act, one of the end results being a thirty-day open boat voyage during which two-thirds of the American seamen in the boat died. The *John Drayton* (Wilmington, December 1942) had cleared the Channel and was making south for Cape Town when lookouts spotted a torpedo. It passed a bare 5ft ahead of the ship. Captain Carl Norman immediately ordered a zigzag course and about forty minutes later another torpedo was seen to pass harmlessly astern. But the third torpedo from the *Da Vinci*, Commander Gazzana, struck squarely amidships, holing the ship below the waterline. With engines and boilers damaged and his ship making water, Captain Norman had no other recourse but to order abandon ship. Some of the crew had been killed, but most got away in two lifeboats and on a raft. The *Da Vinci* surfaced and fired at the ship with her gun before making off. Two days later one of the lifeboats was spotted by the Swedish *Oscar Gorthon* which rescued eleven men. Six days after that, the destroyer HMS *Relentless* came across the raft on which were Captain Norman and thirteen others. The last boat, which had originally held twenty-four men, was at sea for thirty days before being sighted. By then only eight men in it were still alive, and three of those were later to die in hospital at Durban.

A few weeks later the *Relentless* was involved in the rescue of American seamen from another Liberty. The *William King* (Portland, Maine, October 1942) had left Bahrain for Durban carrying 18,000 barrels of oil. She had safely negotiated the Channel and was within two days of her destination when early in the afternoon of 6 June 1943 she was struck by a torpedo. It came from Lieutenant Commander Hartmann's *U-198*. As well as blowing a great hole in the ship's side, the port boiler blew up, and fire soon raged throughout the engine-room and No. 3 hold, then took hold in the midships accommodation. Six men had been killed, but the remainder got away in two lifeboats and on two rafts. A second torpedo then struck, and flames shot several hundred feet into the sky before the ship disappeared stern-first in a cloud of steam. Hartmann surfaced and took the American master, Captain Owen Reed, aboard before leaving the scene. Over the next six days the survivors were picked up either by *Relentless* or by the armed trawler HMS *Northern Chief*. Hartmann landed his prisoner in Malaya and handed him over to the occupying Japanese. Captain Reed did not survive his time in the prison camps.

So far we have concentrated our attention on Liberty ships using the bottleneck of the Mozambique Channel, but Axis submarines were busy in other parts of the Indian Ocean as well. Vice-Admiral Nomura Naokuni of the Imperial Japanese Navy had been one of Japan's representatives on the Axis Tripartite Military Commission in Berlin since 1941. He no doubt felt honoured in the spring of 1943 when he was able to travel home in one of the German submarines being transferred to the Japanese navy. He would have been doubly honoured in fact, because his passage was made in *U-511* which was Hitler's personal gift to Emperor Hirohito. The *U-511* reached Penang safely in mid-July, but not before giving Nomura some extra bonuses on the way.[2]

On the morning of 27 June, Lieutenant Commander Schneewind on *U-511* sighted the *Sebastian Cermeno* (Sausalito, March 1943), which was in mid-Indian Ocean on passage from Mombassa to Bahia, Brazil via Australia. Schneewind fired two torpedoes at the ship, both striking astern of the accommodation on the port side. Captain David Nilsson ordered abandon ship, and the crew, except for four men who had been killed, got away in five lifeboats just before the ship sank stern first. Schneewind surfaced and questioned some of the survivors before leaving the scene. Who can doubt that Admiral Nomura would have been an eager onlooker from the conning tower? The *Cermeno* boats soon became separated. Seventeen days later the Liberty *Theodore Parker* (Los Angeles, March 1943) came across one and rescued the men from it. Over the next ten days British naval vessels found two more boats and took the survivors on board. One boat made it to Madagascar and another to Durban. One man, an officer, died of exposure during one of those boat trips.

There would have been nothing for Nomura to see after the sinking of *U-511*'s second victim. On 9 July when making for the northern tip of Sumatra, the submarine fell in with the *Samuel Heintzelman* (Los Angeles, October 1942). The Liberty under the command of Captain Johann Wilkie was making for Colombo from Fremantle with nearly 6000 tons of munitions on board. Schneewind fired his torpedoes and then dove, and soon afterwards underwater explosions were heard. When the submarine surfaced there was no trace of her victim except some floating debris. All seventy-five men on board had perished. Two months later identifiable wreckage from the ship was reported washed up on the island of Diego Garcia. (At Penang Hitler's gift was handed over to a Japanese crew and then sailed to the Kure Naval Base in the Inland Sea of Japan. In September she was commissioned into the Imperial Navy becoming the *RO-500*. She survived the war and was subsequently scuttled by the Occupation Forces in Japan.)

---

2. Carl Boyd, *The Japanese Submarine Force and World War II*.

Back in the vicinity of Madagascar, July 1943 saw the demise of two more Liberties. Commander Gysae and his *U-177* which had in the previous November sunk the *Pierce Butler,* now got his second Liberty victim, the *Alice F. Palmer* (Los Angeles, March 1943). A torpedo struck the ship's stern causing havoc there and breaking her back so that the after end was drooping at a steep angle. Even before Captain George Pederson ordered abandon ship, some of the crew and Armed Guard began to leave. All on board eventually got away on four boats after which Gysae shelled the ship, which slowly sank. The four boats made sail for Madagascar but soon became separated. The men in one were picked up three days later by an RAF Catalina flying-boat. The other three missed the island altogether but eventually landed on the coast of Mozambique, the last one reaching safety twenty days after the attack. Everyone survived the ordeal.

The second Liberty was the *Robert Bacon* (New Orleans, March 1943) en route from Mombassa to Cape Town. On 14 July a torpedo from *U-178*, Lieutenant Commander Dommes, struck in the vicinity of the deep tank containing fuel oil in No. 2 hold. The explosion blew a mixture of oil and water into the air, which coated everything in sight. Two lifeboats were so full of oil as to be unusable, so the crew apart from two who had been killed got away in the three remaining lifeboats and two rafts. As the survivors cleared the ship another torpedo finished her off. Dommes surfaced and gave some advice on which way to sail, and then sailed off himself. Captain Clyde Henderson in his boat made it safely to the Mozambique coast two days later. Over the next twelve days the men in the other two boats were picked up by British merchant ships. One of the rafts made it to the shore on the fourteenth day, but the final raft only made landfall after being a total of forty-four days at sea. One man aboard the raft had died from exposure.

When, 100 miles north of the equator and five days out from Aden on 21 September on its way to Durban, the *Cornelia P. Spencer* (Wilmington, April 1943) was struck by a torpedo, she and her crew put up a gallant fight for survival. The explosion aft destroyed the propeller shaft, so making the engines useless. Captain Elmer Kirwan sounded the general alarm and as *U-188*, Lieutenant Commander Ludden, surfaced about 100 yards off the ship's port quarter, the Armed Guard manning the ship's two 3in guns fired a total of seventy-five shells at it, forcing it to dive. About half-an-hour later a second torpedo struck aft, blowing up the magazine there, killing two seamen and blowing the after gun crew into the water. As his ship began to settle, Captain Kirwan ordered abandon ship, all the survivors getting away in four boats which then picked up the men in the water. It took a third torpedo to ensure the ship sank. HMS *Relentless* rescued the men from two lifeboats on the following day, the British freighter *Sandown Castle* doing the same for the men in a third boat soon afterwards. The fourth made it safely to the coast of Somalia a fortnight after the attack.

It was the Japanese submarine *I-10*, Commander Tonozuka Kinzo, which gained the next Liberty victim. This Allied loss occurred in the Gulf of Aden on 24 September 1943. The ship involved was the *Elias Howe* (Vancouver, Oregon, July 1942). Under the command of Captain Joseph Dickover the ship was making for Egypt with a cargo of over 9000 tons of nitrate from Chile. A torpedo struck the *Howe* in way of the engine-room, destroying it and the boiler room and killing the men on watch there. Red-hot fire bricks were hurled in the air, to land in various places around the deck. The crew abandoned in the one undamaged lifeboat and four rafts. After the survivors were clear, *I-10* then put another torpedo into the ship. Almost certainly aided by the nitrate cargo the *Howe* then exploded in a fire-ball and disappeared in a matter of minutes. Tonozuka brought his boat to the surface within 200 yards of the survivors before making off. In view of some of the incidents to be described later in this book, it needs to be emphasised that this Japanese commander made no attempt to further harm the men in the boats. As the lifeboat had a motor Captain Dickover decided to make for Aden which was only seventy miles away to get help, but on the following day it was found by an RAF Catalina which took aboard the crew. On the same day another Catalina rescued the men from two rafts and the trawler HMS *Aiglon* rescued the balance of the men the day after that.

The *Sambo* was also carrying nitrates from Chile to Egypt when she struck a mine off the coast of Somalia on 10 November 1943. The ship had been built at Los Angeles as the *Edwin Joseph O'Hara* and named for one of the heroes of the *Stephen Hopkins* (see Chapter 9). She was handed over to the British on 12 August 1943, and managed by Cunard became the *Sambo*. She was commanded by Captain J.D. Smith. Including nine DEMS gunners the ship carried a crew of forty-seven.

Two successive explosions came in the early afternoon, one each in Nos. 4 and 5 holds. After that there was a smaller third explosion right aft, presumably as the after magazine went up. Then, within a space of five minutes, the ship blew up and sank, again probably aided by the nitrate cargo which is not the safest commodity to carry around. Only one boat got away, and after picking up men who had been blown off the ship into the water, it had thirty-five souls on board. All nine gunners, the ship's carpenter and two engine-room hands were missing and believed killed in the explosion. The survivors were picked up before dark by the Norwegian *Helgoy*. It was Captain Smith's considered opinion, one which was supported by other members of the crew, that the initial explosions were caused by a mine rather than a torpedo as they appeared to be under the ship rather than on the side. The Naval Staff Officer at Aden ventured the opinion that the mine may have drifted away from the British minefield off Perim, the edge of which was only ten miles from the scene.

Yet another nitrate-carrying ship was the *Samblade* (built at Los Angeles as *Augustus H. Garland* and handed over to a British Port Line crew on 10 August 1943). While making for the Gulf of Aden on 10 November, five shells were fired at her from a surfaced submarine. She was lucky, for all of them fell short. The ship took evasive action and radioed for help and the submarine disappeared when a Catalina arrived on the scene. A warship made a search of the area but no contact was made.

The sinking of the *Sambridge* (launched as *John L. Wilkie*, Richmond July 1943) on 18 November 1943 involved the breaking of the most golden of the traditions of the sea, and that was followed by two acts, one of which can only be described as cowardice, the other, as one of great gallantry. *Sambridge* managed by T. & J. Brocklebank and commanded by Captain A.S. Bain, was making for Aden from Bombay. Torpedo nets were not streamed as they had previously been damaged in bad weather. It was early evening when the Japanese submarine *I-27*, Commander Fukumura Toshiaki, fired two torpedoes at the ship, the first passing astern, the second exploding in the engine-room killing the Second and Fourth Engineers and two hands. The vessel caught fire and in under two minutes the midships section was burning fiercely. Captain Bain later reported that 'No. 4 boat lowered without my orders and had pulled off with only nine men in it'. With his ship now well ablaze, Bain ordered abandon ship.

His report goes on:

> I got into No.2 lifeboat and ordered it lowered, intending to remain alongside taking only as many of the crew with me as I thought safe, as the boat had a large quantity of water in it. I instructed the Chief Officer and those remaining on board to take to the rafts, adding that I would take them in tow. The boat drifted away from the ship towards the stern. All 4 rafts were successfully released and by 1910 hours . . . everyone was clear of the vessel.[3]

On his own admission, then, Bain had broken the unwritten but golden rule, that the captain should always be last to leave a sinking ship (unless of course, there are special reasons making that impossible, which manifestly was not so in this case).

Some men had been blown into the water by the blast and were picked up, several of them suffering from severe burns. Captain Bain went on:

---

3. ADM199/526, PRO, Kew.

Saw light which we thought was No.4 boat and headed towards it, but saw wake of submarine heading this way. Ship suddenly exploded and sank.

Submarine surfaced and closed and ordered me alongside. I obeyed ... at the same time instructing my crew to deny all knowledge of Captain's whereabouts if questioned. [Author's note. Nothing wrong with that, it was standard procedure.]

In broken English a Japanese asked for Master, Chief Officer and Radio Officer. We replied, they had gone down with the ship. [Again, standard procedure.]

Whilst being questioned our lifeboat washed up on to sub causing it to swamp and throwing out some of the gear including several oars. I ordered painter cut, which did not please the Japanese who ordered us alongside their lee side. Whilst doing this I conferred with the Second Officer and we decided that it looked as though someone would have to board the sub. Having denied all knowledge of the Master and Chief Officer we could not suddenly produce them; I said that failing all else I would go aboard, but my Second Officer bravely volunteered to do so if it became necessary.

By that time the Japanese were scrutinising everyone by torchlight.

Greaser Byrne who was severely burned with the skin hanging off his back, volunteered to board sub. The Japs simply laughed at him and pushed him back. Japanese then asked Second Officer who he was and ordered him aboard. He was ordered to climb to the conning tower and as he did so he called out 'Cheerio', then disappeared from view.

Ordered to cast off and as we were pulling away towards the rafts I heard a burst of machine gun fire. Everyone crouched down, then a second burst was heard which I was afterwards told went over the rafts, one bullet hitting the raft on which the Chief Officer was lying. I do not think any injury was intended – but I consider it was an act of deliberate terrorism. Sub steamed away on surface southerly.

On the following morning the men in the Captain's boat and the rafts were picked up by the SS *Tarantia* and subsequently landed at Aden. The men in No. 4 boat were later rescued by a British frigate and landed at Port Said, where Gunner Zappa, who was apparently in charge, was questioned as to why they had abandoned ship without orders. 'No satisfactory answer was given', said the author of the relevant report.

As well as breaking the golden tradition, Captain Bain had permitted a more junior officer to be taken away aboard a Japanese submarine in his stead, an act of cowardice for which there can be no excuse. It is of little wonder therefore, that at Aden after Bain had made his report to the King's Harbour Master there, that the Navy did not want much to do with him. However, this reaction seems to have come as a surprise to Bain, for he made an official complaint about being treated with discourtesy. Bain also considered that the repatriation arrangements made for him and his crew were unsatisfactory – 'no money for cigarettes or comforts' and, 'The King's Harbour Master was always too busy to see me'. Greaser Michael Byrne, who had volunteered to board the submarine, died from his burns in hospital at Aden. In June 1944 he was given a Posthumous Commendation. Apprentice Hugh Jones who had manned an oar in the captain's boat with a broken arm, was awarded the British Empire Medal on the same date. No one at that time knew what had happened to twenty-seven year-old Second Officer Henry Scurr. In fact he had been landed from the submarine at Penang and became a prisoner of war. He managed to survive that experience and in December 1945 was awarded the MBE. The citation for that medal read, 'For services when the ship was torpedoed and sunk, for identifying himself to the Japanese as a Senior Officer and for his services as a POW'. Henry Scurr also received Lloyd's Bravery Medal. Perhaps none was better deserved.[4]

The demise of the *Robert F. Hoke* (Wilmington, May 1943) was both long and involved. She was on a voyage between Abadan and Mombassa with a cargo consisting mainly of empty oil drums, when on 28 December 1943 a torpedo from *I-26*, Commander Kusaka Toshio, struck between Nos. 4 and 5 holds, destroying the intervening bulkhead. Both holds flooded, and water also entered the engine-room. Captain Frederick MacLean ordered abandon ship; he and his crew did so, but not the Armed Guard, the tradition that the captain is always last to leave his ship being broken in this case because of the dual command structure on board. The Armed Guard opened fire on the submarine's periscope to keep it submerged, and apparently drove it away. Two hours later Captain MacLean and some of his men reboarded but could not raise steam. Then everyone entered the lifeboats. An RAF sea rescue boat picked up survivors from two of the boats that same day. The others landed on Masirah Island a day later. The *Hoke,* probably kept afloat by the empty drums in her cargo, was towed to Aden by the tug HMS *Masterful.* From there she was towed to Suez by the Liberty ship *Mark Keppel* (Los Angeles, April 1943). She was partially repaired and had several adventures throughout 1944 being towed from one port to another in the Red Sea until at last she was declared a constructive total loss. At the end of 1944 she was towed to Bombay where she was used as a training ship for the Royal Indian Navy. In 1949 she was scrapped.

Commander Kusaka and his *I-26* made another Liberty ship kill on 2 January 1944. This time it was the *Albert Gallatin* (Los Angeles, April

---

4. Seedie's Merchant Navy List.

1942). Until then this ship had been deemed a lucky one, for in July 1943 off Savannah she had been struck by no less than three torpedoes, none of which exploded. But the one from *I-26* did, in No. 3 hold. The ship's Armed Guard had a go at the submarine's periscope, firing off over fifty rounds at it. Again the Armed Guard stayed aboard after the captain and crew had abandoned, but this time they had to jump overboard to be picked up by the boats as the ship settled rapidly. The ship actually split in two before sinking. There were no casualties and everyone was picked up by the Norwegian tanker *Britannia*.

Two German submarines of Group Monsoon were working together in late January 1944 in the vicinity of the northern Maldives. The *Fort Buckingham* was sunk there on the 20th with the loss of most of those on board. Then on the 29th, the *Walter Camp* (Richmond, May 1943) sailed into the sights of *U-532*, Lieutenant Commander Junker. The explosion in No. 3 hold caused the ship to take a 30° list and start to settle by the bow. Captain Henry Shutz ordered abandon ship and fifteen minutes later a second torpedo struck the ship which then sank. On the fifth day after the sinking the men in the boats must have been mighty pleased to see a large ship come over the horizon. It was the cruiser HMS *Danae* which took them aboard and landed them at Aden.

If the Mozambique Channel was a happy hunting ground for submarines, so was the Gulf of Aden. This was close to the end of one very long and important Allied line of communication, one over 11,500 miles in length from the United Kingdom via the Cape, and even longer from the United States. So the cargoes of every ship lost in that area entailed months to make good, and no one knew that better than the Axis submarine commanders. One of them had a heyday there. Working his way westward into the Gulf, a submarine, 'apparently a German' wrote the authors of the official British naval history of the war with Japan which was written contemporaneously and before German records had been available for scrutiny, sank three British ships and a Greek in the space of four days between 25 and 29 January 1944, over an area not more than thirty miles in circumference. The first of those ships was the Canadian-built *Fort Le Maune*, the second, the *Samouri* (built as *Manasseh Cutler*, Portland, Oregon, September 1943).[5] *Samouri*, under Captain W.J. Slade and managed by Moss Hutchinson, was proceeding from Bombay to Aden when early in the morning of 26th she was struck by a torpedo. The submarine was indeed German; it was Commander Ludden's *U-188* which in the previous September had sunk *Cornelia P. Spencer* in the southern part of the ocean. Ludden's boat was one of Group Monsoon and was probably the most successful one of all. The torpedo's track was

---

5. *War With Japan*, Vol. IV.

sighted from the ship and although the Chief Officer put the helm hard over, it was too late; it struck in the vicinity of No. 4 hold. Hatches and heavy metal beams were blown off, one of the latter flying through the air to land on the boat deck. The after topmast collapsed into the hold. The Second Engineer had just vacated the shaft tunnel and closed its watertight door, and that prevented the engine-room flooding. Nevertheless, as the after holds began to flood the ship settled by the stern. Only when the after deck was awash and Captain Slade knew his ship was beyond saving, did he give the order to abandon. All the crew got away in four boats and set sail for Socotra some ninety miles away. Three boats were picked up on the following day by the SS *Shahzada*. The fourth under the charge of the Fourth Officer had disappeared in the dark but managed to reach Socotra safely. Captain Slade reported that although his ship was fitted with anti-torpedo net booms, no nets had been supplied. He said that had they been streamed his ship might have been saved. After sinking the fourth in this sequence of kills, which was the Greek *Olga E. Embiricos* on the 29th, the submarine was sighted by an RAF Catalina and a sea search was organised but met with no success. By that time Ludden was moving back eastward and on 4 February he sank the Chinese-flagged Liberty *Chung Cheng* off Socotra. (See Chapter 21.) Moving eastward still, he sank three dhows on the 8th together with the Norwegian freighter *Vivas*. Possibly short of torpedoes, Ludden then made back for Penang.

The horrors of the so-called unlimited warfare campaign waged by submarines during the First World War had caused the Big Five Naval Powers in 1930, the United States, Great Britain, France, Italy and Japan, to include in the Naval Treaty of that year the famous Article 22. It stated that:

> 1. In action against merchant ships submarines must conform to the rules of International Law, to which surface vessels are subject.
> 2. In particular, except in the case of persistent refusal to stop on being duly summoned, or of active resistance to visit and search, warships, whether surface vessel or submarine may not sink or render incapable of navigation a merchant vessel without having first placed passengers, crew and ship's papers in a place of safety. For this purpose the ship's boats are not regarded as a place of safety, unless the safety of the passengers and crew is assured in the existing sea and weather conditions, by proximity of land, or the presence of another vessel which is in position to take them aboard.

The Treaty contained another clause ensuring that Article 22 remained binding on the signatories even should the Treaty expire, which it was allowed to do in 1936. Germany, it should be noted, having in 1930 no Navy of her own, was not a signatory. When the Second World War came along, the main Allies therefore, and Japan and Italy, were still legally bound by Article 22. But no country during the war, Allied or Axis, kept strictly to the provisions of it, but because it pays to be on the winning side, in 1945 it was only the Axis nations who were called to account for Article 22 transgressions.

Upon America's entrance into the war in December 1941, Hitler was not slow to realise that this provided the Allies with an almost inexhaustible shipbuilding capacity. He decided that one way to tackle the prospect of Allied shipping preponderance at some time in the future, was to ensure lack of suitable crews, so he issued instructions that not only should no attempt be made to rescue merchant ship survivors, but that they should be exterminated. It is fortunate that just about all U-boat commanders chose to ignore the latter part of the instruction. Indeed, there is only one recorded German atrocity against merchant seamen.

That was not to be the case with the Japanese when they decided to follow the Fuhrer's lead. The first such atrocity took place off Hawaii on 10 December 1941, and that will be described in the next chapter. The first one to take place in the area covered by this chapter took place in the Dutch East Indies (Indonesia) in January 1942 and concerned a Dutch vessel, the *Langkoeas*. There were at least nine other such incidents carried out by either surface units or submarines of the Imperial Japanese Navy against Allied merchant vessels in the Indian Ocean area. Two of those concerned American-flagged Liberties, and the others, another Dutchman and six British ships. Many merchant seamen lost their lives in these incidents. So bad did the situation become that Admiral Somerville made the following entry in his diary on 1 April 1944:

> I sent a signal to the Admiralty giving a list of the atrocities which had been committed in this Theatre by the Japanese on the crews of torpedoed ships; in every case these were independently sailed ships and I expressed the view that when the news of these atrocities leaked out there might be a reluctance on the part of crews to sail in unescorted ships.

The Admiral followed that up with a list of the additional long-range escort ships he reckoned he needed to rectify the situation.[6]

The first of the two Liberty ships to suffer in the Indian Ocean from such an atrocity, although perhaps attempted atrocity would be a better way to describe this one, was the *Richard Hovey* (Portland, Maine, April 1943). She was sailing independently from Bombay to Aden with torpedo nets streamed when she fell in with Commander Kusaka's *I-26*

---

6. *The Somerville Papers*, p535.

during the afternoon of 29 March 1944. Two torpedo wakes were spotted from the ship and the quick reaction of the helmsman assured that one missed. The other, however, either passed through or under the torpedo net hitting the ship in way of the engine-room. A third undetected torpedo then struck No. 4 hold. The explosions jammed the rudder, wrecked the bridge and caused the port boiler to blow up.

This is how Lieutenant Harry Goudy of the Armed Guard unit described the event.

> I was in my cabin when I felt and heard a terrific explosion. My cabin immediately filled with fumes. . . went to bridge to my battle-station and found all ship's guns manned . . . When I reached the bridge the vessel appeared to be settling in the water by the stern with a slight list to starboard. The Captain and Chief Officer appeared to be checking the damage and seeing to launching of boats and rafts. A short time afterwards another explosion on starboard side No. 3 hold. Before this all the Merchant crew had abandoned the ship and were waiting alongside in the boats. A third torpedo did serious damage to the ship which seemed to buckle up from the fore part of the bridge for'd. As the ship seemed to be breaking in two I thought it time to leave the ship and had received a message from the captain to do so.
>
> I told my men to abandon ship. Some got away on boats, some on rafts. I jumped in the water and swam to a raft . . . in the tow of the Captain's boat. I was the last man to leave the ship.[7]

The report submitted by the ship's Chief Officer R.H. Evans seems to contradict Goudy's report in respect of some of the timings involved, for he stated that it had taken Captain Harry Thorsen ten minutes to escape from his cabin as it had been wrecked when the boiler blew up.

I-26 surfaced and then shelled the ship until it sank. Kusaka then turned his guns on the boats and rafts, and rammed and capsized No. 2 boat. Miraculously, in the hail of machine gun fire no one was killed. Kusaka then closed No. 1 boat and took on board four men from it including Captain Thorsen and Second Officer Turner. He then left the scene. Why Kusaka acted in this way with the *Hovey* when he had not done so earlier with either the *Robert F. Hoke* or the *Albert Gallatin,* or for that matter with two other ships he had sunk in between times, is not known. Perhaps he was merely playing lip-service to his admiral. Nevertheless his actions resulted in the holing of the boats which could have led to the death of many.

Two British-flagged Liberties rescued the survivors. Three days later, the *Samcalia* (built as *Lorrin A. Thurston,* Los Angeles, September 1943),

---

7. ADM199/526

took aboard twenty-five and landed them at Karachi. No. 1 boat was at sea for sixteen days before the thirty-eight survivors in it were picked up by the *Samuta* (launched as *Jesse de Forest*, Baltimore, October 1943). Captain Niblock of Bank Line's *Samuta* noted in his ship's official log-book that the survivors reported that the Japanese submarine had only made off after smoke was sighted on the horizon. He added that the machine-gunning had left the boats full of holes which the survivors had to plug as best they could. Water tanks had also been pierced, which meant that water had to be distilled using the boards of a raft as fuel. It was Captain Niblock's view that another day in the boat would have meant death for some of the rescued men. This group of survivors, which included Lieutenant Goudy, were landed at Cochin.

At that port the survivors presented Captain Niblock with an illuminated address commissioned from a local artist. He valued it greatly for the rest of his life. It read:

> April 24 1944 will forever stand out in the minds and hearts of the undersigned as our 'Red Letter Day' of World War II. Our indebtedness to you can never be repaid in word or deed. We have chosen this wholly inadequate means of expressing our unanimous gratitude. Permit us to say that our short stay aboard your vessel was one of the most pleasant experiences in our lives. It is indeed gratifying to look back upon the feeling of comradeship so readily prevalent between us Americans and the men under your command.[8]

Those sentiments were perhaps a trifle fulsome, but were obviously heartfelt, and they provide an insight into the brotherhood of the sea, a concept that Commander Kusaka apparently knew nothing about or had decided to forget.

Lieutenant Harry Goudy made his initial report before the Senior British Naval Officer, Cochin. On the cover of the file in which the report was stored, the following annotation appears.

> The Jap atrocities are so systematic that it is probable that they are acting under standing instructions. We know that in the case of at least one sub. force, standing instructions to destroy the crews of torpedoed ships have been issued.

The annotation was dated 12 June 1944 and signed C.H.M. Waldeck, Head of British Military Intelligence. The standing instruction mentioned by Waldeck was probably that issued by Rear-Admiral Mito Hisashi, commanding the Japanese 1st Submarine Force at Truk in the

---

8. Article in *Sea Breezes* 15 (1953).

Marshal Islands on 20 March 1943, a copy of which was captured at Truk by the Americans in early 1944. A translation of it reads:

> All submarines will act together in order to concentrate their attacks against enemy convoys and totally destroy them. Do not stop with the sinking of enemy ships and cargoes; at the same time carry out the complete destruction of the crews of the enemy ships; if possible seize part of the crew and endeavour to secure information about the enemy.

Similar orders were issued by other Japanese admirals. The calculated evil of the instructions was matched only by the willingness with which some Japanese submarine commanders, especially those of the 8th Submarine Flotilla based at Penang, carried them out; and none was more avid than Commander (later Captain) Ariizumi Tatsunosuke.

Ariizumi graduated from Etajima Naval College (situated on an island off Kure and very much run on the lines of the Royal Navy's college at Dartmouth) in 1924. His one and only active submarine command in the war was *I-8* which he joined early in 1944. Previously *I-8* had been engaged in blockade-running to Europe. She had reached Singapore safely sixty-four days out from Europe in December 1943 with a cargo of torpedo parts, machine-guns, and chronometers (the timepieces manufactured in Japan in those days being unreliable). She then sailed for Japan where Ariizumi took command.[9] Over the next few months his sadistic treatment of Allied merchant seamen was to earn him the name of 'the Butcher'.

On 26 March 1944 Ariizumi sank the Dutch freighter *Tjisalak* with two torpedoes. Before the ship sank its gunners fired at the now surfaced submarine, shells landing so close to it that it was forced to dive. Maybe that riled Ariizumi, but that was no excuse for what he was about to do. The ship's crew of seventy-five and five passengers including an American Red Cross nurse, Verna Gorden-Britten, abandoned ship in three lifeboats. Most of the officers were Dutch but there were three Britons amongst them, whilst the crew were mainly Hong Kong Chinese with a few Indians. The ten DEMS gunners were all British. Ariizumi surfaced again and ordered the boats alongside, and the people in them to board the submarine. The survivors were forced to squat on the casing as the lifeboats were cut adrift. Captain C. Hen, four of his officers and three passengers including the nurse were then ordered below. As the submarine got under way the killing of the others began. In ones and twos the helpless prisoners were taken abaft the conning tower after which

---

9. *War With Japan*, Vol. IV.

those left behind heard the sound of shooting. When it came to the turn of Second Officer Jan Dekker someone swung at his head with a heavy hammer. The blow was a glancing one and he then found himself staring down the barrel of a gun but managed to twist and throw himself over the side. Chief Officer Frits de Jong, Radio Officer James Blears and Third Engineer Spuybroek had similar experiences. The fifth and last man to survive the massacre was an Indian named Dhange. With only about ten seamen left to kill, the Japanese had apparently grown tired of the original method of slaughter. The remaining men were tied to a long rope attached to the submarine which then dived. Dhange, the one on the very end, was the only man able to free himself. All five men were able to reach one of the lifeboats and two days later they were rescued by the Liberty *James A. Wilder* (Los Angeles, January 1945) but not before that ship had mistaken the lifeboat for a conning tower and fired at it. They were later transferred to HMS *Emerald*. Dhange reported that he had seen Captain Hen killed with a sword on the conning tower. After the war at a War Crimes Trial in Tokyo, one *I-8* crewman testified that the American nurse had been taken up on deck that night and shot. What happened to the others taken below is not known, but they were never heard of again.

When Admiral Somerville was informed of this atrocity, and on the receipt of intelligence that the submarine concerned was proceeding south down the west side of the Maldive Islands, he sent three destroyers and four Catalinas out to hunt for it. Had they found it, it might have prevented Ariizumi's second massacre. En route from San Pedro, California to Colombo via Fremantle, by 2 July 1944 the *Jean Nicolet* (Portland, Oregon, October 1943) had reached a position south of the Maldives. There she had the misfortune to come within torpedo range of Ariizumi's command. After the *Tjisalak* episode he had gone on to sink the British *City of Adelaide* on 30 March, following that on 29 June by sinking the British troopship *Nellore* which had gone down with nearly 200 of her complement of 341. The *Nellore* had been unable to get off a distress message, but 156 survivors in two lifeboats were subsequently picked up by HMS *Lossie*.

Under the command of Captain David Nilsson the *Nicolet* was loaded with a full military cargo and had a complement of ninety-nine persons including thirty army and civilian passengers. The ship was not zigzagging although Nilsson was aware that his ship was passing through a danger area. At seven o'clock in the evening two torpedoes struck in way of No. 3 hold, the ship immediately taking a heavy list to starboard. Captain Nilsson ordered abandon ship, but not before a distress message was sent out. Everyone got away in four lifeboats and on two rafts. Nilsson and the Armed Guard commander, Lieutenant Gerald Deal, made a round of the ship to make sure everyone was off before leaving on a raft

themselves. Nilsson then transferred to the motor lifeboat. At that juncture Ariizumi surfaced and began shelling the ship from a range of about
2000 yards. The *Nicolet* was soon on fire and Nilsson ordered the boats
and rafts to scatter. Soon a powerful searchlight from the submarine,
which had come closer, was playing over the water. As the beam
approached Lieutenant Deal's raft, he ordered everyone over the side.
Then a voice came from the submarine ordering everyone to board it.
Most of the survivors did so, but Lieutenant Deal and five others managed to swim away in the dark.

On board the submarine the hands of the survivors were bound behind
their backs. They were then made to sit down, and as if to enforce the
order, Deck Boy William Musser was shot in the head and his body
dumped overboard. Captain Nilsson, Radio Officer William Tilden, and
Purser Francis J. O'Gara, were taken below. Those left on deck were then
either beaten with iron bars where they sat or made to run the gauntlet.
Whilst this was going on Japanese gun crews riddled the lifeboats with
machine-gun fire. Assistant Engineer Charles Pyle was one of those
made to run the gauntlet, passing along a line of Japanese armed with
'clubs and other blunt instruments'. He remembered being struck 'a terrific blow' on the base of the skull before passing out to fall into 'a white
foamy sea'. Armed Guardsman Robert Butler suffered similarly.

Another Armed Guardsman, Seaman First Class Robert Applegate,
remembered sitting on the casing for about three hours, his head aching
from the blows he had received. Then the submarine's alarm klaxon
sounded as the sound of a plane was heard overhead. By that time about
thirty prisoners were left on the deck, and there was blind panic as they
strove to free themselves as the submarine began to submerge. Able Seaman George Hess had managed earlier to work his bonds free, and using
a knife another survivor had secreted in his pocket, he passed from man
to man freeing as many as possible. But he had freed, or partially freed,
only about half a dozen when they were all dragged down by the suction.
Applegate's hands had been partially freed by Hess, and he managed to
regain the surface along with some others, even some of those with still
bound hands. Applegate saw a plane skimming over the surface towards
the still burning *Nicolet.* It was a Catalina of the Royal Canadian Air
Force, although Applegate would not have known that at the time. Without a life-jacket Applegate kept himself afloat until the following day
when another Catalina dropped a raft, life-jackets and some rations. Yet
another day was to pass before the armed trawler HMIS *Hoxa* arrived on
the scene to pick up the only twenty-three men still alive.

Captain Nilsson and Radio Officer Tilden did not survive internment
in a Japanese prisoner of war camp. But Purser Francis J. O'Gara did. A
former sports writer for the Philadelphia *Inquirer,* he reappeared in late
1945 to find himself something of a celebrity. For in unknowing

contravention of the standing rule that Liberty ships were only to be named after the late and departed, a ship had been launched with his name from the J.A. Jones shipyard at Panama City, Florida, in June 1945. It was the only occasion the standing rule was broken. When that ship was later scrapped, O'Gara was presented with its plaque.

Captain Ariizumi escaped direct Allied retribution at the end of the war. After his service on *I-8* he become Chief of Staff, Submarine Squadron 8 at Penang, the unit whose commanders enacted more atrocities than anyone else. Towards the end of the war he moved on to command Submarine Squadron 1 in the Inland Sea of Japan, flying his flag on a new submarine, *I-401*. After the Japanese capitulation and whilst his squadron was under American naval escort to Yokosuka naval base in Tokyo Bay, Ariizumi, no doubt in the knowledge that he would be called to account for his activities, shot himself.[10]

It was planned that the retaking of Malaya would begin with a British amphibious force being landed at Morib beach on the west coast of Malaya in August 1945. It was called Operation 'Zipper'. In the event it was an unopposed landing because of the Japanese capitulation after the dropping of the atom bombs. Several British-flagged Liberty ships were among the merchant ships involved. The *Samtroy* was one of them, and was off the beachhead on the first day. She was commanded by Captain Niblock, the man who as master of the *Samuta* in April 1944, had saved some of the survivors from the *Richard Hovey*. It was as well perhaps, that 'Zipper' was unopposed. For the staff of the Allied Supreme Commander, South-east Asia, Admiral Mountbatten, had not done their homework properly. Morib beach was not an ideal landing site, for underneath a gleaming layer of sand which appears firm enough to the naked eye, lies a thick layer of mud. Although troops got ashore in good order, much of their heavy equipment did not, trucks, tanks and guns, sinking through the sand and disappearing into the mud below.

---

10. Boyd, op.cit.

CHAPTER 20

Liberties in the Pacific

The Pacific Ocean is the world's largest and many of the longest logistical voyages of the war were made across it. The very vastness of the ocean was a protection for merchant ships, as, providing a ship maintained radio silence, the chance of being spotted by an enemy submarine was small. Most ocean crossings were therefore made independently. In addition to troops, the cargoes carried on these voyages ranged from tanks, trucks, landing craft, guns, and ammunition, down to much more mundane items such as beer supplies for military Post Exchanges. When the *Edwin M. Stanton* (Portland, Oregon, September 1942) left New York on 6 June 1944 for New Guinea, her cargo consisted almost entirely of cartons of beer. 'We arrived at Milne Bay', says Bob Gifford, 'with less than we had when we left New York'. He added that the ship's captain was quite a character. 'At Milne Bay we ran out of coal for the galley stove. He radioed ashore for some, only to be told that the nearest supply was in Australia. 'Request permission to proceed Brisbane', he radioed back. We had our coal within the hour.'[1]

Despite its vastness there were areas of that ocean where the menace from submarines was potentially considerable. The waters surrounding the Hawaiian Islands for example, and at the other end of the ocean passage, the approaches to the islands north-east of Australia and along the eastern seaboard of that continent itself. The nature of General MacArthur's island-hopping campaign in the South-west Pacific and Admiral Nimitz's campaign in the islands to the north and east, with the need to convey troops and supplies from one point of attack to the next, meant that many inter-island voyages had to be made under sustained enemy attack, sometimes from enemy naval units, but mostly from aircraft, the latter attacks not always being of a conventional nature. Even in these danger zones merchant ships very often sailed independently. Convoys were fairly common features off the Australian eastern seaboard but usually only when troops were being carried. The decision by the Allied High Command that there were higher priorities for naval vessels than their utilisation as convoy escorts in this theatre was not

---

1. Correspondence with Robert W. Gifford, 2000.

entirely due to a shortage of such ships. It was also based on a judgement of the risks involved. It was known that the Germans had few submarines available for use in the Pacific (in fact those that did operate there did so only off the eastern and southern coasts of Australia) and that the Japanese did not have sufficient submarines to operate, for example, Atlantic-style wolf-pack systems. Japanese submarines rarely operated in anything more than groups of two or three. In fact neither the Germans nor the Japanese ever used wolf-pack tactics in the Pacific. (The most common Japanese submarine tactic of the war was the picket line. Off Guam in mid-1944 they organised no less than three of these.) On top of everything else, the Allies knew from signals intelligence sources that the efficiency of the radar as fitted to Japanese submarines in 1943, left something to be desired.

Before telling the story of the first Liberty to be lost in the Pacific, for the sake of chronology the first of the two known Japanese atrocities against Allied merchant seamen in Pacific waters must be mentioned. The ship involved was owned by the US Maritime Commission but sailed under the Panamanian flag. She was the *Donerail* of 1924 and on 9 December 1941, two days after the attack on Pearl Harbor, she was south-east of Hawaii on a voyage from Suva to Vancouver with a cargo of sugar and pineapples. On that date she had the misfortune to cross the track of *I-10*, one of the Japanese submarines being sent to patrol off the American coast. At that time she was commanded by Lieutenant Commander Kayahara. *I-10* sank the unarmed freighter with gunfire and then machine-gunned the forty survivors who had taken to the boats. Sixteen men, including the master, died. The survivors drifted for thirty-eight days before being picked up by a Japanese vessel and taken into captivity on Tarawa, the horror of their experiences therefore remaining unknown to the outside world until after the war.

The first Liberty to be lost in the Pacific was voyaging independently northwards up the eastern Australian coast en route from San Francisco to Brisbane via Adelaide. The *William Dawes* (Portland, Oregon, April 1942), under the command of Captain John Froberg was carrying around 7000 tons of ammunition and other military supplies. In late July 1942 two submarines of the Japanese 3rd Flotilla were working the stretch of Australian coast between Sydney and Townsville, with a third member of the flotilla operating off New Caledonia to the north. Between 20 July and 6 August the trio between them claimed ten victims, the third one being the *Dawes*. On 22 July a lookout aboard the Liberty spotted the *I-11*, Commander Izu Hisaichi, surfacing not more than 200 yards away. (One American source states the submarine was *I-24*, but that is incorrect.) There was no time for evasive action before a torpedo struck the ship in the vicinity of her after magazine, the resulting explosion blowing the ship's stern clean off. Water flooding through the wrecked stern tube soon reached the engine-room. Four Armed Guardsmen and an American Army passenger who had been on duty at the after gun were killed. It was now impossible to bring the forward gun to bear because the ship had no steering. Captain Froberg ordered the survivors into the boats but they remained close until a second torpedo struck the ship which then began burning fiercely. The boats made it safely to the nearby coast. Meanwhile, after several explosions in the cargo, the ship sank in fairly shallow waters. In the 1960s, and again in 1970, the wreck and its cargo was offered for sale by auction.

In mid-1942 intelligence reports from coastwatchers reached General MacArthur to the effect that the Japanese were constructing an airstrip at Guadalcanal in the Solomons. Situated at the south-eastern extremity of the Japanese defence perimeter, such an airstrip could have been used by the Japanese as a base from which to launch air attacks against the Allied principal line of communication from the States, via Hawaii to Australia. In consequence in August 1942 the US 1st Marine Division launched an attack there. Taken by surprise, the Japanese were ousted from the airfield, henceforth to be known as Henderson Field, by 8 August. A naval Liberty, the USS *Carina* (built Richmond, November 1942 as the *David Davis* but immediately taken over by the Navy and renamed), carried out sterling work during the Guadalcanal campaign. Later in the war she almost met her end when rammed by a Japanese PT boat on a suicide mission.

The Japanese in the Guadalcanal area had not given up, however, and over the next six months made two attempts to recapture the airfield. Japanese Submarine Force B took part in covering those attempts. One of those submarines damaged the cruiser USS *Chester* on 20 October 1942, and another, the *I-21*, severely damaged the Liberty *Edgar Allen Poe* (Portland, Oregon, April 1942) off Noumea on 8 November. A torpedo struck the Liberty in the engine-room causing both boilers to explode. Commander Matsumura Midori's *I-21* then surfaced, and at a range of 300 yards was fired upon by the ship's Armed Guard using both the 3in gun forward and the 4in aft, two of the shells reportedly hitting the submarine and driving it off. Captain Jack Edgerton ordered about half those on board the *Poe*, including eighteen passengers, into two boats and a raft, but remained on board himself with the balance of the crew. Those in the boats and on the raft drifted off during the night but were soon picked up by an American destroyer. The minesweeper HMNZS *Matai* and a trawler eventually towed the ship into Noumea where she was handed over to the US Navy to become a towed storeship for the remainder of the war.

Whatever damage *I-21* had sustained from the *Poe*'s gunfire it could not have been serious because she was back in business early in the New Year. Off Sydney on 18 January 1943 she torpedoed and badly damaged

the American tanker *Mobilube* then sank the British freighter *Kalingo*.
Four days later *I-21* torpedoed the *Peter H. Burnett* (Los Angeles,
August 1942) which was on its way back to the States with a cargo of
baled wool. The torpedo blew out the ship's side for almost the whole
length of No. 5 hold, throwing bales of wool through the hatch and high
into the air. The explosion also damaged the main shaft, making the
engines useless. Captain Charles Darling ordered abandon ship, but the
Armed Guard officer, some of the engineers and two cadets asked to
remain on board and did so. Possibly because of the nature of her cargo,
the *Burnett* was still afloat on the following morning and the men in all
but one of the lifeboats then reboarded. The missing boat was Captain
Darling's which had drifted off in the dark, to be picked up two days
later by the USS *Zane*. The *Zane* then intercepted the still floating
Burnett and towed her back to Sydney. She too became a floating storeship for the Navy.

It was a night of very rough weather when the *Samuel Gompers* (Los
Angeles, September 1942) went down after being torpedoed by *I-10* (of
the *Donerail* incident mentioned above) which was now under Commander (later Captain) Yamada Takashi. On 30 January 1943 the Liberty
was making for Newcastle, New South Wales, from Noumea and was
only a few hours into the voyage when a torpedo struck at the forward
end of No. 4 hold in way of the deep tanks containing fuel oil. The explosion blew debris, fuel, and cargo 40ft into the air, which then landed all
over the ship. Captain John Lapoint ordered the boats lowered, but
because of the weather only the two starboard boats were properly
launched, the port ones capsizing. The *Gompers* sank within five
minutes. Some of the survivors managed to right one of the upturned
boats and the three craft then set off in company for the nearest land.
Soon they became separated. One boat reached a small island off New
Caledonia four days later, and another reached the main island itself. An
Army crash boat *P-111* rescued the others. Four men lost their lives in
the attack.

Having previously only managed to damage two Liberties, Commander Matsumura's *I-21* had more success on 10 February with the *Starr
King* (Los Angeles, August 1942), but not before the ship had put up a
fight. On the 9th, a day out from Sydney and making for Noumea with
over 9000 tons of military cargo, lookouts on the ship's bridge spotted a
submarine periscope. Captain Gustav Winsens put his stern to the submarine and made a run for it, at first adopting a zigzag course. Later, in
an endeavour to put more distance between his ship and the submarine,
Winsens dropped the zigzag. That proved to be a mistake for Matsumura
had been persistent. As the sun came up on the 10th lookouts on the ship
saw three torpedoes heading their way. Two passed harmlessly ahead and
astern, but one struck in No. 4 hold, rupturing steam lines and starting a

fire there. The engines were closed down and as some crew members began fighting the fire Winsens ordered others to lower the lifeboats and lay off as a precaution. However, confusion seems to have reigned for a time with the Chief Officer unsuccessfully attempting to belay the order. The boats were lying a short distance off when another torpedo passed between them to strike the ship's bunker tanks and so spewing oil everywhere. Those still aboard then vacated the ship as the boats came alongside for them. There had been no casualties. Later that day the destroyer HMAS *Warramunga* arrived and took the crew aboard before attempting to take the *King*, now very low in the water, in tow. But the cable fouled one of the destroyer's screws and the attempt was abandoned. The *Starr King* sank later that night.

From signal intelligence sources the Allies knew that in March 1943 German Foreign Minister von Ribbentrop had stressed, not for the first time, to the Japanese ambassador in Berlin, the importance of submarine campaigns against shipping. He urged the Japanese to deploy more of their submarines to this task. By that date the Japanese had given up all hope of recapturing Guadalcanal where some of their submarines had been operating, and so finally acceded to the German plan. That fact was also picked up by Allied intelligence. When General MacArthur was made aware of the increased danger to his supply routes along the eastern Australian coast he asked 'for more destroyers to combat the menace off his Australian bases'. He was told they could not be spared on account of the concomitant threat in the Fiji-Samoa area.[2]

Despite the Allies being forewarned of the new offensive they could not prevent the Japanese gaining a number of successes. Between 24 April and 17 May, eleven Allied merchant ships, four of them Liberties, were lost or damaged in the two threatened areas. An Allied hospital ship was also sunk. Two of the Liberty incidents in that spate of attacks involved ships launched from the same yard within two months of each other, and both named after ladies. The first to go was *Lydia M. Childs* (Los Angeles, March 1943). After sailing safely across thousands of miles of ocean between San Francisco and Sydney with a full cargo of military supplies including tanks, she was within 100 miles of her destination when she was struck by a torpedo from *I-178*, Commander Utsuki Hidejiro. The ship sank in under ten minutes but not before all the crew got away in lifeboats. They were soon rescued by Australian minesweepers. The crew of the *Phoebe A. Hearst* (Los Angeles, January 1943) were also all rescued when she was sunk by *I-19*, Commander Kinashi Takaichi, but not, however, before some of them had spent a fortnight in

---

2. *War with Japan*, Vol. III.

a boat. Voyaging between Noumea and Pago Pago with a cargo of muni-tions and gasoline, on 30 April the ship was torpedoed between Nos. 2 and 3 holds. She blew up and disintegrated twelve hours later. The crew had got away on two lifeboats and some rafts. A Catalina picked up the men from the rafts on the third day, and one of the boats landed at Tofua Island after five days at sea. The boat containing Captain Stephanos Bacoyanis and twenty-four men was sighted after fourteen days by the rescue boat USS *Dash*.

On 1 May the *William Williams* (Richmond, September 1942) sailed in ballast from Suva, Fiji Islands. On the following day she was severely damaged by a torpedo from *I-19*, Commander Kinashi, fresh from his *Hearst* kill. The *Williams* was so badly damaged aft that her deck was completely awash, so badly in fact, that she has been used as an example of just how much punishment a Liberty could suffer and yet survive. The *Williams* was towed back to Suva with the USS *Dash* acting as one of the escorts. The ship was then towed first to Auckland for emergency repairs, then on to Sydney where she was acquired by the US Navy, becoming the *Venus*. Henceforth she was used in various parts of the Pacific as an accommodation ship.

The *William K. Vanderbilt* (Richmond, October 1942) sailed from the New Hebrides bound for the Panama Canal but instead became another victim of Commander Kinashi. In the early hours of 17 May when west of Suva, a torpedo from *I-19* struck in the vicinity of No. 5 hold, destroy-ing the propeller shaft. Captain William Goldsmith ordered abandon ship but the Armed Guard remained on board. One lifeboat overturned dur-ing the launching process. Twenty minutes later Kinashi fired a second torpedo, this explosion ripping the ship almost in two and engulfing the accommodation in flames. The Armed Guard then left the ship, either by jumping into the sea, or by taking to rafts, or by literally walking off the ship into the waiting lifeboats, for by then the ship was well down by the stern. The ship finally sank stern first. The submarine then surfaced and approached the boats, firing a machine-gun burst at one as it did so. Cap-tain Goldsmith was taken aboard the submarine for questioning but then released. It was the ubiquitous *Dash* which rescued the survivors the fol-lowing day. That burst of machine-gun fire had caused no casualties and quite why Kinashi saw fit to do it was never discovered for he was later to die in action. He certainly did not have the sort of reputation gained later by 'the Butcher', Commander Ariizumi in the Indian Ocean, nor that of a colleague who had been involved in an atrocity only four days earlier off Brisbane. On the night of 13 May the *I-177*, Lieutenant Commander Nakagawa Hajime, torpedoed and sank the Australian hospital ship *Cen-taur*, despite the ship being fully lit and marked in accordance with the Geneva Convention. There were 363 persons on board including a num-ber of Australian army nurses, but only sixty-four survived.

Commander A.C.C. Miers VC was one of the British observers serving with the US Pacific Fleet in 1943. He noted in his report to the Admiralty that most of the ships sunk in the South-west Pacific by Japanese submarines during April and May, including naval ships, had not been employing 'evasive routeing' techniques, zigzagging being the main one, and that he 'envisaged further losses in the future unless drastic anti-submarine precautions were insisted upon'.[3]

Although other merchantmen and naval ships were lost in the interim, it was not until August 1943 when the next Liberty ship casualties occurred in the region. On 11 August two days after sailing from Guadalcanal to the New Hebrides, the *Matthew Lyon* (Richmond, April 1943) was struck by a torpedo from *I-11*, Commander Tagami Akeji. At the time the *Lyon* was in company with another Liberty, the *J.H. Kincaide* (built in the same month and also at Richmond), and with a rare escort in the shape of the USS *Crosby*. Perhaps it was the presence of the naval vessel that ensured that the small convoy was zigzagging at the time. Nevertheless that did not save the *Lyon* from being hit. The explosion blew a 35ft hole in way of No. 3 hold. Three steel beams from that hatch were blown up on to the flying bridge, crippling the steering gear. Captain Jean de Reske Dandel and his crew rigged the emergency steering gear and with all pumps working to control the flooding, the ship reached Espiritu Santo under its own steam several days later. A few months later the ship joined the growing list of damaged Liberties taken over by the US Navy, becoming a 'net cargo' ship and used to recover and install boom defence nets at various harbours in the South Seas.

On 13 August it was the turn of the *M.H. De Young* (Richmond, July 1943). Carrying nearly 4000 tons of construction equipment including pontoon barges in every hold, she was making an independent voyage from California to Espiritu Santo and was about 200 miles south-west of Fiji when a torpedo from Commander Kinashi's *I-19* struck in way of the engine-room. For safety's sake Captain William Munda ordered most of those on board, including all twenty-eight members of a military construction company on board and some injured men, into the boats, although he was aware that due to the pontoons on board, his ship was unlikely to sink as they would act like buoyancy tanks. Together with the Armed Guard unit, the chief engineer and the bosun, Munda remained on board. On the following morning those in the boats re-boarded. Later that day the freighter *Quebec* took the *De Young* in tow, and made the island of Tongatabu two days later. Transferred to the Navy the Liberty became the *Antelope* and was used as a storage hulk.

---

3. *War with Japan*, Vol. IV.

Henderson Field at Guadalcanal became an important air base for the Americans and, of course, the men and aircraft there had to be regularly supplied. The anchorage off the base was not the safest place to be, for there were regular Japanese air attacks. On 11 October 1943 the Japanese gained two successes there within five minutes of each other. The *George H. Himes* (Portland, Oregon, July 1943) was struck aft by an aerial torpedo. The damage was extensive but would probably have been worse had it not been for the lumber cargo on board which somewhat cushioned the effect. As the *Himes* settled by the stern she was beached. She was later salved, repaired and returned to service. The second ship was not nearly so lucky. Whilst discharging her cargo which included petrol, aviation spirit and diesel, as well as explosives, the *John H. Couch* (Portland, Oregon, April 1943) was also struck by an aerial torpedo. It hit at No. 2 hold, blowing several men over the side and hurling blazing drums of oil high into the air. The flames soon spread, and despite the efforts of the ship's fire-fighting parties, the fire was soon blazing out of control. Two destroyers laid alongside and used their foam equipment, but to no avail. As fire engulfed his ship Captain David Welch ordered everyone off into waiting landing craft. The ship burned for four days and was then towed clear of the anchorage by the USS *Pawnee*. During this operation the ship suddenly capsized.

Early in the New Year, as General MacArthur's forces advanced northwards, two Liberties servicing Australian and US troops on New Guinea sustained damage from enemy bombers. Off Finschhafen on the north coast of the island on 24 January the *John Muir* (Sausilito, December 1942) received several hits that injured a number of Seabees on board, several of whom died later in hospital. Five days later and a little way along the coast, the *George Sterling* (Richmond, September 1943) was also damaged by bombers.

An exceedingly unfortunate event occurred on 26 September 1944. On that date in broad daylight whilst voyaging between the New Hebrides and New Caledonia, the *Elihu Thomson* (Richmond, December 1942) ran into a marked minefield near the entrance to Noumea Harbour. She struck two mines, both of which exploded on the port side, forward. The ship was carrying over 200 troops, and thirty-two of them were killed in the double explosion. Captain Frank Waters ordered abandon ship and the survivors got away in lifeboats and rafts and aboard the USS *Apache* which at great risk, laid herself alongside. *Apache* later towed the ship into port where she was partially beached and her cargo discharged. After temporary repairs she was towed to Espiritu Santo and was back in service by January 1945. Captain Waters had his master's license temporarily suspended pending an inquiry into the incident.

Ever since the Battle of Midway in June 1942, the Japanese had been losing more aircraft than they could afford. In both 1943 and 1944, the

Japanese built a massive number of warplanes of one sort or another. But whereas in 1941/1942 Japanese planes were ahead of their time, by 1943 that was no longer the case. There are some indications that production quality control had broken down, and certainly their aircraft maintenance and supply techniques were, by Allied standards, extremely inadequate. Of even greater significance was the loss of many experienced pilots, mostly at the hands of the Americans. From a force that in 1941 had contained some of the world's best and most experienced pilots – a fact that had been largely overlooked or underplayed by the Allies at that time – by 1944 the best that could be said for most Japanese pilots was that they were dedicated. Unfortunately that dedication did not translate into victories. Inexperienced pilots now at the controls of many Japanese planes contributed to ever-growing losses, many pilots not returning from their very first operations. After the fall of Saipan to American marines in June 1944, Vice-Admiral Onishi Takajiro put forward a plan to use suicide pilots. At first the idea did not go down well with other Japanese war leaders, but in the circumstances then confronting the Japanese, the concept made considerable sense. If pilots and planes engaged in conventional combat were going to be lost and to little effect as heretofore, argued Onishi, why not expend those pilots and planes to the best possible effect? The idea was taken up by Rear-Admiral Arima Masafumi. Arima had been raised in England, his father having been attached to the Japanese Embassy in London. After attending an English public school he trained with the Royal Navy, attending the college at Greenwich. When in April 1921 W.F. Forbes-Sempill (Lord Sempill to be), late of the Royal Naval Air Service and the RAF, arrived in Japan as head of the British Aviation Mission to set up and train the fledgling Imperial Naval Air Service, Arima was one of the pilots trained.

As the Americans prepared to assault the Philippines (the Japanese were not aware of where the attack would take place, indeed, at one point they thought that Formosa and not the Philippines would be attacked first), the Japanese fought a series of air battles in mid-October 1944 against planes launched from carriers of the American task force under the command of Admiral Halsey. The Americans lost fewer than 100 planes, the Japanese over 500. In the middle of that period Admiral Arima decided to make his point in the most dramatic and practical way he could. On 13 October flying one of the planes engaged in the second wave of what had been planned as a conventional attack on the American ships, he deliberately crashed his plane into the carrier USS *Franklin*, causing considerable damage. And so it was that the kamikaze operations were born. (Kamikaze, or divine wind, for the typhoon that had dispersed an invading Mongol fleet in the 14th century.) Admiral Onishi Takajiro whose idea it had all been, survived the war – just. On the night of the Japanese surrender he gave a small party for close friends. Then after attiring himself appropriately, he wrote a small poem in accordance with tradition. He followed that with a short letter addressed to the youth of Japan, so many of whom had died as a direct result of what he had set in train. Afterwards he laid down on the tatami-covered floor of his study, drew a short sword, cut across his stomach with it and then slashed upwards. He tried to administer the *coup de grace* himself, but failed, and lay that night in a pool of his own blood. In the morning he was found by a servant, but he refused medical attention. It is said that it took him twelve hours to die, many, many times longer than the fractions of a second his pilots had taken.

An official but 'nominal' British list of ships sunk or damaged by suicide bombers during the Philippines campaign presents twenty-two ships as being sunk and 126 damaged. In fact the total was much higher than that for although the list included some merchant ship victims, it omitted many others including some Liberty ships. From all causes, including kamikaze attacks, during the period 24 October 1944 to 13 January 1945, no less than thirty-four Liberties were either sunk or damaged in the retaking of the Philippines, and a number of others suffered similarly in other parts of the Pacific campaign.

American landings in the Philippines began on 20 October on the east coast of the island of Leyte. On that same day General MacArthur wadded through the surf to the beach, thus having kept his promise to return. Three days after the landings the *Augustus Thomas* (Richmond, September 1943) was lying in San Pedro Bay discharging her cargo of military supplies including ammunition when she was strafed by a Japanese bomber, one Armed Guard being wounded. Early on the following morning the alarm on the ship sounded as another bomber was sighted bearing down on the ship. The Armed Guards set up a hail of gunfire, setting the plane alight. But flying very low it kept on coming. One of its wings struck the funnel of the tug USS *Sonoma* lying alongside the *Thomas*, and the plane then crashed into the ship's side amidships, its bombs detonating on impact. The explosion blew in the side of the *Thomas*, flooding the engine-room and the two after holds. *Sonoma* was ablaze alongside. Although the Liberty was carrying 480 troops, no one aboard was killed. The ship was beached and eventually towed to Newcastle, New South Wales, and then to the States. However, she did not become operational again.

On 26 October off Leyte two near misses from a bomber slightly damaged the *Benjamin Ide Wheeler* (Los Angeles, December 1942). During the evening of the following day a burning bomber suddenly appeared, heading straight for the ship. The *Wheeler*'s Armed Guards managed to shoot off one of its wings but could not prevent it striking the ship. The aircraft hit just above the waterline at No. 5 hold, its bombs tearing a great hole in the ship's side. The explosion blew the plane's engine straight through the hold and out the other side. Drums of gasoline in the hold began blowing up, and soon the after end of the ship was ablaze. In order to prevent the fire from spreading forward, Captain Daniel Coughlin ordered No. 4 hold flooded, and the ship slowly settled on the bottom. In addition to the Japanese pilot, two men lost their lives aboard the ship. The death toll could easily have been much higher for the ship was carrying 500 troops. *Wheeler* was salvaged and towed back to the States but never saw service again.

The *Matthew P. Deady* (Portland, Oregon, July 1942) was also carrying troops at the time she was struck by a kamikaze on 3 November when lying off Tacloban. The plane first dropped bombs which missed, then strafed the ship before turning to come in again. It struck one of the gun tubs and exploded, igniting gasoline and some acetylene tanks stowed on deck which caused a second explosion, the main cause for the twenty-eight deaths among the 300 troops on board. The crew and the remaining troops were able to fight the fire successfully. This ship was eventually repaired and returned to service.

The *Thomas Nelson* (Baltimore, June 1943) was the centre of one of the most tragic of all kamikaze incidents. Whilst the ship was lying off the port off Dulag on 12 November, a Japanese aircraft first strafed the ship before diving into the heavy-lift boom at No. 4 hatch. There was an explosion as the plane struck, followed almost immediately by another as its bomb went off. Fires broke out all over the after end of the ship. Firefighters from ashore joined in the fight to save the ship and some hours later the fires were out. The ship had been carrying 578 troops, and 133 of them perished and another eighty-eight injured. Three of the ship's Armed Guard unit also lost their lives. The ship made it back to San Francisco under its own steam and the fire damage was repaired. She returned to service, and after the war sailed under the Greek flag until she was scrapped in 1970. Seamen are a superstitious lot, and no doubt the Greek sailors were never informed of the Dulag incident.

Later that same day at Dulag three more Liberties were to suffer similarly. In the case of the *Jeremiah M. Daly* (Richmond, August 1943) the kamikaze crashed into the front of the bridge near the wheelhouse destroying much of the accommodation. Parts of the plane ignited drums of fuel stowed on No. 3 hatch, and fire raged for several hours. Three of the ship's officers and 100 of the 550 troops on board lost their lives, another forty-three men being injured. Another Japanese plane dove into the *Alexander Majors* (Richmond, March 1944) striking the ship's mainmast and showering the deck with shrapnel, wreckage and burning gasoline. Luckily this ship was not carrying troops. Nevertheless, two crew members died in the attack. To round off that day of mayhem at Dulag, a plane came in from astern to launch itself at the *Morrison R. Waite* (Richmond, November 1942). Despite being repeatedly hit by the ship's machine-guns, it struck the hull at No. 1 hold, the explosion blowing inward. About a quarter of the 600 troops on board were in the 'tween-deck there. A fire started, but fire-fighting efforts soon brought it under control. Nevertheless, twenty-one troops had lost their lives and about twice that number were severely burned.

A graphic account of that day's events at Dulag is contained in the report made by Ensign Irving N. Goldstein in charge of the *Waite's* Armed Guard unit. He stated that all the attacks on the ships in the harbour seemed to have been well planned, with the planes intent on coming in either from directly ahead or directly astern, before side-slipping in to crash on decks or against hulls. It was clear, wrote Goldstein, that the suicide pilots were keeping to, at least as long as they could, some pre-flight briefing, for that was the way to avoid masts, booms and superstructures and so cause maximum damage. Armed Guardsman Edward Haake of the *Waite* says that the ship sported a large swim-suited, painted pin-up on the after end of the rear gun platform. It had the words Vigilant Virgin around it. 'This was the only pin-up on a Liberty I knew of', he says. As the kamikaze pilot who had dove at the ship had made his approach from that direction, that attractive lady might well have been almost the last thing he saw.

Kamikazes were succeeding on a scale never achieved by more ordinary combat methods. Nevertheless, a few ships were still suffering from the old practices. One was the *Gus W. Darnell* (Houston, May 1944). Off Samar Island on 23 November she was struck by an aerial torpedo at the after end of No. 2 hold. The ship was carrying Army trucks on deck and the ship became an inferno when their gas tanks exploded. Captain George Parsons ordered all those not fighting the fire to abandon. A fire-boat and a tug came to the assistance with foam gear, but by that time the ship was down by the head with a severe list to port. To prevent the ship capsizing she was beached. Subsequently declared a total constructive lost, she was taken over by the Navy as a storeship and renamed *Justin*.

The *Antoine Saugrain* (Richmond, August 1943) was in convoy making for the strait between Mindanao and Leyte when on 5 December she was attacked by a torpedo bomber. The torpedo struck aft, blowing off the rudder and propeller and wrecking the tail shaft. The ship soon lay dead in the water and Captain Anthony Van Cromphaut ordered everyone, including the nearly 400 troops on board, to stand by lifeboat stations. Another plane then roared in, its torpedo striking near No. 2 hold causing the vessel to start settling by the head. The order was then given to abandon, and everyone on board got away in boats, rafts or by jumping overboard. They were soon picked up by naval craft. An Army tug *LT-454* took the ship in tow, but on the 7th the ship was struck by yet another aerial torpedo and sank. The *Marcus Daly* (Richmond, August 1943) was part of that same convoy, and on the same day was

struck by a plane whose pilot was either dead set on becoming a
kamikaze hero, or was turned into one when the ship's guns damaged his
tail section. The plane hit the foremast and crashed through the maindeck
into the forepeak where its bomb exploded, throwing burning debris a
hundred feet into the air. The forepeak contained the bosun's stores
including paint, and that caught fire. It was reported that the explosion
opened holes in both sides of the bows 'big enough to drive a train
through'. However, the ship managed to reach Tarragona Harbour under
its own steam. She was carrying a huge complement of 1200 troops, and
sixty-six of those were lost in the incident. The *Daly* was not a lucky
ship. Having lost her anchors in that incident, she was unable to anchor
at Tarragona, but was held roughly in one position by judicious use of
her engines and with the aid of landing craft moored alongside during the
discharging operation. The troops were disembarked, and by the 10th
some of the cargo had been discharged into landing craft. On that day she
was visited by another kamikaze. This one crashed into the bridge gun
tubs and the boat deck, before striking a landing craft alongside aft, on
the way showering the ship with shrapnel. Eight men on board were
wounded in that attack. Rather surprisingly perhaps, the ship made it
safely back to San Francisco after temporary repairs. The *Daly*'s two
kamikaze attacks was by no means a record. According to historian John
Costello, the *William R. Davie* (Wilmington, July 1942) fought off a total
of seventy-two such attacks without suffering anything more than
superficial damage.[4]

By October 1944 German submarine activities in the Pacific off
Australia were coming to an end. During that month the flotilla based at
Penang was forced to move to Batavia (now Jakarta) because RAF
Liberators had laid many mines off the Malayan port. (The Japanese had
little or no minesweeping facilities in South-east Asia. Indeed, what they
had elsewhere was primitive compared with that of the Allies.) Allied
raids on the Sumatran oilfields had badly affected oil supplies and that
also had an effect on U-boat operations. By that time too, the U-boats'
batteries had deteriorated due to extended cruises under tropical conditions, and no replacements were available. Torpedoes were also in short
supply. In November the survivors of Group Monsoon were ordered to
make for Europe, the last to leave being Lieutenant Commander Timms'
U-862 which sank the Liberties *Robert J. Walker* and *Peter Sylvester* –
the latter in the Indian Ocean – as sort of parting shots which were
described in Chapter 13.

That October brought another Japanese submarine atrocity against
Allied merchant seamen, and as with the *Donerail* the commander

---

4. John Costello, *The Pacific War* (London 1981), p564.

involved was not one of the group operating out of Penang, for this incident too took place on the opposite side of the Pacific. By the middle of 1944 Japanese submarine losses had been so heavy that only twenty-six remained fully operational and morale in the service was correspondingly low. Late in the year, in an endeavour to bolster morale, Vice-Admiral Miwa Shigeyoshi, Commander Submarines, 6th Fleet, decided to send a single submarine to operate against commerce in the approaches to the Hawaiian Islands. The boat chosen for the task was the *I-12,* a relatively new boat that had been launched in the previous year and which had a cruising range of 22,000 miles. Commander Kudo Kameo was given the command. Having graduated from Etajima College in the Class of 1929, he was probably the youngest full commander in the submarine service and this was his fourth boat. *I-12* sailed from Kure on 4 October and a few days before the end of that month took up position about half-way along the route between San Francisco and Hawaii.

The Liberty ship *John A. Johnson* (Portland, Oregon, June 1943) was the unfortunate who sailed into Kudo's sights on the night of the 29th. The ship, managed by American Mail Lines, had sailed from San Francisco five days earlier with a full cargo of military supplies. Captain Arnold Beeken had orders to make for Honolulu where he would be informed of his final destination which would be 'somewhere in the Western Pacific'. There were twenty-eight Armed Guardsmen on the ship and an Army Security Officer, which brought the total complement up to seventy. The ship's course placed her at right-angles to a heavy swell rolling up from the south and she had taken on the usual Liberty roll in such conditions, a violent, stomach-churning heel over to one side, followed by an equally violent one over the other way. It was as the ship rolled heavily to port that a torpedo struck low down on the starboard side of No. 3 hold just forward of the bridge. Not only did the explosion blow a huge hole in the ship's side most of it well below the normal waterline, it virtually broke her back. As the ship 'worked' in the seaway, it seemed that only the deck plating was holding her together. General Alarm was sounded, the engines stopped, and Radio Officer Gordon Brown attempted to get off a distress signal, but in the middle of doing that the generators suddenly packed up.

It was clear that the ship was about to break in two so Captain Beeken ordered abandon ship. One boat had been damaged in the explosion, and another was swamped as soon as it hit the water, but the other two got away, rescuing those from the swamped boat as they did so. Other men left on a raft, and three more jumped into the sea. That left Captain Beeken still on board. He made his way aft looking for anyone who may have inadvertently been left behind, and, sure enough, he found four gunners still stationed at the after gun. At that moment the fore end of the ship broke away and the after end on which Beeken and the gunners were standing began to settle. All five leapt over the side and had the good fortune to find the swamped boat which was still just afloat due to its buoyancy tanks. A few minutes later they were joined by the men who had earlier jumped overboard.

The three boats and the raft were close enough for it to be established that all seventy men had got safely away. But then Commander Kudo brought his submarine to the surface. At full surface speed – a little under 18kts – he bore down upon the boats. The nearest one was under the charge of Third Officer Barber who saw the submarine heading his way and yelled for his crew to go over the side. Some were too late and were thrown out as the boat was rammed, despite the blow being only a glancing one. Then machine-guns opened up sweeping the surrounding sea, and Barber clearly saw a man on deck firing a pistol at the boat and the men in the water. Kudo brought his craft round in a wide sweep and did the same thing again, also firing at the raft on which seventeen men were crouched. He then rammed the raft, and it could have been no accident, for when he missed the first time he completed the job at a second go. Before making off Kudo also attempted to ram the other good lifeboat. He had killed ten men, four of the merchant crew, five Armed Guardsmen, and the Army Security Officer. Some of the other survivors had bullet wounds, and others had injuries caused in the rammings. The survivors were fortunate in that a Pan American Airways flight overflew the scene shortly afterwards, sighted the two burning halves of the ship, and reported in. The sixty men left alive were rescued by the USS *Argus* on the following day. The *Johnson* was Kudo's only victim in a sortie that was to be his last. Authorities differ as to the fate of his submarine (as was the case with several others that were lost with all hands). But it seems likely that it was the combined efforts of the US Coast Guard cutter *Rockford* and the minesweeper USS *Ardent* on 13 November, just fifteen days after the atrocity, that avenged the deaths of those ten victims. On that date, in a position north-east of the Hawaiian island of Kauai, the two warships put paid to a submarine, and after that date Kudo's command was never heard from again.

Kamikaze attacks carried on into 1945. Under the command of Captain John Platt the *Lewis L. Dyche* (Portland, Oregon, December 1943) had spent most of her short life shuttling around the Pacific Islands hauling troops and supplies, almost without incident. On 4 January she was one of a number of ships anchored off Mindoro. Almost as if he knew that the ship was carrying a cargo of bombs and fuses, the pilot of the plane that roared in from seaward only feet above the surface in the early morning, came straight for the ship. It struck amidships and the ship exploded and disintegrated in seconds, parts of it raining down on other ships, killing and wounding men aboard them. Not one member of the *Dyche*'s complement of sixty-nine survived.

The convoy of which *Kyle V. Johnson* (Houston, August 1944) was part on 12 January consisted of forty merchant ships and a similar number of LSTs. Nine destroyers made up the escort, and twenty PT boats also voyaged along under the protection of the larger ships' guns. It was dusk when eight Japanese planes attacked the convoy. One dove at the *Johnson* piercing the hull and ploughing through the 'tween-decks where some of the 506 American troops on board were housed. The ensuing fire was soon extinguished, but not before 130 men had died, all but one of them troops. The *Johnson* was able to make her destination safely.

Later that month a tragic event took place with a Naval Liberty. On 29 January the USS *Serpens* (launched at Los Angeles as the *Benjamin N. Cardozo* before being handed over to the Navy and renamed) was loading depth charges when anchored off Lunga Beach, Guadalcanal. Including military stevedores there were nearly 200 men on board when the ship suddenly blew up. There were no survivors. The cause of the explosion is unknown. At least one source has it that the ship might have been sunk in error by a US submarine. Whether or not that Liberty ship incident was a case of friendly fire, the bombing of the *Harrington Emerson* (Portland, Oregon, January 1944) on 13 March 1945 certainly was. The ship was sailing north off the coast of North Borneo when an American bomber mistook her for an enemy. It happened in broad daylight, so one wonders how such a mistake was possible; by that time there were literally hundreds of these ships, all with the same silhouette and appearance from above, plying Western Pacific waters. Two bombs hit the water close alongside, and although the ship received nothing more than superficial damage, no less than eighty-one of those on board sustained shrapnel injuries. It might have been worse had not two American Corsairs flown in to escort the bomber away.

The Japanese may not have had much in the way of minesweeping abilities, but the same criticism cannot be levelled at their minelaying.[5] On 31 March 1945 the *John C. Fremont,* which in March 1942 had been the first ever Liberty to come off the stocks of Henry Kaiser's Calship facility at Los Angeles, struck a mine while moving between piers at Manila. The ship was extensively damaged and had to be beached. There she was written off. On 1 May the *Henry L. Abbott* (Portland, Oregon, August 1943) also struck a mine in Manila Harbour, which blew a hole in the ship's side in way of the engine-room. The blast killed two engineers. The ship was repaired and re-entered service. In July 1949 she was caught in a typhoon at Hong Kong and grounded and was declared a constructive total loss. A third Liberty ship mine victim at Manila was the *Edmund F. Dickens* (Portland, Oregon, September 1943) on 3 May. She struck a mine

---

5. US Naval Technical Mission to Japan, Report S-25, 1950.

right aft which damaged the hull and bent the tail shaft. The damage to the ship was estimated at $100,000. She was towed right across the Pacific to the Panama Canal and then up to New York where, after the expenditure of all those towing costs, she was declared a constructive total loss. On 8 August, just two days before the war in the east ended, a dredging operation was taking place at Manila not far from where the *Casimir Pulaski* (Savannah, July 1943) was berthed. The dredge exploded a mine that damaged the Liberty's bow section and injured two Armed Guards.

In October 1944 the Allied Joint Chiefs of Staff opted for an amphibious assault on the island of Okinawa rather than Formosa (Taiwan), an assault designed to secure a forward air base for the bombing of Japan, and an assembly area for the troops that it was planned would invade the country later in the year. Okinawa, the largest of the Ryukyu Island chain lying between the Japanese island of Kyushu and Formosa, was within 400 miles flying distance of Japan. The assault was codenamed Operation 'Iceberg' and took place on 1 April 1945. It was made by the 3rd Marine Corps which included the veterans who had taken the Central Pacific strongholds of Eniwetok, Guam and Saipan, and the 24th Army Corps up from the Philippines, so bringing ground force elements of Admiral Nimitz's and General MacArthur's forces together for the first time. The supply ships for this huge amphibious operation came from Seabee-built bases on islands all over the Central Pacific, from the Philippines, and even from as far away as Guadalcanal. It was about this time that MacArthur said of the American Merchant Marine, 'They brought us our lifeblood and they paid for it with their own'. Liberty ships were of course, central to the success of these many supply chains.

The island of Okinawa proved to be another happy hunting ground for Japanese pilots, in both conventional and unconventional attacks. Between 30 March and 10 August 1945, eight Liberties were attacked there, four by kamikazes, one by a bomber, and three by torpedo planes. The kamikaze attacks did not result in any sinkings, only damage. One of those ships was the *Mary A. Livermore* (Richmond, November 1943) which has been cited as the last Liberty to be so damaged. That is not correct. She was damaged at 0500 hours on 28 May, and that incident was followed three hours later by another on the *Josiah Snelling* (Richmond, May 1943). But even that was not the last. That 'honour' goes to the *Walter Colton* (Richmond, December 1942) which was attacked by a kamikaze on 11 June.

Two of the aerial torpedo attacks on Liberties at Okinawa resulted in the loss of both ships. The *John A. Rawlins* (Richmond, December 1942) was badly damaged by a torpedo on 17 June. She was still awaiting repairs on 17 September when a typhoon threw her up on to the shore and she was declared a constructive total loss. The *Jack Singer* (Los Angeles, January 1944) was struck by an aerial torpedo off Naha,

Okinawa, on 10 August 1945. The ship was badly damaged and beached. Fortunately none of the crew were killed or sustained injury. If it is an honour to be last at anything, then *Singer* holds the accolade of being the last merchant ship victim of the Second World War, for five days later on 15 August the Japanese capitulated. The ship was refloated, but on 10 September was blown ashore in a typhoon and became a constructive total loss.

As in Europe the war left legacy of mines in Far Eastern waters. (A Second World War minefield exists to this day in the strait leading to the port of Surabaya in Indonesia.) A fortnight after the Japanese capitulation the *Peter White* (Portland, Oregon, October 1943) struck a mine in Filipino waters on 30 August. There were no casualties and the patched up ship made it safely back to Portland, but never sailed again. On the day after that the *Joseph Carrigan* (Portland, Maine, April 1945), one of the last Liberties ever to be constructed, hit a mine in Brunei Bay, Borneo. There was one fatality, an Australian army major who was struck by a lifeboat shaken loose by the explosion. The ship was later repaired at Manila and was put back into service.

Four of the Baltimore-built Liberties lend-leased to Britain were intended to be commissioned into the Royal Navy as Fleet Train Repair Ships. They were HMS *Assistance, Diligence, Hecla* and *Dutiful*. Because the necessary conversion work took a long time, only the first two were ever commissioned into the Royal Navy. That took place at Baltimore in March 1945. The two then sailed for Britain, the *Assistance* making for Devonport, the *Diligence* for Chatham. Lieutenant Commander Russell Linsell RNR (then with the rank of Temporary Lieutenant (E) RN) was the Senior Engineer in *Diligence*. He says the ships had been fitted out with workshops in the holds, comprehensive enough to service the battleships, cruisers and destroyers of the British Pacific Fleet. The workshops were manned by Admiralty civilian staff. 'The workshop complement were young Dockyard mateys in Engine Room Artificer's uniforms and their Divisional officers were Dockyard Foremen and Inspectors wearing wavy stripes with green distinction cloth'.[6] *Diligence* sailed for the Far East in July 1945, only to celebrate VJ-Day at Port Said. Nevertheless the ship carried on and after calling at Colombo and Singapore, arrived at Hong Kong about two weeks after it had been liberated. In February 1946 the ship steamed to Subic Bay in the Philippines where it was handed back to the Americans.

The British Pacific Fleet had operated alongside, but very much as the junior partner to, the American Pacific Fleet during the last months of the war. Within hours of the cessation of hostilities in the East, units of

---

6. Correspondence with Lieutenant Commander R.F. Linsell, 2000.

that fleet were detached to race for Hong Kong. For it had become known to the British that the Americans had secretly negotiated a deal with Generalissimo Chiang Kai-shek that the colony would be handed over to the Chinese rather than back to the British. In addition to warships, British merchant ships were also sent to the colony, with the ostensible purpose of taking food and supplies to the starving populace there, but also to serve notice on the world, and to China and America in particular, that trade and commerce and the governance of the Crown Colony were back as they had been before the Eastern war began. Two Liberty ships managed by the New Zealand Shipping Company were among the first merchant ships to re-enter Hong Kong. The *Samkey* (built as *Carl Thusgaard*, Baltimore, December 1943), Captain A. Hocken, had sailed from Britain carrying RAF personnel and equipment out to Okinawa, but during a call at Eniwetok in the Marshall Islands the news of Japan's surrender came through. She was then diverted to Hong Kong where the airfield equipment came in very useful indeed. The other ship was the *Samesk* (Baltimore, February 1944), Captain J.W.C. Pring. Also carrying RAF equipment, she was in mid-Pacific when the war came to an end and she was diverted to Singapore, becoming the first British merchantman to enter that port after the surrender. After discharging there she proceeded to India to load supplies for Hong Kong. From there she carried 1400 Japanese prisoners of war back to their homeland. We shall be hearing more about those two ships in a later chapter.

Another British Liberty caught up in the Pacific peace process was the *Samstrule* (Baltimore, February 1944), managed by Elders & Fyffes and commanded by Captain Frederick P. Inch. She too, loaded RAF equipment for Okinawa, in her case at Birkenhead in June 1945. N.S. 'Sand' Gurnell was Third Mate and he says that during the loading operations a high-ranking Air Force officer boarded, took a look down No. 4 Hold, decided that he needed more room for his equipment, and ordered 'that thing' to be removed. Says Gurnell, 'unbeknownst to him "that thing" was the propeller shaft tunnel and more important than him'. The ship arrived at Bilbao, Panama Canal, on VJ-Day. There she received orders for Eniwetok, and then on to Leyte Gulf. Short of fresh water, in the latter place the water supply was replenished whilst laying alongside a naval water boat which gloried in the splendidly apposite name of USS *Tits*. Eventually, that RAF cargo too, was discharged at Singapore.[7] The ship's DEMS gunners were also landed at that port, and after that it was back to peace-time cargoes for *Samstrule*. She loaded a cargo of badly-needed rice for Hong Kong at the Thai port of Go Sichang. It was loaded

---

7. Correspondence in 1999 with N.S. Gurnell, who now lives in California.

from barges, and just as one of them came alongside and before the so-called 'shit-shoots' had been rigged over the ship's discharges, shoots that were designed to prevent that sort of thing happening, 'someone flushed a toilet and the whole bit went on to the bags of rice'. Gurnell was sent to find the culprit, and it turned out to be the Chief Engineer. Apparently he belonged to a religious sect which did not believe in taking medicines, including those for relieving constipation. 'He went into a flaming temper when I told him to take care. This was his first success on the toilet since we left Britain three months before. I guess he was entitled to feel chagrin when all hell breaks loose when you've just had your first crap for a long, long time.'

After Hong Kong *Samstrule* recrossed the Pacific and loaded at Vancouver. If the crew thought they were loading for England, they were unlucky. That cargo was taken to South and East Africa, sailing via Cape Horn to save on Panama Canal dues, a sure sign that peace again reigned and that shipowners were already returning to the old parsimonious ways. In fact the ship did not return home until the ship had criss-crossed around the globe, as was the way of tramp ships, earning much needed foreign-exchange currency for war-impoverished Britain. She finally arrived home in February 1947. 'So ended another successful voyage', wrote Sand Gurnell. 'About nineteen months and 43,000 nautical miles at a steady ten knots.'

CHAPTER 21

The Other Allied Liberties

The British Merchant Navy from September 1939, together with the American Merchant Marine from December 1941, bore the brunt of the war at sea because of the size of their fleets. Elsewhere in this book it has been stated that the wartime services of both those organisations have suffered almost total neglect at the hands of historians. Lest this writer be accused of acting similarly over the services of non Anglo-American ships and seamen, this chapter is dedicated to all the other Allied seamen, whether or not they served in Liberty ships, who also did sterling work during the war, many of them paying with their lives whilst doing so. No one should forget, for example, the sacrifices made by the seamen of many nations who served on Panamanian-registered ships, a country that the uninitiated might not usually associate with the Allied cause. Panamanian-flagged ships plied the seas in that cause, including the northern run to Murmansk, from early on in the war. Also to be remembered are those seamen from officially neutral countries who sailed and sometimes died aboard Allied ships, or aboard ships chartered by the Allies from those countries. In that context Swedish seamen come first to mind.

Perhaps the example that best illustrates the gallantry of non Anglo-American seamen, is the incident that involved the Dutch tanker *Ondina*. Manned by Dutch officers, Hong Kong Chinese ratings, and a DEMS gunnery unit consisting of Australians and Britons, she typified the international make-up of many merchant crews in the war. She was sailing in company with a new minesweeper of the Indian navy, HMIS *Bengal*, when on 11 November 1942 in the Indian Ocean she fell in with two large Japanese raiders. She took them on in an engagement that resembles that of the *Stephen Hopkins*. One of the heavily armed raiders was sunk, the other afterwards making off with the survivors. Both *Ondina* and *Bengal* were badly damaged in the engagement but made it safely to port. Three men died aboard *Ondina*, including Captain Willem Horsman and his Chief Engineer.[1]

Liberty ships were transferred to Norway, Russia, Belgium, Greece, China and Holland during the war, in addition to Britain, and in this

---

1. For a fuller description of this engagement see the author's *Life Line* (London 1999).

chapter we follow the stories of some of these ships. Complete lists of all the foreign flag transfers are to be found in Appendix 3.

Norway

We have seen that Britain had a running dispute with the USA over charterparties for their Liberties. The other Allies did not have the same kind of trouble as they received their ships under different arrangements. The Norwegians, for example, received theirs under bare-boat charters, just like the British, but then unlike the British, immediately re-chartered them back to the Americans on what were called 'concurrent time-charter terms'. The ships were then allocated cargoes and routes by the American War Shipping Administration. So, although they flew foreign flags and were foreign manned and operated under Norwegian shipping laws, they were in effect used like units of the American merchant marine. The twelve Liberties transferred to the Norwegian flag, together with the eight tankers and four larger freighters similarly handed over, were managed by Nortraship, the Norwegian Shipping Mission, initially based in London but then in New York, which during the war took over the management of all Norwegian ships.

The non-Liberty ships all survived the war, but two of the Liberties were lost, the first one on her maiden voyage. The *Christian Michelsen* (built as *John M.T. Finney* at Baltimore) was handed over to a Norwegian crew under Captain Jens Ugland on 31 May 1943. She sailed from New York in convoy on 1 September with a cargo of bombs and ammunition bound for Bizerte. The convoy reached Gibraltar safely, but on 26 September when within 80 miles of its destination, it was attacked by *U-410*, Commander Fenski. It was evening time, and after firing a fan of torpedoes Fenski stayed at periscope depth long enough to see the characteristic fireworks display made by an ammunition ship as it blows up. It took less than a minute for the *Michelsen* to be blown apart, and it is a miracle that any of the fifty men on board survived. But four men did get off although only three of them lived to tell the tale.[2]

Gunner Ole A. Olsen was sleeping aft when the torpedo hit.

> I jumped out of my bunk and tried to get out of the cabin which was filled with smoke. I was at first stopped at the door by heat and fire, but the sea washed in and put out the worst of the fire so I could get out. There were continuous explosions as long as I was on board. I found my way to the rail and dived into the sea. I saw a float and climbed aboard. At 2000 hours I was picked up by an escort ship.

Able Seamen Einar Melbye and Henry Erlandsen were on duty on the after gun platform when the torpedo struck. Melbye later reported that

---

2. Jon Rustang Hegland, *Notraships flate* (Oslo, n.d.).

there had been no warning of the attack. He said that after diving into the sea he was drawn down and had to fight his way back to the surface. He came up close to Erlandsen who was injured and jammed amidst some floating debris. Melbye managed to prise his friend free and then pull him up on to some timber floating nearby. But shortly afterwards Erlandsen died and fell back into the water. Melbye himself was plucked from the sea about an hour later by an escort ship. The last survivor was Ordinary Seaman Knut Egil Berg. He was asleep in his bunk when the explosion blew in the door of his cabin. The next thing he knew he was in the water helping Gunner Olsen on to a float. (Commander Fenski's *U-410* was destroyed in a U.S. Army Air Force attack on the port of Toulon on 11 March 1944.[3])

The second of the two Norwegian Liberty casualties was the *Sverre Helmersen.* Built as the *William Hodson* at Baltimore in April 1944, on being handed over to the Norwegians on the 22nd of that month she was renamed after a Norwegian patriot executed by the Germans earlier in the war. The standard catalogue of Liberty Ships states that this vessel struck a mine in the Dover Strait on 23 April 1945, but that is incorrect. The ship, under the command of Captain August Christian Konow, was off Ramsgate on the night of 22 April when at 2306 hours she was hit and badly damaged by a torpedo from *U-2329,* Lieutenant Commander Schlott. There were no casualties and the ship was towed into Dover and eventually to Falmouth where she was declared a constructive total loss. The hulk was scrapped at Zeebrugge in 1948.

Another of the Norwegian Liberties saw little action during the war but did not fare so well soon afterwards. The *Roald Amundsen* (launched as *William Strong* at Baltimore, April 1943 and handed over on the 24th of that month) made several crossings of the Atlantic, and also carried military cargoes between various Mediterranean ports. Gunner Oddvin Liseth joined the ship at Baltimore and was impressed by his new ship which was much better than his last one, the old *Skottland* dating from 1920 and which had been torpedoed from under him on 17 May 1942 in the Bay of Fundy. 'The *Amundsen* even had a spare barrel for the 3-inch gun in case the original one got too hot,' he recalls. He, along with the other members of the crew, had only one criticism of the ship. 'The crew quarters had not been panelled i.e. no insulation over the steel except for some sprayed cork, and this was in direct violation of hard-won rights of Norwegian seaman, and so had to be righted! Seaman's rights were few enough and not to be trampled on! Although it nearly took a sit-down strike, the matter was taken care of.'[4]

---

3. Eric Grove, *The Defeat of the Enemy Attack on Shipping* (Aldershot 1997).
4. Correspondence with Oddvin Liseth, February 2000. He became an American citizen in the 1950s.

Able Seamen Lief Vetlesen signed on the *Amundsen* at Cardiff, South Wales, on 30 October 1943 and stayed with it for seven months. 'During that time we did not experience any enemy attacks', he reports. The ship's last wartime voyage was to northern Norway after that part of the country had been liberated by Russian troops, reports Ingvald Wahl who was another of the Norwegian Navy gunners on board. The ship was voyaging in that same part of Norway again on 20 November 1947 when she struck a reef off the port of Skudeneshavn. All the crew got safely ashore but the ship was lost.

Another of the Norwegian Liberties built at Baltimore was the *George M. Shriver,* named for a late vice-president of the Baltimore & Ohio Railroad Company. She became the *Viggo Hansteen* on 20 October 1943, under the command of Captain Torbjorn Thorsen. Viggo Hansteen was another of the Norwegian patriots executed by the Germans in 1941. Kornelius Korneliussen joined the ship at Baltimore as one of her six naval gunners under the charge of Anker Kristiansen. Kornelius had served in the Norwegian merchant navy since leaving school in 1938. Having signed off his third ship at New York in 1941 he volunteered for the Royal Norwegian Navy and was sent to Lunenburg, Nova Scotia for gunnery training. He went on to serve as gunner on a freighter and after further training at Trevors Island, New York, was sent to Baltimore to join the *Hansteen.* The ship's complement, including the gunners, numbered forty-seven, much more in line with British manning figures than American. Except for five Canadians, all were Norwegian (although two of those were domiciled in England). The ship's first voyage was through the Mediterranean and Suez to Bandar Shapur carrying supplies for Russia, and then back to New York, and it was largely uneventful. The second voyage, made to Alexandria, was not.

As part of Convoy UGS-28, on the night of 20 April 1944 off the North African coast, those aboard the *Hansteen* were close witnesses to the blowing up of the troop-carrying Liberty *Paul Hamilton* with the loss of all 580 persons on board (see Chapter 13), the sinking of the British freighter *Royal Star,* and the damaging of the Liberties *Samite* and *Stephen F. Austin,* all by aerial torpedoes and all in the space of a few minutes. Gunnery Officer Kristiansen reported that a violent explosion close to the *Hansteen* 'made her vibrate rather heavily'. After discharging at Alexandria, the ship returned to the States, this time to Norfolk, Virginia, where she was joined by Able Seaman Leif Fosse. Another new crew member to join there was Second Radio Officer Maude Steane, an attractive Canadian girl on her very first voyage. The Russian merchant service apart, women 'sailors' were a rarity in Allied merchant fleets at that time except for those serving as stewardess, nurses, and the occasional doctor on passenger and troopships. Apart from the Russians, the Norwegian merchant navy was the only one among the Allied fleets to permit women radio operators, and it had less than a handful. It is unfortunate that in Maude Steane's case that policy was to lead to tragedy.

At Norfolk, then at nearby Newport News, and then at Charleston, the *Hansteen* loaded a cargo of ammunition and high explosives below decks, and a number of crated glider planes as deck cargo. In view of what they had witnessed during the previous voyage, it is unlikely that Captain Thorsen and his crew looked upon the below-decks cargo with aplomb. But the ship made it safely to the Mediterranean by early August 1944. The gliders were discharged at Naples and about 300 American soldiers were 'loaded' in their stead for the short, 150-mile voyage north to Piombino Roads. Leif Fosse says that there the ammunition cargo was discharged into DUKWs by American Army stevedores, 'who were throwing bombs and shells all around the deck, so that some even fell back into the holds'. When remonstrated with, and told they might well blow up the ship if they were not careful, 'they answered they didn't care about that, for they had orders to unload 800 tons a day'.[5]

During the voyage Gunnery Officer Anker Kristiansen had apparently made advances towards Maude Steane which were spurned. On the evening of 9 August Kristiansen went ashore and from all accounts did some heavy drinking. On his return to the ship he somehow lured Maude into his cabin. No one knows exactly what happened after that, but at some juncture Kristiansen shot Maude through the left temple with his pistol and then shot himself. The shots apparently went unheard, and Kornelius Korneliussen found the bodies some time later when routinely checking the ship's blackout precautions. Kristiansen was buried in the American cemetery at nearby Follonica. It is likely that Maude Steane's body was taken back to Canada.[6]

The ship transported some 200 German prisoners of war back to Naples before returning once more to the States. That voyage was followed by several more North Atlantic crossings during one of which, in April 1945, the crew witnessed the sinking of the Liberty *Cyrus H. McCormick* and a British freighter. Then in June 1945 the *Hansteen* was the first Norwegian-flagged vessel to arrive in post-war Norway, and the reception at Bergen afforded Captain Thorsen's ship was nothing short of rapturous. Most of the crew members had not seen their homeland for over five years.

In October 1946 after it had been technically but not physically 'handed back' to the US Government, the *Viggo Hansteen* was purchased by the Norwegians, eventually becoming the property of A/S Asplund, a shipping line based at Moss, a small port south of Oslo. The ship was

5. Correspondence with Leif Fosse, February 2000.
6. Correspondence with Kornelius Korneliussen, February-April, 2000.

then used in world-wide tramping. She went aground off the port of Otago, New Zealand in April 1952, but no great damage was done. In the following year she was sold to Greek shipping interests, becoming the *Alkimos*, although until 1959 she traded under the Costa Rican flag. In that year she was transferred to the Greek registry. Beginning in March 1963 the ship had a run of misfortune. On that date she struck the Beagle Island reef north of Fremantle, Western Australia, damaging the bottom plating and the propeller. A few days later she floated free of the reef and managed to reach Fremantle safely. From that port she was taken in tow by the tug *Pacific Reserve*, bound for Hong Kong, but only a day out the tow parted in heavy weather and the ship drifted ashore on the 31 May 1963. Two months later an attempt was made to refloat her but it failed. In February 1964 the tug *Pacific Star* arrived and managed to pull her into deep water. After being pumped dry, a second attempt was due to be made to tow the ship to Hong Kong, only to be thwarted again, this time by legal action. The ship was arrested on account of moneys owed to the Bank of America and in consequence was anchored off the nearby Eglington Rocks. Two of the Filipino crew of the *Pacific Star* were placed aboard as ship watchers, and the pair were still there when on 2 May the anchor chain parted and the ship went ashore again.

It seems that the Filipino seamen had not much cared for being left alone on the ship, and certainly they did not want to stay aboard any longer. In order to ensure that, they started some stories about seeing a ghost on board, stories that were taken up and developed by local newspaper reporters who were out for a good headline, and later by other writers who should have known better. One of the latter even suggested that the ghost may have been that of the gallant Viggo Hansteen himself. One can only imagine what tales those writers might have come up with had they known about the case of the unfortunate Maude Steane.

The *Alkimos* was finally abandoned as a constructive total loss. Over the years since 1964 the battering effects of the sea and the ravages of corrosion have broken up the hulk until only small portions of it remain visible above water. However, enough is left for any seamen from the old days to recognise her for what she once was.

Belgium

The Belgians received a total of seven Liberties between 1943 and 1945, but only five were brand new from the yards. All survived the war. They were operated by Cie Maritime Belge on behalf of the Belgian Government in exile. Until being handed over to the Belgians in 1945, two of the ships spent the first months of their lives sailing under their original names and under the American flag. They were the *George P. Garrison* (Houston, July 1943) which became the *Belgian Liberty*, and the *Richard Stockton* (Richmond, August 1942) which became the *Belgian Loyalty.* Both were handed back to the United States in 1947.

The *Belgian Unity* was also handed back in 1947. It had once been intended that this ship's American name would be *Bert Williams*, but that was changed for some reason to *Earl A. Bloomquist*, the original name then going to another vessel from the same yard at Portland, Maine. However, when the ship was finally launched in November 1944, the ceremony was carried out under its Belgian name, with sponsorship being carried out by Mrs. Sengier, wife of a prominent Belgian financier in New York. The ship's first master was Captain Jean Prie.

Of the remaining four only one was actually launched under its Belgian name. She was the *Belgian Tenacity* built at Portland, Maine in April 1944. The other three were the *Belgian Dynasty* (launched as *Harry A. Garfield*, Portland, Maine, July 1943), the *Belgian Equality* (*Richard A.Van Pelt*, Brunswick, February 1945) and the *Belgian Amity* (*Lawrence T. Sullivan*, Portland, Maine, April 1945). In 1947 all four of these vessels were purchased by Cie Maritime Belge.[7]

The Netherlands

Two Liberties were handed over to Dutch crews during the war. The first was the *Mohlengraaf* built at Richmond as the *Mary M. Dodge* in September 1943. For reasons that have not been recorded, it seems that this ship sailed under the Stars and Stripes and not under the Dutch flag. The other vessel did sail under the Dutch flag. She was launched at Portland, Maine, also in September 1943 as the *Tobias Lear.* On being handed over to a Dutch crew she became the *Fort Orange.* Both these ships survived the war.[8]

Greece

The Greeks received thirteen Liberties during the war years. All were transferred immediately after being launched under their original American names. The first two handed over, both at Portland, Maine, in September 1943, were the *Ameriki* (previously *William H. Todd*) and the *Hellas* (previously *William De Witt Hyde*). Those new Greek names appropriately commemorated the two participant countries in this particular Lend-Lease arrangement.

Only one of the thirteen did not survive the war. She was the *Eleftheria* launched at Houston in November 1944 as the *I.B. Perrin.* On 23 March 1945 she struck a mine just after leaving the Schelde Estuary for the Thames. She went aground off Ostend, broke in two and was written off as a total loss.

---

7. From information supplied by Cie Maritime Belge.
8. Information from Dick Schouten.

Some of the others did not do so well post-war after they had been purchased by the Greeks. The *John C. Preston* (New Orleans, January 1945) became the *Hydra* on being handed over and subsequently became the *Kostas Michalos*. Under that name she was carrying a cargo of wood pulp from North Russia to Calais, when on 26 October 1962 she went ashore close to the French port. Three weeks later she broke in two. Another unlucky one was the *Navarchos Konturiotis* built as the *Cyril G. Hopkins* (Houston, November 1944). Under that same name she was owned by I.K. Karras when on 20 October 1964 she went aground off Mar del Plata with a cargo of wheat which had been destined for Marseilles. She also broke in two.[9]

Russia

After Britain, Soviet Russia was the largest recipient of Liberty ships, getting a total of forty-three. The intended figure had been forty-one but two were added to compensate for two lost soon after delivery. Three of the ships were Liberty tankers. (Much of the information in this Russian section is appearing here in the English language for the first time.) The forty-three Liberty ships formed but a small proportion of the total of over 900 ships that were transferred by the other Allies to the Soviet Union during the war. Most of the others were naval ships, and most were American, many of them being small craft such as PT boats and landing craft. The largest of all the ships transferred was the battleship HMS *Royal Sovereign,* renamed *Archangelsk;* the next largest was the four-stacker cruiser USS *Milwaukee,* renamed *Murmansk*. Four submarines were included, three British and one American. On the merchant shipping side, over and above the Liberty ships, fifty-seven American cargo vessels dating from around the time of the First World War were transferred, together with ten old tankers. The transfer of the old cargo vessels began with the *West Modus* – renamed *Argun* – on 20 November 1942. That ship dated from 1919 and had been built by Northwest Steel.

The Russian Liberties came under the management of an organisation called Sovtorgflot, which ran every Soviet merchant ship. This organisation had four operational divisions, the Far East based at Vladivostok, the Black Sea, the Baltic, and the North based at Archangel. Forty-one of the Russian Liberties spent their entire war careers running the supply route between the United States and Soviet Siberian ports and therefore came under the control of the Soviet Far East State Sea Shipping Division. It made logistical sense, therefore, for all these ships to have emanated from American west coast yards. In fact, without exception and including the two odd ones to be mentioned later, all forty-three ships were constructed at west coast yards run by Henry Kaiser. Although these ships

---

9. Information from Christos E. Dounis, Hon. Head of Hellenic Coast Guard.

were transferred under Lend-Lease terms, most of them were not handed back after the war or paid for. But three were handed back, and two had been allocated on a non-returnable basis, as we shall see. The first Russian-flagged Liberty was the *Krasnogvardeyets*, formerly the *Charles S. Fairchild*. Built at Richmond, the handing over ceremony took place on 28 January 1943 at San Francisco, after which she loaded and sailed for Vladivostok.

The only Russian Liberty to suffer damage due to enemy action along that North Pacific route was the Richmond-built *Odessa*, formerly the *Mary Cassatt*. Handed over on 31 May 1943 she was on a voyage from Akutan in the Aleutian Islands to Petropavlovsk on the Kamchatka peninsular on 3 October 1943, when she was either torpedoed or struck a mine, probably the latter. She was holed aft but remained afloat. After temporary repairs she returned to the States where proper repairs were carried out and she was soon back in service. The loss of the Richmond-constructed *Valeri Chkalov* (formerly the *Alexander Baranof*), which sustained a structural failure and broke in two in heavy weather in the North Pacific on 12 December 1943, has been described in Chapter 7. Following that incident, on the last day of 1943 in fact, the Americans replaced her with the Portland, Oregon-built *Grant P. Marsh* which became *Valeri Chkalov II*.

Even earlier than that incident another Russian Liberty had broken in two, but on that occasion it came about through grounding. She was the *Kherson*, built at Richmond as the *Joseph C. Avery* and handed over on 3 June 1943. She was on her maiden voyage when on 4 July 1943 she went ashore at Asatcha Bay on the south-west coast of Kamchatka, so badly damaging the bottom plating at the fore end, that Russian salvagers reported that she had taken in close to 2000 tons of water. On 18 July large cracks developed on both sides of the ship, and five days later she split in two. The two sections remained afloat and were towed by tugs of the Soviet Pacific Fleet Rescue Service to Petropavlovsk, arriving on 30/31 July, and there they remained. On 15 October 1949 the damaged fore end was handed over to the Kamchatski-Tchukotsk Shipping Company for use as a ship-repair base. Another damage casualty along this route was the *Dekabrist* (formerly *E.H. Harriman*, Portland, Oregon, 10 March 1943) which was damaged in heavy weather on 29 January 1944 on a voyage from Akutan to Vladivostok. That damage was soon repaired.

Upon the capitulation of Italy in 1943 the Russians had expected to be allocated a few of the ships of the Italian Navy in some recompense for the actions of the Italian troops that had fought alongside the Germans on the Russian front. But those ships were not forthcoming. Instead, and in an attempt to keep the Russians quiet, the United States and Britain agreed to transfer some of their own warships to the Russian flag during

1944. That failed to placate the Russians and so, as an added sop, two American-flagged Liberties that had voyaged north to Murmansk as parts of Convoy JW-57 in February 1944 were gifted to them. These did not come under Lend-Lease arrangements and so were not required to be returned to the USA after the war. Both ships were handed over on 5 April 1944, one at Murmansk, the other at Archangel. The first was the *Charles Gorden Curtis* (Portland, Oregon, November 1942) which became the *Sergei Kirov*. Under the management of the Soviet North State Shipping Division she served out the remainder of the war in the White, Barents, and Kara Seas. On 6 November 1946 this ship was awarded a merit flag by the National Committee Sea Fleet for its war work, and that was followed six days later by a memorial plaque presented by the Soviet Sea Ministry. On 14 February the ship was transferred to the Baltic area and operated there until 11 November 1971 when she was scrapped at Avila in Spain. The other ship in the 1944 transaction was the *John Langdon* (Los Angeles, June 1942) which at Archangel became the *Tbilisi*. On the 30 December 1944 whilst carrying a military cargo from Kurilsk Bay to Petchenga, just west of the Kola Inlet, she was torpedoed by *U-956*. The explosion broke the ship in two and the bow section immediately sank. A Russian tug took the after part in tow and safely reached Murmansk.

One of the incidents related in the chapter on the North Russia convoys was the torpedoing on 14 February 1945 of the *Horace Gray* near Murmansk, the badly damaged Liberty then being towed by a Russian tug and beached at Tyuva Bay where the Americans declared her a constructive total loss. We heard how the Chief Officer of the ship reported that in his opinion she had been abandoned too soon. Perhaps he was right, for Russian records show that the forward end of the ship had later been salved by them. In 1958 at Archangel, that forward end was joined to the salved after end of the *Tbilisi* by the shipbuilding firm of Krasnaya Kuznicza. In the following year this 'new' ship joined the Soviet North State fleet under the name *Tbilisi*. This means that in effect the United States had transferred an additional half ship to the Russians, but without knowing about it! In 1964 *Tbilisi* was transferred to the Arctic Ice-breaking Fleet. By the 13 March 1968 she was plying the Sea of Azov as part of the Black Sea fleet. On 20 January 1977 she was scrapped in Russia.

The Americans did know about another of their wrecks made use of by the Russians. As we saw in Chapter 11, the *Horace Bushnell* as part of Convoy JW-65 to Murmansk on 20 March 1945 was torpedoed by *U-995*, after which she was taken in tow by two Russian tugs and beached near Toroborski. The Americans declared the ship a constructive total loss, but on top of that officially made the wreck over to the Russians. She was later refloated and towed to Murmansk. After the war she was rebuilt as a fish-carrier and renamed *Pamyati Kirova*. She ended her days at a Russian scrapyard in 1978.

The joining-up at Archangel of parts of two different Liberties to form the *Tbilisi* was not the first such operation conducted in Soviet yards. The name *Valeri Chkalov* must have been rather an unlucky one, for on 5 March 1951, the second ship to hold that name suffered a similar fate to her predecessor. Caught in a storm off the west coast of Kamchatka on that date, she broke in two. The stern part sank, but the fore end was towed to the port of Petropavlovsk on the east coast of that peninsular. Laying there ever since July 1943, as mentioned above, were the two parts of the *Kherson*. So when the fore end of *Valeri Chkalov* arrived it was joined to the after end of *Kherson* and sailed again under the former name. The 'new' ship was probably used only in Far Eastern waters. She is mentioned in Russian records as still operating there in 1964. On 30 December 1967 she was deleted from the Russian register and scrapped.

There was yet another Russian Liberty ship reconstruction operation, but in this case the accidents to both ships concerned took place after the war. The *General Vatutin* (formerly the *Jay Cooke*, Richmond, June 1944) was badly damaged on 19 December 1947 by an explosion on board whilst unloading at Nagaevo Bay, Siberia. The ship sank, and although she was salvaged on 22 December 1948, she was deleted from the Russian register. The second vessel was the *Briansk*, formerly the Richmond-built *William E. Ritter,* which had been transferred to the Russians on 11 May 1944. On 9 December 1950 she ran aground in shallow water off Sakhalin Island whilst attempting to assist another vessel that was in difficulties. Whilst being towed off the *Briansk* broke in two, but both parts were salved. According to Russian records the fore part of this ship was then joined to the stern part of a ship 'similar to the *Briansk*'. Where did that unnamed stern part come from? A study of the Russian records indicate that the only possible source was the *General Vatutin*. The 'new' *Briansk* was still sailing into the early 1970s. On 23 July 1974 she was scrapped at Vladivostok.

The three Liberty tankers, all of them constructed at Los Angeles in either October or November 1943, had been transferred to the so-called Soviet Purchasing Commission at San Francisco during July/August 1944. The *Thomas A. Gallaudet* was renamed *Maikop*, the *Charlotte P. Gilman* became the *Apsherson*, and the *Paul Dunbar* was called the *Byelgorod*. They were used to convey petroleum products from the United States to the Kamchatkan port of Petropavlovsk. Two of them were handed back to the American authorities at Yokohama on 24 February 1948, and the third on 1 March 1948.

The war with Japan came to an end on 10 August 1945 after the dropping of the atom bombs on Hiroshima on the 6th, and Nagasaki on the 9th. In between those dates, on 8 August, Russia found a new task for some of the Liberty ships of its Far East fleet. At the Yalta conference held in the previous February, an agreement had been signed by Roosevelt, Churchill and Stalin, detailing the conditions under which the USSR would declare war on Japan. At that time Germany had yet to be beaten and the atom bomb, a deeply-hidden secret, was still being developed. American planners at the time of Yalta estimated that after Germany was beaten, a further eighteen months would be needed to defeat Japan. The Americans, who would take the brunt of any attack on the Japanese islands, also estimated that Allied casualties might run to a million men, and a similar number of Japanese. It was considered that the advent of Russia into the war with Japan, might reduce the casualties, for if Russia was to throw its weight against the Japanese army based in Manchuria, for instance, those troops would not be available to protect the home islands. Of course all this presented Stalin at Yalta with a golden opportunity to extort concessions and, as was his wont, he used the opportunity to the full. In fact Stalin's bargaining power was a bit of a sham, for Russian interests in the Far East in 1945 were no less than they had been in 1900 and in all the years in between, and would most assuredly have brought Russia into the war against Japan without any special concessions.

The conditions exacted by Stalin included the restoration of Russian rights taken away under the Treaty of Portsmouth (the one in New Hampshire, USA, not the one in 'old' Hampshire, England) of 1905, by which she had been forced to give up South Sakhalin to the Japanese. Stalin also demanded that he be given the Kurile Islands, which had never been Russian. These conditions were agreed between Stalin and Roosevelt, Churchill not being consulted until after the event, one of the earlier indications that Roosevelt, not to mention Stalin, was busy downgrading Britain as a major power. Possibly in order to save face Churchill was later to write of that agreement, which he had merely been asked to approve, 'To us [Britain] the problem was remote and secondary. It would have been wrong for us to get in their way unless we had some very solid reason'.

It must be said that Roosevelt made his agreement with Stalin in the face of opposition from some of his advisors as their later writings show. And in the event, the use of the atom bombs made the agreement superfluous, but nevertheless it stood, and it laid the ground for much future trouble in the area. On 8 August the Soviets declared war on Japan, and thenceforth claimed full belligerent rights in the East, even though they had not done much to deserve them. Russian troops advanced into Manchuria and that territory was fully under their control within two weeks. After three weeks of fighting, Admiral Ivan Yumashev and his Russian Pacific Fleet occupied the Kuriles, for good measure also taking the Habomai Islands immediately off the north coast of Hokkaido.

Despite American protests, the Russians claimed the Habomais as part of the Kuriles, which they had never been. Just before the Japanese surrender on the 10th, Russian marines landed at Chongjin in northern Korea, and on the 25th, at Wongsa farther down the coast. The Americans followed that by landing troops in the southern part of Korea and accepted the surrender of all Japanese south of the 38th Parallel; the Russians accepted the surrender of those north of that line. So, although the greatest war the world has ever known had just come to an end, the seeds of the Korean conflict had already been sown.

Seven Russian Liberty ships took part in the operations against Japanese-held territories as troop transports. The *Jean Javres* (*Thomas Nast*), *Nakhoda* (*Irving W. Pratt*) and the *Stalingrad* (*Thomas F. Flaherty*) landed troops on Sakhalin. The *Sutchan* (*Jose Sepulveda*) landed hers in North Korea and whilst doing so on 15 August, struck a mine and was damaged. The Russian authorities must have considered this ship's work as particularly noteworthy for on 24 March 1948 she was awarded a special merit award plaque by the Sea Ministry. The *Novorossisk* (*Edward Eggleston*), the *Emilian Pugachev* (*Louis Agassiz*) and the *General Panilov* (*George E. Goodfellow*) took part in the attacks on the Habomai Islands. One of the above-named ships, the *Emilian Pugachev*, is shown in American records as having suffered deck and side cracking during a voyage in ballast back to the United States on 5 January 1944. Not long after the war, the *Mikhail Kutuzov* (*Graham Taylor*, Portland, Oregon, 28 March 1943) during a voyage between Murmansk and New York on 19 March 1946 also suffered cracking according to Lloyd's List, and was repaired. In January 1958 on a voyage from Vancouver to Nakhoda the *General Panilov* suffered the same malady, in her case in the vicinity of No. 1 hold. She made port and was repaired and carried on trading until she was scrapped in Russia on 26 September 1976.

The last surviving Russian Liberty, which was probably also the last floating working Liberty in the world, was the *Alexander Nevsky*, formerly *Harry W. Corbett* built at Portland, Oregon, and handed over to the Russians on 6 April 1943. On Christmas Eve 1943, whilst voyaging in ballast in heavy seas and a Force 9 wind, she suffered cracks in the deck and hull plates in the vicinity of No. 2 hatch. They were repaired during her next call in the United States, and certainly that had no bad effect on the ship's longevity. After the war some of the Russian Liberties in the Far East were transferred to other sea areas, but that does not seem to have applied to the *Nevsky* and it is likely that she spent the whole of her trading life sailing out of Vladivostok and other Siberian ports. On 26 September 1973 she was taken out of sea service 'for technical reasons', which probably means that she could not by that date be economically brought up to sea-going standards. The ship was moved to the First River in Amur Bay near Vladivostok, and there became a training ship for

Russian seamen and stevedores. She was used for that work into 1997, but lack of proper maintenance over many years at last had taken its toll. Early in 1998 she was towed to a breaker's yard in the Republic of South Korea.[10]

China

Four Liberty ships flew the Chinese flag during the war. All four carried Chinese crewman but the officers were American. Each ship also carried an American Armed Guard unit. The first of the four to be handed over, and the only one to be launched under its Chinese name, was the *Sun Yat-sen* (Sausilito, April 1943). She survived the war as did the *Chung Shan* (*Henry M. Teller*, Richmond, September 1943) and the *Chung Tung* (*William Hodson*, Baltimore, June 1944). Generalissimo Chiang Kai-shek had his formal name perpetuated with *Chung Cheng* (*Murat Halstead*, Richmond, September 1943). That ship did not survive the war. Managed by American President Lines, she was on passage from Cochin to Aden and the United States with a full cargo of ilmenite sand, when just before midnight on 3 February 1944, she was struck on the port side by a torpedo. It came from *U-188*, Lieutenant Commander Ludden. The torpedo track was sighted by a gunner, but too late to save the ship which sank in under five minutes. Six of the American officers including the captain were lost, along with thirteen of the thirty-three Chinese crew members, and one Armed Guardsman. The most senior man to survive was Lieutenant (jg) C.J. Kennedy of the Armed Guard, who later made the official report of the sinking. The survivors were picked up from rafts on the following day by the British freighter *Mahadevi* and landed at Aden.[11]

France

The French allocation of thirteen ships is of particular interest. Although the ships were handed over under Lend-Lease terms, it did not take place until June 1945, a month after the war in Europe had ended. It may be that this late handover was due to the undoubted shortage of Free-French merchant seamen. However, it is also possible that in part at least, it reflected President Roosevelt's well-known antipathy towards General Charles de Gaulle. When handed over, the French ships retained their original American names until purchased by French shipping lines in 1947. (It is also of interest to note that Britain transferred twenty-four of its Empire ships to France, but those too were transferred only after the end of the war in Europe. Mr. Churchill did not much care for de Gaulle either, though that may not have affected this particular issue.)

---

10. Information from Vladimir Chepelev.
11. ADM199/526, PRO, Kew.

In the immediate post-war allocation of shipping space to France it seems that the United States Government was not at all keen on helping the French return to their colonies in Indo-China. A message dated 22 October 1945 sent to Washington from London, mentioned eight Victory ships which had sailed from the States and were being made available to the French authorities at Marseilles. The French had asked for two of them to be diverted 'into Oran en route to Marseilles each to lift approximately 100 tons of wine . . . owing to the extreme shortage of wine at Marseilles'. It afterwards came to light that the wine was not required for Marseilles directly, but to store vessels sailing from that port which were carrying French troops to Saigon. Not only that, the French then asked for another two ships to be similarly diverted, as twice the original quantity of wine was now required. It seems the Americans were not amused.[12]

12. MT59/639, PRO, Kew.

PART III: AFTER THE WAR

CHAPTER 22

The Liberty Ship's Role in Peacetime

Although the end of the Second World War brought to an end the sinking of ships by submarines and aircraft (although mines were to remain a hazard for many years to come), there was the aftermath of the war to contend with. The period from the summer of 1945 until, say, 1947, became a transitional time for merchant shipping. Many of the wartime logistical operations conducted by the major Allied nations had to be maintained to keep the Occupation Forces supplied, although the frequency of those operations was much reduced. On the other hand, the immediate post-war years brought new logistical problems and needs which were direct consequences of the war. And against that background, traditional trading was resumed.

Immediately after the war hungry populations around the world had to be fed, including those of erstwhile enemies. Prisoners of war from both sides required repatriation. Allied armies, except those needed in the occupation forces, had to be transported home. There were several trouble spots, the Dutch East Indies and Greece being two of them, where nationalist or communist guerrillas were taking advantage of the situation to stir up trouble, and which in way or another, involved Allied forces. The stationing of so many American servicemen in Britain, Australia and elsewhere during the war, meant that there were many GI brides to be shipped back to the States. The number of such ladies was to grow after 'non-fraternisation with the enemy' rules were relaxed and soldiers in occupied countries began to get to know their 'hosts' a little better. Some ships were required for more sombre services. The US Army Memorial Service converted some to carry home the bodies of the dead, each ship being fitted to carry 6000 caskets. Other ships were required to make one final voyage, their holds loaded to the coamings with munitions that were no longer needed and for which officialdom had decreed a watery grave.

As a backdrop to all the operations which were direct legacies of the war, normal world trade was being resumed. At the centre of all this merchant ship activity was the ubiquitous Liberty. If there were any ports left in the world that had not been visited by a Liberty in wartime, the demands of normal trade soon rectified the omissions; and of course, the Liberty was now to be seen in German and Japanese ports. Well before the cessation of hostilities, the post-war shipping problem posed by the sheer size of the American merchant fleet, came under discussion and was being argued about on both sides of the Atlantic, as we saw in an earlier chapter. The United States with a merchant fleet that amounted to only some 8.7 million tons in 1939, had by 1946 multiplied almost five-fold to 41 million tons, which was more than all other nations put together.[1]

In consequence the US Government faced a dilemma. On the one hand American maritime interests which, along with the fleet itself, had grown apace during the war years, had to be protected. Not least amongst those interests, and certainly the most vociferous of them all, were the maritime trade unions. On the other hand, the Truman Administration knew that if it tried to keep all the war-built tonnage for America's own use, the decision would have met with world-wide condemnation and opposition. Such opposition would have thrown world trade into utter confusion for some years until overseas shipbuilding could play catch-up. Not only that, and perhaps in the end it was this argument that was the clincher, the Americans knew that such an enormous merchant fleet would need a whole range of subsidies, much as it had during the war itself. It would be a costly business. There was another problem, a lesser one, in that the greater part of the wartime construction was the utilitarian Liberty ship which had not been built to last, and no one in 1946 could have foreseen that some of these 'sea scows' would still be trading thirty years later; so, the question was, if some ships were going to be sold to foreigners, which should they be, the Liberty or the comparatively well-found Victory? In the end most of the ships sold were Liberties, but later some Victory ships were also put up for sale.

Whilst the debate continued, the US Government did not demand the immediate return of those Liberties loaned under Lend-Lease arrangements. The end result of the American deliberations was the Merchant Ship Sales Act of 1946 which outlined the conditions under which wartime construction could be sold off to American shipping interests and to overseas companies. Immediately upon the signing of that Act into law, matters began to move. The Americans asked Britain for the return of the Liberties that had been Lend-Leased, although the return dates were necessarily open-ended for the ships were scattered all over the world. The United States also entered into negotiations with a number of nations over the sale of blocks of Liberties, including its erstwhile enemy Italy. Britain was placed at the bottom of the pecking order, one supposes

---

1. Figures from S.G. Sturmey, *British Shipping* (London 1962).

because American shipping interests were demanding that Britain not be given a fast-lane opportunity to regain its pre-war preponderance. This 'Britain last' attitude was only belatedly relaxed after the American Government was forcibly reminded that one of the wartime agreements between the two leading Allies had been that America would largely concentrate its shipbuilding efforts on merchant ships, whilst Britain would largely concentrate on warship construction, which at the time the agreement had been reached, made sublime sense.

The effect of the magnanimous, if that is what it was, decision to permit the sale of some American ships to foreign owners, was soon somewhat diminished by other legislation. The US Foreign Assistance Act of 1948 decreed that half of all American aid cargoes (made under the famous Marshall Plan), should be carried in American ships. Perhaps that was not so bad, even reasonable, considering that Stateside shipping interests were demanding protection. But in the following year further legislation decreed that the 50 per cent must be computed separately for different trades, with the end result that the ratio carried by American ships was more like 60 per cent.

One of the nations that was given a much easier time than Britain over buying American ships was Greece. During 1946/47 the Greeks were permitted to purchase a block of 100 ships comprising ninety-eight Liberties and two coasters. The twelve surviving Greek Lend-Leased Liberties from the war years were included in this deal. This purchase is of particular interest because historically it marks the beginning of what the Greeks call 'the shipping miracle' which culminated in that country becoming one of the world's foremost maritime nations. It was the foundation stone of the fortunes made by several Greek shipping magnates including Onassis, Coulandris and Niarchos. Stavros Niarchos, for example, purchased two Liberty ships at that time. They were the *James L. Ackerson* (Jacksonville, March 1944) which became the *Captain J. Matarangas*, and the *Thomas L. Haley* (Jacksonville, February 1945, the last Liberty to be launched from that yard) which became the *Captain K. Papazoglou*. From such acorns mighty oaks were to grow, and in the not too distant future Greek shipping interests were to own more Liberties, the ship at the heart of the Greek miracle, than anyone else. It has been estimated that the overall number of Liberties owned by Greek interests was about 800 although not all at the same time of course, and not all of them sailed under the Greek flag.

The initial Greek contingent is of interest for another reason. The first Greek names given to these ships were mostly either the names of the families that owned them, or the names of the Greek islands from whence those families came. According to Christos Dounis, these ships were therefore considered 'community ships' and were colloquially and proprietorially known as, the 'Ithaca ship' or the 'Syros ship', and so on.

Not only that, the ships of this first one hundred were known collectively to Greek seamen as *Vasilovapora*, best translated into English as 'Queen vessels'. This was because the facilities on board were considerably above the standards on pre-war Greek ships.[2]

The conditions set by the Americans for that sale to the Greeks were probably similar to the sales made to other countries, except Britain. The total price of that first hundred was $65 million, averaging $650,000 a vessel. The new Greek owners were allowed to pay 25 per cent down, the balance payable over seventeen years. The balances were subject to an annual interest rate of 3.5 per cent, with the unpaid amounts being guaranteed by the Greek Government. The outstanding sums and the interest payments on each of the vessels were secured by mortgages, one of the conditions being that until all moneys were paid, the vessels must remain under the Greek flag. In fact, such was the shipping boom in the immediate post-war years, that the mortgages were paid off very quickly indeed. (At various times later, Liberty ships were changing hands at much more than the original purchase price, although there were sometimes downturns too.) Most of the original 100 ships enjoyed long trading lives. One of those which did not was the *Kalliopi* (*Robert Dale Owen*, Wilmington, May 1943). She struck a mine in the North Adriatic on 20 December 1947 whilst on a voyage from Charleston to the Yugoslavian port of Rijeka. She broke in three parts before sinking.

The last two Liberties ever to sail in the Greek fleet were both members of the *Vasilovapora*, that famous first hundred, and both were owned by the same family. They were the *Alexandros Koryzis* (built as *I.N. Van Nuys*, Los Angeles, March 1944) and *Georgios F. Andreadis* (*Michael Casey*, Richmond, September 1943). These vessels stayed with the Andreadis family fleet for the whole of their post-war working lives. They were both laid up in the port of Eleusis in the 1970s, and were scrapped together in 1986. Another of that 100 sailed under its original American name for all its life until scrapped in Japan in 1968. She was the *Richard D. Lyons* (Portland, Maine, March 1945) and was owned by the Galaxias Corporation.

In all, including those chartered or sold to American companies, about 900 Liberties traded commercially after the war, most of them in their original condition except for the removal of wartime appurtenances such as guns, gun tubs and magazines. The remaining two-thirds did not trade commercially. Some stayed in the service of the American Army and Navy, but most ending up moored and mothballed in harbours on both sides of the United States as parts of the Reserve Fleet. Because some of the original purchasers of Liberty ships soon sold them on, it is difficult

---

2. Information from Christos E. Dounis.

to sort out the exact numbers that went to individual countries at the time of the 1946/47 sales, apart, that is, from the block that went to the Greeks which is very well documented due to the reverence in which it is held. Research indicates these 'best' estimates for the following countries:

Italy 100
Norway 26
China 18
France 75
Holland 29
Britain 108

Around 450 were allocated to American shipping lines. Some of those were purchased by individual shipping lines, but most seem to have been chartered from the US Maritime Administration. There is another wrinkle concerning the American contingent. Both before and during the war, many American-owned ships sailed under the Panamanian flag because it was financially beneficial for the owners involved to do that; taxes and crew costs, for example, were lower. This policy continued at an enhanced rate after the war, and many of the Liberty ships controlled by American interests were registered in Panama and so sailed under the flag of that country.

The largest single purchase made by any non-American shipping line appears to have been the twenty-seven purchased by the Compagnie Generale Transatlantique of France, over a third of the total number bought by that country. When Britain was given the go-ahead to purchase Liberties in 1947 she paid an average of about £140,000 per ship, about 12 per cent less than the Greeks. In that year Elder Dempster paid exactly £135,261 for the *Samos* ex-*Tench Tilghman* (Baltimore, September 1943) renaming the ship *Zini*. British companies, including prestigious ones like Blue Funnel, P&O, Cunard and Ellermans, who before the war would never have dreamt of buying utility ships, were queuing up to purchase them as interim measures. Some British purchasers, Blue Funnel was one, spent a great deal of extra money in strengthening those they bought. That company, which always self-insured its ships and so was not about to have one crack and sink, for example strengthened every part of the double-bottom arrangement of the *Samarkand* after she became the *Talthybius* in 1947. (She had been built as *Peter Cooper*, Baltimore. September 1943.) Other significant changes to the structure were made including extra special strengthening in the vicinity of No. 3 hatch, the trouble-spot on many Liberties.[3] Blue

---

3. Correspondence with Colin Macdonald, 2000.

Funnel purchased a total of eight Liberties – a sister-company, Glen Line purchased a few more. All eight of the Blue Funnel purchases were ships that had been managed by the company ever since they had been launched. It is perhaps significant in view of that company's self-insurance policy, that all eight had been built at Baltimore, the only Liberty yard to part-rivet their ships.

Blue Funnel did not buy the *Samcree* (Baltimore, January 1944), another of the ships they had managed up to early 1947. Second Mate Ian Jackson was aboard that ship at anchor in Morotai Harbour in the Halmahera Islands (in present day Indonesia, and which had been one of the main jumping off points for General MacArthur's return to the Philippines), in February 1947. He says that he was down No. 3 hold as the last of the ship's inward cargo was being discharged.

> I noticed that there was a ripple in the tank top plating stretching right across the ship, right under the after hatch coaming; just exactly where these ships were reputed to break in two.
>
> The Mate came down to look at it, and didn't like what he saw. The Captain came down to look at it, and agreed with the Mate.[4]

Samcree had been due to sail for Vancouver on the other side of the Pacific; indeed the ship had sailed from Morotai and was within half a day's sailing of Guam, when Captain Robb was told to turn back and head for Singapore, wireless messages about the ripple having flown thick and fast between the ship and the Liverpool head office. The ship was dry-docked at Singapore and surveyed, after which she loaded at Penang for home. Soon after that *Samcree* was returned to the United States.

The British Ministry of Transport bought some Liberties directly from the US Maritime Administration, afterwards selling them on to British shipping lines. Other British shipping companies purchased their ships direct, but as dollar expenditure was involved and Britain had little in the way of dollar reserves, the approval of the Exchequer was required for every purchase. Some lines adopted novel ways to pay for their ships, ways that circumvented the restrictions on dollar expenditure. The *E.H. Sothern* became the *Sammont* after being launched at Los Angeles in September 1943. She was purchased by Ben Line in 1947 becoming that Line's *Salmonier* by an arrangement made with Saguenay Aluminium Company at Chicoutimi, Canada. a subsidiary of an American company. The ship was manned and run by Ben Line for four or five bauxite-carrying voyages between Georgetown, British Guiana and Chicoutimi, after which the ship became Ben Line's property.[5] (It is possible that the

4. Correspondence with Ian Jackson, 1999.

bauxite cargo itself, which could have been paid for with sterling credits as it was mined in what was then a British colony, somehow entered into this transaction.) A similar but longer term arrangement and covering several vessels, seems to have been made by Furness Withy Line, which used Liberties to convey pipes for an American oil company from the States to the Middle East. At the conclusion of the contract the ships belonged to Furness Withy.

The largest block purchase made by any single British shipping line appears to have been the twelve bought by Bank Line (Andrew Weir & Company Limited). That company had managed nine Liberties on behalf of the Ministry of War Transport during the war, and in 1947 purchased eight of that nine, having for some reason already returned the *Samclyde* (Baltimore, January 1944) to the US Maritime Administration in 1946. They also purchased four others which had been managed by other British companies in the war years.

One of the four Liberties purchased by Royal Mail Line in 1947 was renamed *Barranca*. Launched as *Charles A. Broadwater* at Portland, Maine in 1943, she was completed as the *Samthar* and placed under the management of Royal Mail. She cost the company about £140,000. She traded as part of the company's fleet for ten years until she was sold to the Soc. Anon di Nav. Corrado, of Genoa, Italy, in 1957. The ship was then renamed *Cesco Corrado*. The purchase price, probably the world record for a Liberty ship, was £670,000. She traded for the Italian company until 1967 when she was broken up at Spezia.

Of the Liberty ship in general it can be said that it became central to the regeneration of most of the world's merchant navies. Not only did the ship win the war, it played an important role in winning the peace. One of the most urgent uses for the Liberty ship immediately post-war was the conveyance back home of US troops, GI brides and their dependants. Some, but not all, of the ships used in this traffic were those which had earlier been specially fitted out as troopships. Three Liberties earlier converted to US Army Hospital Ships, the *St. Olaf, Dogwood,* and *Jarrett M. Huddleston,* passed through another adaptation before being used to carry GI brides from Britain, Australia and New Zealand. That last-named ship had a rather chequered career until taken over by the army. Launched at Richmond in October 1942 as the *Samuel B. Morse,* in March of the following year she was badly damaged in a collision with two tankers in a transatlantic convoy and was towed to Rothesay Bay, Scotland. Four months later in a convoy going the other way, she was again in collision, this time with another Liberty ship, the *Henry Wilson* (Portland, Maine, May 1943) and had to put back to Belfast.

---

5. Correspondence with Eddie Bruce, 2000.

One US Liberty hospital ship did not undergo further adaptation before being used in 1947 to transport US Army personnel and war brides from Germany to the States. She was the *Zebulon B. Vance* (Wilmington, February 1942) with a capacity for 476 passengers. Oddvin Liseth, serving as an Able Seaman on this ship, says that she also carried some 'hush-hush' Germans from Bremen to New York. It is likely that they had been connected with the German rocket programme, so their expertise was needed in the States.[6] Some GI brides travelled to the States aboard ordinary Liberty ships. Mrs Reta Orsini was one of those ladies. In fact she was the sole GI bride aboard the ship she joined at Plymouth. She had an officer's cabin all to herself and says that everyone made a great fuss of her.[7]

The Americans used a combined total of 104 Liberty ships and LSTs to convey Japanese prisoners of war back to Japan. One of the Liberties was the *James McNeill Whistler* (Portland, Oregon, October 1942). Whilst carrying over 3400 repatriates from Shanghai, the ship struck a reef on 19 June 1946, south-west of Nagasaki. The ship was a total loss but all on board were saved by other vessels. One authority has stated that 5,700,000 Japanese were ferried home, which probably means that taken overall, Liberties conveyed more Japanese soldiers around the seas than they did American. The British also used Liberties for the same purpose. Late in 1945 the *Samesk* (Baltimore, February 1944), managed by the New Zealand Shipping Company, transported 1400 Japanese prisoners home from Hong Kong. Then in June 1946 fourteen Liberty ships were used over a period of three weeks to repatriate 35,000 Japanese from the ports of Moulmein and Rangoon in Burma in an operation code-named Exercise 'Nipoff'. Simple arithmetic shows that each of those Liberties carried around 2500 men, so the ships must have been very crowded indeed. However, the facilities on board would have been infinitely better than those afforded to Allied prisoners of war by the Japanese when they were transported to Japan to work down mines and in factories. (One of the Japanese ships involved in those transportation operations was the *Lisbon Maru*. She was carrying 1816 Allied prisoners from Hong Kong when on 1 October 1942 she was sunk by the US submarine *Grouper*. 843 of the prisoners lost their lives. Another such ship, the *Rakuyo Maru*, was sunk by the US submarine *Sealion II* on 12 September 1944. She was carrying 1350 British and Australian prisoners, only 150 of whom were saved. In both cases the Japanese use of the ships for that purpose was unknown to the unfortunate submarine commanders.)

That initial exodus on Liberty ships from Rangoon still left another

---

6. Correspondence with Oddvin Liseth, 2000.
7. Correspondence with Mrs. Reta Orsini, 1999.

35,000 Japanese in the Burma area to be used for general labouring activities in the ports and elsewhere for the remainder of that year. Then they too were repatriated over four months commencing March 1947. Japanese ships were used this time, so the operation was probably not called 'Nipoff II'.

Other Liberties were used for much sadder personnel purposes, both post-war and even before the war had ended. British seaman Len Farnham was only sixteen when he joined the *Samfairy* (Brunswick, December 1944) at the West India Docks in London in the early months of 1945. The Liberty was much better than his last ship and Len says, 'I felt very proud and would not have traded places with the King of England'. The ship sailed for Antwerp where the ship's 'tween-decks were fitted out with four-tier bunks and then she was loaded with military supplies in the lower holds. That source of rumour known to seamen as the galley wireless, a source that always came close to being infallible probably because the captain's steward acted as a sort of antenna for it, had it that the ship was sailing for San Francisco to load troops for the invasion of Japan. Writes Len,

> Directly abeam of our berth at Antwerp, another Liberty under the American flag lay. Painted stem to stern, truck to deck completely black. She was loading crates containing the coffins of American war dead. Unfortunately, I never knew her name.

Whatever the name of the ship, she must have been part of the Army Memorial Service. The *Samfairy* with Len Farnham aboard never made it to Japan. As the ship neared the Panama Canal the atom bombs were dropped.[8]

Some revisionist historians and others have said since the war that the dropping of the atom bombs was unnecessary. But one cannot help wondering how many more 'black ship' voyages would have been necessary had the bombs not been dropped. It must be remembered that at the time of the Yalta conference of Allied leaders in February 1945, American planners had estimated that there would be at least one million Allied casualties in any attempt to invade the Japanese home islands, together with a similar number of Japanese.

In December 1946 the *James King* (Richmond, November 1943), carried backed to Japan urns containing the ashes of the Japanese pilots shot down at the time of Pearl Harbor. They included those of 'unknown X-1', a pilot who had crash-landed on the Hawaiian island of Niihau. This pilot is reported to have terrorised the local population of that small

---

8. Correspondence with Len Farnham, 1999-2000.

island until troops arrived, upon which he committed suicide. The man was later identified as one Shigonori Nishikaichi.[9]

The Allies found yet other new uses for some Liberties soon after the war, including some war-damaged ones. The *John Harvey* incident at Bari was not to be the last involvement of Liberty ships with chemical weaponry, not by a long chalk. Two Liberties were used to dump unwanted Allied gas bombs and shells a year after the war in Europe ended. The ships were the *Arthur Sewall* and the *George Hawley,* both constructed at Portland, Maine, during the first half of 1944. Both had been torpedoed off the British coast within a month of each other but had managed to reach port. Soon after the war they underwent temporary repairs before being towed to Bremerhaven in June 1946. Over the next three months they were loaded with Allied gas bombs and shells brought in from the places where they had been stock-piled. In October the ships were towed out to sea and scuttled.

Being victorious in war can have its downside. The victory over Germany left the Allies with the problem of disposing of 302,875 tonnes of German chemical weapons containing fourteen different kinds of toxic agents. In the ensuing operations the sea became the depository for these too. However, the 'depositors' concerned were not very far-seeing, for the dumping was carried out in relatively confined waters. The decision had been made that each of the occupying powers would be responsible for disposing of any such weaponry found in its Zone of Occupation. It is reported that the Soviets dumped 35,000 tonnes of artillery gas shells at two sites in the Baltic Sea. The British and Americans loaded their shares on ships, including war-damaged Liberties, which were then scuttled in the Skagerrak and Kattegat Straits. Somewhere between forty and sixty-five ships are supposed to have been used in this exercise. Twenty-seven of them were scuttled in deep water some twenty miles off the western Swedish port of Lysekil, whilst others were sunk at a similar distance off the southern Norwegian port of Arendal. Full and exact details of the American and British operations are still not known as the relevant files have not yet been placed in the public domain. In mid-2000 Russian sources reported that traces of toxins had been found in sediment samples taken from the sea-bed in the areas concerned, indications that the weapons were beginning to corrode and break up. Similar kinds of operations were carried out over many years. In 1964 the *John F. Shafroth* (Richmond, March 1944) was scuttled in a position less than fifty miles west of the Golden Gate Bridge, San Francisco. Her last cargo consisted of bombs, mines, boosters, parts of Polaris missiles, and something extra nasty that went

---

9. From a letter in *Liberty Log,* August 2000, and further correspondence with Robert W. Gifford.

under the euphemism 'cake-mix'. That load of nearly 10,000 tons of material lies at a depth of 8000ft.

In 1967 the US Defense Department devised a series of underwater tests designed to supply information about the effects of such explosions. (It is probably one of those that is referred to in the latest British Reports on the *Richard Montgomery*. See Chapter 18.) One of the tests went a bit wrong. At Bremerton, Washington, the *Robert Louis Stevenson* (Richmond, November 1943) was loaded in August 1967 with 5000 tons of unwanted explosive materials including torpedoes and mines. She was then towed by the Navy to a point about thirty miles off Amchitka, in the Aleutians. The plan was that the ship would be scuttled in 4000ft of water and that a pressure detonator would then set off what would have been the largest non-nuclear explosion in history. Apart from any other scientific value, the measured results would assist in H-bomb explosion detection techniques and would produce seismic wave information. In position on 10 August, the sea-cocks were opened but the ship failed to sink, merely rolling over on to its side. Not only that, she then disappeared into a fog bank. When finally found again, she was monitored until she sank in heavy weather. Unfortunately she went down in much shallower waters than those intended – the depth of 2800ft not being enough to set off the detonator. US Navy bombers were subsequently used in abortive attempts to build up enough pressure above the wreck to set the detonator off. The *Stevenson* is still there, some twenty miles off the nearest land.

A Liberty ship was also involved in a later chemical weapon dumping incident. In August 1970, rockets containing nerve gas were found to be leaking at a military depot in Richmond, Kentucky. In a highly secret operation the rockets – there were 12,540 of them – were conveyed by railway to Anniston, Alabama some 300 miles away as the crow flies but not as a meandering train runs, to the south-west. At Anniston the rockets were encased in a total of 418 concrete blocks. The rockets in all but one of the blocks contained a gas codenamed 'GB' which can kill within minutes. The odd block contained rockets holding an even more deadly gas code-named 'VX'; this was considered so dangerous that the concrete block concerned was specially marked by scientists to ensure that it received extra careful handling on the way to the military port at Sunny Point, North Carolina which, again as the crow flies, is over 500 miles to the east of Anniston. The US Army engineers in charge of the operation subsequently had all the blocks painted silver to reduce the danger from solar heating during the rail transportation, and in the process inadvertently obliterated the special mark. From then on all the blocks had to receive the special treatment that had been originally reserved for only the most lethal one. (The reader, especially if he or she lives in the south-east United States, may conclude that was no bad thing.)

At Sunny Point the blocks were loaded on to the Liberty ship *Le Baron Russell Briggs* (Brunswick, May 1944) in an operation lasting two days. The ship then made for a point some 300 miles off Cape Kennedy, Florida, where she was scuttled in 2700 fathoms of water. As the vessel sank the monitoring vessels lost contact with her. It was calculated that the ship would have taken eight minutes to reach the bottom which she would have struck at a speed causing her to break up on contact. Some months later tests were made in the area for gas leakage. Scientists reckoned that had any gas escaped, the water pressure at that depth would have hydrolysed it, and so rendered it harmless. In that same month the *David E. Hughes* (Los Angeles, June 1943) was loaded with about 5000 tons of obsolete ammunition and scuttled some 100 miles south-east of Sandy Hook, New Jersey. It was reported that she blew up whilst sinking. Much earlier, in 1946, at least two Liberty ships had played roles in Operation 'Crossroads', the US atomic tests at Bikini. The two Liberties had been specially commissioned for the US Navy and were among the comparatively few launched with non-personal names. They were the *Coasters Harbor* (Portland, Maine, November 1944) and the *Avery Island* (same yard, December 1944). Both were used in instrumentation tests.

Of the many Liberties that went into commercial service, some were converted in one way or another. Some had more efficient engines fitted, some were lengthened, and at least one was shortened. One of those lengthened was the *Thomas Nelson* (Baltimore, May 1942). Severely damaged by a kamikaze off Leyte in November 1944, she was eventually returned to San Francisco. In 1956 under what was called the Liberty Ship Conversion Program she was lengthened by about 25ft, the opportunity also being taken to give her finer lines forward. She was fitted with diesel engines, increasing her speed to 15kts. Her derricks were removed and replaced with deck cranes, and she was fitted with sliding hatch covers. She then operated for four years in the Atlantic service of United States Lines, and was then laid up. Before being scrapped in 1981 she was converted again and used for a time in dredging and pipe-laying operations. At least one Liberty was shortened. She was the *Janet Lord Roper* (Baltimore, July 1943). In 1948 her length was reduced forward by about 30ft during conversion into a self-unloading collier. Later she underwent another conversion and was used to carry cement.

Over the years, some Liberties took on strange forms. The *Charles H. Cugle* (Panama City, August 1945) became almost unrecognisable when she was converted into a floating nuclear power plant for the US Army. In 1962 the French converted the *Beauvais* (launched as *John Lawson*, Wilmington, June 1943) into an experimental liquefied gas carrier. Two years after that, in 1964, the *Nadina*, once the *William G. Lee* (Savannah, July 1944), was converted to carry 175 containers. In peace as in war, the Liberty was the maid of all work.

Liberties were involved in several armed conflicts after the Second World War. The first was the Korean War which began in 1950 when a North Korean Army poured across the 38th Parallel, a demarcation line instituted five years earlier. At that date most of the Liberties (and other types of ships) in the American Reserve Fleet were still in good condition and available for fast recommissioning. Amongst those Liberties recommissioned into the merchant marine was the *George Eastman* (Richmond, April 1943), which from December 1951 until mid-1952 was used to convey military supplies to Korea. After that she was transferred to the US Navy and fitted out as robot-operated nuclear fall-out detection ship and was used in the American atomic bomb tests in the Pacific from 1953 until 1956. In 1962, fitted with new instrumentation, she was used for scientific research off the Californian coast. She was finally scrapped in 1977. The *Bert McDowell* was launched at Los Angeles in October 1944 and was immediately transferred to the US Navy as the *Hooper Island*. The Navy converted her into a repair ship, but too late to take an active part in the World War. She was placed in reserve in 1948 but was recommissioned in 1952. In August 1954 she acted in a support role to the ships that evacuated over a quarter of a million persons from the north to the south of Korea in an operation called 'Passage to Freedom'. She was back in the Reserve Fleet in 1959, and was scrapped in 1970. The *Samuel Bowes* (Baltimore, May 1943) was also transferred into the Navy. As the *Luzon* she did see Second World War action, but was subsequently placed in reserve in 1947. She was recommissioned into the navy in 1950 and served in Korean waters. She went to the scrapyard in 1974. Among the other Liberties recommissioned in to the merchant marine from the Reserve Fleet specifically for the Korean crisis, were the *George Vancouver* (Vancouver, Oregon. July 1942) and the splendidly named *Big Foot Wallace* (Houston, December 1942). (William 'Big Foot' Wallace, a Virginian, fought in the Texan independence war against Mexico and later became an army scout. A legendary figure, one of few known facts about him is that he did indeed have oversize feet.)

The British also used Liberties to convey ammunition, explosives and supplies to their troops serving with the United Nations forces in Korea. One of several Glen Line Liberty ships chartered by the British Government for this purpose was the *Glenbeg* (*Samjack*, Baltimore, April 1944) which discharged her cargo of ammunition at Pusan in late 1952.[10]

By the time the Vietnam War came along in the 1960s, there were still 726 standard Liberty ships in the Reserve Fleet, plus a hodge-podge of twenty-four others that were not standard. By that time, however, only

---

10. Correspondence with Captain John Hannay, 1999.

about 150 were 'susceptible for reactivation' wrote Lane C. Kendall, then advisor to the Commander of the Military Sea Transportation Service (MSTS).[11] Unlike the Korean War where the emergency was sudden and ships were needed very quickly indeed, the Vietnam conflict, one of markedly different nature, required only a gradual build-up of logistical strength. This was perhaps just as well considering the then state of the ships in the Reserve Fleet. In fact, most of the ships used for Vietnam were chartered in from the private sector – including some foreign-flagged vessels – and so little call was made on the Liberty side of the reserves.[12] (By 1 July 1965, a year after the United States had begun to expand its military forces in Vietnam, the number of operational Liberty ships in the then 965 ship-strong American merchant marine was down to only twenty-eight according to Lane Kendall.)

A few Liberties were reactivated, however. Amongst them was the *Harry L. Glucksman* (Savannah, May 1944) and she was used in a capacity never envisaged by her builders. In 1966 she was taken out of the Reserve Fleet and specially converted into a minesweeper for the US Navy for use in Vietnamese rivers. She was filled with plastic foam to make her virtually unsinkable and fitted with gadgetry designed to set off pressure mines. She was also fitted with giant deck-mounted outboard engines to be used much like modern bow and stern thrusters, to push the ship sideways, one way or the other. One supposes that this was a highly dangerous operation, and that was probably the reason the crew consisted of only nine men. She was finally scrapped in 1976.

One US Navy Liberty did not need to be reactivated for the Vietnam War for she had been in almost continual commission since being handed over at Baltimore in September 1943. She was the *Tutuila*, launched as the *Arthur P. Gorman*, and then converted into a floating advance base. In 1962 she had been part of the cordon of ships around Cuba during that crisis. In Vietnamese waters she was used as a service ship for other naval units. In 1972 she was transferred to the Taiwanese Navy becoming the *Pien Tai*.

The *James T. Earle* (Baltimore, September 1943) was the *Parvati Jayanti* when on 6 September 1967 she got mixed up in the Arab-Israel dispute. She suffered damage from Israeli shellfire whilst lying at Suez. She sailed again after being repaired. Perhaps the last Liberty to suffer any kind of war damage was the *Robert M. La Follette* (New Orleans, February 1943). Trading as the *Troarn* in December 1971, she was damaged at Chittagong during the war between India and Pakistan. Five months later she was sold for scrapping at Kaohsiung, Taiwan.

---

11. Lane C. Kendall, 'US Merchant Shipping and Vietnam', *Naval Review* (1968).
12. W.J. McNeil, 'The Economic Importance of a US-flag Merchant Marine', *Naval Review* (1968).

CHAPTER 23

Tragedy off Porthcawl: the Loss of the Samtampa

The winter of 1946/1947 was bleak and bitter right across the British Isles in rather more ways than one. The war, out of which Britain had emerged far poorer than she had entered it, had been over for a year or more, but the country remained in the grip of general shortages and food rationing. The most noticeable sights in its cities and towns, sights which stood out like toothless gaps in badly-kept mouths, were still the many stark, rubble-strewn bombsites where buildings had once stood. The country had barely begun the long haul of reconstruction after six hard years of total war. And, as the nation groped its slow way forward that winter, the weather did not help. It was one of the worst in living memory with a seemingly endless run of storms roaring in, one after the other, all around the coast. It was a long winter too, for storms were still raging in from the Atlantic well into April. One of those late storms was the cause of one of the worst peacetime shipping disasters of the century.

The Liberty ship *Samtampa* was managed by Houlder Brothers of London. She sailed from Middlesbrough during the early hours of the 19th of that month, bound south-about Britain for Newport, South Wales. At Newport it was planned for the ship to undergo dry-docking together with an official survey prior to her possible purchase by Houlders from the US Maritime Administration, her legal owners. Launched as the *Peleg Wadsworth* at Portland, Maine in December 1943, *Samtampa* had seen some eighteen months of war service and, since the end of the world conflict, had traded to Australia, India, Italy and Canada. She had arrived at Middlesbrough to discharge a cargo and to undergo some minor repairs. At that port twenty-four of her regular crew of forty had 'signed off'. For the coming coastal voyage their places were taken by replacements from the Teeside area. In fact, when the ship sailed she was one man short, for thirty-six year-old William Dunsmore missed the ship after signing on. A few days later Bill Dunsmore must have considered himself the luckiest man alive. *Samtampa*'s commander was Captain H. Neale Sherwell, a New Zealander from Wellington. Described as 'good looking and well-built but not fat', Sherwell had been in command of the ship since early 1946. His Chief

413

Officer was Donald Lowe. They had joined the ship together and they got on well.

During the ship's stay at Middlesbrough, Donald Lowe's wife Irene, whom he had married in 1943, travelled from their home in Liverpool to spend some time with her husband. Irene Lowe, now Mrs Richmond, says that she and her husband had managed to spend less than a quarter of their married life together, such were the exigencies of a sea career at that time, and so she grabbed at the opportunity to visit the ship. During Irene's stay on board Captain Sherwell suggested she make the voyage around the coast to Newport with the ship. However, family commitments including the recent death of a young daughter, caused her not to take up the offer. The last time she saw her husband was when she waved to him from the train which was taking her back home. In her mind's eye there is still a picture of Donald, dark-haired and of a little less than average height, standing there on the platform and waving back.[1]

Patrick McKenna was one of the men to sign on the ship at Middlesbrough. He had been at sea during the war but when the conflict ended had come ashore to start a business with his wife. When she died suddenly Patrick decided to return to sea and was offered a post on *Samtampa*. He left behind him a nineteen year-old son John, a jockey who once raced in the Lincolnshire Handicap, and a thirteen year-old daughter called Pat. Another of the Middlesbrough men on board was Assistant Second Cook Joseph Griffiths. He had married only seven weeks earlier and this was to be his second voyage since returning from three-and-a-half years of living hell as a prisoner-of-war of the Japanese. Six of the crew were still teenagers, two of them, Apprentice Peter Ferns from Wallasey and Deck Boy Ralph Chester, being only seventeen.

The ship sailed from the Tees in ballast, most of which comprised water carried in the double-bottoms. There was also 182 tons of permanent sand ballast on board but there is no record now of where that was stowed. Her fuel tanks held 608 tons of oil, something which was to play a grim role in the events to come. It was expected that the ship would reach Newport on the morning tide of 22 April but she was delayed by bad weather and poor visibility. She was sighted passing Hartland Point on the North Devon coast (about halfway between Bude and Westward Ho!) at 0800 hours on the 23rd. That morning would have started on board like any other stormy day at sea with the deck crew inspecting and tightening hatch fastenings, turning ventilator cowls away from the wind, and making sure that lifelines were rigged and secure. About halfway through the morning Captain Sherwell radioed that his ship would arrive off Barry Roads in the Bristol Channel at 1400 hours. Although gale

---

1. Correspondence and telephone interviews with Mrs Irene Richmond during 1999.

warnings had been issued from early morning, it was not until after the ship had rounded Hartland Point that the first warning of exceptionally severe weather was broadcast.

The storms blowing up were not confined to the Bristol Channel area. About 100 miles south-westward, over on the other side of the peninsular that forms the county of Cornwall and which sticks out like a finger into the Atlantic, the veteran battleship HMS *Warspite* was under tow to the breakers yard and found herself on a lee shore and in danger. This famous old ship with battle honours ranging from Jutland to Normandy, ran ashore in Prussia Cove that night. Also during the night, but much farther to the north at Fladda Island in Scotland, the Hull trawler *Bengazi* was driven ashore in extremely rough seas.

By mid-afternoon the weather had worsened and Captain Sherwell radioed that he would soon have to heave-to as it was unlikely that in the prevailing conditions a pilot would be able to board. Not long after that he sent an 'urgency' signal – one step down from an SOS – reporting that his ship was rapidly drifting towards the Nash Sands lying off the eastern end of Swansea Bay. Some forty minutes later two radio stations on shore including the one at Land's End, and the radio officer aboard the nearby *Empire Success*, picked up a message from *Samtampa* stating that she had both anchors down but it was doubtful whether she would be able to keep off the Nash. Ten minutes later, a little after 1600 hours, came another urgency signal reporting her position as 290 degrees, 2.5 miles off Porthcawl light. By that time some of the watchers who had gathered on the shore estimated that the south-westerly wind was gusting up to storm force.

Coastguard Officer George Shepherd, always known as 'Shorty', of the station at Porthcawl, was the first official to arrive at the scene. He was soon joined by members of the police force. Shorty, with about twenty-five years of naval service behind him, had a reputation for being unflappable even in the direst situations, so his testimony at the later Court of Inquiry can be relied upon. He stated that when he arrived on the shore a little after 1600 hours, he estimated that the ship was about a mile off, with its bow pointing seaward and into the weather and, as far as he could ascertain, it was stationary and at anchor. He watched as best he could through the wind-swept spray for about ten minutes but saw no signs of the ship dragging, but did see its propeller turning as Captain Sherwell fought to relieve some of the strain on the anchor cables. Shorty then made for the nearby Porthcawl Golf Club from where he sent a standby message for the Mumbles lifeboat situated on the far side of Swansea Bay. Returning to the beach he saw that *Samtampa* was now flying a two-flag signal but in the prevailing conditions with salt spray almost blinding him and everyone else on shore, the flags could not be made out. He took them to be a distress signal and fixed the time of that at 1647 hours.[2]

Meanwhile, at about 1630 hours, *Samtampa* had radioed an SOS message which read, 'Fear cables will not hold much longer. Please send assistance.' Some six minutes later came another message stating that the starboard anchor cable had parted and the ship was now rapidly drifting shorewards. At 1650 hours another SOS reported that the ship's port cable had also carried away. A minute or two later a further message stated that the ship would soon be onshore. There were three more messages after that, the second of which reported that she was now aground, and the last one, sent at 1708 hours, was to the effect that the ship had begun to break up and that the crew were abandoning ship.

The message which said the ship's starboard cable had carried away had been relayed by telephone and by runner to Shorty Shepherd and, soon after receiving it, he saw the ship begin to drift shorewards. He ordered the Life-saving Appliance Company, an auxiliary unit of the coastguard, to stand by, and via his headquarters asked for urgent tug assistance, something the ship had already done, of course.

The ship struck the rocks of the reef at Sker Point, rocks that were being swept by the incoming tide and wind-driven seas. Shepherd began directing the setting up of the Appliance Company's breeches buoy apparatus. At the subsequent Court of Inquiry the point was stressed that as the rocket-gun had only a limited range and, moreover, a range much reduced when fired into the teeth of a storm, the equipment had to be set up as close as possible to the point where the vessel actually struck, and that it would have served no useful purpose to have set up the cumbersome apparatus before the ship had grounded.

The youngest of the group of men struggling in Force 10 winds to set the gear up – he says that the wind was blowing so hard 'you could lean on it' – was seventeen year-old John David. 'I was too young to be in the Life-saving Company proper, but as my father was a member and as I had spent as much time as I was allowed to with the unit, I was quickly signed on as an official helper.'

John reports:

> The weather was terrible. The storm was ferocious and, as we got up to Sker Point, we could see the *Samtampa*. The waves were really pounding at the ship and she eventually broke in three. It all happened very quickly.[3]

2. Ministry of Transport Report No. 7496 dated October 1947 and entitled SS *Samtampa*, Report of Court.
3. Interview with John David at Porthcawl 25 May 1999, and subsequent correspondence and telephone talks with him. John David is one of the volunteer curators of the Porthcawl Town Museum which houses a small *Samtampa* memorial collection.

Confirmation of that evening's terrible weather conditions comes from Eric Gibbs, then a twenty-one year-old auxiliary coastguard on duty at the coastguard station along the coast at Rhossilli, 20 miles to the east. Interviewed in 1997, he said he had never seen weather like it and 'still hasn't until this day'. He went on, 'trying to peer out of the windows of the coastguard hut was impossible, for there was so much salt in the air whipped up by the wind and rain'. Someone else with a vivid recollection of the weather that night was Peggy Moran, who was one day to become the mayoress of Swansea. 'The weather that night was something I will never forget', she said, also in 1997. 'I was down at the front in Langland [close to Mumbles Head]. The storm had been building up all the afternoon and the sea was lashing the beach and everything on it. The waves were towering. They were huge. I've never seen waves like those since that night.'

On the Sker Rocks with the life-saving apparatus set up to his satisfaction, Shorty ordered the line-carrying rocket fired. It failed to reach the wreck. As the tide was coming in fast the laborious task of moving the gear back shorewards had to be undertaken before another rocket could be fired. That too was fired with the same negative result. Again the gear had to be moved, and once more the line did not carry. Afterwards it was reported that because of the wind, only one of the rockets made a flight to the full extent of its 400-yard line, and as *Samtampa* was about 500 yards off, there had never been a chance of any of the rockets reaching her.

Because of the storm the tides reached a phenomenally high level that night as is evidenced by Coastguard Eric Gibbs who said that on the following day he went up the nearby Mewslade valley to be met with what he described as an amazing sight; signs of damage that indicated that 'the sea had come up the valley further than ever before'. In fact that storm-pressed tide forced *Samtampa* so hard against the Sker rocks that within minutes the entire bow section had torn away from forward of the bridge to be swept bodily up on to the ledge of rock, to be followed shortly afterwards by the after end of the ship which had similarly broken away. Only the heavy midships section carrying the bridge superstructure and the engine-room remained pounding against the rock ledge.

Quite a crowd had gathered on shore by that time, and as they watched in helpless horror, figures could vaguely be seen moving about the midship section. Although the ship carried an American Galbraith rocket line-throwing gun, it seems that no attempt was made to fire a line from the ship to the shore. The Court of Inquiry later took the view that this failure was almost certainly due to the extremely heavy pounding suffered by what was left of the ship; anyone on the bridge would have required both hands merely to hold on. One of the ship's lifeboats was swept away soon after the ship grounded and some of the shoreside watchers later reported that they had seen men clambering into one of the other boats although no one saw any attempt to launch it. It was the Court's opinion anyway, that in the sea conditions then raging and given the position of the midship section, any such launching would have been impossible.

Twelve miles away on the other side of Swansea Bay the emergency maroons had gone up and the Mumbles lifeboat *Edward Prince of Wales*, was launched at a little after 1600 hours. The launching was possible only because of the protection afforded the slipway from south-westerly storms by Mumbles Head under whose shelter it lay. The lifeboat's crew of eight was led by forty-two year-old Coxswain William Gammon. An extremely experienced lifeboatman, Gammon was one of only seven men who during the Second World War had been awarded the Royal National Lifeboat Institution's Gold Medal for conspicuous gallantry, a medal often called the lifeboatman's Victoria Cross, and which like the VC itself, is awarded only in very special circumstances. Gammon had earned his in December 1944 when involved in rescuing men from HMCS *Chebogue*. That Canadian frigate, under tow of the corvette HMCS *Chambly* after being torpedoed in the Atlantic, broke away and foundered in heavy weather off Swansea. Although seven men from the frigate were lost, Gammon and his crew were able to save forty-two lives. With but one exception the other crew members of *Edward Prince of Wales* were also well experienced. Even the exception, thirty-four year-old Ronald Thomas for whom this was only the second rescue trip, had served for nearly four years in the Royal Navy, so knew something about boats. The lifeboat itself was 45ft long and fitted with an 80-horsepower engine. Although dating from 1924, she was of a type the RNLI considered among their finest sea boats at the time. As the lifeboat proceeded seaward an attempt was made to signal a message to it from Mumbles Coastguard Station giving the latest information on the *Samtampa* situation. But visibility was so bad the boat had to return to the slipway to receive the update, and so did not finally get away until about 1710 hours by which time *Samtampa* was already ashore. Given the distance between Mumbles and Sker Point, 'it is clear', said the authors of the Official Report, 'there was never any chance of the lifeboat getting to the *Samtampa* before she got on the rocks'. As *Edward Prince of Wales* made towards the south-east she could be seen from the Mumbles until she was about three miles off. Then she was lost to sight.

Conditions back at the scene of the disaster were rapidly growing worse. Fuel oil from *Samtampa*'s fractured tanks had spewed out, some of it mixing with the sand and salt that was blowing in the faces of the watchers on shore. 'When I finally got home in the early hours', says John David, 'my mother had to cut off most of my hair, there was so much oil in it. She had nothing that would get the oil out'. All night those on the shore watched and waited, praying that by some miracle some of the crew would manage to reach shore. Says John David, 'Strangely, despite all the time we were there, we didn't see the Mumbles lifeboat. Although we knew she was out there battling against horrendous conditions, we never saw her'.

As the tide receded members of the rescue party were able to reach parts of the ship, but it was still dark and much too hazardous to venture into the remnants by torchlight. Then, as dawn broke over the scene, the first bodies were discovered and the full extent of the horrors of the night were revealed. Lying on the rocks close to a section of the *Samtampa*, a policeman discovered the upturned and empty *Edward Prince of Wales*. Exactly how and when the lifeboat capsized will forever remain a mystery, but officers of the Royal Lifeboat Institution Inspectorate made certain educated guesses based on the position and condition of the wreckage. It was considered that shortly before high tide at 2200 hours the lifeboat with her engine on half speed and running close in to *Samtampa* had been struck by an exceptionally high wave which turned her over and flung the crew into the sea.

The bodies of several members of the *Samtampa* crew and those of all eight lifeboatmen were found on that first day, all of them either close to the scene or on the sandy beaches lying either side of the rocks. All had died from asphyxia from drowning hastened by oil clogging their noses and mouths. Most of the bodies had sustained injuries from striking against the rocks. Throughout the next few days the bodies of the rest of the ship's crew were found, some so badly battered that no identification was possible. 'By the law of averages someone should have survived', says John David, 'even if it was only one or two'. But not one man did; every man on board the ship losing his life along with those gallant Mumbles lifeboatmen. 'It's terrible to think', said John David recently, 'that had the ship brought up on the beaches which lie either side of the Sker, a matter of a few hundred yards one way or the other, it is likely that some men would have been saved. The thought of that possibility has been with me for over fifty years.' There was a glint of wetness in John's eyes as he spoke.

As if the tragedy itself was not bad enough, the way some of the relatives of the ship's crew found out about it, compounded the horror for them. At her home in Liverpool, Irene Lowe had the horrendous experience of learning about it from a radio news broadcast early on the morning of the 24th. She says that some sense of foreboding had kept her awake for most of the night, and after hearing the broadcast she ran down the road to get a newspaper to find news of the tragedy all over the front page. She then telephoned John Houlder of the shipping line and he confirmed the news. A day or two later Irene travelled to South Wales for the dreadful task of identifying her husband's body. She then brought him home to Liverpool for burial.

The uncle of thirteen year-old Pat McKenna also heard the news over the radio, and rushed round to break the news to the girl. Unfortunately, brother John was not there to comfort her for he was away doing his National Service in the army. Later that day Pat received a visit from the padre of the Seamen's Mission at Middlebrough who had been asked by the shipping line to take on the melancholy task of officially informing all next of kin in the area. Pat's uncle later travelled to Wales to identify the body which was then brought back to Teeside.[4]

Twenty-eight bodies of *Samtampa's* crew were taken away from Porthcawl by their families for burial. But eleven were not, and they lie together in a communal grave in a cemetery just along the coast from Porthcawl. Two of the men are there because they had no close relatives; the other nine lie there because they could not be identified. The bodies of all eight lifeboatmen are buried in the Oystermouth cemetery on the other side of Swansea Bay. Their funeral procession attracted thousands of mourners who lined the streets as the coffins were borne past on tenders supplied by the Royal Air Force.

Although not a man survived the disaster, it is wrong to say that there was no survivor from the ship. Two or three days after the event when it became possible to board the fore end of the ship that had been tossed up on to the reef, the ship's cat was found alive in the bosun's locker. It was rescued and given a home by a local family. It is sad to think that had any members of the crew been on that fore section, instead of all being fore-gathered at lifeboat stations on the midship's section, they too might have lived.[5]

On 21 May 1947, about a month after the disaster and in accordance with one of the traditions of the Lifeboat Institution, a tradition which seems to echo an old Viking burial practice, the hulk of *Edward Prince of Wales* was set alight at the place where it was found. The place on the Sker Rocks where the boat was burned is now marked by a commemorative plinth which is looked after by members of the present Coastguard team. The communal grave in Porthcawl, which is adorned with a stone anchor, is regularly tended by the local unit of the Sea Cadets.

Very early in the following year the British Steel Corporation along the coast at Port Talbot, purchased the remains of the ship for scrap. They awarded the job of breaking up the wreck to the Bristol Channel Salvage Company, run by an American-born but Lancashire-bred engineer called Fred Winstanley. The team virtually set up camp on the beach, and to some extent it was a family undertaking, for Winstanley's mother and father took part. The first task was to construct three 'ways' across

---

4. Telephone interviews with Mrs Pat McKenna June 1999.
5. Correspondence with Jason Winstanley, September 2000.

the rocks from deck plates cut from the ship along which larger cut-away sections from the wreck could be drawn. For hauling the pieces from the sea and across the rocks, Winstanley bought an American Sherman tank, an ideal piece of equipment for the job even though with gun still attached the 'tractor' looked rather incongruous. One of the first portions removed from the ship was part of the *Samtampa*'s deck-house which was fitted out ashore as a galley and in which Mrs. Winstanley prepared food for the team. The job lasted for the best part of a year and was not without its adventures. On one occasion an unexploded mine was washed ashore close to the wreck, and the salvors secured it with ropes until a naval disposal squad arrived on the scene. The salvors left behind one gaunt reminder of the tragedy. A part of *Samtampa*'s boiler is still to be seen at times of very low water off Sker Point.

In 1997 on the 50th anniversary of the tragedy, many relatives of the dead seamen together with people who had been involved on the shore, attended a special service of remembrance at Porthcawl, part of the service being held around the communal grave. Irene Lowe received £600 compensation from the Shipping Federation, the organisation which in those days looked after the interests of shipowners. It seems a rather measly sum for the loss of a husband. (It equates roughly to £12,000 at 2000 prices.)

One of the two motor mechanics who lost his life on *Edward Prince of Wales* was fifty-two year-old Ernest Griffin, a married man with three children. His daughter Joan still asks the question, was her father's sacrifice really necessary and wonders why the boat had not been called out earlier. However, given the timings of all the events as recorded in the Report of the Court of Inquiry, it seems there were no avoidable delays. Had the visibility been better at 1600 hours when the lifeboat first left the slipway, a circumstance which would have enabled the latest information to be signalled across and so obviating the need for the boat to return to base, it is possible that at least part of the tragedy might have been avoided. But little purpose is served in entering the realm of ifs and maybes. The Court of Inquiry held that no one was to blame for the loss of *Samtampa*, and on the facts as given, the same must apply to the loss of *Edward Prince of Wales*.

Captain Sherwell was quite possibly the most unfortunate and tragic of all Liberty ship captains, for the *Samtampa* was the second of his Liberty commands, and the first one had also ended in disaster, although that had been a war induced one. His first Liberty ship was the rather similarly named *Sampa* (launched as *William Smallwood*, Baltimore, September 1943) and was also managed by Houlder Line. Sherwell was on the bridge when she struck a mine off the North Foreland in the English Channel in the late afternoon of 15 February 1945. The explosion blew out part of the ship's port side amidships and broke the ship's back, in the process blowing Captain Sherwell from the bridge into the sea. *Sampa* was carrying a total of sixty-two crew and passengers, and twelve of them lost their lives in the explosion, another four dying later from their wounds. Captain Sherwell was picked up in a dazed and battered condition by an escort ship and subsequently landed at Southend-on-Sea. With the master missing, Chief Officer J. Allerton took command of *Sampa* and transferred all the survivors, including several wounded, to the destroyer HMS *Middleton* which later landed them at Sheerness. *Sampa* sank within fifteen minutes of striking the mine. Chief Officer Allerton was awarded the MBE and Lloyds Medal for his gallantry during the incident. In recognition of his services during the liberation of Belgium aboard *Sampa* prior to her sinking, Captain Sherwell was posthumously awarded two Belgian honours. In April 1948 HRH The Prince Regent of Belgium approved the appointment of Sherwell as Chevalier Honorary of the Order of Leopold with Palme, and he was also awarded the Croix de Guerre with Palme.

CHAPTER 24

Lost Without Trace

In 1948 there were still a few Lend-Leased Liberties sailing under the British flag that had not yet been handed back to the US Maritime Administration nor yet purchased by British shipping lines. Some of them were in the process of being handed back, the others in the process of being purchased. Amongst them was the *Samkey* under the management of the New Zealand Shipping Company, some of whose wartime activities have been described in Chapter 20.

In late January 1948 she was making a crossing of the North Atlantic en route to Cuba from London. She was in ballast. On the 29th she was sighted 'in good order' by a passing vessel. *Samkey* reported her position by radio two days later by which time she was about 150 miles north-east of the Azores, adding that she had run into bad weather. After that message she was never heard from again. When the weather abated a sea and air search was conducted, but the ship and its crew of forty-three had disappeared without trace.

Samkey was one of those ships – any seamen will know of one or two of the kind – which seem destined to be involved in unusual incidents of one sort or another. In March 1945, for example, she had run aground off Flushing and had to be pulled off by the tug *Sea Giant*.[1] Shortly after the war she got into difficulties whilst trying to berth in high winds at Wellington, New Zealand, a port not called 'Windy Wellington' for nothing. It took over four hours for her to berth alongside Aotea Quay. The ship was involved in an adventure of a different kind on 11 June 1947. At that time *Samkey* was on what was called the 'Makatea Run', transporting phosphates from the island of that name near Tahiti, to various destinations in New Zealand and Australia. On that date the ship's master, Captain J.J. Youngs, received a radioed request from the Governor of Tahiti to go to the aid of a large French trading schooner, the *Oiseau des Iles*, which had struck a reef off the island of Mopihaa. The schooner was carrying 140 workers from Rarotonga to work at the Makatea phosphate installation, and it was thought they could be in

---

1. ADM1/17274, PRO, Kew.

423

danger before a French ship could get to the scene. No doubt with thoughts of prospective salvage money on top of the humanitarian aspects of his mission in mind, Captain Youngs hastened to the rescue. He found the schooner well up on the reef with a large hole in her side, and lying very close to what remained of Count Felix von Luckner's *Seeadler,* a German armed raider wrecked there in 1917. The 140 passengers had already been placed ashore, and on the following day they were taken aboard *Samkey* and sleeping space allotted them on deck. The schooner's pumps were barely coping with the ingress of water and Captain Youngs offered to place some of his own pumps aboard, pull the schooner off, and then tow her to Makatea, which, if successful, would have resulted in a salvage award. In the knowledge that a French ship was on its way the French skipper turned down the offer, so *Samkey* went on her way with her passengers to land them safely at Makatea. (The *Oiseau des Iles* was eventually towed to Tahiti by a French ship.)

Samkey returned to Britain in December 1947, and some of her crew then signed-off permanently. They were the lucky ones. Amongst that batch were Seamen Fred Honisett, Alan Lewis, and John Chapman. At that time Honisett was under some pressure from his wife Joan to leave the sea altogether and so decided to take all the leave that was due to him. Lewis says he would have signed on again except that he had not got on with Chief Officer Haines during the previous voyage. Haines, who was leaving the ship himself, therefore advised the new Chief Officer 'don't sign him'. John Chapman, who was studying for his Second Mate's certificate, decided to widen his experience and so signed aboard the *Fort Chambley*. The lives of those three men can be said to have been saved therefore as a consequence of three very different influences, wifely persuasion, officer resistance, and professional ambition.[2]

Other crew members went on leave and then returned to sign on again. One of those was twenty-one year-old Seaman John Gates. The New Zealand Shipping Company was something of a family concern for the Gates family for John's older brother Jim was a bosun on another of the company's ships. Not only that, an uncle was an accountant in the firm's London office. Amongst others to sign on the ship again, were Bosun F.W. West, Senior Ordinary Seaman Frank Ballard, Chief Cook T. Sheville and Second Steward E.N. White. Seaman Tom Lynch also signed on again, but signed off once more only a day before the ship sailed when he discovered that the ship was not returning to Australasian waters. He wanted to go to Australia to marry his girlfriend there. He was on the quayside waving to his erstwhile shipmates when *Samkey* sailed.[3]

---

2. Correspondence and meetings with Fred Honisett, Alan Lewis and Captain John Chapman, 1999–2000.
3. Correspondence and discussions with Jim Gates, 1999-2000.

Some of the ship's officer cadre changed too. Captain Youngs left the ship due to a bout of mumps. His place was taken by Captain C.A. Cremin, a forty-four year-old from Blackheath in South-east London. Cremin was an experienced Liberty ship captain having been master of the *Samkey* itself in early 1946. He had also captained the *Stafford*, formerly the *Samingoy* (Brunswick, May 1944), which had been purchased in 1947 by Federal Steam Navigation Company an off-shoot of New Zealand Shipping. Another new appointee was twenty-two year-old Radio Officer Ernest Harradine. He had been serving in the company ships since 1944.[4] The four youngest members of the crew, all in their teens, were Junior Ordinary Seaman Gerald McAllen, Deck Boy J.J. Martinson, Steward's Boy R. Strong, and Galley Boy G.A. Butterworth. McAllan, from South Dunedin, New Zealand, was only seventeen. The youngest officer on board was Fourth Officer D.M. Gee from Leicester who was twenty. The oldest man on board at sixty was Chief Engineer T.C. Barry, a Londoner.

The *Samkey* sailed from London in ballast for Cuba on 24 January 1948. Before the ship sailed an official group photograph was taken of Captain Cremin and his officers in accordance with the shipping company's usual procedure. The company did this prior to every sailing of one of their ships from Britain, an unusual policy that this author has found no counterpart to in other sections of the British Merchant Navy. It has left posterity with a unique pictorial record.

We have seen that the ballasting of Liberty ships when sailing in the light condition was a matter that concerned both the American and British governments because of the ships' built-in stiffness which caused them to roll excessively. During the war both governments had issued instructions regarding the use of solid ballast over and above the water ballast carried in the ships' double-bottoms and deep tanks. The two sets of instructions differed somewhat in degree. The American rules called for a total of 1500 tons to be divided between the lower holds and 'tween-decks, 450 tons of it to be carried in the latter compartments. The British rules called for a total of 1650 tons, of which 400 was to have 'tween-deck stowage.

New Zealand Shipping Company records show that ballasting arrangements for the Liberty ships they managed during the war and after it, was a matter of concern to some of their captains. That concern had in fact begun with the *Samkey* itself at Oran in April 1944 when Captain A. Hocken insisted on having his ship ballasted with 2000 tons of iron ore, apparently to the annoyance of the British Ministry of War Transport official based at that port. That official had reported the matter to his chief at Algiers and in consequence on 22 April Captain

---

4. Correspondence with Marjorie Bain *nee* Harradine, 2000.

Hocken wrote the following explanatory letter which he copied to his London office.

> Dear Sirs
>
> The MOWT representative in this port has informed me that you require an explanation from myself regarding the quantity of iron ore ballast (2000 tons) shipped in this vessel. . . .
>
> Before leaving the USA on this voyage I received from my owners a copy of the MOWT letter to them concerning the suggested ballast requirements for North Atlantic voyages in which 1500 tons was taken as a yardstick.
>
> I discussed the advisability of keeping to this amount with several other Masters of American Liberty ships whom I met at convoy conferences etc., and they appeared unanimous that it was insufficient for safe handling of their ships in convoy during bad weather. My own observation during the short time we have been in light condition confirms this.
>
> I am aware that many vessels have negotiated the North Atlantic with only 1500 tons but it is possible that they have experienced fine weather, in which case I think the 1500 tons would be enough.
>
> I wish to point out that this ship is fitted with T.N.D. gear which renders steering extremely difficult with strong beam winds, more especially at the slow speeds which are necessary in bad weather. It is with a view of having a small safety margin that I ordered this amount of ballast.

Captain Hocken went on to point out that his ship would have had an inadequate draft aft had he kept to the 1500 tons.[5] (It should be noted that Captain Hocken referred to '1500 tons' as required by the American regulations, and not to the 1650 called for by the British. It seems that at some time after the promulgation of the original British advice to shipmasters, someone in authority decided that the American quantity was sufficient. There appear to be three possible reasons for this change of heart. 1. That the British had reworked their figures; 2. Solid ballast material during the war years was often in short supply, and it took time to load and eventually to off-load, so the least supplied to each ship the better; 3. That because the ships were still the property of the US Maritime Administration, it was thought politic to follow the American rules, for to have deviated from them might have provided cause for an American claim for compensation if such a ship had been lost. Perhaps a combination of all three factors was involved.)

---

5. NZS/31/1–3–7, New Zealand Shipping Company Records held at the National Maritime Museum, London.

During Captain Cremin's previous spell in command of *Samkey,* and after a voyage from Glasgow to St. Johns, Newfoundland, in March 1946, he had made the following report to his Head Office.

A good deal of boisterous weather has been encountered on the Atlantic passage and vessel rolled very heavily at times, as was expected, and this did no harm. But some anxiety was felt at times when pounding and racing took place, and it was necessary on occasions to reduce revolutions, and steering was difficult.

I note from past correspondence in the ship's files that the MOWT took exception to this vessel on one occasion having taken 2000 tons of ballast for a voyage from the Mediterranean to USA, and quoting from their correspondence to Owners, they say, 'It is considered that if double-bottom tanks and other tanks are full, either of oil or water, then 1500 tons of solid ballast is sufficient for North Atlantic ballasting purposes,which is the yardstick, and in general, the most required'.

My own personal view however is that this figure, 1500 tons, is the minimum for this time of year.

In view of the fact that the American wartime regulations (and for that matter the British) called for most of the solid ballast to be carried in the lower holds, the ballast configuration when the *Samkey* sailed from London in January 1948, might seem rather odd. The ship was carrying the recommended 1500 tons of temporary solid ballast, but *all* of it was stowed in the 'tween-decks (300 tons in both Nos. 2 and 5 'tween-decks, 400 in No. 3 and 500 in No. 4). On the other hand, at some time previously, 186 tons of permanent rock ballast had been placed in the bilges under Nos. 2 and 4 holds and the engine-room. When all that is added to the tonnage of water ballast (most of which would have been pumped aboard when the ship got out to sea where the water was cleaner), and the oil fuel on board, the vessel left British waters carrying something like 3700 tons of water and hard ballast, and oil, and although the configuration might have been a little suspect because of the 1500 tons carried high up in the ship in the 'tween-decks, that in itself does not prove that it was a dangerous configuration. In fact the carriage of all 1500 tons of the recommended temporary solid ballast in the 'tween-decks of Liberty ships was not a new departure. Since the war, that practice together with the carrying of approximately 190 tons of permanent ballast in the bilges, had become the norm for Liberties crossing the North Atlantic.[6]

However, *where* solid ballast is stowed in a ship is not the only problem with it. *How* it is stowed is of equal or even greater import. Any bulk

---

6. See J. Bes, *Chartering & Shipping Terms* (London 1975).

material loaded in a ship, be it cargo or ballast, has what is known as a natural angle of repose. Grain for example, when poured on to a level surface, will assume a conical heap form with the sides at an angle of repose of about 23° to the horizontal, and under static conditions will have no tendency to shift. Should that flat surface be inclined more than the angle of repose, however, the grain will shift. It is not quite so simple as that in a ship because the ship is never in a static condition, but is moving in one way or another all the time. Not only that, the farther the surface of the grain is above the centre about which the ship rolls, the greater propensity there is for the grain near the surface to move to the low side as the ship heels over. This can result in a ship capsizing, something that has indeed happened many times over the years. Other bulk cargoes have different angles of repose, but the problem is the same with all of them; they must be prevented from shifting to any great extent. With some bulk cargoes trimming them level is often enough, but with others like grain, as well as being trimmed level, the fitting of what are called shifting boards is required. (Modern bulk-carriers are designed to obviate the necessity for temporary shifting boards.) These are substantial temporary timber constructions erected vertically at the centreline of the ship from top to bottom, effectively dividing the holds into two and so reducing what is called the heeling moment of the cargo (in effect, by a mathematical factor of four). Solid ballast is in a similar category, especially when loaded in the 'tween-deck which is as far above the point about which the ship rolls as it is possible to load any material except deck-cargo. The type of ballast loaded into the 'tween-decks of the *Samkey* was called Thames Ballast, a particular mixture of sand and stone which has an angle of repose of only 18°. It was trimmed level in those spaces, but no shifting boards were fitted.

Six months after the disappearance of the ship an Official Court of Inquiry into its loss was opened in London. The Chairman of the Court, who was assisted by two nautical assessors, opened with a general statement on the loss of the ship during which he stated that at the time of the ship's disappearance, very severe weather prevailed off the Azores.

The weather was indeed atrocious. That particular storm was described by officers aboard other ships in the vicinity as one of the worst Atlantic storms they had ever experienced. Ship after ship caught up in it sent out distress signals. Some reported being hoved-to, others that they had lost propeller or rudder. One had lost two men swept overboard. In that same storm an airliner of British South American Airlines flying under the name *Star Tiger* and on a flight from Lisbon to Bermuda, vanished with thirty-one people on board.

Mr. J.B. Hewson, counsel for the British Ministry of Transport, having outlined the disposition of the ship's ballast arrangements, added,

It may be that the Court may wish to consider the advisability of carrying the whole of the hard ballast in the 'tween-decks, and if so, what precautions should be taken to avoid shifting of ballast.

He went on;

Here was a well-built ship, efficiently manned and surveyed immediately before the voyage, which on or after January 31 this year was overwhelmed by something that was so sudden in its onslaught and so dire in its effect, that no signal of any kind was made from her, and she just vanished from sight.

Experienced seamen would tell the Court that they considered the ship was sufficiently ballasted, and that she was probably overwhelmed by some phenomenon of the sea. But the Ministry's technical officers were more inclined to think that the storage of the ballast may have had something to do with the disaster.

He concluded, however;

There is not one shred of suspicion in this case that anyone was in any way negligent in the stowage of the ballast or the sailing of the ship.

Counsel Hector Hughes, who was representing the next-of-kin of the crew, attempted to make the point that there was something inherently wrong with the seaworthiness of Liberty ships, and recalled the loss of the *Samwater* on 29 January 1947. *Samwater* (launched Baltimore, August 1943 under the name *David De Vries*) had been abandoned after it caught fire off Cape Finesterre after an escape of hot oil from a boiler. He also brought in the loss of the *Samtampa,* driven on the rocks off Porthcawl in April 1947. Captain Hubert Dawson, Marine Superintendent of the New Zealand Shipping Company answered that he had no fault to find with Liberty ships. On the seaworthiness of the *Samkey* in particular, D.W. Jones, a Senior Nautical Surveyor with the Ministry of Transport, reported that he had made a final visit to the ship in the Royal Albert Dock on 12 January, and found all was in order.

Staff Commander Stanley Burnnand of Orient Line was called to give evidence about an incident that took place aboard the *Sameveron* (Baltimore, January 1944) under his command in late 1944. The ship was in convoy off Newfoundland after having nearly completed a westward Atlantic crossing, when bad weather was encountered. She had about 2000 tons of Thames Ballast on board, distributed in the lower holds and 'tween-decks. He said:

Ship rolled very heavily and quickly, and the ballast in lower holds and 'tween-decks shifted, and we listed over to starboard at 55 degrees.

Main induction came out of the water, I lost vacuum and engines stopped. We just lay there. The Chief Engineer got the dynamos running and a certain amount of steam, but not sufficient to move the ship.

A lifeboat washed away and hatches stove in. After trimming the ballast in 'tween-decks and in the holds, the tanks were pumped out and the ship brought back to an 8 degree list to starboard. Weather then moderated and we headed for St. Johns.

There was no structural damage to the ship and I was very satisfied with the way the ship had gone through the ordeal. It was a very nasty affair.

He added that 2000 tons of ballast was ideal, and concluded, 'I don't think this would have happened had there been shifting boards'.

Another witness was from Blue Funnel, Captain Eric Radford. He had commanded a total of three Liberties, and had made two ballast voyages across the North Atlantic in them. On one of those he had carried 1500 tons of phosphate as ballast. 'She rolled heavily as we always expected with Sam ships – we had to hold on to our eyebrows.' At another point in the proceedings W.J.G. Hawkins, a Senior Ship Surveyor with the Ministry, said that he wanted to stress 'that once a movement of ballast had started. the likelihood of it continuing was rather great'.

The last day of the proceedings featured some rather unseemly exchanges between Hector Hughes, counsel for the relatives, and Roland Adams. counsel for the New Zealand Shipping Company. Returning to the matter of the ballasting arrangements, Hughes stated;

> I would be sorry for the ship's master if he differed from the Marine Superintendent on the question of the amount of ballast to be used.

Adams took exception to this, calling it;

> . . . a foul and mischief-making imputation against a company that enjoyed a high reputation for decades before Mr. Hughes was born.

Then addressing the bench he added;

> You have had that insinuation from a Counsel who had not called one single witness before you. On behalf of NZSC I repudiate any such suggestion and I venture to think the Court should make it quite clear that no such imputation should have been made.

To that Mr Hughes replied, 'My friend is using strong language'.
Adams retorted:

> I will use stronger language if you go on this way. What did you intend by saying you would be sorry for a master if he differed from the marine superintendent?

Hughes replied to the effect that there was a conflict of expert opinion, after which he backed down.

The Court held no one to blame for the loss of *Samkey*, but the point was made that as there was a danger of Thames Ballast shifting, there was a case for shifting boards to be fitted in 'tween-decks and that the Ministry should publicise this. The compensation awards granted to the next-of-kin of those lost aboard *Samkey* seem to have been measly in the extreme. The mother of Seaman John Gates was initially awarded only £60, although that was later doubled. For her that low award compounded the horror of the way she found out about her son's fate. The uncle, P.C. Armour, who was an accountant with the Company, telephoned the family with the unconfirmed news of the loss of the ship but advised that Mrs Gates not be told until it had been confirmed. Unfortunately the Press got hold of the story and Mrs Gates read about it in a newspaper. That was bad enough, but then the BBC in a broadcast that same night stated that the ship had, after all, arrived safely at Cuba. Mrs Gates had the horror of going through the agony all over again when on the following day the BBC corrected its first report. Marjorie Harradine (now Mrs Bain), the Radio Officer's sister, had a different but equally disturbing experience. She says that her parents received a letter informing them only that the ship was overdue. That same morning whilst travelling in a train, when the man sitting opposite her opened his newspaper, she read that it was believed that the ship had sunk with all hands in a storm.

On 16 April 1948 a Service of Remembrance was held at the Mariner's Chapel of St. Andrew, at the Mission to Seamen in Victoria Dock Road, London. Then, in the following year, the New Zealand Shipping Company organised a collection among its seagoing and shore staffs, to pay for a stained-glass memorial window to be placed in that chapel. The window, a fine piece of decorative art with nautical motifs and incorporating the names of all the crew members, was dedicated by the Bishop of Barking on 29 April 1949. But *Samkey*'s bad luck continued. With the closing down of the London Docks that mission became disused in 1973, after which the window was vandalised. Only a remnant of it, about one quarter of the whole, and depicting a sailing ship, survived the vandals. That remnant is now displayed as part of a window in the Church of All Hallows by the Tower, which rather appropriately lies just across the road from the Merchant Navy War Memorials on Tower Hill. Under that window in All Hallows, a black marble plaque has been erected which features the names of the *Samkey* crew. But still the ship is unlucky. Although the remnant in the church window is clearly visible, the plaque is not. It is hidden by screens containing parish notices and the like, and paintings by children from a nearby school. Requests to have those screens moved elsewhere are always met with disapproval from the helpers working in the church.

On 16 September 1948 a long letter to the editor appeared in the London *Shipbuilding & Shipping Record* of that date. It was headed '*Samkey* and Thames Ballast'. It was signed by someone calling himself 'Interested', and its contents indicate that either he had served aboard *Sameveron* in 1944 when her ballast shifted, or that he had received detailed information from someone who had. This is the letter:

Some considerable interest has been aroused by the findings of the Court of Inquiry into the loss of the *Samkey,* particularly to the reference made to the failure of the Ministry . . . to give wider publicity to the shift of Thames Ballast which occurred in a sister-ship – the *Sameveron.*

This vessel was carrying 1005 tons of ballast in the 'tween-deck and 1020 tons in the lower holds when she left London for a voyage across the North Atlantic in December 1944. None of the ballast was secured against shifting and the vessel unquestionably had a remarkably lucky escape when, in a severe storm, the whole of the 'tween-deck ballast took charge and carried the vessel over to starboard to an angle of 55 degrees. Only the most strenuous and tenacious efforts enabled the master and crew of the *Sameveron* to transfer ballast from the starboard side of the 'tween-deck to lower deck hatches on the port side, through which it was dumped into the port sides of the lower holds – some into forward holds part equipped with centreline division, and some into the after hold having the shaft tunnel recess along the centreline. This extremely narrow escape appears to have been fully reported to the Ministry of War Transport and, having regard to the fact that – in wartime – the value of every ship is immensely enhanced, it seems extraordinary that no news of this mishap was communicated, even confidentially, to those responsible for managing – and incidentally ballasting – ships engaged in war service.

The omission is noteworthy for two entirely distinct reasons:-

1) The MOWT as representing the owners of these vessels, i.e. the Crown, might well have been expected to take particular note of any and every circumstance likely to cause loss or damage to their charges, and to have insisted upon adequate safeguards being devised and adopted against any and all new risks known to them.

2) The MOWT Mercantile Marine Department . . . have for so long enjoyed the world-wide reputation of being the most alert, experienced and reliable guardians of the rules and regulations which cover 'Safety of Life at Sea', that their silence over the *Sameveron* incident is most difficult to understand.

According to the daily press some inquiries have already been addressed to the Ministry . . . in respect of the Ministry's failure to take some form of 'safe-guarding' action on learning of the near loss of the *Sameveron.*

It will be interesting to learn of the official reaction to these developments.

The date of that letter, 16 September 1948, is interesting. For on that very day another British Liberty got into serious difficulties when its Thames Ballast shifted. The ship was the *Leicester,* previously the *Samesk* and which like the *Samkey,* had been managed by the New Zealand Shipping Company during the war. At the time of the incident she was owned by Federal Steam Navigation.

Leicester was on a voyage from Tilbury to New York and was nearing the American coast when she ran into a hurricane. The ballast in the ship's 'tween-decks was secured with shifting boards but these gave way, and as the ballast shifted, this ship like the *Sameveron* before it, took on a great list, except that this one was 40° to port instead of 55° to starboard. The crew abandoned ship, six lives being lost in the process. The rest of the crew were picked up by another Liberty, the American-flagged *Cecil N. Bean* (New Orleans, April, 1944).

Once again a Liberty was to prove its basic ruggedness, for the *Leicester* refused to sink. She was sighted adrift five days later and was taken in tow by the salvage tug *Samsonia,* Captain Jack Cowley, working out of Bermuda. The boarding party had a mammoth task in connecting a towing wire to the listing vessel, but finally made it and towed the ship to Bermuda. On 3 October tug and charge anchored safely in the Sound. 'There was no time for congratulations,' says Captain Bill Stewart, who got the story from his friend Jack Cowley, 'because a hurricane struck both vessels and they were both severely damaged when they were blown ashore and pounded on rocks. The salvage award to *Samsonia* was very poor because *Leicester* was declared a constructive total loss'.[7] However, the *Leicester* was later refloated and towed to Baltimore where she was repaired. After that she traded under various names and ownerships until 1966 when as the *Viking Liberty* she was scrapped at Santander, Spain. (The tug *Samsonia* was also refloated and repaired. In 1948 Jack Cowley was appointed Deck Superintendent of Foundation Salvage Company at Halifax, Nova Scotia. It was probably on his advice that the company purchased the tug. She then became *Foundation Josephine.*)

Fred Honisett, one of the men who had so luckily signed off the *Samkey,* joined the *Leicester* as his next ship. He was away for about six months on that ship which then returned to England. On the day before he was to leave home to rejoin *Leicester* he was looking at his reflection in the bathroom mirror and noticed some spots on his chest. He called out to his wife Joan, who took one look and said, 'Oh good, that's chicken pox. You must have caught it from my sister. You won't be able to go back now'. 'Imagine,' says Fred, 'when later in the month I opened

---

7. Captain Bill Stewart, correspondence, etc., 1999–2000.

the newspaper to find out what had happened to *Leicester*. Twice in a year was too much for my wife who told me I must not tempt fate. So I left the sea.'

It is of interest that sometimes and for short voyages, ballast was stowed on the decks of Liberty ships. This happened with the *Clan MacFadyen* (*Samderwent*, Portland, Maine, March 1944). On a voyage back from India in 1956, the ship was nearly lost in a storm off Crete when the steering gear failed. Gerald Smith was the Second Officer, and he says that during that storm a crack appeared in the deck near No. 3 hatch. After discharging at Dundee the ship sailed northabout Scotland to Glasgow for repairs, 'and because the screw was half out of the water we took on 400 tons of Dundee sand on the after deck as ballast, then had to shovel it all over the side in the Minches before reaching Glasgow. Those were the days!'[8]

Samkey was not the only Liberty ship to be lost at sea without survivors in post-war years. Another was the Greek-owned *Thrasyvoulos* (*Roger Williams*, Wilmington, September 1942). She was heading for the Suez Canal with a cargo of iron ore for Constanza and was somewhere south-east of Aden on 29 June 1965 when some sort of disaster struck. On that date she reported leaks in No. 1 hold, and after that was never heard from again. There were no survivors. Yet another was the *Captain G* (originally *Ammla*, Baltimore, December 1943). She was on the way to the Shanghai breakers yard when on 21 August 1968 she was caught in a typhoon about sixty miles south of Hong Kong. Distress messages were received to the effect that the engines had been damaged and the ship was flooding. After that there was silence. Some wreckage identified as having come from the ship was eventually found.

---

8. Captain Gerald Smith, correspondence, 2000. After his sea-going days Gerald Smith handled many Liberty ships, first as an Aden pilot, then as a Trinity House pilot on the River Thames. He says, 'Liberty ships, in a light condition with any kind of wind, were like balloons'.

CHAPTER 25

More Post-war Disasters, Trials and Tribulations

Most peacetime Liberty voyages were, of course, completed successfully and without major incident. But the sea can never be taken for granted; anyone who does so is asking for trouble. On top of that there are always the 'normal' hazards and woes of shipboard life with which sailors have to contend, including the tensions stemming from being holed up, sometimes for weeks on end in those old days, with only one's immediate shipmates for company. To paraphrase a line from Doctor Samuel Johnson, being in a ship is like being in a jail, with the added chance of being drowned. The good doctor was talking in the days when the Press Gang was rife, but had he lived in the twentieth century he might well have wondered why it was that such seaborne prisoners were there of their own volition.

To illustrate some of these 'normal' hazards, the author recalls the days when he was serving as Senior Cadet aboard the *Harpagon* (*Samderry*, Portland, Maine, March 1944). That ship's captain probably had a bad war, for in 1949/1950, he was still a bundle of nerves. The difference between what sailors know as a 'happy ship' and the opposite kind, is usually the behaviour and attitudes of the master, and *Harpagon* was not at all a happy one. Furthermore, superstitious seamen will tell you that an unhappy ship has the propensity to turn into an unlucky one, and that is exactly what happened to *Harpagon*. During a voyage that spanned some fifteen months and two circumnavigations of the globe, the ship suffered a grounding incident and was once fired upon by insurgents when passing up the Saigon River. There were other untoward incidents, but none was more tragic than when leaving Port Said on the way back to England, the ship lost a man overboard in bad weather. The only good thing to come out of that incident was the insight it presented into the camaraderie of the sea. The captain had radioed a message asking all ships in the vicinity to keep a lookout for the lost man, and within the hour a Dutch ship ranged up and after an exchange of signals, joined us in cruising up and down a search pattern that lasted all day. The search was called off as dusk came – there had been little chance of ever finding the man for

435

he had been wearing heavy seaboots and he could not swim – and the Dutchman then went on its way. The lost man, a seaman of only twenty, had probably been the most popular man on the ship, but it was not only that which left scarcely a dry eye amongst the rest of the crew members as we watched the Dutch ship sail off. All the post-war sailors amongst us had learnt a valuable lesson, one already learned by most of those that had served during the war; that a seaman is a seaman, and when one is in distress, nationality rarely enters the equation.

Cadet Ian Hopkinson, who joined the Royal Mail Liberty ship *Barranca* as his first ship in March 1956, presents us with a humorous story about certain shipboard woes. He talks about the daily ritual of determining the noon position, sun sights being taken by the Captain, the Chief Officer, the Navigating Officer, and the Cadets. 'The Junior Cadet was the first to announce his findings, and these findings were announced by all in reverse order of seniority. One might suppose that the noon position was arrived at by the process of democratic vote. Such was not the case, however. Seniority played its part and more often than not the findings of the cadets were discounted as being beyond reason.'

Chris Sturke was Third Officer of *Balantia* (*Samfaithful*, Baltimore, April 1944) in January 1958 when she loaded a cargo of sugar at Matanzas, Cuba. His story illustrates that merchant seaman are sometimes the foreigners that get closest to the world's trouble spots. He says the port was in a state of tension due to the 'Batista regime taking some stick from a bearded communist revolutionary named Fidel Castro'. Not all the tensions on that ship came from outside. Sturke says that a rum-crazed seaman on board had to be subdued and handcuffed to an awning stanchion on the boat deck until he cooled off.[1]

Liberty ships around the globe suffered many mishaps after the war. In three months alone, in early 1946, four Liberty ships were involved in three separate dangerous incidents. In its 1 March edition, *Lloyd's List* reported that the *Sambanka* (Portland, Maine, April 1944) had arrived at Diego Suarez, Madagascar, on 25 February 1946 in tow of the steamer *Cape Wrath*. On a voyage from Rangoon to Lorenco Marques the Liberty had lost its propeller and suffered a broken tail-end shaft. The ship had no spares on board and there were none at Diego Suarez so she was then towed by the freighter *Empire Kinsman* to Durban and eventually repaired there.

In early morning dense fog off the entrance to the River Humber on England's east coast on 1 May 1946, two Liberties were in collision. The British *Samgaudie* (Baltimore, March 1944) was proceeding out of the Humber from Hull when she ran into the side of the American *Andrew*

---

1. Extracted from various editions of the Royal Mail Association *Newsletter* kindly supplied by George Monk.

Furuseth (Richmond, October 1942). The *Furuseth* was severely damaged with a great hole in its side, whilst the *Samgaudie*'s bow had been
set back. Both vessels safely berthed at Hull on the following day. (The
American-flagged vessel had been named for a maritime labour leader
who had been largely responsible for the passing of what has been called
the Seaman's Bill of Rights in the States in 1915.)

Nine days later on 10 May the *Samhope* (Baltimore, April 1944)
radioed that she was ashore and fast on a rock ledge in about as remote a
place one can find on the face of the globe. It was near the Pritchard
Islands at the southern extremity of Chile. Fortunately the captain was
able to extricate his ship three days later and then proceeded to Punta
Arenas for emergency repairs.[2]

Two years later, in thick monsoonal weather on 10 December 1948, the
American *Amelia Earhart* (Houston, December 1942) piled up on an
island in the South Natuna Group off the Sarawak coast of Borneo, in the
same general part of the world from which the aviatrix after which the
ship had been named, had made her last take-off before disappearing forever. (Amelia Earhart and her navigator, in an attempt to fly around the
world, had taken off from New Guinea to head for remote Howland
Island, but were not heard from after 3 July 1937.) The tug *Griper*, out
of Singapore, pulled the ship off the reef ten days later and towed her
back to that port. She was declared a constructive total loss. But afterwards she was sold and repaired and was back trading by 1951. By 1965
she was sailing under the Chinese flag as the *Jiading*. In 1967 she arrived
at Liverpool emblazoned with placards proclaiming some of the
'thoughts of Mao'. The thoughts were in Chinese so probably had no
great effect upon the local populace, except perhaps on some of the
residents of that city's Chinatown.

Those incidents were all of a minor nature compared with the one that
occurred on 16 April 1947. The Liberty *Grandcamp* was one of the vessels purchased directly from the Americans by the French Government
in that year. She had originally been the *Benjamin R. Curtis* (Los
Angeles, November 1942) named after a former Justice of the American
Supreme Court. Immediately after the purchase was concluded she was
sent to Texas City to load a cargo for Dunkirk and Bordeaux. Texas City
was then a town of some 15,000 people. It lay in Galveston Bay between
Galveston and Houston, about a dozen miles north-west of the former
place. It was not a town noted for its beauty. Developed only in the twentieth century, the topography was flat with the land lying only a few feet
above sea level. It was an industrial town, and all around were oil tanks,
chemical plants and grain elevators. The *Grandcamp* arrived at the port

---

2. Various editions *Lloyd's List*.

on 11 April 1947 and began loading a cargo of ammonium nitrate, a chemical used as a fertiliser. Ammonium nitrate is rather an innocuous-looking substance and although it was widely used as a fertiliser, few people in 1947 knew that it also had an awesome explosive potential. A warning of sorts had been given at a factory at Oppau in Germany in September 1921 when, in an endeavour to break up a rock-hard crystal-line mass of the same substance that had formed on the inside of some tanks, dynamite was used on it, resulting in a terrible explosion that reportedly killed 500 people and destroyed over 2000 buildings. The accident was put down to being caused by a sympathetic explosion, and did not get much international publicity.

Grandcamp lay alongside Pier O in what was called the North Slip. Luckily, as it turned out, there were only two other ships of any size in port on the morning of the 16th. In the Main Slip immediately to the south, the American-flagged Liberty *Wilson B. Keene* (Portland, Maine, October 1944) lay alongside Pier B. Moored alongside Pier A just across from the *Keene* was the slightly smaller 6214-ton American freighter, *Highflyer*. By 0800 hours on the 16th *Grandcamp* had loaded about 2300 tons of the fertiliser, all packed in 100lb bags, mainly in Nos. 2 and 4 holds. The ship's engineers had taken advantage of the ship's stay in port to carry out some maintenance on the engines, so the ship was incapable of movement without tugs. The stevedores who boarded that morning began work at No. 4 hatch, and nothing untoward was noticed when they removed the hatch covers. But about fifteen minutes later, smoke was seen rising from one of the gaps between the vertical frames at the ship's side. Apparently thinking that the fire was small the stevedores and crew members at first tried putting it out with canisters of drinking water, then with portable fire-extinguishers, but within few minutes the smoke was so dense that everyone had to evacuate the hold. A hose was rigged from the ship's water supply but the chief officer refused its use for fear of damaging the cargo. Instead he ordered the hatch covered and steam injected into the now-enclosed space. Then came an explosion which blew the hatch covers off, and flames and smoke began pouring from the hatch. Only then did someone think of calling the Texas City Fire Department. Stevedores and crewmen had been ordered off the ship before the firemen arrived, and were gathered on the quay along with a number of spectators who had arrived from nearby installations. There were twenty-seven fireman in the group, and they began setting up their equipment from the shore, apparently running out of hoses whilst doing so. A press photographer appeared on the scene, took a picture and then rushed away to make the noon edition. By doing so he saved his life.

At exactly 0912 hours the *Grandcamp* disintegrated in a huge explosion. All the fireman, crewmen, and spectators on the quay were killed instantaneously. The blast flattened buildings, and blazing parts of the ship landed all around the port and industrial area. A tidal wave swept through the port tearing *Highflyer* from her moorings and smashing her up against the *Wilson B. Keene,* the two vessels becoming locked together by twisted metal parts from both. The wave swept a 150ft barge ashore, leaving it high and dry on the quay. Two private planes which had the misfortune to be flying overhead at the time of the explosion were blown from the sky. The giant Monsanto Chemical Works just across the North Slip from where the *Grandcamp* had once been, suffered most in that explosion, with buildings and other structures either razed to the ground or set afire. Many of the sheds and tanks contained combustibles, including polystyrenes. Directly in line with Pier O was an oil-tank farm owned by the Stone Oil Company; the tanks there caught the full blast and were soon on fire. It is thought that 400 people lost their lives in that initial explosion.

With half of the Texas City Fire Brigade dead and the port's water mains now out of commission, volunteer fireman were called in from far and wide, including from Houston about fifty miles away to the north. The US Army base at Fort Crocker sent in its fire-fighting teams. The oil companies' own firefighters strove to keep the fires away from the tanks that were not yet burning. Tugs arrived from Galveston, but were unable to enter the port immediately because of floating debris, and the dense smoke and sulphur fumes that were hanging over everything. The fire-fighting efforts went on all that afternoon and into the night.

Over at Pier B those crew members of *Highflyer* and *Wilson B. Keene* who had not been injured were fighting a losing battle against the fires that had broken out on board both ships. The initial explosion had blown off *Highflyer*'s hatches, exposing the 2000 tons of sulphur on board and 360 tons of ammonium nitrate. Late that night the tugs from Galveston at last forced their way through and secured lines to *Highflyer* with the intention of towing her out into the bay. Men in breathing apparatus boarded the freighter to cut away its anchor cable. But the towing attempt failed, *Highflyer* being inextricably linked with the *Keene.* The last man to leave the ship saw smoke rising from the hold containing the fertiliser. A few minutes after one in the morning of the 17th the *Highflyer* blew up and disappeared, red-hot fragments from it shooting thousands of feet into the night sky. The *Keene* also disintegrated, only her bow section being left lying above water. As all the rescue workers had been withdrawn in time, only one man lost his life in the second explosion. However, that explosion finished off the work begun by the first one. Many more warehouses were destroyed, reinforced concrete buildings reduced to rubble, and storage tanks everywhere were burning, many of them containing chemicals of a noxious nature.

The Governor of Texas declared a State of Emergency and state authorities took charge of all subsequent rescue and fire-fighting operations. The number of known dead by the time the last fire had been extinguished was 468, but over 100 others were posted as missing and they have not been accounted for since. About 3000 people were injured, 800 of them seriously. The monetary cost of the whole affair has been estimated at $67 million.[3] A number of lessons were learnt from what has come to be called The Great Texas City Explosion. One of them is that the French chief officer unbeknowingly made a grave error when he insisted upon closing the hatch and using steam injection. Water and only water, and in vast quantities, must be used to fight fires involving ammonium nitrate. And if when dealing with a ship, that means flooding the holds until she sinks alongside the berth, then so be it. That is better than the Texas City alternative.

Lessons take time to learn, and they had not been learned at the Port of Brest in France four months later. On 28 July 1947, the Norwegian-flagged half-sister to the Liberties, the *Ocean Liberty,* the first Ocean to be launched at Portland, Maine, took fire whilst carrying a cargo that included over 3000 tons of ammonium nitrate. Despite Texas City, attempts were made to use steam smothering and in consequence the fire spread. Fortunately the ship was being towed clear of the quays when the cargo exploded and the ship sank. Had she still been at her original berth the death toll might have matched that at Texas City; as it was twenty-one people lost their lives. *Ocean Liberty* was later salved, and lived to trade into the 1960s.

The Greek *Nicolaos Epiphaniades* (*George H. Himes,* Portland, Oregon, July 1943) a veteran of Guadalcanal, exploded and caught fire on 15 March 1961 whilst loading a cargo of anthracite at the Ukrainian port of Odessa. She grounded and was abandoned by her crew. She was later refloated and then seized by the Soviet authorities because of the damage the explosion had caused to parts of the port. Repaired, the ship sailed under the Russian flag for several years until she was scrapped.

The name *Captain George* was twice used for Greek Liberties, the second time for a ship that suffered a chemical explosion at sea. The first *Captain George* (*James H. Lane,* Portland, Oregon, November 1943) had also came to an untimely end when she ran aground in October 1957 at the Cape Verde Islands and was declared a constructive total loss. The second ship of that name (built as *W.W. McCracken,* Portland, Oregon, October 1943), had loaded a cargo of sulphur and nitrate at New Orleans and then topped off with 400 tons of mining explosives at Houston for Tripoli, Libya. On 14 November 1962 when about 300 miles north-east of Bermuda, Captain G. Karamezis reported that his ship was on fire after an explosion in a hold containing sulphur. He also

---

3. (a) Contemporary reports in *The Houston Chronicle.* (b) Information supplied by Senator Louis de Catuelan, 2000. Senator de Catuelan sailed in a few French-flagged Liberty ships post-war.

reported that the sea was rough. In a later message he said the fire could not be controlled so he was dumping some of the explosives. On the 15th two Liberian tankers, the *Virginia* and *Trinity Navigator* arrived at the scene but were unable to get close because of the weather conditions. An aircraft flying overhead reported that the crew of the *Captain George* had abandoned ship in two boats, one with five men on board, the other with twenty. The second boat capsized, and the plane dropped life-floats to the men in the water. The *Trinity Navigator* was able to pick up the five men from the remaining lifeboat, but only two of the other crew members were found by the *Virginia*. The Liberty sank three days later.[4]

On several post-war occasions, Liberty ships were involved in salvage operations. Alex Clarke was Second Cook and Baker aboard County Ship Management's *Stamford Hill* (*Samneagh,* Baltimore, April 1944) when she loaded tractors, cement, and other cargo at Gravesend for Mombassa towards the end of 1948. (The cargo was destined for the famous Ground Nut Scheme which the British Government thought would revitalise the Kenyan economy, but which instead turned into an economic fiasco.) The ship was at Mombassa when, off nearby Pemba Island on 26 February 1949, the company's *Akri Hill* reported that she was in trouble having suffered a complete engine breakdown. *Stamford Hill* sailed to the rescue, and four days later successfully towed the ship into port. Two years later, Alex Clarke received his portion of the salvage award, amounting to a little under £53. As is the way with salvage awards, the captain's portion was much larger, Captain Church receiving £1000.[5]

There was no salvage award after the incident which took place in January 1953 involving two Liberty ships owned by Britain's Bank Line. It took place at Ocean Island in the Pacific, then part of the British colony called the Gilbert and Ellice Islands; now it is part of Kiribati. Like nearby Nauru, it is rich in phosphates, guano produced by countless numbers of sea birds. The deposits at that time were controlled by the British Phosphate Commission, which had chartered several Bank Line vessels to convey cargoes of it from both those islands to Australia and New Zealand. Nauru had proper berthing facilities and the phosphate was loaded via a pair of cantilever bridges. Ocean Island had no such facilities. Instead ships moored to buoys off the island and the phosphate was brought out to them in barges and then the ship's own cargo-handling gear was used, with 2-ton buckets, to load the ship. The moorings at Ocean were exposed to the weather, so when onshore winds blew up, moorings would be slipped and the ship steam away and stand off until there was an improvement.

---

4. Information supplied by Christos Dounis.
5. Correspondence with Alex Clarke, 1999.

On the evening of 5 January 1953 the *Kelvinbank* (launched as *Jesse de Forest,* Baltimore, October 1943, which had become the *Samuta* when handed over to the British), had done just that. Captain Shorthouse had stood off all night, but on the following morning on making back to the moorings he misjudged his approach and the ship ended up on a reef at Sydney Point. Not only that, the ship was sitting on top of what was left of a wreck dating from 1926. The wreck was that of the British *Ooma.* The only major part of it left was the tail-shaft and propeller assembly, and that had penetrated *Kelvinbank*'s hull in way of No. 3 hold, effectively pinning the ship to the reef. With the after end of the ship still afloat and a heavy swell running, the ship was 'working' in the seaway, causing yet more damage.

Captain Shorthouse radioed that he required assistance to the sistership *Titanbank* (*Samnegros,* Baltimore, June 1944) which was at Nauru. *Titanbank,* Captain E. Craig, sailed that afternoon and arrived off Ocean the following morning. By that time the crew of *Kelvinbank* had used the lifeboats to get off the ship and on to the island. Bank Line chartered a seaplane in Australia and flew in a salvage expert named Captain Herd. With the assistance of the crews of both ships Herd went about trying to save the stricken vessel. Apprentice John Burtt was one of the *Titanbank* crew. He says that the only way to get on board *Kelvinbank* at first, was to shin up the lifeboat falls. 'I was a lot younger and fitter in those days!' He says it was difficult to keep to one's feet on board as the swell was pounding the ship which was being pushed ever further onto the reef.[6]

As Herd organised the attempt at salvage over the next few days, John Burtt says he learnt more seamanship than in the rest of his time at sea. Emergency pumps were dismantled aboard *Titanbank* and transferred over, as were anchors and sections of anchor chains, using the Phosphate Company's barges, lashed together and fitted with a platform, for conveying the heavy material over. At the first attempt there was a mishap, and the anchors and cables ended up at the bottom of the sea, fortunately in shallow water. Island divers swam down, secured wires, and the whole lot was dragged back aboard *Titanbank* where the job began over again. Ground tackles were laid leading from *Kelvinbank* to anchors, and using blocks, wires, and shackles stripped from *Titanbank*'s heavy-lift derrick, two giant purchases were rigged, which according to Captain Herd would give a pull of over 100 tons. That was about three times more than the largest and most powerful salvage tug of those times. Herd's idea was to haul the ship bodily around until it faced the sea, and then haul her off the reef.

The gear had taken four days to set up during which two pumps were used to try and reduce the water level in No. 3 hold. Despite the pumps,

---

6. Correspondence with John Burtt, 1999.

the water had not gone down, and the movement of the ship had caused further hull and bottom damage. However, the ground tackle did its job, and the *Kelvinbank* was turned to face the sea. But then, after a further inspection and to the disappointment of all, Captain Herd concluded that the ship would sink if she was pulled off the reef. He then radioed his verdict to the insurers and the ship was declared a constructive total loss. After stripping *Kelvinbank* of everything of value, the *Titanbank* then sailed for New Zealand with two crews on board. As the attempt at salvage had ended in failure, there were no salvage awards.

The dangers of war, mines apart, might have been over by 1948, but Liberty ships, with their propensity to roll heavily, could still scare the living daylights out of experienced seamen, let alone a then uncertificated Fourth Mate. John R. Jones was serving in that capacity in January 1948 aboard Blue Funnel's *Eurymedon* (built as *Matthew Brush*, Baltimore, August 1943, before becoming *Samoa*). The ship sailed from Glasgow for New York, and says, John Jones, 'it turned out to be one of the most horrendous passages I have ever experienced'.

He goes on:

From the moment we passed into the Atlantic, we hit bad weather. Every weather report forecast depression after depression, and the ship pitched and rolled in a manner such that I had never experienced before or since.

About ten days out when in mid-Atlantic we were in difficulties. The problem was that if we maintained a speed sufficient to keep our bow to the weather, she was pitching so much that we were in danger of losing our propeller (through racing) and, if we reduced our engine revs, she kept falling into the 'trough' [between wave peaks] where we were on our beam-ends for minutes at a time. One member of the crew, who shall be nameless, became hysterical and had to be restrained in his cabin.

We received an SOS from another Liberty a few miles to the north of us but such was our own plight we were unable to offer any assistance.

Captain G.I. Thomas then took the only decision that was open to him – that is – to go about and head for the Azores, as we were now short of fuel. All the ship's company were informed of what we were about to do and the order was given to 'go about'. As we fell into the trough, I estimated that our angle of heel was about 70 degrees and there she lay for about four minutes! When she finally came about and righted herself, everyone cheered with relief, and I suppose, with the easing of tension.

John Jones says that if his memory is correct, that crossing of the Atlantic which should have taken about ten days, took three and a half weeks. It was an experience he never forgot. He says that he was working in

Freetown, Sierra Leone in 1964, when an old battered Greek Liberty berthed alongside. 'On her stern, under layers of paint, I could just make out the name *Eurymedon*!' (At that time the ship was called *Mimosa*, She had two more names after that before being scrapped at Bilbao in 1971.)[7]

T. & J. Harrison of Liverpool purchased ten Liberties during 1947-8, two of which were the *Samgaudie* and *Samhope* both of which have been mentioned earlier in this chapter as being involved in incidents. Four of the total came from the bulk purchase of Liberties made by the British Ministry of Transport, and four of the others were purchased through the agency of Mollers Limited, a shipping company based at Hong Kong where the stringent British conditions over the use of dollar reserves did not apply. T. & J. Harrison always named their ships after trades, professions, and other ways of describing human endeavours, and no exceptions were made with the Liberties. They called the first one they bought, in honour of its country of build, *Senator (Anton M. Holter/Sambay,* Portland, Oregon, August 1943).

The *Samhope* that became *Successor* was one of the ships purchased by way of Mollers of Hong Kong. On 15 May 1951 *Successor* was proceeding up the Mississippi river with a pilot aboard when evasive action had to be taken to avoid the American freighter *Tillie Lykes,* action that was only partially successful for the freighter struck *Successor*'s stern. In the process the Liberty hit another American ship, the *Andrew Jackson Higgins,* which was lying alongside a riverside wharf. All three ships suffered extensive damage, but there were no casualties.

The crew of the Greek *Irini (Hugh L. Kerwin,* Baltimore, December 1943) had what can only be described as a lucky escape when she was in collision on 10 June 1967. Loaded with sulphate the ship was in collision off Cape Spartel with the tanker *Russell N. Green* owned by Naess Shipping. *Irini* managed to limp into Cadiz where she was adjudged to be beyond economic repair. She was towed to Valencia and broken up there. Another unlucky Greek Liberty was the *Archon Gabriel (Vernon L. Kellog,* Los Angeles, July 1943). On 8 January 1958 she was carrying a cargo of iron ore from Rio de Janeiro to Szczecin when she grounded off Greifswald Lighthouse, East Germany. Over the next two weeks East German tugs made several attempts to pull the ship off and finally succeeded in towing the ship into Szczecin where her cargo was discharged. The details of the grounding and of the salvage work, were never examined before a court, and the ship's Greek owners would not, or could not, pay the salvage bills presented to them. In consequence the East German authorities confiscated the ship. She was repaired and then taken over by VEB Deutshe Seereederei, a shipping company based at Rostock. In

---

7. Information from John R. Jones, 2000.

the process she became the only Liberty ship ever to sail under the East German flag. She was renamed *Ernst Moritz Arndt*. During the repairs carried out at the Stettiner Werft Shipyard (Szczecin was once called Stettin), no great changes were made although new generators were fitted, and the radio room was equipped anew. The ship was sold on in 1968 and eventually scrapped in Taiwan in 1971.[8]

Structural failures on Liberty ships continued to be a problem throughout their careers, despite the extra strengthening that all of them received from time to time. After the sale of many to overseas interests in 1946-1947, American authorities discontinued keeping a check on them, so no central record is available. Four ships that broke in two and sank after springing leaks that may have been attributable to the old problem, or maybe to their then old age, met their respective ends between January 1965 and November 1967. The first was the Taiwanese-flagged *Grand* (*W. Walter Husband*, Baltimore, October 1943). She was carrying a cargo of scrap iron to Japan and on 13 January 1965 was about 300 miles east of Tokyo Bay when she sprung a leak, broke in two and sank. The Liberian *Tradeways II* (*William H. Dall*, Portland, Oregon, November 1943) sprung a leak in heavy weather north of the Azores on 21 October 1965. Carrying a cargo of steel products she broke in two and sank on the following day. Next was the Greek *Eleni K* (*John Hopkins*, Baltimore, March 1943). On 29 October 1966 in heavy weather eight miles off the South Australian coast, she sank after breaking in two. The fourth vessel was the Cypriot-flagged *Artemida* (*Fremont Older*, Richmond, June 1943). On 5 October 1967 she was in the Malacca Strait and making for China with a cargo of phosphate rock, when she developed severe leaks. The ship's master beached her at Sungei Muar on the Malayan coast. A fortnight later she was refloated and towed first to Singapore, then to Shanghai. When at anchor off Woosung on 30 November she broke adrift in the aftermath of a storm, drifted ashore and broke in two.

---

8. Information from Wolfgang Siegert, September 2000.

CHAPTER 26

The Last Years of the Trading Liberties

Although some Liberty ships were to sail into the 1970s and 1980s it was the 1960s that really brought an end to an era in which they had been familiar sights on every ocean and in most ports. As they had grown older it had become more and more expensive to maintain them to the Class requirements of ship registration societies such as Lloyd's Register, the American Bureau of Shipping, and Bureau Veritas. Unless they were so maintained and had the appropriate certification, no insurance underwriter would touch them with a bargepole, quite apart from any Government legislation they might then have offended. By 1965 even the last batch of Liberties built in 1945 were due for their fifth special survey, a four-yearly experience of the utmost importance, during which surveyors descend upon a ship and inspect every last inch of her, the usual result being significant repair and rectification costs. The ships had also become uneconomic in fuel consumption when compared with modern diesel-powered vessels of similar cargo-carrying capacity. By the mid-1960s therefore, it was becoming less and less desirable to own these ships and the bottom had fallen out of the market for them. In those circumstances a Total or Constructive Total Loss situation could be the most financially attractive way for an owner to dispose of his Liberty ship properties. In consequence many underwriters at that time viewed any such claims with what can be described as a rather jaundiced eye.

Some of the more unscrupulous owners may have been tempted to 'arrange' such a loss. However, to do so is not easy. There is a very real risk to life involved, whether the 'arrangement' is by grounding, scuttling, or by an engine-room fire. In addition, at least one of the crew must be involved, probably the captain, and others may suspect what is going on and may give the game away. Because of these factors this kind of insurance scam was probably uncommon, and if underwriters ever did pay out on such a suspect or dubious claim, they are not talking. It was much more common whenever a Liberty ship sustained reasonably extensive damage, for the shipowner to try very hard to prove to underwriters, by fair means or foul, that the cost of the damage repairs would be in excess of the insured value of the ship. By these means the owner would hope to obtain a settlement with underwriters on the basis of a

Constructive Total Loss, after which he could go off whistling to the bank. Needless to say, some of these attempts resulted in heated and rather acrimonious discussions between surveyors representing the owners and others representing the underwriters concerned.

Sometimes spurious claims were made for repair costs not amounting to a Constructive Total Loss. Andrew Sinclair, one-time Chief Surveyor to the Salvage Association, remembers one such case very well. He had been asked to attend a Greek-owned Liberty that had been laid up for a time in the River Blackwater in Britain. The ship had previously reported a rudder problem when at Colombo, and certain repairs had been carried out in the dockyard there, under the supervision of the ship's own engineers. Further rudder problems were experienced on the way back to Europe, and the Greek owners had put in a claim citing bad weather damage on the way, as the proximate cause for the still malfunctioning rudder. When Andrew Sinclair examined the rudder he found not only that there was much corrosion in the area, but that the bush on which the lower rudder pintle (one of the pins about which the rudder rotates) should have been resting upon was missing. The owner's Marine Superintendent, an affable but devious Greek who Sinclair knew quite well from previous experience, was in attendance. He said the bush must have been lost as a result of the heavy weather. It was a statement Sinclair doubted, reckoning that the bush had been left off in error at Colombo, so he asked the Superintendent to provide photographs. The necessary repairs were carried out even while the claim was in dispute, and when it came to settling the accounts the Superintendent produced some beautifully produced photographs of a newly-machined pintle sitting very nicely on its brand new bush. When it was pointed out that the photos were of the current work, the Superintendent said, 'But, Mr. Sinclair, you did not tell me from *when* you wanted the photographs!' So the claim remained in dispute. When Sinclair next met the Greek Superintendent, the man was all smiles. His company had changed the basis of the claim from weather damage to engineers' negligence, something also covered by the insurance policy.[1]

The Salvage Association for which Andrew Sinclair worked, investigated many of the claims made by Liberty ship owners. That organisation had been set up in Britain under Royal Charter in 1856 by Lloyd's underwriters and the Royal Mail, in order to protect the interests of underwriters and shipowners. Later, the shipowning influence disappeared, after which the Association's Committee comprised equal numbers of so-called Company underwriters and others from Lloyd's. Over the years it built up a high reputation, and with offices the world over, was called in to investigate shipping claims everywhere. Its function was to establish the cause,

---

1. Interview and correspondence with C. Andrew Sinclair OBE, August 2000.

nature, and extent of damages to ships, with complete objectivity. As Andrew Sinclair made a point of telling all new Association surveyors when they first entered his office, 'You don't give a damn who pays so long as it is the right person'. One of the earlier Liberty incidents in which the Salvation Association became involved was when the *Armar* (*E.H. Sothern/Sammont*, Los Angeles, September 1943) went aground off Cuba in December 1952. George Emmerson, from the Association's New York office, was sent down to survey the ship at Savannah after the ship had been towed there. There was a dispute over the extent of the damage. (Usually this meant that additional earlier structural damage had been discovered that had nothing whatsoever to do with the proximate cause, but which the owner was trying to throw into the pot.) The repair methods to be used were also in dispute. As a result of Emmerson's report the case went to court in New York some eighteen months later and settlement was finally made in favour of the underwriters.[2]

In the mid-1960s when the youngest of the Liberty ships still trading was some twenty years old, which is rather ancient for a ship, there was a spate of Liberty ship losses. Professor Frank Bull has provided a list of unknown origin which shows that between February 1964 and December 1967, a period of less than four years, a total of sixty-four Liberties were lost either by shipwreck or after having sprung leaks at sea. A note at the end of the list says that during that same period a further twenty-one Liberties were stranded then refloated but subsequently were either broken up or condemned. So in that period, a total of eighty-five Liberties met their fates from direct or indirect consequences of accidents of one sort or another.[3] That works out at nearly two a month.

Not all the cases investigated were necessarily of a suspicious nature. Sometimes investigations were conducted when it was thought that the loss might have come about through faults built into the structure right at the beginning, faults that had nothing to do with 'notch sensitive' steel. As one of the world's leading experts on stresses in ships, Professor Bull was once called upon to advise in the Salvage Association's investigation into the loss of a Liberty off the South Australian coast. The ship was the Greek *Eleni K* (*John Hopkins*, Baltimore, March 1943) which cracked and then foundered in shallow water on 29 June 1966, but was then refloated and finally grounded on Goat Island where she broke in two. She had suffered complete buckling of the bottom structure, almost certainly due to the bottom plates having originally been welded together not exactly in line, this 'unfairness', as it is called, having grown worse over the years.

---

2. Correspondence with George Emmerson, April 2000.
3. Frank Bull may have obtained the list from a Salvage Association representative, but he cannot now recall how it came into his hands.

In the 1960s the Salvage Association did not have an office at Singapore, so when a casualty came along in South-east Asian waters they usually requested the firm of Ritchie & Bisset to act for them. That firm of Consulting Engineers and Marine Surveyors had long been established in the city. Stuart Walker was a young engineer surveyor with them, and being young tended to be sent on the more gruelling jobs that occurred in out-of-the-way places. At Singapore he had carried out 'countless Liberty ship boiler, machinery, hull and safety equipment surveys' on behalf Bureau Veritas and other organisations and so knew the ships very well.[4] In August 1967 he was asked to inspect the *Angelina* which had arrived at the Singapore Eastern Roads under tow of the tug *Friesland*. Since being launched at Baltimore as the *Melvil Dewey*, and completed as *Samsacola* in December 1945, this ship had sailed under four different names before being renamed for the last time in 1965. Her final owner was Transocean Navigation Corporation of Monrovia, Liberia.

On 31 July 1967 that ship was on a ballast passage to Madras when a serious fire occurred in the engine-room. The crew of twenty-five including the master abandoned ship and were picked up by the British *Golden Phoenix*, one fireman being lost in the incident. On 4 August the tug *Friesland* intercepted the derelict vessel and reported that it was expected that the fire would be out and towing arrangements completed by the 6th, when the tow would begin to Madras. The destination was changed when the Madras Port Authority refused to accept the disabled vessel on the grounds that the port was congested and that the ship would be unsafe in the anchorage because of the onset of the monsoon. It was decided to tow the ship to Singapore instead. Stuart Walker boarded the ship on 20 August together with the owner's Marine Consultant who had flown in from New York. They found the entire accommodation block completely gutted, with decks and bulkheads heavily distorted, and on the bridge, all navigation and radio equipment destroyed. Shell plating on both sides of the engine-room had buckled in the heat of the fire, and there was fire damage in both Nos. 3 and 4 holds. The next day was spent ascertaining the extent of the damage in the engine-room and in attempting to find the source of the fire. The deck inspection had already shown deposits of semi-burned fuel close to the starboard fuel settling tank air pipe, which suggested that the tank had overflowed at some time prior to the fire. In the engine-room around the starboard settling tank they discovered more deposits of carbonised and partly burned fuel oil, and the securing bolts on the manhole cover of that tank were found to be loose. In Liberty ships the Babcock & Wilcox boilers faced inwards towards each other, and the rear of each boiler was

---

4. Correspondence and talks with Stuart S. Walker, August-November 2000.

very close to the inboard side of its nearest settling tank. This meant that heavy fuel leakage from one of the tanks would almost inevitably come into contact with the rear casing of the nearest boiler. The findings clearly showed that the starboard settling tank had been over filled, causing oil to spill out of the loose manhole cover and eventually to splash onto the casing of the starboard boiler. Any 'hot spots' on the boiler casing caused by missing or defective refractory brickwork inside it, would have resulted in auto-ignition of the spilled oil. It was not at all unknown for twenty-odd years of wear and tear to have caused localised failure of the refractory boiler lining in Liberty ships, so causing these hot spots. (These would be discovered, hopefully, at the annual boiler surveys, and rectified.)

After having ascertained what seemed to be the certain cause of the fire and the extent of the damage it had caused, it was then necessary to estimate the cost of the repairs. That exercise quickly showed that the cost would exceed the vessel's insured value. Underwriters were informed and advised that the fire had probably been caused by a combination of accidental overfilling of the starboard settling tank and crew negligence in failing to properly secure the manhole cover. The ship was declared a Constructive Total Loss. Several weeks later, says Stuart Walker, 'the *Angelina* was towed off to the ship breakers'.

It was not long after that when he became involved in his first Liberty ship Total Loss case. This time the ship was not handy in the Singapore Roadstead, but instead ashore and burning on remote Great Coco Island, just north of the slightly less remote Andaman Islands. Great Coco, some 250 miles south-west of Rangoon, lay not only at the back of beyond, it belonged to Burma, which since gaining independence from Britain in 1948, and more especially since the military coup d'etat there of 1962, had steadily been turning inwards upon itself. The country did not much care for visitors. As if all that was not enough, Great Coco happened to be a restricted area off-limits to all, because it was the site of a detention centre housing political prisoners and dissidents. The ship involved was the *Kostis A. Georgilis* (*Samconstant*, Baltimore, May 1944). Its then registered owners, although the ship sailed under the Greek flag, was the Okeanoporos Shipping Corporation of Panama. It was named after its captain. The ship had arrived at Rangoon in ballast from Chinwangtao, north China, and had loaded a full cargo of bagged rice for Colombo. She sailed from Rangoon on 2 November 1967 and on the following day a fire broke out in the engine-room, close to the boiler fronts, much like the one on *Angelina*. The vessel was by then close to Great Coco Island and Captain Georgilis decided to run in close so that should the fire get out of control he could beach his ship on the island. In fact the engine-room had been rapidly abandoned and so the Captain ran the ship ashore whilst there was still power on the main engines.

After beaching, the crew, which included the Captain's wife and small daughter, took to the lifeboats and landed safely on shore. Before abandoning the ship a distress call had been sent out, but it had not been acknowledged by any shore station or ship in the vicinity. The Radio Officer had brought the ship's emergency transmitter ashore and was about to use it to transmit another signal when an armed party of the Burmese Navy descended upon them, confiscated the radio and placed everyone under arrest. The distress message had not got through, and Captain Georgilis, his family and crew, were about to embark on two miserable weeks in a couple of wooden huts made available to them, and existing on a diet mainly of rice that the Burmese supplied. The Navy had informed Rangoon of their unexpected visitors and the news eventually filtered through to the ship's agents there, then to Greece and to the underwriters in London. The latter appointed the Salvage Association to investigate, and that body in turn appointed Ritchie & Bisset, and so Stuart Walker got elected for the job. It took a week for him to get a visa, and he eventually arrived at Rangoon on 15 November. To get to Great Coco a DC-3 belonging to Burma Airlines had to be specially chartered, 'a very large aircraft for just four passengers', and the flight was made the following day. As the aircraft circled the island before landing, it passed over the beached ship from which plumes of smoke were still rising. After landing, the party consisting of Stuart Walker, the ship's agent, the charterer and an official from the Burmese Navy, were transported to the beach by tractor and trailer. Captain Georgilis, his chief engineer, and first mate, were there to greet them. Says Walker, 'I need hardly say they were extremely glad to see us'.

The ship's motor lifeboat was then used to convey them out to the ship.

> The stern was in approximately 25 feet of water and at high water there was some movement in the after half of the vessel. The fore end was firmly aground and almost dried out at low tide. As we approached we could see that the midship house was completely burned out. Large areas of paint work on the side shell plating in way of the engine-room and Nos. 2, 3, and 4 holds had been burned off with the steel work . . . buckled to varying degrees. The acrid stench from the burned paint, accommodation, and rice cargo hung over the ship . . .

The party got aboard by climbing up the lifeboat falls. They found the midships accommodation completely destroyed. Stuart Walker then made for the door to the engine-room and stepped through on to upper gratings and looked down. About 20ft below he saw 'an inky liquid surface sloshing gently from side to side'. It was fuel oil. Clearly there was no chance of examining the boilers or anything else down there, to establish the cause of the fire. In the forward cross alleyway he took note that the remote control device situated there for closing down the fuel supply to the engines was heavily distorted. Out on deck again, and negotiating a deck very hot to the touch, he looked down No. 3 hold and was met by a wave of heat like the blast from a furnace. All he could see was an incandescent glow coming from the burning rice. It was the same in Nos. 2 and 4 holds.

> There was no doubt that *Kostis A. Georgilas* was well beyond economical salvage and repair. The vessel had been reduced to a burned out hulk. I forget now what estimated cost I subsequently passed to underwriters but it would have been well in excess of the insured value.

Back onshore and after informing all and sundry of his decision, Walker was asked by Captain Georgilis if he and his crew could return in the plane to Rangoon. Perhaps influenced by the presence of Mrs Georgilis and her daughter, the Burmese authorities gave permission for this. Back in Rangoon and after having contacted the underwriters, Walker was advised by them that they were suspicious of the circumstances surrounding the casualty. As no physical evidence was obtainable, he was asked to interview the crew to try to establish the exact sequence of events surrounding the fire outbreak.

The only items of importance that came out of the following two days of interviews was the timing and circumstances of the fire outbreak. It had been about 1100 hours when the duty engineer and fireman first saw flames dancing about the furnace front of the starboard boiler. After informing the Bridge and Chief Engineer, an attempt was made to put the fire out by using the 10-gallon, semi-portable foam extinguisher kept nearby for just that purpose. For whatever reason, that was not successful, and the fire spread rapidly and threatened to engulf the fire-fighters. It was at that stage, it seemed, that the engine-room had been abandoned, with the boilers still steaming and with the main engine and auxiliary machinery still running.

> The action the engine-room crew should have taken once it became clear that they were unable to control the fire locally, was to shut down the main engine and close the fuel supply to the boilers by closing the starboard settling tank outlet valve. The steam supply valves to the fuel oil burning system, and the forced draught fan, should also have been closed. These valves were provided with extended spindles so that they could be operated from outside the engine-room in just such an emergency. With the fuel supply isolated, the engine-room vents and skylights should then have been closed and the steam smothering system activated.

None of that had happened, said the interviewees, because the Master wished to make towards the island and therefore needed steam on the main engines as long as possible. As the two witnesses to the start of the fire were adamant that the first flames they saw had been at the furnace front of the starboard boiler it seemed that the fire could not have been caused by an *Angelina*-style overflow of oil because then the flames would have been at the rear of the boiler.

At the end of the day Stuart Walker did not obtain any real evidence as to the prime cause of the fire, or as to whether or not the loss was a deliberate stranding on a remote island. However, he was of the opinion that as the Master had his wife and child with him, it was unlikely that this had been a 'deliberate' Total Loss claim. However, underwriters and their London solicitors were yet to be convinced of this, and correspondence went on for many months. An attempt was made to engage a salvage contractor to attend the ship and pump out the fuel oil in the engine-room so that a proper examination could be carried out. However, the Burmese Government refused permission.

> It maybe that underwriters were justified in being uneasy about this case. Was it just a coincidence that the fire occurred conveniently in the middle of the morning when the ship was nicely positioned close to the island? It also seemed a little strange that, with most of the crew available at that convenient hour, there seems to have been no serious attempt to fight the fire. Looking at it from that point of view, it did look a bit odd. But still, would the Master have really placed his wife and daughter in danger? I don't think so. No, I think the balance of probabilities is that the fire was the result of leakage from some part of the boiler fuel burning system.

When Stuart Walker got the call in March 1968 to investigate the stranding of a ship on the Little Basses, reefs off the south-east coast of Ceylon, now Sri Lanka, he must have thought he was becoming a sort of double-specialist; Liberty ships ashore in remote places. The *Edward K. Collins* (Brunswick, August 1944) had been one of the famous first hundred Liberty ships sold to Greece in 1947, becoming the *Helatros*. In 1963 she became the *Universal Trader* and at the time of the stranding was owned by the Universal Shipping Company of Monrovia, and was sailing under the Liberian flag. She had loaded a full cargo of grain at Gdynia for Chittagong.

On the night of 8-9 March the ship ran onto the Little Basses. The men manning a nearby lighthouse on Great Basses picked up a distress message from the ship and soon afterwards saw her silhouetted in the glow from the burning accommodation block. The crew had abandoned ship and were picked up at first light by the *Ocean Enterprise* which had answered the distress call. They were eventually landed at Karachi. *Ocean Enterprise* must have stayed around long enough for its Master to make some kind of long-distance examination of the *Trader*, for added to the information he had obviously received from his new passengers, he was able to radio in a pretty complete description of the condition of the hapless vessel and what had happened after she struck. All three forward holds were flooded and oil leaking from ruptured tanks had caught fire in the engine-room, a fire which had then spread into the accommodation. Dense smoke on deck had made fire-fighting impossible so the crew had abandoned ship.

Stuart Walker flew to Colombo, then travelled down to the southern port of Galle by car, and then eastward along tracks into the Yala National Park and Game Reserve. A boat of the Ceylon Lighthouse Service was then used to take him out to the wreck, a few miles off the coast. As they approached a number of small craft were seen to be alongside the wreck with people clambering all over it. 'Bloody looters!', exclaimed the Lighthouse officer in charge, 'I'll soon get rid of them.' A seaman handed over a canvas bag from which was drawn a Lee Enfield rifle. Five rounds fired over the funnel of the stricken Liberty did the trick and the looters vanished. 'Boarding the wreck was no problem,' says Walker, 'as our now departed friends had left a pilot ladder rigged over the side.'

By then the *Trader* was in a very bad state. She had broken in two, with the after section including the accommodation block and engine-room sitting firmly upright on the reef. The fore part had partly slid off the reef and slewed to port, with only the masts, derricks and ventilator cowls above water. The grain cargo in Nos. 4 and 5 holds was still burning. The bulkhead at the point where the ship had broken in two had collapsed and the sea was rushing in to smash against the boilers and main engine. Every now and then the after section would shudder as an extra high swell rolled in. 'It was clear that the *Universal Trader* was a Total Loss in every sense, salvage was not an option'. Soundings around the ship showed that had the ship been just 50 metres east, she would have missed the reef altogether.

Walker was then taken over to the Great Basses Lighthouse two or three miles away, from whence the wreck had first been sighted. He got ashore by Breeches Buoy, the landing stage being unsafe because of the swell. He got the story of that sighting at first hand from the keeper, who then provided some additional information that aroused Walker's investigative instincts.

The lighthouse keeper told me that he had heard reports on his radio of an unidentified vessel being sighted close inshore at Batticola on 6 March and at Arugam Bay on 7 March. These locations were some 120 and 40 miles respectively to the north of Great Basses. This certainly sounded rather suspicious, was this ship the *Universal Trader* and if so, what was she doing sailing southwards down the coast when she was bound to the north for Chittagong? Were they looking for a suitable location to arrange a phoney Total Loss grounding?

Walker decided to investigate, and the next day set off up the coast in a Land Rover making for Arugam Bay, having informed London of the information he had received from the lighthouse keeper. At Arugam several people were interviewed who said that they had sighted the mystery ship, but the evidence was confusing. Some said it was a large ship, some a small coaster. Next day it was up to Batticola, where the Harbour Master was interviewed. He too had seen the ship but confirmed that it had been a small coaster, with bridge and accommodation aft. Whoever she was, she was not the *Trader.*

> Well, that was that. My hopes of cracking a case of maritime fraud, with visions of being congratulated by the Chairman of Lloyd's, suddenly evaporated into the thin tropical air.

Stuart Walker ends by saying, 'It had been an interesting trip around the southern half of Ceylon, the sort of safari-like expedition that today's tourists pay thousands of pounds for.' And Scotsman Stuart Walker had got it for free, and had a ride in a Breeches Buoy! It was around this time that underwriters, according to Andrew Sinclair, decided they would not accept any Liberty claims over and above the scrap value of the ship.

In 1959 the Sunderland shipyard of Austin & Pickersgill had introduced a large standard bulk carrier ship, an innovation that at the time had been largely ridiculed by many other shipbuilders and by many shipowners. However, it had proved a success and builders everywhere had since jumped on the bandwagon. But there were a number of shallow-water ports world-wide where these 'bulkers' could not get in. Into the 1960s that gap was still largely being filled by the 800 or so Liberty ships remaining in operation. Around that time and in the knowledge that the dreaded fifth special survey for the Liberties was on the horizon, which could mean repair bills of £90,000 for a ship with the then scrap value of only £25,000, Austins under managing director Kenneth Douglas, began thinking about a replacement vessel for the Liberty. Ken Douglas writes:

> To cater for the likely demand, of course, there was no point in just producing a tin-type replica of the existing [Liberty] design. To have any chance of success economically it would need to be faster and to have a larger deadweight [carrying capacity].[5]

After lengthy deliberations it was finally decided to go for a 14,000-ton vessel with a speed of 14kts, using as a basis a ship of about that size that

---

5. Letter to author dated June 1999 from Kenneth Douglas.

Douglas had built in 1954 when in charge of Gray's Shipyard at West Hartlepool. That ship, the *Atlantic Countess,* had been built for Greek shipowner Stavros Livanos, who had been owner or part owner of no less than ten of the original 100 Greek-owned Liberty ships. Douglas says the *Atlantic Countess* was 'normal' for 1954 in having the engine amidships, but now he told his naval architect that he wanted the new design to have the machinery aft, a particular fad of his. He told the designer, 'we're building ships to carry cargo, not loads of reciprocating pig-iron!'

Preliminary market research, directed mainly at the Greek market, indicated that Douglas' broad parameters were about right, and by 1965 Austins had produced the plans and detailed production schedules of a ship they called the SD.14 Liberty Replacement. Furthermore, they planned to build it in eight weeks from keel to launch, with six weeks fitting out, a total of only fourteen weeks. The first two ships, were finally built to the order of London & Overseas Freighters. The very first one was delivered in February 1968 right on schedule. She was called the *Nicola.*

It is perhaps entirely appropriate that this British designed replacement for the Liberty came from a shipyard on the River Wear at Sunderland, not far from the yard where the Liberty story all began about thirty years earlier. Not only that, although SD.14 was nearly twice the size of a Liberty, the scheduled time of build was not much longer than the average overall construction time of all those Liberties. The world had changed however, far fewer ships being required, so the number constructed was much smaller. By 1983, the year Ken Douglas retired, 124 SD.14's had been built on the Wear, and around another 240 under licence abroad.

CHAPTER 27

Treasure Hunt

The ocean floor is littered with the remains of ships, and no equivalent period in world history added more to the number down there than the six-year long Second World War. Some of the ships sunk during that war were bullion carriers, and at least one Liberty ship may have been amongst them. No one knows the total value of bullion, precious stones, specie and banknotes that were moved between countries during the war years. Some bullion, such as that used for payment for strategically important ball-bearings from Sweden which were brought out on British blockade runners, was flown into Sweden. At neutral Sweden's insistence, the fast naval motor gunboats used for part of this operation were manned by British Merchant Navy crews, and the unarmed Mosquito aircraft used to fly the bullion in, were manned by British civilian airline pilots. Both the sea and air sides of this operation were extremely dangerous and both sustained casualties.[1]

Sometimes naval vessels were used. Lieutenant (later Rear-Admiral) Colin Madden took part in Operation 'XD' in May 1940 when Royal Navy demolition parties were landed at various ports in Holland in the face of the German advance into that country. They had orders to destroy port facilities, to evacuate members of the Dutch Royal Family, and to bring away as many valuables as possible. Madden and his party were landed from the destroyer HMS *Whitshed* at Ijmuiden and at one juncture he was handed two boxes containing a fortune in diamonds which were later to help finance the Dutch government-in-exile. Other ships successfully carried away much heavier consignments of bullion.

Another British warship so engaged was less lucky. In April 1942 HMS *Edinburgh* made a run to Murmansk, arriving at the Kola Inlet with steel plates needed for repairs to the damaged cruiser HMS *Trinidad*. Before leaving Russia one of her magazines was loaded with five tons of gold bullion. She was heading southwards with Convoy QP-11 when on 30 April in the Barents Sea she was attacked by a U-boat. One of a pair of

---

1. See the author's *Life Line* for fuller details.

457

torpedoes fired from *U-456*, Lieutenant Commander Tiechert, struck in way of the engine-room, the other blowing off her stern. Four destroyers, two British and two Russian, hastened to assist, and one of them, HMS *Forester*, attempted a tow but it failed. Further attempts were made to save the disabled cruiser over the next two days. However, on 2 May she was attacked by three German destroyers, and although one was sunk, another managed to fire off a salvo of torpedoes one of which struck, and after which *Edinburgh* began to settle. Most of the crew of 760 were saved but there were about eighty casualties. To ensure the ship and its treasure sank, HMS *Foresight* was ordered to finish off the job with a torpedo. The loss of this gold was largely kept under wraps until 1981 when a British salvage team under Keith 'Goldfinger' Jessop recovered £35 million of gold bars from the wreck.

Most valuable cargoes were carried not in naval vessels but in merchant ships and most arrived at their destinations safely. Some of these cargoes were carried in Liberties. Ken Maguire was serving in *John J. McGraw* in the late summer of 1944. This Baltimore-built ship had been handed over to a British crew under the management of Lamport & Holt on 1 October 1943 as the *Samariz*. After representations from the McGraw family, the ship had quickly reverted to her original name and so became one of the few Liberties to sail under the Red Ensign without a 'Sam' name. Throughout the summer of 1944 the *McGraw* was used in the Eastern Mediterranean to ferry troops and supplies from Alexandria to Greece and Italy. On one of the trips to Piraeus, made under the escort of a small Italian warship, the Italians by then having changed sides, the *McGraw* carried a fortune in Greek drachma notes to replace the German Occupation money that had been in circulation there. Says Maguire, 'Walking around Athens later it was interesting to see the old German money lying around the streets and pavements as the local people had thrown it away. It made me realize that it is just paper after all!' (He added that at that time near the end of the war, previously unidentifiable grey-painted Allied merchant ships were beginning to sport self-made emblems on their funnels. Chief Officer Eric Spooner had done some research and discovered that his ship was named after a past manager of the New York Giants. Consequently, that ship's emblem became crossed baseball bats incorporating the letters NYG. In harbours sometimes crowded with seemingly cloned ships, such identification marks would have made one's own ship more easy to find.)[2]

The *John Barry* was launched at Portland, Oregon in February 1942, the fifth Liberty to come off the stocks at the Kaiser facility there. (She was named for Commodore John Barry, a former Irishman who

---

2. Correspondence with Ken Maguire, November 1999.

commanded American ships during the Revolution. In command of the *Lexington* and *Raleigh* he had his ups-and-downs but they were mostly ups, and when the US Navy was reorganised in 1794, he was made its senior officer.) Under the management of Lykes Line, *John Barry*'s war had been largely routine and uneventful until the summer of 1944. Then, newly under the command of Captain Joseph Ellerwald the ship sailed from Philadelphia on 19 July. According to a later statement by Eller-wald, the ship had 8233 tons of cargo on board. Including the Captain, who was in his late twenties and had held a master's licence for two years, there were seventy-one men on board, forty-four merchant seamen and twenty-seven Armed Guards. Five days later she joined a convoy in Chesapeake Bay. *Barry* was bound for Ras Tanura on the Persian Gulf side of Saudi Arabia and then to another unidentified Gulf port, accord-ing to a sailing report made by the ship's agents. Because an attempt has been made to make something of a mystery out of this reference to an 'unidentified port', it needs to be said that no mystery was involved here. The greater part of the ship's cargo was for Russia and was to be unloaded at one of the 'back-door' ports in the Gulf that were being used for that purpose, ports that often became congested. In such a situation destinations were often undesignated at the time of sailing, the port to be decided upon later. *Barry* was to voyage via the Mediterranean, Suez and Aden. On 26 August the ship called at the latter port to pick up sailing instructions from the naval authorities there for the final leg to the Gulf.

The ship was on a zigzag course in rough weather when at 2200 hours on 29 August she was struck by a torpedo from Commander Jan Jebsen's *U-859*. According to an affidavit signed later by Captain Ellerwald, as his ship was going rapidly down by the head, he ordered abandon ship, he himself leaving at 2220 hours. Only two lifeboats were available as the others had been destroyed in the explosion, but life-rafts were also launched. One of the good lifeboats capsized whilst being launched fling-ing its occupants into the water. That boat was soon righted and although it was swamped, that was the one that Captain Ellerwald went down into. He stated that the Chief Engineer and Radio Officer 'followed soon after', another example of a master not being the last to leave his ship. Two men, Chief Officer Gordon Lyons and Messman Tan See Jee, did not make it to the boats and were not seen again.[3] Commander Jebsen waited for the crew to clear before putting another torpedo into the ship which then broke in two and sank. On the following day all the survivors were rescued by either the American Liberty ship *Benjamin Bourn* (Houston, August 1942) which landed its contingent at Khorramshahr,

---

3. Statement sworn by Captain Ellerwald and supported by Chief Engineer William Watler before Notary Public A.W. Paulsen, Kings County, New York, 17 October 1944.

or by the Dutch tanker *Sanetta* which landed its contingent at Aden. (*U-859* was sunk in the Malacca Strait by HM submarine *Trenchant* less than four weeks later on 23 September 1944. Lieutenant Commander A.R. Hezlett commanding the British submarine knew the U-boat's exact position from information received by the Admiralty from deciphered Enigma messages. Of the U-boat's crew of sixty-nine only nineteen survived and Commander Jebsen was not amongst them.)

In the context of total war there was nothing particularly extraordinary about all that. However, the *John Barry* might have been an out of the ordinary ship. For she might have been carrying silver bullion from America to the value of $26 million; she certainly was carrying a much smaller fortune in the form of 750 wooden boxes containing 3 million Saudi silver riyals worth about $500,000 in 1944. It was obscure references to the silver bullion lying in a wreck at the bottom of the Arabian Sea that, many years after the war, caught the imagination of some prospective salvors and treasure hunters in America, and subsequently in Arabia. The references were not in official files, but in two books, one published in 1972 and the other in 1988, both concerning certain aspects of the American merchant marine during the war.[4] Both references were probably based on information contained in survivors' reports after they were interviewed at Aden. A Naval Intelligence report dated 3 September 1944 from a US Naval Observer at that port at the time the first survivors were interviewed, specifically states that the cargo included $26 million in silver.

According to an article in Britain's *Mail on Sunday* of 12 November 1995, an article based on a book written on the subject, those book references brought the matter of the *Barry* bullion to the notice of retired US Navy Captain Brian Shoemaker an expert in recovering ditched helicopters from the sea.[5] He in turn gained the interest of Jay Fiondella the owner of a celebrated Santa Monica restaurant who had long been interested in wrecks, and whose business provided him with contacts who might be persuaded to back a salvage project. To salvage anything from the ship was going to be very expensive indeed and not at all easy. For although the approximate position in the Arabian Sea where the *John Barry* had gone down was known, the wreck had still to be pinpointed. Not only that, the sea in the vicinity was 8500ft, or about a mile and a half, deep, and for six months of the year during the south-west monsoon, no salvage operations of any kind would be possible.

---

4. John G. Bunker, *Liberty Ships; The Ugly Ducklings of WWII* (Annapolis 1972), and Arthur Moore, *A Careless Word , A Needless Sinking* (Kings Point 1988).
5. (a) Jane Preston, *Stalin's £200m Lost Treasure*. (b) John Beasant, *Stalin's Silver* (London 1995).

After agreement in principle had been reached between the two men, Fiondella began the task of attempting to interest financial backers, whilst Shoemaker set about trying to find confirmation from official sources that the treasure had indeed been carried in the ship. Very soon Shoemaker dug out the ship survivors' reports, including one made by Captain Ellerwald dated 23 March 1945, which referred specifically to $26 million of bullion. He found that those references had in part been supported by research carried out by an earlier prospective salvor who referred to having seen a copy of the ship's cargo manifest in the Maritime Administration archives in 1967 which mentioned a large but unquantified quantity of silver bullion being on board the ship. Unfortunately that manifest had subsequently gone missing.

Although Shoemaker found no documentation that provided irrefutable proof that the silver bullion had ever been loaded on the ship, he did find proof that the consignment of Saudi silver riyals had been loaded. He went on to interview some surviving crewmen, two of whom said they remembered seeing a special vault being built in No. 3 'tween-deck, starboard side. As official documentation showed that the Saudi coins had been loaded in No. 2 hold, Shoemaker took this as evidence that the bullion must have been loaded in No. 3.

In 1989 the US Maritime Administration, perhaps spurred on by the interest Shoemaker was showing in the official files pertaining to the ship, decided to put the *Barry* and its cargo up for auction. The bid made by the John Barry Group formed by Shoemaker, Fiondella and their backers succeeded. But a few months later the consortium was advised that the Sultanate of Oman had declared an interest in the wreck as it lay 127 miles off its coast and therefore within that country's Exclusive Economic Zone. After protracted negotiations, Omani interests in the person of Sheikh Ahmed Farid al Aulaqi of Yemen who was residing in the Oman and who had formed the Ocean Group for this very purpose, purchased the John Barry Group's rights in the ship, although its members retained some interest.

Much of the circumstantial evidence unearthed by Captain Shoemaker indicated the possibility that if the bullion was aboard the ship, then India was likely to have been its intended final destination. This was because it was known that only a month prior to the silver supposedly having been loaded aboard the *John Barry,* an agreement had been signed in Washington, on 8 June 1944 to be precise, between representatives of the United States, Britain and British India, for the transfer of silver amounting to $50 million to India to help pay for that country's war effort, which would have included the wages of the Indian Army. (The contribution that India made to the Allied war effort is often overlooked. The Indian Army ended the war with well over two million men under arms; in fact it was the largest volunteer army the world has ever known, for it contained not a single conscript. Units of that army fought in the Far East, North Africa, and Italy.)

Had Shoemaker extended his researches wider he might have discovered that, beginning four days after that Washington agreement, a total of four new British-flagged Liberties had been presented for loading at either New York or Baltimore, their destinations listed as being India. The four with dates of presentation were the *Samspeed* 12 June, *Samtana* 14 June, and *Samsylarna* and *Samlamu,* both on 2 July. All were therefore within the time-frame for loading consignments of that silver for the Indian sub-continent. One could argue a case that it would have been more likely that British-flagged vessels would have been used for that transportation to British India, than any others, if for no other reason than if any of it had been lost aboard a British ship, then liability would have lain with the British. However, one does not really need to present that argument. One of the four, the *Samsylarna* was torpedoed en route, and that is how we know for certain that she at least was carrying a consignment of millions of dollars worth of silver bullion from New York to India. After the ship was torpedoed in the Mediterranean on 4 August 1944 she was beached and the silver on board salvaged (see Chapter 16). It is very likely, therefore, that the balance of that 'Indian silver' would also have been shipped in British ships. A side issue is that it made logistical sense to spread the whole shipment over several ships, not stick it all aboard one and so risk losing the lot.

Ocean Group's search for the wreck began in November 1990 using a sonar scanner aboard a reconnaissance vessel. The position given by Captain Ellerwald proved to be a good one for within a few days the scanner showed the remains of a ship in two halves on the ocean floor, an identification made even more positive when a remote controlled vehicle with cameras aboard and belonging to Eastport International of Florida, was lowered over the wreck in March 1991. Meanwhile Captain Shoemaker had carried out additional research which led him to conclude that the silver bullion had been stowed, not in No. 3 hold as he had previously thought, but in the deep tanks at the bottom of No. 1 hold, such deep tanks being a feature of all standard Liberty ships.

In November 1992, Ifremer, a French organisation that had in the previous decade worked on the wreck of the *Titanic,* was brought in to the operation along with salvage expert Keith Jessop, the man who had rescued the Russian gold from the wreck of the *Edinburgh.* Ifremer's manned submersible *Cyana* made a dive down to the ship on 23rd of that month, and using its pincer arm, ripped off the builder's plate affixed to the front of the bridge, a plate that always identifies the ship concerned. Back on deck, it confirmed that the *John Barry* had indeed been found. *Cyana* made several more dives, one of the survey runs indicating that No. 1 hold, in which Shoemaker now thought the bullion had been stowed, lay partially buried in the seabed. Explosives experts therefore decided to blow open No. 2 'tween-deck where it was known for sure that the Saudi riyals had been stowed. Unfortunately, when *Cyana* submerged after the explosions, all that could be seen was a great stirring-up of the sediment in the area. Then the cameras on the craft malfunctioned and so operations were abandoned. In fact a decision was made not to proceed any farther until Ifremer technicians had come up with an improved type of underwater grab that would facilitate the operations.

It was not until late October 1994 that a former oil-drill ship, the *Flex LD*, was positioned over the site of the wreck with its newly designed 50-ton grab. Ifremer engineers then began the laborious task of joining the lengths of pipe that pushed the grab out through the craft's water chamber and, controlled by monitors, down 8500ft to a point above the deck of *Barry*'s No. 2 hold. In a series of difficult operations the deck there was ripped open by the grab, after which it entered that compartment to scoop up samples of whatever was there. The first load brought to the surface was nothing but junk. At the second attempt made the following day, cameras on the grab revealed that a gun was being lifted towards the surface, but then a section of pipe buckled which caused the grab to open, sending the gun back to where it had laid for the past fifty years. However, four days later when the grab opened on deck, out poured around a million and half silver riyals, half of the original total. All were badly discoloured, but still recognisable for what they were. In the knowledge that the other half of the Saudi cache would be even more difficult to reach, and with expenses rising by the day, Sheikh Ahmed Farid decided to call it a day. Robert Hudson, a Briton working for the Sheikh, later recorded that the presence of the riyals on board was well documented, but that no one could be certain that silver bullion ever had been on board. He added that his own researches indicated that the 'Indian silver' had reached India on other vessels.

The only firm indications available that silver bullion, whatever its final destination may have been, had ever been loaded aboard *John Barry* were those survivors' reports. Those reports were very precise as to the value of the bullion on board, so precise that it gives them considerable credence. But if silver bullion in addition to the silver coins was aboard *John Barry*, and it was not silver for India, to what other nation could the bullion have been consigned? John Beasant, author of the book on the *John Barry* affair, has come up with a different destination for the silver. He says that it was meant for Russia, and that makes considerable sense because most of the ship's cargo was also for that country.

It is when he goes on to elaborate that Beasant rather spoils his thesis. He makes mention of what was known as the Third Protocol, one of four such documents all dating from October 1943, which governed the supply of Lend-Lease aid to Russia. Specifically he draws our attention to one item worth $25 million 'which is very close to the recorded value of the bullion carried by the *John Barry*'. It is close, but that closeness is not as he says it is, 'beyond the bounds of credible coincidence', especially as that value appeared against an item listed as 'urgently required equipment', with no mention of bullion. The fact that a Russian diplomat in the 1990s told Beasant that the words 'urgently required equipment' was obviously meant as a disguise, is really no proof that it was a cover for silver, and certainly no proof that any such consignment was aboard the *John Barry*.

The Protocol governed all Lend-Lease aid to Russia, whether it travelled along the Pacific route via Vladivostok, the Persian Gulf route via several ports there, or the most dangerous of all, the Murmansk route. An official archivist in Moscow informed Beasant that not all the goods agreed to be supplied under the Protocol actually arrived. Indeed it did not, and most of the shortfall still litters the bottom of the Barents Sea. The archivist's remark is again no proof that 'Russian silver' was part of that shortfall or that it was aboard the *John Barry*, although Beasant seems to think it was an indication in that direction.

For good measure he then throws other 'mysteries' into the pot. He says that the installation of a 30-ton boom at *John Barry*'s No. 4 hold before she sailed, is a crucial piece of evidence proving that cargo of considerable weight and secrecy was stowed there. This does not really stand up to scrutiny. Heavy-lift booms are certainly fitted to lift heavy weights, but to suggest that silver was loaded into ships in 30-ton lifts in 1944 (well before modern containers were in use) is just not acceptable. At that time bullion was shipped in small boxes of a size that could be man-handled. On the quay a number of these would have been stowed on lifting boards, in lifts up to five tons which was the safe working load of a Liberty's normal booms. Far from being used to lift silver, that heavy-lift boom was almost certainly installed so that it could be used at the final destination to lift off the heavy tractors and half-tracks which are known to have been on board. There was a shortage of heavy crane facilities in all of the Gulf ports used for Russian cargoes, and discharging would have been facilitated if the ship had its own heavy-lift gear. The fact that the *John Barry* was issued with a new official log book for what turned out to be its final voyage is also looked upon as being a mystery, when it was really nothing of the sort. Every ship starts every voyage from a *home* port with a new official log-book. That is standard procedure in case the ship is lost and the record lost with it. The old log is lodged with the authorities ashore as a matter of course, as well as a matter of law.

On balance and in view of the precise valuation of the silver bullion mentioned in the survivor's reports, it seems likely that the *Barry* was carrying silver bullion. But where was it stowed? Some of the riyals were recovered because the salvors knew precisely where to look for them. To rummage around a two-part wreck under 8500ft of water without some indication of where to search, is rather like looking for a needle in a haystack. If ever additional information is discovered that will make a new salvage attempt seem worth the financial risk, it must be hoped that those engaged in it will not use as a guide the outlines of a Liberty ship that appeared in both Beasant's book and the *Mail on Sunday* article. Those drawings indicate the Liberty as having two holds instead of three forward of the bridge, and two aft of it, a total of four holds instead of five. (*John Barry* was not one of the four-hold specials built to carry boxed aircraft.) No. 3 hold is missing all together in the drawing, although its booms are depicted. Only the positions of holds 1 and 2 are depicted accurately.

CHAPTER 28

The Surviving Liberties

Liberty ship memorials and mementoes of various kinds abound in the United States. They range from builder's plates to bridge structures and engines, and are held at various museums, colleges, and other official buildings. On 31 May 1999, a 'Liberty Ship Memorial Plaza' was dedicated at the Mary Ross Waterfront Park at Brunswick, Georgia. not far from the site of the J.A. Jones Construction Company's shipyard which produced eighty-five of the ships during the war. The centre-piece of the Plaza is a 23ft scale model of a Liberty, one twentieth of the size of the original. The model was built as an exercise in welding techniques by students of the vocational-technical division of Brunswick College.[1]

Liberty ship bits and pieces are scattered in many places, some still having a practical use. The superstructure of the *William H. Allen* (Richmond, August 1943) for instance, reportedly lies within the campus of a Texas University where it used for training in marine fire-fighting. Much more than a piece of the *Albert M. Boe,* a product of the New England Shipbuilding Corporation at Portland, Maine, exists at Kodiak, Alaska. Not completed until 30 October 1945, this was the last Liberty ever to be constructed. Under the name *Star of Kodiak* she now lies within an in-filled area so is no longer afloat. Used as a fish cannery, access holes for vehicles have been cut in her hull and some of the superstructure has been removed. But she is still recognisable for what once she was.

Many Liberties form parts of artificial fish reefs off the Gulf, Atlantic and Pacific coasts of America. Visited by skin-divers and sport fishermen, these 'reefs' provide an almost perfect habitat for marine wildlife. Off the Texas shoreline along the 300-mile stretch of coast between Brownsville and Freeport, there are six of these reefs, constructed from a total of fourteen ships, twelve of them Liberties. Four of the reefs are three-ship reefs, and are named after a town or geographical feature on shore. The other two are single-ship reefs. One is called John Worthington after the non-Liberty ship down there. The last one is the Vancouver

---

1. *The Brunswick News,* 1 July 1991.

Liberty Ship Reef after the *George Vancouver* (Portland, Oregon, July 1942). All the ships were acquired under what was called the Appropriations Authorization-Maritime Programs Bill of 1972, which allowed the transfer of some ships from the US Reserve Fleet to individual States for use for this specific purpose. As with all other ships used for these reefs, the Texas ships had first to go through an extensive preparation process. They had to be cleaned of all contaminants such as oil, and then any non-ferrous materials were removed. After that the ships were cut down to 'tween-deck level. Finally the hulks were towed to the designated positions and scuttled using explosive charges. The Texas reefs are under the care of the State body called Texas Parks and Wildlife.

Liberty ship memorials of sorts exist in other countries. In Australia, the country which provided temporary 'home ports' for so many Liberties during General MacArthur's push northwards during the war, the Museum at Largs Bay, South Australia, has a small Liberty ship display including the builder's plate from *Samoresby* (Portland, Maine, April 1944). That ship's name had derived from Port Moresby in Papua, New Guinea, and was one of several British-flagged Liberties delivered in April and May 1944 whose names referred to places or features in the Pacific theatre of war. (*Sambanka, Samleyte, Samcebu, Samsuva* and *Samidway* are others.) She was managed during the war by the South American Saint Line but was not one of the ships later purchased by the British, and so was handed back to the United States in 1948. The builder's plate was removed at Baltimore in 1960 and presented to the Consul-General of the Commonwealth of Australia. Some 'undeliberate' mementoes of Liberty ships, in the form of wrecks that adorn remote parts of Australian territory, have been mentioned elsewhere in this book.

Britain, which during the war had more Lend-Lease Liberties than any other country, has little in the way of Liberty legacies. Two or three museums possess models of Liberty ships and two, at Sunderland and Newcastle, have models of the *Empire Liberty*. (Another *Empire Liberty* model is in the Maritime Museum at Bergen in Norway. All three of these models were presented by Cyril Thompson in the years before his death.) The site where the North Sands Shipyard once stood at the entrance to the River Wear, is now part of the University of Sunderland campus, and the road leading down into it is called Liberty Way. Then there is the remnant of the *Samkey* window now in the Church of All Hallows By The Tower. Apart from those items, that seems to be about it, except of course, for the unwanted wreck of the ammunition-carrying *Richard Montgomery* off Sheerness. The Medway Ports Authority is presently trying (with the help of this author) to find a suitable home for the heavy-lift blocks recently removed from that vessel. If a museum can be found to accept them, they will constitute the only artefacts from a Liberty ship to feature in any British museum.

Due to the dedication of two groups of people in the United States, two Liberty ships have been preserved for posterity. They are the *Jeremiah O'Brien* at San Francisco, and the *John W. Brown* at Baltimore. The *Jeremiah O'Brien* was completed at Portland, Maine, in June 1943 and after sea trials was handed over to her managers, Grace Line, on the last day of that month. Her maiden voyage, under the command of Captain Oscar Southerland, was to London and back to the States and was uneventful except that during the return trip the ship developed boiler trouble and had to turn back to Scotland for repairs. That was followed by three more trans-Atlantic voyages, during the second of which Southerland left the ship, command being taken by Captain A. De Smedt. Deck Cadet Coleman 'Coke' Schneider made his first trip to sea aboard the *O'Brien* at this time. He says that his war experience aboard the ship was 'simply wonderful', and that 'we never saw a torpedo or a sinking, and we were never bombed'. From June to October 1944 *O'Brien* was one of the great armada of ships that ferried troops and supplies from Britain to the Normandy beachheads, making a total of eleven such crossings. After returning to the States that October she made voyages to South America and the Pacific until the end of the war and beyond. On 17 January 1946 she was taken out of commission and placed in the Reserve Fleet moored in Suisun Bay, California, one of the three designated Reserve Fleet areas on the Pacific coast. (The others were at Olympia, Washington, and Astoria, Oregon.)[2]

The *O'Brien* was still at Suisun Bay in 1962 when she fell under the purview of Captain (later Rear-Admiral) Thomas J. Patterson. He was then one of a Maritime Administration team of captains and chief engineers whose job it was to survey the 300 or so Liberty ships that lay at the Pacific sites. (Another team was engaged in doing the same sort of thing with the 500 Liberties in similar sites on the Atlantic coast.) What particularly interested Patterson about the *O'Brien* was her condition which, except for the guns having been removed, was exactly as it had been on the day she left the builder's yard. Everything was in place even down to the charts in the chartroom. Apart from a few indents and some minor corrosion, the hull was in good condition. 'The ship was a time capsule', Patterson later reported, and it was at that time he began wondering whether she could be saved. Wonder he might, for the purpose behind the surveys he was conducting was to assess the condition of each ship and then allocate it a position on the 'to be scrapped list'. Although the *O'Brien* was in excellent condition she was not one of the ships that during the war had been fitted with crack-arresters, and that fact on its own should properly have made her a candidate for the first

---

2. Details from Coleman Schneider, *The Voyage of the Jeremiah O'Brien* (Tenafly, New Jersey 1994).

group to be scrapped. Nevertheless said Patterson, 'we kept moving the *Jeremiah O'Brien* down the scrap list ... kept shoving her back ... kept dropping her name down'.[3]

That was not all. The US Navy still had some working Liberty ships and habitually raided the lines of the Reserve Fleet to cannibalise spare parts for them. Patterson managed to keep the *O'Brien* from being raided, a game that went on for years. Finally, when the *O'Brien* was close to being the only one left, something had to be done quickly if the ship was to be saved. In 1977 Patterson and his fellow campaigners managed to get commercial and industrial leaders interested in preserving the ship, and eventually also the government in Washington. The campaign group, including Harry Allendorfer, Tom Crowley, Bob Blake, Barney Evans and others too numerous to mention, finally obtained a large grant from the National Trust for Historical Preservation. There was one snag; the grant was conditional on it being matched by funds, labour, services and materials from the private sector. Patterson and other enthusiasts set about the task of doing exactly that.

Although all regular maintenance on the ship had ceased as long ago as 1963, a team led by Chief Engineer Harry Morgan managed to get steam up after four months of hard, continuous slog, so that in October 1979, almost thirty-four years since the ship's engines had last moved, the ship was able to move to the Bethlehem shipyard in San Francisco for repairs and refurbishment. That work included sandblasting every inch of her hull down to the bare metal before it was re-coated with paint. Gayne Marriner, the yard's general manager, not only did not insist on payment up front, but took a personal interest in the project. So much so that the work was finished in time for the ship to become the centre-piece of National Liberty Ship Day in 1980, becoming the designated National Liberty Ship Memorial. Thanks to Admiral Patterson and his team, the *Jeremiah O'Brien* had been saved. The ship now lies alongside a berth at the Fort Mason Center, San Francisco.

The story of the *John W. Brown* is in some respects very different, but it is one with an equally happy ending. The ship was launched at Baltimore on 7 September 1942. Named after a prominent figure in the labour movement in the States, she was appropriately sponsored by Mrs Annie Green, wife of the leader of the Union of Marine and Shipbuilding Workers of America. During the war the ship was managed by the States Marine Corporation. In October 1942, under the command of Captain Matt R. Crawford she set out on her maiden voyage loaded with Lend-Lease cargo for Russia, via the Persian Gulf. One of the crew was fifty-eight year-old Bosun Matts Oman, a Finn, who was destined

---

3. Admiral Patterson as told to Karl Kortum, *Sea History* (Winter 1987/1988).

to stay on board longer than anyone else, not leaving the ship until November 1945. Oman must have been quite a guy, for he made a distinct impression on Navy Armed Guardsman Vernon Joyce, who said, 'The crewman who most impressed me was the Bosun . . . a master seaman if there ever was one. As a 19-year old kid I idolized him, and he taught me a lot of seamanship that I never forgot.'[4] The Mediterranean route not being open at that time, the ship voyaged via the Panama Canal, down the west coast of South America, around Cape Horn, across the South Atlantic to Cape Town, then northwards up the Indian Ocean. After two and a half months and having travelled well over 14,000 miles, the ship arrived in the Gulf on Christmas Day 1942. The Gulf ports had few facilities and were congested, and it was almost three months before the *Brown* completed discharging. Then it was back to New York arriving there in May 1943 after a maiden voyage that had taken eight months.

The *Brown* then underwent modifications to enable her to carry troops and prisoners of war in her forward 'tween-decks. When she sailed from New York on 24 June 1943 for the Mediterranean under the command of Captain William Carley, there were nearly 400 men on board. In addition to the crew and Armed Guard, she carried over 150 US Military Policemen and about an equal number of Royal Navy personnel, survivors of a torpedoed warship who were now on a circuitous route back to Britain. Cargo and passengers were discharged at Algiers except for a contingent of the MPs who were left to guard the 500 German prisoners of war who were embarked, destination Hampton Roads. A further troop carrying voyage followed, this time to Oran. After that the *Brown* made several shuttles with troops and equipment between North African ports and Naples. Some of the troops carried at this juncture were Free-French. At Naples on 27 December 1943 she was struck on the starboard side by the *Zebulon Pike* (Los Angeles, May 1942) which was shifting anchorages. The damage was extensive but not bad enough to put her out of action; in fact repairs were delayed until the ship eventually arrived back in the States.

The *John W. Brown* was amongst that great majority of Liberty ships that, despite sailing in and out of war zones and across U-boat infested waters, were to escape virtually unscathed for the entire war. The nearest she came to disaster was on the day after she sailed in Convoy GUS-31 from Bizerte for home with a cargo of scrap metal and personal effects of American troops who had been killed in battle. One day out of Bizerte, on 22 February 1944, the convoy was attacked by *U-969*, Lieutenant Commander Dobbert. Torpedoes struck two Liberties, one of them

---

4. Quoted in Sherod Cooper, *Baltimore's Living Liberty* (Baltimore 1991).

immediately in line ahead of *Brown*, the other just four cables off her starboard bow. Both victims, the *Peter Skene Ogden* (Portland, Oregon, November 1942) and *George Cleeve* (Portland, Maine, June 1943) were later beached and written off as constructive total losses. The *Brown* itself reached New York safely three weeks later.

With a new master on board, the almost eponymous Captain George Brown, the *Brown's* next voyage was also to the Mediterranean. Then began another series of shuttle trips, conveying troops, prisoners of war, and supplies around the area. The Allied troops carried included French Colonials and, since Italy was now one of the Allies, Italian soldiers. In early August the *Brown* took part in the invasion of Southern France. Able Seaman Wilfred Goslin was on board during that period and he reported that the ship laid off the beachhead at St. Tropez in mid-August without firing a shot. Then, on the ship's sailing day, a lone German plane flew over and was shot down. 'The *John W. Brown* along with every other Liberty in the armada claimed the downing and painted a swastika on its stack.'[5] At the end of September the ship arrived home, again carrying prisoners of war.

It was back to the Mediterranean once more in October 1944, this time with black troops of the US 758th Tank Battalion. After a few more shuttle trips, the ship returned to the States for more troops and cargo for the Mediterranean theatre. This was the last one she was to make to that destination whilst the war in Europe was still on. In April 1945, and now under the command of Captain Andrew Lihz, she left the States bound for Antwerp, arriving at The Downs in the English Channel just in time to celebrate VE Day on 8 May 1945. After discharging at Antwerp it was down to Le Havre to pick up American troops, including some who had been prisoners of the Germans, for repatriation. That homeward voyage was made in convoy, but for the first time in six years the ships were able to use their running lights at night and not bother about blacking out.

No longer with an Armed Guard unit on board, the *Brown* made several more voyages to Europe with cargoes, sometimes returning with troops. The ship's last voyage, her thirteenth, with Captain Alfred Hudnall in command, was to England. She arrived back in New York in November 1946. The *Brown* was still on that final voyage when the City of New York asked the US Maritime Administration for the loan of a Liberty ship for educational purposes. The City required a ship as a floating annex for the nautical trade's side of the Metropolitan Vocational High School. The *Brown*, with its 'tween-deck conversion, seemed ideal for the job, and so became the selected ship. For the next thirty-six years, until 1982, she was used to train sometimes up to 450 students a year.

---

5. Quoted in *Sea History* (Autumn 1986).

Some of the students were receiving marine engineering training, so the ship's engines got to be regularly serviced and 'turned over'.

Warren McConnell was a tutor on the schoolship for thirty years, and was proud of the fact that former students had not only gone into the merchant marine, but into every branch of service that was marine related. Former student Kurt B. Ostlund, who became a ship's officer, had fond memories of the ship which he says was always known to students as KHJL, the vessel's international call sign. In 1978, in the knowledge that the *Brown*'s days as a schoolship might soon be drawing to a close, a seminar backed by the National Maritime Historical Society of America, on the ship's future was held in the Seaman's Church Institute, New York. That seminar saw the birth of what came to be called Project Liberty Ship, an organisation determined to save a Liberty for the Atlantic coast now that the *Jeremiah O'Brien*'s survival on the Pacific coast was well in hand. The only real candidate left was the *Brown*; the few other Liberties remaining at that time had either been cannibalised or altered out of all recognition. Funds were needed, so a membership drive was instituted and a regular newsletter issued. However, when the schoolship was finally shut down in 1982, no berth in New York Harbor would accept the ship. In consequence the *Brown* was handed back to the Maritime Administration and was towed down to Chesapeake Bay to join the ships of the Reserve Fleet in the James River.

But matters were beginning to move on the political front and in 1983 Congress passed a Bill, subsequently signed into law by President Ronald Reagan, transferring the ownership of the *Brown* to the Project. The ship was also listed in the National Register of Historic Places. Eventually, in early 1988, a berth was found for the ship, not at New York, but instead at Baltimore. This was arguably a more suitable place, for it was there at the nearby Bethlehem-Fairfield yard that the ship had been constructed. Moreover, it was the yard that had built the *Patrick Henry*, the first Liberty of them all. After being towed out of Reserve and dry-docked at Norfolk for preliminary restoration work and a lick of paint, the *Brown* was towed up to Baltimore to its new home alongside Pier 1, arriving there on 13 August 1988. If there had been any doubts about the enthusiasm of that city to have the ship, they were laid to rest by the welcome the old warrior received. Civic dignitaries, Coast Guard fire-boats, ships of the United States Navy, pilot boats, and a host of privately owned craft were on hand to greet her. The *John W. Brown* had arrived home.

Ships nowadays have small crews and so much ship maintenance is therefore carried out by shore gangs. But in days gone by most maintenance was carried out by crew members and, as any seaman from those days will recall, such maintenance was a continuous job that, aside from watch-keeping, took up the better part of the crew-time available. Apart from labour costs, it was expensive in materials too. Ship restoration and preservation projects are no different; plenty of labour is required and lots of money. Fortunately for the world's maritime heritage there are people around ready to supply those, in addition to that extra ingredient needed which can only adequately be described as love. The two surviving Liberty ships are fortunate in having a full share of the latter. Since the early days of restoration both ships have been able to rely upon the ministrations of armies of volunteers for regular maintenance tasks, administration, and to man them whenever the ships leave their berths for whatever reason, be it for cruises or trips to the repair yard. None of the volunteers are paid. Although some refurbishment and maintenance materials are received as gifts, some have to be paid for out of monetary donations, the sale of souvenirs, visitors' admission fees, and the fees charged for cruises. To keep the ships up to the standards required by the US Coast Guard, regular surveys and regular visits to repair yards and dry-docks are required, and that is a very expensive business indeed.

In 1992, with the 50th Anniversary of the D-Day landings looming on the horizon, an event that was to be commemorated internationally in June 1994, the idea was floated that the two Liberty ships together with the *Lane Victory*, another preserved merchant vessel from the Second World War, should sail in convoy to Normandy. It would be a very costly operation so a Bill was pushed through Congress that provided for six ships from the Reserve Fleet to be sold, the money received for them then being divided among the three participating vessels. Even with that money, other substantial funds had to be found. To the great disappointment of many people, when the *John W. Brown* went into dry-dock to be prepared for the voyage it was discovered that many of the rivets in the bottom plates – being Baltimore-built, she was part riveted – needed to be replaced, and the money for that could not be found quickly enough. She was pulled out of the project. The Victory ship *Lane Victory* left San Pedro on schedule but then developed serious engine problems, and so she also had to pull out.

The *Jeremiah O'Brien*, the one of the trio with the greatest distance to sail, did make it. Sailing with an wholly volunteer crew under Captain George Jahn, and with Admiral Tom Patterson on board as commodore, the ship made it to England and then to Normandy. There was considerable competition for places on the voyage and volunteers were prepared to take any position that was going. Coleman Schneider, a certificated deck officer, signed on as Assistant Steward.

Arriving at Portsmouth on 21 May 1994, where many of an international host of ships were to foregather for the crossing to Normandy, it was reported that the *Jeremiah O'Brien*, the only merchant ship in that gathering, stole the show. The daily average number of visitors to board the ship there exceeded by far the highest attendance ever achieved at San

Francisco. For a brief period the Ugly Duckling had almost become a Swan.

On 2 June 1994 the *O'Brien* paid a brief visit to Southampton, the port from whence she had sailed for Normandy exactly fifty years previously. Amongst the visitors to board there were two ladies who had been war babies, the offspring of romances between English girls and American soldiers. Pauline Natividad's father might have sailed off to Normandy on a ship just like the *O'Brien* which is why she visited the ship. She told reporters of how many years later and well after her mother's death, she had managed to trace her father and a half brother in the States. Margrit Morton, had a similar story to tell except that her mother and father met just after the war. She too had managed to trace her father; not only that, he had flown over to England to visit her.

Anchored with a host of other ships in the Solent on 5 June, but in a place of honour as the only ship there to have actually participated in the Normandy landings, those aboard the *O'Brien* cheered as the Royal Yacht *Britannia* with Queen Elizabeth on board, steamed by. After that the ship was visited by President and Mrs. Clinton. 'This is the greatest day of my life', said Admiral Patterson, the man who had more to do with saving the ship from the scrap yard than any other. On the following day, 6 June, the *Jeremiah O'Brien* returned to Normandy, almost certainly for the last time ever. She was surrounded by ships, but there was no vast armada as there had been fifty years before, and it was far, far less noisy. The day was spent in ceremonies, wreath-laying, and in memories. The French coast looked peaceful and ordinary, and not a bit as it had looked on that morning half a century before. Coleman Schneider says that the total experience, the voyage, the visit to England and then to Normandy, was fantastic. 'It is a chance at 70 to do what we did at 19', a sentiment echoed by other crew members. It was a great day for the veterans on board. But off that Normandy coast on 6 June 1994, using a pair of binoculars, the white headstones of graves could be seen not far from what had been called Omaha Beach. The men lying there never had the chance of one day returning as veterans.

By no means all the volunteers who carry out work for free aboard the Liberties in their home ports are Americans. Many come from overseas, most from Britain. The *John W. Brown* probably receives more of these expatriate workers than the *Jeremiah O'Brien* because Baltimore is much nearer Britain than San Francisco. To encourage these British visitors to the *Brown* an unofficial arrangement has been set up between Ray Witt in Britain, and Derek Brierley of Joppatowne, Maryland. Brierley was originally from Britain and both he and Witt served in the Merchant Navy. Briton Denys Lomax served in the *Samfoyle* (Brunswick, March 1944) during the war having joined her at Brunswick for her maiden voyage. He later left the sea and worked in an industry far removed from his earlier calling. That did not stop him in 1994 taking the medical required by the US Coast Guard and then joining the *John W. Brown* for a sea voyage. It was a voyage the Coast Guard permitted the *Brown* to make in some recompense for the missed Normandy voyage of that year. The high point of the voyage for Lomax was the historic meeting at sea, when the *Brown* heading north for Halifax passed the *Jeremiah O'Brien* heading south for Portland, Maine, on its way back from Normandy. That meeting off Cape Cod of two Liberty ships at sea, might well be the last one ever to take place.[6]

When another British ex-merchant seaman joined the *John W. Brown* as a crewman in August 1998 for a voyage to Charleston, it was his second cruise on the ship. This time Thomas Tinkner had a special mission in mind. He had been serving aboard the British freighter *Margot* as a cabin boy on 23 May 1942 when she was torpedoed and sunk with the loss of about half of her crew somewhere off Cape Hatteras. It was his intention to purchase a wreath at Charleston and on the return voyage to Baltimore, drop it overboard in honour of his long dead shipmates. But that was not to be; instead Tommy Tinkner was to join his comrades. At Charleston Tinkner was taken ill and two days later he died in hospital there. His family in England were informed and they requested that he be cremated and his ashes consigned to the sea from the deck of the ship of which he had been so fond. So, on the voyage back to Baltimore in a ceremony conducted by the ship's chaplain, the Rev. Ramon Reno, Tinkner's ashes in a receptacle covered in a Red Ensign, were consigned to the deep, accompanied by the wreath he had bought for others. On that same day his family held a memorial service for him in London. Ron Quested of London and his twin Len, now of Melbourne, Australia, were both radio operators in the British Merchant Navy during the war. In 1998 they came together to work aboard the *Brown*. They found themselves in familiar territory when they visited the ship's radio room, for most of the equipment there is original.

On 29 August 2000, the *John W. Brown* returned to her berth at Baltimore after a voyage of 5000 miles to the Great Lakes and back, her longest voyage since 1946. She had been away for three and a half months. Ship riveters are a rare breed these days, and in 1997 a rivet crew from Toledo, Ohio, had travelled to Baltimore to replace several hundred rivets in the ship. As 13,000 more needed to be replaced, the Toledo shipyard suggested bringing the ship there where the job could be completed in one dry-docking. And that is what happened. On the way back the ship called at various ports en route and became a centre of attraction for many visitors.

---

6. Correspondence with Denys Lomax, March 2000.

In the past, the two preserved Liberty ships have both been recipients of American awards. In 2000 it was announced that they were jointly to receive the prestigious Maritime Heritage Award of the World Ship Trust, which has headquarters in London. These awards, which were instituted in 1980, are always presented by Heads of State on behalf of the Trust. Queen Elizabeth, for example, presented one to *Mary Rose* in 1983, and President Ronald Reagan to the USS *Constitution* in 1987. It is hoped that the joint Liberty ship award will be made in 2002 and that an international group of Liberty ship ex-mariners will be in attendance at the ceremony. Those awards will mark not only the excellent preservation efforts of all those who have been involved with the two surviving Liberties, but also the crucial role the Liberty played in the Second World War and its rightful place in the history of that conflict.

In his Report to Congress on 23 August 1944, President Roosevelt had a great deal to say about the efficacy and costs of the Lend-Lease arrangements. To placate critics of the programme – even at that stage of the war there were still plenty of those around – he also gave some fascinating details and costings of what he called 'reverse Lend-Lease'. These were goods and services supplied absolutely free of charge to American forces, mainly by Britain, but also by Australia, New Zealand and India. He gave many specific examples, including the fact that every American tank shipped to Normandy from Britain had been waterproofed in Britain for landing in surf conditions, all at a cost to the British taxpayer. In that same overall context the President also mentioned that the barracks, camps, and airfields built in Britain for the American forces had not cost the Americans one single dollar, nor had the use of the world's two largest liners, the *Queen Mary* and the *Queen Elizabeth* for conveying American troops to Britain. There was much more, including the use without cash payment of a US Naval Base in Britain, and the transfer of over of 1100 Spitfires and other British aircraft to the United States Army Air Force.

Then he said,

> We have also benefited greatly from British engineering and research in new weapons. No money evaluation is put on this type of aid, but it is made freely available to us. For, example, rockets based on a British design are now being used by American forces against the Japanese in the Pacific; a British-developed radio set has been widely used in American tanks built for Britain and Russia; and the jet propulsion plane uses an engine based on the Whittle design developed in Britain.

Had President Roosevelt not been constrained by secrecy he could also have mentioned other 'reverse flows' amongst them radar, anotherBritish invention. (A British-made radar set had been installed before the United States was in the war on the north-east coast of the Hawaiian island of

Oahu, on which Pearl Harbor lies. Had the radar station been manned on a continuous basis, the attack on Pearl Harbor might not have been such a disaster.)

There was no secrecy over another east to west benefit that, for whatever reason, President Roosevelt did not mention in his report. That was the plans for the vessel that was eventually to develop into the Liberty ship. As this ship was central to the winning of the Battle of the Atlantic and was at the heart of all the logistical operations of the war from 1943 onwards, logistical operations without which the war could not have been won, the transfer of those plans was arguably the most important of the lot.

Peter Guy was a junior officer aboard the *Samur* (*Charles C. Long*, Baltimore, September 1943) during the war and later served on another one. He says, 'many things have been said about the Liberties – some of them uncomplimentary – but I can only say from my own experience that they were damn good ships'.

They were, and they won the war.

Appendix 1

From File ADM1/10278
British Admiralty Instruction.

SECRET   *11/9/40*

MERCHANT SHIPBUILDING MISSION TO USA

1. The Merchant Shipbuilding Mission will consist of:-

(i)   *Mr. R. Cyril Thompson BA* (Managing Director of Messrs Joseph L. Thompson & Sons Ltd., Sunderland and a Director of Messrs Sir James Laing & Sons Ltd., Sunderland) as head of the Mission, acting in full consultation with the undernamed, but with the power to make all decisions on behalf of the Controller of Merchant Ship-building.

(ii) *Mr. Harry Hunter OBE B.Sc.* (Technical Director, Messrs North Eastern Marine Engineering Co Ltd., Wallsend-on-Tyne.)

(iii) *Mr. William Bennett B.Sc.* (Principal Surveyor of Lloyd's Register of Shipping for the United States and Canada.)

(iv) *Mr. J.S. Heck* (Principal Engineer Surveyor of Lloyd's Register of Shipping, New York.)

(v)   *Mr. R.R. Powell* (An Assistant Secretary, Admiralty now in North America with the British Admiralty Technical Mission, to be trans-ferred temporarily.) as Secretary to the Merchant Shipbuilding Mission. His principal duties will be to link up with the Purchasing Commission in New York on all subjects of general policy.

2) The object of the Merchant Shipbuilding Commission is to endeavour to obtain at the earliest possible moment the delivery of Merchant ton-nage from USA shipyards at the rate per annum of about 60 vessels of the Tramp type each averaging about 10,000 tons deadweight and of 10.5 knots service speed, loaded, in fair weather and to make immediate pro-vision for the building of 30 such vessels within the financial limits referred to in the following.

478

As an alternative to some vessels of the Tramp type two vessels of the Cargo Liner type and of 15 or 16 knots speed, and two vessels of the Tanker type, can be taken but, having regard to the high prices of such vessels in USA, action should be limited to two vessels each of these types. This limit can be extended from time to time by special authority asked for and granted by cable.

3) The Merchant Shipbuilding Mission is associated with that which is about to leave under the charge of Sir Walter Layton and it is, in fact, to be regarded as being under the auspices of Sir Walter Layton, and, of course, the Purvis Mission in USA, for all matters of general policy and those concerning the drawing up of financial propositions, actual purchases, etc. The Merchant Shipbuilding Mission shall have full authority to make all decisions and take actions concerning all technical aspects, within the limit of expenditure of £10,000,000.

4) The principal duties of Mr. Thompson as head of the Mission, will be:-
(i)   to ascertain the types, sizes, and numbers of Merchant ships that can be built in USA shipyards for delivery by:-
30th June 1941
31st December 1941
30th June 1942
(ii) to approve the various yards as being suitable and capable of our work.
(iii) to approve the types and sizes of ships, modifications, alternatives, and all technical details concerning design, construction and equipment.
(In this connection it is recognised that the types of ships and propelling machinery which ordinarily would be built at Home, are not available to any extent in USA, and the position is therefore, one in which we must take what we can get. In particular we must be prepared to take geared turbines in place of reciprocating engines and water-tube boilers in place of Scotch boilers.)
(iv) to report on the possibility of building tankers of commercial type;
(This class of vessel, mostly equipped with geared turbines and water-tube boilers, has been a fairly regular product of USA yards even throughout the period when the USA shipbuilding industry was in low-water.) Also to report on the possibility of building vessels of Cargo Liner type, being if necessary, repeats or approximate repeats of the vessels now building for the Maritime Commission or such vessels of other design.
(The authority given in (2) for the immediate placing of two vessels, each of these types is intended for the purpose of making a link which can subsequently be developed.)

(v) to agree plans and specifications with Shipbuilders.

(vi) to approve prices and terms and conditions of contract, but these not to exceed a condition in which more than 25% of the price is paid as a 'signing instalment' and the total amount to be paid in the form of 'signing' or subsequent instalments is not to exceed £5,000,000 up to 28th February 1941.

(vii) to give all necessary information to Lloyd's Register with whom the vessels will be classed and by whose Surveyors the superintendence of the carrying-out of the specifications etc., will be done.

(viii)to provide Mr. Powell with a note of the technical features concerning each propsed contract, in such a form that Mr Powell can communicate the necessary information to the Purchasing Commission for action in regard to the completion of contracts and for transmission to the Admiralty, London.

(5) As advised by the USA Ambassador, London, the Merchant Shipbuilding Mission should, as early as possible after arrival in USA, contact with the United States Maritime Commission. (The Ambassador has already made valuable contacts on our behalf by cable and transatlantic telephone, and the Maritime Commission is, in fact, holding off to let us in.)

Having regard to the position so far created with the valuable assistance of the Ambassador in London, and of Mr. Harvey Klemmer, Special Attaché, it will be desirable to keep the Maritime Commission fully acquainted with all movements and actions, including contract settlements. It may be that the Maritime Commission will have an interest in maintaining a fair and reasonable price level in the interests of their own large programme.

(6) A further contact should be made with:-
Mr. H. Gerrish-Smith
National Council of American Shipbuilders
21 West Street
New York
who may be able to advise where suitable merchant shipbuilding capacity can be obtained.

(7) In dealing with prices, the Merchant Shipbuilding Mission may be faced with proposals to include in the price of vessels the capital expenditure on new or extended yards and plant. This should be carefully handled, and it may be found to be a subject regarding which the Maritime Commission are closely interested. It should also be remembered that a USA Government organisation, The Reconstruction Finance Corporation (RFC) exists for the purpose of financing extensions or new plant. If

shipyards etc. can be looked upon (perhaps in the view of the Maritime Commission) as being defence measures, it may not be necessary for us to meet or contribute to the capital expenditure referred to above.

(8) To facilitate the work of the Merchant Shipbuilding Mission relative to its contact with the British Purchasing Commission, Mr. Purvis, of the latter organisation, will be requested to attach a responsible member of its staff to the Merchant Shipbuilding Mission during the course of the visits to and negotiations with the various shipbuilding establishments.

(9) It may be possible to arrange, subject to the approval of the USA Ambassador in London, that Mr. Harvey Klemmer (Special Attaché) will accompany the Mission and provide a most valuable link for the Mission with the Maritime Commission and the USA Shipbuilding Industry generally. (Mr. Klemmer was associated with the Ambassador during the latter's chairmanship of the Maritime Commission during the period when the USA Shipbuilding Programme was developed.)

(10) The work of the Merchant Shipbuilding Mission will have been completed at the stage at which orders will have been placed (or provisionally placed) for the various types of vessels and settlements made as to technical details. Subsequently, further orders will be given, as repeats, by the British Purchasing Commission and any further questions arising as to technicalities will be dealt with by the Principal Surveyor of Lloyd's Register of Shipping, New York, acting on behalf of the Controller of Merchant Shipbuilding and Repairs, Admiralty

Appendix 2
The Liberty Shipyards and their Geographical Spread

Atlantic Coast
Bethlehem-Fairfield Shipyards Inc., Baltimore, Maryland
J.A. Jones Construction Company, Brunswick, Georgia
New England Shipbuilding Corporation, Portland, Maine.
(A two-yard facility, East and West.)
North Carolina Shipbuilding Company, Wilmington, North Carolina
St. Johns River Shipbuilding Company, Jacksonville, Florida
Southeastern Shipbuilding Company, Savannah, Georgia
Walsh-Kaiser Company, Providence, Rhode Island*

Gulf Coast
Alabama Dry Dock Company, Mobile, Alabama
Delta Shipbuilding Company, New Orleans, Louisiana
J.A. Jones Construction Company, Panama City, Florida
Todd Houston Shipbuilding Corporation, Houston, Texas

Pacific Coast
California Shipbuilding Corporation, Los Angeles, California *
Kaiser Company, Vancouver, Washington*
Marinship Corporation, Sausilito, California
Oregon Shipbuilding Corporation, Portland, Oregon*
Permanente Metals Corporation, Richmond, California.* (A two-yard facility, No.1 and No.2)

Those marked thus * were yards owned by Henry Kaiser or yards he had an interest in. The site at Providence, RI, had originally been allocated to Rheem Manufacturing. That firm constructed only one ship, the *William Coddington*, after which the yard was reallocated to the Walsh-Kaiser Combine.

Appendix 3
Non-American-flagged Liberty Lists

A. The British Lend-Leased Liberty Ships *in order of date of delivery*
Abbreviations used in list:- M.East = Middle East, CMA = Central
Mediterranean Area, P.Gulf = Persian Gulf.
* The vessels marked thus did not load in the United States. Instead they
proceeded to Chile in ballast from the port listed to load nitates.

British Name	American Name	Delivered	1st Loading Port	Destination	Company
Samholt	*Jacob Riis*	17 July 43	Los Angeles	India	Cunard
Samson	*John H. Ingalis*	21 July 43	Los Angeles	India	Cunard
Sambridge	*John E. Wilkie*	21 July 43	San Francisco	India	Brocklebank
Sampler	*Wm.C. Lane*	21 July 43	Puget Sound	India	Port Line
Samaritan*	*Granville Stuart*	23 July 43	Los Angeles	M. East	Cunard
Samovar	*Frank Phinney*	30 July 43	San Francisco	M.East	Brocklebank
Samsurf	*Cornelius Cole*	5 Aug 43	Los Angeles	India	Cunard
Sambay*	*Anton M. Holter*	5 Aug 43	Puget Sound	M.East	Glen Line
Samblade*	*Augustus Garland*	8 Aug 43	Los Angeles	M. East	Glen Line
Sambre	*George Innis*	9 Aug 43	San Francisco	India	Cunard
Sambo*	*Edwin Joseph O'Hara*	12 Aug 43	Los Angeles	M. East	Cunard
Samana	*Wm. F. Vilas*	12 Aug 43	San Francisco	India	Lamport&Holt
Samsteel	*James H. Robinson*	15 Aug 43	Los Angeles	India	Union Castle
Samwater	*David de Vries*	16 Aug 43	Baltimore	M. East	Glen Line
Sampan	*Wm. T. Kip*	18 Aug 43	Los Angeles	India	Union Castle
Sambrake	*Lionel Copley*	20 Aug 43	Baltimore	M. East	Ellerman
Samarovsk	*Henry M. Robinson*	21 Aug 43	Los Angeles	India	Lamport&Holt
Sambut	*C.J. Jones*	21 Aug 43	Puget Sound	India	P.Henderson
Samphire	*Montford Stokes*	22 Aug 43	Baltimore	M. East	P.Henderson
Samhain	*Henry Van Dyck*	23 Aug 43	Baltimore	M. East	Ellerman
Samoa	*Matthew Brush*	23 Aug 43	New York	P. Gulf	Blue Funnel
Samite	*Howland Thompson*	26 Aug 43	Baltimore	M.East	Blue Funnel
Sambrian	*John Branch*	27 Aug 43	Philadelphia	P. Gulf	Clan Line
Samshire (ex-*Samara*)	*Emma Lazarus*	30 Aug 43	Baltimore	M. East	Ellerman
Samos	*Tench Tilgliman*	30 Aug 43	Baltimore	M.East	Elder Dempster
Samur	*Chas. C. Long*	1 Sept 43	Baltimore	M.East	Lamport&Holt
Sampep	*Victor F. Lawson*	1 Sept 43	Los Angeles	India	Houlders
Samarkand	*Peter Cooper*	2 Sept 43	Philadelphia	P. Gulf	Blue Funnel
Samarina	*James Blair*	3 Sept 43	Baltimore	M. East	Ellerman
Sampa	*Wm. Smallwood*	6 Sept 43	Baltimore	M. East	Houlders
Samthar	*Chas. A. Broadwater*	6 Sept 43	Vancouver	India	Royal Mail
Sampenn (ex-*Samora*)	*John H. Halton*	7 Sept 43	Baltimore	M. East	Clan Line
Samaye	*James T. Earle*	8 Sept 43	Baltimore	M. East	Clan Line
Samothrace	*Orville Taylor*	11 Sept 43	Baltimore	M. East	Pacific SNC
Sampford	*John Reed*	12 Sept 43	San Francisco	India	Bank Line
Samwash	*Herman Judson*	13 Sept 43	San Francisco	India	Bank Line
Sambur (later *Samwharfe*)	*Dwight D. Heard*	14 Sept 43	Los Angeles	India	Ellerman
Samarinda	*Samson Occum*	17 Sept 43	Los Angeles	India	T & J. Harrison
Samzona	*Victor C. Vaughan*	19 Sept 43	Tacoma	India	Royal Mail
Samdel (ex-*Samore*)	*Charles Devens*	20 Sept 43	San Francisco	India	Ellerman
Samtredy	*John Tipton*	21 Sept 43	Los Angeles	India	Prince Line

British Name	American Name	Delivered	1st Loading Port	Destination	Company
Samcalia	Lorrin A. Thurstin	23 Sept 43	Los Angeles	India	Furness Withy
Samida	Annie Oakley	25 Sept 43	Los Angeles	India	P & O
Samneva	Henry M. Stanley	27 Sept 43	Los Angeles	India	Blue Funnel
Sammont	E.H. Southern	30 Sept 43	Los Angeles	India	Ben Line
John J.McGraw (ex-*Samariz*)	John J.McGraw	1 Oct 43	Baltimore	M. East	Lamport&Holt
Samouri	Mannesseh Cutler	2 Oct 43	Puget Sound	India	Moss Hutchinson
Adolph S. Ochs (ex-*Samwyo*)	Adolph S. Ochs	2 Oct 43	Baltimore	M. East	Clan Line
Samkansa	Nikola Tesla	4 Oct 43	Baltimore	M. East	Hadley SC.
Sammex	Franz Boas	5 Oct 43	Baltimore	M. East	Sheaf Line
Samdak	John Russell Pope	6 Oct 43	Baltimore	M. East	Moss Hutchinson
Samark	John North	6 Oct 43	San Francisco	India	Ellerman
Samota	Adolph Lewisholm	13 Oct 43	Baltimore	M. East	Elder Dempster
Samwis	Edward Cook	15 Oct 43	Philadelphia	India	T.&J.Harrison
Samnebra	Lyon G. Tyler	18 Oct 43	Baltimore	M. East	Clan Line
Samnesse	Simon B. Elliott	18 Oct 43	Philadelphia	India	Blue Funnel
Samsylvan	J. Whittridge Williams	27 Oct 43	Baltimore	M. East	Shaw Savill
Samvern	Edith Wharton	28 Oct 43	New York	P. Gulf	Ben Line
Samyork	W. Walter Husband	29 Oct 43	New York	India	Bank Line
Samtucky	Wm. Blackstone	30 Oct 43	Philadelphia	India	Prince Line
Samokla	Jose Artigas	3 Nov 43	New York	India	Clan Line
Samlouis	Priscilla Alden	5 Nov 43	Philadelphia	India	Ellerman
Samois	Sam H. Ralston	8 Nov 43	Baltimore	M. East	Ellerman
Samakron	Jeremiah Chaplin	9 Nov 43	New York	India	Royal Mail
Samsip	Edward A. Robinson	9 Nov 43	New York	India	NZ Shipping
Samphill	Barrett Wendell	9 Nov 43	Philadelphia	India	Royal Mail
Samuta	Jesse De Forrest	12 Nov 43	Baltimore	M. East	Bank Line
Samsette	Augustine Herman	12 Nov 43	Baltimore	M. East	Blue Funnel
Edward Bruce (ex-*Samoine*)	Edward Bruce	15 Nov 43	Baltimore	M. East	Silver Line
Samflora	Israel J. Merritt	17 Nov 43	Baltimore	M. East	Union Castle
Samlong	Elias H. Derby	17 Nov 43	New York	India	Orient Line
Frank A. Vanderlip (ex-*Sambuff*)	Frank A. Vanderlip	20 Nov 43	Baltimore	M. East	Union Castle
Samrich	Wm. Pitt Preble	20 Nov 43	Philadelphia	India	Shaw Savill
Samburgh	Jacob C. Schiff	22 Nov 43	Baltimore	M. East	Bank Line
Samcleve	John T. Clark	23 Nov 43	Baltimore	M. East	Blue Funnel
Samgara	James Carroll	25 Nov 43	Baltimore	M. East	Blue Funnel
Samfield	Daniel Appleton	29 Nov 43	New York	C.M.A.	Runciman
Samboston	Willis J. Abbott	30 Nov 43	New York	C.M.A	Ellerman
Samtrent	Percy D. Haughton	30 Nov 43	New York	India	Union Castle
Samtroy	Ross G. Marvin	7 Dec 43	New York	C.M.A.	Bank Line
Ammla (ex-*Samvard*)	Ammla	13 Dec 43	New York	M. East	Ben Line
Samport	Israel Wheeler	14 Dec 43	Baltimore	M. East	Clan Line
Samspring	Chas. A. Young	16 Dec 43	New York	C.M.A.	Royal Mail
Samyale	Hugh L. Kerwin	17 Dec 43	Baltimore	M. East	Booth Line
Samdee	Patrick H. Morrissey	17 Dec 43	Baltimore	M. East	Brocklebank
Sambalt	Robert Wyckliffe	18 Dec 43	New York	P. Gulf	Clan Line
Ben H. Miller (ex-*Samroan*)	Ben H. Miller	20 Dec 43	New York	C.M.A.	Ellerman
Samtampa	Peleg Wadsworth	22 Dec 43	New York	C.M.A.	Houlder
Samharle	Martha C. Thomas	23 Dec 43	New York	C.M.A.	Blue Funnel
Samkey	Carl Thusgaard	24 Dec 43	New York	C.M.A.	NZ Shipping
Samsacola	Melville Dewey	29 Dec 43	Philadelphia	India	Silver Line
Samavon	Bronson Alcott	30 Dec 43	New York	India	Prince Line
Samvannah	Louis A. Godney	30 Dec 43	Baltimore	M. East	Anchor Line
Frederick Banting (ex-*Samspey*)	Frederick Banting	30 Dec 43	New York	C.M.A.	Ellerman

British Name	American Name	Delivered	1st Loading Port	Destination	Company
Samtweed	*Wm. R. Cox*	30 Dec 43	New York	C.M.A.	Ellerman
Samdon	—	31 Dec 43	New York	C.M.A.	Clan Line
Samforth	—	6 Jan 44	New York	C.M.A.	Blue Funnel
Samclyde	—	10 Jan 44	New York	C.M.A.	Bank Line
Samettrick	—	12 Jan 44	New York	C.M.A	P & O
Samcree	—	14 Jan 44	Baltimore	M.East	Blue Funnel
Sameveron	—	17 Jan 44	New York	C.M.A	Orient
Samfeugh	—	19 Jan 44	Baltimore	M. East	Charles Hill
Samtay	—	20 Jan 44	New York	M. East	Blue Star
Samythian	—	21 Jan 44	New York	C.M.A	Kaye
Samnid	—	24 Jan 44	Baltimore	M. East	Blue Star
Samouse	—	26 Jan 44	New York	C.M.A.	Cunard
Samchess	—	29 Jan 44	New York	C.M.A.	Clan Line
Samearn	—	31 Jan 44	New York	C.M.A.	Houlders
Samesk	—	5 Feb 44	Baltimore	M.East	NZ Shipping
Samteviot	—	8 Feb 44	New York	C.M.A.	TrinderAnderson
Samleven	—	14 Feb 44	New York	C.M.A.	Port Line
Samannan	—	15 Feb 44	New York	C.M.A.	Blue Star
Samstrule	—	16 Feb 44	New York	C.M.A.	Elders & Fyffe
Samlyth	—	21 Feb 44	Baltimore	M.East	Moss Hutchinson
Saminiver	—	22 Feb 44	Baltimore	U.K.	Blue Star
Samlossie	—	22 Feb 44	New York	India	P. Henderson
Samhorn	—	23 Feb 44	Baltimore	M.East	Donaldson
Samtyne	—	24 Feb 44	New York	C.M.A	Royal Mail
Samstrae	—	29 Feb 44	New York	C.M.A.	Headlam
Samconan	—	29 Feb 44	New York	C.M.A.	S.Am.Saint Line
Samgaudie	—	8 Mar 44	Philadelphia	India	Brocklebank
Samaffric	—	8 Mar 44	New York	C.M.A.	Ben Line
Samwye	—	8 Mar 44	New York	C.M.A.	Bank Line
Samnethy	—	10 Mar 44	New York	C.M.A.	ER Management
Samalness	—	10 Mar 44	Baltimore	M. East	Halden Phillips
Samdart	—	13 Mar 44	New York	C.M.A.	Munro Campbell
Samderwent	—	14 Mar 44	New York	C.M.A.	Clan Line
Sameden	—	14 Mar 44	New York	C.M.A.	Port Line
Samcolne	—	16. Mar 44	New York	C.M.A.	Anchor Line
Samsperrin	—	18 Mar 44	New York	C.M.A.	Hain
Samshee	—	21 Mar 44	Philadelphia	India	Hain
Samlea	—	22 Mar 44	New York	India	Ellerman
Samdaring	—	23 Mar 44	New York	P. Gulf	Prince Line
Samspelga	—	25 Mar 44	New York	P. Gulf	J. Morrison
Samjack	—	27 Mar 44	New York	India	Blue Funnel
Samfairy	—	28 Mar 44	New York	M. East	Court Line
Samdonard	—	29 Mar 44	New York	C.M.A.	McCowenGross
Samgallion	—	31 Mar 44	New York	C.M.A.	E.J. Sutton
Samfoyle	—	31 Mar 44	Boston	U.K.	Cunard
Samderry	—	31 Mar 44	New York	C.M.A.	J.&C. Harrison
Samhope	—	5 Apr 44	New York	C.M.A.	Reardon Smith
Samneagh	—	6 Apr 44	Portland	UK	P. Henderson
Samsturdy	—	12 Apr 44	Baltimore	UK	Common Bros
Samfinn	—	13 Apr 44	New York	UK	Donaldson
Samadre	—	14 Apr 44	New York	India	Hain
Samdauntless	—	15 Apr 44	Philadelphia	UK	Ben Line
Samtrusty	—	22 Apr 44	New York	India	Donaldson
Sambanka	—	22 Apr 44	New York	C.M.A.	Hogarth
Samvigna	—	24 Apr 44	New York	India	Hain
Samselbu	—	26 Apr 44	Savannah	UK	Runciman
Samconstant	—	26 Apr 44	Hampton Rds.	UK	Furness Withy
Samwake	—	28 Apr 44	Boston	UK	Silver Line
Samglory	—	29 Apr 44	Baltimore	M.East	DoddThomson
Samloyal	—	29 Apr 44	Baltimore	UK	S.Am. Saint Line

British Name	American Name	Delivered	1st Loading Port	Destination	Company
Samoresby	—	29 Apr 44	New York	India	S.Am. Saint Line
Samadang	—	29 Apr 44	New York	India	Stag Line
Samwinged	—	30 Apr 44	New York	UK	Reardon Smith
Samleyte	—	1 May 44	Baltimore	M.East	C.T.Bowring
Samfleet	—	6 May 44	New York	M. East	Bank Line
Samfaithful	—	9 May 44	New York	C.M.A.	Royal Mail
Samcebu	—	10 May 44	Savannah	UK	Bolton
Samaustral	—	13 May 44	Savannah	UK	J.&C. Harrison
Samsuva	—	13 May 44	Portland	UK	Ropner
Samingoy	—	13 May 44	Baltimore	M.East	NZ Shipping
Samcrest	—	15 May 44	New York	C.M.A.	Ellerman
Samidway	—	17 May 44	Portland	UK	Glen Line
Samlorian	—	20 May 44	Savannah	UK	ER Management
Samfreedom	—	23 May 44	New York	P.Gulf	Counties
Samsmola	—	25 May 44	New York	India	Ellerman
Samtruth	—	25 May 44	New York	M. East	HaldinPhilipps
Samsoaring	—	29 May 44	New York	C.M.A.	P & O
Samtorch	—	31 May 44	Baltimore	India	Ellerman
Samlister	—	31 May 44	Baltimore	India	Munro Campbell
Samspeed	—	3 Jun 44	New York	India	Lyle
Samoland	—	9 Jun 44	New York	C.M.A.	Watts Watts
Samtana	—	9 Jun 44	Baltimore	India	Lyle
Samluzon	—	12 Jun 44	New York	C.M.A.	Morel
Samskern	—	15 Jun 44	New York	C.M.A.	ER Management
Samindoro	—	17 Jun 44	New York	C.M.A.	Headlam
Samnegros	—	22 Jun 44	New York	C.M.A	G. Nisbet
Samsylarna	—	24 Jun 44	New York	India	Ropners
Samlamu	—	26 Jun 44	Baltimore	India	Reardon Smith

B. The Russian Lend-Leased Liberty Ships

Russian Name	US Name	Delivered
Alexandr Nevsky	Henry W. Corbett	6 Apr 1943
Alexandr Suvorov	Elijah P. Lovejoy	27 Mar 1943
Askold	Henry L. Pittock	27 Mar 1943
Baku	David Douglas	'Summer' 1943
Bryansk	Wm. E. Ritter	11 May 1944
Valeri Chkalov (I)	Alexander Baronof	17 Apr 1943
Valeri Chkalov (II)	Grant P. Marsh	31 Dec 1943
Vitbesk	John Minto	5 Jun 1943
Vladivostok	Pleasant Armstrong	7 Jun 1943
Voykov	Samuel P. Langley	9 Feb 1943
General Vatutin	Jay Cooke	Jun 1944
General Panilov	George E. Goodfellow	Jun 1944
Dekabrist	E.H. Harriman	10 Mar 1943
Emelyan Pugachov	Louis Agassiz	21 Apr 1943
Erevan	Joseph Watt	13 Jul 1943
Jean Javres	Thomas Nast	7 Feb 1943
Ingul	Emmet D. Boyle	3 May 1944
Kamenets-Podolsk	Robert S. Abbott	Apr 1944
Kolhoznik	Charles Wilkes	Jun 1944
Krasnogv Ardeyets	Charles S. Fairchild	28 Jan 1943
Kuban	William G.T. Vault	Jun 1943
Leningrad	Gouverneur Morris	26 Jun 1943
Mikhail Kutuzov	Graham Taylor	28 Mar 1943
Nahodka	Irving W. Pratt	28 Mar 1943
Novorossisk	Edward Eggleston	23 May 1943
Odessa	Mary Cossat	31 May 1943
Oreol	Charles E. Duyea	Apr 1943
Pskov	George L. Shoup	'Summer' 1943
Rodina	Henry I. Waters	8 May 1944
Sevastopol	De Witt Clinton	28 Apr 1943
Sergei Kirov	Charles Gordon Curtis	28 Feb 1944
Sovetskaya Gavan	Samual A. Worcester	22 Jun 1943
Stalinabad	Willis C. Hawley	31 Jul 1943
Stalingrad	Thomas F. Flaherty	Apr 1944
Stepan Razin	Cass Gilbert	24 Apr 1943
Suhona	George Coggeshall	Apr 1944
Sutchan	Jose Sepulveda	7 Feb 1943
Tbilisi	John Langdon	29 Feb 1944
Tungus	Sieur Duluth	5 Mar 1943
Herson (or Kherson)	Joseph C. Avery	3 Jun 1943
Apsherson (tanker)	Charlotte P. Gilman	26 Aug 1944
Byelgorod (tanker)	Paul Dunbar	26 Aug 1944
Maikop (tanker)	Thomas H. Gallaudet	Jul 1943

C. The Greek Lend-Lease Liberty Ships

Greek Name	US Name	Delivered
Ameriki	*William H. Todd*	1943
Kerkyra	*William Grayson*	1945
Hellas	*William De Witt Hyde*	1943
Thermistokles	*Francis S. Barton*	1944
Kalliopi	*Robert Dale Owen*	1943
Spetsae	*Thomas L. Haley*	1945
Hydra	*John C. Preston*	1945
Lesvos	*Charles H. Shaw*	1945
Miaoulis	*Lot Morrill*	1944
Navarchos Konturiotis	*Cyril G. Hopkins*	1944
Dodekanisos	*Frederick Austin*	1945
Niki	*James H. Courts*	1945
Psara	*Mark A. Davis*	1945

D. The Norwegian Lend-Lease Liberty Ships

Norwegian Name	US Name	Delivered
Liev Eiriksson	*John Wright Stanley*	29 Jan 1943
Fridtjof Nansen	*Francis Nash*	31 Jan 1943
Roald Amundsen	*William Strong*	24 Apr 1943
Ole Bull	*Sallie S. Cotton*	14 May 1943
Edvard Grieg	*Thomas F. Bayard*	31 May 1943
Christian Michelsen	*John M.T. Finney*	31 May 1943
Viggo Hansteen	*George M. Shriver*	20 Oct 1943
Sverre Helmersen	*William Hodson*	22 Apr 1944
Harald Torsvik	*Henry B. Plant*	6 Nov 1944
Vadso	*Robert J. Banks*	20 Dec 1944
Lektor Garbo	*Alfred L. Baxlay*	7 Mar 1945
Carl Oftedal	*George N. Drake*	28 Mar 1945

E. The Belgian Lend-Lease Liberty Ships

Belgian Name	US Name	Delivered
Belgian Unity	*Earl A. Bloomquist*	1944
Belgian Tenacity	—	Apr 1944
Belgian Dynasty	*Harry A. Garfield*	1945
Belgian Equality	*Richard A, Van Pelt*	1945
Belgian Amity	*Lawrence T. Sullivan*	7 Apr 1945
Belgian Liberty	*George P. Garrison*	1945
Belgian Loyalty	*Richard Stockton*	1945

F. The Chinese Lend-Lease Liberty Ships

Chinese Name	US Name	Delivered
Chung Cheng	*Murat Halstead*	Sep 1943
Chung Shan	*Henry M. Teller*	Sep1943

Chinese Name	US Name	Delivered
Chung Tung	*William Hodson*	Jun 1944
Sun Yat-sen	—	Apr 1943

G. The Dutch Lend-Lease Liberty Ships

Dutch Name	US Name	Delivered
Fort Orange	*Tobias Lear*	Sep 1943
Molengraaf	*Mary M. Dodge*	Sep 1943

Notes:

a) In addition to the 182 merchant Liberties listed above Britain had five additional Liberties allocated in June 1944 as Repair Ships for the Royal Navy. They were *Diligence, Assistance, Hecla, Dutiful* and *Faithful*.

b) Some Liberty ships were operated by more than one managing shipping company in the war years. Sometimes managers were changed when the ship arrived back in the UK. It depended upon which companies had crews to spare.

c) Between October 1943 and January 1944, 13 Landing Ship Infantry (Large) were also allocated to Britain. They were, in order of delivery, *Empire Battleaxe, Empire Cutlass, Empire Halberd, Empire Broadsword, Empire Lance, Empire Mace, Empire Rapier, Empire Anvil, Empire Javelin, Empire Spearhead, Empire Aquebus, Empire Gauntlet* and *Empire Crossbow*. These LSI(L)s were manned by Merchant Navy crews.

Bibliography

Anderson, E.P., *Audel's Marine Engineers Handy Book* (New York 1943)

Anon, *The Battle of the Atlantic* (HMSO, London 1946)

Anon, *Army Veterinary and Remount Services, 1939–1945* (HMSO, London 1961)

Anon, *The Royal Marines 1939–1943* (HMSO, London 1944)

Anon, *War With Japan* (Ministry of Defence Naval Historical Branch, HMSO, London 1995), 6 vols

Anon (Owen Rutter), *Merchantmen at War* (HMSO, London 1944)

Anon (Frank Owen), *The Campaign in Burma* (HMSO, London 1946)

Anon, *British Vessels Lost at Sea 1939–1945* (Cambridge 1983)

Anon, *The Works of Gibbs & Co* (New York 1946)

Arnold, J Barto III and others, *Texas' Liberty Ships*, Texas Parks & Wildlife Bulletin No. 99–1 (Austin, Texas 1998)

Beasant, John, *Stalin's Silver* (London 1995)

Berezhnoy, S.S., *The Ships and Vessels of Lend-Lease* (St. Petersburg 1994). (Russian text. Complete listing of all ships, naval and merchant, transferred to the Russian flag by the other Allies in the Second World War.)

Bes, J, *Chartering & Shipping Terms* (London 1975)

Bourneuf, Gus, *Workhorse of the Fleet*

Bradley, Professor Melvin, *The Missouri Mule: His Origins and Times* (Columbia 1993)

Braynard, Frank, *By Their Works Ye Shall Know Them* (New York 1968)

Braynard, Frank & Miller, W.H., *Fifty Famous Liners* (Cambridge 1982)

Broome, Jack, *Convoy is to Scatter* (London 1972)

Browning R.M., *US Merchant Vessel War Casualties of World War II* (Annapolis 1996)

Bunker, John G., *Liberty Ships; the Ugly Ducklings of World War II* (Annapolis 1972)

Burgess, R.H., *This Was Chesapeake Bay* (Baltimore 1982)

Burrell D.C.E., *The Thistle Boats* (Kendal 1987)

Bushell, T.E., *Eight Bells* (London 1950)

Chapman, Professor J.W., *The Price of Admiralty*, 4 vols (Ripe, East Sussex 1989)

Colledge, J.J., *Ships of the Royal Navy*, 2 vols (Newton Abbot 1969)

Costello, John, *The Pacific War* (London 1981)

Cowden, James E & Duffy, John, *The Elder Dempster Fleet History 1852–1985* (Norwich 1986)

Crisp, Dorothy, *Truth Too Near the Heels* (London 1986)

Davis, Hunter, *Born 1900* (London 1998)

Dear, Ian, *The Ropner Story* (London 1986)

Denham, Henry, *Inside The Nazi Ring – A Naval Attaché in Sweden 1940–1945* (London 1984)

Devos, Prof. Dr. Greta & Elewaut, Guy, *CMB 100: A Century of Commitment to Shipping* (Antwerp 1995)

Dilkes, David (ed.), *The Diaries of Sir Alexander Cadogan* (London 1971)

Dougan, David, *History of North East Shipbuilding* (London 1968)

Dounis, Christos, *In Memory of Sailors & Ships Lost in the Second World War* (Athens n.d.)

Edwards, Bernard, *Blood & Bushido* (Worcester 1991)

Eisenhower, Dwight D., *Crusade in Europe* (London 1948)

Elphick, Peter, *Life Line; The Merchant Navy at War 1939–1945* (London 1999)

    "   *Far Eastern File* (London 1997)

Fasset, Professor F.G. Jnr (ed.), *The Shipbuilding Business in the USA*, Vol.1 (New York 1948)

Foster, Mark S, *Henry J Kaiser:Builder in the Modern American West* (Austin 1989)

Gasaway, E.B., *Grey Wolf, Grey Sea* (London 1972)

Gibson, Charles, *Death of a Phantom Raider* (London 1987)

Gilbert, Martin, *Finest Hour: Winston S. Churchill 1939–1941* (London 1983)

    "   *Road to Victory: Winston S. Churchill 1942–1945* (London 1986)

Gleichauf, Justin F., *Unsung Sailors: The Naval Armed Guard in WWII* (Annapolis 1990)

Grove, Eric J., *The Defeat of the Enemy Attack on Shipping 1939–1945* (Aldershot 1997)

Guttman, Jon, *Defiance at Sea* (London 1995)

Hannan, Bill, *Fifty Years of Tugs* (Maritime Books 1985)

Harper, Stephen, *Capturing the Enigma*

Harris, Robert & Paxman, Jeremy, *A Higher Form of Killing* (London 1982)

Hegland, Jon Rustang, *Notraships flate* (Norwegian text) (Oslo, n.d.)

Herring, George C., *Aid to Russia: 1941–1946* (New York 1973)

Hervey, Rear-Admiral John, *Submarines* (London 1994)

Hicks, Peter, *Sailors Don't Cry* (Oxford, n.d. but 1990s)

Hocking, Charles, *Dictionary of Disasters at Sea 1824–1962*, 2 vols (London 1969)

Hoehling, A.A., *The Fighting Liberty Ships* (Kent State U.P., 1990)

Hogg, Robert S., *Naval Architecture & Ship Construction* (London 1956)

Hope, Dr Ronald, *A New History of British Shipping* (London 1990)

Howard, Michael, *Grand Strategy*, Vol. 4 (HMSO, London 1970)

Hoyt, Edwin P., *The Death of the U-boats* (London 1988)

Hull, Cordell, *Memoirs* (New York 1948)

Humphreys, Lansdale, *Merlin's Man* (Gwent 1995)

Infield, Glen B., *Disaster at Bari* (London 1974)

Jaffe, Walter W.m *The Last Liberty – Biography of the SS Jeremiah O'Brien* (Palo Alto, California 1993)

Jones, G., *U-Boat Aces and Their Fates* (London 1988)

Kahn, David, *Seizing the Enigma*

Kelshall, Gaylord, *The U-Boat War in the Caribbean* (Annapolis 1994)

King, Rear-Admiral R.W. USN (ed.), *Naval Engineering and American Seapower*, (Baltimore n.d.)

Land, Emory Scott, *Winning the War with Ships* (New York 1958)

Lane, Frederic, *et al*, *Ships for Victory; a History of Shipbuilding Under the U.S. Maritime Commission* (Baltimore 1951)

Lash, Joseph P., *Roosevelt & Churchill 1939–1941, The Partnership that saved the West* (London 1977)

Laskier, Frank, *My Name is Frank, a Merchant Seaman talks* (London 1941)

Loewenheim, Francis L. *et al* (eds.), *Roosevelt and Churchill, Their Secret Wartime Correspondence* (London 1976)

Masters, David, *Wonders of Salvage* (London 1946)

McEnery, John H., *Epilogue in Burma 1945–48* (Tunbridge Wells 1990)

McDowell, William, *The Shape of Ships* (London 1950)

McKay, C.G., *From Information To Intrigue – Studies in Secret Service Based on the Swedish Experience, 1939–1945* (London 1993)

Middlebrook, Martin, *Convoy* (London 1992)

Middlemiss, Norman L., *Travels of the Tramps*, 3 vols (Newcastle, various from 1989)

Mitchell, C. Bradford, *Every Kind of Shipwork, A History of Todd Shipyards Corporation* (New York 1981)

Moore, Arthur, *A Careless Word, a Needless Sinking* (Kings Point 1988)

Muggenthaler, Auguste Karl, *German Raiders of WWII* (New York 1977)

Nichols, Ray, *Changing Tide* (Sunderland & Hartlepool 1990)

Nolte, Carl, *Destination D-Day* (San Francisco 1994)

Pursey, H. J., *Merchant Ship Stability* (Glasgow 1977)

Pursey, H. J., *Merchant Ship Construction* (Glasgow 1978)

Rohwer, Professor J. & Hummelchen, G., *Chronology of the War at Sea 1939–1945*, 2 vols (London 1972)

Roskill, Stephen, *Churchill & the Admirals* (London 1977)
      "   *The War at Sea*, 3 vols in 4 parts (HMSO, London 1961)
      "   *A Merchant Fleet In War (Alfred Holt & Company)1939–1945* (London 1962)

Rushbrook, Frank, *Fire Aboard* (Glasgow 1961)

Russell, Lord, *The Knights of Bushido* (London 1958)

Rutter, Owen, *Red Ensign* (London 1943)

Sawyer & Mitchell, *The Empire Ships* (Colchester 1990)
      "   *Empire Ships of World War 1* (Liverpool 1968)
      "   *The Liberty Ships* (Newton Abbot 1970)
      "   *Oceans, Forts & Parks* (Newton Abbot 1970)
      "   *Victory Ships & Tankers* (Newton Abbot 1974)

Schneider, Coleman, *The Voyage of the* SS Jeremiah O'Brien 1994 (Tenafly, New Jersey 1994)

Simpson, Michael, *The Somerville Papers* (Aldershot 1996)

Slader, John, *The Fourth Service, Merchantmen at War 1939–45* (Wimborne Minster 1995)

Smith, Beth L. & Kluever, Karen T., *Jones Construction Centennial 1890–1990* (Charlotte, North Carolina n.d.)

Smith, J.W. & Holden, T.S., *Where Ships Are Born – Sunderland 1346–1946* (3rd Ed., Sunderland 1953)

Somner, Graeme, *Ben Line* (Kendal 1980)Stewart, Ian G., *Liberty Ships in Peacetime* (Rockingham Beach, Western Australia 1992)

Sturmey, Professor S.G., *British Shipping and World Competiton* (London 1962)

Syrett, David, *The Battle of the Atlantic and Signals Intelligence; U-boat Situations and Trends 1941–1945* (Aldershot 1998)

Taylor, James, *Ellermans, A Wealth of Shipping* (London 1976)

Thomas, Lowell, *Road to Mandalay* (London 1952)

Thompson. Julian, *War Behind Enemy Line* (London 1998)

Tipper, C.F., *The Brittle Fracture Story* (Cambridge 1962)

Truman, Harry, *Memoirs* (New York 1955)

Uhlig, Frank (ed.), *Naval Review 1968* (Annapolis 1968)

Walton, Thomas & Baxter, B., *Know Your Own Ship* (London 1970)

Waters, Sydney D., *Ordeal By Sea* (London 1949)

Watson, A.D., *Wilmington* (Wilmington 1967)

Weinberg, Gerhard L., *A World at Arms* (Cambridge 1994)

Wheeler, William R, Editor, *The Road to Victory, A History of the Hampton Roads Port of Embarkation in World War II* (Newport News 1946)

Williams, David L, *Liners in Battledress* (London 1989)

Williams, J.A. & Gray, J.B., *HM Rescue Tugs in World War II*, HMRT Veterans Association, n.d. circa 1992

Wollenberg, Charles, *Marinship at War* (Berkeley, California 1990)

Woodman, Richard, *Arctic Convoys* (London 1984)

Young, J.M., *Britain's Sea War – A Diary of Ship Losses 1939–1945* (London 1989)

Articles

Ayre, Sir Amos & Boyd, G.M., 'The Work of the Admiralty Ship-Welding Committee', *Transactions of the Institution of Naval Architects* (1946)

Chapelay, Frederique, 'Le Dernier Liberty', *Cols Bleus* No 2497 (4 September 1999)

Bond, Brian, 'The Theseus Experience:One Merchant Ship and 485 Mules go to War', *Army Defence Quarterly Journal*, Vol 124, No 4 (October 1995)

Britton, Beverley L., Lt.Cmdr USNR, 'Navy Stepchildren:The Armed Guard', *US Naval Institute Proceedings*, Vol 73, No 12 (December 1947)

Bull, F.B., Shepheard R.B., & Turnbull, James, 'Structural Investigation in Still Water on the Welded Tanker *Neverita*', *Transactions of the Institution of Naval Architects* (1946)

MacCutcheon, E.M., *Structural Alterations in Liberty Ships*, Society of Naval Architects & Marine Engineers, Chesapeake Section, March 1946

Malcolm, Ian M., 'Voyage 1 of the Samite', *Nautical Magazine* (Sept 1994-Feb 1995)

McNeill, David M., 'Rebuilding Broken Liberty Ship *Valery Chkalov*', Society of Naval Architects & Marine Engineers, August 1951, Pacific North West Section,

Robson, John, 'Merchant Shipbuilding in Canada', *Transactions of the Institution of Naval Architects*, Vol. 88 (1946)

Simpson, Major K. S., 'From Far Cathay', *Journal of the Royal Army Veterinary Corps* (1939)

Stanford, Peter, 'How an Ugly Duckling Fought Back', *Sea History*, No 35 (Spring 1985)

Vasta, John, 'Structural Tests on the Liberty Ship ss *Philip Schuyler*', *Transactions of the Society of Naval Architects & Marine Engineers*, No.55 (1947)

Vedeler, G., 'The Torsion of Ships', Institution of Naval Architects, London, 1924

Magazines and Journals

The Arctic Lookout, Winter 1997, No.30. Russian Convoy Club magazine.

The Ugly Duckling, various editions, Project Liberty Ship, Baltimore.

The Liberty Log, various editions, Project Liberty Ship, Baltimore

The Pointer & The Plane Shooter, various editions, Armed Guard Veterans, Rolesville, NC

The Wainwright Liberator, various editions, Jones & Company in-house magazine during the Second World War

The Brunswick Mariner, various editions, Jones & Company in-house magazine during the Second World War

The Link, the works magazine of Richardsons Westgarth Group, No. 2, August 1956

Royal Mail News, Newsletter of the Royal Mail Association, various editions

Journal of the Honourable Company of Master Mariners, various editions

Sea Breezes, various editions.

Nautical Magazine, various editions

Mountain Artillery Dinner Club Report, 1999

Monographs

Allison, Thomas M, *Convoy WS12* (n/d). Reproduced for its members by the Japanese Labour Camp Survivors Association.

Anon, *One Hundred Years, Joseph L Thompson & Sons Ltd 1846–1946* (Sunderland 1946)

Beyle, Noel W., *The Target Ship in Cape Cod Bay* (Falmouth, Massachusetts 1978)

Bull, Professor F B, *Stresses in Ships,* University of Queensland Press, 1962

Cooper, Sherod, *ss John W Brown, Baltimore's Living Liberty,* Project Liberty Ship, (Baltimore 1991)

Witt, R.J., & Heaton, P.M., *The Gallant Ship Stephen Hopkins* (privately published, nd)

Material on Film and Video

1. *The Men who Sailed the Liberty Ships,* PBS Home Video, San Jose, California, 1994

2. *Dangerous Coast,* Downwood Film Productions, Swansea, South Wales, 1997

3. *Seabed Visualisation Services,* SRD Limited, Beverley, East Yorkshire, n.d.

4. *Inspection of the ss Richard Montgomery 1995–1998,* SRD/U.K.Coastguard Agency, 1998

5. *Last of the Liberties.* Part of course:- *Failure of Stressed Materials.* Open University, Milton Keynes
6. *Ocean Vulcan Sea Trials.* The British Admiralty Ship Welding Committee filmed much of their ground-breaking work on this ship. During the editing of the film, parts of it ended up on the cutting-room floor from where they were retreived by Professor Frank Bull. This video is a compilation of those cuts and is therefore unique.
7. *Capture Enigma, the True Story,* DD Video, North Harrow, 2000

German archives
1. Die Handelsflotten der Welt 1942, Oberkommando der Kriegsmarine (Intelligence Division, OKM 3/Skl)
2. Anlage zu O.K.M. 1375/42. Briefing by Admiral Donitz
3. Nauticus. (Semi-official publication) Editions for 1943 and 1944.
4 Oberkommando der Marine – Kriegstagebuch der Seekriegsleitung (1/Skl). (War Diary, excerpts from.)

Unpublished material in British archives
1. FE.4/146 Admiralty Ship Welding Sub-Committee Preliminary Report on Analysis of Casualty Reports to 1st September 1944. Dated November 1945.
2. Value of Pre-Heating in Welded Ship Construction, by James W. Wilson, of the U.S. Maritime Commission and a member of the U.S. Welding Advisory Committee. Report in File MT9/3882, PRO, London.
3. Many Admiralty convoy files have been consulted at the Public Record Office, Kew. Among the most important are ADM199/72, ADM199/440, ADM199/524. ADM199/526, ADM199/758, ADM ADM199/1709, ADM199/2130–2149, ADM234/369, ADM237/168, ADM237/169
4. R. Holubowicz, memoir, Imperial War Museum, 91/31/1
5. G.E. Dale, memoir, Imperial War Museum, 76/132/1

United States Archives
1. Second Interim Report of a Board of Investigation convened by Order of the Secretary of the Navy to inquire into the Design and Methods of Construction of Welded Steel Merchant Vessels 1 May 1945.
2. Final Report (as in 1. above), 15 July 1946
3. CG140, A1706, *The Structural Alterations on Liberty Ships*, (Treasury Department) United States Coast Guard, April 1946.
4. Navships 250–641, Code 641, *Ship Contracts Awarded 1 January 1934 – 1 July 1955* (Treasury Department) Bureau of Ships, Washington D.C.

Unpublished material in private hands

1. Bull, Professor Frank, extracts from *Worst Things Happen at Sea*, part of personal reminiscences under the title *Gravitas Tauri.*

2. Anon, International List of Liberty Ship Casualities during the period 1964–1967. From the files of Professor Frank Bull.

3. Thompson, R. Cyril, diaries.

4. Thompson, Doreen, diaries.

5. White, Harry D., Memorandum for U.S. Treasury Secretary's Files, Franklin D. Roosevelt Library, Quebec Box, 13 September 1944, Hyde Park, New York.

6. Hicks, Peter, Apprentices Journal 1945–1946 aboard *Samettrick*

7. Jordan, R., *The Romance of a Century of Shipbuilding on the River Wear*, a history of J.L. Thompson and Company from 1846–1946, in two parts.

Abbreviations

ATS	Auxiliary Territorial Service (Women's Auxiliary Army Unit, Britain)
BEM	British Empire Medal (a decoration lower in order than the MBE – see under CBE)
BIS	British Information Service in the US during the war. An offshoot of MI6
BPC	British Purchasing Commission in the United States
CBE	Commander of the Order of the British Empire. (British decoration. Lower ranks are Order - OBE and Member – MBE)
C-in-C	Commander-in-Chief
CO	Commanding Officer
DEMS	Defensively Equipped Merchant Ships (DEMS gunners, equivalent to US Navy Armed Guard)
EWOMN	Essential Work Order, Merchant Navy (Britain)
ft	foot/feet
HMAS	His Majesty's Australian Ship
HMCS	His Majesty's Canadian Ship
HMIS	His Majesty's Indian Ship
HMNZS	His Majesty's New Zealand Ship
HMSAS	His Majesty's South African Ship
IHP	Indicated Horse Power (a measure of a ship's engine power)
in(s)	inch(es)
kt(s)	knot(s)
LSI(L)	Landing Ship Infantry, Large
LST	Landing Ship Tanks
MOWT	Ministry of War Transport (Britain)
MRA	Maritime Regiment, Royal Artillery
NAAFI	Navy Army Air Force Institute (British Forces canteens etc.)
OSS	Office of Strategic Services (United States. Predecessor of CIA)
POW	Prisoner of War
PRO	Public Record Office at Kew, England
PX	Post Exchange (US Forces canteens, etc.)
RAF	Royal Air Force
RN	Royal Navy
RNR	Royal Navy Reserve
RNZNVR	Royal New Zealand Navy Reserve
RPN	Report on Preliminary Purchasing Negotiations (United States)
TND	Torpedo Net Defense
USN	United States Navy
USNR	United States Navy Reserve
WSA	War Shipping Administration. (The ship-operating arm of the US Maritime Administration)

Index

For individual ships' names, see under 'Ships' and sub-entries.

Abbreviations:
Adm. = Admiral; Arg = Argentina; Belg = Belgium; Br = Britain; Braz = Brazil; Brig. = Brigadier; Can = Canada; Capt. = Captain; Cdr. = Commander; Ch = China; Ch. Eng. = Chief Engineer; Cmdre = Commodore; Dan = Danish; Du = Dutch; Fr = France; Ger = Germany; Gr = Greece; Hond = Honduras; Ind = India; It = Italy; Jap = Japan; Lib = Liberia; Lt. = Lieutenant; Lt. Cdr. = Lieutenant Commander; Nor = Norway; Pan = Panama; Pol = Poland; Prof. = Professor; R/A = Rear-Admiral; Ru = Russia; Sp = Spain; Sub. Lt. = Sub-Lieutenant; Sw = Sweden; Tai = Taiwan; US = United States; V/A = Vice-Admiral

Index

Index